Effectual Entrepreneurship

Whether you come to this book as an entrepreneurship student, a corporate manager, someone seeking regenerative social change, or a seasoned creator of new ventures, you already know that entrepreneurship is the primary engine of growth, innovation, and financial self-reliance.

What you will discover in this book is that there is a science to entrepreneurship—a shared logic that can be observed in expert entrepreneurs across industries, geographic locations, and time. We call this logic *effectuation*—which means working with things already within your control to co-create valuable new futures with people who want to work with you.

At the heart of the book you will find the four core principles of effectuation that expert entrepreneurs follow when creating new ventures, products, and markets:

- Start with your means
- Set affordable loss
- Form partnerships
- Leverage contingencies

In this book, each of these core principles is explained through cases, stories, thought exercises, and a variety of practical applications.

Presented in the concise, modular, graphical form made popular in previous editions, *Effectual Entrepreneurship* is perfect both for those seeking to become entrepreneurs, and those already in the thick of things!

A wealth of thought-provoking material, expert advice, and practical techniques resides in these pages and on the accompanying website: www.effectuation.org.

Saras Sarasvathy is the Paul M. Hammaker Professor of Business Administration at the Darden School of Business, University of Virginia, USA.

Glen B. Wheatley is Managing Director of Best Solutions International Group, entrepreneur, thought and cultural nomad, and adjunct academic at the University of Adelaide, Australia.

Previous editions of this book were co-created with:

Stuart Read, retired Professor of Strategic Management at the Atkinson School of Management, Willamette University, Washington, USA.

Nick Dew, a Professor of Strategic Management at the Naval Postgraduate School in Monterey, California, USA.

Robert Wiltbank, CEO of Galois, a software firm based in Portland, Oregon, USA.

Praise for This Edition

'*Effectual Entrepreneurship* successfully demystifies the concept and practice of entrepreneurship through uniquely highlighting important understandings and perspectives. Examples of the entrepreneurial process are featured through insightful cases and contexts. Furthermore, the book's principles-based approach also illustrates the nature of entrepreneurship, its eventual interactions and ongoing challenges, towards economic, social, and technological considerations critical for entrepreneurial success.'

Dr. Robert J. Crammond, *Senior Lecturer in Enterprise and Co-Director of the Transformative Enterprise Research Group, University of the West of Scotland, UK; Visiting Professor in Entrepreneurship, CBS International Business School, Germany*

'An entrepreneurship text with a very different feel, a definite win for students.'

Katie Pascoe, *Senior Lecturer, University of Northampton*

'Effectual entrepreneurship explores the creative power of people—the soft factor of economic production, which is often difficult to tackle in classical theories.'

Dr. Irina Heim, *Henley Business School, University of Reading, UK*

'A practical guide to innovate the business; a different approach to get a different solution.'

Dr. Ruud Koopman, *Saxion University, Netherlands*

'This book is the book for entrepreneurs—both those who are considering becoming one and those who already are. It is research inspired but practical oriented. It is able to turn highly abstract theoretical constructs into something easily understood and implemented. It is action oriented. A highly positive and inspirational book.'

Professor Mariarosa Scarlata, *University of Bergamo, Italy*

Effectual Entrepreneurship

Third Edition

Saras Sarasvathy and Glen B. Wheatley

Routledge
Taylor & Francis Group
LONDON AND NEW YORK

Designed cover image: Getty © melitas

Third edition published 2025
by Routledge
4 Park Square, Milton Park, Abingdon, Oxon, OX14 4RN

and by Routledge
605 Third Avenue, New York, NY 10158

Routledge is an imprint of the Taylor & Francis Group, an informa business

First edition published by Routledge 2011
Second edition published by Routledge 2017

British Library Cataloguing-in-Publication Data
A catalogue record for this book is available from the British Library

Library of Congress Cataloging-in-Publication Data
Names: Sarasvathy, Saras D., 1959- author. | Wheatley, Glen B., author.
Title: Effectual entrepreneurship / Saras Sarasvathy and Glen B. Wheatley.
Description: Third edition. | Abingdon, Oxon ; New York, NY : Routledge, 2025.
Identifiers: LCCN 2024037013 (print) | LCCN 2024037014 (ebook) |
ISBN 9781032427300 (hardback) | ISBN 9781032427287 (paperback) |
ISBN 9781003364016 (ebook)
Subjects: LCSH: Entrepreneurship. | New business enterprises. |
Success in business.
Classification: LCC HB615 .E453 2025 (print) | LCC HB615 (ebook) |
DDC 658.1/1—dc23/eng/20240905
LC record available at https://lccn.loc.gov/2024037013
LC ebook record available at https://lccn.loc.gov/2024037014

ISBN: 9781032427300 (hbk)
ISBN: 9781032427287 (pbk)
ISBN: 9781003364016 (ebk)

DOI: 10.4324/9781003364016

Typeset in Minion Pro
by codeMantra

Access the Support Material: www.effectuation.org

MIX
Paper | Supporting responsible forestry
FSC™ C013985
FSC www.fsc.org

Printed in the United Kingdom
by Henry Ling Limited

Contents

Acknowledgments

Writing any textbook is an effort that extends well beyond a team of authors. And writing one about effectuation involves an enormous network of self-selected stakeholders, many of whom we would like to recognize here.

First, we would like to thank our families for their enduring patience as we talk endlessly about this topic and then disappear endlessly to write about it.

This being the third edition of the book, we would like to thank our previous co-authors, namely, Stuart Read, Nick Dew, and Robert Wiltbank, for their herculean lifting with the first two editions and who generously handed over the wheel for this new stage of our adventure.

In the same vein, we thank all those people who contributed to the first and second editions, including Jack Roseman, Artie Buerk, Andy Dale, Anne-Valérie Ohlsson, Beverley Lennox, Amy Halliday, Andreea Rosca, Catherine Egli, Kevin Baumer, Emma Brown, Sinead Waldron, Leigh Wilkerson Ayers, Abby Skolits, Terry Clague, and Elisabet Sinkie.

We would like to recognize all those who provided rich examples of effectual logic and entrepreneurial action. As you read this book and enjoy the uniqueness, diversity, and texture of their stories, please appreciate that this was only possible because they shared their experience with others.

In this edition we tapped into the global community of the Society for Effectual Action and feature the work of many co-creators in Practically Speaking and Research Roots. Hence, a special thank-you to Sophia Marie Braun, Aline Winckler Brufato, Moataz Darwish, Gonzalo Jiménez-Seminario, Nobuo Kanai, Edmilson Lima, Rose Mary Almeida Lopes, Frédéric Ooms, Isabella Nunes Pereira,

Javiera Salvo Porras, Yuriko Sawatani, Philippe Silberzahn, Bernard Surlemont, Patricia Cabero Tapia, Dominique Vian, and Kwabena Obiri Yeboah.

Furthermore, we appreciate the input we received from users of the previous editions. We have done our best to incorporate your valuable suggestions and hope you can see your own mark on this edition.

A particular thank you goes to Terry Clague, Andrew Harrison, and Helena Parkinson at Taylor & Francis for their endless patience in the particularly long gestation of this third edition while breaking in a new author.

A final thank-you goes to Jim Zuffoletti for being a very long and supportive bridge between Charlottesville, Virginia (Saras) and Adelaide, South Australia (Glen). Your wise and patient backing enabled us to maintain our wits and keep chipping away at the project.

That said, all errors and omissions are completely our responsibility, and as entrepreneurs, we will use any unexpected surprises to inform and improve the next revision.

Effectually yours,
Saras Sarasvathy and Glen B. Wheatley

Introduction

The Science of Entrepreneurship

DEAR READER,

Whether you come to this book as an entrepreneurship student, a corporate manager, or a seasoned creator of new ventures, you already know that entrepreneurship is the primary engine of growth, innovation, and that most delicious of personal freedoms—financial self-reliance.

What you will discover in this book is that there is a science to entrepreneurship—a common logic we observe in expert entrepreneurs across industries, geographic locations, and time. We call this logic "effectuation," a word you probably don't run into every day.

The concept, though, isn't new. In fact, the underlying principles are the same ones that:

- Enabled Josiah Wedgwood in the eighteenth century to transform a pottery business into an enduring brand
- Helped Kiran Mazumdar-Shaw turn approximately 120 US dollars into a 2.8 billion US dollar global pharmaceuticals firm
- Were the basis for Oprah Winfrey to turn a traumatic childhood and distinct empathetic interviewing style into a globally recognized media empire
- Allowed Muhammed Yunus, the Nobel Laureate founder of the Grameen Bank and microfinance pioneer, to transform the lives of millions of women in Bangladesh

In a nutshell, effectual entrepreneurs work with things already within their control to co-create valuable new futures with people who want to work with them.

As you begin the book, you will come face-to-face with some common misconceptions about entrepreneurship, as well as some of the fears entrepreneurs face. In the heart of the book, you will find the four core principles of effectuation expert entrepreneurs have learned in the process of creating new ventures, products, and markets.

Each will be explained through cases, stories, thought exercises, and a variety of practical applications. Though simple and easy to put into action, these principles challenge and even invert the traditional logic mature organizations follow:

1. **Start with your means.** Don't wait for the perfect opportunity. Start taking action based on what you have readily available: who you are, what you know, and who you know.
2. **Set affordable loss.** Evaluate opportunities based on whether the downside is acceptable, rather than on the attractiveness of the predicted upside.
3. **Leverage contingencies.** Embrace surprises that arise from uncertain situations, remaining flexible rather than tethered to existing goals.
4. **Form partnerships.** Form partnerships with people and organizations willing to make a real commitment to jointly creating the future—product, firm, market—with you. Don't worry so much about competitive analyses and strategic planning.

Together, these principles enable entrepreneurs to co-create opportunities with other people who choose to work with them. When you can make the future happen by working with people who want to work with you and working with things you control, you don't need to worry about predicting the future, determining the perfect timing, or finding the optimal opportunity.

We have included entrepreneurial stories from a wide diversity of people, backgrounds, venture types and locations, hoping that you will find many examples which speak to you and your available means and thus inspire you to take action.

As you reach the conclusion of the book, you will find applications of these principles in contexts ranging from social entrepreneurship to large firms. And you will understand the challenges entrepreneurs face, as their lovingly created ventures become mature businesses.

When you start a new venture—for-profit or not, individually or within an existing organization—you are not only trying to make a good living but also expanding the horizon of valuable new economic opportunities. This book is designed to help you do that from start to finish. And, in form and content, the book embodies the expert entrepreneur's logic—bold, systematic, pragmatic, and, always, full of energy, mischief, and fun.

We wrote this book for you and are keen to hear what you think of it: what you like, what you don't like, suggestions for future editions, and what impact it has had on your entrepreneurial story. Visit https://effectuation.org/EE3/feedback or scan the following QR code. Thank you in advance for sharing and co-creating with us!

How to Use This Book

We designed this to be much more than a textbook. Certainly, it can accompany you through a course in entrepreneurship, and we hope it will.

But it is also prepared to venture outside the academic environment into the uncertain world of startup creation.

As much as the chapters, in sequence, tell a story, each chapter is designed to stand on its own. So, whether you start at the beginning and read through, or jump to the chapter (15) on partnerships in the moments before a meeting with a prospective stakeholder, we intend this book to be your partner in creating new opportunities.

As you read through, you will also find different special topics, outlined below, which provide more detail on the material in the chapter. Each is designed to help with a specific aspect of thinking about or starting a new venture:

Practically Speaking

In every chapter, you will find brief stories of new ventures. Every entrepreneurial story illustrates at least one of the principles described in this book. You will find stories matched with topics in each chapter. But if you choose to focus on just the "Practically Speaking" stories, you can skip from one to the next and quite literally tour the entrepreneurial world. Alternatively, use the overview to select specific stories based on their description, entrepreneur, or geography.

Research Roots

There is an enormous body of academic research on entrepreneurship—far too much for us to include in a book you could actually carry in your hand. So, we searched for foundational research that has shaped thinking over the years and contemporary research that reflects current knowledge to date. In the context of a chapter, we summarize the key points of a research stream in "Research Roots" to give you an idea of what other scholars are working on and to offer directions for further reading.

What Now?

Let's face it, entrepreneurs like to do things. So, at the end of each chapter, we have prepared a series of things you can do to put the ideas in the chapter into practice. Like everything else in the book, these are designed to accompany the sequential story or to stand alone. So, create your roadmap as you read, or review the entire "Now What?" inventory to get a feel for what a complete new-venture journey might look like.

So What?

Impatient? Eager? Want the bottom line? We have tried to summarize the one idea we hope you will take away from each chapter in "So What?" The goal is not to encourage you to skip the chapter. Quite the contrary. If you are wondering whether a chapter is worth your time, skip to "So What?" If the idea seems relevant to the challenge you face, know that you will find a whole lot more detail in the chapter.

Think It Through

Collectively, the authors of this book have many new ventures under their belts. So, we understand the need for practical, immediate, and relevant material. At the same time, we have provided space to consider some of the larger topics entrepreneurship opens up: the more intellectual questions that you may not find appealing when you have to close a financing round, but you might appreciate on a long contemplative hike with your partner during the weekend. We keep these for the very end of each chapter so as not to distract from the business of getting a venture going. But we hope you will enjoy taking the time to step back every once in a while and consider the broader implications of what you are accomplishing.

CONNECTING TO MORE

We have much more to share with you than we could include in this book, so throughout the book you will find the words "To learn more, visit …" accompanied by a web address and a QR code. This connects the content in the book directly to a dedicated page in the Society for Effectual Action website where you will find more information, from texts and images to videos and web links.

The world of entrepreneurship is diverse and fascinating, so we hope you will see use these pathways to new (ad-)ventures.

To learn more, visit: https://effectuation.org/EE3/userguide or scan this code.

About the Co-Authors

Saras Sarasvathy

Paul M. Hammaker Professor of Business Administration, Darden School of Business, University of Virginia

Saras Sarasvathy is a distinguished scholar and an influential figure in the field of entrepreneurship, best known for her groundbreaking work on effectuation, a logic of entrepreneurial expertise that has significantly shaped contemporary understanding of the entrepreneurial process. As the author of several pivotal texts on entrepreneurship, including the seminal book *Effectuation: Elements of Entrepreneurial Expertise,* Sarasvathy has made profound contributions to entrepreneurship education, research, and practice.

Born and raised in India, Sarasvathy's academic journey led her to the United States, where she completed her Ph.D. in Information Systems at Carnegie Mellon University, under the guidance of Nobel Laureate Herbert A. Simon. This diverse international background has imbued her with a unique perspective on entrepreneurship, which is evident in her research and teaching methodologies.

Sarasvathy is currently a Professor at the Darden School of Business, University of Virginia, and has held visiting positions at various prestigious institutions around the world, showcasing her international influence in the field.

Sarasvathy's work is characterized by a blend of rigorous research and practical relevance. She has contributed to numerous articles in top academic journals, served on editorial boards, and been an active member of entrepreneurial networks globally.

Her international experience and personal entrepreneurial journey have enabled her to foster a global dialogue on entrepreneurship, mentor aspiring entrepreneurs, and contribute to the development of entrepreneurial ecosystems in various countries.

ORCID: 0000-0001-9135-0150

Glen B. Wheatley

Managing Director, Best Solutions International Group

Glen B. Wheatley is an adjunct academic at the University of Adelaide teaching postgraduate and undergraduate courses in entrepreneurship, innovation, leadership, and corporate social responsibility.

Glen also founded and leads the advisory firm Best Solutions International, tapping into his extensive experience in both manufacturing and services. He has worked with many types of organizations: from startups and sole traders to some of the largest global companies.

His career has taken him on project and long-term assignments in Europe, Australasia, and the Americas, including Greater China, Germany, and Mexico.

His entrepreneurship and innovation experience is extensive, having co-founded an angel-financed startup in Germany, and been involved in various startups as advisor, board member, and angel investor.

Glen is a Fellow of the Australian Institute of Company Directors and holds a BA (University of Michigan); MBA (Thunderbird School of Global Management); Graduate Certificate in Science and Technology Commercialisation; and a Master of Applied Innovation and Entrepreneurship (University of Adelaide).

ORCID: 0000-0001-7506-4242

Co-Creators

In this edition we tapped into the global community of the Society for Effectual Action and feature the work of the following co-creators in Practically Speaking and Research Roots.

Sophia Marie Braun

Research Fellow, ESCP Business School

Sophia Braun is passionate about entrepreneurial action and sustainable innovation. In her Ph.D., she conducted research on uncertainty, effectuation, and institutional transformation. Specifically, she studied uncertainty as a context for entrepreneurship and effectuation as a mode of action and a method for corporate and policy change.

ORCID: 0000-0002-4746-633X

Aline Winckler Brufato

Ph.D. Candidate in Production Engineering at the COPPE of the Federal University of Rio de Janeiro (UFRJ)

Aline Winckler Brufato has a Master's Degree in Production Engineering from COPPE/UFRJ, with 20 years of experience as an entrepreneur. She is researcher and project executive at the Laboratory Technologies, Dialogues and Sites (LTDS) at COPPE/UFRJ. Aline led the organizing committee for "Effectuation in Rio" in December 2022, which headlined with Professor Saras Sarasvathy.

ORCID: 0000-0002-6379-4990

Moataz Darwish

Associate Professor of Practice, AUC School of Business, The American University in Cairo

Moataz Darwish is an Associate Professor of Practice at the American University in Cairo School of Business and a former senior executive at Shell Oil. Moataz is also an energy consultant, startups mentor, and angel investor. He is conducting doctorate research in the field of strategy and entrepreneurship to explore and compare the mental and business models of startups and big corporates.

ORCID: 0009-0002-7934-5345

Gonzalo Jiménez-Seminario

Founder, Proteus Management, Governance and Effectuation

Gonzalo Jiménez Seminario is a prominent figure in the field of governance, strategy, and family business. He holds a Doctorate in Governance from the University of Liverpool and is the Founding Partner at PROTEUS, a Strategy & Governance Consulting Firm in Chile. Additionally, he is a Professor of Governance, Strategy & Family Business at the Pontificia Universidad Católica de Chile.

ORCID: 0000-0002-4983-2583

Nobuo Kanai

Research Fellow, Design for ALL Co., Ltd.

Nobuo Kanai holds a Master of Science degree in Information Science and Technology from Tokyo Institute of Technology and a Master of Arts degree in Social Studies—Investment & Finance from the University of Exeter, UK. His extensive finance experience includes Nomura Asset Management, Schroder Investment Management, Goldman Sachs Asset Management, Barclays Capital Fund Solutions, and East Spring Investments.

ORCID: 0009-0005-6376-7553

Edmilson Lima

Professor, Master and Doctoral Programs in Administration—Universidade Nove de Julho, Brazil

Edmilson Lima has a Ph.D. in Administration (HEC Montreal, Canada); is professor and researcher (Master and Doctoral Program in Administration at Universidade Nove de Julho—UNINOVE, Brazil); Co-founder and scientific director (National Association for the Study of Entrepreneurship and Small Business Management—ANEGEPE); and scientific editor of the journal *PODIUM Sport, Leisure and Tourism Review.*

ORCID: 0000-0002-1833-8742

Rose Mary Almeida Lopes

Vice-President at ANEGEPE—National Association of Studies on Entrepreneurship and Small Business Management

Rose Mary Almeida Lopes is Vice-President at ANEGEPE, and Global Entrepreneurship Monitor (GEM) Project Manager. She has a Ph.D. in Social Psychology from São Paulo University (USP, Brazil). She was a professor and coordinator of Entrepreneurship activities at the business school ESPM/SP. She also co-leads the SaSS project dedicated to creating video-cases for teaching effectuation theory.

ORCID: 0000-0003-2359-7519

Isabella Nunes Pereira

Brazilian Official Institute of Statistics

Isabella Nunes Pereira is a Brazilian economist with a background in entrepreneurship from the Federal University of Rio de Janeiro, where she got her Ph.D. on the nature of business in favelas. With over 35 years of experience researching large companies at the Brazilian Official Institute of Statistics (IBGE), Isabella Nunes currently leads an unprecedented project studying entrepreneurship in small and medium-sized companies.

ORCID: 0000-0003-3920-3107

Javiera Salvo Porras

Executive

Javiera Salvo Porras is a professional with 12 years of experience at the CODELCO—Corporación Nacional del Cobre de Chile as well as other international mining corporations. Her expertise and background make her a valuable contributor to an entrepreneurship textbook, providing real-world insights into business leadership and management. Her experience in a prominent national corporation adds a unique perspective to the textbook's content.

Yuriko Sawatani

Professor, NUCB Business School

Yuriko Sawatani is professor at NUCB Business School, and director at Entrepreneurship Center. She received her Ph.D. at The University of Tokyo. After working at IBM Research, she received a professor position at Waseda University in 2013 and obtained the current position in April 2018. Her research investigates the design function of companies focusing on service design, innovation management, and entrepreneurship.

ORCID: 0000-0003-4921-3966

Philippe Silberzahn

Professor, Emlyon Business School

Philippe Silberzahn is Associate Professor at Emlyon Business School (France). His research interests lie at the intersection of strategy, innovation, and entrepreneurship. He studies how businesses deal with radical uncertainty. He has over 20 years of prior industry experience as an entrepreneur and CEO.

ORCID: 0000-0002-6608-5559

Patricia Cabero Tapia

Professor, Business School of Production and Competitiveness, Bolivian Catholic University

Patty Cabero is a specialist in information technologies and holds a Ph.D. in Economics from the Technical University of Berlin. Her research focuses on entrepreneurship, the development of digital skills, digital business ecosystems, and the gender gap in STEM. She enjoys teaching, mentoring, and working with tech companies.

ORCID: 0009-0008-2955-4839

Dominique Vian

Associate Professor, SKEMA Business School and Université Côte d'Azur

Dominique Vian is Associate Professor at Skema Business School, Doctor in Management Sciences, graduate from Télécom ParisTech, a specialist in entrepreneurial cognition, and author of six effectual methods that take advantage of the near decomposability property of complex systems. They can be used to identify the means and effects of any complex situation.

ORCID: 0000-0002-5783-3690

Kwabena Obiri Yeboah

Dr., Catholic University of Ghana

Kwabena Obiri Yeboah, Ph.D., is a researcher, effectual entrepreneur, and capacity builder driving sustainable development in Africa and Europe. With years of experience in academia and the startup ecosystem, he founded the Social Entrepreneurship Hub in Ghana, supporting entrepreneurs to transform innovative ideas into successful businesses addressing social and environmental challenges.

ORCID: 0000-0002-6413-3393

To learn more, visit: https://effectuation.org/EE3/co-creators or scan this code:

EFFECTUAL ENTREPRENEURSHIP

What Are You Waiting For?

Whether you're dreaming about starting a business, learning about entrepreneurship, or on the brink of creating a new opportunity right now, don't wait. Open this updated bestseller. Inside you'll find everything you need, including:

- A new, interactive, and popular way to learn about and practice entrepreneurship
- New practical exercises, questions, and activities for each step in your process
- Specific principles derived from the methods of expert entrepreneurs
- Updated and expanded (now 112) "Practically Speaking" case briefs of entrepreneurs across industries, locations (34 countries), and time
- Applications to social entrepreneurship, technology, and to the creation of opportunities in large enterprises
- Expanded (now 70) and updated "Research Roots": connections to current and foundational research in the field
- Significantly more women entrepreneurs are featured throughout the book
- Expanded chapter on "the ask"—strategies for initiating the process of co-creating with partners
- Expanded and completely re-built chapter on socially responsible entrepreneurship and social change
- Data that challenges conventional entrepreneurship wisdom
- A broader perspective about the science of entrepreneurship and the ways in which individuals shape their own situations

In this vibrant updated edition, you will find these ideas presented in a concise, modular, graphical form made popular in the first and second editions, perfect for those learning to be entrepreneurs or already in the thick of things.

If you want to learn about entrepreneurship in a way that emphasizes action, this new edition is vital reading.

If you have already launched your entrepreneurial career and are looking for new perspectives, and want to challenge the traditional approach and think effectually, this book is for you!

If you feel you are no longer creating anything novel or valuable in your day job, and you're wondering how to change things, this book is for you!

Anyone using entrepreneurial thinking to create the change they want to see in the world will find a wealth of thought-provoking material, expert advice, and practical techniques in these pages and on the accompanying website. Visit www.effectuation.org or scan this code:

PART I

What We Know About Entrepreneurs and Entrepreneurship

The five chapters that constitute the first part of the book present common myths about entrepreneurship and the associated and pragmatic questions that hold individuals back from starting a new venture—namely, "I don't have an idea, the money, I'm afraid to fail, I'm not the type, and I don't know where to start."

These fears arise from misconceptions similar to those ascribed to the pioneering explorers who set sail on the open seas several hundred years ago. History has stylized these early adventurers as visionary heroes, possessing superhuman abilities and extraordinary luck.

In fact, the process of drawing the map of the world is similar to the process an entrepreneur employs in starting a new venture. Both explorers and entrepreneurs do what they can with the things they have available. Both embrace surprise as an asset. And both create new maps that define our world for generations to come.

We encourage you to look past the glamorous retelling of entrepreneurial lore and instead focus on the systematic principles that experts follow—principles detailed in this book that you can apply yourself as you create your own map.

> Hold up a mirror and ask yourself what you are capable of doing, and what you really care about. Then take the initiative—don't wait for someone else to ask you to act.
>
> *Sylvia Earle*, marine biologist and explorer

DOI: 10.4324/9781003364016-1

CHAPTER 1

Figure 1.1 A mythical map to a sunny future on the Bahamas.

Roadmaps, Myths, and the Bahamas

In This Chapter

Popular entrepreneurship myths have created barriers that hold people back from becoming entrepreneurs.

Entrepreneurs are often seen as the daring visionaries of our business culture—conquering new markets, thriving on risk, and pursuing opportunities others simply could not see.

Comprehensive data, however, indicates that the mythical entrepreneur's roadmap is a fantasy.

Most great entrepreneurial stories don't involve business plans and huge venture capital investments. Most enduring companies actually start with an idea that has little relation to the venture which eventually emerges from hard work, experimentation, and co-creation.

DOI: 10.4324/9781003364016-2

ROADMAP TO SUCCESS?

If you are reading this, you are most likely looking for a roadmap to success. You are, of course, not alone. Most human beings whose basic needs are satisfied share this quest with you. Each may define success differently. For some it may be to make a meaningful difference in the world, for others it may be power and fame, and for yet others it might simply be independence, dignity, and the opportunity to achieve the creative potential within themselves. And, perhaps, make plenty of money in the process.

There are countless ways to define and achieve success, just as there are countless individuals. No matter how you personally define success, the principles of entrepreneurship you will learn from this book can help you achieve it. Entrepreneurship is about creating new paths that can become innovative roadmaps to creating benefit for those along the way.

As you read this book, we encourage you to actively consider your own roadmap. Yours may be based on existing paths that work well or new ones that reshape the terrain and perhaps even create new worlds altogether.

Regardless, we hope you are prepared for an adventure of mind-bending possibilities rooted in street-smart realities, all culled from rigorous academic research.

THE MYTHICAL ENTREPRENEUR

Entrepreneurs are heroes of our times. Arianna Huffington, Jack Ma, and Richard Branson are often seen as the daring visionaries of our business culture—conquering new markets, thriving on risk, and pursuing opportunities others simply could not see.

THE FAIRY TALE JOURNEY

How do they do it? Let's begin by sketching out a ten-step roadmap generally ascribed to the mythical entrepreneur, who:

1. Searches for a "new, high potential" opportunity
2. In a lightbulb moment, discovers something nobody has thought of before
3. Writes a business plan
4. Raises lots of investment money—especially from venture capitalists (VCs)
5. Hires a great team
6. Builds a product
7. Orchestrates a big launch
8. Achieves steady, or, better yet, hockey-stick growth
9. Sells the venture or has an initial public offering (IPO)
10. … and, finally, retires to the Bahamas

This all sounds great, but there's a problem: when we look at the startup histories of companies and the biographies of the entrepreneurs who founded them, this roadmap has no bearing on their actual course.

Consider just a few data points along this journey.

- One academic study found that only 28% of a sample of Inc. 500 firms had completed a formal business plan (Bhidé, 2000).
- Only about 0.1% of all startups are funded by venture capital (Lerner & Nanda, 2020).
- A detailed calculation by the company Lending Tree is based on data from the United States Census Bureau's "2016 Survey of Entrepreneurs" and found that the median startup costs across all industries was under 30,000 US dollars. The costs in mainstream industries, however, range from 10,000 US dollars for professional, technical, and scientific services to 94,000 US dollars for accommodation and food services.

These data suggest that the mythical entrepreneur's roadmap is a fantasy. But if many great entrepreneurial stories don't involve business plans and huge venture capital investments, how do entrepreneurs actually create enduring companies?

For more than 20 years, we, along with many collaborators around the world, have been engaged in research to answer that question and identify specific techniques people actually use to create valuable new firms. The results of our investigations point to the principles detailed in this book. The results challenge us to rethink several key aspects about how great entrepreneurship happens. The core insight is that anyone who wants to be an entrepreneur can (learn to) be an entrepreneur.

THE REAL ENTREPRENEUR

Let's put the popular media aside for a moment and reconsider the waypoints on the real, as opposed to the fantasy, path to success. As we examine each, see if you can begin to diagram for yourself the real entrepreneurial journey.

Search or Divine Inspiration

The fantasy path started with an entrepreneur searching for an opportunity and having a lightbulb moment. Which means that the opportunity could be found by anyone smart enough or alert enough. It means our mythical entrepreneur's clients would recognize the solution when she presented it to them. It also means that our entrepreneur could assess the value of and calculate the risks in the opportunity when she discovered it.

But imagine trying to predict the pathway and returns of creating a new "airline we hope you love" in an industry which has been notoriously unprofitable. Or creating an opinion and news website to compete with the biggest names. Or building an online store in a country where credit cards were few and far between. Or two blind friends building a PC-based screen reader from home.

Only with the benefit of hindsight, Virgin Air, Huffington Post, Alibaba, NVDA, and countless others appear brilliant. Only with the benefit of hindsight is it also possible to distinguish those successful businesses from the spectacular failures of Theranos (never delivered on promised medical technology), Pebble (an early smartwatch), or Quibi (video streaming service that raised 1.8 billion US dollars in equity).

Furthermore, as you will discover in Chapter 2, there is little magic in the initial idea anyway. Ideas are cheap and plentiful. And because most ventures start with an idea that has little relation to the company which subsequently emerges, success is in the active perspiration, not the divine inspiration.

In reality, many companies you know are based on ideas that were co-created by the entrepreneur and her partners; ideas not anticipated even by the entrepreneur who started the venture; ideas that might have looked dubious in the form of an initial business plan.

> Genius is one percent inspiration, ninety-nine percent perspiration.
>
> *Thomas Edison*, inventor

Figure 1.2

Money

To shake you off your journey through mythology, we investigate the actual data on new venture financing in Chapter 3. The National Venture Capital Association reports that in 2021, there were 10,873 venture capital deals made in the US, with a total of almost 326 billion US dollars in venture capital invested (National Venture Capital Association, 2022).

Meanwhile, the number of new businesses started in the United States in 2021 was 5.4 million (US Census Bureau, 2022). A little quick math shows that only about 0.2% of new firms received venture funding in 2021, while the vast majority of US entrepreneurs (99.8%) managed to start a new business without investment money from venture capitalists.

Failure

Nobody sets out to fail, yet despite every effort, some ventures don't make it. Coming back to the legendary Richard Branson, even he is not as invincible as you might imagine. Having 16 businesses fail along the way to creating his constantly evolving entrepreneurial empire, Branson says, "Business opportunities are like buses, there's always another one coming."

So as obvious as it may feel to hire a team, scale up operations, and take big chances on a big idea, even Richard Branson manages things conservatively enough so that he is always ready for the next bus.

Barriers

We share the roadmap and its flaws with you not to pick on venture capitalists or even Sir Richard Branson, but to shed light on the barriers that can keep prospective entrepreneurs from starting a new venture. As you compare the mythical roadmap with the data summarized here and detailed in the chapters in this section, it is easy to see where those barriers come from. And it is also easy to see why they are false.

More specifically, if you are not starting your dream venture because you think:

"I don't have a good idea."

… you now know that this false assessment came from the mythical entrepreneur, but real entrepreneurs simply start with something doable, then iterate and co-create until they generate an opportunity worth pursuing, as we discuss in Chapter 2.

If you think:

"I don't have the money"

… you only get this feeling from stories about firms securing millions of US dollars in venture funding. These are the ones that make the news, perhaps because they are so rare. Most real entrepreneurs start firms with little or no capital. More information on the truth about investments in new ventures is in Chapter 3.

If you believe:

"I'm not the type"

… you have bought into the hype about superhero entrepreneurs, who, like unicorns, actually don't exist. Read the many entrepreneurial stories in this book, which describe what passions, personalities, and perseverance successful everyday entrepreneurs demonstrate.

And you believe:

"I don't know where to start"

… you will see we wrote this book for you. Because once we break through the barriers that hold people back from starting a new venture, the idea of taking the plunge into entrepreneurship (Chapter 4) is not so scary. In fact, you can learn how to get going. Effectuation offers tools to do just that: a simple, pragmatic approach to starting up.

And finally, if your worry is:

"I'm afraid to fail"

… you will find both good company in failure and good learning from failure. Described in more detail in Chapter 5, you will understand that failure is part of the entrepreneurial process. It is not a question of whether ventures fail (as some do), but how you set yourself up to survive and learn from venture failure to become a successful entrepreneur.

The following stories of regular people finding their own unique entrepreneurial pathway provide a contrast to the mythical ten-step process and demonstrate the inherent messiness (and adventure) of the entrepreneurial method.

The Bahamas

We have addressed or will address the first nine steps in the mythical roadmap with data and examples to show why that map leads people to imagine artificial barriers to starting a company. But what about the tenth step?

… and, finally, retires to the Bahamas

Retirement isn't really the topic of this book. Everyone's journey takes them to a different place. For some that place may be a warm sandy beach in the Bahamas. But not for many entrepreneurs. There is such a deep sense of personal satisfaction that comes from creating your own venture that it also creates the serial entrepreneur—that person who creates multiple, perhaps even dozens, of ventures over the course of a lifetime.

Of all the myths around entrepreneurship, the stories of the individual organizing her next business while she is selling—or even running—her current one seems one of the most accurate.

TAKEAWAY: ENTREPRENEURSHIP IS ACCESSIBLE

We will not advocate that everyone should become an entrepreneur. Our purpose is far more specific: to cast light on the realities of starting a new venture so those people who want to become entrepreneurs understand the facts. And while more complete information may make people more or less likely to start a new venture, those who do understand the facts should have a better sense of the real barriers, heuristics, and practicalities associated with entrepreneurship.

Also, while you may not actually want to become an entrepreneur, sometimes you may have to—because life is uncertain. Entrepreneurship is the ultimate backup option. And learning it makes it available for you whenever you or someone you care about needs it.

■ ■ ■

Research Roots

WHAT IS ENTREPRENEURSHIP, REALLY?

One issue that has caused a lot of debate among entrepreneurship researchers over the years is the question of "What is entrepreneurship, really?" If you do it, what are you doing? And if you study it, what are you studying? What is the central phenomenon?

Though this issue may seem silly, it isn't atypical; it turns out that biologists have a surprisingly hard time defining "life" and physicists have a hard time agreeing on what "matter" really is. Perhaps understandably then scholars have had some difficulty defining precisely what entrepreneurship is—and isn't.

One way to tackle the question of what entrepreneurship is (really) is to focus on what entrepreneurs do—the activities they undertake. This is how we approach it in this textbook. The emphasis is on the actions and behaviors of entrepreneurs. One key entrepreneurial activity is creating new ventures. Other key activities include developing new markets, discovering and creating opportunities, and enabling new ways of doing things inside corporations.

An important implication of defining entrepreneurship in terms of activities is that it shifts the focus away from seeing entrepreneurs as special people with particular personality characteristics. Instead, we can focus on the central activities that are involved in entrepreneurship and look at how these activities can be learned and done well (Gartner, 1988).

Practically Speaking

Asma Khan: From Arranged Bride to Social Force

Who could have predicted that a newly married woman homesick for her native India and unable to cook would end up becoming one of the United Kingdom's most beloved celebrity chefs?

Asma Khan is a British-Indian chef who has made a name for herself in the culinary world. She is the founder of Darjeeling Express, an acclaimed Indian restaurant in London, and the first British chef to be featured in the Netflix series *Chef's Table*.

Homesick for Flavors of Home

Khan's journey is extraordinary because she began her new life in London as an arranged bride, arriving there completely homesick and unable to cook. She was thrust into a foreign culture with no connections and no knowledge of Western cuisine.

Khan did not begin with a grand plan to become a successful chef. Rather, she began by learning how to cook to combat homesickness. Her desire to recreate the flavors of home led her to culinary experimentation, using family recipes to gradually hone her skills.

Word got around and Asma started hosting modest supper clubs in her home, where she could receive feedback on her dishes. One important aspect of these supper clubs was that Khan employed an all-women team of cooks, many of whom were homemakers like her. It was a low-risk approach, which allowed her to explore her newfound interest in cooking while getting to meet people.

A Turning Point: The Visit of a Food Critic

A crucial moment in Khan's journey occurred when a well-known food critic attended one of her supper clubs. The positive review from the critic helped boost her profile in London's culinary scene, leading to increased attention and recognition. The success and growing demand encouraged her to take the next step: low-risk, temporary pop-up restaurants at various locations across London.

Khan's now famous Darjeeling Express started as a pop-up restaurant and in 2015 became a permanent fixture in what is called the "epicenter of culture and lifestyle": London's trendy West End. Khan continues to employ an all-female kitchen staff, many of whom had no formal culinary training, echoing her own journey.

Impact Beyond Food

The story of Asma Khan demonstrates that grand plans and massive investments are not necessary. In fact, homesickness and longing combined with her family's recipes, experimentation, and hard work with others willing to work together all served to carve out a unique niche in London's culinary scene.

Practically Speaking *(continued)*

Beyond the restaurant's culinary achievements, Khan has been recognized for her social impact, including mentoring women and her philanthropic efforts in India. Darjeeling Express has continued to thrive, and Khan's influence has expanded through appearances in media, such as the Netflix series *Chef's Table*.

Her journey also challenges traditional gender roles and cultural norms, showcasing how determination and creativity can overcome significant barriers.

To learn more, visit: https://effectuation.org/EE3/asma or scan Figure 1.3.

Figure 1.3

Practically Speaking

Howard Schultz and His Rising Star

Murky Brew

Perhaps over a grandé mocha nonfat latte, it is useful to consider the insight that created today's fabulously successful Starbucks.

Interestingly, the alternatives suggested by the mythical journey do not get us there: market analysis cannot be credited with helping Howard Schultz discover the opportunity in Starbucks. Daily per capita coffee consumption in the United States had declined from 3.1 cups in the 1960s to 2 cups when Schultz was assembling the ingredients for Starbucks.

Nor did a functional prototype point to the opportunity. The original Starbucks, founded in 1971, was a shop that sold beans, tea, and supplies, but not coffee by the cup.

Furthermore, Shultz's vision of bringing the Italian espresso bar format to the United States has little relationship to a Starbucks store today. In fact, when Schultz joined Starbucks in 1982 as head of marketing, he was unable to talk the founders into serving drinks, so he built his own coffee bar and called it Il Giornale (merged with Starbucks in 1987).

The Daily Grind

In its original form, Il Giornale struggled. Customers did not like nonstop opera music. They wanted chairs. Some asked for flavored coffee. A menu printed mainly in Italian was inaccessible. The baristas' bow ties were untidy.

Schultz adjusted in response to those customers who chose to buy from him and those employees who chose to work for him, providing chairs and playing more varied music. The baristas stopped wearing ties.

Practically Speaking *(continued)*

"We fixed a lot of mistakes," Schultz said, although for many years he chose not to grant the request for flavored coffee. After all, it was his venture too, not only the customers'.

Figure 1.4 This type of greeting at morning coffee was too much for Il Giornale customers.

Making Your Own Cup

So, the story of Starbucks, like the story of many enterprises, is full of stakeholder (customers, investors, employees, strategic partners, and of course, the founders themselves) input and entrepreneurial action. This is the insight from the story of Starbucks, and it highlights two elements of the real entrepreneurial journey.

First, based on market information at the time, Starbucks was not an opportunity waiting to be found. Had Schultz not taken the series of actions to create and shape the firm, there might not be a mainstream market for premium coffee cafés today.

Second, it informs you what actually needs doing. If opportunities are created, as opposed to found, then taking action is more important than doing research. So, stop looking and start doing!

To learn more, visit: https://effectuation.org/EE3/starbucks or scan Figure 1.5.

Figure 1.5

Practically Speaking

Arianna Huffington: A Woman With New(s) Perspectives

As much as we don't know what the future will bring, looking at one's past can help you take your next steps, which might even become a new pathway. This is true for Arianna Huffington, a high-profile commentator in the internet age.

Once you know that she is the daughter of a newspaper publisher in Greece, it seems perfectly reasonable that she would go on to study in England and become the first foreign-born president of the highly respected Cambridge Union, a debating society.

Arianna later moved to California, where she married a conservative politician. Her journalism and debating skills were deployed in print and broadcast media, not least supporting her husband's candidacy for the United States Senate.

Making sense of local, national, and world events shaped Huffington's perspective, shifting her from the conservative end of the spectrum more to the center. She even ran as an independent candidate for governor of California. Not having made it into the Governor's Mansion, but wanting to have wider influence, she co-founded the Huffington Post in 2005.

Practically Speaking *(continued)*

To address the challenge of content creation, Huffington leveraged her existing connections in the media industry to build a team of content contributors. This meant that literally hundreds of guest authors were featured each week, making for an attractive and diverse collection of ideas, perspectives, and stories, many of which linked to mainstream media outlets.

She was on to something, so much so that it was acquired by the media giant AOL for 315 million US dollars in 2011.

Huffington's journey was not an easy one, as her own words show:

> My own wake-up call came in 2007, two years into building The Huffington Post, when I collapsed from exhaustion and burnout, breaking my cheekbone, and waking up in a pool of blood. After going around to various doctors, what I learned was that nothing was wrong—except everything was wrong. "Is this what success looks like?" I asked myself. This was the moment when the seed of Thrive Global was planted.
>
> (*Huffington*, 2016)

We see the interweaving of Huffington's pathways of her media company and her dealing with the "wake up call" of a breakdown to focus more on health and well-being. So, when it was time to move on from the Huffington Post, the pump was primed to start a new venture focused on health and wellness called Thrive Global.

Arianna Huffington couldn't have known as a little girl that one day she would be a respected international voice. She didn't follow a mythical plan, but rather did what all entrepreneurs do: start small, experiment with and combine different ideas, adjust along the way, and learn from setbacks and surprises.

To learn more, visit: https://effectuation.org/EE3/arianna or scan Figure 1.6.

Figure 1.6

Practically Speaking

The Blind Leading the Blind

Jamie Teh laughs when he remembers being with his friend, Mick Curran, at summer camp, referring to it as "the blind leading the blind."

Jamie is not being cruel; he is stating a fact. Jamie lost his sight as a baby and Mick had limited vision as a child and later lost it completely as a teenager. That was a huge blow for Mick, who became depressed. He describes how he moved on:

> I think what brought me out of my depression was identifying and throwing myself into skills that I already had and enjoyed doing. So, when I was 16, I decided to go back to music camp and that's where I ran into Jamie.
>
> (Australian Broadcasting Corporation, 2023)

Practically Speaking *(continued)*

Shared Problem Becomes Shared Solution

The friendship blossomed based on their shared love for music and technology, just like so many teenagers. But unlike most teenagers, they encountered significant hurdles.

> For a blind person to use a computer you need a screen reader which is essentially software which reads the text on the computer screen in synthetic speech. That screen reading software costs a lot of money—it was between a thousand and two thousand dollars.
>
> (Australian Broadcasting Corporation, 2023)

Mick had always had an interest in computers and asked his father to read him a programming book from cover to cover. With that, Mick set out to solve the expensive screen reader problem.

> My overall dream is that I can pick up a computer and use it as soon as I get home and so we designed software—that we've made free—which allows blind and vision impaired people to access computers.
>
> I was on a blind pension [and] I wanted to try my hand at writing free screen reading software. I named the software NVDA which stands for non-visual desktop access.
>
> (Australian Broadcasting Corporation, 2023)

The Solution Goes Global

Mick and Jamie created a registered charity to house the project and protect the NVDA product. Their work gained recognition from some big names such as the Mozilla Foundation and Microsoft.

But they truly began to understand the importance of the project when they started getting emails from people overseas asking if they could translate it and use it in their country. Today Mick and Jamie's screen reader is used by 275,000 people in 175 countries.

> I'm very proud that I can give back or should say "give forward" the gift that I had been given: Firstly of life, to be honest, and the chance to succeed.
>
> (Australian Broadcasting Corporation, 2023)

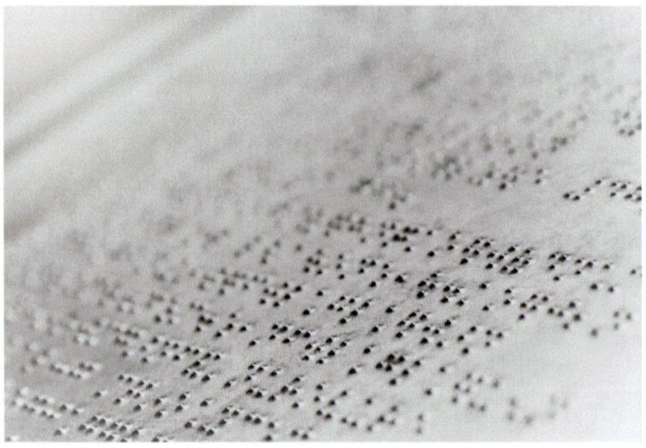

Figure 1.7 Braille enables vision impaired to read physical text and NVDA is the equivalent for computer screens reading out text.

Mick's brother, Chris, is not surprised:

> Watching this over the last however many years just completely blows my mind but doesn't surprise me. No matter what obstacle is thrown in along the way, he's gonna get over it. That's just what Mick does and that's what he's always done.
>
> (Australian Broadcasting Corporation, 2023

Mick and Jamie demonstrate that you don't have to see the path before you (or even see at all!) to move forward and make a difference.

To learn more, visit: https://effectuation.org/EE3/blind or scan Figure 1.8.

Figure 1.8

So What?

Many of the issues that hold people back from starting a new venture are not based in reality. As a result, potential entrepreneurs may be distracted from the real issues, or might be hesitating for no good reason at all.

Think It Through

Beyond the immediate topic of this chapter, think about the following questions:

- If real entrepreneurs aren't working through the ten steps in the mythical roadmap at the start of this chapter, what are the real steps associated with creating a new venture?
- What do entrepreneurs really do each day?
- If you had to start a venture right now, what are the first three things you'd do? Write them down and keep reading.

What Now?

- Identify what you believe are the three biggest things holding you back from launching your new venture. Look within each to find ways around, under, and over it.
- Identify one thing that, if true, would immediately make you start. Are you thinking lack of money? Think again!
- See for yourself. Go talk to an entrepreneur or three; ask them about their path and how they started.
- On your path through this book, will it be helpful to read Chapters 2–5 about barriers to getting started, or are you ready to skip to Part II to get into the details of entrepreneurial thinking?

REFERENCES

Albert, M. (2023). Arianna Huffington. In *Encyclopedia Britannica*. https://www.britannica.com/biography/Arianna-Huffington

Australian Broadcasting Corporation. (2023). Best friends don't want a cent from their big tech idea. This is why | Australian Story. In *Australian Story*. Australian Broadcasting Corporation. https://www.youtube.com/watch?v=jwHbXh3WzSw

Bhidé, A. (2000). *The Origin and Evolution of New Businesses*. Oxford University Press.

Gartner, W. B. (1988). Who is the entrepreneur? Is the wrong question. *American Journal of Small Business*, *12*, 11–32. https://doi.org/10.1177/104225878801200040

Gompers, P., & Lerner, J. (2001). The venture capital revolution. *The Journal of Economic Perspectives*, *15*(2), 145–168. https://doi.org/10.1257/jep.15.2.145

Huffington, A. (2016). *From Arianna Huffington: Welcome to Thrive Global*. https://medium.com/thrive-global/arianna-huffington-welcome-to-thrive-global-bbdaea4aa455

Lending Tree. (2023). *Startup Costs by Industry*. https://www.lendingtree.com/business/startup-costs-by-industry/

Lerner, J., & Nanda, R. (2020). Venture capital's role in financing innovation: What we know and how much we still need to learn. *The Journal of Economic Perspectives*, *34*(3), 237–261. https://doi.org/10.1257/jep.34.3.237

National Venture Capital Association. (2022). Venture Monitor Q4 2022. https://nvca.org/pitchbook-nvca-venture-monitor/

Rauch, A., & Frese, M. (2007). Let's put the person back into entrepreneurship research: A meta-analysis on the relationship between business owners' personality traits, business creation, and success. *European Journal of Work and Organizational Psychology*, *16*(4), 353–385. https://doi.org/10.1080/13594320701595438

US Census Bureau (Ed.). (2022). *Not Seasonally Adjusted Business Applications [Units]—2021*. https://www.census.gov/econ/currentdata/

Figure 2.1 Venture ideas are as plentiful as stars on a clear night—and everyone can see them.

CHAPTER 2

Good Ideas Are Everywhere

In This Chapter

Many people who want to start a venture say they haven't yet because they don't have a good idea. The fact is that ideas are cheap, plentiful, and constantly emerging. It's what you do with them that matters.

It is important to emphasize that there is no such thing as a "good" idea upfront—there are only ideas we implement and ones we don't. A good idea can be wasted, just like a bad idea can be turned into an opportunity.

Successful entrepreneurs and experienced investors state that there is only one way to determine whether a given idea is a good business opportunity: go ahead and give it a try.

Finally, an opportunity is transformed into a viable business through commitment.

DOI: 10.4324/9781003364016-3

One clear fact emerges from research into entrepreneurial expertise and initial phases of new ventures—it is not possible to know with any certainty whether an idea will turn out to be a good business opportunity.

Successful entrepreneurs and experienced investors state that there is only one way to determine whether a given idea is a good business opportunity: go ahead and give it a try. Implement it creatively with very low levels of investment and either find real customers who are willing to buy the product or service at a reasonable price or locate partners willing to commit resources to the venture early on—or, ideally, both.

Understandably, most first-time entrepreneurs, especially those who have good job market prospects, worry a lot about finding the "right" opportunity—hence the concern about waiting for an idea that is "good."

What is a good idea? Where do ideas come from? Who decides whether an idea is good? When and how do you recognize if an idea is feasible?

As you think about these questions, consider the company Medtronic. In 1949, inspired by the impact of electricity on life, as depicted in the 1931 movie *Frankenstein*, Earl Bakken founded the medical devices firm. But it was a long time until he conceived the cardiac pacemaker, the company's first breakthrough product.

Bakken spent his first eight years working as a medical equipment repair technician. In 1957, after years of interactions with doctors and the medical industry, he began developing the pacemaker. Even then, the device was much more a collection of knowledge from his repair work than a flash of visionary genius.

Once the device was introduced, a medical industry analyst organization predicted a world market for pacemakers of, at most, 10,000 units—not per year—but 10,000 units in total. Although the analysts considered that a small market, Bakken and his team rejoiced—they were selling fewer than 100 units a year at the time! Today, Medtronic is a 31.2 billion US dollar business (FY2023 revenue) and a leader in the medical devices field.

So, set aside your worries about having a good idea. Instead, work on whatever ideas you have.

Where Do Ideas Come From?

In theory:

- Patent Office Gazette
- Government (NASA, CERN)
- Technology transfer
- Trade shows
- Doctoral dissertations
- Invention expositions
- Brainstorming
- Industry experts, including futurists

In practice:

- A personal satisfaction or dissatisfaction
- Market knowledge from prior job
- Hobbies
- Other people
- Acquisition of a company or product already launched
- The news
- Rejects from employer or other company
- Customers

Useful Contacts for Generating Ideas

- Lawyers
- Other entrepreneurs
- Accountants
- Venture capitalists
- Bankers
- R&D professionals
- Patent attorneys
- Purchasing agents
- Businesspeople
- Salespeople or distributors
- Trade associations
- Executives
- Potential customers

IDEAS ARE A DIME A DOZEN

One simple way to come up with an idea is to think of things we like and things we don't like, things we wish we had, things we would like to get rid of, things we care about, and so on. In fact, like the queen in *Alice in Wonderland*, who came up with six "impossible things" before breakfast, most of us can come up with six new venture ideas before going to bed tonight. But we don't necessarily know what to do with them. Or even whether we want to do anything with them at all.

It is important to reiterate here that there is no such thing as a "good" idea upfront—there are only ideas we implement and ones we don't. A good idea can be wasted, just like a bad idea can be turned into an opportunity.

Think of successful ventures you know and where their ideas came from. Throughout this book, there are examples of ventures that grew out of mundane, even silly, ideas. Ventures like Agilyx and unsicht-Bar were formed on top of things we might label as negatives—trash and disability.

IDEAS EVOLVE

Not only are ideas everywhere; new ideas are constantly emerging in response to changes around us. Heraclitus, a Greek philosopher, pointed this out thousands of years ago with his quote "The only constant in life is change."

It is therefore logical that some companies have had enduring success by changing their business to take advantage of evolving opportunities. In fact, there are many examples of companies that moved away from their original business idea: some prominent examples are given in Table 2.1. What we see in the stories of these firms is the relative importance of the entrepreneur and the action over the idea.

With the rate of technological change increasing, pressure has increased on companies to adapt their business model to changing circumstances, as is shown in Table 2.1.

While it seems perfectly logical that Netflix got its start capitalizing on the move away from video rental locations, their solution of physically mailing out DVDs also wouldn't last once video streaming technology became mainstream.

And Marvel's move from just the printed page to moving pictures is not without precedent if we consider the effect television had on newspaper sales.

Amazon's evolution is less obvious and came from the expertise it built up in expanding its online store. Offering cloud computing services is akin to renting out the spare bedroom, but in Amazon's case, its cloud business is now a freestanding entity: a way for people to build stores within Amazon and is not just a way for Amazon to make some extra cash.

These examples remind us that ideas are everywhere, so what separates "just an idea" from successful ventures? We'll look at that next.

Table 2.1 Prominent Examples of Radical Business Model Change

Company	Where they started	Transformation
Tiffany & Co.	Started as a provider of stationery in 1837.	Not until 1853 did the firm shift over to jewelry.
Colgate	Soap, candles, and starch were the first products.	Founded in 1806, Colgate did not make toothpaste for nearly 70 years.
Nokia	Since its founding in 1865, Nokia has been in industries from rubber to paper.	More than 100 years after founding, in the 1980s, Nokia started to make phones. It sold its phone business to Microsoft in 2014 and now focuses on mobile networks.
Hasbro	Textile remnants were the first offering from the Hassenfeld Brothers.	Toys were not offered until 1952, some 30 years after founding.
John Deere	Started as a blacksmith, making plows.	A full range of farm products, but best known for making its iconic green tractors.

Recent Examples of Business Model Evolution

Company	Where they started	Evolution
Apple	Began as one of the first personal computer companies.	Today Apple is one of the best-known brands for consumer electronics, such as smartphones, tablets, and wearables, which tap into its proprietary music streaming and software marketplaces.
Marvel	Started as a comic book publisher.	Marvel has evolved into a multimedia entertainment company. Its expansion beyond comics began in the 1990s with the launch of its Marvel Studios division, which has since produced a series of blockbuster films based on Marvel's iconic characters.
Netflix	Began as a DVD-by-mail rental service as an alternative to physical video rental locations.	Today Netflix is a global leader in streaming media which produces its own content as well as licensing content from other creators. It sent out its last DVD by mail in 2023.
IBM	Started as a computer hardware and services company selling to blue chip (major) companies.	IBM is now focused on software and services and has since become a leader in areas such as artificial intelligence and cloud computing.
Amazon	Started as an online bookseller in the late 1990s.	In addition to being a major online marketplace for all types of goods, Amazon is one of the top global cloud computing companies. It has even extended its reach to healthcare and entertainment production.

THE IDEA-TO-VENTURE FORMULA

So now that you know divine revelation is not the source of opportunities, where do viable ventures come from? In this section, we outline the kinds of transformations an idea goes through on its way to becoming something valuable.

You may well find more steps in your own process. But this is the point where you begin to create your own roadmap. So perhaps the steps here offer initial waypoints—the beginnings of how you will make sense of how this book can help you fill in the details of your roadmap.

We start the idea-to-venture formula by acknowledging that ideas are a good and important first step. Viable ventures often start with an idea. And ideas generally start with a transformation of the means you already have.

IDEA = ANYTHING + YOU

But we also know that ideas are plentiful and commonplace. It is action that turns an idea into a valuable opportunity:

OPPORTUNITY = IDEA + ACTION

At this point, we need to be clear. Gathering information does not count as action. Action is proposing a deal with a client. Action is getting a supplier to assemble a prototype. Action is asking a co-founder to join the business. Action goes beyond observation and calculation to invoke transformation, manipulation, fabrication—it's a function of interaction with the world:

ACTION = FUNCTION (INTERACTION) ON MONEY, PRODUCT, PARTNERS …

Finally, opportunity is transformed into a viable business through commitment. Commitments result in revenue, hiring, and production lines starting up at suppliers:

VIABLE VENTURE = OPPORTUNITY + COMMITMENT

When putting together all the pieces of this formula, starting with you, it is important to see that at every point, there exists the possibility that your actions combined with the means and commitments of others may slightly or significantly redirect the course of your venture. Most enduring firms start very differently from where they end up. Their founders repeatedly act to create more valuable opportunities than would have been expected from their original ideas.

ON THE IMPORTANCE OF COMMITMENT

We will look at partnerships, asking, and commitments in greater detail in Chapters 14 and 15, but there is at least one thing you need to consider at the outset: if you can't find anyone besides yourself who thinks it's a good enough idea that they are willing to make some kind of commitment (time, money, etc.), maybe it's not a good idea. And don't be too easy on yourself or your idea. There is no such thing as tentative commitment.

But how long do you look for others to commit to your idea before dropping it? That question depends on how much you can afford to lose (more on this in Chapter 12). Maybe you can afford to wait for years for your idea to come of age. Early investors in video-conferencing technology waited over two decades. Sometimes ideas, especially technology-based ideas, such as certain kinds of renewable energy today, stew on the back burner for a long time. Affordable loss puts a limit on how much time you commit.

And other people's commitments shape what venture you end up building.

TAKEAWAY: EVERYBODY HAS A GOOD IDEA

Eric von Hippel (1988) at MIT examined the sources of successful invention in large corporations. He found that most new ideas that turned out to be profitable product lines came not out of research and development departments, but out of customer inputs such as complaints and suggestions gathered by support and service departments. More recently, social media has provided an ideal platform to collect such ideas in real-time.

The ability to act, learn, and change is critical as well. FedEx began with the idea of delivering spare parts, and RealNetworks began as an interactive television channel. Most successful entrepreneurs find that it makes sense to abandon the ideas they first perceived and be willing to change their "vision" in response to feedback and stakeholder negotiations, both in the early stages of their venture and as they grow.

Sticking close to who you are, what you know, and who you know tells you not only what to do, but also what not to do. The problem with most novice entrepreneurs is not that they do not have great new ideas for ventures—it's that they have too many ideas and are too excited by them. In their excitement, they often linger on the ideas and don't move into action to gather commitments.

Inexperienced entrepreneurs, especially those with resources, feel tempted to expand production too soon, or jump into too many new market segments all at once. Even more so, if they have some initial success, it is easy to feel prescient (i.e. believe they can predict the future) as well as omnipotent (i.e. believe they are invincible). But good ideas are often a lot less glamorous than that.

Robert Reiss, founder of R&R, a company that brought games like Trivial Pursuit to the United States, once said:

> **People think they shouldn't go into business unless they have a blockbuster idea that's going to change the world. It doesn't really work that way. There are few new blockbuster ideas. There are just mundane kinds of ideas. You do something better than someone else. You take an existing thing and you add a new twist. It is just like Scrabble. You take an existing word, you put one letter on it and you get credit for the whole word—your letter plus the whole word.**

Implicit in Reiss' statement is that you have to be in the game in the first place. You have to be playing Scrabble in order to be in a position to add that extra letter which makes a great venture.

Research Roots

INNOVATION ADOPTION

Everett Rogers (2003) identified five attributes of an innovation that are highly predictive of whether it will be adopted. They include:

- Relative advantage. Is the innovation perceived as better than what it replaces?
- Compatibility. Is the innovation consistent with the values, experiences, and needs of potential adopters?
- Complexity. Is the innovation perceived as difficult to use?
- Trialability. Is the user able to experiment with the innovation?
- Observability. Are the results of an innovation visible to users?

Whether or not you like the words, these research-based tests provide a good common-sense basis for making an idea more likely to gain adoption.

Practically Speaking

Turning a Hobby Into a Business

When John Vence sent his son Michael off to college, he equipped the young man with a loft bed to maximize tight space in the campus dormitory. Word of mouth soon spread, and Vence was delivering loft beds hundreds of miles from his home in Horseheads, New York. Demand became so great that Vence investigated what was necessary to ship his beds nationally and turned the hobby into a full-time business. Today, College Bed Lofts employs 18 people, making and selling about 5,000 unfinished wood lofts a year to customers coast to coast.

To learn more, visit: https://effectuation.org/EE3/hobby or scan Figure 2.3.

Figure 2.2

Figure 2.3

Practically Speaking

Old Godmother Spices Things Up

Tao Huabi's remarkable story began in an unremarkable rural village in the Chinese province of Guizhou with an everyday product (chili sauce). Simply by doing normal things—taking action, experimenting, and integrating customer feedback—today, Tao Huabi is one of the richest women in China, thanks to her famous Lao Gan Ma ("Old Godmother") chili sauce.

A Hot Opportunity!

In 1989, Tao was a widow selling rice, tofu, and cold noodles as a street vendor to provide for her two sons. Over time she noticed that customers really enjoyed her chili sauce, which she served to spice up the bland noodles and tofu. This led her to launching the Lao Gan Ma branded chili sauce in 1996. Tao turned watchful observation of customer preferences into a business opportunity.

"One of the most-striking things about her business is that she was able to control and manage the sourcing of the product," says Dali Yang, professor of China's political economy at the University of Chicago. "The company gained a significant reputation because she priced the product very inexpensively. It's very accessible to the average consumer, in fact, to low-income people as well."

Until only recently, a bottle of Lao Gan Ma sauce cost less than 2 US dollars in China. No wonder it is particularly popular among students seeking a quick meal of steamed rice and a dab of the "Old Godmother."

The Spicy Taste of Success

Tao's success is shared in her hometown, with her company reportedly signing supply contracts with 180,000 local chili farmers and hiring thousands of workers in her factories. It is no surprise that this has led to praise from local authorities.

Lao Gan Ma chili sauce is not just a beloved household staple, but also a symbol of China's entrepreneurial spirit, and Tao is hailed as the embodiment of the Chinese success story.

Tao Huabi's journey from an illiterate widow in a rural village to becoming one of the richest women in China is living proof that a successful business idea can come from anywhere. And the taste of success need not always be sweet. Sometimes spicy noodles do the trick.

To learn more, visit: https://effectuation.org/EE3/godmother or scan Figure 2.4.

Figure 2.4

Practically Speaking

Focus on the Food, Just Not With Your Eyes

Ever been on a blind date? Most people say it's simultaneously scary and exciting, and it's always memorable. Which is also what people say about Axel Rudolph's unsicht-Bar, a small Cologne eatery run by the blind where patrons enjoy wine, cuisine, and conversation in the pitch dark. Even the glow of a mobile phone is not permitted in this establishment. Diners are attended by blind waiters/guides who describe the food in terms of both its preparation and its location on the plate.

Success Without Looking

Since its opening in 2002, unsicht-Bar has won acclaim from critics and restaurateurs alike. In addition to the novel yet empathic experience of spending the evening with someone who can't see, eliminating the sense of sight intensifies the rest of the senses so that unsicht-Bar's simple fare (the chef seasons with only salt, pepper, garlic, onions, and herbs) comes alive in a way you might never have tasted before. According to Rudolph: "You smell better, you are more receptive to differences in texture, consistency and temperature … it's a holistic experience."

unsicht-Bar's popularity led Rudolph to open additional locations and has brought an intriguing innovation to the restaurant industry.

Vision Inversion

Rudolph's venture embodies a powerful insight into the source of many successful innovations. Blindness is generally considered a liability—a handicap. Rudolph inverts it. unsicht-Bar makes blindness a point of differentiation and a basis for advantage. It takes a negative and makes it a positive.

Seeing Upside Down

Inversions like this are everywhere. Take Post-it Notes. Who would have thought you could develop a blockbuster product from a glue that wasn't very sticky? Or consider violent video games. Criticized for their disruptive psychological effects on minors, games like Full Spectrum Warrior are now the basis for an emerging software market in treating war veterans with post-traumatic stress disorder. Retro styles are an inversion of the idea that clothing goes out of fashion. And celebrities who drive inexpensive, compact Toyota Priuses invert the notion that wealth and prestige are embodied in an enormous luxury car.

Figure 2.5 Seeing is not believing, tasting is believing!

An Eye to Opportunity

The next time you feel you are on a blind date with destiny, look around you. Look for things that evoke a negative response. And think about transforming them into a positive basis for a new venture. For, as experienced entrepreneurs will tell you, opportunities are usually blind dates—simultaneously scary and exciting, yet memorable and, more often than you might think, worth embracing.

To learn more, visit: https://effectuation.org/EE3/unsichtbar or scan Figure 2.6.

Figure 2.6

Practically Speaking

Trash to Cash

Good ideas for new companies can come from anywhere—from a frustrated customer, a breakthrough invention, or, as Kevin DeWhitt would tell you, from the trash. In 2004, he and his wife founded Agilyx Corporation (originally Plas2Fuel) with the idea of taking plastic waste and turning it into something better than money—crude oil.

From a chemical engineering perspective, it makes perfect sense. Plastic is a petroleum product. Why not reverse the process when you're done with the plastic? Simple enough, in theory. In practice, the science turned out to be difficult, and the business even more difficult.

Converting the Idea Into Action

You need customers to generate revenues. You need a product to attract customers. And you need cash to build a product. DeWhitt had none of these at the start. The team's solution was to partner with a customer willing to make an angel investment and at the same time assist in the development of an operational prototype. By creating with its customer, Agilyx built a working system that could be demonstrated to potential new customers, provide real-time environmental data to regulators, and give the team ideas for optimizing the system for full commercial deployment.

Using Action for More Action

Today, Agilyx can convert several thousand pounds of mixed waste plastic into hundreds of gallons of sweet synthetic crude oil each day. While this is exciting, it is utterly dwarfed by the fact that 26 million tons of plastic are sent to landfills annually in the US, and more than three times that amount is disposed of in Europe and China. Having proven the concept, Agilyx is now scaling the business up to be able to handle this enormous quantity of fuel.

Figure 2.7 Bottles which held many drops of liquid return to being drops of oil.

Ideas From Nothing

If you think Agilyx is unique, consider that eBay's 2022 sales volume was 4.6 billion US dollars—much derived from sales of someone's unwanted items (i.e. their trash). Like Agilyx, eBay has turned waste into a business. So, if you are looking for a good idea, one of your assets might just be another person's trash. Or your own.

To learn more, visit: https://effectuation.org/EE3/agilyx or scan Figure 2.8.

Figure 2.8

Practically Speaking

Everyone Is Doing It

There has been much research directed at discovering the unique characteristics of entrepreneurs. In particular, we might want to know whether entrepreneurs are psychologically different from the general population. But perhaps we are asking the wrong question. Instead of asking how psychology makes entrepreneurs, we may want to ask how entrepreneurs make psychology work for them.

Peer Power

Generating more energy and using energy more efficiently have become central issues of our time. One interesting approach to the problem seeks to turn psychology into energy savings. Dan Yates and Alex Laskey founded Opower in 2007 to help their public utility customers reduce consumer peak-power usage, build fewer power plants, and better utilize existing facilities. Opower is effective. About 85% of its clients' residential customers cut home power consumption by about 3.5%. But where did such a good idea come from?

Fueled by Competition

The results of a 2007 experiment make the psychology behind Opower transparent. Researchers hung announcements on the doors of 1,207 homes in San Marcos, California. All urged residents to use fans instead of air conditioning, offering one of four reasons. Some informed residents they could save $54 a month on their energy bill. Others indicated that using fans would eliminate 262 pounds of greenhouse gases per month. A third notice described fans as the socially responsible option. And the last group was told that 77% of their neighbors already used fans instead of air conditioning, closing with a caption of "San Marcos' popular choice!" Subsequent meter readings found that recipients of the "everyone's doing it" notice reduced their energy consumption by 10%, while no other group reduced their energy use by more than 3%.

Mind in Hand

Yates and Laskey combined this information with other means they already had. Dan Yates, a computer scientist, learned first-hand about environmental issues during a yearlong expedition to South America and Alex Laskey had experience in politics and public policy. Seeing the foundation for Opower illustrates how the firm is more of a natural synthesis of the founders' means than it is an unexpected flash of inspiration.

Mighty Mail

Opower puts homeowners into competition with other homeowners. The company produces customized data reports that let people know how much energy they're using compared to their neighbors and follows up with suggestions for a course of action. Total energy reduction from Opower's activities with just their existing utility customers is equivalent to one-third of the US's entire solar energy generation. No hydrogen fuel cells needed. No cold fusion. Just comparison data on your monthly electricity bill.

Figure 2.9 The flow of information enables the conscious flow of energy.

Practically Speaking *(continued)*

The firm issued an IPO in April 2014 and was valued at up to half a billion dollars before it was acquired by Oracle in 2016, who has since rolled its system out to hundreds of utilities. Apparently, it takes an entrepreneur to create the future, print it out, and mail it.

To learn more, visit: https://effectuation.org/EE3/opower or scan Figure 2.10.

Figure 2.10

So What?

You can begin with a simple problem for which you see an implementable solution—or even something that you believe would be fun to attempt—and start. Waiting for that blockbuster idea or "billion-dollar" opportunity is more likely to hold you back than to carry you to new heights.

Think It Through

Beyond the immediate topic of this chapter, think about the following questions:

- If it's unrealistic to identify the best idea ever, what would it take to recognize one that's just good enough?
- Do we live in societies that encourage innovation? How would one know?
- Now that we realize that the magic of entrepreneurship is not in the idea, where is it?

What Now?

As you work toward taking the plunge into a venture:

- List five ideas that you think are really good and five that you think are terrible. What is the difference between them?
- Think of an idea you love, identify the critical hurdle to making it happen. How would you overcome that one hurdle? This may change the scope and nature of your idea. Why is that hurdle there?
- Consider the extreme case: how about becoming an entrepreneur without having any ideas at all? What would be the first step?

REFERENCES

Agilyx. (n.d.). Plastic Recycling Technologies—Chemical Recycling. Retrieved September 21, 2023, from https://www.agilyx.com/

eBay. (2023). eBay Inc. reports better than expected fourth quarter 2022 results. Retrieved September 21, 2023, from https://investors.ebayinc.com/investor-news/press-release-details/2023/eBay-Inc.-Reports-Better-Than-Expected-Fourth-Quarter-2022-Results/default.aspx

Food Channel China. (n.d.). Lao Gan Ma: Product exports exceed 80 countries and regions. Retrieved September 21, 2023, from http://food.china.com.cn/2018-01/25/content_50302123.htm

Kuang, W. (2022, December 24). The woman behind your favourite supermarket chilli sauce is one of China's richest women. ABC News. https://www.abc.net.au/news/2022-12-25/tao-huabi-laogama-chilli-sauce-empire/101802986

Medtronic. (2023). Medtronic reports full year and fourth quarter fiscal 2023 financial results; announces dividend increase. Retrieved October 4, 2023, from https://news.medtronic.com/2023-05-25-Medtronic-reports-full-year-and-fourth-quarter-fiscal-2023-financial-results-announces-dividend-increase

Oracle. (n.d.). How can Oracle help consumers make better energy decisions? Retrieved September 21, 2023, from https://www.oracle.com/au/utilities/opower-energy-efficiency/

Ries, E. (2011). *The Lean Startup: How Constant Innovation Creates Radically Successful Businesses*. Portfolio Penguin.

Rogers, Everett M. (2003). *Diffusion of Innovations*. The Free Press.

Von Hippel, E. (1988). *The Sources of Innovation*. Oxford University Press.

Figure 3.1 Entrepreneurs don't need to turn to gambling to amass cash, they get started with very little money and seek other inputs from co-creators at the table.

CHAPTER 3

Most Ventures Require Little Startup Capital

In This Chapter

Most firms operate without any outside funding, making decisions with an eye to what they can afford to lose.

Starting without invested capital forces you to try to make a sale as quickly as possible, which is when you learn whether you really have a business or not. It also means that you get the feedback and cash you need from customers and other stakeholders, so you refine your idea and develop new and productive partnerships with people.

Put simply, starting without money is more challenging than starting with money, which is exactly why starting with little money generates strong and enduring new ventures.

DOI: 10.4324/9781003364016-4

In This Chapter *(continued)*

WHEN 90 MILLION US DOLLARS IS NOT ENOUGH

Of all the reasons wannabe entrepreneurs give for why they haven't already started their ventures, one that often tops the list is the lack of adequate startup capital. So, how much money is enough to get started? One of the most promising startups of all time in Silicon Valley was a company called Zaplet. In early 1999, Brian Axe and David Roberts created the concept of Zaplets—dynamic, updateable, web-like messages and applications delivered through email. Zaplet's history followed the textbook path for high-tech ventures—from two techies in a garage to pitching to venture capitalists in the Valley, using systematic market research leading to the perfect plan focused on delivering a financial home run that every new entrepreneur naively dreams of and every investor hopes for.

Zaplet did everything right. Venture capitalists fell in love with the product. Silicon Valley buzzed with the market possibilities for Zaplet. Wall Street could not get enough of the story. By July 2000, Zaplet had hired 27 product managers, and 30 developers were writing code for six independent, potentially revenue-generating product areas.

> **How much does it take to start a business?**
>
> Dell Computer Corporation launched in 1984 with 1,000 US dollars.
>
> Calculations completed by the company Lending Tree and based on data from the United States Census Bureau's "2016 Survey of Entrepreneurs" found that 21% of businesses are launched with less than 5,000 US dollars.
>
> In fact, almost half (48.4%) of businesses in the United States start out with less than 25,000 US dollars.

Before it began its descent into oblivion in 2001, Zaplet had raised, and consumed, a total of 90 million US dollars in venture funding.

... YET 5,000 US DOLLARS IS PLENTY

Around the same time, in the small town of Bozeman, Montana, Greg Gianforte built RightNow Technologies to commercialize a software product that helped companies respond to their customers' emails quickly and effectively.

Starting with a goal of creating 2,000 jobs in his beloved Bozeman, Gianforte invested 5,000 US dollars of his own money and booked about 20,000 US dollars in revenue in the first year.

Working alone, coding a bare-bones product with specifications derived from a series of cold calls to customers, Gianforte often took price out of the equation by offering bargain-basement deals such as a few thousand dollars for a two-year lease of his software to early customers. Because his costs were so low, he could even afford to give the product away for free in return for actual early adoption and detailed real-time feedback-in-use.

Once he had about 40 users, Gianforte hired five employees. With his relentless focus on revenue, all of his first hires were salespeople. Gianforte does not believe cold calling is disreputable work, nor does he believe fundraising or even product building has to precede sales. Instead, he waxes poetic about selling. For example, he told Professor William Sahlman and Research Associate Dan Heath of the Harvard Business School:

> **The little venture grew from an investment of 5,000 US Dollars and sales of 20,000 US Dollars in its first year to revenues of over 35 million US Dollars and a post-money valuation of 100 million US Dollars in its third year. In 2011, the firm was acquired by Oracle Corporation for 1.5 billion US Dollars.**
>
> **(Gianforte & Gibson, 2007)**

Selling: Sleazy or Noble?

Some entrepreneurs don't like sales very much. They do it only because they have to, and as soon as they can, they hire someone else to do the selling. They may even feel that there's something a little bit sleazy about calling up strangers for money. Yes, sales can be hard work. No one likes making cold calls. But sleazy? On the contrary, sales is actually the noblest part of business since it provides a solution to the customer's need.

> Nothing happens until somebody sells something.
>
> *Greg Gianforte*, Founder, RightNow Technologies

MONEY MATCHING

To stay in business, every venture (profit and non-profit alike) must take in at least as much cash as it spends, and in the case of for-profit ventures, ideally a bit more. It's true that "it takes money to make money," but taking investment money at the outset starts a new venture off in a deficit position. As far as the venture is concerned, any money it does not generate through sales is money it owes someone. This is what we call the "money matching principle." Simply put, any cash out needs to be matched with cash in.

While our mythical entrepreneur may seek to raise 10 million US dollars in venture capital as part of her roadmap to success, we take a different tack. We encourage you to try to think about not having money as an asset in itself—an asset that challenges you to build a more robust business, forces you to be more creative in how you deal with customers and partners, and allows you to maintain more control over your venture.

MONEY MATCHING: ACCOUNTANTS VERSUS ENTREPRENEURS

Accounting works to extend the money matching principle over time. For example, if it costs 500,000 US dollars to buy a new machine, accountants don't put that entire amount in the expense column of the balance sheet that year. Instead, they spread it out over the number of years the machine will be producing product revenue—say, ten years. Through this process, accountants match the expenses and the revenues using the idea of depreciation.

How can this possibly matter to an entrepreneur? The answer is that depreciation happens only on paper. Where accountants rationalize actually paying out the 500,000 US dollars in full for the machine, and writing it off on paper over ten years, entrepreneurs seek to find ways to pay out only a fraction of the cash up front for the same machine—and work hard to match funding to actual use in each time period.

This difference in matching mirrors the difference in Zaplet and RightNow. It is the difference between matching funding to a vision and matching it to actual implementation. It is the difference between selecting courses of action based on five-year return projections fueled by imagined uses for a technology or focusing on the immediate next step that is underwritten by current commitments from actual stakeholders.

To match expenses and revenue, ask yourself questions like these:

- How much output do I need right now?
- Are there ways to get cash for that output before actually producing it?
- What are the ways I can delay cash outflows and accelerate cash inflows?
- Can a customer pay half up front?
- Will suppliers let me pay in 60 days instead of 30? Would they be willing to go to 90?
- Can I focus on non-cash-intensive parts of the business first so I don't need funding now and can raise money on better terms later?
- How can I use technology (of all types) to make the most of my limited capital?

CREATIVE CAPITAL

One of the most common ways to match expenses and revenue—and thus reduce the need for cash—is to convert fixed costs into variable costs. Instead of buying the 500,000 US dollar machine, you might find someone who owns a similar machine and is willing to sell you units from it. You may have to pay a premium for this option, but now you don't have to raise 500,000 US dollars to buy the machine yourself.

Creative thinking along these lines often leads to the discovery of slack resources (i.e. resources lying around) such as periods when an existing factory is underutilized. You may be able to access this capacity at a discount or even for free on a trial basis.

Move from asking, "Can I raise 500,000 US dollars to pay for the new machine?" to asking, "How can I make the 500,000 US dollars without incurring the fixed costs of buying and owning the machine?"

CREATIVE CAPITAL VERSUS INVESTED CAPITAL

Entrepreneurs don't always see all the costs associated with capital and make two common mistakes:

High Cost of Invested Capital

They do not take opportunities to convert fixed costs into variable costs, because it is more expensive in the short term, yet are willing to sell a large percentage of their firm to an investor to obtain expensive capital.

Not Considering Creative Capital

They weigh the cost of one type of invested capital against the cost of another, overlooking the cost of invested capital versus the cost of creative capital.

Costs of Creative Capital

At the same time, there are caveats with the creative capital approach. Creative financing gives entrepreneurs more time—but at a cost. Contrary to what you might have learned in a finance course, the cost of capital is not just the interest rate or the return your investors require. The cost of creative capital also includes:

- Paying a premium variable price (for example, paying top rental rates for a factory) in order to avoid a major fixed cost investment (for example, building your own factory)
- Exposure to renegotiated terms from suppliers if you turn out to be successful
- Exposure to opportunistic partners if you don't control the parts of your business that are most competitively valuable (At the start, it's not always clear what will end up being your competitive advantage.)

If you make all your fixed costs variable, the total cost might be too high to make a profit. If the asset you decide not to buy—say, the 500,000 US dollar machine—turns out to be critically necessary to the business, will the owner of that asset have you over a barrel, perhaps forcing you to buy output at a premium price?

The answer is that these things can happen, and each entrepreneur needs to make these trade-offs idiosyncratically, according to his or her own level of affordable loss, staying focused on keeping the venture going, and working hard on keeping relationships working well. Early in the life of a venture, the greatest threat is survival. When time and money run out, the venture stops.

We have yet to see the cost of creative capital kill a new venture. Many ventures, however, have ended in the pursuit of invested capital. The simple fact is that the market for lending and investing surrounding new ventures is far from easily accessible.

Even if you effectively evaluate the true costs of your sources of invested capital, and venture capital comes out as the most cost-effective source, the reality of striking a deal for venture capital is another thing entirely.

Furthermore, chasing venture funding may be expensive in terms of the cost of your time, since you miss all the venture building you could have been doing (customers you do not talk to, suppliers you do not negotiate with, employees you do not build long-term relationships with) while you are out chasing venture capitalists.

You may spend six months chasing that cost-effective capital source unsuccessfully, leaving you without time and capital, which results in the end of the venture. The cost of obtaining investment capital, even well managed, can be higher than the cost of NOT getting it.

In the event of venture growth and success, the cost of creative financing tends to go down even more. At the same time, the cost of invested capital becomes higher, because the investors claim a fraction of the total value created in the venture. As a result, setting up milestones for addressing success as well as failure, "alternative" contracts, and even pre-negotiated changes that are different for "good" versus "bad" situations, can be an important part of your effort to use those creative sources of capital.

Beware, of course, that you don't let your predictions of the future take over in these moments. For example, your predictions of the assets you think are most strategic (and those that you don't) can lead you to seek narrow control rights over those assets, rather than continue to work creatively with potential partners.

BOOTSTRAPPING BENEFITS

In their book *Bootstrapping Your Business*, Gianforte and Gibson (2007) make the case that starting with nothing is a good idea. We agree, and summarize the highlights:

- *You can start now.* Instead of waiting for a prospective funder to come along, be inspired by your business and write you a check, you can start your business today. There is nothing holding you back.
- *You can start learning now.* Most ventures we know and love were created through entrepreneurs' interactions with suppliers, customers, partners, and employees. Cash can encourage you not to engage in those interactions and, thus, not learn as quickly.
- *Cut your waste.* When you have money, it is easy to waste it on speculative ideas. But if you have none, it's hard to throw it out the window.
- *Limit your downside.* If you do not have a huge amount of cash invested in the venture, the mistakes you will inevitably make will likely be proportionately smaller.
- *Increase your upside.* Taking investment generally means selling equity. And the more you sell, the less you have when it comes time to realize the value created in your venture.
- *Increase your creativity.* Studies show that constraints increase creativity. When you have money, you'll spend it. When you don't have money, you add a constraint that makes you more creative.

And the business environment has evolved since *Bootstrapping Your Business* came out. For example, cloud-based systems can provide needed business functions at relatively low monthly fees, avoiding major upfront purchases of hardware and software. And crowdfunding sites can get customers to pre-order and help underwrite your initial product runs.

TAKEAWAY: HAVING NOTHING IS A GOOD THING

The reality is that most firms in the world operate without any outside funding; instead, they make decisions with an eye to what they can afford to lose. Their priority is to stay in business, and so they make sure the downside risks are acceptable.

Starting without invested capital means that you work harder to work with people who have what you need. Since you cannot pay them with money, they begin to be emotionally invested in your success. It is then easier to transform them into partners than merely vendors or paid workers.

Practically Speaking

Dragon Lady

What would you guess happens to this book after you read it? If you are a social person, you might share it with a friend. If you are a resourceful person, you might resell it. And if you recycle it, chances are good it will end up with Yan Cheung of Nine Dragons Paper Holdings Limited in China. It won't take long, either. "The newspaper that you put in your newspaper bin—three weeks later, it's in the hands of someone in China," explains Bill Moore of Moore & Associates in Atlanta, a consultant on recovered paper. Amazing—but how does this happen?

Resourceful Recycler

Rewind to 1990. In that year, Cheung created America Chung Nam (ACN) with just 3,800 US dollars. Her plan was to buy recycled paper in the United States and export it to China. She observed that Americans love to consume paper, using more than 700 pounds per person each year. And the Chinese desperately need to produce paper-based cardboard boxes in which to export domestically manufactured goods to the world.

Driving around the US from dump to recycling facility in a minivan, Cheung and her husband filled containers (likely ones that had just arrived from China) with wastepaper and sent them to China. It wasn't long before they were filling a lot of containers.

Printing Money

Five years later, armed with the new means of a strong cash flow from ACN, a reliable source of high-quality recycled paper, and a clear understanding of the appetite for packaging materials in China, Cheung returned to Hong Kong. There she launched Nine Dragons to take that stream of wastepaper and process it into kraft linerboard, test linerboard, or corrugating medium—the basic papers used to make a cardboard box.

Practically Speaking *(continued)*

Nine Dragons has steadily built capacity to become the largest producer in China and among the largest globally, employing over 20,000 employees as of 2022. This empire built on waste paper makes Cheung the self-crowned "Queen of Waste Paper" and one of the richest women in the world.

Paper Trail

There are two useful insights from Nine Dragons that can be boxed up and shipped to entrepreneurs everywhere.

The first is that new ventures can be created with things that already exist. It is easy to believe that in order to start a company, you need a technological innovation or a huge investment. But Cheung started with nothing more than trash.

Second, ideas don't become opportunities until somebody acts. The fact that Americans were generating paper waste and that China needed massive amounts of cardboard was no secret to anyone, even in 1990. Yet someone, an entrepreneur, had to get into her minivan and make the opportunity happen.

Figure 3.2 One woman's waste is another woman's treasure, as Yan Cheung has shown us.

Packaged Solution

Also contained in this story is a bigger idea. It's about where solutions to big problems come from. The problem of paper waste is huge. Every 120 pounds of recycled paper saves a tree. Paper made from recycled paper requires 64% less energy than paper made from raw materials.

While governments try to convince people to recycle, Cheung gets the job done, using an average of 85% to 90% recovered paper in the manufacturing process. That's a lot of trees and a lot of watts. She and entrepreneurs like her build businesses and sustainability.

To learn more, visit: https://effectuation.org/EE3/dragon or scan Figure 3.3.

Figure 3.3

Practically Speaking

Business in a Bowl

Munching on your breakfast and thinking about your plans for the day, you might not be paying much attention to what you are eating. In 1992, as an 18-year-old first-year university student of history and sociology in Melbourne, Carolyn Creswell did put thought into her breakfast, and her future. Here's how she describes it:

> It's amazing where life can lead you … One day I was told that I was to lose my job as the business was to be sold. I immediately thought, "You could buy this little business! You love the muesli and you make it already!"
>
> My offer of $1,000 was eventually accepted and Carman's was born. It was a life changing decision. Finishing my degree proved challenging as I made deliveries before morning lectures and balanced the books in the library during lunch breaks.

(*Waters*, 2022)

Within two years Carolyn had bought out her partner (who had also put in 1,000 Australian dollars) and by 1997 was selling her Carman's brand muesli in supermarkets. In 2002, she expanded into the snack food market, introducing a range of nut and muesli bars.

Figure 3.4 Nowadays, Carolyn Creswell can take time to savor her healthy (and lucrative) breakfast muesli.

Queen of Muesli

The next step was into the wider world in 2007, starting with exports to the United Kingdom. By 2012, Carman's could be found in 32 countries.

In 2021, Carman's had sales of over 110 million Australian dollars, and is a leader in the healthier foods category, competing with global brands such as Nestlé and Kellogg's.

Carolyn Creswell is considered the Australian Queen of Muesli, but she had humble beginnings with the threat of losing her part-time job and thus making a 1,000 Australian dollar bid to save it by buying the company!

To learn more, visit: https://effectuation.org/EE3/muesli or scan Figure 3.5.

Figure 3.5

Research Roots

THE LEAN STARTUP

Few popular books on entrepreneurship have proven to be as well liked as Eric Ries' *Lean Startup*. Published in the wake of the global financial crisis of 2009, *The Lean Startup* was very much the right book, with the right message at the right time.

Central to the book's message is the notion of "lean," which borrows from the lean manufacturing philosophy pioneered by Japanese auto manufacturers such as Toyota. To make a production process "lean" means to eliminate all the waste in it.

Leaning a startup means eliminating the need for elaborate business plans, fancy product development, and large amounts of outside funding. Instead, Ries urges founders to focus on just the necessary things to get a new venture going.

Therefore, in place of attempting to develop the perfect product or service, just develop the "minimal viable product" (MVP) version. In place of doing elaborate market research, validate the MVP by getting direct customer feedback on it. In place of investing heavily in a particular direction, stay flexible and "pivot" when necessary.

Lean Startup may not be based on a careful program of published research in the way that effectuation is, but the popularity of the terms "lean," "pivot," and "MVP" suggests that Eric Ries has written a book that many entrepreneurs find exceedingly useful (Ries, 2011).

Since the book's appearance, the terms "pivot," "iteration," and "innovation" have even become buzzwords in large companies, which can sometimes lead to what is called "innovation theater," making lots of noise about supporting innovation, but without significant results.

Steve Blank, mentor and colleague of Eric Ries, responds to this critique in his 2019 *Harvard Business Review* article: "Instead, what organizations need is an Innovation Doctrine that addresses culture, mindset, and process and guides the organization's efforts to achieve real innovations."

Research Roots

FUNDING VIA THE MASSES

Crowdfunding is a unique category of fundraising that draws on practices in micro-finance and crowdsourcing. It refers to efforts by for-profit, social, and cultural ventures to fund projects by amalgamating small contributions from a large number of individuals, usually via internet crowdfunding sites.

A 2014 research paper by Ethan Mollick of Wharton investigated data on 48,526 US projects crowdfunded on Kickstarter, an internet crowdfunding site, totaling 237 million US dollars in funding (averaging around 5,000 US dollars per project).

Research Roots *(continued)*

Mollick's analyses showed that several interesting patterns exist in crowdfunding. First, success in crowdfunding a project appears to be linked to the perceived quality of the project, with higher quality projects more likely to achieve funding.

Second, a bigger presence on social networking sites such as Facebook was linked to more success in achieving funding. Third, there is a strong association between projects and the culture of the places they come from. For example, crowdfunded projects in Los Angeles were likely to be in the film industry, whereas projects in Nashville were mainly music-based.

Lastly, Mollick found very little fraud among the projects, but around 75% of crowdfunded projects were delayed, with the bigger, more complicated projects being more likely to be delayed (Mollick, 2014).

More recent work by Moysidou and Hausberg (2020) looks at the age-old connection of trust and risk related to crowdfunding and concluded that:

> Trust enables crowdfunders to overcome perceptions of risk and uncertainty, and thus influences their intentions to support a project financially. Hence, building crowdfunders' trust in a lending crowdfunding project is a strategic imperative not only for fund-seekers, but also for crowdfunding platforms.

Practically Speaking

Chill Out in Tradition

The next time you reach for an energy drink to deal with stress, ask yourself if perhaps a relaxation drink might be better. Ask Fiji Kava founder Zane Yoshida, who swears by the non-alcoholic, but sedative ceremonial drink from the South Pacific called kava (piper methysticum).

Zane Yoshida seeks to root his venture in an ancient tradition, one which travels with people, even (or particularly) when they leave their homeland. Anau Mesui Henry, whose parents migrated from Tonga to New Zealand, were faced with many challenges in their new home. Causes for tension included, as she describes, the following: "[They faced] different cultural norms and social constructs … And in order to look after the family, my parents just went back to kava, that's what they knew."

Back to the Roots

Anau remembers many trips to Tonga to grow and process the kava roots: "We had a kava pounding machine ... And it was their way of looking after the family."

Looking back, she now sees the role kava played besides maintaining tradition: "Now I'm like, 'oh, they are business people' but they never saw themselves as that. They were just immigrants trying to make sure their family was looked after."

Practically Speaking *(continued)*

Ceremonial Lounging

Anau is not just maintaining the tradition, but is also a "businessperson" running a kava lounge in Auckland, New Zealand. According to Zane Yoshida, Anau is part of an international kava wave.

> There's been an explosion of demand for kava and an explosion of growth of kava bars throughout the US. When I started this project 10 years ago, we estimated that there were 50-odd kava bars in the US; that number is now in excess of 450.
>
> (*Salamasina & Boucher*, 2023)

The opportunities created by this increase in demand for kava range from very low investment kava cultivation to kava processing, to export and kava-focused hospitality.

Alosio Ray, a kava farmer from Fiji's Vanua Levu Island, shares the impact the root has had on his family:

> We get lots of money with the kava, a lot more money than we had before, … We achieved [sic] to buy material for our houses, and before we don't have this kind of solar [power] we have now.
>
> (*Salamasina & Boucher*, 2023)

Figure 3.6 Women in Samoa preparing kava in approximately 1890. Photographer unknown.

Feed the Roots and They Feed You

The story of kava is an example of how deep cultural roots can grow into income that feeds the family while also soothing its users, as Zane Yoshida points out: "I think timing is right to take kava to the masses in the West, given the stresses of everyday life right now that we're facing."

To learn more, visit: https://effectuation.org/EE3/kava or scan Figure 3.7.

Figure 3.7

Research Roots

KEEPING COOL UNDER (FINANCIAL) PRESSURE

Do you remember when you were a kid and had just a little bit of pocket money and thought long and hard about what you would spend it on? It turns out that is how adults under financial pressure also think and act.

A 2023 study by Sharma, Tully, and Wang concluded that despite scarce resources, most people make reasonable decisions, weighing both short- and long-term benefits. Contrast this finding with the common perception that people under financial pressure make impulsive decisions.

As much as this finding might not make us feel any better about our bank balance, it does reassure us that we can keep a clear head despite the bank balance being low … or when we are starting a venture on a shoestring.

So What?

The most important inputs come from you: who you are, what you know, and who you know. You plus a customer and a shared solution gives substance to the venture, not external investment. So no need to wait around for investment to build your venture. You can start today.

Think It Through

- What would happen if a rich aunt died and left you several million dollars? Would you still want to start a venture?
- What is it about money that makes it valuable? If it's about what it can buy, think about how you can get those things without having to use money to buy them.

What Now?

- Take stock of your monthly expenses and ask yourself how much you could do without.
- What slack resources (not money, but capabilities) could you tap into that belong to other people?
- Imagine that it is illegal to raise money for you to develop your new venture. How would you then take on the challenge of starting your new venture?
- Find resources on the web that will get you started in creating your own budget: www.inc.com/encyclopedia/businessbudget.html.

REFERENCES

American Psychological Association. (2023, September 14). Take the money now or later? Financial scarcity doesn't lead to poor decision making. Retrieved October 13, 2023, from https://www.sciencedaily.com/releases/2023/09/230914103317.htm

Bartlett, S. (2002, October). Seat of their pants. Inc. Magazine. http://www.inc.com/magazine/20021015/24772.html

Bhidé, A. (2000). *The Origin and Evolution of New Businesses.* Oxford University Press.

Blank, S. (2019, October 7). Why companies do "innovation theater" instead of actual innovation. *Harvard Business Review.* https://hbr.org/2019/10/why-companies-do-innovation-theater-instead-of-actual-innovation

Carman's Kitchen. (n.d.). Carolyn Creswell. Retrieved October 13, 2023, from https://carmanskitchen.com.au/our-story/carolyn-creswell/

Dennis Jr., W. J. (1997). Wells Fargo/NFIB study shows 14% drop in new business starts; despite slower pace, 3 million new firms launched in 1996. www.nfibonline.com

Fitzsimmons, Caitlin. (2017). Muesli queen Carolyn Creswell is taking Carman's to China. *Sydney Morning Herald.* Retrieved October 13, 2023, from https://www.smh.com.au/business/why-australias-museli-queen-carolyn-creswell-has-set-her-sight-on-a-nuttier-challenge-20170802-gxns8t.html

Gianforte, G., & Gibson, M. (2007). *Bootstrapping Your Business: Start and Grow a Successful Company With Almost No Money.* Adams Media.

Hurst, E., & Lusardi, A. (2004). Liquidity constraints, household wealth, and entrepreneurship. *The Journal of Political Economy, 112*(2), 319–347. https://doi.org/10.1086/381478

Kauffman Foundation. (2009). *Business Dynamics Statistics: An Overview.* https://www.kauffman.org/entrepreneurship/reports/business-dynamics-statistics/business-dynamics-statistics-an-overview/

Lending Tree. (2023). Startup costs by industry. https://www.lendingtree.com/business/startup-costs-by-industry/

Mollick, E. (2014). The dynamics of crowdfunding: An exploratory study. *Journal of Business Venturing, 29*(1), 1–16. https://doi.org/10.1016/j.jbusvent.2013.06.005

Moysidou, K., & Hausberg, J. P. (2020). In crowdfunding we trust: A trust-building model in lending crowdfunding. *Journal of Small Business Management, 58*(3), 511–543. https://doi.org/10.1080/00472778.2019.1661682

Nine Dragons Paper (Holdings) Limited. (n.d.). Retrieved October 4, 2023, from http://www.ndpaper.com/en/global/home.php

Ries, E. (2011). *The Lean Startup: How Constant Innovation Creates Radically Successful Businesses.* Portfolio Penguin.

Salamasina, S., & Boucher, D. L. (2023, September 20). "Kava is alive." But as it goes global, can you export the mana of kava as well as the product? *ABC Pacific.* https://www.abc.net.au/pacific/kava-is-a-staple-in-places-like-fiji-vanuatu-and-tonga/102869984

Sharma, E., Tully, S. M., & Wang, X. (2023). Scarcity and intertemporal choice. *Journal of Personality and Social Psychology.* https://doi.org/10.1037/pspa0000353

Straight, K. (2023, August 4). This relaxation drink, touted as a non-alcoholic substitute, tastes like "muddy water"—But that's about to change. *ABC News.* https://www.abc.net.au/news/2023-08-05/australian-kava-company-takes-on-muddy-water-reputation/102674924

Waters, C. (2022, July 22). The $1000 buy that made Carolyn Creswell a breakfast food queen. Retrieved October 13, 2023, from https://www.theage.com.au/national/victoria/the-1000-buy-that-made-carolyn-creswell-a-breakfast-food-queen-20220621-p5avhp.html

Figure 4.1

CHAPTER 4

The Plunge Doesn't Have to Be a Plunge at All

In This Chapter

Should you plunge in, wade in, or dip in? Entry into entrepreneurship can occur in as many different ways as the diversity of entrepreneurs themselves.

Many of us nervously measure our current situation against what is needed to chase an opportunity, often exaggerating the stability of our current position and underestimating the potential losses of not taking action.

Experienced entrepreneurs rarely take an "all or nothing" approach to new ventures. They start small and incrementally, only risking what they can afford to lose.

The following quote from the author Charles Dubois summarizes this idea eloquently: "The important thing is this: To be able at any moment to sacrifice what we are for what we could become."

DOI: 10.4324/9781003364016-5

We have all heard of people who jumped ship and started their own businesses. Ask any group, from undergraduate students to mid-career executives, if they want to start a venture, and two-thirds will say yes. Most, though, never will.

The reasons we don't do it are varied. Some reasons are cultural, while some are specific to the individual.

Most of us, faced with the decision of whether to take the plunge, instinctively compare what we know and have with what we think it will take to pursue an opportunity.

Moreover, we look at our current job, salary, location, and comfort, and believe it is so stable that we can map our future. We then see entrepreneurship as shaky and cannot discern a path forward.

Even in a world where job security is a thing of the past, there is a perception that certain situations (a full-time job in a stable industry, for instance) will lead to a comfortable future. We balk at the idea of plunging into the unknown or the unknowable, seeing it as a realm where we might fail.

What people (perhaps mistakenly) think about statistics on new venture success and failure (Chapter 5) could bias the decision. Other biases from this first section of the book could influence prospective entrepreneurs as well. Taking all the myths together, only overconfident, risk-seeking, or mildly crazy people, it seems, would become entrepreneurs.

> Entrepreneurship is about creating something new, something different, something better. It's about having a vision for the future and then doing whatever it takes to make that vision a reality. It's about taking risks, making mistakes, and learning from them. It's about being persistent and never giving up, even when the odds are against you. It's about having the courage to follow your dreams and the determination to make them come true.
>
> *Tony Hsieh*, former CEO of Zappos

So, what kind of decision process leads potential entrepreneurs to feel comfortable taking the plunge? Researchers have spent a lot of time studying this question. The answer is important to governments and economic development organizations that spend large amounts of money trying to increase entrepreneurship. It's also important to the thriving industry of entrepreneurial educators who, either directly or indirectly, teach potential entrepreneurs how best to make the plunge decision.

Over the next few pages, we will dissect the decision-making process behind the plunge decision. As you read the following stories of entrepreneurs, decide for yourself whether a plunge is really a plunge.

FIVE STORIES AND FIVE PLUNGES

Why plunge? The answer depends in large part on where you are in your life and on your entrepreneurial motivation. In this chapter, we share five stories, each of which shows us an entrepreneur at a particular stage in life and with a particular motivation.

Contrast the story of Larry Hench (Boing-Boing) with that of Pierre Omidyar. Hench entered entrepreneurship at the end of a successful career; for Omidyar, entrepreneurship provided the start of a successful career.

Contrasting those two stories, not all entrepreneurship is born of success. Judi Henderson-Townsend (Mannequin Madness) had time on her hands to try a new venture because her dot-com venture had gone out of business.

And though she and Richard Sears (Sears and Roebuck) shared similar circumstances around the founding of their respective ventures, Sears had clearly been looking for entrepreneurial opportunities and had already dipped his toe in the water, providing coal and wood outside of his day job as a railway station agent.

And then there is the singer Annie Lennox, who after plunging into (and not liking) classical music, went on to become a pop music success. Always moving to her own beat, she later went on to apply entrepreneurial thinking to her activism.

Clearly, there are more stages in life and more motivations for entrepreneurship than those we mention. The point is to see how perspectives change with context. Where would you situate yourself? What might motivate you?

Why NOT Plunge?

Many people fall into the trap of delaying their true-life plan, settling for jobs or activities that don't align with their passions or purpose. They convince themselves that sacrificing their current happiness will eventually pay off in the form of a better future. However, this approach has two major flaws.

First, there's no guarantee that this delay will ever pay off in gratification. Nobody is going to tap you on the shoulder and say, "now's the time to start living your best life."

Second, we all have a finite amount of time on this earth, and we don't know how much of it we have left. It's important to ask yourself: Do you want to spend the majority of your limited time doing something you don't enjoy, or do you want to take the plunge and pursue your passions now?

ANATOMY OF THE PLUNGE DECISION

There are at least four ways to think about the plunge decision and, ultimately, to take the plunge. They are closely related to the affordable loss principle, which we discuss in Chapter 12. Consider each to figure out which works best for the way you should think about the decision.

1. What You Can Lose

This is a twist on the standard business textbook approach. Instead of calculating the opportunity cost of starting a business in terms of your current salary and future earnings potential, you calculate two relatively simple values.

First, estimate the absolute maximum amount you are willing to lose. Second, decide on the absolute minimum you want to earn. Now evaluate only those opportunities you can afford with your maximum investment that will pay you at least the minimum earnings you need.

This approach—called the min–max or max–min approach—provides a useful filter that reduces the number of ventures you can seriously consider and then leads you to a go/no-go decision on each of them.

2. Toes First (Start Small)

There are usually several plausible ways of pursuing an idea. One way to go about taking the plunge is to always choose the option that involves the least risk—for example, running a venture "on the side" while continuing to work at one's job, rather than launching a venture with all the associated costs right at the start. This is what Pierre Omidyar, the founder of eBay, did. Research indicates that about 50% of entrepreneurs start this way.

3. Opportunity Cost

Just as there are opportunity costs associated with starting a new business, there are opportunity costs associated with not starting one. People often overlook these costs. There are costs to staying in your current job and forgoing both the potential financial upside and the psychological returns of starting the new business venture. These costs, many of which are psychological or emotional, are often difficult to quantify.

For someone who believes the costs of not becoming an entrepreneur outweigh the calculable costs of taking the plunge, it's critical to understand that you can start small and proceed step-by-step in the direction you have chosen. And remember, not starting at all guarantees you will never build a successful venture.

It is important to realize also that failing can have very positive side effects. For one, it helps you build relationships with people who are willing to walk through failure with you. If you don't try, you won't know who these people are.

And there are larger implications. Many would-be entrepreneurs say they cannot fail because they live in a cultural setting that does not look kindly on failure. But research shows that in every country there are pockets of entrepreneurship and support groups. By refusing to take the plunge, would-be entrepreneurs turn their fears into self-fulfilling prophecies, encouraging the further stigmatization of fear.

4. Walk Before You Jump

Every company we know today was started by an entrepreneur. So, clearly, others have successfully created their own maps where none might have existed before they set out on their entrepreneurial journey.

The examples in this chapter demonstrate that the plunge decision is not about a sudden dive into unfathomable depths. It is a process that happens step-by-step, depending on your means and what you are willing to lose. In fact, it is not a plunge at all. It is just another way for you to incrementally achieve things, including things you might not even imagine possible today.

Practically Speaking

Boing-Boing

Larry Hench, a scientist and inventor, spent decades developing Bioglass, a revolutionary material used in the repair of bone damage that has helped millions of people.

The Right Time Is Now

Despite his success and truly having reached typical retirement age, Hench felt a desire to explore new areas and extend his creativity. He took stock of his life's means, including his understanding of core scientific research, his strong writing abilities, and his interest in educating children.

Using these seemingly unrelated means, Hench created Boing-Boing, a series of children's books that combine storytelling with technology and science education.

Hench's approach highlights two insights into entrepreneurship. First, there is no single right moment to take the plunge or a single perfect opportunity to pursue. At any time, entrepreneurs can generate multiple options based on their current means. Second, by starting with their personal means, entrepreneurs can gain a unique insight, a differentiated approach, and a competitive advantage.

Practically Speaking *(continued)*

The Bionic Power of How

Boing-Boing began as a robotic "cat substitute" for a boy with allergies but has since expanded to include a product line of educational materials such as workbooks, experiment books, and hands-on kits for schoolchildren. By starting with his means, Hench was able to take an easy plunge into entrepreneurship with Boing-Boing, and he has now added children's book publisher, brand owner, and children's science educator to his set of means.

Figure 4.2 "Boing-Boing", the adventuresome robotic cat.

Bouncing Ahead, Not Plunging Down

While many people his age are slowing down, Hench continued bouncing ahead, exploring new possibilities, showcasing the power of combining personal means to create novel and exciting opportunities until his death at age 87 in 2015.

To learn more, visit: https://effectuation.org/EE3/boing or scan Figure 4.3.

Figure 4.3

Practically Speaking

Billions Without Blank Checks

> Back when I launched eBay on Labor Day 1995, eBay wasn't my business—it was my hobby. I had to build a system that was self-sustaining … because I had a real job to go to every morning. I was working as a software engineer from 10 to 7, and I wanted to have a life on the weekends. So I built a system that could keep working—catching complaints and capturing feedback—even when Pam and I were out mountain biking, and the only one home was our cat.
>
> If I had had a blank check from a big VC (venture capitalist), and a big staff running around—things might have gone much worse. I would have probably put together a very complex, elaborate system—something that justified all the investment. But because I had to operate on a tight budget—tight in terms of money and tight in terms of time—necessity focused me on simplicity: So, I built a system simple enough to sustain itself.
>
> By building a simple system, with just a few guiding principles, eBay was open to organic growth—it could achieve a certain degree of self-organization. So, I guess what I'm trying to tell you is: Whatever future you're building … don't try to program everything. Five-year plans never worked for the Soviet Union—in fact, if anything, central planning contributed to its fall. Chances are that central planning won't work any better for any of us.
>
> *Pierre Omidyar*, eBay Founder

To learn more, visit: https://effectuation.org/EE3/ebay or scan Figure 4.4.

Figure 4.4

Practically Speaking

A Model Business

Judi Henderson-Townsend had never worked in retail. She had done no market research on the demand for mannequins. In fact, she had never actually touched a mannequin prior to getting into the business. All she wanted was a creative art project—to mosaic a mannequin for her garden. But instead of buying a single mannequin, she impulsively bought 50 from a vendor who was closing his mannequin rental business and leaving the state. Cost of startup: 2,500 US dollars.

Paying Guests

Though it didn't cost an arm and a leg for Judi to get into business, she then had to figure out the rest of the equation. After explaining to her husband Jay that they would have 50 unusual guests in their basement, Judi went about creating the market.

Her online marketing skills enabled her to attract customers all over the US and Canada. After acquiring 500 additional mannequins from a retail chain that was remodeling, she expanded her customer base from trade-show vendors to small retailers, artists, eBayers, event planners, and even to Industrial Light & Magic—the visual effects behind Lucas Films.

Saving Face

Her hard work has taken on a life of its own. Judi started running her firm, Mannequin Madness (www.mannequinmadness.com), at the end of 2001 after being let go from a failing dot-com. Today, she earns between 100 and 1,000 US dollars for a used mannequin based on its condition and style and handles thousands of mannequins a year. She sources most of her inventory from retailers that close or remodel and discard existing mannequins to bring in the latest styles. Mannequin Madness also repairs mannequins, has a blog about mannequins and became a distributor for new mannequins.

Saving Earth

Creating a firm from an initial investment of 2,500 US dollars, Judi clearly has a head for business. However, she has another persona—one that's remarkably green. Because while she is making money, she is also keeping used mannequins out of landfills. Mannequins are bulky and typically made of materials that do not biodegrade easily. Her business recycles more than 100,000 pounds of heads, limbs and torsos every year that would otherwise be waste. So, in addition to a good living, she has earned a special achievement award from the United States' Environmental Protection Agency.

Her Own Way

Judi has earned something more than success—something less tangible, but perhaps more important. She has earned the right to do what she wants. She has much more contact with the creative people she enjoys. She works with her husband, who joined the business as it has grown. While Judi has not mastered the "four-hour work week" popularized by Timothy Ferris, she does have a flexible work schedule.

Practically Speaking *(continued)*

Figure 4.5 Judi Henderson-Townsend has no shortage of helping hands. © Mannequin Madness.

To learn more, visit: https://effectuation.org/EE3/mannequin or scan Figure 4.6.

Figure 4.6

Practically Speaking

The Making of Sears

In 1886, when a Chicago jewelry company shipped some watches to an unsuspecting jeweler in the Minnesota hamlet of Redwood Falls, it started a chain of events that led to the founding of an American icon.

Watch Out! Here Comes an Opportunity

Richard Sears was an agent of the Minneapolis and St. Louis railway station in the neighboring hamlet of North Redwood. To earn extra income on the side, he sold lumber and coal. When the shipment of watches arrived, unwanted, at the Redwood Falls station, Sears went into action. He purchased them himself and sold the watches at a nice profit to other station agents up and down the line. It went so well that he ordered more.

The following year, Sears moved his business to Chicago and placed an ad in the newspaper looking for a watchmaker. Alvah C. Roebuck answered the ad, which began the association of two young men, both still in their 20s. In 1893, Sears, Roebuck and Co. was formally established, and they were off.

Time for Change

In that era, farmers in rural America were selling their crops for cash and buying what they needed from rural general stores. But exchanging low-value commodities for high-value finished goods was a losing proposition. In 1891, the wholesale price of a barrel of flour was reported to be 3.47 US dollars, while the retail price was at least 7.00 US dollars, a 100% difference. Farmers formed protest movements, such as the Grange, to do battle against high prices and the "middleman."

Practically Speaking *(continued)*

Going Bigtime

Sears, Roebuck and Co. and other mail-order companies provided the answer. Through a combination of volume buying and making use of the railroads, the post office, and, later, rural free delivery and parcel post, they offered an attractive alternative to the high-priced rural stores.

Sears prospered in the 1890s, and over the next 100 years, the company built a huge product line, created countless successful brands, rolled out retail locations around the world, and added insurance and investment services, ultimately making a tremendous impact on the world of retail.

Acting in Time

Was it market research? Deliberation? Luck? Opportunism? Richard Sears took advantage of a chance occurrence, and rather than focus on learning before doing, he learned while doing.

Sometimes the best way to figure out whether an idea is really a good idea for a business, or the "right" opportunity for you, is to buy the box of watches and try to sell them. Richard couldn't envision what his venture would become, but the initial opportunity was one that he was able to take on, and he made good things happen from there.

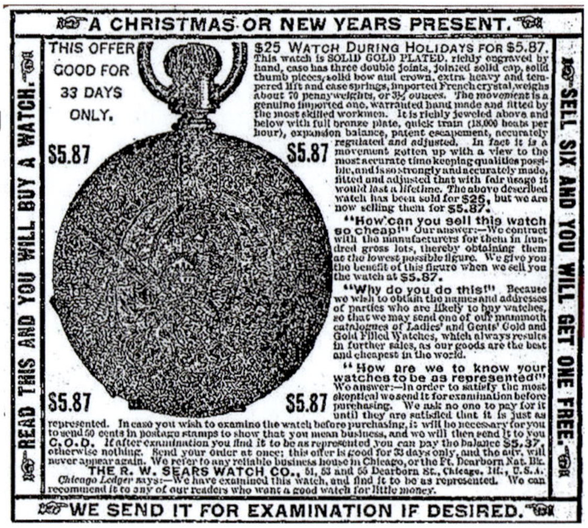

Figure 4.7 Advertising an early chapter of what would become the Sears retail empire.

End of Times?

For a good century, Sears and Roebuck stood the test of time, taking advantage of market opportunities as they came and expanding greatly into a wide variety of services and locations.

But the internet era has been difficult for many retailers, including Sears. And even a pocket watch vendor can suffer from bad timing and missteps, which resulted in a series of bankruptcies, ownership changes, and legal challenges. As of December 2024, the once giant is a shadow of itself, with only 8 retail locations still open. Watch this space.

To learn more, visit: https://effectuation.org/EE3/sears or scan Figure 4.8.

Figure 4.8

Practically Speaking

Venturing In Sync

Plunging Out

Annie Lennox's journey began with a plunge into classical music studies at the Royal Academy of Music in London. She quickly realized she was out of sync. Classical music was not her tune. As she stated in an interview in 2023 with Amna Nawaz of the PBS Newshour, "I knew from the very first day that I stepped in the building that it wasn't right for me."

Chance Harmony

This realization could have been discouraging, but Lennox's willingness to take risks and try new things led her down a different path.

It was a chance encounter with Joni Mitchell's music that inspired Lennox to pursue a career in music. She recounts, "So he came in with a Joni Mitchell album, which I think was probably 'Court and Spark.' It was something else. And what I identified with was this extraordinary lyrical aspect, this poetic aspect of visual painting, but in sound and in word. It sort of made everything come together."

Rhythming Forward

Lennox took action on this inspiration and formed the band, The Tourists, before eventually founding the more successful group Eurythmics.

Annie Lennox's success as an entrepreneur can also be attributed to her ability to stay true to her creative identity. When asked about her androgynous style, she replied, "If you are a creative person, then you're always kind of looking outside the box. So, it's partly decision. But it's also something intuitive. It just happens to be who you are."

Powerful Resonance

Lennox did not try to predict the market or cater to mainstream fashion trends. Instead, she focused on what felt right to her, and this authenticity translated into her brand image. By staying true to her unique identity, Lennox created a distinct brand that resonated with her audience and contributed to her entrepreneurial success.

Lennox's entrepreneurial spirit also led her to work with Comic Relief, a UK-based charity, where she made films about projects in Africa. Through this experience, Lennox saw the disparity of rights for women and girls and was inspired to start The Circle, a global NGO that promotes female empowerment around the world.

Practically Speaking *(continued)*

As Lennox stated in the PBS Newshour interview, "I saw that young girls are not getting education, not getting access to education, young girls becoming pregnant because they have been raped or abused." Well into her fifties, this plunge into philanthropy allowed Lennox to use the platform she had built during her long music career to make a positive impact on the world. In fact, you could argue that her powerful voice reaches well beyond music to global activism.

To learn more, visit: https://effectuation.org/EE3/lennox or scan Figure 4.10.

Figure 4.10

Figure 4.9

Practically Speaking

How to Learn to Let Go

Moonlighting

Tom Fatjo was an accountant in Houston in 1967 when a meeting in his community challenged him to take up the garbage collection problem the neighborhood was facing. He borrowed 7,000 US dollars for his first truck.

Every day, Fatjo woke at 4 a.m. to collect garbage for two hours before changing into a suit to go to work in his accounting office. This went on for over a year before Tom sat down to make the hard decision of whether to go on his own.

Tax Man or Garbage Man

> The pressure just kept building. Even though it was cold, my body was damp from continuous perspiration. Since so much of what I was doing in the accounting firm had to be done by the end of the tax year and involved important decisions with key clients, I needed to spend time thinking through problems and consulting with them as they made decisions. I was caught in a triangle of pressing demands, and I felt my throat constricting as if there were wires around my neck.
>
> (*Fatjo & Miller*, 1981)

Practically Speaking *(continued)*

Whatever It Takes

> That night I was exhausted, but I couldn't sleep. As I stared at the ceiling, I fantasized all our trucks breaking down at the same time. I was trying to push each of them myself in order to get them going.
>
> My heart began beating faster in the darkness and my body was chilled. The horrible thought that we might fail almost paralyzed me. I wanted to quit and run away. I was scared to death, very lonely, sick of the whole deal. As hard as I tried to think about my life and what was important to me, my mind was just a confused mass of muddled images … I remembered committing myself to make it in the garbage business "whatever it takes!" I lay back on my pillow and felt a deep sigh within myself—"Good Lord, so this is what it takes," I thought, then rolled over and got some restless sleep.
>
> (*Fatjo & Miller*, 1981)

Getting to Letting Go

When Fatjo let go of the security blanket of a white-collar profession to start the waste management giant Browning-Ferris Industries (originally American Refuse Systems), he had no way of knowing he would end up building a billion-dollar enterprise that shaped an entire industry. But what he did know was his worst-case scenario. For him, making the commitment to take the plunge meant understanding what he could lose, and coming to terms with that possibility.

Affordable Loss

Fatjo's decision embodies the principle of affordable loss. Instead of considering the potential upside opportunity in waste management, the important information in Fatjo's decision was what the possible downside looked like, and whether he could tolerate it, should the worst happen. By focusing on the prospect of the negative, entrepreneurs effectively manage the risk inherent in a new venture down to only what they find personally acceptable.

To learn more, visit: https://effectuation.org/EE3/waste or scan Figure 4.11.

Figure 4.11

Research Roots

WHO ACTUALLY PLUNGES?

The Global Entrepreneurship Monitor is the most extensive international survey of entrepreneurship activity, with over 120 countries having participated in their research since 1999. As an indicator of entrepreneurship, they track the percentage of adults aged 18–64 involved in new entrepreneurial activities, calling it the "Total Early-Stage Entrepreneurial Activity (TEA)" score.

According to their 2022/2023 Global Report, the average TEA scores for countries with a gross domestic product (GDP) per capita below 20,000 US dollars (group C) is the highest, averaging 15.1% of the adult population.

Research Roots *(continued)*

In Group B countries (GDP from 20,000 to 40,000 US dollars), 13.7% of adults are involved in entrepreneurial activity. And in the high-income countries (GDP per capita over 40,000 US dollars), only 11.1% of adults are active in early-stage entrepreneurial activities.

One explanation for the higher entrepreneurial activity in lower-income countries is the lack of employment, resulting in people creating their own source of income through entrepreneurship.

Table 4.1 shows the five most active countries for each income category in 2022/2023.

Table 4.1

By income classification, sorted from highest to lowest percentage	**Income Classification**	**Total Early-Stage Entrepreneurial Activity (TEA) Percentage**
Guatemala	C	29.4
Colombia	C	28.0
Togo	C	24.1
Brazil	C	20.0
Tunisia	C	17.1
Panama	B	27.9
Chile	B	27.0
Uruguay	B	26.3
Puerto Rico	B	20.0
Latvia	B	14.2
United Arab Emirates	A	25.5
Saudi Arabia	A	19.2
United States	A	19.2
Canada	A	16.5
United Kingdom	A	12.9

To learn more, visit: https://effectuation.org/EE3/gem or scan Figure 4.13.

Figure 4.13

Figure 4.12

TAKEAWAY: ACTION TRUMPS ANALYSIS

In general, we observe that expert entrepreneurs emphasize action rather than analysis. The history of entrepreneurship includes many examples of entrepreneurs whose ideas were not considered blockbuster opportunities, but who went ahead and built successful businesses simply by doing the next thing and the next thing and the next.

Expert entrepreneurs are means-driven, not goal-driven in formulating their ventures. The more experienced they are, the better they become at using readily available bits and pieces of ideas to create new possibilities, including new strategies, new business models, rapid responses to changes in the environment, valuable new applications for mundane technologies and even new markets no one quite knew could exist.

In their view, action trumps analysis. It also removes the need to "plunge."

Think It Through

- If you start with a toe in the water, rather than diving in headfirst, are you limiting how "big" the venture can/will become?
- Is it "moonlighting" to start a venture on the side of a full-time job? Does it matter?
- If this approach to getting started makes it easier to take action, how might more formal planning get in the way of taking action?

So What?

The plunge doesn't have to be, and usually isn't, a plunge. It's often a series of smaller steps, driven by your means and what you are willing to lose, rather than what you hope to gain. By this design, getting started is much less daunting.

What Now?

- Figure out your own max–min. What's the max you can afford to lose? Over what time frame? What is the minimum you need to earn to meet your needs?
- What can you do today to get started? It could be something as simple as coming up with a name for your venture and getting a business card printed.
- Is there anything you need to let go of before you can take just the next step?

REFERENCES

Benz, M., & Frey, B. S. (2008). Being independent is a great thing: Subjective evaluations of self-employment and hierarchy. *Economica* (London), *75*(298), 362–383. https://doi.org/10.1111/j.1468-0335.2007.00594.x

Fatjo, T. J., & Miller, K. (1981). *With No Fear of Failure: Recapturing Your Dreams Through Creative Enterprise*. Word Books.

GEM Global Entrepreneurship Monitor. (2023). Global Entrepreneurship Monitor 2022/2023 Global Report: Adapting to a "New Normal." Retrieved October 14, 2023, from https://gemconsortium.org/report/20222023-global-entrepreneurship-monitor-global-report-adapting-to-a-new-normal-2

PBS NewsHour. (2023, April 1). Annie Lennox on her success in music and dedication to activism (A. Nawaz, Interviewer). https://youtu.be/PLQlYoe0e5o

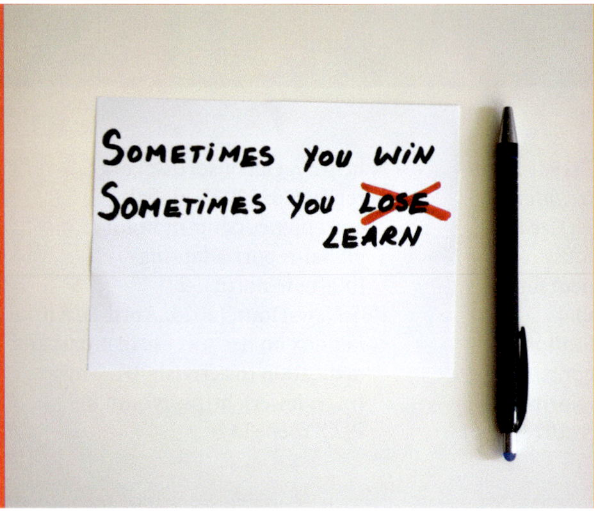

Figure 5.1

CHAPTER 5

Failing as the Way Forward

In This Chapter

There are many myths around failure. One of the most common is that failure is the end. If you can overcome the grief of a failed business and learn from it, then you have a fair chance of doing better (and smarter) the next time.

A tangible measure of failure can be seen in companies that close owing money to creditors, which represent only a small percentage of all the venture closures. With the lessons in this book, outstanding debts can be avoided. But not all failures need or should be avoided. In fact, some may argue that you are a successful entrepreneur only if you have failed once and continue to want to risk failing again and again.

DOI: 10.4324/9781003364016-6

SUCCESS IS LEARNING FROM FAILURE

No entrepreneur sets out to fail. But what, exactly, constitutes failure? And what counts as success? The answers to these questions are not as straightforward as you might think.

Most people would agree that a failed venture is one that closes owing money to creditors. But most would also say that there are other kinds of failure, too. Success is just as hard to pin down. We all have different personal definitions of success and failure.

For some, quitting is the only form of failure. For others, earning less than they could working for someone else is equivalent to failing.

Similarly, for some, only an initial public offering (IPO) can be considered a true success, while for others, simply being able to make a decent living without answering to a boss is a sign of having truly made it.

The matter is further complicated by cultural differences. In some parts of the world, an entrepreneur whose venture doesn't work out may find it difficult to get married and move forward with a productive life. But in Silicon Valley, if you are an entrepreneur who hasn't failed, you're a suspicious creature, an oddity.

The fear of failure, whatever it means, certainly looms large for many of us considering starting a business. But it shouldn't. If you are among those hesitating to dip your toe in the water for fear of being burned, consider these equations:

- Success ≠ Success
- Success ≠ Money
- Failed Venture ≠ Failed Individual
- Failure = Learning

In this chapter, we'll discuss each of those equations, take a look at some spectacular failures, and investigate how entrepreneurs learn to make failure part of the process and, importantly, a necessary learning experience.

Figure 5.2

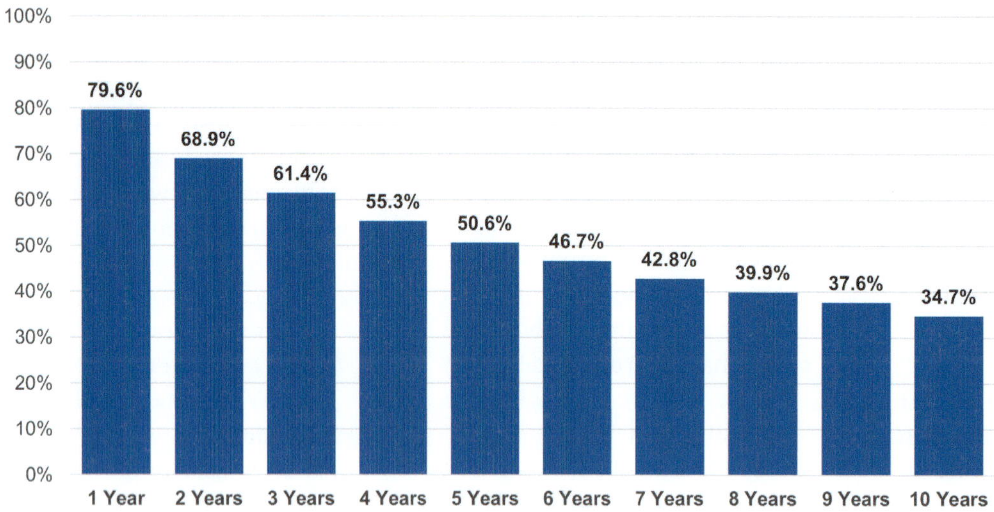

Figure 5.3 Survival Rates of US Businesses Started in 2013 (US Bureau of Statistics, 2024, www.bls.gov/bdm/us_age_naics_00_table7.txt).

SUCCESS ≠ SUCCESS

We know, this first equation looks nonsensical. We're not trying to be difficult, but are suggesting that success (and failure, too) is a slippery concept. If we need to overcome our fear of failure by reconsidering what failure actually means, then we should do the same for success.

Small Milestones—And Big Learning

Let's start with small milestones of success in the business world: making it to the first anniversary. In Figure 5.3 you will see that according to the US Bureau of Labor Statistics (n.d.), 79.6% of the private sector establishments opened in 2013 made it to their first birthday in 2014.

Imagine you are in that group that had a 50/50 chance of making it to their fifth birthday in 2018. That is probably long enough to have the experience of being your own boss, learn a few things, and maybe even stash away a bit of money. If you continued on and made it to the venture's tenth birthday in 2023, you would only be in the remaining 34.7% of the original "Class of 2013" business founders. Or you could be working on your second venture after having closed your first one without making it to its fifth birthday.

More importantly, we should not assume that an enterprise closure is necessarily a financial failure. Most statistics track only firm closures, so we don't know if they could be considered financial failures, in other words whether they were losing money, breaking even, or even profitable at the time when they stopped operating.

Just as importantly, economic viability is not the only reason people close a business. Maybe the owner retired, moved, was brought into the fold of a larger enterprise, accepted a job offer elsewhere, or simply got bored.

If Only the Big League Counts …

You might have heard that nine out of ten startups fail. For example, according to research done by Startup Genome (2022), 90% of new ventures will fail and only 1.5% will exit with a value of more than 50 million US dollars. Remember, however, that this number is not for all businesses, only for startups funded by venture capitalists (VC). And remember less than one-hundredth of one percent of new ventures are funded by VCs.

For the other (more than 99% of all) ventures, the survival

rate is 50% or more. And even out of the 50% that have exited, one-third of those were profitable at the time of exit (Headd, 2003).

That exit could be through a sale to new owners ("merger and acquisition," or "trade sale"). But then, you might think that only VC-funded firms will achieve the best of all exits, selling to many new shareholders through an initial public offering (IPO), which requires listing the venture on a stock market. But only 27% of IPOs are VC-funded! (Gompers & Lerner, 2001).

If you are dreaming of ringing the session starting bell in the New York Stock Exchange as part of your IPO, then you have a lot of work ahead and might want to rethink your assumptions.

According to the advisory firm EY Private (2023), only 130 companies completed an IPO in 2022. Even if we generously assume that those companies only came from the same pool which were born in 2013 and survived through 2022 (thus 236,663 enterprises according to the US Bureau of Labor Statistics), only 0.055% of them made it to IPO.

Three Stories: Success or Failure?

Now, make up your own mind about what success is and isn't, read the following short stories. Think about whether each demonstrates a success or a failure and tick the appropriate response.

Story 1

Lucy launched four ventures that failed before she moved onto her fifth one. Her fifth and sixth ventures were enormously successful, financially. Unfortunately, however, the sixth venture was wiped out by a natural disaster in which Lucy lost everything.

❑ Success ❑ Failure

Story 2

Mark meets a venture capitalist (VC) to pitch his next idea. He is feeling confident. His previous venture sold after only 18 months, making over four times its original investment for its founders and stakeholders. The VC looks at the previous venture as a failure. Their argument: Mark sold too soon and could have made more money.

❑ Success ❑ Failure

Story 3

Jacqueline, a serial entrepreneur, looks at the company she founded 15 years ago. It makes an 8% return for its shareholders, pays the bills, and is highly respected in its industry. Jacqueline quit the company seven years ago, selling her shares to the management team because she knew she could never take it public.

❑ Success ❑ Failure

That may have felt like a quiz, but it wasn't. There are no right or wrong answers. Clearly, how you view success (and failure) depends on your environment and on the expectations of others who are involved. It also depends on your role in the process.

If you are a venture capitalist (VC), you want at least ten times the money you invested. If you are a supplier, you only worry about whether the startup will pay their bills.

The fact that success and failure mean different things to different people makes the statistics we discussed earlier a lot less alarming because whether you succeed or fail really depends on what your objectives are and what your committed stakeholders want. This takes us to our next equation—success and the reasons why entrepreneurs start businesses must deal with more than just the financial return.

Celebrating Failures

Failures can be confusing, particularly when you are stuck in the emotion and details of the situation. One way to gain perspective (and see how failing is a normal part of trying) is to attend events designed to bring together people to share their failure stories.

To find an event close to you, start with the organization F**kUp Nights (acronym: FUN), which will show up when you search the internet (replace the asterisks in the name to reach "full spice"). Or approach organizations that support entrepreneurship in your community and ask about their programs. Or take entrepreneurial action and host your own failure event.

An online version of failure events can be found in the AdmittingFailure community (www.admittingfailure.org/).

These seriously fun events can help you celebrate the learning of failures with like-minded, courageous entrepreneurs.

To learn more, visit: https://effectuation.org/EE3/failure or scan Figure 5.4.

Figure 5.4

Research Roots

AMY EDMONDSON: "RIGHT KIND OF WRONG"

You might have heard about Harvard Professor Amy Edmondson in connection with her work on psychological safety (being able to speak up in a group without punishment), so it makes sense that Edmondson has gone on to deeply investigate the concept of failure.

Her latest book, *Right Kind of Wrong: Why Learning to Fail Can Teach Us to Thrive* (2023) urges us to "fail well"—not avoid failure, but also to move beyond "fail fast, fail often."

So how can we fail well? Edmondson explains: "Good failures are those that bring us valuable new information that simply could not have been gained any other way" (2023, p. 16).

She also puts failures into three categories:

- Intelligent: These are the good failures which provide an opportunity to learn and move forward. Pioneers carefully make many intelligent failures.
- Basic: These are failures due to mistakes, ones which could have been avoided by being more careful.
- Complex: These are failures which come from multiple causes which might have been preventable if small, initial problems (basic failures) had been addressed.

Getting a detailed understanding of failures can help you increase the number of intelligent failures you make (to move you ahead) and hopefully decrease other failures, which, left unchecked, can become complex failures.

For example, there might not be immediate consequences from the basic failure of ignoring the blinking light on your car dashboard, but not acting, particularly when the engine starts making noise, could lead to the complex (and expensive!) motor failure.

To learn more, visit: https://effectuation.org/EE3/rightwrong or scan Figure 5.5.

Figure 5.5

Practically Speaking

Persist Easy; Swerve Hard

The city of Bangalore, India, has over 200,000 three-wheel auto rickshaws—short-distance, open taxis that provide critical transportation in a metropolis of more than 13 million (2023) and a limited two-line metro rail system covering only 74 kilometers.

Efficiently ferrying both people and goods, these simple rickshaws challenge the urban environment. Their entrepreneurial drivers cruise the edges of the streets eagerly soliciting passengers, choking traffic, and adding smog to an already congested city. Meanwhile, frustrated businesspeople, merchants, and families await rides in other locations without an available auto rickshaw in sight.

Smooth Solution

When the commissioner of traffic police approached Padmasree Harish, an entrepreneur and self-taught web designer, to build a software system that would connect available auto rickshaws with waiting passengers, Harish saw both a natural answer to her city's problem as well as a good business opportunity.

The system would receive SMS messages from drivers indicating location and availability, as well as calls from passengers with their current location and desired destination. The system would match passengers with the closest auto rickshaw and dispatch the vehicle to the passenger. Harish could charge a setup fee for each driver and a small fee for each fare her system was able to connect. All she had to do was let the software do the work while the rupees rolled in. And so, in 2007, Easy Auto kicked into gear. In theory, that is.

Hard Stop

In practice, after the announcement of the initiative, the system never got beyond the rave press write-ups of its potential. This left Harish with a software system she and her team had spent six months developing, a call center filled with people hired to take calls from passengers, a tech team ready to roll out the system, extra uniforms for the drivers of the spruced-up rickshaws, and even 50,000 rupees worth of coolers and inventory from Pepsi for in-transit sales and additional revenue.

The bumps in the road seemed never-ending. Drivers were reluctant to pay a setup fee and were unwilling to send SMS messages with their current location. But the unseen pothole that derailed Harish was the regulatory environment. It turned out that the traffic commissioner who initiated the project did not have permission from the branch of the bureaucracy that oversaw auto rickshaws. So, the entire project was brought to a screeching halt.

U-Turn?

Harish's inclination was to return to her profitable web hosting and design business, leaving physical traffic to someone else. But her personal cell phone was one of the three numbers provided in the Easy Auto announcement for passengers to call an auto rickshaw on demand. And whenever it rained, as it often does in Bangalore, Harish would get 200 to 250 trip requests. The market had her number, and it simply would not hang up. But when does tenacity become foolishness? And how does an entrepreneur know when to quit?

Practically Speaking *(continued)*

A New Route

Harish started looking for work-arounds. She took courses in entrepreneurship so she could get others to chew on her problems. She actively observed every auto rickshaw she rode in and then some. In one, she saw an advertisement. She saw taxis with GPS units.

Nearly every website she saw offered free services to end users but made money from someone else. So, when the head of transportation came back to her in 2009 and asked her about getting Easy Auto going again, she was ready to negotiate: the approvals had to be complete before she would spend a rupee.

- The auto rickshaws would have to be equipped with units containing LCD screens showing promotional videos and GPS units for precise location information.
- The video would be funded by a company that builds the auto rickshaws.
- The drivers would receive compensation for signing up with Easy Auto.
- The GPS and LCD hardware would be provided by the manufacturers in advance with payment once the system started generating income.
- The call center would be outsourced to a firm willing to set it up at no charge.

Harish was prepared to do everything differently than she had on her first try. She left behind the choice between the straight road of persistence and the sad U-turn. She had learned to swerve hard.

Figure 5.6

Enduring Logic

Conventional wisdom describes the doggedly determined entrepreneur enduring in the face of adversity. But a closer look reveals an unexpected combination of persistence and flexibility. Persisting hard for a particular solution can be counterproductive and even end in despair.

But hard-headed flexibility may transform the problem into an opportunity that attracts unexpected shareholders. Especially when problems persist, entrepreneurs need to be able to swerve hard to co-create new answers that can form the basis of new firms, new products, new markets, or even that unlikeliest of novelties—smoother traffic flow in Bangalore.

To learn more, visit: https://effectuation.org/EE3/easyauto or scan Figure 5.7.

Figure 5.7

How Many Rejections Are One Too Many?

Within a month of submitting the first manuscript to publishing houses, the creative team behind the multimillion-dollar book series *Chicken Soup for the Soul* (Canfield & Hansen, 1993) got turned down 33 consecutive times. Publishers claimed that "anthologies don't sell" and that the book was "too positive."

Canfield and Hansen continued their quest and collected a total of 140 rejections before finally, in 1993, the president of a company called Health Communications took a chance on the collection of poems, stories, and titbits of encouragement.

In the more than 30 years since, *Chicken Soup for the Soul* has become a stand-alone publisher with a collection of more than 275 titles translated into 42 languages, selling over 500 million copies worldwide.

The company has moved beyond print to include podcasts and video and curate collections for specific audiences. And for the pet needing some tender loving care, the company even has a pet food line!

At what point in the sea of rejections would you have quit? If never, how would you sustain your energy to keep on going against the tide?

Research Roots

PERSIST, BUT KNOW WHEN TO QUIT

Persistence is often said to be an important trait of entrepreneurs. But is it possible to be too persistent; in other words, can it sometimes be better to (using the old adage) "quit while you are ahead"?

Annie Duke, former professional poker champion and now holder of a Ph.D. in cognitive psychology, knows some things about when to quit (versus persisting), which she shares in her 2022 book *Quit: The Power of Knowing When to Walk Away*. She builds on the work of the Nobel Prize laureates Daniel Kahneman and Richard Thaler, who deal with the topic of holding on too long.

Her core learning from the poker world is (Duke, 2022, p. 18):

> Optimal quitting might be the most important skill separating great players from amateurs.
>
> and
>
> In the battle of whether to hold 'em or fold 'em, amateurs usually hold 'em. Professionals usually fold 'em.

Moving from the poker table to the marketplace, Duke emphasizes the importance of knowing when to abandon a failing venture, which involves:

- Assessing opportunity costs: understanding what other opportunities might be missed by continuing in a failing venture can guide the decision to quit.
- Embracing uncertainty: accepting uncertainty and being willing to pivot when necessary is vital.

Research Roots ***(continued)***

- Evaluating progress: regularly assessing progress toward goals and recognizing when those goals are no longer attainable is crucial for making the decision to quit.

Effectually speaking, know your affordable loss and quit when you have lost that. And keep going only when someone else fully prepays for or underwrites your next step.

It is also important to note that pivoting and quitting are not the same thing. A recent study by Hampel et al. (2020) provides clues as to why pivoting "too much" could be detrimental: the authors highlight that multiple pivots can upset stakeholder relationships. Their suggested remedy is to communicate experiences of shared challenges to strengthen the bond.

To learn more, visit: https://effectuation.org/EE3/quitpoker or scan Figure 5.8.

Figure 5.8

Figure 5.9

SUCCESS ≠ MONEY

Before you launch your venture, hoping to become a multimillionaire, consider the following:

- On average, the self-employed earn about the same as those employed and working for a wage.
- Having said that, the distribution of earnings is skewed by a few superstar entrepreneurs who make incredible amounts of money (e.g. Jeff Bezos). Most entrepreneurs earn below the average.
- Those who earn below average officially earn about one-third less than a comparable employed person does.
- Research by Hurst et al. (2010) suggests that this pattern is reversed when income under-reporting is considered. Large companies have a strong incentive to ensure accurate reporting of employee income. Entrepreneurs are not as visible to tax authorities, opening up the possibility to "optimize" their declared income and hence taxes paid.

Of course, there are things other than money that matter to entrepreneurs (such as being your own boss, doing something that's important to you, or even just trying to solve a problem that bothers you).

Success is a lousy teacher. It seduces smart people into thinking they can't lose.

Bill Gates, Microsoft co-founder and philanthropist

Twain on Learning

We should be careful to get out of an experience only the wisdom that is in it—and stop there; lest we be like the cat that sits down on a hot stove lid. She will never sit down on a hot stove lid again—and that is well; but also she will never sit down on a cold one.

Mark Twain, American entrepreneur and author

FAILED VENTURE ≠ FAILED INDIVIDUAL

Entrepreneurial performance is almost always confused with firm performance—the success or failure of the company is the success or failure of the individual. This is a mistake for several reasons.

First, as we have seen, although market entry is common, survival in the market is less common. Second, many companies enter a market in its infancy. As the market matures, only the fittest survive. A lot of work has been done on the corporation, looking, for example, for a correlation between the age of the firm and survival rates. (Do firms die young or degenerate with age?) Unfortunately, little is known of the success or failure rates of entrepreneurs.

The primary reason is that evidence on failed firms is hard to obtain (the data usually disappears along with the firm), while evidence on individual entrepreneurs who have failed a firm is almost impossible to come by. People simply do not walk around with business cards that say, "Failed entrepreneur."

Two-thirds of entrepreneurs quit after their first venture fails. The other third dust themselves off and go on to start other firms. And almost all of them succeed sooner or later. In any case, entrepreneurs tend not to mention their failed firms, except long after the fact as part of uplifting anecdotes in public speeches.

Practically Speaking

Making Sweet Success Out of Bitter Failure: Milton Hershey

Born September 13, 1857, on a farm near Derry Church, a small Pennsylvania community, Milton Hershey was the only surviving child of Fannie and Henry Hershey. His mother raised him in the strict discipline of the Mennonite faith. Frequent family moves interrupted his schooling and left him with a limited education. He only completed the fourth grade.

A Bitter Start

Following a four-year apprenticeship with a Lancaster candy maker, he established his first candy-making business in Philadelphia. That initial effort failed, and his next two attempts, in Chicago and New York, went bankrupt as well. Returning to Lancaster, Pennsylvania, in 1883, Hershey established the Lancaster Caramel Company, which quickly became an outstanding success. It was this business that established him as a candy maker and set the stage for future accomplishments.

New Ingredients

Hershey became fascinated with German chocolate-making machinery exhibited at the 1893 World's Columbian Exposition in Chicago. He bought the equipment for his Lancaster plant and soon began producing a variety of chocolate creations.

Hershey sold the Lancaster Caramel Co. for 1 million US dollars in 1900 (the equivalent of 35 million US dollars today) to concentrate exclusively on his chocolate business. Three years later, he returned to his birthplace of Derry Church to build a new factory. There he could obtain the large supplies of fresh milk needed to perfect and produce fine milk chocolate.

Practically Speaking *(continued)*

Sweet Success

Excited by the potential of milk chocolate, which at that time was a Swiss luxury product, Milton Hershey was determined to develop a formula for milk chocolate and sell it to the American public. Through trial and error, he created his own formula for milk chocolate. In 1903, he found success and began construction on what was to become the largest chocolate manufacturing plant in the United States.

To learn more, visit: https://effectuation.org/EE3/hershey or scan Figure 5.11.

Figure 5.10

Figure 5.11

Figure 5.12 Hershey, Pennsylvania where the streetlamps are shaped like chocolate kisses and the street names are unmistakable.

Practically Speaking

Sheila Johnson: Under the Thorns

As we have mentioned earlier in the book and this chapter, fairy tales of entrepreneurial success abound in the media. But they are just that—fairy tales. In reality, the stories often gloss over the harder patches, the challenges, the failures, the moments of great doubt and insecurity.

No Longer a Perfect Crown

By any standard, Sheila Johnson is an extremely successful entrepreneur—in media, sports management, and more recently in hospitality. In 2023, after years of silence, she published her biography, entitled *Walk Through Fire: A Memoir of Love, Loss, and Triumph.*

Why did she do this? Why not keep the "perfect image" of a media queen? Here's Sheila's response to Amna Nawaz, who interviewed her for the PBS Newshour (2023):

> Because the silence was killing me inside. And it was time for me to open up those wounds, and it was time for them to heal. It's been a journey. I have been through three acts of my life, and each one of them carried certain problems, the second act especially, and unusually painful problems. And now I'm in my third act, and I'm healing and I'm happier than I have ever been.

Let's begin with the sanitized version of her success story—the fairy tale queen with the perfect crown. Then we will start adding the thorns—the "wounds" she suffered and how she healed.

Princess of Music

The daughter to an accountant mother and neurosurgeon father, Sheila fell in love with music and worked hard to become an accomplished violinist, winning a major competition in her home state of Illinois. Johnson graduated from high school and went on to complete a Bachelor of Arts degree in music at the University of Illinois.

She then became a music teacher at one of the most exclusive schools in Washington, DC, Sidwell Friends, known for educating the children of many US presidents and politicians.

Johnson founded a youth orchestra, Young Strings in Action, and was invited to perform in the Kingdom of Jordan, which resulted in Johnson receiving an educational award from Jordan's King Hussein.

Fairy Tale Thrones …

With the intention of creating a television version of *Ebony Magazine* (focused on African American readers), in 1980 Johnson and her husband, Bob, started a cable television channel called Black Entertainment Television (BET), which was sold 20 years later to the cable giant Viacom for 1.3 billion US dollars, easily making the Johnsons multimillionaires.

Since then, Johnson has taken management and ownership roles in various sports teams and founded Salamander Hospitality, which has properties in several US states, Jamaica, and the British West Indies. Johnson is also an active philanthropist in the arts, education, and fighting poverty.

In mid-2023, the business magazine *Forbes* estimated Sheila Johnson's net worth to be 840 million US dollars.

Practically Speaking *(continued)*

… and Reality Thorns

When Sheila was a teenager her father abandoned the family, taking with him the family income, bank accounts, and credit cards. Sheila had to step up to support her mother in rebuilding their life. Memories of that painful transition still linger.

Black Silence

There was another factor which made Sheila's childhood difficult: skin color. Her neurosurgeon father was only permitted to treat black patients. Once those patients were served, he had to relocate to a new hospital. This resulted in the family moving house 13 times before they finally were able to set down roots outside Chicago.

The racism affected Sheila's daily life as well, as she describes:

> And even as a young person, they were saying you should be seen and not heard. And it just went against who I am. It's not in my DNA. And I love challenges. I'm a risk-taker. So it was just important that I just—these doors would open. And I said, why can't I go through them? And I decided I was going to go through every door that came my way.
>
> (PBS NewsHour, 2023)

BETween the Thorns

Johnson's challenges were compounded by her business success and the fact that she had co-founded her company BET with her husband Bob. When the marriage wasn't going well, those around her discouraged her from ending the marriage, as Johnson explains:

> I think, because of how successful BET was—and you're the king and queen of media. You're the first black company on television. And they were proud of the fact that there was that representation there, and for it to have scandal, where we would break up, it sort of shatters the image of what we were trying to build.
>
> (PBS NewsHour, 2023)

Some people insisted she should be "the good wife," so she supported him in public, but that didn't work either:

> But I was doing so much work in the background. And I was literally erased, literally erased out of that company. And I got fired by my own husband because I found out what was really going on. And as I—when I confronted him, he wanted to get rid of me.
>
> (PBS NewsHour, 2023)

Walls Closing In

All of these circumstances and the loss of a child led Johnson to a conclusion many people have when things are particularly difficult with their partner: That it was her fault, that she was somehow a failure, sharing a perspective known to many women:

> When people read the book, the thread that kind of goes through that, because from the emotional abuse, I felt like a failure. I felt like a failure in everything that I did, the way I looked. I was either too fat or too thin. I was too outspoken, or I didn't speak enough. It was this constant berating of who I really was.
>
> (PBS NewsHour, 2023)

Practically Speaking *(continued)*

The Johnson's marriage ended in 2002, and as you will note from the description above, Sheila Johnson had re-built her career by 2005, including with the available means of strength, resilience, and courage she had developed over many years of dealing with racism, misogyny, and failure.

Doors Opening Again

What's next for Sheila Johnson? She's expanding her collection of properties and with confidence in her abilities to master just about anything, she is open: "It's just whatever comes towards me. And, instinctively, if it's the right thing, I will embrace it. I just don't want life to be over, because I'm enjoying it more than ever now" (PBS NewsHour, 2023).

That sounds like someone who has learned how to move forward through failure. Not only to success, which can turn out to be a crown of thorns, but also beyond success to living well.

To learn more, visit: https://effectuation.org/EE3/sheilajohnson or scan Figure 5.13.

Figure 5.13

Separating Entrepreneur From Firm

The corporation was invented to separate the success or failure of the firm from that of the individual. If an individual closes the business to pursue a new opportunity, does that constitute individual failure? Too often, we think that if the business fails the individual has failed.

Remember that this is not the case, as the Hershey story illustrates. Milton Hershey's early business missteps did not destroy him; some of his ventures may have failed, but he, as chocolate fans in the United States know, did not. In fact, there is an entire town in Pennsylvania that still bears his name.

Kintsugi: Broken Joy

In many places, particularly in so-called "throw-away societies" that rely on single-use items, when something is broken, it is sent to recycling, or worse, to landfill.

The Japanese culture sees things differently. Knowing that breaks and cracks are part of life, they seek to give broken ceramic items a new life and new meaning with a process called Kintsugi (golden repair).

Figure 5.14

The broken pieces are re-attached with lacquer and gold, making the piece whole again, and in fact much more unique and special.

The entrepreneurial process, too, can be a work of Kintsugi.

Practically Speaking

Failing Up to the Top: Apple Computer

Apple is well known for its innovativeness and its incredible product successes—creating a mass market where there was none. Yet did you know that Apple has survived a series of failed products over the years?

Table 5.1

Product	Date	Apple's product failures: Lessons learned
Lisa	1983	The Lisa was the first computer to boast a graphical interface and a mouse. Aimed at the business community, it was priced at today's equivalent of more than 20,000 US dollars. Unsurprisingly, the business community voted for the cheaper IBMs. Lesson learned: Price does matter.
Apple IIc	1984	The Apple IIc was hailed as the first portable computer. It had a carrying case, external power supply, built-in floppy drive, and peripheral expansion ports. But it lacked upgradeability, and it had an extremely short-lived LCD display. The lessons learned from the Apple IIc's shortcomings would drive the design of the Macintosh.
Mac TV	1993	A combination of a Sony Trinitron and an Apple Performa 520, the product lasted barely 12 months before it was discontinued. Its major problem? It was incapable of showing TV feeds in a desktop window. Although only 10,000 units were produced, it was the precursor to today's Apple TV.
Newton	1993	The best known of Apple flops is probably the Newton. Released in 1993 as a revolutionary personal digital assistant (PDA) (but not as revolutionary as its first prototypes), it was available for four years with nearly no sales. When Steve Jobs returned to Apple in 1997, he axed the product he had tried so hard to launch. The Newton was bulky and relied on handwriting recognition software, which wasn't yet very good. Once Apple got those deficiencies fixed in the form of an iPad, the Newton became a good example of a product ahead of its time.
Pippin	1996	With the Pippin, Apple tried (once again) to enter the video game market with a product that was co-marketed with toymaker Bandai. The Pippin was sold as a cheap machine on which one could play games, but it also served as a network computer—one of the first multimedia platforms. It failed for several reasons, including a lack of software and competition in a market dominated by players such as Sega, Sony PlayStation, and Nintendo.
Hockey Puck Mouse	1998	The mouse that was shipped with the first iMacs was small, not ergonomic and awkward to control. It was almost immediately phased out and replaced by the Mighty Mouse. Lesson learned: sometimes a classical shape is good.
G4 Cube	2000	While the Cube was meant to fill the gap between the iMac G3 and the PowerMac G4, it was killed by the critics before it got anywhere. Its major problems: it lacked a monitor, and it had a high price tag. Apart from its design, it also set the stage for fanless cooling in PCs. The G4 was also an improvement on the NeXT computer, which Jobs had designed based on another major learning: don't build in proprietary software. The G4 won several international design awards and its designer, Jonathan Ive, stayed with Apple until 2019, designing many highly successful products along the way.

Practically Speaking *(continued)*

iPod Hi-Fi	2006	This high-end speaker system was designed to work with Apple's iPod music players but failed to catch on due to its high price point and limited compatibility with other devices. Lesson learned: Apple realized that it needed to focus on more universal products that could work with a wider range of devices and platforms.
MobileMe	2008	MobileMe was a subscription-based service that was intended to provide email, calendar, and contact syncing across Apple devices, but was plagued by technical issues and poor user reviews. Lesson learned: Apple realized that it needed to invest more in cloud services and infrastructure to ensure that its products and services could work seamlessly together.
Apple Maps	2012	This mapping app was intended to replace Google Maps on Apple devices, but was criticized for its inaccuracies, missing features, and poor user interface. Lesson learned: Apple realized that it needed to prioritize quality and user experience over speed of development and that it should focus on its core competencies rather than trying to compete with other tech giants in every area.
Apple Watch	2015	The Apple Watch was initially criticized for its high price point and limited functionality compared to other smartwatches on the market. Lesson learned: Apple realized that it needed to focus on delivering more value to customers and building a better ecosystem of apps and services to support its hardware. In the meantime, however, Apple Watches have become more ubiquitous.
AirPower	2017	The AirPower wireless charging mat was announced in 2017, but faced many technical issues and was canceled in 2019, never having been sold to consumers.
Apple TV+	2019	Although it is not a complete failure, Apple TV+ continues to struggle to gain significant market share in the highly competitive streaming market.

To learn more, visit: https://effectuation.org/EE3/appleflops or scan Figure 5.15.

Figure 5.15

Figure 5.16

FAILURE = LEARNING

There are smart ways to fail and not so smart ways. Without failure, there would be no learning, no progress. In fact, the essence of the scientific method—the most rigorous learning process we humans have—is the design of well-thought-out failures—experiments that seek to disprove hypotheses. As some hypotheses are shown to be incorrect and others continue unscathed, we begin to get closer to workable truths that lead to valuable technologies and cures for diseases.

The same is true of good engineering. In a book entitled *Success Through Failure: The Paradox of Design*, Henry Petroski (2006) shows how success often masks potential modes of failure and how throughout history failures have led to technological progress and better design.

The key to learning from failures is to fail cheap and fail fast. The affordable loss principle, which we'll learn more about in Chapter 12, is useful here. The idea is to limit your investment in a new opportunity to what you have consciously chosen as an acceptable level of loss. This has the benefit of reducing the magnitude of failure as well as limiting the psychological hit likely to come with unanticipated failures.

GRIEVING AFTER FAILURE

Failure is never easy. Dean Shepherd (2009) suggests that the emotions associated with having to close a business are somewhat similar to those we feel when we lose someone dear to us. Business owners see the closure of their business as a personal loss and experience feelings of grief.

The ability to learn from the loss of a business depends on recovering from that grief. Shepherd suggests that confronting the reality of the loss and acknowledging the emotions as normal while suppressing them enough to move on may be helpful for entrepreneurs.

It's also crucial to keep in mind what is perhaps the most important rule of failure: don't fail alone. Failure is more palatable and success is sweeter when we have supportive people around us who share in the ups and downs. More on this in Chapter 14 and Chapter 16.

And interestingly, people who have gone through adversity together tend to strengthen their bonds of trust and friendship. As the founder of Teledyne remarked, "My co-founders and I are blood brothers. We have been through failed ventures in the past."

David Shrank, the founder of PupCups, a promising startup that he was forced to close due to a cash crunch, said this about his entire team, "The PupCups alumni meet regularly and exchange memories and hopes. The question is not whether I would start another venture with them. I don't think I would start another venture without them."

When you ask expert entrepreneurs about failures, they will say:

- Keep 'em small
- Kill 'em young
- Don't fail alone

Deciding and Learning

"Sir, what is the secret of your success?" a reporter asked a successful businessman.

"Two words."

"And what are they, sir?"

"Right decisions."

"And how do you make right decisions?"

"One word."

"And what is that, sir?"

"Experience."

"And how do you get experience?"

"Two words."

"And what are they, sir?"

"Wrong decisions."

TAKEAWAY: FAILURE IS THE WAY FORWARD

The failure equations show us that some of the most common notions about failure are actually myths.

The most pernicious of these is that failure is about the end of something. We urge you instead to think of it as a beginning. And actually the way forward.

For billions of people around the world, entrepreneurship is the only option. If they do not make something and sell something, their children will starve. Even in the developed world where lots of well-paying jobs are available, people get downsized and even lose their homes, as in the financial crisis of 2008 or due to the COVID-19 pandemic.

Entrepreneurship is the ultimate backup option. For everyone. And the set of lessons entrepreneurship teaches about failure is the way forward. For all societies. At all times.

So What?

By creating more companies, trying more often, your probability of success will increase because each experience will add to your learning. Think of yourself as an emerging chess master, learning new moves with each game and using them in the next.

Think It Through

- How much does our ego get in the way of risking failure?
- Is the failure of a public firm different in important ways from the failure of a privately (independently) owned business?
- How do we deal with the cultural aspect of failure? Does it mean that it's easier to be an entrepreneur in some countries than in others?

What Now?

As you step forward, consider what you might lose if you don't try. How does that compare to what you might lose if you try and fail? The following questions can help you make sense of this.

- What are your options after each situation? Which experience will put you in a stronger position?
- Think of failure not as an option, but as the norm. Paint the picture of everything consistently going wrong. How bad is it?
- In your current effort, what and how much would you need to learn to decide that it was time to stop?
- What could be the next thing for you to try at that point?

REFERENCES

24–7 Press Release Newswire. (n.d.). Barclays reveals SME owners plan to stay in business longer than they'll be married. Retrieved September 23, 2023, from https://www.24-7pressrelease.com/press-release/58172/barclays-reveals-sme-owners-plan-to-stay-in-business-longer-than-theyll-be-married

Aldridge Foundation—Empowering future generations. (n.d.). Aldridge Foundation. Retrieved September 23, 2023, from https://www.aldridgefoundation.com/

Åstebro, T. (2014, January 14). Earnings from entrepreneurship: Less than salaried employment or just less measurable? HEC Paris. https://www.hec.edu/en/knowledge/articles/earnings-entrepreneurship-less-salaried-employment-or-just-less-measurable

Berends, H., van Burg, E., & Garud, R. (2021). Pivoting or persevering with venture ideas: Recalibrating temporal commitments. *Journal of Business Venturing, 36*(4), 106126. https://doi.org/10.1016/j.jbusvent.2021.106126

Burnell, D., & Stevenson, R. M. (2019). To pivot or not to pivot? How core venture identity inhibits early business model revision. *Academy of Management Proceedings, 2019*(1), 19449. https://doi.org/10.5465/AMBPP.2019.19449abstract

Bygrave, W. D. (1997). *The Portable MBA in Entrepreneurship*. Wiley.

Canfield, J., & Hansen, M. V. (1993). *Chicken Soup for the Soul*. Health Communications.

Chicken Soup for the Soul Website. (n.d.). Chicken Soup for the Soul. Retrieved January 13, 2024, from https://www.chickensoup.com/

Cottle, G. W. (2020). *Capturing the Strategic Pivot: Identifying the Performance Outcomes of New Venture Pivots*. ProQuest Dissertations Publishing.

Duke, A. (2022). *Quit: The Power of Knowing When to Walk Away*. Penguin Books.

Earle, A. G., Merenda, M. J., & Davis, J. M. (2019). Strategy-as-process in a technology venture: A case study of pivots, pauses, partners, and progress. *Technology Innovation Management Review, 9*(1), 9–19. https://doi.org/10.22215/timreview/1208

Edmondson, A. C. (2023). *Right Kind of Wrong*. Simon & Schuster.

EY Private. (2023). EY global IPO trends 2022. EY. https://www.ey.com/en_jp/ipo/how-can-you-prepare-to-seize-the-right-moment

Forbes. (n.d.). Sheila Johnson—Profile. Retrieved January 13, 2024, from https://www.forbes.com/profile/sheila-johnson/

Fernández-Bastidas, R. (2023). Entrepreneurship and tax evasion. *Economic Modelling, 128*, 106488. https://doi.org/10.1016/j.econmod.2023.106488

Gompers, P., & Lerner, J. (2001). The venture capital revolution. *The Journal of Economic Perspectives, 15*(2), 145–168. https://doi.org/10.1257/jep.15.2.145

Grove, L. (2010, April 29). Sheila Johnson slams BET. The Daily Beast. https://www.thedailybeast.com/articles/2010/04/29/sheila-johnsons-fight-against-hiv-in-dc

Gur, F. A., Mooney, C. H., & Mathias, B. D. (2022). The co-evolutionary process of venture identity formation in the era of pivots. *Academy of Management Proceedings*. https://doi.org/10.5465/AMBPP.2022.123

Guynn, J. (2018, April 20). Exclusive: Flickr bought by SmugMug, which vows to revitalize the photo service. *USA TODAY*. https://www.usatoday.com/story/tech/2018/04/20/smugmug-buys-flickr-verizon-oath/537377002/

Hampel, C. E., Tracey, P., & Weber, K. (2020). The art of the pivot: How new ventures manage identification relationships with stakeholders as they change direction. *Academy of Management Journal, 63*(2), 440–471. https://doi.org/10.5465/amj.2017.0460

Headd, B. (2003). Redefining business success: Distinguishing between closure and failure. *Small Business Economics, 21*(1), 51–61. https://doi.org/10.1023/A:1024433630958

Hernbroth, M., & Hartmans, A. (2020, December 4). The life and career of Stewart Butterfield, the Flickr cofounder and Slack CEO who just sold his company to Salesforce for $27.7 billion. Business Insider. https://www.businessinsider.com/amazing-life-of-slack-ceo-stewart-butterfield-2015-9

Hoffman, R. (n.d.). Highlights to inspire your 2024. Retrieved January 6, 2024, from https://mastersofscale.com/episode/highlights-to-inspire-your-2024/

Huang, R., Ritter, J. R., & Zhang, D. (2023). IPOs and SPACs: Recent developments (SSRN Scholarly Paper 4319577). https://doi.org/10.2139/ssrn.4319577

Hurst, E., Li, G., & Pugsley, B. (2010). Are household surveys like tax forms? Evidence from income underreporting of the self-employed. *Review of Economics and Statistics, 96*, 19–33. https://doi.org/10.1162/REST_a_00363.

Johnson, S. (2023). *Walk Through Fire: A Memoir of Love, Loss, and Triumph*. Simon & Schuster.

Kessler, G. (2014, January 27). Analysis | Do nine out of 10 new businesses fail, as Rand Paul claims? *Washington Post*. https://www.washingtonpost.com/news/fact-checker/wp/2014/01/27/do-9-out-of-10-new-businesses-fail-as-rand-paul-claims/

Kintsugi. (2023). Wikipedia. https://en.wikipedia.org/w/index.php?title=Kintsugi&oldid=1191913995

Kirtley, J., & O'Mahony, S. (2023). What is a pivot? Explaining when and how entrepreneurial firms decide to make strategic change and pivot. *Strategic Management Journal*, *44*(1), 197–230. https://doi.org/10.1002/smj.3131

Knaup, A. E. (2005). Survival and longevity in the business employment dynamics data. *Monthly Lab. Rev.*, *128*, 50.

Lapinski, Z. (2023a). How to succeed at failing, part 1: The chain of events. Freakonomics. Retrieved October 12, 2023, from https://freakonomics.com/podcast/how-to-succeed-at-failing-part-1-the-chain-of-events/

Lapinski, Z. (2023b). How to succeed at failing, part 2: Life and death. Freakonomics. Retrieved November 4, 2023, from https://freakonomics.com/podcast/how-to-succeed-at-failing-part-2-life-and-death/

Lapinski, Z. (2023c). How to succeed at failing, part 3: Grit vs. quit. Freakonomics. Retrieved November 4, 2023, from https://freakonomics.com/podcast/how-to-succeed-at-failing-part-3-grit-vs-quit/

Lapinski, Z. (2023d). How to succeed at failing, part 4: Extreme resiliency. Freakonomics. Retrieved November 4, 2023, from https://freakonomics.com/podcast/how-to-succeed-at-failing-part-4-extreme-resiliency/

Leswing, K. (2019, March 29). Apple cancels AirPower, the wireless charging pad it announced over a year ago. CNBC. https://www.cnbc.com/2019/03/29/apple-cancels-airpower.html

Marvel, M. R., Wolfe, M. T., Kuratko, D. F., & Fisher, G. (2022). Examining entrepreneurial experience in relation to pre-launch and post-launch learning activities affecting venture performance. *Journal of Small Business Management*, *60*(4), 759–785. https://doi.org/10.1080/00472778.2020.1762626

McDonald, R., & Gao, C. (2019). Pivoting isn't enough? Managing strategic reorientation in new ventures. *Organization Science*, *30*(6), 1289–1318. https://doi.org/10.1287/orsc.2019.1287

McMullen, J. S. (2017). Are you pivoting away your passion? The hidden danger of assuming customer sovereignty in entrepreneurial value creation. *Business Horizons*, *60*(4), 427–430. https://doi.org/10.1016/j.bushor.2017.03.012

Milton Hershey. (n.d.). Retrieved January 5, 2024, from https://www.thehersheycompany.com/content/hershey-corporate/en-us/home/about-us/milton-hershey.html

PBS NewsHour. (2023b, September 26). Sheila Johnson discusses her groundbreaking career and new memoir "Walk Through Fire" (A. Nawaz, Interviewer). https://www.youtube.com/watch?v=hMyguIdhYnY

Petroski, H. (2006). *Success Through Failure: The Paradox of Design*. Princeton University Press. https://doi.org/10.1515/9781400849116

Pozin, I. (2012, November 28). How to avoid being a startup failure. Forbes. Retrieved September 23, 2023, from https://www.forbes.com/sites/ilyapozin/2012/11/28/how-to-avoid-being-a-startup-failure/

Sandage, S. A. (2005). *Born Losers: A History of Failure in America*. Harvard University Press. https://doi.org/10.4159/9780674043053

Shepherd, D. A. (2003). Learning from business failure: Propositions of grief recovery for the self-employed. *The Academy of Management Review*, *28*(2), 318. https://doi.org/10.2307/30040715

Shepherd, D. A. (2009). *From Lemons to Lemonade: Squeeze Every Last Drop of Success Out of Your Mistakes*. Pearson Prentice Hall.

Snihur, Y., & Clarysse, B. (2022). Sowing the seeds of failure: Organizational identity dynamics in new venture pivoting. *Journal of Business Venturing*, *37*(1), 106164. https://doi.org/10.1016/j.jbusvent.2021.106164

Startup Genome. (2011). Why startups fail—Premature scaling. Startup Genome LLC. https://startupgenome.com/reports/startup-genome-why-startups-fail-premature-scaling

Startup Genome. (2022). *The Global Startup Ecosystem Report 2022*. Startup Genome LLC. https://startupgenome.com/article/the-state-of-the-global-startup-economy

Statista Daily Data. (2023, December 21). Infographic: How big is Apple's supporting cast? https://www.statista.com/chart/14433/apples-other-products-revenue

Tanveer, L. (2019). *Entrepreneurs, Pivots and Shocks: An Exploration of Organizational Learning Processes in Nascent Ventures*. ProQuest Dissertations Publishing.

The HistoryMakers. (n.d.). Sheila C. Johnson's Biography. Retrieved January 13, 2024, from https://www.thehistorymakers.org/biography/sheila-c-johnson-41

Twain, M. (1897). *Pudd'nhead Wilson's New Calendar*, in *Following the Equator*. American Publishing Company.

US Bureau of Labor Statistics. (n.d.). Survival of private sector establishments by opening year. Retrieved January 12, 2024, from https://www.bls.gov/bdm/us_age_naics_00_table7.txt

Wagner, E. T. (2013, September 12). Five reasons 8 out of 10 businesses fail. Forbes. https://www.forbes.com/sites/ericwagner/2013/09/12/five-reasons-8-out-of-10-businesses-fail/

Wikipedia. (2023). Stewart Butterfield. https://en.wikipedia.org/w/index.php?title=Stewart_Butterfield&oldid=1187629070

PART II

How (Expert) Entrepreneurs Think

Systematic study of expertise in areas that range from chess to taxi driving shows that experts are not different from the rest of us except in how they have learned to think about and solve problems. These differences are what enable the extraordinary performance we have come to associate with experts across domains.

This section is dedicated to explaining those differences within the domain of entrepreneurship. Here, you should expect to find a clear explanation of what makes the entrepreneurial problem space unique, and fundamental strategies expert entrepreneurs have learned for operating effectively within that problem space.

As you work through it, we hope you will begin constructing a clear and precise way of looking at the world, so that you can see the world in the same way that expert entrepreneurs have learned to see it. In their view, the world is both uncertain and shapeable at the same time.

Understanding this perspective helps explain the relationship between the effectual principles we introduce in this section, and the ways that expert entrepreneurs seek to control outcomes through their own actions.

> I think a great entrepreneur is learning every day. An entrepreneur is somebody that doesn't take no for an answer—they're going to figure something out. They also take responsibility. They don't blame anybody else. And they're dreamers in one sense but they're also realistic and they take affordable steps when they can.
>
> *Daymond John*, serial entrepreneur and investor

DOI: 10.4324/9781003364016-7

To learn more about Daymond John, visit https://effectuation.org/EE3/daymond or scan this code:

REFERENCE

Nance-Nash, S. (2012, September 24). FUBU founder Daymond John Stages his next act. DailyFinance. https://web.archive.org/web/20120924141410/http://www.dailyfinance.com/2010/07/24/fubu-founder-daymond-john-stages-his-next-act/

Figure 6.1 Clouds form over the Grand Canyon (USA): An illustration of prediction, risk, and uncertainty.

CHAPTER 6

Prediction, Risk, and Uncertainty

In This Chapter

Economist Frank Knight argued that entrepreneurs bear the uncertainty of bringing new products and services to the market and should therefore be rewarded for this.

Extensive research has shown that expert entrepreneurs shape new opportunities within uncertainty, and instead of seeking to predict outcomes, they take actions within their control.

This mindset is called "effectuation" and is reflected in the words of Helen Keller, the author and activist who lost her sight and hearing as a baby: "Security is mostly a superstition. It does not exist in nature, nor do the children of men as a whole experience it. Avoiding danger is no safer in the long run than outright exposure. Life is either a daring adventure or it is nothing."

DOI: 10.4324/9781003364016-8

Is risk-taking an attribute—something people are born with? Or can it be taught and learned? Is risk inherent to all entrepreneurial ventures, or is it a characteristic of the environment in which entrepreneurship occurs? Are all risks created equal? If not, what metrics can we use to classify different types of risk? Do all people perceive the same risk in the same venture? If not, why not?

FACTORS OF PRODUCTION

Let's explore a framework that can help us tackle these questions, namely, one of the first and most exciting dissertations in entrepreneurship, published in 1921 by a doctoral student named Frank Knight (Knight, 1921).

Take any simple product—say, a pen. If you ask yourself, "Where does the value or price of this pen come from?" you will get at least three types of answers—these can be mapped onto the three "factors of production" that are listed in every foundational economics textbook. They are as follows:

- The value of the pen comes from the raw materials that go into it—the factor of production here is "land," and the price of land is usually termed "rent."
- The value of the pen also comes from the people who actually produced it—their time, effort, and skills. This factor is "labor," and the price of labor is usually termed "wages."
- The value of the pen also includes the ideas, creativity, and design of the technologists who invented it and the machinery and business processes that were used to produce it. This is considered "capital," and the price of capital is usually termed "interest" or "return on investment."

If the market is efficient, classical economists argue that these three factors of production—land, labor, and capital—cover all the value that goes into the making of the pen, and the pen should cost no more and no less than the prices paid for the three factors. Ergo, when demand and supply are in sync with each other in an open, efficient market, profit should equal zero.

THE FOURTH FACTOR OF PRODUCTION: ENTREPRENEURS

It was this utopian view of microeconomics that Knight (1921) assaulted when he argued, in essence, that human capital (which includes entrepreneurship) is a necessary fourth factor of production, and that profit is the price paid for it.

What Do Entrepreneurs Contribute?

So, what do entrepreneurs bring to supply and demand? And why do they appear to keep such a big share of the price of the products and services that, after all, are made up of the raw materials, labor, and investments belonging to their stakeholders?

The answer lies in the simple fact that after the other three factors are paid for, there may or may not be anything left over. In other words, before new products or services are produced and sold, there is no guarantee that they can indeed be produced, nor is there any assurance that they will indeed be bought at a price above the cost of production.

Someone has to bear the uncertainties involved in bringing new products and services to the market—and in creating markets where none existed before. In other words, demand and supply cannot always be known before the entrepreneur acts.

Why Are Entrepreneurs Entitled to Profit?

Most entrepreneurs have never even heard of Knight—and that's okay. But imagine you started an IT firm that needs to hire a chief technology officer. Many technical people do not understand how the price of a product is determined. Not because they are not smart, but because good technical people spend their time and energy on technical skills. And often even the best technology education does not include exposure to business concepts or the role of entrepreneurship in economics.

Hence, good technologists, even when they perceive the technical "value" of a product (or think they do), may wonder why products are priced so high, or why the marketing person often makes more money than the techie, or even why the founding entrepreneur gets the lion's share of the pie. Pointing to Knight's thesis not only makes a credible case to them, but also provides an easy way to approach otherwise delicate issues such as negotiating relevant and just compensation—not to mention the necessity to share in the risk.

Most people, not just technical folks, assume that price, customers, and markets can be analyzed, and outcomes predicted. Or they go to the other extreme and fear vague and undefined "risks" associated with starting a company—based on the oft-repeated phrase "most firms fail." We have already tackled this combination of misconceptions in the first section.

This means that now we can return to Knight for a useful way to actually understand problems of risk in the entrepreneurial setting. We will explore important differences between prediction, risk, and uncertainty—terms that at first glance may seem very closely related.

A JAR FULL OF RISK

Imagine a game where you win if you pick a red ball. There are three jars in front of you. One has an equal number of red balls and green balls. The second contains balls, but you do not know how many balls are red. And you have no idea what the third jar contains. Which jar would you choose?

In 1961, Ellsberg used this jar game, described in Knight's (1921) dissertation, to investigate preferences and found that most people prefer the jar whose proportion of balls they know to the one whose proportion of balls they don't know. That seems intuitive enough. But now, ask yourself, "Which jar would an entrepreneur choose?" Researchers speculated that entrepreneurs might prefer the unknown to the known—i.e. they are risk takers and hence might pick the second jar.

But all those years ago, Knight had already argued implicitly that entrepreneurs, by definition of operating in the unknowable, would choose the third jar; that there are so many dimensions to the entrepreneurial problem and each dimension is likely to vary in so many different ways, making the prediction problem impossible even to attempt, let alone solve.

To put this into context, few business situations are represented by the first jar. Nothing is cleanly predictable. Educators believe that most business situations fall into the second jar. All the forecasting, prediction and scenario analysis tools taught in school are approaches for determining the distribution contained in the second jar. But when you understand that entrepreneurs are drawing from a completely different jar, it's easy to see why a set of completely different principles apply to how they learn to make decisions.

Research Roots

FRANK KNIGHT

Frank Knight was born in 1885 in McLean County, Illinois. The son of Christian farmers, he never completed high school, but went on anyway to American University in Tennessee in 1905. By 1916, he had completed his doctoral studies in economics with a dissertation entitled "Cost, Value, and Profit."

This was the start of a brilliant academic career. In addition to teaching many of the Nobel Laureates of the current era (Milton Friedman, Kenneth Arrow, and Herbert Simon among them), Knight was a prolific publisher. In his work, he creates the notion of entrepreneurship as the fourth factor of production; that in addition to land, labor, and capital, the entrepreneur manages uncertainty and in exchange is justified a profit.

Without arguing about whether expert entrepreneurs actually view the world through the lens of uncertainty described by Knight (or "Knightian uncertainty"), we can find examples of the three types of jars. Once we describe, understand, and play with this notion enough, we can begin to think about how to make decisions and act in the face of true uncertainty. In fact, a substantial portion of this book is devoted to methods used to play the game in Knight's third jar.

PREDICTION, RISK, AND UNCERTAINTY

We will use the terms prediction, risk, and uncertainty to identify the types of problems that the three jars represent. It is important to understand the difference between the three concepts, because each requires a different approach.

When the future is predictable (i.e. we know the distribution of balls within the jar), we can use our knowledge of the past—of common recurring patterns—to predict the future.

When the future is risky (i.e. when we are dealing with an unknown distribution of balls), we can still use the past and our instincts about the future, but we also need to test the waters as we go, look out for new patterns, find ways to adapt to the new patterns wherever possible, and hedge our bets any way we can.

However, it is the third jar that is the most difficult, and maybe the most interesting. Representing a future that is truly uncertain, the distribution of balls in that jar can never be known, no matter how long you play.

> Prediction is very difficult, especially about the future.
>
> *Niels Bohr*

The Difference Between Prediction, Risk, and Uncertainty

Table 6.1

	Prediction An environment with enough stability that future events can be determined based on past recurring patterns.	**Risk** An environment characterized by general trends and local variance. The decision-maker seeks to model these data to tolerances that meaningfully inform decision-making.	**Uncertainty** A situation in which no historical data exists to help the decision-maker. Uncertainty cannot be modeled or predicted. It is a future that is not only unknown but also unknowable.
What matters	Data, information that was collected in the past	Variance and possibility	Expertise, influence, and control
How you move ahead	Refine prior efforts—strive for a perfect business plan	Robustness, preparedness—scenarios	Co-creation and affordable loss
Dealing with surprises	Quality checking (must have been my mistake)	Weather the storm, work to stay on track/on plan	Embrace and rethink: it provides new opportunities
Measuring success	Actual versus plan, execution	Actual versus plan, closeness to the vision, within margin	Valued novelty, getting to somewhere that has potential

You Can't Predict Who Will Change the World

The American system of trial and error produces doers: black swan–hunting, dreamchasing entrepreneurs, with a tolerance for a certain class of risk taking and for making plenty of small errors on the road to success or knowledge ... It is high time to recognize that we humans are far better at doing than understanding, and better at tinkering than inventing. But we don't know it. We truly live under the illusion of order, believing that planning and forecasting are possible. We are scared of the random, yet we live from its fruits. We are so scared of the random that we create disciplines that try to make sense of the past—but we ultimately fail to understand it, just as we fail to see the future.

(*Taleb*, 2007)

Research Roots

Adam Smith

Adam Smith was a key figure in the intellectual movement known as the Scottish Enlightenment. He gained international attention when his examination of societal ethics—*The Theory of Moral Sentiments*—was published in 1759. But it was his book *An Inquiry into the Nature and Causes of the Wealth of Nations* (1776) that secured his fame and went on to become a classic of modern economics. Widely acknowledged as the "father of economics," Smith is known for his explanation of how rational self-interest and competition can lead to economic well-being and prosperity. He also coined the metaphor "invisible hand of the market," which is a term economists use to describe the self-regulating nature of the marketplace. His work helped to create the modern academic discipline of economics and provided one of the best-known rationales for free trade and capitalism. And his writings on supply and demand encouraged academics and businesspeople to believe that many economic activities could be modeled and predicted.

Prediction (the First Jar)

Classical economists (and most business schools) teach us that markets exist, are predictable to a greater or lesser degree, and that sooner or later every market reaches a point of perfect equilibrium, where supply and demand intersect.

Since Adam Smith (1759) introduced the notion of the invisible hand of the market that helps allocate scarce resources to the best possible use through individuals who make decisions based on their self-interest, countless academics and managers have found ways to predict the behavior of that invisible hand. Underlying virtually every management tool today, from the sales forecast to expected value calculations to real options analyses, is the belief that Adam Smith's insight can be applied to estimate the future based on historical information of one sort or another.

In recent times, there has been a greater appreciation of the fact that not all elements of the market are known or even knowable in any meaningful manner. Therefore, our models cannot rely on prediction alone; instead, they have to allow for risk—the idea that not all the actors would necessarily behave in a predetermined manner, nor would everyone even have access to the information necessary to make good decisions. Therefore, notions such as risk and imperfect information have become more common in economic analysis today.

The limits of prediction

We all know great stories of failed predictions. There are countless websites dedicated to failed predictions and end-of-world stories, including the "Millenium 2000 computer bug" prior to the shift from the last century to this one. Some other examples include:

- "That idea is so damn nonsensical that I'm willing to stand on the bridge of a battleship while that nitwit tries to hit it from the air."—Newton Baker, Secretary of War, 1910, responding to the suggestion that airplanes might sink battleships by dropping bombs on them
- "We don't like their sound. Groups of guitars are on the way out."—Mike Smith, Decca Recording Co. executive, turning down The Beatles in 1962
- "With over 50 foreign cars already on sale here, the Japanese auto industry isn't likely to carve out a big slice of the US market for itself."—*Business Week*, August 2, 1968

Those stories are only funny if you didn't lose time or money based on those predictions. But they are also good examples of why you would not want to build a business based on a prediction in an uncertain environment.

Look at some of the predictions you have made in your own environment. How many of these came true? What did you lose when they didn't come true? Did they apply to uncertain environments?

Figure 6.2

Figure 6.3

Figure 6.4

Research Roots

The Future That's Already Happened

Did you know that there's a way to predict the future with a fair amount of accuracy? No, it's not a crystal ball or a psychic hotline—it's demography! That's right, according to the management guru Peter Drucker, demography predictions have been surprisingly reliable for the past 650 years. He even called it "the future that's already happened."

What does that mean for entrepreneurs like you? Well, it means that there's an opportunity to take this reliable predictive information and use it to your advantage.

For example, if you know that there's going to be a significant increase in the number of elderly people in a certain area over the next decade, you could start a business that caters to their unique needs and preferences.

Practically Speaking

The Unlikely Story of Freitag

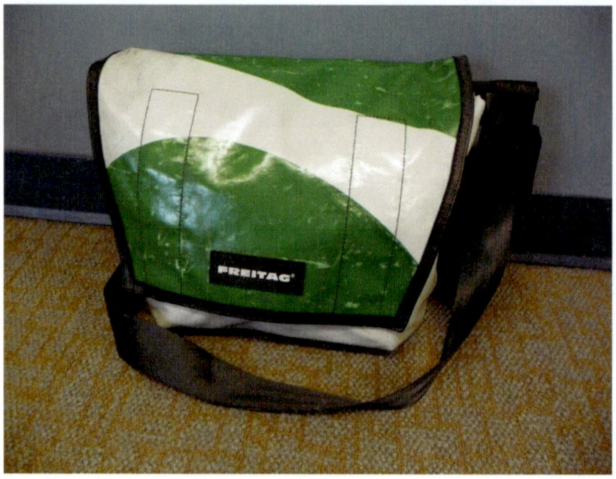

Figure 6.5

In Zurich, Switzerland, Markus and Daniel Freitag started thinking about a new business from their apartment overlooking the main Zurich truck route at Hardbrücke. Dissatisfied with the durability of available bicycle messenger bags, the pair wanted to create a heavy-duty, water-repellent product. So, in 1993 they started prototyping bags and formed Freitag AG. But instead of sourcing the latest high-tech materials, they formed bags from used truck tarpaulins, using second-hand car seatbelts as straps and used bicycle inner tubes for edging. Recycling materials keeps input costs low while taking advantage of the emerging environmental trend, and guaranteeing that every Freitag bag is as original, customized, and personal as the truck that hauled its skin in the first place.

A Predictable Success?

Freitag and its line of bags have done remarkably well. It currently sells about 400,000 bags per year, online and through a network of 300 stores around the world. The average price for a bag well exceeds 275 US dollars. But ask yourself this: if Freitag hadn't done it, would consumers pay high-fashion prices for bags made of commercial waste—or would such bags even exist at all? Likely not. Entrepreneurs do more than just meet existing market needs and discover business opportunities; they narrate novelty and uncertainty in the market.

To learn more, visit: https://effectuation.org/EE3/freitag or scan Figure 6.6.

Figure 6.6

Risk (the Second Jar)

Unlike problems of prediction, which require only extrapolation, problems of risk call for the estimation of likely changes under multiple scenarios over time. Decision-making under risk involves calculating the odds of a specific outcome using not only existing information, but also trial and error, which yields additional information. In other words, whereas prediction allows only defensive tactics, risk can be managed through more proactive measures.

Countries assess risk—for example, in the Cold War, the superpowers attempted to use scenario planning to assess a range of possible outcomes. This approach was picked up and improved upon by companies such as Shell, who used scenario planning to determine the risks associated with fluctuations in oil production and prices. It then made its way to financial derivatives (options, futures, and the like) before becoming a tool for all sorts of decision-making.

Risk Taking: Comparing Entrepreneurs and Bankers

Which would you say is the most risk-averse profession? Until the financial crisis of 2008, most of us would probably have answered "bankers" (while secretly thinking, they had better be—after all, they are managing my account). We decided to test the risk aversion of bankers and entrepreneurs. A group of bankers and entrepreneurs were given a series of problems to solve, all in the context of managing a manufacturing plant. The problems included financial risk, risk to human life and health, and risk of a natural disaster. For each problem, we looked for similarities and differences in the ways bankers and entrepreneurs reacted.

When it came to purely financial problems (investing in a new product), the entrepreneurs and bankers seemed to have very different perceptions of what could be controlled: the entrepreneurs seemed to accept risk as a given—as a result, they worked on controlling the returns rather than the risk.

Their approach was to pick an acceptable level of risk and then push for larger profits, selecting the project with the best worst-case scenario. They also expressed confidence that they could make the reality better than the worst-case probability.

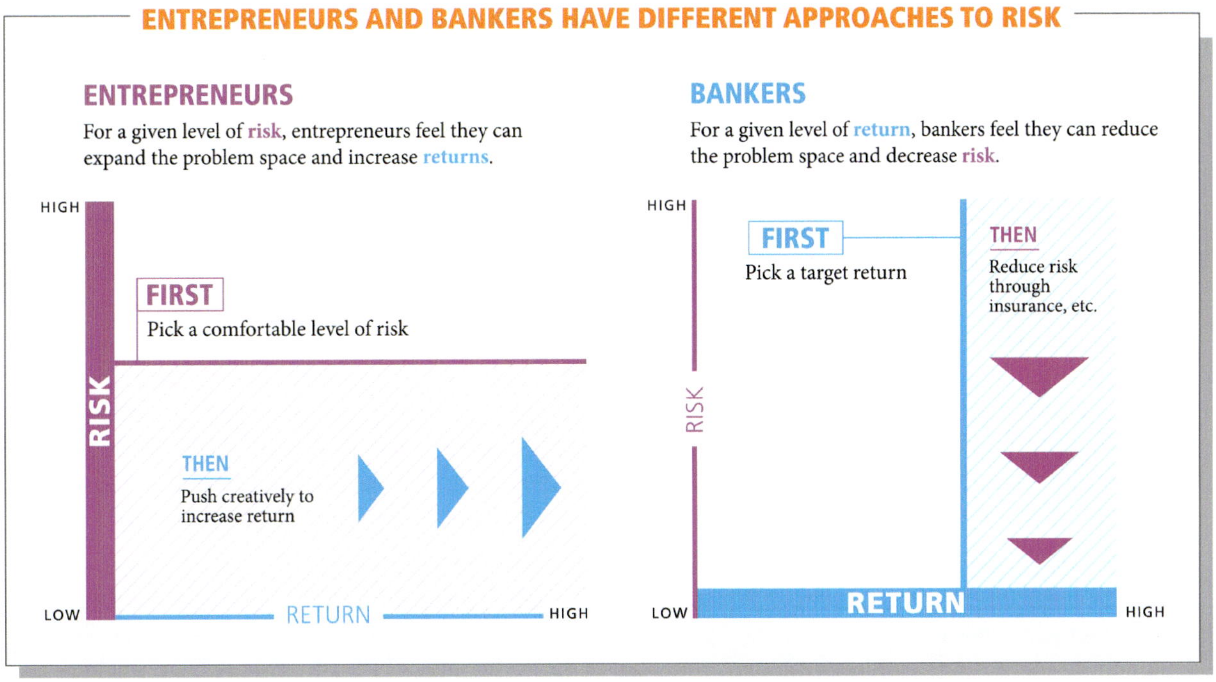

Figure 6.7

In contrast, bankers suggested many ways of controlling risk and practically no measures to increase returns. They seemed to believe that they could generate the highest possible returns and somehow work on minimizing the risks.

The next set of problems involved decisions around human life and health. The context was the following: the factory's industrial hygiene consultant recommended an investment of 3 million US dollars to put a hood and special ventilation apparatus over the production area. The consultant concluded that a rupture of a pipe could spill an extremely toxic chemical, endangering the workers. When questioned closely, the consultant expected the pipe would rupture less often than once every ten years, a rupture could cause the death of eight workers, and that putting up the hood and ventilation system would mean that only four workers would die if a pipe ruptured.

A second option would require a 10 million US dollar investment to put in special pipes and enclose the area so there would be a much lower chance of a pipe bursting, and there would be no worker exposure if the pipe did rupture.

In this situation, where the trade-off was between a 3 million US dollar option that reduced but did not eliminate the risk to the workers' lives and a 10 million US dollar option that eliminated risk, but the firm could not afford it, all the entrepreneurs rejected the 3 million US dollar option outright and came up with creative suggestions to pay for the 10 million US dollar option. Besides possible technical suggestions, they also considered asking for volunteers and giving up equity, selling to a larger company, or cooperating with competitors to increase prices.

None of the bankers made a decision—their suggestions were doubtful and evasive. All of them said they would invest the proposed 3 million US dollars, because that was better than doing nothing. They did not make creative suggestions for raising the 10 million US dollars. Their reactions focused on trying to delay or avoid the decision, suggesting that more information was needed. The way both groups saw their decision spaces can be schematized, as illustrated in Figure 6.7.

Research Roots

Expert in Forecasting? An Oxymoron

Entrepreneurs who end up on the cover of business magazines are often hailed as visionaries who had an ability to see what the next big thing was going to be. However, such accolades fly in the face of everything we know from studying human beings' ability to predict, including the forecasting ability of people who are considered experts in their domains.

In a painstakingly constructed multi-year study, researcher Phil Tetlock gathered data on thousands of predictions made by experts in politics and economics. The results showed that on average, the experts fared no better in their forecasting results than novices, and both were essentially no different to coin flipping. Moreover, people who successfully forecast extreme events have been shown to be, on average, poor forecasters who rank lower on forecasting than their peers. One can conclude that no one has an upper hand in forecasting the future, whatever claims are made retrospectively.

Such research suggests that claims regarding a particular entrepreneur's prescience as a forecaster may be misattributing the sources of their success. Alternative factors may better explain why they achieved what they did. The most important of these explanations may be the capabilities and skills in entrepreneurship that they developed. These are skills in the process of entrepreneurship. Having

Research Roots *(continued)*

these skills may make expert entrepreneurs less dependent on making accurate forecasts. If this is the case, then prediction and forecasting abilities—which research shows to be a myth anyway—may have very limited relevance for explaining entrepreneurial success (Tetlock, 2005).

Later work by Mousavi and Gigerenzer (2014) investigated top adaptive decision-making heuristics and came to a similar conclusion that, "In an uncertain world, less often proves to be more" (Mousavi & Gigerenzer, 2014, p. 1671). This is based on the idea that in the face of uncertainty, there is simply not enough data to apply rigid decision-making rules and hence experimentation will yield concrete results on which to base future action.

Uncertainty (the Third Jar)

Uncertainty exists with any new product, new market, or new technology, and it can happen at any level—from the macro (climate change and resource depletion) all the way to the micro (the CEO has a heart attack). Who can predict the future of antibiotic resistance? Or the impact of artificial intelligence?

When low demand due to the pandemic pushed the price of oil below 20 US dollars per barrel in April 2020, it seemed unimaginable that by June 2022 the price would jump to over 110 US dollars. Nor could anyone have predicted that Steve Jobs, the iconic founder of Apple, would be fired by his board in May 1985, only to come back in December 1997, or that Apple would become even more successful his second time around.

Keeping these examples in mind, it is clear that uncertainty is not confined to startups in budding industries. Consider the implications of the fact that one in every four firms on the *Fortune 500* list simply did not exist 30 years ago. That means that every 88 days, a new firm is created that will replace one of the existing *Fortune 500* firms. What new competitors, products, and business models that have yet to be imagined will suddenly make headlines?

Research Roots

Blue Ocean Strategy

Kim and Mauborgne (2005) coined the term "blue ocean strategy" in their book *Blue Ocean Strategy*. The metaphor of red and blue oceans describes the market universe. Red oceans are industries in existence today—the known market space. In the red oceans, industry boundaries are defined and accepted, and the competitive rules of the game are known.

Blue oceans, in contrast, represent all the industries not in existence today—the unknown market space, where standards, expectations, and competition don't yet exist. In blue oceans, demand is created rather than fought over. There is ample opportunity for growth that is both profitable and rapid. In blue oceans, competition is irrelevant because the rules of the game are yet to be set.

Blue ocean strategies are about playing a different game—with the aim of creating markets. These strategies generate uncertainty in the environment. They can be contrasted with strategies that react to uncertainties in the environment, as is the case with uncertainties posed by disruptive technologies.

Influential business writers such as Clayton Christensen (1997) and Chan Kim and Renée Mauborgne (2005) have looked at uncertainty in the context of innovation and new markets. Christensen focused primarily on how to help managers who are the "victims" of uncertainty, while Kim and Mauborgne have looked at how managers can turn the existing environment upside down, in effect creating uncertainty for others. While both approaches help us consider uncertainty as a given in the business environment, they do not provide an overall perspective on how to work with uncertainty as an opportunity.

EXPERT ENTREPRENEURS DEAL WITH UNCERTAINTY, NOT RISK

Entrepreneurs face uncertainty. What have they learned through the accumulation of their expertise in this unique setting that is teachable and learnable?

To better understand, we not only studied experts themselves, as described in the section comparing bankers and entrepreneurs, but also conducted follow-on studies with business novices and managers with expertise in large multinational corporations. We describe these studies in more detail later in the book. Here, we briefly summarize what we found.

The most important difference between the expert entrepreneurs and the other two groups was in their decision-making strategies. The novices and expert managers wanted desperately to predict.

The expert entrepreneurs did not try to predict, but neither did they shoot from the hip or exhibit divine insight into the future. Instead, they had developed workable and sometimes even winning strategies for the game embodied in Knight's third jar. In terms of that jar, experts had learned something like the following: work with the first few things you draw from the jar and ignore the rest of what's in it; or add red balls to the jar so you are more likely to win; or rebuild the jar from what you have and persuade others to play a different game altogether.

In sum, expert entrepreneurs appear to have developed a set of techniques that effectively answers the question, "How do I control a future I cannot predict?" This pattern of decision-making behavior is what we call "effectuation." Throughout the third section of the book, we explore the principles of effectuation and understand how each works at different stages of the life cycle of new ventures as well as in a variety of other settings, such as large corporations and the social sector.

Research Roots

Entrepreneurs and Risk: It's Complicated ...

Risk is a perennial topic of interest in entrepreneurship research, with a long history dating all the way back to the very origin of the term "entrepreneur" in French. The early writings of the French economist Cantillon describe entrepreneurs as individuals who assume the risk of running a firm.

So, are entrepreneurs distinguished as having a higher risk tolerance than non-entrepreneurs? The usual practice in research on this topic is to compare entrepreneurs to a control group typically made up of managers. Miner and Raju meta-analyzed the results of 28 studies like this, concluding that the combined results indicate that entrepreneurs may not have a propensity for risk. However, the interesting result is that the studies split depending on how risk was measured.

Research Roots *(continued)*

Studies in which entrepreneurs self-reported their risk proneness suggest that they are risk tolerant; whereas studies that measure entrepreneurs' behavior show them to be strongly risk avoidant. This makes it tempting to conclude that biased self-perceptions may play a distorting role in our image of risk taking in entrepreneurship. It may be that entrepreneurs perceive themselves as risk takers even though they actually score as more risk avoidant than managers (Miner & Raju, 2004).

Wu and Knott (2006) took a different approach, investigating the acceptance of two different types of uncertainty, namely, market uncertainty and uncertainty regarding their own ability. While not very tolerant of market uncertainty, entrepreneurs are willing to accept uncertainty about their own ability, perhaps because that is within their own control.

Extending the entrepreneur's perception of ability to overconfidence was explored by Salamouris (2013), who concluded that in contrast to the general public, entrepreneurs didn't let their self-perception of skill be affected by a lack of information, hence uncertainty. This could be what gives the courage to experiment in the face of uncertainty.

Research Roots

Real Options

Faced with the problems of making investments in uncertain technologies and ventures, one intuitive approach is to think of yourself as making initial small investments in order to "buy" an "option" on making larger investments later. This approach helps manage the risk of failure by keeping initial investments small, and delaying significant investments until you have more information about how the initial steps worked out. One of the biggest upsides of starting with a small investment is that "options" may emerge in the process that you couldn't have imagined when you started (McGrath, 1999).

Practically Speaking

Your Amigo: Navigating Uncertainty Without Maps

Co-Creator: Isabella Nunes Pereira

When you buy something online, you can be quite certain that before long, it will be delivered right to your door. But what about people who live in a chaotic jumble of buildings with no standardized addresses?

Pedro, Elaine, and Silas lived in this uncertain reality: they were born and raised in Rocinha, one of the largest favelas (shantytowns) in Brazil. Favelas are home to millions of people, but their dense population and maze of informally named laneways pose significant obstacles for traditional delivery companies.

Practically Speaking *(continued)*

In 1998 the trio joined a community cleaning project in Rocinha. Despite being an enormous job, it didn't pay enough to live on. So, seeking to increase their income, they got temporary jobs as census takers in Rocinha for the 2000 Census.

Something to Get Going

This new task deepened their experience in the territory, introduced them to surveying and mapping technology, and put them in direct contact with the entire population of Rocinha. Knowing that home delivery services were unavailable, the trio started asking residents if they would pay a monthly fee to have this service.

The positive responses, the trio's understanding of Rocinha, and their newfound skills were enough for them to get started, despite not even having much equipment, as one co-founder recalls: "And we didn't even have a computer. That is, if we wait for our things to happen, other things will happen first, so it is essential to have initiative" (Silas Vieira co-founder). They didn't have money either, but convinced a friend to allow them to use his small shop in exchange for future profits.

And so, in 2000, the first physical store of Carteiro Amigo Express appeared in Rocinha.

Someone for All …

Despite a shopfront, and their increasing customer base, the fledgling business was not profitable. Since the trio still needed money to live, they took a group decision that Elaine would keep her day job to guarantee a minimum income for their project: Carteiro Amigo. Pedro and Silas quit their day jobs and received six months of unemployment benefits.

Within a year, Carteiro Amigo was generating enough revenue to become the trio's only source of income. Moreover, their innovative approach has revolutionized the logistics industry by addressing the challenges of last-mile delivery in favelas.

Figure 6.8 The Carteiro Amigo team in Rocinha, Brazil.

… and All for All

Their success attracted public funding, allowing Carteiro Amigo to expand to other communities in the city, and develop direct partnerships with big e-commerce sellers interested in selling their products in the favela.

The mobile app they are now building may end up mapping the unmappable. Way to go, Amigo!

To learn more, visit: https://effectuation.org/EE3/amigo or scan Figure 6.9.

Figure 6.9

Practically Speaking

U-Haul, or Transforming Uncertainty Into Success

In 1945, newly married and with barely 5,000 US dollars in the bank, Anna and Leonard Shoen initiated a sequence of events that led to the creation of U-Haul. Within four years, the duo had founded a company that made it possible to rent a trailer one-way from city to city throughout most of the United States.

Examining these events, we find that this could not have been accomplished by using prediction or by trying to measure risk. In fact, if you tried to write a business plan for this venture, you would conclude that the plan is financially infeasible, since it requires a large and risky capital outlay for a network of relatively low-value assets such as trucks and rental locations spread across the country.

Moreover, the logistics of starting the business on a much smaller scale and growing it as fast as U-Haul did, overwhelms the analytical prowess of the best of forecasters. The lack of any entry barriers to imitators with deep pockets is seen as another insurmountable obstacle to success.

Means Over Prediction

The Shoens, however, did not do elaborate market research or detailed forecasting and fundraising. Instead, using who they were, what they knew, and who they knew (what we call "effectual means"), they plunged into action, creating the market as they grew the business, working from the observation that people kept coming to Anna's father asking whether they could borrow the truck that was parked in the back.

In Leonard's own words:

> Since my fortune was just about enough to make the down payment on a home and furnish it, and knowing that if I did this we would be sunk, we started the life of nomads by putting our belongings in a trailer and living between in-laws and parents for the next six months. I barbered part time and bought the kind of trailers I thought we needed to rent from anybody who happened to have one at a price I thought was right. By the fall of 1945, I was so deep into the trailer rental deal economically that it was either make it or lose the whole thing.

Building With Partners

The couple moved with their young child to the ranch of Anna's family in Ridgefield, Washington where they started building the first trailers in the fall of 1945. They painted them in striking orange with the evocative name U-Haul on the sides, and they used the ranch's automobile garage (and milk house) as the first manufacturing plant.

To spread their idea, the Shoens offered discounts to renters who agreed to find a reputable service station at their destination which would rent out U-Haul trailers. This was the beginning of the U-Haul dealer network, which facilitated partnerships with service stations across the country. U-Haul provided the trailers (trucks were added later), and the service station provided the unused land and labor to service U-Haul customers. U-Haul benefited from new business, and the service station owner benefited from a second source of income.

In the 1950s, the company established a fleet ownership program that enabled investors (including dealers and eventually employees) to purchase trailers for the U-Haul fleet in return for future dividends.

Practically Speaking *(continued)*

Blocking Competitors With Partners

Together, this vast network of stakeholders formed a substantial entry barrier to any imitator, who would have to risk a large capital outlay to compete. Advertising was entirely limited to phone books and to the growing number of bright orange vehicles on the highways of the country.

Managing Affordable Loss

At any given moment, U-Haul could have failed, but the resulting financial fallout would not have been a disaster since the investments were spread across so many stakeholders.

Looking at the story of U-Haul's creation, we see that Anna and Leonard Shoen dealt with uncertainty step by step, using effectual principles—starting from their means, developing partnerships, and limiting the potential downside loss by sharing it with others.

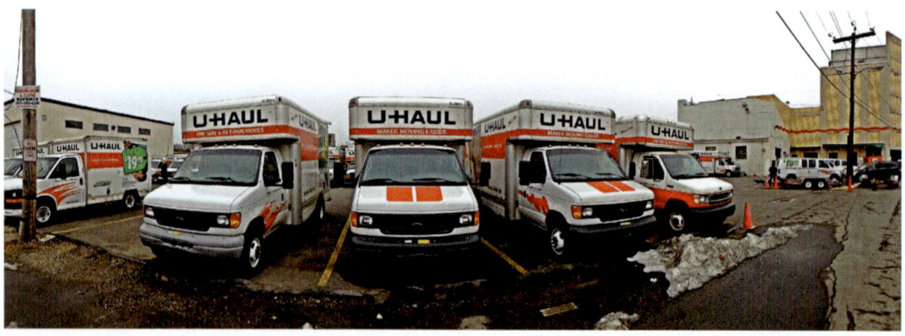

Figure 6.10 UHaul trucks with their famous orange branding.

Of course, we could rewrite history and suggest that they could have done market research, found out about the migration of populations in the US in the late 1940s, borrowed money from investors to set up locations, and so on. But the sheer challenge of it probably would have prevented Anna and Leonard from taking action. Instead, because they could not and would not measure the risk, they managed the uncertainty with each step forward.

To learn more, visit: https://effectuation.org/EE3/uhaul or scan Figure 6.11.

Figure 6.11

Think It Through

- How does one know what is and isn't predictable? That is, how do I know I'm operating in an unknowable situation?
- Which error is better? To mistake a predictable situation for an unpredictable one? Or to believe you can predict an unpredictable one?
- Choose your favorite new product. Is its market risky, predictable, or uncertain? Why?
- What have you learned over the years about HOW to create the future? Have you learned more about how to research and predict, or to control and create?

So What?

Prediction can be useful in certain places and times, but it does not work well when creating new markets and new ventures. Handling uncertainty is at the very core of why entrepreneurs are able to create wealth, but betting on predictions isn't how they do it. Instead, they look for ways to control the future rather than predict it.

What Now?

- In your current job, how much time do you spend trying to predict versus trying to control? Is that mix of prediction and control a good match for the environment in which you are operating?
- Think about the last market research report you read. How useful would it have been for a company in that environment? How predictable or uncertain was that company's environment?
- How critical are predictions to the moves you have in mind? If those predictions are wrong, does everything fall apart?
- How might you more actively create the future you desire for your ventures?

REFERENCES

Christensen, C. (1997). *The Innovator's Dilemma: When New Technologies Cause Great Firms to Fail.* Harvard Business School Press.

Drucker, P. (2007). *Innovation and Entrepreneurship.* Routledge. https://doi.org/10.4324/9780080549415

Ellsberg, D. (1961). Risk, ambiguity, and the savage axioms. *Quarterly Journal of Economics, 75*, 643–669. https://doi.org/10.2307/1884324

Kim, W. C., & Mauborgne, R. (2005). *Blue Ocean Strategy: How to Create Uncontested Market Space and Make Competition Irrelevant.* Harvard Business School Press.

Knight, F. H. (1921). *Risk, Uncertainty and Profit* (Vol. 31). Houghton Mifflin.

McGrath, R. (1999). Falling forward: Real options reasoning and entrepreneurial failure. *Academy of Management Review, 24*(1), 13–30. https://doi.org/10.2307/259034

Miner, J. B., & Raju, N. S. (2004). Risk propensity differences between managers and entrepreneurs and between low- and high-growth entrepreneurs: A reply in a more conservative vein. *Journal of Applied Psychology, 89*(1), 3–13. https://doi.org/10.1037/0021-9010.89.1.3

Mousavi, S., & Gigerenzer, G. (2014). Risk, uncertainty, and heuristics. *Journal of Business Research, 67*(8), 1671–1678. https://doi.org/10.1016/j.jbusres.2014.02.013

Salamouris, I. S. (2013). How overconfidence influences entrepreneurship. *Journal of Innovation and Entrepreneurship, 2*(1), 8–8. https://doi.org/10.1186/2192-5372-2-8

Smith, A. (1759). *The Theory of Moral Sentiments.* Millar. https://doi.org/10.1093/oseo/instance.00042831

Smith, A. (1776). *An Inquiry Into the Nature and Causes of the Wealth of Nations.* W. Strahan and T. Cadell. https://doi.org/10.1093/oseo/instance.00043218

Taleb, N. N. (2007, May 23). You can't predict who will change the world. *Forbes.* https://www.forbes.com/2007/05/23/nicholas-taleb-innovation-tech-cz_07rev_nt_0524taleb.html

Tetlock, P. (2005). *Expert Political Judgment: How Good Is It? How Can We Know?* Princeton University Press. https://doi.org/10.1515/9781400888818-014

Wu, B., & Knott, A. M. (2006). Entrepreneurial risk and market entry. *Management Science, 52*(9), 1315–1330. https://doi.org/10.1287/mnsc.1050.0543

CHAPTER 7

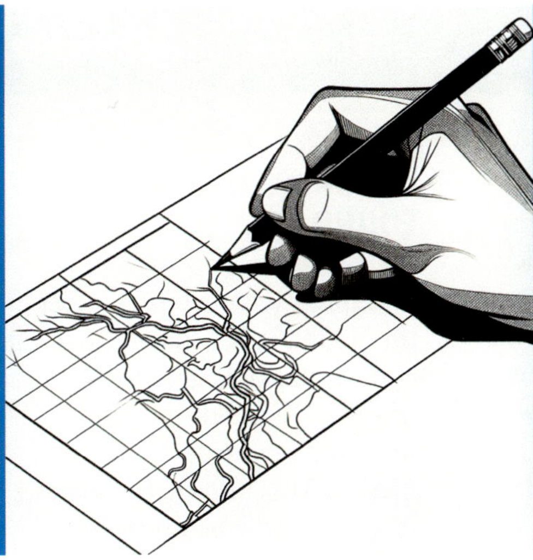

Figure 7.1 Using our hands to create opportunities is an age-old approach of taking action and being entrepreneurial.

Opportunities Are Created as Well as Discovered

In This Chapter

Entrepreneurial opportunities are either found or created.

Finding opportunities (causal logic) is a methodology typically taught in business school programs and ascribed to by managers around the world. The idea is that you first discover an opportunity and then chart an optimal path to exploit it.

Effectual logic, which adopts a create-and-transform approach, is the inverse: instead of beginning with a specific opportunity, you begin with a given set of means, and you allow opportunities to emerge and form through co-creative action.

Surprising as it may seem to aspiring entrepreneurs, expert entrepreneurs who master uncertainty do what the actor and comedian Milton Berle suggested, "If opportunity doesn't knock, build a door."

DOI: 10.4324/9781003364016-9

In the first chapter, we made the argument that entrepreneurship is about the very creation of new roadmaps. We hesitated in doing this because the analogy of a roadmap is misleading in two ways. First, it suggests a clear destination. And second, with the help of the map and perhaps additional navigational aid, there might be an optimal way to arrive at that destination.

Before we talk about where opportunities come from, we would like to set the record straight in terms of how we view a map. Our view is not new. We see a map not as a static image of a fixed environment, but as a dynamic reflection of your activities, with paths that are constantly changing, and destinations shaped by your own actions. No two maps are alike, and the number of possible paths and destinations is infinite.

A similar concept can be seen in the way people navigate and explore cities. A person's experience of a city is shaped by their interests, preferences, and activities. Two people can visit the same city and have vastly different experiences based on the neighborhoods they choose to explore, the restaurants they eat at, and the attractions they visit. Each person's "map" of the city is unique, and the number of possible paths and destinations is infinite.

WHERE OPPORTUNITIES COME FROM

The question of where opportunities come from may seem abstract, academic, and about as useful as a blank sheet of paper. But it may help explain the way those interested in starting a business think about opportunity (maybe not even consciously) and offer insight into what they do as they pursue a venture.

OPPORTUNITY CREATION AND DISCOVERY

To be clear, there is no right or wrong answer to the question of whether opportunities already exist and if they can be discovered or if they must be created—that is, whether they are found or made.

OPPORTUNITIES ARE FOUND

Entrepreneurs operating under the "found" view start by looking at the traditional growth areas of a market and the largest unserved segments in that market. This information helps them select the best possible opportunity. Once they've made their choice, they develop a business plan based on extensive market research and detailed competitive analysis. They then look to acquire the resources and stakeholders required to implement the plan. Over time, entrepreneurs adapt the venture to the environment in an attempt to build and maintain a competitive edge.

The "found" view assumes that the budding venture is sufficiently similar to an existing business for historical information to inform decisions, and the environment is sufficiently stable for outcomes from the past to be relevant to the current situation and to the future. One way of identifying opportunities is to look at existing solutions to needs and seek alternatives, such as Uber did in the transport sector.

Practically Speaking

Duh! Why Doesn't This Exist Already?

Travis Kalanick and Garrett Camp were attending the major European technology conference LeWeb in Paris in 2008 and shivering in the cold night; they couldn't get a taxi. They questioned the traditional system and dreamed of using their mobile phone to quickly hail a ride.

Practically Speaking *(continued)*

Both returned to California, where Camp started developing the idea in his free time. Eventually he convinced Kalanick to join him in his efforts and together they founded UberCab in 2009.

Despite there being many ways of getting from point A to point B, and that included carpooling and other usually informal ways of travelling together, no formal systems existed for ride-sharing up to that point.

Bumpy Ride

Challenging the status quo is hard work, as Camp and Kalanick soon found out. One of the biggest hurdles was regulatory restrictions. The taxi industry in most cities was highly regulated, with strict requirements for licensing and insurance. Kalanick and Camp realized that they couldn't just enter the market and compete with traditional taxis on their own terms. Instead, they had to find a way to make a new market within the existing regulatory framework.

Trust was another bump on the road. The idea of getting into a car with a stranger was not something that most people were comfortable with at the time. Kalanick and Camp had to find a way to build trust with their customers and drivers, which they did through a combination of user reviews, background checks, and insurance policies.

Making, as Well as Finding

Kalanick and Camp had to transform existing resources and create new ones. They didn't just rely on existing taxi fleets, but instead recruited ordinary drivers who were willing to use their own cars to provide rides. They also created new mobile phone software that made it easy for customers to hail a ride and pay for it without ever having to exchange cash.

Riding High and Low

On the way to success, problems continued: pricing questions, driver compensation, passenger safety, corporate culture failings, and, importantly, sustainability. It took 14 years for Uber to become profitable in 2023. Now it's available in over 10,000 cities around the globe and its market value has topped 63 billion US dollars.

More interesting are the opportunities Uber has created for people to travel conveniently and inexpensively, turn their private car into a new income source, and help co-create the sharing economy.

To learn more, visit: https://effectuation.org/EE3/uber or scan Figure 7.2.

Figure 7.2

Search and Select in Music

The range of approaches used to find opportunities, generally referred to as search and select, is useful in explaining the success of new ventures in predictable environments.

In the 1970s, the only way to listen to music while on the move was using a car radio. So when the company Sony developed a portable cassette player called Walkman, there was no market and no historical data to guide its creation.

The idea that possibilities are transformed into opportunities (opportunities are made) is useful in exactly those situations where the past cannot help predict the future.

Some years later, the Sony Walkman had demonstrated that people wanted to listen to music on the move and the internet became widely available. This allowed Apple to complete a search and select process and come up with the software and a device to access music libraries on the move: the Apple iPod.

Figure 7.3

Figure 7.4

Practically Speaking

Something From Nothing

While some entrepreneurs discover their business plans are unintentionally full of excrement, Tom Szaky's was designed around it; worm dung, in fact. Inspired by his friends' success using red wiggler worms to process compost and feeding the resulting dung to plants, Szaky felt there could be a business in commercially producing and distributing a product he would call "Worm Poop." Emboldened by taking fifth place in the Princeton Business Plan Contest, he quit Princeton after two years to form TerraCycle and devote himself to delivering Worm Poop to households everywhere.

The Smell of Success

With 20,000 US dollars—the sum of all of Szaky's bank accounts and credit cards—he purchased a processing machine and began shoveling Princeton University's food waste into it to feed an ever-growing colony of worms. A worm can consume twice its body weight each day, so Szaky was soon up to his knees in product. Committed to a fully sustainable offering, he packaged his prized Worm Poop in paper bags and took it to gardening stores inviting them to stock it. The polite response was that the product looked good, but the aroma was not consumer compatible.

Recycled Idea

The answer to his stinky packaging problem already existed—plastic bottles. The product was made from waste, so why not package it in waste as well? Szaky developed a process to mix his Worm Poop with water, strain out the solids to leave a nutrient-rich liquid, then fill recycled bottles with it and seal them with waste spray tops. The idea was so good that Szaky took top honors at the Carrot Capital Business Plan Challenge in 2003, recognition that came with a 1 million US dollar investment prize. A good thing, since TerraCycle had only 500 US dollars in the bank at the time.

Committed to Waste

For some entrepreneurs, this would define the moment of success—validation of an idea combined with the financial resources to make it happen. For Szaky, it was a defining dilemma.

The investors wanted to direct TerraCycle into plant foods without the eco-friendly mission and its founders. So Szaky refused the investment. Instead, he redoubled his efforts with big retailers and brought in a more benevolent form of capital: revenue. By 2004, Walmart and The Home Depot were stocking his products in Canada, and he was negotiating to expand into the United States.

Upcycling

Under Szaky's direction, more and more trash fed more and more worms, which fed more and more plants, and, with Americans throwing out 2.5 million plastic bottles an hour, packaging was also readily available. As TerraCycle grew, Szaky saw opportunities everywhere. Trash was something to be "upcycled" into an offering more valuable than the original product.

Practically Speaking *(continued)*

He started with seed starters and potting mix, made from and packaged in waste. Then he offered the Urban Art Pot, made from electronic waste. Then came plastic products, from kites to clipboards, all completely recycled.

Partnerships with Target, Walmart, Nabisco, and Kraft closed the cycle. Today, these firms participate in "Sponsored Waste" programs where TerraCycle pays "brigades" of consumers (often school communities) to collect used packaging manufactured by and distributed by these firms, which TerraCycle turns into new products and into sales. By 2021, the firm was active in 22 countries and generating 70 million US dollars in revenue.

Learning From Trash

Szaky teaches us that opportunities are more a function of what you already have than a function of convincing a venture capitalist to invest large sums to turn your business plan into reality. And that some people are paying to get rid of resources that can form the basis of new and valuable offerings.

While building a business on trash might not top the glamor charts, it also offers one more lesson: the word sustainability can apply equally to the business and to the planet when spoken by an entrepreneur.

To learn more, visit: https://effectuation.org/EE3/terracycle or scan Figure 7.6.

Figure 7.6

Figure 7.5

OPPORTUNITIES ARE MADE

Under the "made" approach, the information available to entrepreneurs at the start of the venture creation process is both incomplete and overwhelming. The market cannot be defined. Consumers are not aware of their future preferences. New technologies may emerge. Available data is confusing and conflicting. All this implies that entrepreneurs do more than simply recombine existing resources or transfer them from their current use to one that yields better returns. In reality, they create or transform, thereby generating new opportunities from mere possibilities.

Research Roots

New Combinations

Joseph Schumpeter (2021, originally published in 1934) theorized that demand could be created, proposing that innovations took the form of "new combinations" that combined existing things in new ways. These transformations could result in new markets, new production processes, new products, new ways of organizing, and new methods of distribution. Schumpeter defined "the carrying out of new combinations" as the essence of entrepreneurship.

Because New Ventures are Uncertain, Effectual Logic Often Prevails

Surprising as it may seem to aspiring entrepreneurs, the "made" view often prevails in the world of expert entrepreneurs. This view is guided by what we call the logic of effectuation—a logic particularly suited to moving forward in uncertain situations. To understand how we're using this funky word, let's think about the difference between cause and effect—or between causal and effectual.

Search and select (the "found" view) is guided by a causal or predictive logic—the kind that is typically taught in business school programs and ascribed to by managers around the world. The idea is that you start with a goal in mind, and you find the optimal way to reach it.

Effectual logic, which adopts a create-and-transform approach, is the inverse: instead of beginning with a specific goal, you begin with a given set of means, and you allow goals, or effects, to emerge as you work with your means. (We outline the principles of effectuation in Chapter 9 and detail them in Part III.)

Table 7.1

The approach	The approach	The logic	The heuristics
Search and select	Markets are fixed. Part of any given market may be served, underserved, or latent.	Explore a finite set of possibilities to find unserved, underserved, or latent areas of the market.	**Causation** Predict to identify a goal. Focus is on achieving that goal by accumulating the necessary means. Surprises are bad.
Create and transform	Markets can be created. Creation can be intentional or an unanticipated consequence of people just doing things they think are possible and worth doing.	Knowing it is possible to create demand, let interactions give rise to an infinite set of possibilities, which can then be prioritized by self-selected stakeholders.	**Effectuation** Start taking action. Focus is on transforming a set of evolving means to generate goals that emerge along the way. Surprises are good.

We can see an effectual logic at work in the stories of many of the firms we admire—firms that started out doing nothing close to what they do today (see Chapter 2). Opportunities were made over time and through interactions with customers, partners, and employees. The "Curry in a Hurry" example gives us two ways—one "found" (causal) the other "made" (effectual)—to pursue the same possibility.

Practically Speaking

Curry in a Hurry

Imagine an entrepreneur who wants to start an Indian restaurant. Using a search and select approach, she would start by doing market research in the restaurant industry in the city of her choice. Based on the market research, she would carefully select a location, segment the market in a meaningful way, select target segments based on estimates of potential return, design a restaurant to appeal to her target segments, raise the required funding, bring her team together, and, finally, implement specific marketing strategies and manage daily operations to make her restaurant a success.

It's the Skills, Not the Venue

If our entrepreneur instead followed a create-and-transform approach, the outcome would depend on who she is, what she knows, and who she knows. For the sake of understanding the process here, let us say she is a good Indian chef considering starting an independent business.

Assuming she has little money of her own, what are some of the ways she can bring her idea to market? She might partner with an existing restaurant, participate in food fairs, set up a catering service, and so on. Let us say she decides to pursue starting a business and persuades friends who work downtown to allow her to bring lunch for their office colleagues to sample. Some of those people sign up for a lunch service, and she begins preparing the lunches at home and delivering them personally. Eventually, she could save up enough money to rent a location and start a restaurant.

Same Ingredients, Different Meal

It is equally plausible that the lunch business does not take off beyond the first few customers. However, using a creative and transformative logic, our entrepreneur could co-create other enterprises depending on whatever her customers are actually interested in, besides her cooking. For example, maybe it is her personality that is interesting; she could then produce a cooking video or maybe start a cooking school.

Figure 7.7

Contingent on who is interested in what, our entrepreneur could go into any one of several businesses. Her eventual successful enterprise could be in entertainment, education, travel, manufacturing, packaging, retail, interior decoration, or self-help and motivation—to name just a few possibilities.

Tasting Platters Reduce the Risk

The myriad of possibilities through create and transform provide her with many more chances to try an idea out, failing cheaply, and moving on to the next one. This increases her likelihood of winning. If she chooses search and select, it is much more difficult to fail cheaply.

To learn more, visit: https://effectuation.org/EE3/curry or scan Figure 7.8.

Figure 7.8

> Never doubt that a small group of thoughtful, committed citizens can change the world. Indeed, it is the only thing that ever has.
>
> *Margaret Mead,* anthropologist and progressive thinker

THE CENTRAL PREMISE OF EFFECTUATION

The "Curry in a Hurry" example illustrates what we describe as the "pilot in the plane" principle. Core to effectual logic, it conceives the entrepreneur as the person at the controls. The person who, to some greater or lesser degree, creates the course a venture will take. The course of the venture is just as likely to be created in the process of doing as it is to be preconceived. While Columbus set a course for discovering India, his mission was transformed when he was surprised by a new continent.

A modern-day example can be found in the Laos Buffalo Dairy. Its founders, Susie and Rachel, initially were just seeking fresh buffalo milk curd to serve their guests, but ended up teaching local residents the power of buffalo dairy products to nourish their children and make extra income.

Practically Speaking

An Overwhelming Urge

According to her husband, Susie Martin "has an overwhelming urge to eat cheese." Susie admits this, stating "Because looking for cheese is my life's mission, I called my daughter 'Brie', like the cheese, so I kind of like it."

Did You Say "Cheese"?

When Susie, her husband Steven, and a friend, Rachel, moved to the Luang Prabang region of Laos (recognized for its blend of traditional and European colonial architecture) to run a guest house, they insisted on including cheese and yoghurt on the menu.

With over 700,000 buffalo in Laos, Susie became excited at the prospect of buffalo curd, a type of yoghurt, which she had enjoyed previously in Sri Lanka. But she was in for a surprise, as she tells the story: "We wanted to serve guests fresh curd in the morning. I asked a local farmer if we could buy milk from their buffalo, and they looked at me like I was mad."

May I Borrow Your Buffalo?

Buffalo milk and the products that can be made from it are not a traditional part of the local Laotian culture, so this potential source of protein was going untapped. Being dairy-obsessed, Susie didn't let go. Her professional background in corporate leasing helped her cook up a creative offer to "rent" buffalo from their owner:

> So, when we said, Well, we're going to bring them to the farm, we're going to pay you an income, we're going to feed them. You won't have to worry about them for six to eight months, I think they

Practically Speaking *(continued)*

> probably thought it was too good to be true. We pay them 100 Dollars every time they bring a buffalo to the farm—so, that's almost the equivalent of a month's salary here.

Understandably the locals were suspicious, says Susie: "for about the first 18 months they were pretty sure we're going to barbecue them. They really didn't know what we were going to do with their buffalo. They didn't know anything about dairy."

From 1 to 18: The Business Comes of Age

The trade paid off for the first courageous buffalo owners, who six months later received their buffalo back, now pregnant, vaccinated, and with a healthy calf at its side. This additional income has made a big difference for that first family, allowing them to spend the funds on educating the children, acquire a loom to manufacture textiles, and buy a sugar cane juicer. In the meantime, the family has 18 buffalo, renting out all their pregnant female buffalos to Susie and her dairy.

The Buffa-Learning Curve

Being new to agriculture, Susie learned a lot of skills online and experimenting on the ground, including how to manage hungry newborn calves. Susie explains:

> All the experts said you separate them, and that's how you do it, and you feed them with bottles. Then, when they would go back to the village, the babies didn't know the mothers, so they wouldn't follow the mothers back into the herds. And the farmers were like, that's a bit of a problem for us!
>
> So we changed our whole system. The milk yield actually didn't drop that much, it's much less work, babies get the milk they need from their mums …
>
> I think, not being a farmer, you're more open to different ways of doing things.

Slack in Cheese

> And what about all the buffalo milk Susie and her team produce? Her partner Rachel picked up that part of the chain, producing yogurt, ricotta, mozzarella, burrata, feta, and marinated feta cheeses, which have found eager consumers in the hospitality sector.

Although Rachel is a trained chef, she came into the project without cheesemaking skills—something that online resources and experimentation quickly changed. She also adapted several local recipes to include buffalo milk and is encouraging families to tap into this source of protein, which is readily available in their own pasture.

Practically Speaking *(continued)*

Opportunities for Life

In seeking a solution to their yogurt and cheese problem, Susie and Rachel created a business opportunity, one which addresses poor outcomes previously accepted by buffalo owners, including an only 50% survival rate for newly born calves. Susie explains: "Buffalo ownership here is kind of more like a lottery than an investment, because there's a lot that can happen. Disease is rampant: foot & mouth and various other diseases."

Figure 7.9 View of the ancient capital of Luang Prabang city, a World Heritage Site known for its synergy of traditional and European colonial architecture.

It's not only the buffaloes that don't make it. Inflation in Laos is high, causing food insecurity and malnutrition, particularly for children, resulting in lasting physical and cognitive impacts. Buffalo milk, being an excellent source of protein, is now helping local children thrive.

To learn more, visit: https://effectuation.org/EE3/buffalo or scan Figure 7.10.

Figure 7.10

A particularly amusing example of a market that could not have been anticipated or preconceived is the Pet Rock. And it highlights another important aspect of effectual logic: success or failure does not hinge on how accurate the original vision turns out to be or how well the strategies crafted to deliver that vision are executed.

Success is individually defined and may change as the process evolves. The relationships formed in creating new products, new ventures, or even new markets (such as the Pet Rock) also influence what those outcomes look like and how success is defined.

Practically Speaking

Making a Market Out of a Joke

Figure 7.11

Gary Dahl was out one evening having a few drinks with his buddies when the conversation turned to pets. Dahl, a California advertising man, joined in by claiming he had a pet rock—an ideal pet with a great personality that was easy and cheap to care for. His friends laughed at the idea. Little did they know that a pop-culture fad was about to be born.

It was April 1975, and Dahl's initial idea was to write a book—*The Care and Training of Your Pet Rock*—a step-by-step guide to having a happy relationship with your geological pet. He spent the next few weeks writing the book, which included instructions on training the Pet Rock to do tricks, such as roll over (best taught on a hillside) and play dead (which the rocks love to practice on their own). As the book took shape, Dahl decided to add some props—an actual rock nestled in some straw and packaged in a little carrying case, equipped with breathing holes. Dahl found his Pet Rock in a builder's supply store in San Jose. At a penny apiece, it was the most expensive rock in the place.

After introducing the Pet Rock at the San Francisco gift show in August, and then later in New York, Neiman-Marcus placed an order for 500. Then, based on a homemade news release that showed a picture of Dahl surrounded by his Pet Rocks in their carrying cases, Dahl was able to attract some great publicity, including a half-page story in the magazine *Newsweek*. He was also invited to be a guest on the popular television show *The Tonight Show* twice. By the end of October, he was shipping 10,000 Pet Rocks a day, and by Christmas, when 2.5 tons of rocks had been sold, three-quarters of all the daily newspapers in the US had run Pet Rock stories.

Just a few months after unleashing his Pet Rock, he had sold more than one million units at 3.95 US dollars each. Dahl—who, from the very beginning had decided to make at least one dollar from every rock—had become an instant millionaire.

To learn more, visit: https://effectuation.org/EE3/petrock or scan Figure 7.12.

Figure 7.12

CREATE YOUR OWN OPPORTUNITIES

Casual readers of history often see heroes, visionaries, and explorers as possessing superhuman qualities. This impression is reinforced by the larger-than-life descriptions of successful entrepreneurs we read about in the news. In this chapter, we separate these myths from reality.

Entrepreneurs are not necessarily visionaries who are better, faster, or smarter than others are at seizing and exploiting opportunities that no one else can see. Instead, in many cases, they make their own opportunities using mundane means. While entrepreneurs have traditionally been described as discoverers, we view them also as creators—terraforming as well as map-making.

TAKEAWAY: IT'S UP TO YOU

What does this mean for you?

The answer is that you do not need to sit and wait for a unique opportunity to come hurtling at you from the sky. On the contrary, it is up to you to create that opportunity. This calls for a much more active role on your part and for you to feel comfortable with a blank map that you will fill in according to your tastes, abilities and means, what you know and who you know. You are not alone. Our early explorers were in this situation. Entrepreneurship is what happens when you don't rely on luck.

Think It Through

- If you develop opportunities as the pilot in the plane, rather than a discoverer with a map, how might your actions and decisions differ?
- What might be the unintended consequences of becoming an entrepreneur with no map and no rules?
- Where does one begin without any roadmap at all?

So What?

Opportunities are created by entrepreneurs, not just found "out there" in the market. Often, the pilot in the plane actively and accidentally creates the roadmap, in addition to goals, partners, and products. Entrepreneurs rarely have a clear vision, clear goals, or a clear roadmap as they launch.

What Now?

- Look into four of your favorite companies and identify what aspects of their opportunities were made vs. found?
- For those that were made, what were the key ingredients in how they were made?
- Now that you can see where those companies ended up, i.e. their roadmap has been created, identify one complete alternative route to the same destination. How ELSE might they have more "efficiently" reached that same destination? This is similar to causation.
- Conversely, now that you can see what those companies became good at, identify one alternative destination that they might have happened upon if a couple of moments changed in their history. This is more like effectual thinking.

REFERENCES

ABC News. (2023, July 8). Australian agribusinesses utilise innovative strategies to empower farmers in Laos. https://www.abc.net.au/news/2023-07-09/australian-agribusinesses-empower-farmers-laos/102566370

ABC News In-depth. (2023, July 12). Australian know-how growing better buffalo in Laos. https://www.youtube.com/watch?v=4XFxxOehG_0

asiatraveltips. (2020, July 9). Churning a dream into reality—Interview with CEO of Laos buffalo dairy, Susie Martin. https://www.youtube.com/watch?v=gVLUVUBb_zM

Bloomberg. (n.d.). The warehouses of plastic behind TerraCycle's recycling dream. Retrieved October 24, 2023, from https://www.bloomberg.com/features/2022-terracycle-tom-szaky/

Green, T. (2023, August 2). Uber is profitable. For real this time. *The Motley Fool*. https://www.fool.com/investing/2023/08/02/uber-is-profitable-for-real-this-time/

Investopedia. (n.d.). The history of Uber. Retrieved October 29, 2023, from https://www.investopedia.com/articles/personal-finance/111015/story-uber.asp

Lagorio-Chafkin, C. (2022, August 11). From selling worm poop to reforming recycling around the world. Inc. Australia. https://www.inc.com/christine-lagorio-chafkin/terracycle-tom-szaky-recycling-loop.html

Laos Buffalo Dairy. (n.d.). Retrieved October 26, 2023, from https://www.youtube.com/watch?v=n12YAx-V-Es

Laos Buffalo Dairy. (2021, March 13). Healthy buffalo, healthier people and climate. https://www.youtube.com/watch?v=NSZGeU2s4CU

Laos Buffalo Dairy. (2023, October 10). Laos Buffalo Dairy. http://www.laosbuffalodairy.com/home

Loop. (n.d.). Eliminating the idea of waste. Retrieved October 24, 2023, from https://exploreloop.com/purpose/

Schumpeter, J. A. (2021). *The Theory of Economic Development*. Routledge. https://doi.org/10.4324/9781003146766

TerraCycle. (n.d.). TerraCycle. Retrieved October 24, 2023, from https://www.terracycle.com/en-US

TerraCycle—Funding, Financials, Valuation & Investors. (n.d.). Crunchbase. Retrieved October 24, 2023, from https://www.crunchbase.com/organization/terracycle/company_financials

Uber Technologies, Inc.—Investor Relations. (n.d.). Retrieved October 29, 2023, from https://investor.uber.com/home/default.aspx

CHAPTER 8

Figure 8.1 A girl flying a fantasy kite on a wintry day: Taking control despite the uncertainty of the world around her.

Managing Uncertainty Through Control

In This Chapter

It is important to know both what you can control, or influence, and what you cannot. You can then tailor your strategies to the situation at hand:

- Predict when it's useful, but be aware that you are predicting.
- Control and influence what you can.
- Heighten the controllability of your situation by working as much as possible with factors you can influence. This reduces your dependence on prediction and puts you on an overall firmer footing.
- Do not sweat what you cannot control. Be aware, but not worried. Work around instead.

People vary in their assumptions about the power of human action to control processes and outcomes in different domains at different times. Effectuators vary too. But they do not wait to know perfectly ahead of time whether they are right or wrong about what seems within their control. By actually putting to work what they perceive within their control, they know they will keep shaping things to their advantage and to the well-being of those they care about.

DOI: 10.4324/9781003364016-10

In This Chapter ***(continued)***

Or in the words of Kevin Plank, CEO of Under Armour: "Put the pen down. Work hard and get your product out there."

In this chapter, we explain how the concept of control fits with situations of prediction and uncertainty, exactly what is controllable, and how entrepreneurs control the destiny of their ventures in uncertain environments.

As you read this chapter, consider how empowering the idea of control is in the context of starting a new venture, and in a more general sense, the power of taking action in uncertain situations.

Destiny in Your Hands

This chapter focuses on the idea that successful entrepreneurs take action to control their future. Consider these voices from the past, which reflect the same idea:

> It is not in the stars to hold our destiny but in ourselves.
>
> *William Shakespeare*, playwright and poet

> The best way to predict your future is to create it.
>
> *Abraham Lincoln*, United States president and emancipator

> The secret of getting ahead is getting started.
>
> *Mark Twain,* writer and humorist
>
> The future depends on what you do today.
>
> *Mahatma Gandhi,* Indian independence leader and civil rights activist
>
> Your life does not get better by chance, it gets better by change.
>
> *Jim Rohn,* entrepreneur and author

You and the World Around You

If you are inspired to act by the quotes above, what is the right thing to do right now, considering you are not alone, and there is a whole world around you? Here are some ways to connect your action to your environment:

> The reasonable man adapts himself to the world; the unreasonable one persists in trying to adapt the world to himself. Therefore all progress depends on the unreasonable man.
>
> *George Bernard Shaw,* playwright and critic
>
> Complete adaptation to environment means death. The essential point in all response is the desire to control environment.
>
> *John Dewey,* philosopher and education reformer
>
> Adaptability is not imitation. It means power of resistance and assimilation.
>
> *Mahatma Gandhi,* Indian independence leader and civil rights activist
>
> The world as we have created it is a process of our thinking. It cannot be changed without changing our thinking.
>
> *Albert Einstein,* physicist and Nobel Prize winner

WHY CONTROL?

The struggle for personal control is as old as humankind itself—primitive and innate. There is abundant evidence that most people desire control of the events in their lives, indeed over their lives, and that such strivings for control span history and cultures as the previous quotes indicate.

The venues, mechanisms, and instruments for control-striving today are different than they used to be, but the issue remains. In fact, psychological research suggests that an enormous range of human behaviors relate to control-striving in some way and are intrinsically linked to healthy human functioning.

For example, personal control is linked to the development of self-esteem and the reduction of stress, whereas loss of control increases the likelihood of feelings of helplessness and depression. In other words, having a desire for control over your life doesn't make you a "control freak" (despite what your friends may say!). Instead, it is normal and healthy.

Many entrepreneurs instinctively recognize the importance of personal control: fundamentally, many chose entrepreneurship because they want to be their own boss and choose their own course. Control enables entrepreneurs to work on things they think are important, set their own schedules, and work with whom they want.

Many entrepreneurs assert that they feel differently about running a business they own as compared with working for a wage, and that they value being in control. For them, the experience of personal control is closely associated with freedom, self-direction, and autonomy.

The strength of a person's desire for control can be thought of as an element of his or her means: "Who you are." While most of us have no control over who we are—height, weight, DNA, family and cultural background, economic circumstances we are born into, and so on—control still begins with who we are at the moment. Knowing that we can still change things within ourselves and our environment helps us reduce fear of uncertainty and things outside our control.

Everyone has some desire for control, and the intensity of that desire varies among individuals and over the course of a lifetime. For example, a feeling of lack of control in one's job may motivate someone to become an entrepreneur, but the experience of working for herself may strengthen the desire for control—she may not be able to imagine working for anyone else again.

Research Roots

ON THE IMPORTANCE OF CONTROL

Research (Peterson et al., 1995, p. 305) is ongoing on how people learn and use that knowledge to guide their actions to control their world. What is clear is that people want a sense of control by knowing what they can and cannot change—including everything from bodily functions to global issues.

A need for control extends from the workplace to the meaning of life, as the following research indicates:

- Bakker et al. (2004) found that individuals who had a greater sense of control over their work environment had lower levels of stress and were less likely to experience burnout.
- Another study (Steger et al., 2006) found that individuals who had a greater sense of control over their lives had a greater sense of purpose and meaning in life, leading to greater life satisfaction and happiness.

Yes, control provides peace of mind at work and home!

WHAT IS CONTROL?

To some extent, prediction will allow you a certain degree of control, as long as you are operating in a stable environment. But the type of control we discuss here is particularly useful in uncertain, entrepreneurial situations because it does not rely on the past to predict the future.

The control you exercise can be either exogenous (you shape the environment) or endogenous (you shape yourself).

Obviously, not everything is controllable, but the entrepreneur focuses on the elements they can control to create desired outcomes.

MORE PERSONAL CONTROL TODAY?

Changing social attitudes in the latter half of the twentieth century have influenced individual perceptions of personal control. These perceptions are embedded in broader social belief systems, such as beliefs about individual freedom and choice, which have been legitimized by social movements in democratic societies.

The feeling of personal control has also been affected by shifting of economic and political power due to globalization and communications technology.

Research Roots

A SHORT HISTORY OF CONTEMPORARY HUMAN RIGHTS

The concept of human rights has evolved over centuries, driven by individuals and groups advocating for basic freedoms and dignity.

The modern human rights movement gained significant momentum after World War II, with the adoption of the Universal Declaration of Human Rights (UDHR) at the United Nations General Assembly in Paris in December 1948. The declaration outlines fundamental rights and freedoms that belong to all people, regardless of race, color, creed, or other distinctions.

The Origins of Human Rights

The UDHR formalized human rights on a global scale based on ideas with deep historical roots. Concepts of justice, equality, and human dignity have been part of various societies throughout history. Landmark developments like the Magna Carta (1215), the Habeas Corpus Act (1679), and the Bill of Rights (1689) in Britain laid the groundwork for recognizing basic human rights and freedoms.

The atrocities of World War II, including the Holocaust, highlighted the urgent need for an international framework to protect human rights. The newly formed United Nations made human rights a core priority, leading to the drafting and adoption of the UDHR.

The Evolution of Human Rights

The UDHR served as a foundation for subsequent human rights treaties and instruments, both at the international and regional levels. The International Covenant on Civil and Political Rights (1966a) and the International Covenant on Economic, Social and Cultural Rights (1966b), together with the UDHR, form the International Bill of Human Rights.

Over time, new rights have been recognized to address emerging challenges and changing societal values. These include the right to development, the right to a healthy environment, and the right to humanitarian assistance, often referred to as "third-generation rights" or "solidarity rights." This evolution reflects a deeper understanding of the interdependence of rights and the collective responsibility to ensure their realization.

The Role of Individuals and Grassroots Movements

Progress in human rights has been driven by individuals and grassroots movements advocating for change within their own means and contexts. From the abolitionists fighting against slavery to the civil rights activists challenging racial segregation, individuals have played a crucial role in advancing human rights.

Research Roots *(continued)*

Ordinary citizens have taken action through peaceful protests, civil disobedience, and advocacy campaigns, raising awareness and pressuring governments and institutions to uphold human rights principles. Human rights defenders, often at great personal risk, have exposed violations and demanded accountability.

The numerous people you might (or might not have) have heard of include: Leymah Gbowee (Liberia), Malala Yousafzai (Pakistan), Domitila Barrios de Chungara (Bolivia), Kailash Satyarthi (India), Rosa Parks (United States of America), Václav Havel (former Czechoslovakia), Eddie Mabo (Australia), and Zin Mar Aung (Myanmar).

PREDICTION, RISK, UNCERTAINTY, AND CONTROL

Thousands of books about business strategy generally suggest two levers that enable decision-making. The first is prediction based on the notion that if the future can be predicted, the decision-maker can steer the company toward a position where it will have an advantage.

The second lever is control, based on the notion that if the future can be controlled, the business leader can work to create a situation that provides their venture an advantage.

These levers are not alternatives, but rather tools managers that can be applied to improve the chances of making good decisions. Figure 8.3 illustrates the relationship between the environment and the combination of levers. Let's look at the logic for determining decision-making strategies for the environments represented in the different quadrants.

In the planning and adaptation quadrants on the left-hand side of the matrix, to respond to changes companies must either plan more (predict better) or be more flexible and faster (better) in adapting. Both approaches rely on the firm's ability to sense and make sense out of the environment, either in the longer term (planning) or in the shorter term (adapting).

In a mature, stable environment, planning, as the source of strategy-making, can be effective. Planning assumes that information—particularly historical information from the environment—is reliable enough to provide a base for decision-making (prediction is possible).

If strategy is based on adapting and learning, the ability to react and iterate quickly is key, with the intent of outpacing the competition in response to changes in the environment.

The visionary (market power) and effectuation quadrants on the right-hand side of the matrix call for a more proactive approach to the environment. If a company has market power (government-regulated markets or quasi-monopolistic status such as that achieved by Google in the search engine market), it can try to dictate what will happen in that environment,

Figure 8.2

imposing its view (visionary) on the landscape and ensuring the position of the organization within that environment.

The effectuation quadrant calls for a different approach. Because the company does not have market power, it needs to co-create (with partners, customers, suppliers, and other self-selected stakeholders) elements of its environment by, for example, developing a new product or market from which all the players involved will benefit. Effectuation assumes you can shape the environment by creating new elements using your means, partnerships, and actions.

Some may argue that managing uncertainty is possible through a combination of predicting better and adapting faster. But consider some examples you may already know. Because they were working on predicting better, Coca-Cola and Pepsi missed the opportunity that allowed Red Bull to create a new category (energy drinks) and develop a new market in soft drinks—those who connect a high-caffeine beverage with sports. By contrast, trying to adapt to market research led to the spectacular failure and subsequent costly termination of New Coke.

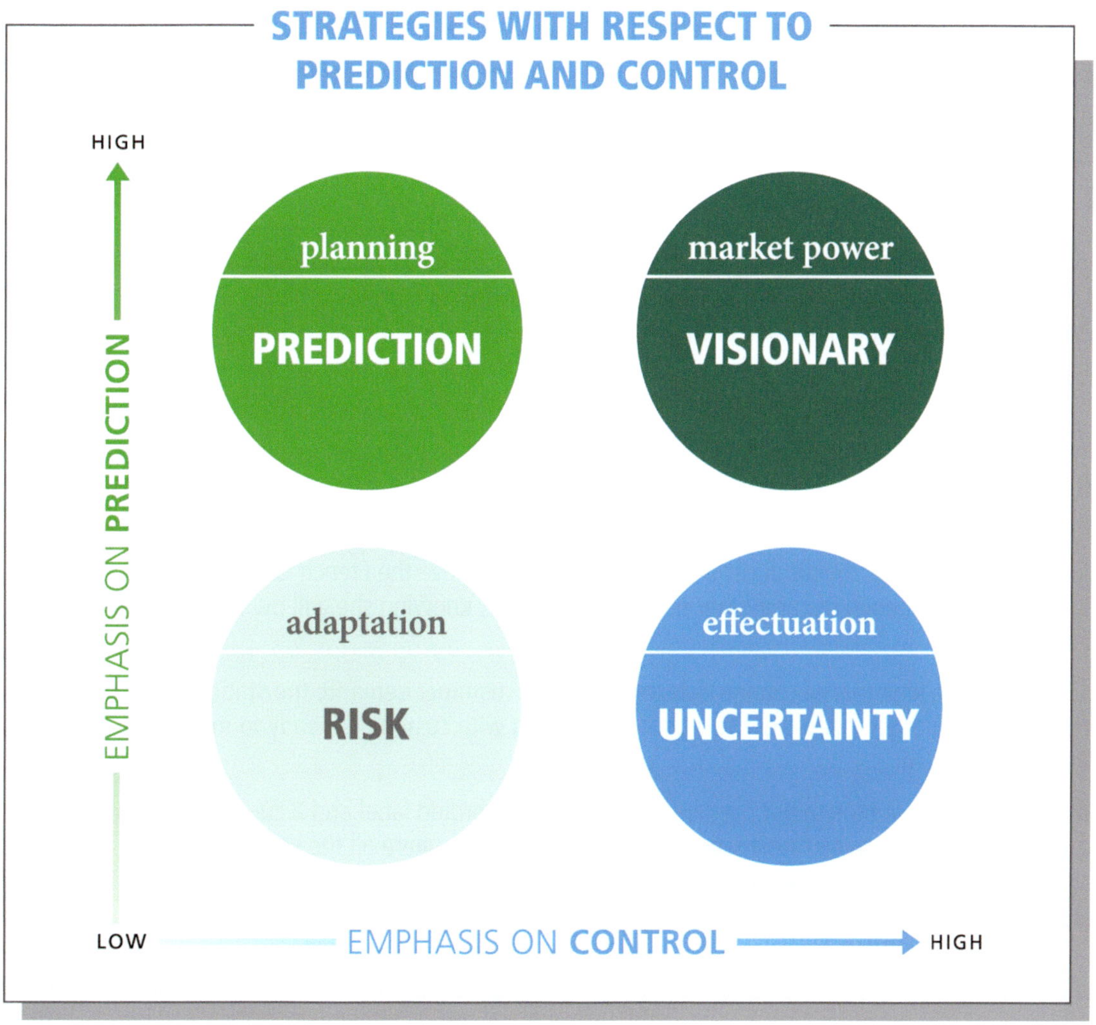

Figure 8.3

Research Roots

SLOW DISRUPTION

In his popular book *The Innovator's Dilemma*, Clayton Christensen puts forward the idea that innovation is not a sudden, revolutionary event, but a series of incremental advancements which can cumulatively result in significant disruption within an industry.

The "dilemma" Christensen refers to arises when established companies, despite market uncertainty, tend to take a more predictive approach which aligns with their existing business models and predictions, potentially creating a false sense of security based on previous success.

Successful entrepreneurs, on the other hand, take an action-oriented approach to navigating uncertainty: developing and constantly improving products based on feedback from customers.

By the time the major players notice that the entrepreneur has taken away market share, it is often too late to change course. While Coca-Cola was trying to make New Coke a success, Red Bull and others had created a whole new drinks category, one sip at a time.

Theory in Practice: KEEP180

Imagine a popular independent radio station, KEEP180, which plays a wide range of new music, from country and western to French rap. The station broadcasts locally and has a growing online audience. The station is funded by donations from listeners and it is facing a strategic decision about where to invest its limited resources as it moves ahead. Let's think about how the radio station would evolve in each of these environments:

- Planning. The station might carry out market research and predict an explosion in a new genre of French music. It could then invest in bringing that music to its audience and consequently capitalize on higher ratings.
- Market power. Alternatively, the producer at KEEP180 may simply love the French language and may build a format exclusively on French rap and other novel French music, knowing she will own the category if she can establish it.
- Adaptation. Given the high rate of change in technology and customer demand, the station might devote its efforts to watching other independent stations and talking with customers, ready to move quickly as new trends are identified.
- Effectuation. Finally, the station might partner with a French recording label and a current American music icon to create a French rap music scene, selling music online, where all the self-selected stakeholders benefit from the new environment they create together.

YOU CAN CHOOSE YOUR ENVIRONMENT

People often assume they can only adjust or adapt to their environment. They may feel helpless about the environment they are born into or find themselves stuck in. But you do not need to accept your environment as given and outside your control.

The entrepreneur, or manager more generally, always has a choice about what kind of environment to operate in, and what kind of decision-making to use in that environment.

Choosing to offer a competitive product in an existing market means the environment is more predictable than creating a venture to introduce something completely new. As such, the choice to use prediction or control can be driven by the stage of the market or the stage of the company. During the early startup phase (of a market or firm), there is very little that is predictable.

While control strategies connect naturally with uncertainty and predictive strategies connect with maturity, entrepreneurial managers might also choose control strategies as a foundation for new ways of competing and innovating in mature markets.

CHANGE OVER TIME

Neither environment nor strategy is static. For example, as an entrepreneurial opportunity develops from nothing, venture capitalists and other potential funders may ask for a business plan, reflecting their expectations of some degree of prediction (sometimes regardless of whether that expectation has any bearing on reality).

Many successful new markets do become more predictable and stable over time and, therefore, more amenable to prediction and planning. In fact, effectuation is a useful tool to transform the uncertain into the predictable. When a venture reaches a more mature stage, even an effectual venture, it can become very reliant on prediction, and managers can choose to base decisions mainly on predictive inputs.

In this situation, it is easy for a firm to be surprised by uncertainty in its environment, making it vulnerable to innovative new products. Ironically, these surprises are created using the same (effectual) logic from which the large firm's foundation was constructed in the first place.

Figure 8.4

Practically Speaking

The Seasons of Bar Semente (Seed Bar)

Co-Creator: Aline Brufato

Bar Semente ("Seed Bar") first became known as a health food restaurant, but after changing hands, started hosting music events, following in the bohemian past of the neighborhood called "Lapa."

Lapa was at the core of Rio's cultural life in the early 20th century, witnessing and fomenting the development of music genres such as samba and choro. By the turn of the century, however, Lapa had fallen into disrepair and was completely excluded from the city's cultural scene. Bar Semente suffered from this decline and closed its doors in 2002.

Entrepreneurs Are Gardeners

Music entrepreneur Aline Brufato sees entrepreneurs as gardeners. "If you are a gardener," she says, "you will be familiar with the relationship of circumstances and the actions you take to cultivate your beloved plants. It starts with the seeds (or seedlings), which require the gardener to take control and plant them in the soil."

Regardless of the season and the weather, there is the work of tending to your plants: watering, fertilizing, moving potted plants to balance growth toward the sun, pruning back long growth to increase the mass of foliage, etc. Gardeners, like entrepreneurs, consider the environment and soil needed to nurture change.

Change of Seasons

Bar Semente has experienced many seasons, many storms, and many changes.

"Just" a customer at the time, Aline Brufato was there on the last day of that season of Bar Semente's life. Her love for the venue and the magic created there motivated Brufato to lead a collective effort called "Comuna de Semente," representing a diverse group of stakeholders, including musicians, patrons, and friends.

The Comuna was instrumental in the re-establishment and transformation of the brand and orchestrated the relaunch of Bar Semente in January 2004, opening its doors once or twice a week. The dedication of the "Seed Bar gardeners" was so intense that within three months they were able to transform the rejuvenated seedling into a viable business and establish itself in the Brazilian music scene.

True to its name, the Comuna operated in a very organic way, bringing together a diverse mix of intergenerational musicians to share and discover new sounds and styles.

Coming to Fruition

The freshness of Bar Semente's entertainment drew hungry music fans from far and wide, but the small stage and capacity of 80 people was not viable without the support of the Comuna project.

Practically Speaking *(continued)*

To overcome the initial limitations of its small stage, Semente formed a partnership with the traditional and rather dated "Clube dos Democráticos" just two blocks away, offering a larger stage with a 1,000-person capacity on Friday nights. This collaboration gave rise to the Semente da Música Brasileira project, evolving into a curated music label. New artists and innovative performances debuted on the small stage before transitioning to the larger one, ensuring economic viability for the distinctive Semente atmosphere.

This partnership attracted established and successful Brazilian artists, strengthening the Semente brand and facilitating Bar Semente's relocation in 2010 to a larger venue (next door to the original location) with a 200-person capacity.

Progress seemed unstoppable with the team well prepared to take on the next project in 2016, becoming a stage for the Villa-Lobos Festival, one of the oldest music festivals in Brazil. The content for the next "canning" project was set: a video collection about the Semente generation, co-produced by Canal Brasil, and including special editions of the Festival Semente da Música Brasileira.

Storms Loom

As all gardeners know from experience, blue skies can suddenly change. In 2016 Brazil was hit with a severe economic downturn. Bar Semente was forced to close its doors. As Brufato describes (Phillips, 2018): "It was the most difficult decision— … so difficult and so lonely." Yet, as Alexander Graham Bell (US inventor) reminds us: "When one door closes another door opens; but we often look so long and so regretfully upon the closed door that we do not see the ones which open for us." Just a week after closing the physical stage, the bar forged a partnership with the legendary New York jazz club Blue Note to bring Semente shows to Blue Note Rio, its first venture into Latin America.

Figure 8.5 Jamming at the Bar Semente in the bohemian Lapa neighborhood of Rio di Janeiro.

Preserved for Export: The Essence of Bar Semente

In 2018, Semente launched the documentary Semente da Música Brasileira, co-produced by Canal Brasil, which was broadcast on television and shown in cinemas and later in national and international film festivals. The home-grown produce from Rio had reached as far as Spain, Germany, and India.

During the pandemic, Brufato won several awards, produced online festivals with prominent national and international musicians, and redesigned Semente's business model as an agency that produces special editions of music and is now in talks to license its brand.

To learn more, visit: https://effectuation.org/EE3/semente or scan Figure 8.6.

Figure 8.6

WHAT IS CONTROLLABLE?

Part of learning how to create new ventures is learning where the more—and less—controllable elements are and how best to leverage them. While prediction and control have different roles at different stages in the life of a venture, our focus here is on the startup and what can be controlled as it launches into existence. There are many factors involved in a firm's success. Some can be directly controlled or managed by the firm, others can only be influenced, and some are completely out of the firm's control.

Figure 8.7 illustrates some elements institutional investors use to determine the "investability" or viability of a venture.

Imagine you are ready to build a venture. Where do you start? What action do you take first? Since you can't do everything at the same time, you need to prioritize.

The answer is simple: start with actions relating to elements over which you have the greatest degree of control. And accept those elements which you cannot control.

At all times, be open to the possibility that your perceptions are wrong. There are probably more factors within your control than you imagine. But even if your perceptions are not accurate, starting with where you believe you have some control gets you going with manageable risk and accessible resources.

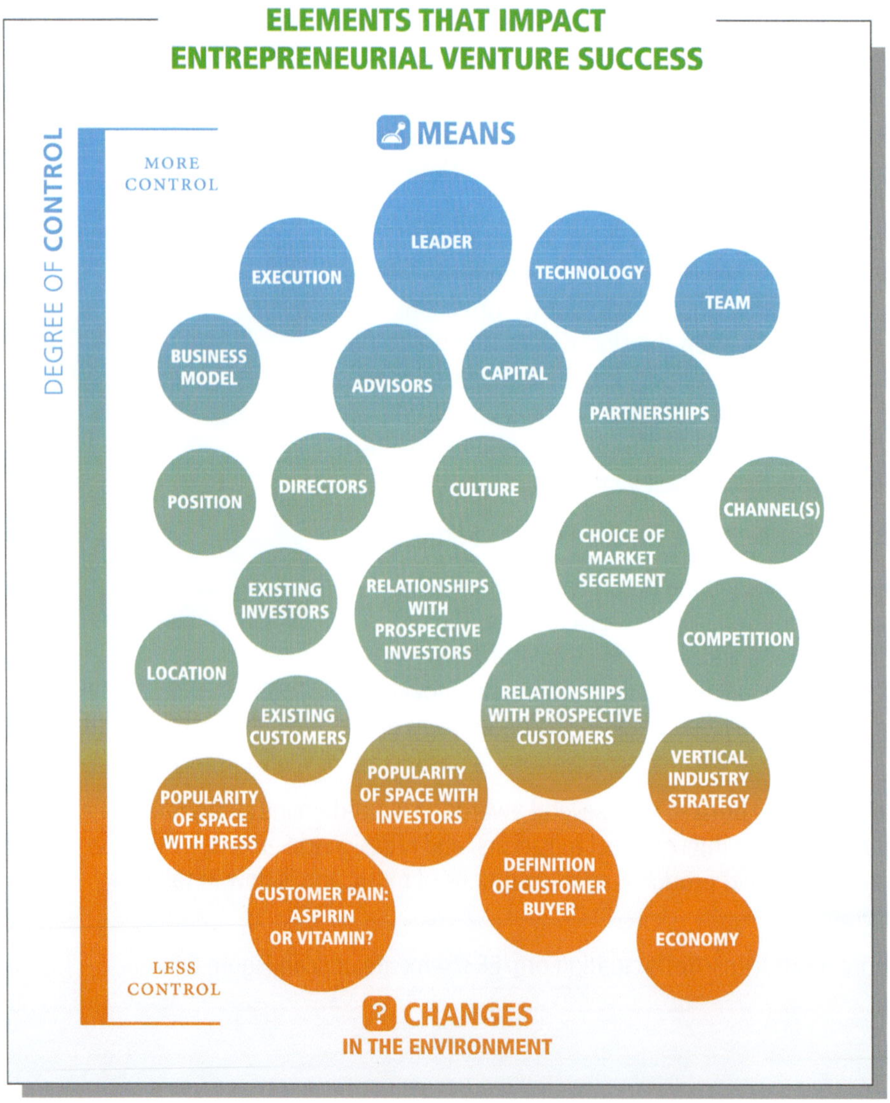

Figure 8.7

Practically Speaking

The Magic of Control at the Circus

What does someone who, as a street performer, ate fire and walked on stilts and later took up professional poker and spent more than ten days in space, know about uncertainty and control? His entrepreneurial success indicates that he is very good at managing uncertainty through control.

We're talking about Guy Laliberté, co-founder (with Gilles Ste-Croix) of the Canadian Cirque du Soleil, which has adoring fans around the world.

Control Through Tunes

Laliberté started developing a sense of the power of control at an early age. As a seven-year-old Guy Laliberté was exposed to a whole new world of people from diverse backgrounds at the World Exposition 1967 in Montreal and wanted to learn more and travel the world. He recounts this in an interview in 2012 (IMD):

> I wanted to discover the world, so the fastest way that I found to discover and go see those people was to pick up the accordion of my father, learn a couple tunes, and hit the road being a busker.
>
> Then I discovered the pleasure of entertaining people, and this is where I started to say to myself, maybe I could combine the two: traveling and entertaining people. And this is where I start to get involved in entertainment—organizing theater troupes, festivals, and then in 1984, founded Cirque du Soleil.

Not Controlling Animals

Taking control to reduce the uncertainty (and expense) of dealing with animals in a traveling performance ended up becoming a hallmark of the Cirque du Soleil brand and is a radical departure from traditional circuses, which usually focus on animal acts and clowns.

At Cirque du Soleil, audiences are kept at the edge of the seats with highly choreographed, artistic, and acrobatic human performers: control is maintained, even if the performers might talk back (unlike animals) backstage.

Keeping Creative Control

Imagine the sense of control (like the Wizard of Oz behind the curtain) Laliberté must have felt when Cirque du Soleil became an international sensation. This didn't go unnoticed, and Laliberté (again) chose control over the alternative. This is how he describes it in the 2012 IMD interview:

> You know, so many times I've been approached by companies who want to buy me, and I said no. I didn't say no because of the money—the money was very tempting—but it's always when it came down to creative control that I said, wait a minute, I'm not selling my soul. I still have things to create. I always believe that if I was selling the company or letting a certain decision-making out of my hand, then I will have no more fun and passion of doing what I did so I didn't want to compromise on that part.

Practically Speaking *(continued)*

The Kids Should Control Their Future

But even for those who are good at controlling their business, uncertainty is never far away, and Cirque du Soleil has gone through its share of challenges. In 2015, after years of turbulent growth, Laliberté sold 90% of Cirque du Soleil to an international consortium of investors, explaining his decision as follows in an interview with the *Montreal Gazette* (2015): "But in all consciousness and with a rigorous reflection—personal reflection or corporate reflection—I believe today I'm making the best decision for a significant future and the best decision for myself and my family."

Many exiting founders focus on the money (1.5 billion Canadian dollars in this case) or what they would be doing next, but again Laliberté framed his decision in terms of control. He focused on the implications for his children, making clear that he wanted them to have the control to determine their own future. In his words (*Montreal Gazette*, 2015):

> As a person, I truly don't believe in second generation entrepreneurship.
>
> Imagine for two seconds to be able to be there as a guide, as a supporter. Being a gardener, the seed you planted in life and having them achieve their dream and not having to carry on the dream of their father is so precious, and this is the opportunity that I have been giving them through this transaction.

Since Laliberté had experienced many ups and downs of building a venture, he is also aware of the potential downside of passing Cirque du Soleil on to the next generation. He prefers to exit, considering the alternative: "instead of just throwing them in the jungle—because this is the jungle … and it's a lot of pressure and I don't want to give them that as a starting point."

Leaving as Ultimate Control

Cirque du Soleil went through a particularly rough period of changing market conditions and an almost clown-like series of changing investors after Laliberté's departure—so much so that he sold his remaining share of 10% in February 2020.

Figure 8.8 Acrobats demonstrate a strong sense of control in the face of uncertainty.

Did Laliberté, as a master of control, sense that the pandemic (officially called a month later in March 2020) would decimate the travel and entertainment industries? Perhaps it was his intuition as a poker player demonstrating the sixth sense made popular in Kenny Rogers' 1978 song "The Gambler," as to when you should keep playing and when you move on.

Standing up and leaving the stage is the ultimate form of control, even if the audience wants more.

To learn more, visit: https://effectuation.org/EE3/cirque or scan Figure 8.9.

Figure 8.9

> Immense power is acquired by assuring yourself in your secret reveries that you were born to control affairs.
>
> *Andrew Carnegie*, business titan and philanthropist

CONTROL AND VENTURE SUCCESS

Success within an entrepreneurial venture is determined by the ability of the organization to define, shape, and optimize the elements shown in Figure 8.7 as the industry, venture, market, and customers emerge and evolve. Think about how you will approach each—we discuss three examples here.

Competition

Should a new venture deal with competition using prediction or control? Decisions managers or entrepreneurs in other firms make about how they want to compete, particularly in new and undefined markets, are quite hard to predict. But does that mean you have no control? We place competition in the bottom third of Figure 8.7 to reflect that the actions of competitors are largely out of our control.

At the same time, we do not place it on the far left-hand edge of controllability, as there are many competitive factors that are shapeable, including the ability to collaborate and co-create with competitors. Determining the differentiator(s) (technology, business model, or distribution strategy) that make your venture unique provides you with significant latitude to determine the dimensions of the competition (and give you a chance to select ones where you have an advantage). As you start your business, think carefully about how to make your venture distinctive.

Economy

Economic climate is relevant to the success of most new ventures for two reasons. In general, a good economy allows even mediocre companies to succeed and helps good companies flourish.

In other words: "A rising tide lifts all boats." The US president John F. Kennedy is credited with popularizing this aphorism and the legendary investor Warren Buffet has added his experience in this version: "A rising tide floats all boats … only when the tide goes out do you discover who's been swimming naked."

Interestingly, there are some products and services that become more attractive in a bad economy (see Chapter 16 on surprise for examples). Unfortunately, such economic cycles are almost always both unpredictable and outside our control. That acknowledged, we generally observe offerings that help people make money perform better in a good economy. And those that help people save money perform better in a bad economy. So, if you direct your efforts toward offerings that might support both value propositions, you give yourself more potential control in responding to any development in the economy.

> [Control is] the characteristic of probability alterability. That is, if a participant could take steps to favorably alter the success rate in subsequent administrations of the task (not in the current administration), then the task is said to be characterized by control.
>
> (*Goodie*, 2003, p. 598)

LEADER: THE META-CONTROLLER

We place the leader, usually the entrepreneur, on the far right of Figure 8.7 because leaders can steer the approach used by the rest of the organization.

Leaders may choose to use control strategies sometimes and other times use prediction strategies. For example, leaders can guide the organization in applying the resources available to create something new (a control strategy), or to embark on market research and seek resources from others (a strategy that offers much less control).

CONTROL IN ACTION: WEIGHT-LOSS CLINIC

Imagine, for a moment, that you want to start a business in the health and fitness industry by opening a weight-loss clinic. You observe a big market in helping people lose weight, but the fact is that nine out of ten people quickly regain that weight, ultimately making them unsatisfied.

What are some ways you can use this data in your business? You could observe that there is a nine-out-of-ten probability of recidivism and decide that:

- Considering the high rate of recidivism, you start a body image counseling service to help people accept their situation.
- Weight-loss programs are an excellent business because customers inevitably will end up coming back, thus bringing you repeat business.
- Partnering with a very wealthy foundation which controls half of the processed food industry is the way to develop a long-term program to change the nutritional profile of popular foods.
- Weight-loss programs offer an excellent opportunity to compete for business because all you have to do is decrease the recidivism rate slightly and your weight-loss centers will be a runaway success with customers.

Now, what's the difference between the way prediction and control are used in these options?

In the first option, you see the business opportunity in not seeking to predict or change the market, but rather take advantage by adapting the service you offer.

Figure 8.10

By using the information on the recidivism rate in a predictive way in the second option, you decide what kind of venture to get into.

In the third option, you take a visionary approach and seek to use market power to influence customer behavior.

By contrast, in the fourth option, information is taken as a control lever, a point of intervention, a statistic that the entrepreneur may be able to change. Instead of taking the nine-out-of-ten ratio as given, the entrepreneur sees it as something she might be able to influence in order to control the success of the venture.

The history of human action has proven time and time again the power of human beings to change the odds of events. Consider, for example, the odds of being crippled by polio. Globally, these odds are dramatically different now than they were 50 years ago owing to efforts by the World Health Organization and individual country organizations to eradicate the disease. In other words, we have collectively changed a child's probability of getting polio.

The weight-loss clinic example challenges us to think about what might be controllable and what truly is not. It also allows us to look at the relationship between prediction and control in a more "active" way.

For controllers, understanding probabilities is valuable to the extent that you can find a way of changing them. Controllers thus use knowledge of probabilities differently than predictors do. For controllers, probabilities are opportunities to intervene, to manipulate events; for predictors, they are an opportunity to make a bet. Or to change and adapt to predicted circumstances.

While the predictor is working on the assumption that no one else will be successful in changing the probabilities, the entrepreneur is working on the assumption that other entrepreneurs out there, like them, are trying to find some way to change the world.

HOW CONTROL WORKS: YOU AND YOUR STAKEHOLDERS

Why should you work directly with stakeholders? Why do seasoned entrepreneurs say they prefer first-hand market input, derived from personally going out and trying to sell a product, rather than gathering data about the potential market?

The answer is that working with self-selected stakeholders enables controllability.

- You control who you interact with. Stakeholders select you, and you select them—the process is mutual. If you don't get along, you can decide to move on and do business with someone else.
- Any relationship that is to some extent negotiable is more controllable than a relationship that is not. Negotiations happen in many different ways, including bargaining, haggling, manipulating, influencing, etc. These methods of interacting with other human beings involve some sharing of control.
- You can be confident your stakeholders also desire control. That means it makes sense to join forces with them and try to shape the future together, rather than spend your time trying to predict what everyone else might do.
- A large part of the method of control relies on the fact that human beings generally prefer control to prediction; therefore, they are willing to work with others to integrate their goals and plans, and also to shape and co-create new goals worth pursuing.

It should be clear from the foregoing discussion that controlling with and through others requires an acceptance of a shared role for those stakeholders. It involves the entrepreneur and stakeholders working together to co-create a non-zero-sum game in which everyone benefits in the future together.

Practically Speaking

The Power of Control

Close your eyes and imagine life without electricity. Entertainment and communications are generally what people think of first. No iPad. No mobile phone. No television or computer. It's very quiet. But electricity also drives more fundamental services we take for granted, such as running water (an electric pump is usually required) and lighting. Now multiply by 329 million. That's the number of people in India in 2007 who were living without electricity. Sounds like the basis for a charitable effort that should command the attention of citizens in the world's wealthier countries.

Time for a Switch

It is the year 2007 and you are Gyanesh Pandey, a young electrical engineer who learned he could generate electricity from rice husks, a waste product heaped along the rural roads of his native state of Bihar.

Would you be tempted to apply for government grants, approach international aid agencies, and seek donations from private foundations? Maybe. But with the input of a couple of MBAs from the Darden School in the USA, Manoj Sinha and Charles (Chip) Ransler, might you consider the heretical notion that you could actually make money from this thing?

What Profit?

With grants and donations, you could do it the right way—import gasification plants from the US, employ trained technicians, and set up a power grid, probably on a rationally justifiable five-year plan. But when you entertain the notion of "profit," you can only begin with what you have or, if you are clever, maybe build a working proof of concept with resources you can afford to lose.

The specifications for your prototype are clear: the solution has to be cheap. Or free. Or cheaper than free. That means you have to make machinery locally and train local talent to put it together and maintain it. And you have to figure out how to get paid. It's just about possible. Except for a few small details. You are in Bihar, one of the poorest states in India. The local population is not educated, often not literate. And the notion of "paying" for electric power is not customary. Tapping into grids and stealing it is more the norm.

Twice Illuminated

The team set out to design a business model based on village systems, not power grids. Small, cheap and prepaid would describe it, like the mobile phones pervasive in rural Bihar. Make technicians, salespersons, and even business leaders out of local people—those hungry to learn, even if only to pay the bills. As the team spins out this unlikely tapestry, they learn that a community's emotional ownership in a business is a powerful thing. And that a functional business model is worth a thousand grandiose plans that gobble cash and go nowhere. It is the same lesson that so-called social entrepreneurs who dare to do it for profit are learning all over the world. Ask Muhammed Yunus, founder of Grameen Bank. Ask Matt Flannery, founder of Kiva. Ask Bill Drayton, founder of Ashoka.

Practically Speaking *(continued)*

Bright Future

Husk makes a profit selling power at 0.07 US dollars per kilowatt-hour. That's a bargain compared with buying kerosene for a lamp. And it's a bargain compared with buying electricity from the national power company. Could a social venture out-compete a state subsidized monopoly? If so, Husk could expand from social startup venture into social multinational firm. That, indeed, would be powerful progress. In the meantime, a lot has happened in Bihar and Husk Power Systems. As of late 2023, they had built 200 mini-grids in Nigeria and India. Their co-founder and CEO, Manoj Sinha, announced that the company is launching an "Africa Sunshot" plan to expand their network with 2,500 solar-powered mini-grids in six African nations including Nigeria and the Democratic Republic of Congo. The five-year project has the goal of bringing clean power to 7.7 million people and several hundred thousand businesses.

Figure 8.11 These tiny waste rice husks have brightened the future of many students studying late into the night with lights powered by Husk Energy.

And all this started with an enlightened and alternative entrepreneurial approach.

To learn more, visit: https://effectuation.org/EE3/husk or scan Figure 8.12.

Figure 8.12

Research Roots

The Power of Networks

The concept of effectuation has received increasing research attention, including the way entrepreneurs create new ventures by relying on their own resources and networks rather than predicting and controlling future outcomes.

Two recent articles by Kerr and Coviello (2019, 2020) explore the role of networks in effectuation. The first article presents a systematic review and synthesis of the literature on effectual networks, focusing on how entrepreneurs form and maintain networks based on their goals and available resources. The authors argue that effectual networks are characterized by a high level of diversity, flexibility, and trust, and that they enable entrepreneurs to achieve their goals through co-creation and mutual support.

The second article builds on this framework by integrating network theory into effectuation. The authors propose a multi-level reconceptualization of effectual dynamics, arguing that effectuation occurs not only at the individual level, but also at the network and ecosystem levels. They identify four key network processes that enable effectuation: (1) creating and maintaining network ties, (2) mobilizing network resources, (3) co-creating value, and (4) managing network tensions.

The articles suggest that entrepreneurs should focus on building diverse, flexible, and trust-based networks in order to achieve their goals. They also suggest that network dynamics play a key role in effectuation, and that entrepreneurs should be aware of the network processes that enable them to create and maintain their ventures. By integrating network theory into effectuation, these articles contribute to a deeper understanding of the complex and dynamic processes that underlie entrepreneurial success.

PERCEPTION OF CONTROL

Thus far in the chapter, we have addressed things you can do—actions you can take that will increase your level of control. But detailed research from psychology tells us that underlying your willingness to act is your perception of control.

Perceptions of control are important only when we're considering outcomes that offer some resistance, outcomes that probably will not happen in the absence of human intervention. So, control, for our purposes, is about attempting to influence things contingent not only on what you do, but also on what others do. Your influence might be 1% or 99%. Low-control activities are those with cause–effect relationships that you can't influence much; high-control activities are ones you have some significant influence over.

We focus our attention on what we will call effectual control techniques. In general, effectuation works with elements where a significant contingency relationship exists between you and the element. An example would be pre-selling a prospective product to a client, where your actions significantly influence how the sale turns out, i.e. the management of the client relationship and the delivery of the promised product, which is in your hands. Not everything is controllable, but the effectual entrepreneur focuses on what they can control. And then expand the horizon into larger spheres of control.

This approach clearly contrasts with causal control techniques that work with elements where there is a low- or no-contingency relationship between you and the element. An example would be developing a business plan on your prediction of the results of an election: "I'm going to invest in a construction company because I predict that the government election will result in more government spending that will spur demand for construction." You can't control the election results; precisely for this reason, you have to predict them and then make a bet based on your prediction.

CONTROL OVER INPUTS AND CONTROL OVER OUTCOMES

To increase our understanding of how control is linked to action, we must consider not only control over outcomes, but also control over inputs. For example, some people feel they could control outcomes if only they had the "correct" inputs. In contrast, effectuators (those who apply effectual logic) act based on inputs within their control on environments they believe they can influence through their actions.

Effectually speaking, the "correct" inputs are the inputs you already have within your control.

Limited control over outcomes

When people are unsure about how much they can influence outcomes, they may try to compensate with elaborate planning and calculated bets. This can lead to "analysis paralysis" if they are relying on prediction. The alternative to this is applying the effectual principle of affordable loss to drive action, especially when there is a willingness to change goals as new stakeholders come on board.

Limited Control Over Inputs

When people do not have the means they believe are required to achieve desired outcomes, they become susceptible to inertia induced by the "if onlys"—if only I had the money; if only my personal circumstances were different; if only I had access to the technology; and so on.

If they do decide to act under these circumstances, and choose a causal approach, they face the prospect of chasing resources outside their control. If they take an effectual approach, they need to be open to self-selected stakeholders because these stakeholders can increase the available means (inputs).

They can act using either approach, but effectuation lowers the cost by reducing resource requirements to affordable loss levels. And it increases incomes by bringing more people on board whose affordable loss resources help expand the sphere of control for the venture.

Figure 8.13

Control Over Neither Inputs nor Outcomes

Perceiving both inputs and outcomes as unpredictable and outside one's control can lead to a state that psychologists call "learned helplessness." This is a serious danger associated with using prediction in uncertain circumstances, and it highlights why effectuators begin with the inputs they control—their means.

In sum, focusing on control strategies can have a positive impact on the likelihood of action because it does not rely on predictability, upfront investments in planning, and the pursuit of resources to deliver on the plans.

Research Roots

Learning Helplessness and Optimism

Martin Seligman, often called the "Father of Positive Psychology," introduced the concepts of "learned helplessness" and "learned optimism" through his extensive research on human behavior. These concepts are particularly relevant for entrepreneurs since uncertainty is a constant and personal control is vital for success.

Learned Helplessness

Learned helplessness is a psychological condition in which individuals believe that they have no control over the outcomes of their actions, often leading to a state of passivity and depression. This concept emerged from Seligman's experiments with dogs in the 1960s, where he observed that animals subjected to uncontrollable shocks eventually stopped trying to escape, even when escape was possible. This behavior was attributed to the belief that their actions were futile.

Research Roots *(continued)*

In humans, learned helplessness manifests when individuals face repeated failures or uncontrollable situations, leading them to generalize the belief that they are incapable of influencing outcomes. This mindset can severely impair an entrepreneur's ability to take risks, make decisions, and persist in the face of challenges. Entrepreneurs who succumb to learned helplessness may avoid taking necessary actions, believing that their efforts will not change the outcome. This can result in missed opportunities and stagnation.

Learned Optimism

In contrast, Seligman also introduced the concept of learned optimism, which is the idea that individuals can train themselves to adopt a more positive and proactive mindset. Learned optimism is based on the notion that our explanatory style, or the way we interpret events, influences our ability to cope with adversity. People with an optimistic explanatory style see negative events as temporary, specific to a situation, and external to themselves. This perspective fosters resilience and a sense of control.

Seligman proposed that by changing one's explanatory style from pessimistic to optimistic, individuals can enhance their mental well-being and performance. For entrepreneurs, Learned Optimism is a crucial trait. It enables them to view setbacks as learning experiences rather than insurmountable obstacles. This optimistic outlook promotes persistence, creativity, and the willingness to take calculated risks, all of which are essential for entrepreneurial success.

Gaining Control Through Individual Action

The interplay between learned helplessness and learned optimism highlights the importance of individual action in gaining control in the face of uncertainty. Seligman's work forms the basis of the following suggestions:

1. Awareness and mindset shift: the first step in countering learned helplessness is awareness. Entrepreneurs need to recognize patterns of negative thinking and consciously shift toward a more optimistic explanatory style. This involves reframing challenges as opportunities for growth and viewing failures as temporary setbacks.
2. Goal setting and incremental progress: setting clear, achievable goals is crucial. Breaking down larger objectives into smaller, manageable tasks can help entrepreneurs regain a sense of control. Celebrating incremental progress reinforces the belief that their actions have a direct impact on outcomes.
3. Skill development and adaptability: continual learning and skill development are essential for maintaining control. Entrepreneurs should invest in their personal and professional growth to adapt to changing circumstances. This proactive approach reduces the feeling of helplessness and enhances their ability to navigate uncertainty.
4. Support systems and collaboration: building a supportive network is vital. Mentors, peers, and advisors can provide valuable feedback and encouragement, helping entrepreneurs maintain an optimistic outlook. Collaboration also allows for shared problem-solving, reducing the burden of uncertainty.
5. Resilience and persistence: developing resilience is key to overcoming setbacks. Entrepreneurs must cultivate the ability to bounce back from failures and persist in the face of adversity. This resilience is often bolstered by a strong sense of purpose and commitment to their goals.

By fostering an optimistic mindset and taking deliberate actions to gain control, entrepreneurs can effectively navigate uncertainty and enhance their chances of success.

TAKEAWAY: CONTROL THE CONTROLLABLE

It is important to know both what you can control, or influence, and what you cannot. The magic of continually working with and building on what is within your control is that you don't have to wait to start a process that helps expand your sphere of control. Moreover, you can reshape and change that sphere even as the world changes.

Venturing, and life itself, becomes more like a dance than a duck-and-grab tug-of-war.

What Now?

- For the opportunity you are developing, work through Figure 8.7 showing elements of entrepreneurial success and detail where and how you are focusing your efforts to control.
- Now identify three moves you could make to exert control of additional elements in that figure.
- Actions enable control. Are your actions consistent with your ideas on what might be controlled? What important action are you postponing today that might enable more control of your future?

Think It Through

- The ideas presented in this chapter are complex and can be confusing. But they are fundamental to understanding effectual logic, so consider re-reading this chapter and discussing it with someone.

So What?

- Action enables entrepreneurs to exert control on things that are otherwise impossible to predict.
- With control-driven strategies, you do not need full control—you only need sufficient control so that you can move on to the next step and the next stakeholder.
- Expert entrepreneurs don't often seek unilateral control of people or markets, but they work hard to control the controllable, often with partners (see Figure 8.7).

REFERENCES

Abramson, L. Y., Seligman, M. E., & Teasdale, J. D. (1978). Learned helplessness in humans: Critique and reformulation. *Journal of Abnormal Psychology*, *87*(1), 49.

Akcigit, U., Ates, S. T., & Chikis, C. A. (n.d.). *Trends in U.S. Business Dynamism and the Innovation Landscape*. https://eig.org/wp-content/uploads/2023/09/Trends-in-U.S.-Business-Dynamism-and-the-Innovation-Landscape.pdf

Alliance for Decision Educators. (2023, September 27). *Episode 027: Too Many Choices With Dr. Sheena Iyengar*. Retrieved September 30, 2023, from https://alliancefordecisioneducation.org/podcasts/episode-027-too-many-choices-with-dr-sheena-iyengar/

Austen, I. (2015, April 20). Sale of Cirque du Soleil aims to open doors in China. *The New York Times*. https://www.nytimes.com/2015/04/21/business/dealbook/cirque-de-soleil-deal.html

Bakker, A. B., Demerouti, E., & Verbeke, W. (2004). Using the job demands-resources model to predict burnout and performance. *Human Resource Management*, *43*(1), 83–104. https://doi.org/10.1002/hrm.20004

Bandura, A., & Cervone, D. (1986). Differential engagement of self-reactive influences in cognitive motivation. *Organizational Behavior and Human Decision Processes*, *38*(1), 92–113.

Bilefsky, D. (2021, May 9). Cirque du Soleil's return could be its most challenging feat yet. *The New York Times*. https://www.nytimes.com/2021/05/09/world/canada/cirque-du-soleil-returns.html

Christensen, C. (1997). *The Innovator's Dilemma: When New Technologies Cause Great Firms to Fail*. Harvard Business School Press.

Decker, R. A., & Haltiwanger, J. (2023). *Surging Business Formation in the Pandemic: Causes and Consequences?* https://www.brookings.edu/wp-content/uploads/2023/09/4_Decker-Haltiwanger_unembargoed.pdf

Goodie, A. S. (2003). The effects of control on betting: Paradoxical betting on items of high confidence with low value. *Journal of Experimental Psychology: Learning, Memory, and Cognition*, *29*(4), 598.

Institute for Management Development (IMD). (2012, August 28). An interview with Guy Laliberté. https://www.youtube.com/watch?v=YLrzvrGBiBY

Kerr, J., & Coviello, N. (2019). Formation and constitution of effectual networks: A systematic review and synthesis. *International Journal of Management Reviews*, *21*(3), 370–397. https://doi.org/10.1111/ijmr.12194

Kerr, J., & Coviello, N. (2020). Weaving network theory into effectuation: A multi-level reconceptualization of effectual dynamics. *Journal of Business Venturing*, *35*(2), 105937. https://doi.org/10.1016/j.jbusvent.2019.05.001

Lyengar, S. (2023). *Think Bigger: How to Innovate*. Columbia University Press.

Lyengar, S. S., & Lepper, M. R. (2000). When choice is demotivating: Can one desire too much of a good thing? *Journal of Personality and Social Psychology*, *79*(6), 995–1006. https://doi.org/10.1037/0022-3514.79.6.995

Macrotrends. (2023a). India electricity access 1993–2023. Retrieved October 24, 2023, from https://www.macrotrends.net/countries/IND/india/electricity-access-statistics

Macrotrends. (2023b) India population 1950–2023. Retrieved October 24, 2023, from https://www.macrotrends.net/countries/IND/india/population

Mishra, A. (2022, June 28). Husk power: Solar energy is key to replacing diesel and advancing sustainable growth in Africa. *Forbes*. Retrieved October 16, 2023, from https://www.forbes.com/sites/ankitmishra/2022/06/28/husk-power-solar-innovation-is-the-best-way-to-deploy-clean-energy-and-advance-sustainable-growth/

Montreal Gazette. (2015, April 21). Guy Laliberté explains the sale of Cirque du Soleil. https://www.youtube.com/watch?v=-rqJ3PstXHU

Moore, D. A., & Healy, P. J. (2008). The trouble with overconfidence. *Psychological Review*, *115*(2), 502.

Peterson, C., Maier, S. F., & Seligman, M. E. (1995). *Learned Helplessness: A Theory for the Age of Personal Control*. Oxford University Press.

Phillips, T. (2018, June 26). "More dead than alive": Rio's closure of legendary club reflects cultural crisis. *The Guardian*. https://www.theguardian.com/world/2018/jun/26/more-dead-than-alive-rios-closure-of-legendary-club-reflects-cultural-crisis

Reeves, M., Love, C., & Tillmanns, P. (2012). Your strategy needs a strategy. *Harvard Business Review*, *90*(9), 76.

Seligman, M. E. (2006). *Learned Optimism: How to Change Your Mind and Your Life*. Vintage.

Sguazzin, A. (2023, September 5). Biggest mini-grid owner in Africa, Asia sets $500 million target. *Bloomberg*. https://www.bloomberg.com/news/articles/2023-09-05/biggest-mini-grid-owner-in-africa-asia-sets-500-million-target

Steger, M. F., Frazier, P., Oishi, S., & Kaler, M. (2006). The meaning in life questionnaire: Assessing the presence of and search for meaning in life. *Journal of Counseling Psychology*, *53*(1), 80–93. https://doi.org/10.1037/0022-0167.53.1.80

Tankersley, J. (2023, September 29). A silver lining from the pandemic:

A surge in start-ups. *The New York Times*. https://www.nytimes.com/2023/09/29/us/politics/pandemic-economy-surge-start-ups.html

United Nations. (1948). Universal Declaration of Human Rights. OHCHR. https://www.ohchr.org/en/universal-declaration-of-human-rights

United Nations. (1966a). International Covenant on Civil and Political Rights. OHCHR. https://www.ohchr.org/en/instruments-mechanisms/instruments/international-covenant-civil-and-political-rights

United Nations. (1966b). International Covenant on Economic, Social and Cultural Rights. OHCHR. https://www.ohchr.org/en/instruments-mechanisms/instruments/international-covenant-economic-social-and-cultural-rights

CHAPTER 9

Figure 9.1 The principles of effectual logic work together to form the mindset of taking control by taking action with the means at hand, within affordable loss, co-creating with others and turning surprises into opportunities.

The Effectual Logic of Expert Entrepreneurs

In This Chapter

Despite the widespread perception that successful entrepreneurs have a great idea, grand vision, and lots of resources, financial and otherwise, this is not true. Extensive research has shown that highly successful entrepreneurs (called "expert entrepreneurs") don't have them. Instead, they build them using a different set of principles:

- Start with your means.
- Don't risk what you can't afford to lose.
- Build the future together with partners.
- Be open to surprise as an opportunity.

This way of thinking and acting leads to certain beliefs about the world, including that the world is something to be shaped, particularly through the actions of human beings. A variety of stakeholders are part of the co-creation that expert entrepreneurs orchestrate, everyone from customers and suppliers to employees, family, friends, strangers, investors, and even the government.

DOI: 10.4324/9781003364016-11

In This Chapter *(continued)*

So, entrepreneurs—even expert entrepreneurs—aren't any different from the rest of us. But they do operate in a unique problem space characterized by uncertainty. Without the ability to predict in that problem space, entrepreneurs seek to shape or control outcomes as much as they can, together with their stakeholders. We contrast this difference between their fundamental assumptions about the future with those of a novice:

- *Novice.* To the extent that we can predict the future, we can control it.
- *Expert.* To the extent that we can control the future, we do not need to predict it.

Research Roots

WHY STUDY EXPERT ENTREPRENEURS?

Psychologists have studied expertise for years, starting by watching chess experts play. What the psychologists learned is that experts develop unique heuristics for pattern matching and problem-solving within their domains but are otherwise no smarter or otherwise different from the general population (Ericsson et al., 2006). Studying expert entrepreneurs using methods from cognitive science studies of expertise and two decades of research on effectuation have identified and fleshed out heuristics for making opportunities in uncertain environments.

The novice's view reflects a causal logic; the expert's view reflects an effectual one. While causal reasoning may or may not involve creative thinking, effectual reasoning is inherently creative. And co-creative. Both logics can be taught and learned. In other words, everybody can learn to think and act like an entrepreneur.

Our claim is not that we can produce entrepreneurial genius on cue, just that everyone can learn to become a better entrepreneur—if we know what principles to apply.

But how? As interesting, lofty, or maybe even inspirational as the idea of co-creating the future may be, it doesn't answer the question of where to start and what to do. In this chapter, we begin getting specific.

In addition to identifying the concept of control as central for dealing with uncertainty as we saw in Chapter 8, our research also identified specific heuristics that expert entrepreneurs use for control instead of predicting.

These are a set of four principles, which together with the "pilot in the plane" principle constitute the logic of effectuation. As we look closely at each in Part III of the book, here we give you a feel for effectuation with the hope that you begin to add detail as you work your way through the book and build your own effectual roadmap for action.

Practically Speaking

A Clean Start (Means)

What do you do when you wake up one day in San Francisco and realize you actually want to be living on a sparsely populated Estonian island in the middle of the Baltic Sea? You make sure you will be able to support yourself by starting a company there, of course. That is what Stephen and Ea (pronounced e-ah) Greenwood did when they moved to the island of Saaremaa in 2004.

But with the move came questions about their idea: what kind of company, where to start, and how to make it work?

Opportunity Bubbles

The Greenwoods took stock of their assets, means already within their control:

- A derelict farmhouse on 4 hectares on Saaremaa
- The island of Saaremaa with its numerous beaches and spas, and their town of Kaarma
- Access to 10,000 euro in seed investment, through a friend managing an EU entrepreneur incubator
- An appreciation of a sustainable, organic lifestyle

We can now easily imagine several ventures that might work for the Greenwoods, for instance, organic farming, eco-tourism, or promotion of Estonia to potential US visitors.

Washing Up

With a strict affordable loss level of the 10,000-euro funding from the EU, the Greenwoods needed to build a business that would have year-round revenue potential. So they decided to make organic soap. Potential customers needed to wash all year long, the business required no expensive equipment, and the product would meet their personal desires for a pure and healthy offering.

Testing the Water

Once they secured EU funding, the Greenwoods started renovation of the farmhouse (their production facility and first retail location). They also started experimenting with soap manufacture (using less expensive non-organic ingredients for practice).

Stephen learned computer programming so he could set up a website for the company. The couple named the firm GoodKaarma, after the local town Kaarma. And then they began partnering.

Practically Speaking *(continued)*

Ea and Stephen approached local spas to develop customized soap products which would enhance spa goers' experience. And they worked with local designers and printers to create packaging using organic local materials.

Scrubbing Sensation

Still today the Greenwoods produce all of their soap in the farmhouse kitchen using simple household equipment and wooden molds the Greenwoods made. The soaps are created by hand (using certified organic ingredients) in small batches of about 7 kilograms. Production is year-round with a variety of soaps, body scrubs, and essential oils available via their website and exported to retail outlets in Ireland, UK, Sweden, Finland, Denmark, and Germany.

Figure 9.2 The product of effectual entrepreneurship: Organic GoodKaarma soap.

The soaps are also available throughout Estonia and under private label at many of Saaremaa's best spas. Thousands of people visit the GoodKaarma Talu (farm) each summer to buy soap, enjoy their café, and participate in hands-on soap-making classes. GoodKaarma was recognized by Estonian President Toomas Hendrik as a model of sustainable entrepreneurship. And perhaps most importantly, the Greenwoods are now permanent residents of Kaarma.

To learn more, visit: https://effectuation.org/EE3/kaarma or scan Figure 9.3.

Figure 9.3

FIRST PRINCIPLE: START WITH YOUR MEANS

When expert entrepreneurs seek to build a new venture, they start with their means. These means can be grouped into three categories:

- *Who I am*—my traits, tastes, and abilities
- *What I know*—my education, training, expertise, and experience
- *Who I know*—my social and professional networks

Using a combination of these means, the entrepreneur begins to imagine possibilities and take action. Most often, she starts very small with the closest means and moves almost directly into implementation without elaborate planning ("fire, aim" instead of "aim, fire").

With each action, possible outcomes are reconfigured. Eventually, certain emerging effects coalesce into clearly achievable and desirable goals—landmarks begin to form on the blank map. The end goals are the combined result of the imagination and aspirations of the entrepreneur and the people she has interacted with during the process.

Practically Speaking

Drawing the Future, Sketch by Sketch (Affordable Loss)

Growing up, did you always understand the guidance of your mother? Wendy McNaughton didn't. Only later did she appreciate her mother's advice: "In life you have a basket, and you walk along with your basket, and you have all these experiences, and you put your experiences in the basket. And then eventually you get to the place you're going, and you have all of these riches that you didn't expect. And that is what you have to work with in your life."

In fact, Wendy attributes her success as an artist to that "basket": "There's no way I could be doing the work I'm doing without having gone through all of that."

Sketchy Start

After getting a fine arts degree, when Wendy was working as a copywriter in an advertising agency in San Francisco, California, she spent her long commute on public transport sketching fellow commuters. Eventually she worked up the courage to start sharing those drawings online, turning her singular journey into a shared one.

Wendy is process-focused rather than goal-focused. For example, she used drawing to process her grief as her aunt was dying, which led to an offer to be Artist-in-Residence for a hospice program. Sketch by sketch, Wendy realized that her co-creators were actually the volunteers caring for those dying and their families.

One of Wendy's best-known projects, the bestselling cookbook *Salt Fat Acid Heat*, is a true co-creation with the book's author, Samin Nosrat. Out of the blue in 2011, Samin sent Wendy an email which started:

> You might be wondering … if I'm stalking you. Well, the answer [is] yes. I'm obsessed with your work. Obsessed, and I have a secret dream, about to be not so secret, that we can collaborate and that you'll illustrate the cookbook.
>
> (*Nosrat & MacNaughton*, 2020)

That was the beginning of a years-long shared project to fill Samin's cookbook with Wendy's drawings and not a single photograph.

Drawing Her Way Out

When the pandemic hit and everyday life became more uncertain, Wendy's process focus and comfort with mistakes came in handy. And at the urging of her wise mother, Wendy again dipped into her basket.

Drawing out her skills from the basket, including a wicked sense of humor, an iPhone, and social media, Wendy started a daily livestreamed drawing class for children called "DrawTogether."

Drawing People In

The success of "DrawTogether" attracted backers who helped fund a new set for her show. With another grant, Wendy also launched DrawTogether Classrooms, which has grown into a non-profit serving thousands of children across the United States of America.

Thanks to these ventures, thousands of kids around the world process their emotions (including trauma and confusion related to the pandemic) through drawing. And Wendy's affordable loss has been transformed into invaluable joy and possibility.

To learn more, visit: https://effectuation.org/EE3/drawtogether or scan Figure 9.4.

Figure 9.4

Research Roots

Measuring Effectuation

In addition to the initial work by the authors of the first editions of this book (Read, Sarasvathy, Dew, & Wiltbank), several researchers have developed and validated survey tools to measure effectual approaches in the context of new ventures, new products, corporate settings, as well as to contrast effectuation with traditional causal approaches.

Chandler et al. (2011) developed a methodology to measure the use of both effectual and causal logic in creating new ventures.

Blauth et al. (2014) found that the use of effectual logic positively affected product development in German firms. In a later study, Blauth et al. (2015) determined that the use of effectual logic in the face of uncertainty can speed up problem-solving and be a competitive advantage.

SECOND PRINCIPLE: SET AFFORDABLE LOSS

In much of the business world, the manager in charge of launching a new product analyzes the market and chooses segments with the highest expected value. It is a natural reflex that is the result of years of training around a single mantra: maximize returns by selecting the optimal strategy for your target.

Expert entrepreneurs turn this logic on its head—they think in terms of affordable loss rather than expected returns. They decide what they are willing to lose, rather than what they expect to gain. Instead of calculating upfront how much money they will need to launch their project and investing time, effort, and energy in raising that money, the effectual entrepreneur tries to estimate the downside and examines what she is willing to lose.

The effectual entrepreneur then uses the process of building the project to bring other stakeholders on board and leverage what they can afford to lose together. For Wendy McNaughton (DrawTogether), this was a smartphone, a social media account, and the intention to help children process the uncertainty of the pandemic through drawing.

An estimate of affordable loss does not depend on the venture, but on the person. It varies from person to person and even across their life stages and circumstances. In the Pet Rock example (Chapter 6), Dahl had time on his hands and enough cash to prototype his idea. For the Greenwoods (GoodKaarma), affordable loss did not permit the use of cash, but did include the use of their old farmhouse.

By allowing estimates of affordable loss to drive decisions about which venture to start, entrepreneurs stop depending on prediction. Instead, they focus on cultivating opportunities that have a low failure cost and that generate more options for the future. The combination enables cheap failure and learning that can be applied to the next iteration of the opportunity.

This does not mean that entrepreneurs choose projects that won't cost a lot if they fail—or that they do not expect to make a lot of money. It simply acknowledges that uncertain new venture opportunities are difficult to value upfront, whereas the investment of time, money, and other resources is quantifiable, manageable, and controllable.

Practically Speaking

Surprise in a Glass (Contingencies)

Think "innovation" and whisky isn't the first market that comes to mind. Yet, in the moist cellars where distillers are patiently waiting for their current batch to reach a delicious age in exotic oak barrels, they are also dreaming up new combinations. For William Grant and Sons, that dream is the perfect beer-finished blended whisky. This is why the firm engaged Dougal Sharp, the head brewer at Scotland's largest craft brewery, to create a special brew that would infuse the oak barrels with a malty, hoppy flavor that could become part of a whisky during the aging process.

Opportunity in the Drain

William Grant and Sons were pleased with the results. The Grant's Ale Cask Reserve whisky that had rested in the barrels after the beer had been discarded had an exciting and distinctive taste. But as the ever-diligent distillery staff discovered during the process of emptying the barrels, so did the beer itself. So Sharp arranged a partnership with William Grant and Sons that enabled him to take the waste beer from the whiskey manufacture and bring it to market under a new label bearing the middle names of Sharp and his brother, Innis & Gunn.

Flowing Success

From there, things have gone well for Innis & Gunn. What started with an advance commitment from the leading supermarket chains Safeway and Sainsbury's even before the brand had been introduced is now the number one craft beer in Scotland and a top three brand in the United Kingdom. The experts agree, having awarded Innis & Gunn in 2021 with 21 international industry awards for the beer's taste, quality, and package design.

Figure 9.5 Dougal Sharp and a bottle of his best-selling Innis & Gun Original.

It's in the Combination

The story of Innis & Gunn offers two insights into innovation. The first is that many innovations are not true inventions—created from scratch—but rather new combinations of things we already have. The second is the role of surprise. Had the employees of William Grant and Sons not sampled the waste beer, the world would have missed out on a delicious new combination.

Even more interesting is how many of the products we know and love today came from accidents and unintended results of completely different ideas. Often, the winning new combination is readily available with the unexpected and even unwanted.

To learn more, visit: https://effectuation.org/EE3/innis or scan Figure 9.6.

Figure 9.6

THIRD PRINCIPLE: LEVERAGE CONTINGENCIES

If you come across lemons, make lemonade! The third principle of effectual reasoning is particularly useful to the expert entrepreneur's mindset—the ability to turn the unexpected into the profitable. With that effectual mindset, uncertainly becomes a source of new opportunities, not a hurdle to be overcome.

Expert entrepreneurs learn not only to work with surprises, but also to take advantage of them. In most contingency plans, surprises are bad—the worst-case scenarios. But because entrepreneurs do not tie their idea to any theorized or preconceived "market," any and all surprises can lead to valuable opportunities.

To accompany the story of Innis & Gunn, consider these three beer-compatible products:

Crisp Surprise

At the pub, you might enjoy potato chips with your beer. Legend describes these popular snacks as born of customer complaint. In 1853, at Moon's Lake House near Saratoga Springs, New York, George Crum was tired of having fried potatoes sent back to the kitchen because they were soggy. Out of frustration, George sliced potatoes as thinly as he could and then fried and salted them. The intent was to challenge the complainers by making the potatoes too thin to be picked up with a fork. But the result has gone on to please beer consumers around the world. Not to mention couch potatoes everywhere.

Figure 9.7

Transparent Surprise

Perhaps after a pint in the lab, French scientist Edouard Benedictus accidentally broke a glass container and observed that the shattered pieces remained bound due to a thin film on the inside of the container left over from a previous experiment. The year was 1903, and safety glass was born.

Figure 9.8

Romantic Surprise

While we will leave the connection with beer to the imagination of the reader, Viagra, the first oral treatment for men with erectile dysfunction, was also discovered by accident. The active ingredient, sildenafil, never met its intended use against angina (chest pain resulting from insufficient blood flow to the heart muscle), but in clinical trials, new applications popped up.

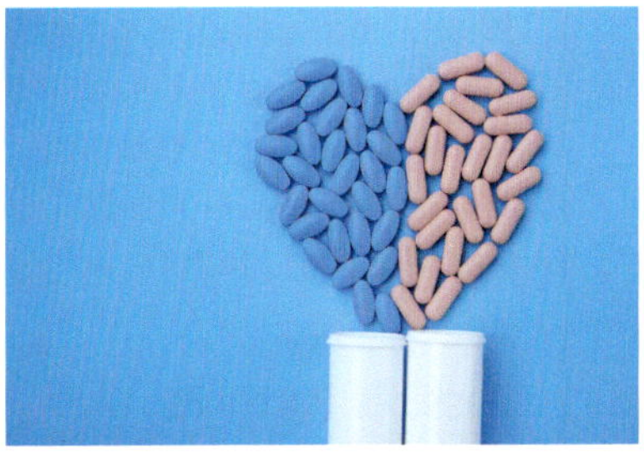

Figure 9.9

The Surprising Entrepreneur

While we love to tell stories of divine inspiration, the actual origins of many products are surprises or accidents that an entrepreneur was able to transform into an opportunity. The implication is clear: while those waiting for the perfect idea sip their beer anxiously, those taking action grab all kinds of things life throws at them to brew up a business. Maybe that will change the way you see your next surprise.

> It is not the mountain we conquer but ourselves.
>
> *Edmund Hillary*

Practically Speaking

Good Pill Hunting (Partnerships)

Bright Simons began his career as an activist at an early age. As a secondary student in Ghana, he organized his friends to protest a change in the school menu with a mass appeal through a popular radio talk show. Upon graduation, he followed his early success by campaigning to drive political change that would open opportunities for people to migrate freely around the world. But, as glamorous as it sounds to be a card-carrying professional activist, governments proved difficult to influence, progress was slow, and Simons soon became interested in more impact, and maybe even a salary. So, reluctantly, he turned to business.

Phony Pharmaceuticals

Unsurprisingly, Simons began to work on opportunities at the intersection of his home country of Ghana and his interest in creating positive social change. When he came across UN estimates that roughly half of the anti-malarial drugs sold in Africa are counterfeits, Simons decided that fake drugs might be an effort worthy of his attention.

Phony anti-malarials generate 270 million pounds sterling per year in sales on his continent alone. Simons wanted to create a business to stop sales of fake pills. Worthy indeed—counterfeit drugs are responsible for an estimated 2,000 deaths a day globally and represent a grey industry estimated by Terry Hisey of Deloitte to be worth between 45 billion pounds sterling and 125 billion pounds sterling a year, touching Europe, America, and Japan as it does emerging markets.

Possible Partners

But how do you set up a business to stop people from selling things? Clearly, legitimate pharmaceutical companies might be interested in curbing fake drug trade. But their willingness to listen to a retired activist with no technology, no product, and no experience in the industry was limited.

So, Simons started talking with more people. He talked with people in the laser hologram and RFID industries to see whether those technologies would enable him to tag genuine drug packages. He talked with pharmacists to understand the supply chain and the consumer buying patterns. But it was talking on his mobile phone that showed him he already had all the technology he needed for a solution right in his handset.

Practically Speaking *(continued)*

Scratching the Surface

In 2007, Simons set up a company called mPedigree. The idea was based on a simple service. Together with a pharmaceutical manufacturer, he would tag individual boxes of legitimate medications with a ten-digit non-duplicable code, covered by a scratch-off surface used on lottery tickets and prepaid mobile phone cards.

The end user could dial a toll-free four-digit text message number listed on the package, enter the medication code hidden under the scratch-off surface, and, within a couple of seconds, receive a validation that the medication was authentic (or not), as well as information about when and where it was manufactured.

Furthermore, the manufacturer could trace where and when the medication was sold and even the buyer's mobile phone number. The system could close the loop on fake drugs and ensure authenticity to large numbers of patients at a very low cost, virtually anywhere in the world.

Real Impact

Simons' first commercial pharmaceutical partner was May & Baker, tagging packages of Easadol, Loxagyl, and Artelum and validating them against a database set up in partnership with HP.

The system proved so effective that mPedigree quickly expanded from Ghana into Nigeria and Kenya, and it now serves 12 countries in Africa, the Middle East, and South Asia. Today, mPedigree collaborates with more than two dozen telecom companies.

Figure 9.10 Are these the real deal? Just text in the code to check.

Being in the business of stopping illegal business has generated one recognition after another for Simons and mPedigree, including the prestigious Ashoka Fellowship in 2008, the Archbishop Desmond Tutu Award by the African Leadership Institute in 2010, Fortune Global 50 Greatest Leaders in 2016, and the 2019 Skoll Award for Social Entrepreneurship.

But, most importantly, it turned his activist aspirations into impact for real pharmacists, real manufacturers, and real patients. And in the meantime, mPedigree is a leader in technologies to control counterfeiting and increase trust for genuine products. Here is just one data point, of many: in the decade since mPedigree started out, the prevalence of counterfeited drugs in Nigeria has dropped from around 30% of the total to less than 10%.

Who knows? Might entrepreneurship be the secret weapon of the idealist after all?

To learn more, visit: https://effectuation.org/EE3/mpedigree or scan Figure 9.11.

Figure 9.11

FOURTH PRINCIPLE: FORM PARTNERSHIPS

The final principle of effectual reasoning, which we touched upon in Chapter 2, is the focus on building partnerships rather than beating competitors. Since entrepreneurs tend to start the process without assuming the existence of a predetermined market for their idea, they don't know who their competitors will be, so detailed competitive analyses have little value. Instead, entrepreneurs generally take the product to the nearest potential customer. Some of the people they interact with make a commitment to the venture, dedicating time and/or money and/or resources and, thus, self-select into the new-venture creation process.

The partnership principle dovetails well with the affordable loss principle to bring the entrepreneur's idea to market with very little cash expenditure. Obtaining pre-commitments from key stakeholders, suppliers, or customers helps reduce uncertainty in the early stages of creating an enterprise.

Finally, since the entrepreneur is not wedded to any particular market for their idea, the expanding network of strategic partnerships determines, to a great extent, which market or markets the venture will eventually end up entering or creating.

Research Roots

Supersizing the Entrepreneurial Mind

Cognition research is something that is usually associated with trying to understand what is going on inside people's heads when they say and do things. There is, however, a growing awareness that this view is incomplete because it ignores one of the human brain's most powerful characteristics, which is its ability to take advantage of its physical environment, including the human body. Cognition, therefore, extends itself in three ways; it is:

- Embedded in the natural environment. For instance, much new product development involves hands-on tinkering with prototypes and mock-ups. These are not outcomes of previously formed ideas, but instead examples of how entrepreneurs think by physically manipulating objects to "see" what works.
- Embodied in the sense that our conceptual systems are at least partially indexed to our perceptual experiences in the world. For example, our notion of "pivoting" a venture is based on our experiences of bodily movement.
- Extended by being spread across multiple agents. For example, in a new venture, different team members provide specialized cognitive resources to one another, thus enabling the venture to "think."

The upshot of these insights is that entrepreneurs are adept at supersizing their minds by opportunistically co-opting aspects of their material, physical, and social context (Dew et al., 2015).

Research Roots

Entrepreneurs Made Through Education

Vivek Wadhwa and colleagues (2009) looked at 549 successful entrepreneurs and did not find a connection with even the few things prior research had suggested might be associated with successful entrepreneurs—entrepreneurial parentage and early entrepreneurial activity.

In his study, he found that 52% of successful entrepreneurs were the first in their immediate families to start a business. Furthermore, only a quarter were interested in entrepreneurship in college. Half didn't think about it and had little interest in it when in school.

Wadhwa's main finding was that education was the biggest predictor of success. Education enabled a huge advantage. Interestingly, the source of that education was not important. Firms founded by Ivy League graduates and those started by graduates of other universities experienced reasonably similar success.

Research Roots

The Surprising Differences Between Expert and Novice Decision-Making

To make a decision, generate several options, and compare them to pick the best one.

Obviously true, right? Gary Klein has spent his career researching such obvious claims and, indeed, when Klein surveyed 160 students, managers, and military officers, they strongly endorsed this claim. Such claims are not only widely accepted as appropriate but also form the basis of formal, rational decision theory. What could be wrong with that?

But in one study, Klein tested this claim, asking 26 highly experienced firefighters how they actually make decisions when fighting a fire. The firefighters insisted they didn't compare options. Commanders with an average of 23 years' experience fighting fires—experts in firefighting—said that when they look at an incident, they just recognize what to do, handily upending the conventional wisdom about the roots of effective decision-making.

Why is this? Klein points out that this result is, in fact, typical. The more skilled a person is at a task the less they need to consider options. Experienced people immediately recognize familiar situations and apply an option that they already know is a good one. In contrast, novices juggle options precisely because they don't have the experience to know what works well.

Such examples show us that many conventional norms about how to make decisions are at best situational, and at worst get in the way of effective decision-making processes. We can do better by learning from how experts in a domain actually make decisions in that domain (Klein, 2009).

Research Roots

Talent Is Overrated?

Asked why some people succeed in their endeavors while others fail, one explanation commonly offered is that successful people had a talent for it. The notion that some people are just born into the world with certain natural gifts that, once discovered, give them superior abilities is a deeply entrenched and socially endorsed answer to why some people do extraordinarily well. It could be in sports, in music … or in business.

Fortune magazine's senior editor Geoff Colvin wants you to wholeheartedly reject this story about the roots of extraordinary performance and replace it with a different story based on the notion that people develop superior abilities by deliberately practicing them.

Colvin reminds us that talent researchers have a surprisingly difficult time explaining what natural factors actually make someone a world-class brain surgeon or chess player, leading some researchers to argue that the idea of innate talent is simply fiction. Instead, the idea that people develop talents by practicing deliberately seems much more plausible, and a great deal of research supports this view by examining in detail what exceptionally talented people actually did to get, and stay, on top of their game.

Then what is the role of talent in entrepreneurship? Despite the simplistic appeal of explaining entrepreneurial success in terms of natural born talents, it seems more likely that entrepreneurial talents are developed the same way that talents in other areas are developed: by deep experience and practice in the domain. Being very good at the specific tasks that are needed to start new ventures successfully is more likely to come from putting in the hard work and effort to learn these skills than by hoping that it's something you were born with (Colvin, 2008).

PRINCIPLES ROOTED IN REALITY

Using effectuation, entrepreneurs begin with who they are, what they know, and who they know. From there, they stitch together a network of stakeholders, each of whom makes commitments that, on the one hand, increase the resources available to the network, but on the other hand, add constraints to the budding businesses in exchange for their commitment. As commitments collect, so do salaries, customer promises, supplier terms, and the like. Effectual commitment impacts the process of creating a venture in important ways:

- It focuses on what is controllable about the future and the external environment.
- The entrepreneur and her stakeholders commit only what they can afford to lose.
- The goals of the venture are determined by whoever makes commitments and what they negotiate.
- All surprises are welcomed and transformed into opportunities.
- The key to the process is not the selection among alternatives but the transformation of existing realities into new alternatives.

Going back to our example of jars in Chapter 6, the entrepreneur using effectual logic says,

> **Whatever the initial distribution of balls in the jar, I will continue to acquire red balls and put them in the jar. I will look for other people who own red balls and induce them to become partners and add to the red balls in the jar. As time goes**

by, there will be so many red balls in the jar that almost every draw will obtain one. On the other hand, if my acquaintances and I have only green balls, we will put them in the jar, and when there are enough, we will create a new game where green balls win.

Of course, such a view may express hopes rather than realities, and many entrepreneurs do fail. At the same time, unpredictable markets are often an advantage for entrepreneurs because they believe they can shape the market through their own decisions and actions, working with pre-committed stakeholders and customer-partners. Together they use contingencies, the surprises along the way, as part of the raw materials that constitute Knight's urn (Chapter 6) to build the future they are constructing.

Unlike causal reasoning, which comes to life through careful planning and subsequent execution, effectual reasoning lives and breathes action. Plans are made, unmade, revised, and recast through ongoing action and interaction with others. Yet, at any given moment, there is always a meaningful picture that keeps the team together, a compelling story that brings more stakeholders and continues the journey that maps uncharted territories. By consciously disregarding the past, the entrepreneur effectually creates the future of their dreams.

Figure 9.12 Expert entrepreneurs keep their eyes open for different perspectives.

TAKEAWAY: A DIFFERENT WAY OF LOOKING AT THE WORLD

Beyond mapping the future, effectuation carries certain assumptions about the world. Effectual thinkers:

- See the world as open, still in the making. They see human action as having a genuine role. They see firms and markets as human artifacts.
- Do not see opportunities as given or outside their control. On the contrary, they believe in creating, as well as recognizing and discovering opportunities.
- Have an interactive view of the world and an instrumental view of business. They see companies as tools that allow them to create novelty for themselves and the world; they see markets as made rather than found; and consider stakeholders to be partners in co-creation, rather than simply customers or suppliers or competitors.
- Work on making success happen rather than trying to avoid failure. They see failing as a normal part of venturing. Because they are willing to fail, they often create portfolios of ventures, knowing and learning to kill those that will lead nowhere and nurture those with potential.

Now you have a complete overview of the logic underlying effectuation. The next section of this book will dot the "i"s and cross the "t"s of the principles outlined here and explicitly relate them to the nitty-gritty details of starting a new venture.

So What?

- Start with your means.
- Set your affordable loss.
- Leverage contingencies.
- Develop committed partners.

Expert entrepreneurs regularly turn our MBA lessons upside down.

Think It Through

- What are the consequences of using only one or two of the effectual principles?
- How do the principles outlined in this chapter reinforce or undermine the concept of control in the prior chapter?
- What might be the consequence of using these principles in a setting that is very predictable?

What Now?

- Think about the companies you admire. To what extent did the principles in this chapter contribute to their creation/success?
- For the opportunity you are working on, detail your thoughts on the use of each of the principles. Where do you have momentum?
- Is the opportunity you are developing an expression of YOU?
- Do others understand how your means and the opportunity deeply connect?
- Do you know in detail how much time/money you can afford to lose in its pursuit?
- What has surprised you as you've developed the opportunity? Did it change you or your approach?
- What partners have truly joined the cause? Have you asked them for concrete support of the cause?

REFERENCES

Blauth, M., Mauer, R., & Brettel, M. (2014). Fostering creativity in new product development through entrepreneurial decision making. *Creativity and Innovation Management*, *23*(4), 495–509. https://doi.org/10.1111/caim.12094

Blauth, M., Mauer, R., & Brettel, M. (2015). Competitive advantage through entrepreneurial decision-making: Effectuation for fast problem-solving. *Die Betriebswirtschaft*, *75*(4), 233.

Chandler, G. N., DeTienne, D. R., McKelvie, A., & Mumford, T. V. (2011). Causation and effectuation processes: A validation study. *Journal of Business Venturing*, *26*(3), 375–390. https://doi.org/10.1016/j.jbusvent.2009.10.006

Colvin, G. (2008). *Talent Is Overrated: What Really Separates World-Class Performers From Everybody Else*. Portfolio.

Dew, N., Grichnik, D. Mayer-Haug, K., Read, S., & Brinckmann, J. (2015). Situated entrepreneurial cognition. *International Journal of Management Reviews*, *17*(2), 143–164. https://doi.org/10.1111/ijmr.12051

Ericsson, K. A., Charness, N., Feltovich, P. J., & Hoffman, R. R. (2006). *The Cambridge Handbook of Expertise and Expert Performance*. Cambridge University Press. https://doi.org/10.1017/CBO9780511816796.001

Klein, G. (2009). *Streetlights and Shadows: Searching for the Keys to Adaptive Decision Making*. MIT Press. https://doi.org/10.7551/mitpress/8369.001.0001

Nosrat, S., & MacNaughton, W. (2020, February 5). Samin Nosrat & Wendy MacNaughton—Partners Podcast [Interview]. https://partners.show/episodes/samin-and-wendy

United Nations Office on Drugs and Crime. (2022). *Trafficking in Medical Products in the Sahel*. https://www.unodc.org/documents/data-and-analysis/tocta_sahel/TOCTA_Sahel_medical_2023.pdf

Wadhwa, V., Holly, K., Aggarwal, R., & Salkever, A. (2009). *Anatomy of an Entrepreneur: Family Background and Motivation*. Kauffman Foundation Small Research Projects Research. https://doi.org/10.2139/ssrn.1431263

Werhahn, D., Mauer, R., Flatten, T. C., & Brettel, M. (2015). Validating effectual orientation as strategic direction in the corporate context. *European Management Journal*, *33*(5), 305–313. https://doi.org/10.1016/j.emj.2015.03.002

PART III

The Nuts and Bolts of Venturing

Effectuation in Action

This section is the heart of the book—the point where the venture gets started. We hope you notice the change in tone from one that is more thoughtful in the first two sections to one that is more action-oriented in this section.

Each of the effectual principles is laid out in detail in the odd-numbered chapters, while the even-numbered chapters explain how to put the principles to use. So, whether you use this section to organize yourself for your venture, or you navigate through the section as you navigate through the first steps of starting up, we wish you a steady hand and an endless palette of colors.

> We have come to think of the actual as one among many possible worlds.
> We need to repaint that picture.
> All possible worlds lie within the actual.
> *Nelson Goodman* (1983)

REFERENCE

Goodman, N. (1983). *Fact, Fiction, and Forecast*. Harvard University Press.

DOI: 10.4324/9781003364016-12

CHAPTER 10

Figure 10.1 Perhaps you know an expert cook who can work wonders with whatever ingredients they have at hand.

The Bird-in-Hand Principle

Start With What You Have

In This Chapter

Effectual logic shifts the focus from "How do I build a successful firm?" or "How can I become a successful entrepreneur?" to "What types of ideas and opportunities should I pursue, given who I am, what I know, and who I know?" and "Given my means, what can I create?"

This is called the means-driven or bird-in-hand principle.

When you use the bird-in-hand principle, starting a new venture is no longer an incredibly risky act of heroism. It is something you can do within the constraints and possibilities of your normal life. You can start a new venture anytime you want. You can get started now.

DOI: 10.4324/9781003364016-13

After years of anticipation, huge investments, and months of preparation, the ancient mariners had to face the day of reckoning: the day they cast free of the dock where their vessel was safely tied and ventured forth into the uncertain sea.

When facing the prospect of entering the entrepreneurial world, you may feel the same sense of leaving a safe harbor. But it need not be so.

So far, we've dispelled several myths about entrepreneurship—myths that make creating a venture seem like a much more daunting endeavor than it is. We've seen that opportunities are not lying around waiting to be found, but are created by the entrepreneur and their partners, so it's not critical or even necessary to have the perfect idea when you leave the dock. The idea will more likely be developed as you are underway on your journey.

We've learned that entrepreneurs aren't looking to take huge risks, nor are they genius forecasters; instead, they risk only what they can afford to lose, and they seek to control and shape the future rather than making futile predictions.

We've learned that many entrepreneurs don't necessarily "take the plunge"; they set out gradually, constructing the business in components while preserving the ability to return to the dock. Finally, we've seen that success and failure are a matter of perspective—how you define those terms depends on what you and your partners want to do.

Expert entrepreneurs, we've seen, follow a logic of effectuation, working with readily available resources and taking small steps into uncertainty, thus shaping the future as they go. Core principles guide the effectual entrepreneur.

In this chapter, we explore the first principle of means-driven action—working with the means already at your disposal. We call this the bird-in-hand principle after the old saying that "a bird in the hand is worth two in the bush."

We begin by looking at how effectual entrepreneurs start with means, while causal entrepreneurs start with goals, and the difference between the two approaches. We then explore the idea of means in greater detail, helping you work with what you already have (but may not be aware that you have it).

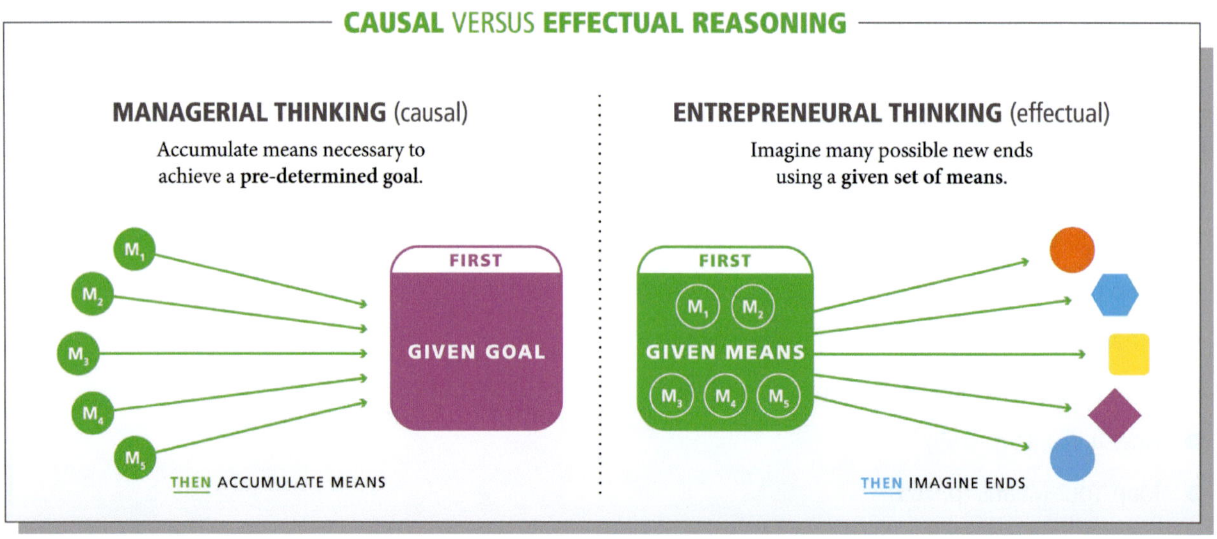

Figure 10.2 Comparison of traditional managerial approach, which is based on finding a way to reach a predetermined goal, and entrepreneurial thinking, which moves forward based on already available means.

WHAT DO WE MEAN BY "START WITH YOUR MEANS?"

People focus so much on whether they will be successful in some specific and ultimate sense or not (in other words, reach the specific goal they set out for themselves), and whether their idea is a good one or not, that they forget about all the things they could be doing with what they already have—their means.

There are three categories of means available to all of us: who we are (traits, preferences, attributes), what we know (expertise and experience), and who we know (social networks).

For the effectual entrepreneur, the fundamental question is, "What effects can I create, given who I am, what I know, and who I know?" They begin by imagining several possible courses of action, the consequences of which are, for the most part, uncertain. The entrepreneur evaluates these courses of action in terms of what resources need to be put at risk to pursue each.

Any course of action needs to have the possibility of becoming valuable. But rather than choosing a course based on expected upside, the entrepreneur prioritizes them according to which possibility is associated with the most acceptable downside.

The entrepreneur's decision about what to pursue is also co-determined by stakeholders willing to commit resources. As they contribute various resources, according to their own means and affordable loss, stakeholders set immediate agendas and generate new sub-goals for the venture, thus helping shape it.

This effectual approach stands in stark contrast to the causal approach. One fundamental difference between the two is how you think about goals and means. As Figure 10.2 illustrates, with the causal approach, you begin with clear goals. These goals may be externally imposed (for instance, maximization of shareholder value in a public corporation), or self-imposed (e.g. I want to make 10 million US dollars before I am 40 years old).

In the causal case, the goals are given, so the focus is on how to accumulate the resources necessary to achieve the goals. Often, this question leads to the formation of a vision that will induce the stakeholders who possess those resources to come on board. The accumulation of resources becomes the predominant initial purpose of the venture, and stakeholders are seen primarily as resource providers.

So, while effectuation is means-driven, the causal approach is goals-driven.

But aren't entrepreneurs highly goal-driven individuals? Yes. And the important thing to realize is that goals exist in hierarchies.

It is not that effectual entrepreneurs have no goals; indeed, they may have quite ambitious higher-level goals. But when the pressure is on and the choice is to be tethered either to means or to specific lower-level goals, effectual entrepreneurs are more likely to change those goals rather than chase means they have no control over.

Understanding that goals exist in hierarchies leads to two important insights: (1) higher-level goals, such as wanting to be a millionaire by age 40, do not tell you what you should do on the first day of your new venture; and (2) tying yourself down to specific lower-level goals, such as starting an upscale restaurant in a high-income neighborhood, drives your entrepreneurial actions toward pursuing resources you currently do not possess.

Starting with what you can do with your readily available means is a practical approach, helping you take action now toward building your new enterprise without giving up your higher-level, longer-term goals, such as becoming financially successful or being your own boss or changing the world.

Key Advantages of Being Means-Driven

How Does Being Means-Driven Compare to Being Goals-Driven?

- You are not chasing investors.
- You are not waiting for the perfect opportunity or the perfect set of resources.
- You are working with your strengths without having to overcome your weaknesses first.
- You attract co-creative stakeholders, who want to shape goals, not just provide resources.
- You are increasing the possible slate of stakeholders who can self-select into your venture.
- You are increasing the probability of innovative surprises.
- You are increasing the likelihood of finding or creating opportunities that are a better fit for you.
- You are decreasing the cost of possible failure, as you only risk means that are affordable to lose, and by doing that:
- You are increasing the likelihood that failures will be learning experiences that you can recover from faster and build on when you are ready to try again.
- You are forcing yourself to get creative with meager resources, including slack resources and even waste.

WHO I AM: THE UNBEATABLE COMPETITIVE ADVANTAGE

We do not usually think of ourselves as the primary source of valuable new opportunities or as the basis for unique competitive advantages. Yet, a little reflection will show this can indeed be true and often is.

One of the most beautiful things about entrepreneurship is that there are probably as many high-potential opportunities as there are individuals. Unlike other professions, such as medicine, accounting, dance, or sports, there is no one specific set of skills, abilities, or personality types necessary and sufficient for entrepreneurial success.

An accountancy-based enterprise, such as H&R Block, can coexist with an athletics-based firm, such as Nike, on the list of the most successful companies ever built. Similarly, a flamboyant risk taker, such as Mark Cuban, and a prudent calculator, such as Daniel Snyder, can both build thriving entrepreneurial careers resulting in eventual ownership of sports teams (the Dallas Mavericks in the case of Cuban and the Washington Commanders in the case of Snyder).

If we begin with the premise that who we are and what makes us unique could be not only the starting point, but also the basic ingredient of the venture and market opportunity we set out to create, we throw open the door to courses of action we would otherwise be blind to. In fact, the success of many enterprises can be traced to the idiosyncratic circumstances and eccentric quirks of their founders.

Practically Speaking

Many Happy Returns

Entrepreneurs begin the venture creation process with a body of knowledge, but their knowledge grows along the way and shapes their course of action. Ann DeLaVergne started with a very small idea—one the size of an envelope. While looking at the stack of used envelopes in her recycling bin, it occurred to her that a lot of small envelopes could have a big impact.

Back of the Envelope Math

Through further investigation, Ann learned that as of the year 2000, at least 81 billion return envelopes were produced and sent through the United States Postal Service each year. This is tough on the environment—using 800 thousand metric tons of wood, generating 450 thousand metric tons of greenhouse gases, and requiring more than 71 trillion BTUs of energy to process and transport. It's tough on the bottom line too, as return envelopes represent between 15% and 45% of direct mailing costs for a business.

Bulk Post

An organic farmer with a philosophy of reuse, Ann already saved large envelopes to send out again herself. But what if she could apply that thinking to 81 billion return envelopes? With that idea, Ann founded EcoEnvelopes, a firm built on the simple goal of using one envelope instead of two for round-trip business mail transactions.

Pen Pals

Figuring out how to transform her small idea into an opportunity that would have a big impact, however, was not obvious. So, Ann, who had also worked as a graphic designer, sat down at her kitchen table with some office supplies and a sewing machine (to make perforations in paper) and prototyped her reusable envelope idea. Her first effort yielded ten envelopes, which she mailed off to friends around the country. When all ten came back, she knew she was on to something.

Direct Mail Community

Partnerships and communities can provide the critical mass for an entrepreneurial idea. Ann began extending her community beyond her friends to include businesses that both use the mail and have an environmental mission. The first were the Land Stewardship Project and the Minnesota Landscape Arboretum. In addition to feeling better about their direct mail efforts and saving money, these organizations increased response rates to their direct mail campaigns to as high as 8% (roughly ten times the average) using EcoEnvelopes.

The Check in the Mail

In January 2008, EcoEnvelopes received a 570,000 US dollar investment from TC Angels—the largest single investment the group had made to date—to help Ann hire employees, secure patents, and take her invention to companies around the globe. Just a month later, the US Postal Service granted Ann a National Consumer Ruling, making EcoEnvelopes the first reusable envelope certified for standard mail.

Practically Speaking *(continued)*

Figure 10.3

Today, in addition to EcoEnvelopes, Ann DeLaVergne, her business partner Gale Ward, and their team at EcoThynk offer a range of ecologically responsible postal solutions—from paper to envelopes to labels, even complete mailing solutions. Many years later, the check is still in the mail!

To learn more, visit: https://effectuation.org/EE3/ecoenvelopes or scan Figure 10.4

Figure 10.4

Practically Speaking

New Venture Recipe

If you were going into the restaurant business, you'd probably want to be Claus Meyer. He co-founded Noma in Copenhagen, which after gaining Michelin Star status, was hailed as one of the Top 50 restaurants again in 2021.

Featuring Nordic cuisine that includes fresh seafood, local herbs, and radishes in edible "soil," Noma draws superlatives from critics that go way beyond delicious and mouthwatering. So, what are the ingredients behind its success?

Practically Speaking *(continued)*

Without a Recipe

Meyer grew up in Denmark, an environment where food was neither pleasure nor luxury, but necessity. Intending to become a banker when he was a student, Meyer spent a year in the south of France. There, the purpose of food took on new meaning. It was more than nutrition—it was beauty. At the age of 21, he returned to Denmark and "knew deeply inside that I wanted to change Danish food culture … and I believed I could do it." It was a grand vision for someone yet to finish university, and one with no clear starting point.

From the Fridge

Cooking meals and starting new ventures have a lot in common, as Meyer himself points out. One way is to start with a tried and tested recipe, get the necessary ingredients, follow instructions carefully and produce a company.

The other is to open the refrigerator, peer inside, and create something—a new dish—an unexpected business model—an entirely innovative venture no one involved could have predicted in advance. Meyer took the second path, capitalizing on the availability of the university kitchen to launch his first venture, a catering and delivery business for students run with the benefit of his Raleigh bicycle.

Into the Kitchen

Like many meals, new ventures often start like Meyer's: a function of what is available and who wants to don an apron. Indeed, cooks of every kind and even non-cooks have since joined with him and contributed their own ingredients and flavors to the mix.

The result is that Meyer and his partners have launched nearly a venture a year over the last 25 years. The Meyer Group imports chocolate to Scandinavia with partner Søren Sylvest, a relationship that cooked up ventures in coffee importing as well as cafés.

With Mette Martinussen, Meyer created a theatre-like restaurant and also built a factory to manufacture soy cakes. He has hosted a television cookery show and yet more collaboration has taken him into the hotel business, corporate catering, food consulting, and a non-profit food laboratory.

And that's not all. Meyer has established a micro vinegar brewery, an organic commercial orchard, and a boutique bakery. He has authored several cookbooks, gives lectures, and he is active in health and wellness research.

Even the famed Noma, which has done much to counter jokes about Nordic cuisine being an oxymoron, is a partnership with chef René Redzepi. Noma recently announced that it is evolving, which is true to their innovative entrepreneurial spirit:

> To continue being Noma, we must change. We are beginning a new chapter; Noma 3.0. In 2025, our restaurant is transforming into a giant lab—a pioneering test kitchen dedicated to the work of food innovation and the development of new flavors, one that will share the fruits of our efforts more widely than ever before.
>
> (*Noma* 3.0, 2022)

Practically Speaking *(continued)*

Venture à la Mode

In many ways, Meyer has come full circle. Many years later, he can fairly claim a recipe for his vision. Not through any one of his ventures, though, but through the process that led to the accumulation of them all. Whether it's changing Danish food culture or changing the world, real entrepreneurship kneads together an enormous amount of information culled from the experiences of large numbers of people, such as those who contributed in some greater or lesser way to the runaway success of Noma.

Figure 10.5 The Noma Team turns their available means into edible Nordic wonders.

The vision imbibes the resultant flavors into a heady blend that appears to have always been part of the recipe. Entrepreneurship is not an all-or-nothing heroic act associated with the unique insight of a single chef. It is about learning, interaction, and application combined through acts of continual co-creation. It starts with Meyer taking the first step and then pushing onward step after step, partner by partner—not informed by a plan, but by the previous step, the people around him, and the available resources at each stage. So now that your appetite is whetted, what's in your fridge?

To learn more, visit: https://effectuation.org/EE3/clausmeyer or scan Figure 10.6.

Figure 10.6

Practically Speaking

The Bird not in Hand

Often called the Hermit Kingdom, the repressive regime of North Korea makes everyday life hard. Ju Chang Yang, who now lives in South Korea, describes her former life: "In North Korea life was a challenge. It was a life and death challenge" (ABC News, 2023).

It is hard to imagine that such conditions would prove to be a training ground for future entrepreneurs, but Sokeel Park, Director of Research & Strategy and South Korea Country Director for Liberty in North Korea (LiNK), an international non-governmental organization, explains:

> The North Korean economy was one of the most demonetized, the most tightly controlled government planned economies of the twentieth century. But with the famine of the 1990s, that government control system and government provision system broke down, and it meant that North Korean people had to fend for themselves.

Practically Speaking *(continued)*

Surviving on Slack

When her father fled to South Korea, 17-year-old Ju had to get entrepreneurial simply to survive. She sorted through leftover soybeans at a nearby factory and sold them at the markets. When she had saved up enough, she started selling candy.

In her own words, on the ABC website: "I had to survive. I was able to earn enough to not starve to death. Besides that, it was also fun to make money," she said.

The next year, when her father sent her some money, Ju used it to bribe a soldier. As she later acknowledged, the border guard could have shot her or arrested her. Instead, he delivered on his commitment, and helped her cross the border to South Korea.

Ju and several other young North Koreans who made it out recount their experiences in North Korean black markets—the Janmadang—that sold all kinds of things from smuggled South Koream movies to everyday items such as food, apparel, and cosmetics.

The School of Hard Knocks

As Ju put it in an interview with *The Korea Herald*, "In South Korea, we have the Generation MZ, but I'd like to say that, in North Korea, we have the Jangmadang Generation. I also jumped into trading from middle school to earn money."

Ju's available means—a mix of skills, attitude, and fortitude—enabled her to set up a café, wellness center, and a side business selling jewelry. She is quick to acknowledge help from a number of people who helped her resettle and overcome other challenges in her new country.

And a decade since her arrival in the South, Ju has established herself on the outskirts of Seoul, running a cooperative venture that bridges North and South Korean businesses and people.

Sometimes it is misfortune, even the non-availability of means, that forms the bird-in-hand for a life of effectual entrepreneurship.

To learn more, visit: https://effectuation.org/EE3/northkorea or scan Figure 10.7.

Figure 10.7

WHAT I KNOW: BRINGING LEARNING TO THE VENTURE

Think about all you know, the facts, wisdom, and insight you've gained from your idiosyncratic life experiences. Now consider that everyone has their own distinct stock of knowledge, informed by their own experiences. It's no wonder that two entrepreneurs, at the same starting point and in the same environment, will come up with two completely different ventures.

Because of the corridor principle—embarking on the voyage exposes the entrepreneur to new opportunities (Ronstadt, 1988), entrepreneurs may be better off simply getting started and developing opportunities as they walk down the corridor. And getting started is easier with the advantage of resources, information, and knowledge you already have.

Research Roots

The Corridor Principle

Robert Ronstadt (1988, pp. 31–40) developed the corridor principle to describe how new and unintended opportunities often arise for entrepreneurs when they are launching a new venture. Picture yourself standing at the entrance of a corridor. Until you proceed down the corridor, it is impossible to know what it holds, but as you move along you gain knowledge and insight.

The corridor principle explains how entrepreneurs, simply by opening a door and pursuing one opportunity, create other opportunities (other corridors) they otherwise would not or could not have imagined.

Research Roots

Six Degrees of Separation

A 1929 short story by a Hungarian writer (Karinthy, 1929) suggested that all individuals are connected to all others by a maximum of six other individuals. Human relationships are both fascinating and important to understanding how we interact, and in 1967, Stanley Milgram (1967, pp. 61–67) addressed the idea of how interconnected human beings are in an academic publication.

Countless studies have since been conducted to measure connectedness. While the exact number of links between people differs depending on the population and the types of links, it is generally found to be relatively small. So, whether you want to call it "six degrees of separation" or the "small-world" phenomenon, your network and the network of your network extends to everyone on the planet.

Newer research by Lin (2011) indicates that people with stronger networks are more likely to use modern communication tools to keep in touch. Or is this a chicken or egg dilemma?

Inventory your means					
Who you know		**What you know**		**Who you are**	
Your networks (online and in-person)		Your prior knowledge and education		Tastes, values, and preferences	
Classmates, alumni		Knowledge from your job		Passions	
Serendipitous encounters		Knowledge from your life		Hobbies	
The strangers in your life		Informal learning, hobbies		Interests	

Figure 10.8

Research Roots

ONE TECHNOLOGY → EIGHT ENTREPRENEURS → EIGHT DIFFERENT IDEAS

Consider a study of eight entrepreneurs who sought to commercialize a 3DP (three-dimensional printing) technology when it was being developed at MIT.

All eight entrepreneurs heard about 3DP technology from someone directly involved in its development. None of the entrepreneurs contacted MIT's Technology Licensing Office. And none of the entrepreneurs contacted each other.

The fascinating thing was that each of the eight entrepreneurs envisioned a different idea for what to do with three-dimensional printing—differences that could be traced back to unique knowledge or experiences specific to each of the individuals (Shane, 2000).

WHO I KNOW: SIX DEGREES OF SEPARATION

Expert entrepreneurs build firms by building stakeholder networks—adding other people's means to their own.

In thinking about creating such a network, consider three sources of stakeholders. The first source is the people who are directly and perhaps immediately accessible to you: friends, family, and acquaintances.

The second is people you meet serendipitously, by chance or accident. And the third source is those you don't know directly, but they are linked to you through people you do know. We all exist in a network of connections: we know people who know people who know people (and on and on) who could become helpful partners.

If you believe the "six degrees of separation" theory, you'd need to move only six steps out to be connected to everyone in the world. Distant contacts can be some of the most valuable because they may offer perspectives and ideas you've never encountered before. This is what's known as "the strength of weak ties."

HOW IT WORKS

To see how this means-driven process works, consider examples from the history of entrepreneurship. The entrepreneurs who founded Toyota, Nestlé, Tata, Starbucks, and many other companies used their means to shape, step-by-step, their opportunities. Their enduring ventures mostly started small, without prespecified grandiose visions or large predicted market opportunities or highly specified goals.

The entrepreneurs wove together the mundane realities of who they were, what they knew, and who they knew into projects that they believed were worth doing. They then continually added to their projects, pushing them outward, reshaping them to work with new stakeholders, stretching themselves—just a bit at a time to reach higher and farther—until eventually they transformed both their means and ends into extraordinary new possibilities.

MAP YOUR MEANS

Start by printing off a one-page version of your résumé. Then add the means you have. Be creative about what you consider; it needn't be things you would normally include in a résumé. To get started, look back at your life. What means did you acquire or build:

- As a teenager?
- At school?
- At university?
- In your first, second, third, ... job?
- In your private life?

- With your hobbies, activities?
- From your parents?

How would your friends, colleagues, family, or acquaintances describe your means?

Be as broad as you can. You will certainly need more room than we provide in Figure 10.8, but we hope this gives you a place to start.

RESOURCES YOU DON'T EVEN KNOW YOU HAVE

The core of the bird-in-hand principle is that the entrepreneur builds on *already* available means. But what if you don't recognize what you have as a resource or see how they might be combined with other resources and people to create something of value?

The destinations of many entrepreneurial stories seem obvious in hindsight because they show clear patterns in the pathways and skills leading up to venture creation. For example, the co-founder of Apple Computer, Inc., Steve Jobs, partly attributes his success to a strong sense of design, which he developed after dropping out of college and taking a calligraphy course.

In the case of José Andrés, starting World Central Kitchen, a quick response team to prepare food for victims and emergency workers in natural disasters and other crisis situations seems obvious when you consider his pathway.

As a boy, Andrés helped his father cook for large groups, went on to cook for the military, developed skills to manage the "chaos" of large kitchens, built a network of restaurants, started volunteering, watched the moments of inaction in response to Hurricane Katrina in 2005, and helped a friend distribute solar cooking equipment in response to the earthquake in Haiti in 2010.

We cannot see into the future, but we can take a closer look at our past and identify available means we have collected, particularly those that might not be obviously connected to a venture. Then consider how we might better use them to build ventures.

And going forward, we can build an eclectic collection of additional available means by staying open to new experiences and skills with the possibility of weaving them into our projects and ad(ventures).

SLACK RESOURCES

The world is full of "slack"—resources left over from other uses or simply lying around because nobody has paid attention to them.

Slack can include anything from waste to empty space to loopholes in the law to buffers created for emergencies.

Consider the story of billionaire J. R. Simplot, the founder of potato processing plants and creator of the first frozen French fries. He began his career by collecting pigs set for slaughter by farmers who feared a pork surplus. Simplot fed the pigs until demand returned and when he sold them to the meat companies, made enough money to buy an electric potato sorter.

Throughout his career, Simplot was quick at picking up slack resources which he then transformed into valuable products, often appearing to snatch opportunities right from under the noses of his competition.

We also saw the use of slack resources in the story of U-Haul (Chapter 6), when Leonard Shoen made a deal with a national service station chain to locate U-Haul dealerships in the stations' unused space. Shoen leveraged that slack resource, making it valuable not only for himself, but also for the service station owners.

Similarly, Mrs. Cheung (Chapter 3) used shipping containers returning empty to China to export used paper for her recycling giant Nine Dragons Paper.

Another example of space being a slack resource is the living room floor of Brian Chesky

Practically Speaking

Connecting the Dots

Even in the inflationary world of social media, more than 43 million views of a video, particularly a recording of a speech at a university graduation ceremony in 2005, is exceptional.

Figure 10.9

Apparently, the message being communicated in the video by the creative genius and co-founder of Apple, Steve Jobs, resonates. Having dropped out of college and with spare time on his hands, he decided to learn about something he was really interested in: calligraphy. The history, theory, and structures behind beautiful typography fascinated him. But he didn't have any illusions about the practicality of what he was learning.

Many years later, however, when he and his team were working on the typefaces and fonts for the new Apple Mac computer, the calligraphy course was foundational in creating the first computer with beautiful typography. And since that beginning, Apple has built its brand around unique and uniquely functional product design.

Jobs reflects on the significance of this:

> If I had never dropped out, I would have never dropped in on this calligraphy class, and personal computers might not have the wonderful typography that they do. Of course, it was impossible to connect the dots looking forward when I was in college. But it was very, very clear looking backwards ten years later.
>
> Again, you can't connect the dots looking forward; you can only connect them looking backwards. So, you have to trust that the dots will somehow connect in your future.
>
> (*Stanford University*, 2005)

Figure 10.10

To learn more, visit: https://effectuation.org/EE3/jobs or scan Figure 10.10.

and Joe Gebbia, the founders of Airbnb, who rented it out to conference delegates needing a place to sleep.

For Estée Lauder, the slack resource was not space but time. Early in her career, she noticed that women sitting under hair dryers in beauty parlors had nothing to do. So, she offered them a free makeover using Estée Lauder creams and lotions. Most would accept, and many would end up buying some of the products to use at home.

Sometimes a slack resource comes in the guise of misfortune, as in the case of Dr. Fad. Ken Hakuta, a jobless Harvard Medical School graduate, had one of the most flexible slack resources of all—his time. If he had found a plush job as his classmates did, chances are he would be working for a living just like the rest of us.

Practically Speaking

Cordon Blue

The French phrase "cordon bleu" means "exceptional cook." But José Andrés is exceptional as a different kind of chef, one who shows up when you are disastrously "blue"—whether you are in war-torn Ukraine or it is Ramadan in your refugee camp in Syria, or your beloved New Orleans was devastated by Hurricane Katrina.

Born and raised in Spain, Andrés founded the Washington, DC–based non-profit organization World Central Kitchen (WCK), which brings food to people affected by natural disasters and other crises around the world.

Cordon Disaster

José Ramón Andrés Puerta's (known internationally as José Andrés) interest in cooking came from his father, who regularly made paella, a traditional dish from Valencia, for large groups of people. José was responsible for gathering the wood and building the fire.

Young José's interest in cooking (and poor performance in high school) led him to move to a culinary school in Barcelona, which was excellent preparation to cook in the Spanish Navy. His tour of duty included his first encounters with abject poverty in the favelas of Brazil and the Ivory Coast.

After completing military service, Andrés joined the kitchen team of the famous Spanish modernist Michelin-starred restaurant "El Bullí," where he spent three years. Still young and seeking adventure, Andrés migrated to the United States, reportedly arriving in New York City with only 50 US dollars in his pocket.

Called to Serve

As a successful chef in 2005, he was watching TV, when his calling woke him to better things:

> I think the moment began really in the moments of inaction, watching what happened in Katrina, when we had thousands of American citizens at the Superdome, and it seemed nobody was there feeding them, bringing them water, bringing them hope.
>
> I think I got tired of watching through TV in the comfort of my home. Actually, big problems have very simple solutions. I don't know how to fix every problem that we face in humanity, but let me tell you, cooks like me, food we know! So, if we start showing up, can we bring relief? That's how it began.
>
> (*Late Show*, 2022)

Co-Cooking Hope

The WCK website summarizes how his life has unfolded since. In 2010, Andrés headed to Haiti following a devastating earthquake. Cooking alongside displaced families in a camp, he was guided on the proper way to cook black beans the way Haitians like to eat them: mashed and sieved into a creamy sauce.

Practically Speaking *(continued)*

It wasn't just about feeding people in need—it was about listening, learning, and cooking side by side with the people impacted by the crisis. This is the real meaning of comfort food, and it's the core value that José, along with his wife Patricia, used at the center of founding World Central Kitchen.

Figure 10.11 World Central Kitchen team member distributing food after a severe earthquake in Morocco, September 2023.

Andrés explains his approach, which very much relies on co-creation with the network of people he has cooked with and worked with over the years: "We are a small organization, but it's created by chefs. Obviously, I'm one of them and it's restaurants and chefs everywhere. So technically we have no infrastructure anywhere, but then in my eyes, we have infrastructure everywhere" (NPR, 2021).

Simply doing the doable with skills you already have and people who are willing to work with you, you can indeed feed the world, not only food, but also hope, in its bluest moments.

To learn more, visit: https://effectuation.org/EE3/wckitchen or scan Figure 10.12.

Figure 10.12

Practically Speaking

Destination Unknown

The story of Airbnb illustrates how not having any means can even provide the basis for a new venture. Born of the need to pay their rent, Joe Gebbia and Brian Chesky started offering lodging on air mattresses and breakfast in their apartment. To their surprise, three people showed up, and an idea was born.

But in order to achieve the success that Airbnb enjoys today, the pair employed many types of available means in the early phases, including:

- Knowledge that local hotels were booked out due to a trade conference
- Ability (Joe and Brian) to set up a simple blog site to promote their "Airbed & Breakfast"
- A friend (Nathan Blecharczyk) to help develop a more attractive website and, as technical wizard, become a venture co-founder
- A small amount of cash to purchase air mattresses and breakfast supplies
- Hosting skills (breakfast preparation, setting up space, sharing relevant local information)
- Ability to nicely photograph listed houses, as the service grows

Practically Speaking *(continued)*

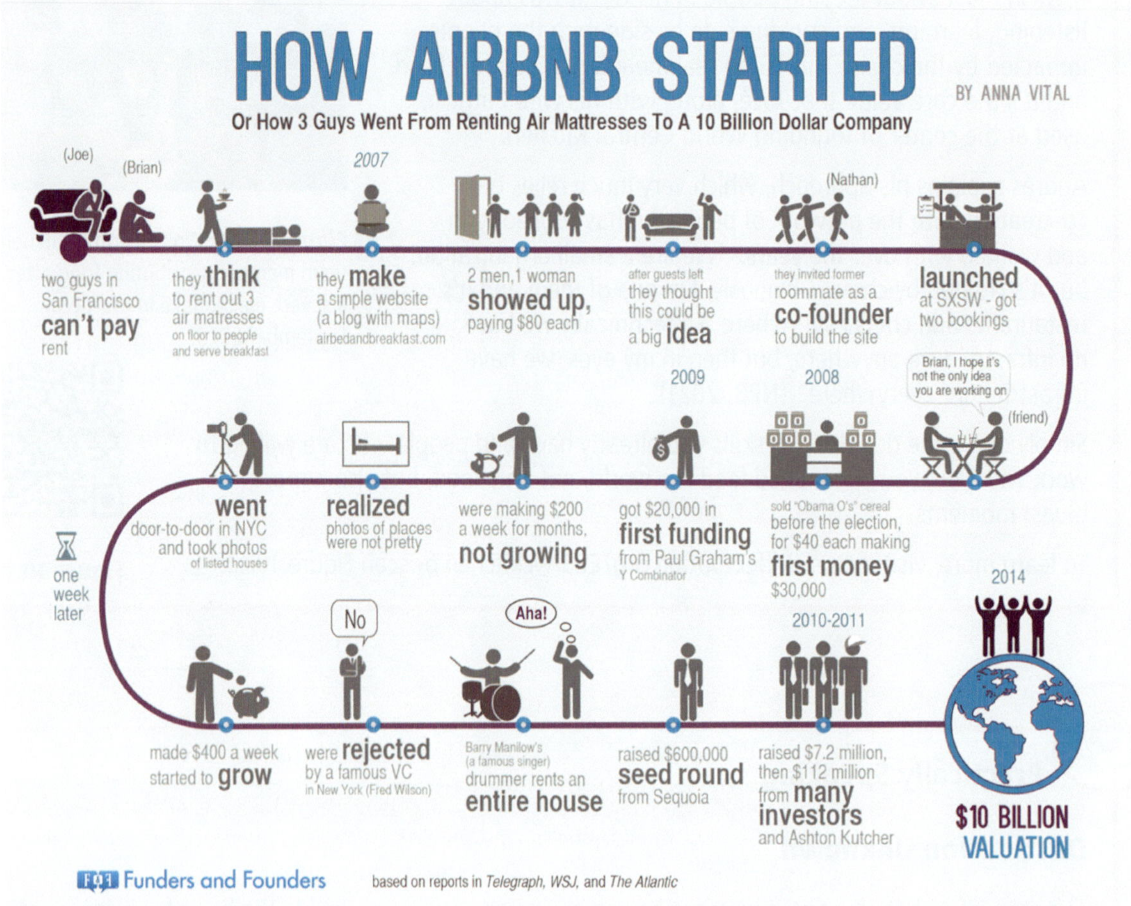

Figure 10.13

Who could have imagined that in 2007 with this starting list of available means, the three friends were building the foundations of a company that would bring in 8.4 billion US dollars in turnover in 2022?

Figure 10.13 provides a graphic view of selected twists and turns of the entrepreneurial journey of Airbnb.

To learn more, visit: https://effectuation.org/EE3/airbnb or scan Figure 10.14.

Figure 10.14

Practically Speaking

Up the Wall

Dr. Fad started out as Ken Hakuta, a Harvard Medical School graduate who was disgruntled by the fact that his classmates all seemed to have better job offers than he did. As he mulled over his situation, he nonchalantly threw around a slimy, sticky, octopus-shaped rubber toy that his mother had sent from Japan for his children. In 1982, they were the only toys that could climb down walls.

Ken bought 100,000 US dollars' worth of the toys, thinking that if his venture failed, he could go back to Japan. He started selling them to small gift shops and toy stores in Washington, DC, where he lived.

And then one day a major television channel featured Wacky WallWalkers in their evening news show, turning the toy into an overnight hit. Over 240 million Wacky WallWalkers were sold, making it one of the biggest selling fads ever. Dr. Fad ran his own shows about fads and published a bestseller called *How to Create Your Own Fad and Make a Million Dollars* (1989).

To learn more, visit: https://effectuation.org/EE3/wallwalkers or scan Figure 10.15.

Figure 10.15

TAKEAWAY: YOU CAN GET STARTED NOW

Effectuation shifts the focus from "How do I build a successful firm?" or "How can I become a successful entrepreneur?" to "What types of ideas and opportunities can and should I pursue, given who I am, what I know, and who I know?" and "Given my means, what can I create?"

Sticking closely to who you are, what you know, and who you know not only tells you what to do, but also tells you what not to do. It helps focus attention on ideas where you have an advantage. Working with what you have and what you know also discourages big and risky leaps; instead, it directs entrepreneurs to take manageable steps with available resources.

To sum things up, the bird-in-hand principle (starting with your means) tells you that you can get going inexpensively, and that your means form the basis of your own competitive advantage. Combined with your partners' means and commitments, the venture you create will be both feasible and unique.

When you use the bird-in-hand principle, starting a new venture is no longer an incredibly risky act of heroism. It is something you can do within the constraints and possibilities of your normal life. You can start a new venture anytime you want. You can get started now.

So What?

Everyone has means—and everyone is different—which explains how even starting with the same idea, each person who begins taking action toward it creates something that is in some way unique.

Forget about what you don't have and focus on finding ways you can take advantage of who you are, who you know, and what you know.

Think It Through

- In goal-oriented societies, how can you develop a means-oriented mindset?
- In what ways might having specific goals for your venture impede your progress?
- Without goals, how can you know if you are successful?
- What if you can't imagine anything worth pursuing from your current means (hint: that's what Chapter 11 is about)?

What Now?

- If you are having trouble deciding on an idea, how about starting with more than one idea at once? You can decide later which path gains the most support from stakeholder commitments.
- Create an elevator pitch for yourself—if you had to sell stock in yourself, what would your prospectus look like? Think means, not goals.
- Who are you? What sorts of things do you do and work on when you can do anything?
- Whom do you know?
- What sort of slack resources might you use together?
- What do you know? It's not just expertise in doing things, it can also be knowing about people, and who needs what, or how to combine slack resources in new ways.

REFERENCES

ABC News. (2023, June 20). North Korea's millennial defectors are thriving. https://www.youtube.com/watch?v=4dZvfj1xpJA

Andrés, J. (2015, October 21). José Andrés: Food has the power to change the world. *Time*. https://time.com/collection-post/4080585/jose-andres-food-haiti/

Andrés, José. (2019, April 23). "Stop planning and start cooking." José Andrés on the power of food in the midst of tragedy. *Time*. https://time.com/5574152/jose-andres-time-100-summit/

Burt, R., Kilduff, M., & Tasselli, S. (2013). Social network analysis: Foundations and frontiers on advantage. *Annual Review of Psychology*, *64*(1), 527–547.

Hakuta, K. (1989). *How to Create Your Own Fad and Make a Million Dollars*. HarperCollins.

Karinthy, F. (1929). *Everything Is Different*. Athenaeum Press.

Late Show. (2022, May 4). An origin story for World Central Kitchen—Chef José Andrés & Ron Howard on "we feed people." https://www.youtube.com/watch?v=BVS-FTVNbcU

Lin, C.-P. (2011). Assessing the mediating role of online social capital between social support and instant messaging usage. *Electronic Commerce Research and Applications*, *10*(1), 105–114. https://doi.org/10.1016/j.elerap.2010.08.003

Mashed. (2022, April 14). The untold truth of Chef José Andrés. https://www.youtube.com/watch?v=O35F3B1S9W8

Milgram, S. (1967). The small world problem. *Psychology Today*, *2*(1), 60–67.

Montalbine, M. (2024, February 27). Interview with Mary Montalbine (A. Kupstats, Interviewer) [Personal communication].

NPR. (2006, November 23). José Andrés: "Boiling point." https://www.npr.org/templates/story/story.php?storyId=6530383

NPR. (2016, November 14). Celebrity chef: José Andrés. https://www.npr.org/2016/11/14/501487330/celebrity-chef-jos-andr-s

NPR. (2018, September 10). After Hurricane Maria, Chef José Andrés had a "crazy dream" to feed Puerto Rico. https://www.npr.org/sections/thesalt/2018/09/10/646242247/after-hurricane-maria-chef-jos-andr-s-had-a-crazy-dream-to-feed-puerto-rico

NPR. (2020, April 30). How I built resilience: Live with José Andrés. https://www.npr.org/2020/04/28/847492651/how-i-built-resilience-live-with-guy-and-jos-andr-s

Noma 3.0. (2022, December 7). https://noma.dk/nomathreepointzero/

PBS NewsHour. (2018, September 21). When disaster strikes, José Andrés brings hot food and hope. https://www.youtube.com/watch?v=f95RTc-avXQ

PBS NewsHour. (2020, April 10). Celebrity chef José Andrés on why food is a national security issue. https://www.youtube.com/watch?v=XDnryKd85Nk

Repanich, J. (2021, October 5). Copenhagen's Noma is named the world's best restaurant (again). Robb Report. https://robbreport.com/food-drink/dining/world-50-best-restaurants-noma-wins-1234639228/

Ronstadt, R. (1988). The corridor principle. *Journal of Business Venturing*, *3*(1), 31–40. https://doi.org/10.1016/0883-9026(88)90028-6

Shaer, M. (2018, April 10). How Chef José Andrés turns impulsiveness into an asset. Fast Company. https://www.fastcompany.com/40547831/how-chef-jose-andres-turns-impulsiveness-into-an-asset

Shane, S. (2000). Prior knowledge and the discovery of entrepreneurial opportunities. *Organization Science*, *11*(4), 448–469. https://doi.org/10.1287/orsc.11.4.448.14602

Skoll.org. (2021, April 14). Chef José Andrés Martin (World Central Kitchen) & Rachel Martin (NPR). https://www.youtube.com/watch?v=ctkzijxYAmE

Stanford University. (2005) Steve Jobs' 2005 Stanford Commencement Address. https://www.youtube.com/watch?v=UF8uR6Z6KLc

Statista. (2023). Airbnb revenue worldwide 2022. Retrieved November 17, 2023, from https://www.statista.com/statistics/1193134/airbnb-revenue-worldwide/

TEDx Talks. (2011, December 2). Creativity in cooking can solve our biggest challenges: José Andrés at TEDxMidAtlantic 2011. https://www.youtube.com/watch?v=j0QS9euiewo

Wikipedia. (2023). José Andrés. https://en.wikipedia.org/w/index.php?title=Jos%C3%A9_Andr%C3%A9s&oldid=1185062652

CHAPTER 11

Figure 11.1 Many hands transform available means into tasty food.

Transforming Means Into Something Valuable

In This Chapter

In this chapter, we outline the mechanisms behind the process of transformation—importantly, the transformation of ideas based on existing means into valuable new opportunities. The value here derives from the role of co-creative stakeholders. A great mind in economics put it this way: "Innovation is not mysterious. There are simple approaches that can be easily learned and applied" (Schumpeter, 1942, p. 84).

DOI: 10.4324/9781003364016-14

TRANSFORMING MUNDANE MEANS INTO OPPORTUNITIES

You've taken stock of your means—you know who you are, what you know, and who you know. But how do you turn all that into something valuable—into a new product, a new venture, or even a new market? Clearly, critical steps are involved, but it's not magic. It's transformation.

How do entrepreneurs transform mundane means into valuable results? To answer that question, we created an experiment—*Venturing*—which we describe in this chapter. The Venturing experiment allowed us to watch entrepreneurs transform ideas into opportunities. And in doing so, we were able to remove some of the mystery that surrounds entrepreneurs.

From the Venturing experiment, we observed general types of transformations. In this chapter, we describe the Venturing experiment, describe each type of transformation, provide real-world examples, and look at how you can create your own transformations.

As you work your way through the chapter, stop at each transformation type and look at the things around you—everything from the features of the chair you are sitting in … to the water you are drinking.

Imagine the transformations that are at the heart of the things you use every day. What pieces came together to join hydraulics with office furniture so it's easy to change the height of your office chair? How did sports equipment and kitchenware merge to put that designer re-useable water bottle on your desk?

Once you start looking, you will see transformations everywhere, because, of course, everything was created from something.

The Venturing Scenario (Exactly as It Was Presented in the Experiment)

Introduction

In the following experiment, you will solve two decision problems. These problems arise in the context of building a new company for an imaginary product. A detailed description of the product follows this introduction.

Although the product is imaginary, it is technically feasible and financially viable. The data for the problems have been obtained through realistic market research—the kind of market research used in developing a real-world business plan. So far, the entrepreneurs who have participated in this study found the project both interesting and feasible.

Before you start on the product description and the problems, I do need one act of creative imagination on your part. I request you to put yourself in the role of the lead entrepreneur in building this company—i.e. you have very little money of your own to start this company, and you have your experience.

Description of the Product

You have created a computer game of entrepreneurship. You believe you can combine this game with some educational material and profiles of successful entrepreneurs to make an excellent teaching tool for entrepreneurship. Your inspiration for the product came from several reports in the newspapers and magazines about the increasing demand for entrepreneurship education and the fact that a curriculum involving entrepreneurship, even at the junior high or high school level, induces students to learn not only business-related topics, but math, science, and communication skills as well.

The Venturing Scenario (Exactly as It Was Presented in the Experiment) *(continued)*

The game part of the product consists of a simulated environment for starting and running a company. There are separate sub-simulations of markets, competitors, regulators, macroeconomic factors, and a random factor for "luck."

The game has a sophisticated multimedia interface—for example, a 3D office where phones ring with messages from the market, a TV that will provide macroeconomic information when switched on and simulated managerial staff whom the player (CEO) can consult in making decisions.

At the beginning of the game, the player can choose from a variety of businesses and the type of business she wants to start (e.g. manufacturing, personal services, software) and has to make decisions such as which market segment to sell to, how many people to hire, and what type of financing to go for.

During the game, the player has to make production decisions such as how much to produce, whether to build new warehouses or negotiate with trucking companies, etc.; marketing decisions such as which distribution channels to use, which media to advertise in, etc.; and management decisions involving hiring, training, promoting and firing of employees, etc.

An accounting subroutine tracks and computes the implications of the various decisions for the bottom line. The simulation's responses to the player's decisions permit a range of possible outcomes—from bankruptcy to a "hockey stick."

You have taken all possible precautions regarding intellectual property. The name of your company is Entrepreneurship, Inc. The name of the product is Venturing.

THE VENTURING EXPERIMENT

The Venturing experiment presented people with an uncertain business situation which allowed a wide range of possible strategies and outcomes. We asked people to talk their way through how they would develop an imaginary company preparing to offer an imaginary entrepreneurship game called Venturing.

Based on the description of the idea, people were asked to answer a set of questions pertaining to the development of an initial market for the product and think aloud continuously during the task. Their comments were collected on tape and transcribed for coding and analysis.

In order to see strategies unique to expert entrepreneurs, we carefully identified three groups of participants to compare the differences. Expert entrepreneurs had, either as individuals or as part of a team, founded one or more companies, remained with at least one company they founded for more than ten years, and taken it public.

We compared the expert entrepreneurs with a sample of MBA students and with a sample of expert corporate managers who had spent a minimum of ten years operating in a multinational organization consisting of more than 500 individuals.

A BIG DIFFERENCE: TRANSFORMATION TYPES

The results of the Venturing experiment clearly showed that expert entrepreneurs had acquired a unique set of decision-making strategies that form the basis of the effectual logic described in this book.

In addition to those strategies (means, affordable loss, partnerships, and contingency), the experts were very creative in the way they used the strategies to transform situations into opportunities.

Let's look at the four most common transformation types we observed from our expert entrepreneurs (we'll offer a more complete list later in the chapter).

Deleting/Supplementing

In the context of a new venture, deleting/supplementing involves looking at a product or service and thinking about which features you may want to remove or add to increase its attractiveness. There is really no limit to the possibilities for adding and removing product or service features to transform an offering. New elements can be related to the original offering in some way or from a completely unrelated domain.

Ruth Owades (Chapter 15) provides a good example of deleting. Her company, Calyx and Corolla, weeded out florists from the fresh flower delivery process by mailing flowers direct from the growers to the customers via courier. By doing so, she not only eliminated the intermediary, but also provided her customers with fresher, longer-lasting flowers.

Composing/Decomposing

Reorganizing material that is already there (in contrast to the first approach, which takes away or adds material to or from the existing set) is what we mean by composing and decomposing.

In the context of a new venture, this means taking stock of what you have to offer—a product, a service, a process—and pulling it apart to recombine the elements in a new way. It's a process similar to pulling apart Lego blocks and putting them together to create something new.

Figure 11.2

Consider Yang Bing-Yi, founder of Din Tai Fung, who, as a struggling supplier of cooking oils, combined his available means of a shop on a busy street, customers hungry for snacks, and ability to learn to create a whole new revenue stream. The result of his composition: an open kitchen which allows eager customers to watch how tasty treats are carefully assembled.

Practically Speaking

A Window Into Precision Dumplings

It seems that virtually all cuisines feature dumplings (small pockets of dough filled with vegetables, meat, or fruit), which truly makes them a universal food. So, you might think that something so ubiquitous hardly has the potential of turning readily available means (a struggling shopfront on a busy street, hungry shop customers, and a keen interest in learning) into innovation and entrepreneurial success.

Think again. Yang Bing-Yi certainly put some thought into humble dumplings, innovated, and built an international chain of dumpling restaurants called Din Tai Fung.

Born in Shanxi Province, China, Yang moved to Taipei in 1948 and found work as a deliveryman for the small cooking oil shop "Heng Tai Fung." He was soon promoted to manage inventory and accounts. His commitment increased when he married his co-worker, Lai Pen-Mei.

When the previous owner left the business, the couple took it over, renaming it Din Tai Fung (loosely translated to mean "wok of peace and abundance"). In the 1970s, when vegetable oils in tin containers overtook the market, the couple felt compelled to diversify.

The basis for this diversification was re-combining his existing available means (shopfront and customers buying cooking oil) into selling dumplings as a snack to existing customers. This exercise in composing a new product required expanding his toolbox, as Yang told *Taiwan Today* (1997): "At first, I knew nothing about the skills necessary for making dumplings and other Shanghai snacks, but I set out to learn."

The couple started selling steamed soup dumplings (Xiao Long Bao), which became so popular that Din Tai Fung decided to focus just on serving food. They later introduced innovations like sparkling clean restaurants and glass windows to the kitchen to show diners the work and precision that goes into composing the multitude of dumplings and other treats.

Figure 11.3

Today people snap photos of their food and share them via social media, but in 1972, when Yang opened up his kitchen to eager viewers, it was unheard of to show the less-than-glamorous work of a restaurant kitchen to diners.

Practically Speaking *(continued)*

These innovations differentiated Din Tai Fung from other dumpling restaurants and the resulting market success allowed Yang to expand from Taipei to Mainland China, Korea, Japan, Singapore, Indonesia, Malaysia, Thailand, Philippines, Australia, the United Arab Emirates, and the United Kingdom.

To learn more, visit: https://effectuation.org/EE3/dumpling or scan Figure 11.4.

Figure 11.4

Research Roots

Creative Templates

Jacob Goldenberg (Goldenberg et al., 1999, p. 200), who researches creativity and innovation, writes about creative templates, similar to the transformation types we discuss in this chapter. He describes five templates, which his research indicates are the basis of about 70% of all new product ideas:

- Subtraction, multiplication, and division, each of which is a specific approach to deleting and supplementing we have described here
- Task unification (making some aspect of an artifact do more than one task) and attribute dependency change (changing a linkage between the artifact and the environment), which are both similar to exaptation in that they involve changing what a product or component is capable of doing

So, regardless of what you call them, it is useful to know that scholars consistently observe the systematic nature of idea generation. It's not magic; it's method.

Research Roots

Exaptation

How did feathers evolve, allowing birds to fly? One explanation is that they initially served to regulate temperature in some creatures and were later "exapted" for a different purpose—flight. This is the notion of exaptation, a term that was originally coined by the evolutionary biologists Gould and Vrba (1982, pp. 4–15). These researchers noticed that biologists paid a lot of attention to the adaptation of species, which makes them better suited to their environments. However, they had paid less attention to the features of organisms that had initially evolved for one reason, or for no identifiable reason, and were later used for a new purpose. In entrepreneurship, the same idea can be used to describe the process of converting an artifact (which could be anything) from one use to another. Therefore, entrepreneurs faced with a hammer ask themselves not only, "What can we do with a hammer?" but also, "What else can we do with a hammer besides hit nails on their heads?" The process of exaptation, of asking "what else?" over and over again, is natural for many entrepreneurs.

Exaptation

Exaptation is a term evolutionary biologists use to describe the use of something for a purpose for which it was not originally designed or intended.

In the new venture setting, exaptation involves employing existing technologies, products, services, or elements thereof, for a use they were not intended to serve.

Consider the humble aspirin tablet. In 1897 researchers at Bayer, a drug company, found acetylsalicylic acid to be an excellent painkiller and fever reducer. They decided to call it aspirin, and by 1899, a brand was born. The product was immensely successful, particularly once its effectiveness was demonstrated during the flu pandemic of 1918. When the patent expired in 1917, copies flooded the market. But the product's popularity fell with the launch of alternative painkillers paracetamol (1956) and ibuprofen (1969). Aspirin appeared to be doomed.

But in the 1970s, clinical trials showed the product's efficacy in reducing clotting in blood and thus reduced clotting diseases. Aspirin sales grew once more, spurred by its use as a preventative treatment for heart attacks and strokes—far from its original use!

Re-Weighting

Re-weighting involves increasing or decreasing the emphasis of features or attributes of a product or market.

BMW, for example, gradually increased its emphasis on "driver appeal" when it launched new product designs during its "The Ultimate Driving Machine" marketing campaign. Volvo, in contrast, emphasizes the safety features of its cars.

Sarah Marquis and her team at Mollydooker took re-weighting seriously by introducing fun and light-hearted marketing to the rather dusty, stuffy wine industry, but only after she used science and innovation to produce exceptional, award-winning wines. This is an example of a sophisticated re-weighting task—when re-weighting in one part of the business (winemaking in Sarah's case) has consequences for other aspects of the organization (marketing and sales).

Take another look at Figure 11.5 and imagine you are that tiny farmer in the foreground. Being entrepreneurial, what opportunities do the re-weighed elements of your situation make available and what do you need to do to turn them into revenue? Despite the dominance of the cow, let your mind move beyond the massive amounts of milk she produces and consider other options.

Figure 11.5 A whimsical re-weighted farm scene filled with mythical barnyard animals.

Research Roots

Adam Smith and Novel Combinations

> Many improvements have been made by the ingenuity of the makers of the machines, when to make them became the business of a peculiar trade; and some by that of those who are called philosophers or men of speculation, whose trade it is, not to do anything, but to observe everything; and who, upon that account, are often capable of combining together the powers of the most distant and dissimilar objects.
>
> (*Adam Smith*, 1776)

Practically Speaking

Mollydooker: The Serious Science of Fun

Imagine this: you are in a shop, getting supplies for a very special dinner with a special friend. You know that they drink wine, so you want to get a special bottle. You are nervous that you are not a very sophisticated (snooty) wine connoisseur.

You head over to the wine section and immediately one bottle almost jumps off the shelf. The label is colorful, playful, and enticing. It's called "Carnival of Love" from an Australian winery called "Mollydooker." Hmm, you think, that sounds interesting.

Unsnooty Flavors?

So, you pick up the bottle, admire the hand-drawn figures of people having fun in Venetian-style costumes. You are compelled to know more and turn the bottle to read the back label:

> What is the Carnival of Love?
>
> This is as life should be—a Carnival of Love. A place where everyone wants to be, and no one wants to leave.
>
> Tasting Notes:
>
> Intense in colour, flavour and aroma, our 2021 Carnival of Love Shiraz captivates the palate from the first sip. Powerful yet delicate, lifted aromas of red cherry, blackberry and turkish delight evolve, while subtle hints of mocha linger. Infectious chocolate cherry, fresh plum and liquorice add to the complexity, while creating a seamless structure and lingering finish.
>
> (*Mollydooker*, 2023)

Snootful of Spin?

You've bought wine before and know how compelling marketing spin can be. You are a bit skeptical, but also intrigued, particularly when you see the price: 90 Australian dollars (for one bottle!). Yes, you want a really special bottle for the special dinner with your special friend, but 90 dollars?

Practically Speaking ***(continued)***

You need more information, so you pull out your smartphone and head to the winery's website to convince yourself that the price is worth it.

First off, you notice that a famous wine magazine has given "Carnival of Love" 93 points—sounds promising. Then you see the following text in the online description: "The required Marquis Fruit Weight™ for the Love Series is 85%–95%. The Actual Fruit Weight for 2021 Carnival of Love 88%" (Mollydooker, 2023).

Comparison Dance

You check out the other wines for alternatives. You are curious about one called "Two Left Feet," with this description and technical note:

> What is Two Left Feet?
>
> Two Left Feet is what can happen when you dance after a glass or two of Mollydooker.
>
> The required Marquis Fruit Weight™ for the Lefty Series is 65%–75%. The Actual Fruit Weight for 2021 Two Left Feet is 68%
>
> (*Mollydooker*, 2023)

The price of "Two Left Feet"? 30 Australian dollars per bottle. Hmmm, this "Fruit Weight" thing probably explains the price difference. More fruit is better, more fruit costs more.

Shake It, Baby!

As you scroll through the Mollydooker website, you see a section "About the Mollydooker Difference" and are curious about the "Mollydooker Shake" and see the following explanation:

> We use nitrogen in our winemaking process to protect the wine and to minimise sulphites. If you think of flavour like a big round ball, nitrogen flattens that ball. So by doing the shake, the nitrogen is released and the flavour ball pops back out to its full size!
>
> (*Mollydooker*, 2023)

Your special friend has made comments about trying to avoid sulphites in wines, so it looks like, "advantage Mollydooker." Plus, getting things shaking early is exactly what you want tonight …

So, what will it be "Two Left Feet" or "Carnival of Love"? It's a stretch for your budget, but the "Carnival of Love" beckons. It's a special dinner with a special friend, after all!

Mollydookered!

What just happened?

Welcome to the wine world of Sarah Marquis and her crew at Mollydooker in McLaren Vale, South Australia. All the fun and lightness of wine that her label communicates is intentional, as are all the systems and science behind her exceptional wine quality.

Practically Speaking *(continued)*

Sarah started working with grapes as a 14-year-old, helping out her father in his hobby vineyard. At 17, Sarah signed up for a winemaking program and on the first day met her future (and now former) husband, Sparky.

Figure 11.6 Mollydooker's "Carnival of Love" being served at your special dinner for your special friend. You made the right choice!

Sarah and Sparky worked hard on their studies, which culminated in a thesis about the effects of canopy (leaf cover) management on the color and flavor of the finished wine. This evolved into a tailored vineyard watering program, which Mollydooker uses today. Sarah explains the effects of these two programs: "So it's what's responsible for the incredible color, flavor, and texture in our wines and makes them really unique. And it's a program that we've invented and perfected over the years" (Marquis & Marquis, 2023).

The experts agree. Only a day before receiving their sales license, Sarah & Sparky's very first wine won an important local award (beating out many very well-qualified and experienced entrants). This set Sarah & Sparky on a path to the United States, where the famed wine critic Robert Parker later gave their wines rave reviews, such as "run don't walk, these are the greatest wines in existence in the world!" (Marquis & Marquis, 2023). Sarah & Sparky's first vintage sold out in 17 days.

Composing Fun Needs Decomposing Science

From the Mollydooker website: "Our seriously fun, juicy wines are the result of what happens when you combine science, innovation and dedication to create wines with a difference" (Mollydooker, 2023).

Reviewing Sarah's story, we can find at least four different transformation types, as is set out in Table 11.1.

Table 11.1

Transformation type	Description	How Mollydooker transformed traditional winemaking and marketing
Deleting/ supplementing	Subtracting from or adding to an existing offering	By removing (or at least minimizing) the use of sulfur in the production and bottling process, the winemakers supplemented with nitrogen to keep the wine fresh. Getting wine drinkers to slosh the nitrogen out of the wine in the glass would be messy, so the Mollydooker team supplemented their marketing with a playful "Mollydooker Shake."

Practically Speaking *(continued)*

(Continued)

Composing/ decomposing	Reorganizing material that is already available; decomposing and recomposing it	Sarah and her team composed a system to assess the fruit weight in wines as an indicator for quality and pricing. Initially this was just for their use, but when consumers wanted to understand the vast range of prices, the Marquis Fruit Weight™ system was included in the marketing of wines.
Re-weighting	Increasing or decreasing the emphasis of features or attributes	Usually wines are sold as a "serious" product (check out most wine labels!) and much of the production follows traditional practices. Mollydooker re-weights these elements, moving all the seriousness, system, and science (innovation) to the process required to get high-quality wine in the bottle. That leaves room for the playfulness in naming and labels and all elements involving the customer.
Manipulation	Inverting, mirroring, twisting, turning an idea or artifact inside out	Sarah & Sparky's academic thesis focused on the manipulation of the growing process (canopy management) and further evolved into a strict watering program to maximize grape quality. This has produced exceptional quality and significantly higher grape yields.

To learn more, visit: https://effectuation.org/EE3/mollydooker or scan Figure 11.7.

Figure 11.7

ONGOING TRANSFORMATION

The previous sections outline only some of the ways expert entrepreneurs transform their means into ideas. If you need inspiration on more, Table 11.2 provides additional transformation types we observed expert entrepreneurs using in the Venturing scenario.

Table 11.2

Transformation type	Description	How our expert entrepreneurs use this transformation in Venturing
Deleting/ supplementing	Subtracting from or adding to an existing offering	Adding features to use the software to teach skills beyond entrepreneurship such as marketing and sales
Composing/ decomposing	Reorganizing material that is already available; decomposing and recomposing it	Looking at just the negotiation aspect of the experiment to focus on that

(Continued)

Exaptation	Transforming existing artifacts by converting them to new uses	Using the software as a self-assessment tool for prospective entrepreneurs instead of as a game
Re-weighting	Increasing or decreasing the emphasis of features or attributes	In Venturing, re-weighting was preceded with a statement such as "What we're really talking about ..." and then focusing in on one aspect of Venturing
Manipulation	Inverting, mirroring, twisting, turning an idea or artifact inside out	Instead of marketing to people who might want to become entrepreneurs—market to those who *don't*, a group one person called "Pretendsters"
Deformation	Deliberately deforming the original idea or concept; analogous to melody deformation in jazz	Use Venturing not as a product but as a platform for a family of different products that might range from crowdfunding to distribution software
Localization/ regionalization/ globalization	Changing the scope of the market by proposing smaller or larger markets	Ideas ranged from selling Venturing to regional development agencies to use in global entrepreneurship competitions
Ad hoc associating	Drawing on prior experience and memory by associating the current venture with some previous problem or opportunity	One entrepreneur who had experience in licensing worked through the process of turning Venturing into a cross-licensed product

Research Roots

Design Thinking

Perhaps formally originating in the Bauhaus Movement (1919), there is an expectation that design requires a specific way of thinking. That perspective has generated a great deal of related academic work (Simon, 1969), the creation of a global industrial design firm named IDEO, and the establishment of an entire school at Stanford University that teaches "design thinking" (it is called the d.school).

Effectuation can work very well with design thinking, particularly as it relates to the topic of this chapter. Research into the topic began with looking at very specific theories of design (Agogué et al., 2015), and more recently the work of Klenner et al. (2021, p. 67) provides confirmation of the hands-on nature of the two theories:

Practitioner Points

- Design thinking practices bring the cognitive principles of effectuation to life.
- Design thinking is an effective practical approach for entrepreneurial innovation.
- Design thinking adds a normative dimension to effectual decision-making.

Research continues to explore the relationship between design thinking and effectuation, so watch this space!

Research Roots

How to Fly a Horse

In his book, *How to Fly a Horse: The Secret History of Creation, Invention, and Discovery* (2015, p. 90), Kevin Ashton summarizes his insights on innovation as: "What determines whether we will succeed as creators is not how intelligent we are, how talented we are, or how hard we work, but how we respond to the adversity of creation."

Practically Speaking

Transforming Stone Into Water: The Birth of the Zen Gardens

Co-Creators: Nobuo Kanai and Yuriko Sawatani

Have you ever felt mesmerized by gazing at a Zen Garden? As the calm washes over you, you observe a "flow" of beauty in the arrangement of stones. How and why did this come to be?

The style of Zen gardens known today as "Karesansui" or Japanese rock gardens was created in the Muromachi period (1336–1573). Karesansui were laid out in small spaces of temples, which were often surrounded by monks' living quarters.

This innovation of Karesansui gardens consists in the minimalism that can be easily understood by comparing them with gardens such as Tenryu-ji Temple Garden (Figure 11.8), which is the pinnacle of Japanese water gardens established in the early fourteenth century.

Disturbed Start

In the late Muromachi period (sixteenth century), the authority of the imperial court, led by the emperor, was on the wane and conflicts among the samurai powers intensified. The Onin War (1485–1493) turned Kyoto into a land of turmoil, and the city was devastated by warfare. However, as the reconstruction began after the war, Zen temples were also rebuilt.

One such example is Daisen-in of Daitoku-ji Temple, erected by Kogaku Soutan in 1513. Daisen-in (Figure 11.9), one of the independent monks' quarters built within Daitoku-ji temple, is a head temple complex.

Being a very small area of the head temple without a source of water to create a pond and few available materials for landscaping, it would be a challenging task for Soutan and his Zen monks colleagues to create a "Zen garden," such as the established one in Tenryu-ji Temple.

Figure 11.8 Tenryu-ji Temple Garden, the pinnacle of Zen gardens.

Practically Speaking *(continued)*

Waves Without Water

After contemplation, the Zen monks declared, "We can create an island without a pond. Even if there is no water, we can create currents and waves."

Figure 11.9 Panoramic view of Karesansui, Daisen-in Temple.

Using the Karesansui technique, a waterfall formation was created using stones that were available on the spot, and together with a small raised area, Turtle Island and Crane Island were created. Here, the planting was also used as an expression of the deep mountains and valleys. The gravel used in the front garden of the temple was spread over the small garden, and a stream pattern was drawn on the surface to represent the flow of water.

Zen ∞ Effectuation

Karesansui was established as a garden style with Zen spirituality that accepted such a difficult task as a form of cultivation. Although it is difficult to understand and succinctly explain the spirituality of Zen, it emphasizes "investigation of the true self" as a form of cultivation for attaining enlightenment.

Zen also teaches that accepting one's own circumstances and taking independent action is the way to truth. Both Zen and effectuation also emphasize transformation and an open embrace of change.

To learn more, visit: https://effectuation.org/EE3/zengarden or scan Figure 11.10.

Figure 11.10

Practically Speaking

Dust, Sweat, and New Ventures

In 1992, you would not have called Mario Moretti Polegato an entrepreneur. He was a vintner, bottling wines from Italy's Treviso region. In that year, business took Polegato to Reno, Nevada, for a meeting of international wine producers. Seeking to make the most of his visit to the United States' scenic west, he took a hike in the mountains and found himself with sweaty feet from the summer heat. His solution? Cut holes in the soles of his shoes so his feet could breathe. He did this on the spot and still has both the shoes and a scar to show for it.

Practically Speaking *(continued)*

Not a Sole Sufferer

Polegato was simultaneously delighted and dissatisfied with his innovation. On the one hand, he could not be the only person in the world afflicted with the discomfort of sweaty feet. Surely, his idea would be of interest to a potential consumer audience.

On the other hand, the innovation had an obvious defect. What was fantastic in the dry desert would be downright damp on a rainy street in London. He still had work to do before he could leave the winery and pursue his newfound mission of making feet around the world more comfortable.

Novel Combinations

Then Polegato started doing something often seen in the world of new ventures. He put things together that had never been put together before. Two of his more fruitful, though not initially obvious, inputs came from NASA and academia.

Anxious to find a material that would let sweat out, while keeping rainwater from getting in, Polegato headed to NASA in Houston, Texas, where he found a material developed to perform exactly that—but for space suits. And, at the universities of Padua, in Italy, and Trondheim, in Norway, he found researchers in materials science working on membrane technology to manage water transfer.

Making the connection to his own needs, Polegato engaged them in the development of his new shoe. Combining these unusual partners with a bit of investment money and some assistance with footwear design from a small ski-boot company, Polegato stepped out with something truly novel—a shoe that breathes.

Stepping Up the Pace

Polegato's story offers three useful tips for any entrepreneur. The first is that opportunities abound, and the second is that an easy way to create opportunities is simply to look for problems people need solved. The third is that innovation is more often a process of combination than invention. Everything Polegato needed to create breathable shoes existed—but nobody had put the pieces together to create a shoe.

Best Foot Forward

Apparently, Polegato was not the only foot-sweater in the world, with Geox (his shoe-producing firm) sales racing forward.

But like any climb in the Dolomite mountains of Polegato's home, the trek has had its ups and downs, with Geox sales peaking at 885 million euros in 2017, dropping slightly in the years after, and plummeting into a ravine to 535 million euros in 2020, with the pandemic restricting movement.

Figure 11.11

Practically Speaking *(continued)*

But as of late 2023, Geox was again tracking well, with sales stepping up to around 750 million euros, somewhere between the valley of 2016 (619 million euros) and the peak of 2017.

So why this relay race of numbers? It demonstrates the naturally bumpy nature of doing business and how this puts demands on the venture team. Thankfully as founder and innovator to the core, Polegato still leads his winning team and is stepping forward (with dry, comfortable feet), finding new ways for Geox to compete as the world changes around him.

To learn more, visit: https://effectuation.org/EE3/geox or scan Figure 11.12.

Figure 11.12

TAKEAWAY: COMMITMENT TRANSFORMS AN IDEA INTO A GOOD IDEA

The notion of turning "something into something" can be found at the heart of Schumpeter's definition of entrepreneurship from his 1911 book, *The Theory of Economic Development*: "Our assumption is that he who makes new combinations is an entrepreneur."

But while making new combinations is easy because there are an infinite number of possible new combinations, it is immensely difficult to find valuable new combinations, for exactly the same reason.

Most scholars of entrepreneurship, including Knight (1921), Schumpeter (2021), and contemporary researchers conclude that entrepreneurs have some kind of intuition or judgment that enables them to instinctively pick good combinations from the infinite set of all possible combinations.

In this chapter, we have outlined the clinical mechanisms behind this process, but thus far, we omit one element common to them all—the importance of interaction.

The interaction sequence is a relatively easy one: I have an idea, so I talk to someone about it and together we transform it into something meaningful. While the transformation types here may allow you to generate ideas on your own, they also allow you to transform ideas collaboratively with others.

Also critical to interaction is the importance of commitment. While you may be able to generate many ideas with these transformation types, what separates ideas from good ideas is whether key stakeholders such as employees, partners, and customers are willing to make a commitment to them.

Expert entrepreneurs make transformations based on stakeholder commitments, not merely new combinations pulled out of a hat. Transformations, as mathematicians know, require interactions in space—in the case of expert entrepreneurs, this interaction happens in the space where stakeholders reside.

So What?

Entrepreneurs who use transformational processes produce more new market ideas than those who search and select for an existing opportunity. If you're struggling to create an opportunity, you don't have to invent something from nothing. Instead, transform something or several somethings into something else.

Think It Through

- Is it possible to create something genuinely new by transforming things that already exist?
- If you're just recombining things, are your efforts really transforming the world? Examples?
- In the venture you dream about, are you adapting to the world or is it adapting to you?

What Now?

- For an opportunity you have in mind, use the transformation concepts from expert entrepreneurs, and imagine three new ways to create value for different audiences.
- Decompose what you've got into its most basic elements and imagine different audiences that could connect to those elements.
- Imagine that a component of your idea, which you consider to be the most irrelevant, turned out to be the most valuable. How would you adjust?
- Develop a way to describe some of these new ideas to someone who might actually value what you assumed to be irrelevant.
- Borrow the idea from a product you most love. How might you make it valuable to the audiences you imagined in the first two points?

REFERENCES

Agogué, M., Lundqvist, M., & Middleton, K. W. (2015). Mindful deviation through combining causation and effectuation: A design theory-based study of technology entrepreneurship. *Creativity and Innovation Management*, *24*(4), 629–644. https://doi.org/10.1111/caim.12134

Amabile, T. M., Barsade, S. G., Mueller, J. S., & Staw, B. M. (2005). Affect and creativity at work. *Administrative Science Quarterly*, *50*(3), 367–403. https://doi.org/10.2189/asqu.2005.50.3.367

Ashton, K. (2015). *How to Fly a Horse: The Secret History of Creation, Invention, and Discovery*. Anchor.

Goldenberg, J., Mazursky, D., & Solomon, S. (1999). Toward identifying the inventive templates of new products: A channeled ideation approach. *Journal of Marketing Research*, *36*(2), 200–210. https://doi.org/10.1177/002224379903600205

Gould, S. J., & Vrba, E. S. (1982). Exaptation—A missing term in the science of form. *Paleobiology*, *8*(1), 4–15.

Investor Relations—Geox.biz. (n.d.). Retrieved January 3, 2024, from https://www.geox.biz/en/investor-relations/investor-relations.html

Klenner, N. F., Gemser, G., & Karpen, I. O. (2021). Entrepreneurial ways of designing and designerly ways of entrepreneuring: Exploring the relationship between design thinking and effectuation theory. *Journal of Product Innovation Management*, *39*(1), 66–94. https://doi.org/10.1111/jpim.12587

Knight, F. H. (1921). *Risk, Uncertainty and Profit* (Vol. 31). Houghton Mifflin.

Marquis, S., & Marquis, H. (2023, March 15). Sarah & Holly Marquis of Mollydooker (G. Wheatley, Interviewer).

Mollydooker. (2023, January 23). https://mollydookerwines.com.au/

Schumpeter, J. (1942). *Capitalism, Socialism and Democracy*. Pinter.

Schumpeter, J. A. (2021). *The Theory of Economic Development*. Routledge. https://doi.org/10.4324/9781003146766

Simon, H. A. (1969). *The Sciences of the Artificial*. MIT Press.

Smith, A. (1776). An *Inquiry Into the Nature and Causes of the Wealth of Nations*. W. Strahan and T. Cadell. https://doi.org/10.1093/oseo/instance.00043218

Szambelan, S., Jiang, Y., & Mauer, R. (2020). Breaking through innovation barriers: Linking effectuation orientation to innovation performance. *European Management Journal*, *38*(3), 425–434. https://doi.org/10.1016/j.emj.2019.11.001

Taiwan Today. (1997, December 1). Steaming to Shanghai. https://taiwantoday.tw/print.php?unit=12,29,33,45&post=21822

CHAPTER 12

Figure 12.1

The Affordable Loss Principle

Invest Little, Learn a Lot

In This Chapter

Expert entrepreneurs take an "affordable loss" approach, which does not rely on predictions. Like the other principles of effectuation, affordable loss turns traditional business practice on its head. Instead of deciding whether to pursue an opportunity based on expected returns, effectual entrepreneurs set the amount they are willing to lose. They base their decisions on what downside risk they find acceptable rather than on a prediction of the potential return.

DOI: 10.4324/9781003364016-15

To explore the affordable loss principle, the second principle we see at work in the decision-making approach of expert entrepreneurs, let's start with a thought experiment.

Imagine you are an entrepreneur. During your 12-year tenure as an engineer at a major computer manufacturer, outside of work you invent a device that recognizes and responds to eye movements. You imagine it to be an attractive alternative to the computer mouse. You can make it rest on the user's head much like headphones and set it up so that point-and-click navigation is accomplished with even the most minor head and eye movements. You are convinced the device has huge potential. But when you attempt to interest your current employer in licensing the idea from you, they don't bite.

There are no firms currently offering anything similar to this device, and you possess all the technical skills needed to create the product effectively and efficiently. You quit your job to develop this idea further by, among other things, conducting initial market research on selling the device through the retail channel as an upgrade to existing or new computers. You win a business plan competition and develop a prototype. And then you face a big decision.

A venture capitalist who was one of the judges in the business plan competition likes your idea and believes that with an initial investment of 10 million US dollars you could realistically capture 1% of the personal computer market worldwide. She believes your product should sell for 30 US dollars and generate a 20% net profit margin. In return for her investment, the venture capitalist would expect to own 40% of your company.

In the meantime, you have been speaking with a friend of your father who runs a large manufacturing facility. He is willing to pay you 1 million US dollars to adapt your technology to create a hands-free device that enables blue-collar factory workers to control industrial manufacturing systems from secure, protected work areas. The adaptation of your product, integration with the factory systems, and commercialization will cost you about 950,000 US dollars. He is willing to pay you up front.

CHOOSING THE BEST OPPORTUNITY

Because of the time required to develop these opportunities, you cannot do both simultaneously. You must choose. Here are some questions you might reasonably ask to make this decision:

- Which is the bigger opportunity?
- What is the net present value of each opportunity?
- What would you be personally investing in each alternative?
- What is the downside risk of each alternative?

As you look at these questions, you will probably recognize that the first two are the more causal, or predictive, ways of thinking about the decision, and the second two are more in line with the logic of effectuation, which we have been discussing in this book. Let us look at each question in turn to get a better grip on what might—and what might not—help you make a good choice between the venture capitalist and the father's friend.

Which Is the Bigger Opportunity?

This seems like an obvious question to ask, but how can you possibly know the answer? Take the case of the highly unlikely venture of Airbnb, discussed in Chapter 10. Until 2008, the world got along without a company helping people rent out their spare bedrooms to perfect strangers.

However, considering the growing success of what is now called the "sharing economy," one could argue that there was latent demand that simply went unnoticed until Brian Chesky, Joe Gebbia, and Nathan Blecharczyk came along. But if we wind back to 2008, what would their elevator pitch have been to potential investors? Or, for that matter, what would Starbucks' pitch have been in 1980, when US coffee consumption had been declining for 20 years straight?

What Goes Into Making a Net Present Value (NPV) Prediction?

A lot of forward-looking details. Let's unpack some of them.

Most NPV calculations are anchored with a demand forecast. This typically involves gathering information to form a consensus on the high side and the low side of demand for the product, given certain price assumptions. The price assumptions, similarly, rely on predictions about product features and competitors' actions.

The next step is to estimate the costs it takes to deliver. Costs must be organized into materials and labor, and again according to which are fixed and variable. Each of these costs as well as margins change over time, impacted by your own actions (improving the product or scaling quantities up or down), and your competitors' actions.

Atop those assumptions, you need to discount the cost of capital and assess the variability in the forecast. Put this together, and you can see all the dimensions in NPV that introduce variance and the resulting wide margins of error when forecasting the activity of an uncertain new venture.

Practically Speaking

Delivering a Venture

It only takes a minute of Steve Kiruri's story to see where entrepreneurial opportunities originate. A recent university graduate in his native Kenya, Kiruri was quick to inventory the things he didn't have: a job, cash, or any assets that might be used to secure a loan. Instead, in his own words, "I didn't sit back and moan. I focused on things right there in front of me."

He identified the following: his education, relatives asking him to take care of their errands, available space, a government with bureaucratic and time-consuming processes, voluntary labor from high-school graduates and dropouts who were jobless, friends willing to give him a chance, and a national media willing to broadcast his story to the world.

Transforming this assortment of resources, Kiruri launched a venture called "Petty Errands." His value proposition assured his clients (initially friends and relatives) that he would take care of the small tasks that consume a lot of time because of Kenya's developing infrastructure.

Unplanned Route

Instead of a business plan and 5 million US dollars in venture capital, Kiruri started right away using what was readily available. And the venture developed as a function of the next resource he added to his list—his clients. Once he had renewed a driver's license for a client, they might ask him if he could pay a bill—a task that can still require a personal visit in Kenya—or courier a package across Nairobi, a chore that could easily cost a morning amid traffic, confusion, and construction. New requests grew into new business opportunities, and Petty Errands became more than a petty business.

Practically Speaking *(continued)*

Next Stop

That was 1995. Since then, the firm has added corporations, non-governmental organizations (NGOs), and government bodies to its client base. Petty Errands is licensed by the Communication Commission of Kenya (CCK) as an Intra-City Operator, and Steve has been recognized as the "Most Inspiring Business Person" by Kenya Television Networks.

Figure 12.2 Mr. Steve Kiruri, in blue jacket, of Petty Errands at his firm's offices.

Today, the firm handles thousands of "errands" in a year. But Steve's story isn't over, and neither is the story of where opportunities originate. Because today, Steve's list of things to work with is much longer than it was in 1995.

In addition to certifications, clients, and employees, he has also added things such as a respected brand, knowledge of the current needs (and issues) of clients, operations and motorcycle transportation expertise, extensive contacts within the Kenya courier industry, and good relations with bankers. Indeed, the story of creating opportunities is one that starts again and again as new resources are found, acquired, used, and lost through business activity, meeting new people and learning new skills. Similarly, Steve's own story is still very much in the writing.

Expanding the Path

Over time many entrepreneurs seek to offer their existing service to a larger geographic area. Steve's has taken a different tack, keeping his focus on Nairobi, but offering a wider range of higher-value services, including business registration, banking, and printing services. The primary goal is to satisfy the needs of existing customers instead of seeking to gain new customers.

This is based on the insight that the source of opportunity is already here. Taking what is readily available and transforming what are seemingly mundane resources into something valuable is the ongoing errand of the committed entrepreneur.

To learn more, visit: https://effectuation.org/EE3/petty or scan Figure 12.3

Figure 12.3

Common sense suggests that while you might be able to calculate what you could lose by investing in a venture (namely, everything that you put into it), it is much harder to calculate the potential upside—that is, the size of the opportunity.

What Is the Net Present Value of Each Opportunity?

Just because calculating the upside of an opportunity is difficult, it doesn't mean people don't try. Net present value (NPV) is a formula widely used in the business world to predict the current value of a future project. To calculate the NPV of your two options, you'll need to answer several questions:

- What is your forecasted demand?
- What is your product cost?
- What are your overheads?
- How will these costs change over time?

Put this together, and you can see the interrelated system of interrelated prediction involved in trying to assess the value of an opportunity. And you can also see how, as the assumptions accumulate, the calculation becomes much closer to guesswork than science.

What Would You Be Personally Investing in Each Alternative?

Both options, the one from the venture capitalist and the one from your father's friend, require you to invest a variety of resources. Spend a moment thinking about how the options differ in terms of the following:

- Your time commitment
- Your reputation
- Your opportunity cost
- Your knowledge
- Your emotional commitment

How would you measure these? How would you decide what constitutes an appropriate level of investment? These are highly subjective and personal assessments that change over time, just as tangible costs do.

What is the downside risk of each alternative?

Let's assume you choose the venture capital option. Here are some possible scenarios:

- The market is not there, and the venture capitalist pulls the plug on the company.
- The market is there, but the venture capitalist takes control of the firm and fires you.
- You don't get along with the venture capitalist, but you can't buy her out.
- The market ends up being 25,000 units per year, just enough to break even, but leaving you managing a firm turned into the "living dead."

Now, assuming you have decided to work with your father's friend, consider these scenarios:

- You miss a critical deadline that costs your father's friend a week's manufacturing output. Your father's friend is unhappy with your father.
- You deliver something defective, and an employee is hurt as a result.
- It costs you twice as much to implement the solution as you estimated.
- While you are working with your father's friend, a new company releases a product very similar to yours, and it is a runaway success.

For each option, which scenario is the worst and why? Which scenarios are within your control? Which are not? What do you do next in each case?

Starting by organizing the issues in this way is the first step in assessing "affordable loss."

Affordable Loss and Its Use as a Decision Tool

NPV offers useful projections in situations where the information that goes into the calculation is relatively stable. Managers in mature markets ranging from energy to carbonated drinks make frequent use of NPV. But in the uncertain setting of new venture creation, the information necessary to perform an NPV calculation is either unavailable, or the ranges are so broad that results are not helpful in planning or running a new venture.

Assessing affordable loss

	Venture capitalist	My father's friend
Time		
Reputation		
Opportunity cost		
Knowledge		

The research upon which this book is based suggests that instead of trying to calculate the upside of an opportunity, using NPV, expert entrepreneurs take what we call an "affordable loss" approach. Fundamentally, affordable loss is based on things they know and can control, whereas NPV is based on predictions they don't trust and can't control.

Like the other principles of effectuation, affordable loss turns traditional business practice on its head. Instead of deciding whether to pursue an opportunity based on potential returns, effectual entrepreneurs look at potential losses. They base their decisions on what downside risk they find acceptable rather than on what they guess the upsides might be.

So instead of calculating up front how much money they need to launch their project and then investing time, effort, and energy into raising that money, effectual entrepreneurs determine what they are willing to lose. As they pursue the opportunity, they bring stakeholders on board, reducing resources the entrepreneur and the stakeholders need to commit to the venture and better controlling risks through the effort, commitment, and resources of self-selected stakeholders.

As we walk through how to think in terms of affordable loss, the important point to remember is that affordable loss puts the entrepreneur front and center. Traditional business planning puts the venture front and center, asking what financing the venture needs to get off the ground independent of the entrepreneur's available means.

Affordable loss starts with the entrepreneur's concrete situation, not abstract estimates of venture financing needs. As such, the emphasis is on taking the entrepreneur's context into account. Big decisions like taking the plunge into entrepreneurship depend a lot on your family, your stage of life, and the social norms around you—for example, attitudes toward failure in your community and industry.

> To ponder:
>
> A loser doesn't know what he'll do if he loses, but talks about what he'll do if he wins. A winner doesn't talk about what he'll do if he wins, but knows what he'll do if he loses.
>
> (*Berne*, 1975)

Research Roots

Mental Accounting

The notion of mental accounting was first developed in a paper by Thaler (1985, p. 199) and later summarized in another paper (Thaler, 1999). Mental accounting emerges relatively directly from the idea of bounded rationality: creatures with limited cognitive processing capabilities (human beings, that is) require ways of keeping track of their money.

Thaler theorized that people do so by categorizing their resources, as accountants do. For example, they create separate mental compartments for long-term savings (such as retirement and children's education) and short-term expenses (such as entertainment and leisure activities).

A key implication of mental accounting is the violation of the fungibility premise of economics—i.e. that resources are automatically arbitraged across accounts (Thaler, 1999, p. 183). A simple way to think about this is that for Homo economicus, "Money by any other name is still money" but for most Homo sapiens, "Money in one mental account is simply not the same as money in another account."

Because of this non-fungibility characteristic, mental accounting suggests that consumers may borrow at high interest rates in some accounts even while they save at much lower interest rates in others.

How About Sixteen Years of Affordable Loss?

The online retailer and cloud services provider Amazon serves as an outstanding example of shared affordable loss on a grand scale. The company's journey reflects the willingness of its founders, shareholders, and other stakeholders to invest substantial amounts of money, time, and patience, hoping for, but unsure if there would be a return on, their investment.

This timeline shows that Amazon was not an "overnight success."

Event	Year	Age of company (years)
Amazon is founded	1994	0
Company lists on stock exchange (IPO) with opening price of 18 US dollars per share	1997	3
Company becomes cash flow positive	2001	7
First full-year profit	2003	9
Cumulative profits exceed cumulative losses	2010	16
Share price exceeds initial offer price of 18 US dollars	2013	19
Share price exceeds 100 US dollars	2018	24
Historical maximum share price of 189 US dollars	2024	30

To figure out your affordable loss, you must consider your life situation, current commitments, aspirations, and risk propensity. It is helpful to think of this as a two-step process:

1. The first step is to ask how much you really need to start your business—the less you need, the less you need to worry about losing. You can greatly reduce your upfront cash needs by getting creative about different ways of bringing your idea to market using all the means that are available to you. The vast majority of new businesses are started with small sums of money, and rely heavily on nonfinancial contributions, such as the entrepreneur's time and (often) family support as well as slack resources from partners.
2. The second step is to ask what you are really able and willing to lose to start your business. This means taking an inventory of your available resources and gauging your risk tolerance.

> You can't always control the wind, but you can control your sails.
>
> *Anthony Robbins*, motivational speaker

Practically Speaking

Partners' Affordable Loss

It would be fair to say that Marius Tudosiei had more aspirations than tangible resources. Growing up in the northern part of Romania, his childhood was spent in and around a big kitchen, where traditional food was cooked using fresh and natural ingredients.

But when Marius arrived in the capital city of Bucharest, the availability of such artisanal cuisine was very limited. So, in 2009, Marius quit his job in the media industry to build "something dedicated to good food"—though he had no idea what that something might ultimately look like, and no capital to fund the project.

Aspiration to Action

Marius started with what was available and free. He built a social media page and asked his friends to tell him about food and about what his business should be. Soon, he had 1,000 friends advising him to open a restaurant. But he said no. Not enough money, not enough expertise. Instead, he decided to offer his friends good food from his small network of suppliers—opening a small and highly specialized grocery store as a means of distribution.

Action to Interaction

Though less expensive to start than a restaurant, a grocery store still required capital Marius didn't have. Until a mentor asked him how much he needed. "10,000 euros," he replied, "and I do not have any idea where I could get that much money." To which the mentor responded, "But do you have ten friends to give you 1,000 euros each?" Before he was done, he had raised a total of 25,000 euros in small bits and pieces from a number of friends.

Interaction to Creation

Marius founded Bacania Veche (The Old Grocery Store) in 2010, which quickly became one of the most popular small food enterprises in Romania, dedicated to good and healthy food. From that starting point, he has gone on to open a restaurant and a TV cooking show. He delivers food daily for 200 children in five nurseries, has a corporate catering business, and employs 20 people.

Figure 12.4 Marius Tudosiei in his shop Bacania Veche.

Practically Speaking *(continued)*

Secret Ingredient

There is no way to get the recipes which generated this comment on Tripadvisor; "It is the greatest shop that I have ever seen. Cookies and bread cooked on the spot give the flavor and enchant the visitor."

But the secret that enabled Marius to get going is understanding his partners' affordable loss. While an investment of 10,000 euros is a meaningful sum for many individuals, providing 1,000 euros to a friend starting the business changes the proposition. If the business fails, losing 1,000 euros is not a crushing loss. But if the business is successful, the 1,000 euros will return a profit and perhaps all sorts of other benefits. A good recipe for bringing people into a venture.

To learn more, visit: https://effectuation.org/EE3/marius or scan Figure 12.5.

Figure 12.5

DECIDING ON YOUR AFFORDABLE LOSS: SOME GUIDELINES

Once you have gone through the process of doing everything possible to lower the amount of money you need to get your venture off the ground, you are left with the question of what downside risk is acceptable to you. Here, the key thing is to ask yourself the right questions. It's helpful to think through both what you can afford to lose and what you are willing to lose. We'll look at each of these in turn.

Different Kinds of Losses

People "mentally account" for different resources in different ways. For example, many individuals are willing to invest loads of time in a new business, but carefully limit how much cash they put into it. Evidently, people account for their time differently than they account for their cash.

Similarly, some resources are mentally accounted for in ways that preclude them from being put at risk. A good example is savings accumulated by parents to fund their children's education. These monies are often considered "out of bounds" for risking on a new business venture.

To figure out what you can afford to lose, you have to know what your resources are, and you have to make some decisions about what belongs in the category of "riskable" and what doesn't. As you are thinking about this, remember that some psychologists have argued that rational people never put at risk what is truly valuable to them.

Consider the following categories of resources as you think through what you can afford to lose and what is "out of bounds" for you.

Time

The time entrepreneurs put into a new venture is often referred to as "sweat equity." A good proportion of entrepreneurs sweat it out over long periods. However, this may make sense to them because time is a different "currency" from cash and, therefore, it is often accounted for in a different way. Moreover, because time is perishable, people feel differently about contributing it—after all, they might have wasted it anyway. Therefore, you may be able to afford losing time more than you can afford losing money.

Windfalls

As Fred Smith was creating the business plan for FedEx, his father died, leaving 8 million US dollars to Fred and his sister—money that was used to fund the new company. This seems like a rather high level of affordable loss, but it's not surprising. Many people put inherited money into a different mental account than earned income—they are willing to risk the former, but not the latter. Other kinds of windfalls that can significantly increase an individual's affordable loss are lottery winnings and big upswings in the value of assets such as stock.

In retrospect, Fred Smith's decision to invest his and his sister's inheritance into the fledgling FedEx looks prescient. But had he been a seasoned entrepreneur, he might have first tried to start the firm with no money of his own.

Long-Term Savings

Research suggests that most people apply rules of thumb to borrowing against or spending certain resources that are mentally accounted for as belonging to other parts of their life. Examples include funds set aside for their own retirement and for the care of dependents, for instance, children and parents.

The Family Home/Home Equity

There are many instances in which people use home equity loans to fund a business startup. However, some individuals are unwilling to put their home at risk, as the loss would not be "affordable."

Credit Cards

We've all heard stories about companies initially financed on credit cards—EDS and Home Depot come to mind.

There is some evidence that people mentally account for credit card expenses differently from other expenses because credit cards weaken the link between making the decision to purchase something and actually paying for it.

Loans From Family and Friends

Other examples of weak links between purchasing and paying may include loans from family members that have flexible or unspecified payback terms. Descriptions of family business, for example, refer to the relatives' money as "patient capital." Such funds may seem more affordable to use and to lose than funds with heavy pressure to repay at specific deadlines.

Practically Speaking

Affordable Loss for an Unaffordable Loss

Greta Thunberg, the Swedish environmental activist, has become a symbol of youth advocacy for climate change, building awareness of the fact that we cannot afford to lose our planet.

Skipping School

Greta's activism began with her protest outside the Swedish Parliament in August 2018. Her parents' support of her skipping school made it affordable loss for her to start on this journey which became known as "Fridays for the Future."

Living with Asperger's syndrome, OCD, and selective mutism would hardly count as assets useful to her endeavor. Yet, her family's support and understanding allowed Greta to travel extensively for her cause, impacting their daily lives.

Practically Speaking *(continued)*

The Slow Boat for the Climate

On her journeys, Greta learned to deal with loss of privacy and various forms of criticism. Another calculation of affordable loss resulted in the decision to travel by train or sail to keep her carbon emissions as low as possible. These choices entailed inconvenience and loss of time. But on the upside, they aligned with her cause.

Affording a Criminal Record

When her losses extended to being arrested in 2023 for protesting in Malmö, Greta showed the lessons she had learned. She leveraged her arrest, along with others, as a way to amplify the message she shared via social media: "Activism works. So act."

Sometimes the cost to act is affordable, simply because the cost not to act is unaffordable. Every effectual entrepreneur who wishes to tackle massive social problems needs to learn these new calculations of risk and return.

To learn more, visit: https://effectuation.org/EE3/greta or scan Figure 12.6.

Figure 12.6

What Am I Willing to Lose?

Once you have decided what you can afford to lose in general, you still need to decide what you are willing to lose on this particular venture. Figuring this out will mean assessing the degree and intensity of your desire to start this particular venture.

It will also mean creating thresholds, since if the downside case for your venture hits a key threshold you have set, this will dictate your course of action. Ultimately, the question you to ask yourself is, "Is the venture worth doing even if I lose what I invest?"

Regardless of whether your motivation to become an entrepreneur is largely pecuniary or non-pecuniary, there are several ways reasoning through the plunge decision using the idea of affordable loss is likely to increase the chances that you'll decide to go ahead:

- It reduces the financial risk. Going through the exercise of minimizing startup costs lowers the risk of starting your venture.
- It allows you to focus on things within your control (the downside loss) and proceed in spite of things outside your control, which increases your confidence.
- It makes explicit that the upside potential for the venture is in large part contingent on your actions and the actions of your stakeholders, which again increases the perceived controllability of the venture and, therefore, its attractiveness.
- It encourages you to consider an opportunity from the perspective of what matters to you in ways beyond the economic upside. Bringing in factors that lie beyond financial calculation makes the decision more realistic, and in tune with how most people actually make major decisions.

In short, using the principle of affordable loss will provide you with more reasons for taking the plunge into entrepreneurship and fewer reasons for saying no.

Research Roots

Affordable Loss

The economist George Shackle refers to the concept of affordable loss in a paper in which he postulates that the entrepreneur might characterize each venture opportunity according to the possible gains and possible losses and suggests that the latter can help the entrepreneur evaluate which opportunity to pursue.

> It is practical and reasonable to regard the focus loss, in absolute terms, as depending on the nature and scale of the enterprise concerned. Thus, by choice of an appropriate kind, or an appropriate size, of plant or enterprise, he can adjust the greatest amount he stands to lose, that is, his focus loss, to the amount which, given the size and character of his assets, he can afford to lose.
>
> (*Shackle*, 1966 [2010], p. 765)

Practically Speaking

Diving Deep in Affordable Loss

In June 2018, an unusual rescue mission unfolded in the Tham Luang cave in Thailand, where 12 boys and their football coach were trapped.

A Rare Bird

The rescue mission called for individuals with a really rare bird-in-hand. Dr. Richard Harris, an Australian anesthetist and experienced cave diver, was one of them. His rescue technique involved trading one risk for another.

Disastrous Choice

Later Dr. Harris explained in an interview how sedating the boys for the three-hour underwater journey out of the cave was really the only alternative:

> And even though right up till, pretty much till the last boy came out that I thought that they would not survive what I was doing. Essentially, I felt like I was probably euthanizing them.
>
> And you would say, well, why would you ever embark on something if that's what you genuinely believed? And the answer is that the alternative was even worse and that was that they would die over weeks, probably from starvation or infection, and suffocate because the oxygen levels in the cave were falling.

Realizing that doing nothing was not an option, Dr, Harris acted: "So that left one option. Give this thing a go even though I thought it was, you know, almost certainly courting disaster."

Lose and Learn

Dr. Harris was not new to the fear of loss or the awesome responsibility that went along with it. From anesthetizing patients to cave diving, he had learned courage as a way to work with fear, starting small and building slow:

Practically Speaking *(continued)*

> You broaden your experience slowly, you go further, you go deeper, you become more complex in your diving, and you have small frights regularly to broaden your kind of comfort zone, your sphere of, you know, experience or if that's the way to put it. Until you look back and you go, gosh, look at what I'm doing now. Like this cave in Thailand compared to my first few cave dives 20 something years ago.

Figure 12.7 Sign at the entrance of Khun Nam Nang Non Forest Park in Chiang Rai Province Thailand, the location of the Tham Luang cave where the junior football team was rescued.

Like all expert entrepreneurs, Dr. Harris isn't a swashbuckling risk taker:

> You know, I'm not a courageous person in my view, I'm not brave. I don't enjoy danger. I don't get out of bed going to thinking to myself, I'm going cave diving. There's a good chance I'll die today.
>
> But what I've learned is that, you know, doing things that are difficult in life and again, not physical risk, but doing stuff that is, is confronting or emotionally challenging is, is really empowering and I have felt so much stronger for it.

To learn more, visit: https://effectuation.org/EE3/cave or scan Figure 12.8.

Figure 12.8

TAKEAWAY: UN-RISKY BUSINESS

Statistics would seem to suggest that budding entrepreneurs would have a bias against starting new ventures, simply because a large number of new firms fail. Affordable loss lessens the impact of failure—it makes failure clearly survivable by constraining the loss to something the entrepreneur is in fact willing to lose in order to pursue the venture. If the entrepreneur reduces the downside risk to an acceptable level, he or she is likely to lose less in the event of failure than an entrepreneur who invests based on his or her guess about the venture's upside potential.

So What?

Using affordable loss to reason through the plunge decision helps you see how to get started right now, while managing your risk. The decision to start a business doesn't have to be about predicting whether the upside is big enough; instead, it can be about whether the downside is "life-threatening."

Think It Through

- How do notions of affordable loss differ in various parts of the world?
- How might affordable loss encourage or discourage commitment?
- If investment in an opportunity is constrained by affordable loss, can it lead to a "point-scoring goal"?

What Now?

For the opportunity you are developing, work these through from the perspective of affordable loss:

- Do I hire at all? Whom specifically should I hire? How should I hire them?
- How much, if any, do I invest in longer-term investments such as research and development?
- Can I quantify the levels of time, reputation, money, and other resources I am willing to lose to advance my idea to the next step?
- Who benefits from my idea, and how can I bring them on board to share the expense and risk as well as the benefit?

REFERENCES

Berne, E. (1968). *Games People Play: The Psychology of Human Relationships*. Penguin.

Berne, E. (1975). *What Do You Say After You Say Hello? The Psychology of Human Destiny*. Random House.

Harris, R. (2023). Dr. Richard Harris "That Thing in Thailand" (H. van Cuylenberg, Interviewer). Retrieved August 7, 2023, from https://theresilienceproject.com.au/at-home/podcasts/season-5-episode-25-dr-richard-harris-risk-and-thailand-cave-rescue/

Shackle, G. L. S. (1966[2010]). *The Nature of Economic Thought*. Cambridge University Press.

Thaler, R. H. (1985). Mental accounting and consumer choice. *Marketing Science*, *4*(3), 199–214. https://doi.org/10.1287/mksc.4.3.199

Thaler, R. H. (1999). Mental accounting matters. *Journal of Behavioral Decision Making*, *12*(3), 183–206. https://doi.org/10.1002/(SICI)1099-0771(199909)12:3<183::AID-BDM318>3.0.CO;2-F

CHAPTER 13

Figure 13.1 These boots are made for walking!

Using Slack for Bootstrap Financing

In This Chapter

Aspiring entrepreneurs need to keep in mind that there are countless ways, beyond investment money, to grow a business.

In general, experienced entrepreneurs prefer the cheapest option, so they come up with creative ways of doing things at little cost and risk to themselves. When they do have to seek outside investment, they think carefully about what and whom they need.

By figuring out how to do the most with the least, and what type of outside capital is taken, entrepreneurs can better maintain control over their ventures.

In other words, follow the advice from Professor Venkataraman (2002):

- *Do not buy new what you can buy used.*
- *Do not buy used what you can lease or rent.*
- *Do not lease or rent what you can borrow.*

DOI: 10.4324/9781003364016-16

As we saw in Chapter 3, "I don't have enough money" is a common refrain among aspiring entrepreneurs. Lulled by the stories of venture capitalists and angel investors who pour millions of dollars into small startups with barely a business plan to their name, the budding entrepreneur naturally assumes that the first step is to look for money, preferably a lot of it. But before you embark on that quest, think about the following:

- How much do you want?
- How much do you need?
- What do you need money for?
- What can you do without money?
- What does money cost?
- What are you willing to give up in return for money?

This chapter and Chapters 18 (ownership) and 19 (business plans) will help you answer those questions and offer alternative views on startup financing—views that reflect the effectual logic we observe among expert entrepreneurs.

In this chapter, we look at bootstrapping—that is, starting a business without taking on external funding (or taking on as little as possible). It's a practice that embodies the principle of affordable loss, discussed in Chapter 12.

To explore the nuts and bolts of bootstrapping, we'll consider in this chapter a real-life case of a young couple who decided to launch their own business. At each decision point in the story, think back to the questions listed here and how you, as the founder of this business, would have answered them.

The base assumption throughout the case is, not surprisingly, when you start a business, the amount of cash coming in must be greater than or equal to the amount going out (the idea of money matching, described in Chapter 3).

Graphical Practically Speaking

Stacy's Pita Chips

Who I am, what I know, who I know

The year is 1996. Stacy and Mark are a couple, living in Boston. Mark is a psychologist and Stacy a social worker. They both have experience in the Californian food industry, having worked in restaurants. They know trends in the US often move from west to east. They believe Boston might soon acquire an appetite for Californian style food. They are strong believers in the healthy diets they experienced in the West. They know they want to be their own boss. Together they have debt of US$370,000.

Mark and Stacy are attracted to the food/restaurant business. Ideally, they would like to start a healthy bistro, but that dream is squelched by their debt and the lack of enthusiasm by their immediate family to support the venture. So they start selling sausages and hot dogs from a pushcart in the streets of Boston. It isn't exactly the healthy diet they had in mind, but it is a profitable and cash positive living.

What should they do next?

Keep selling sausages from the pushcart: it's making money?	Quit selling junk food and look for jobs?	Make healthier sandwiches Californian style?	Do something else (remember Curry in a Hurry, Chapter 7?)
Not consistent with values	Not consistent with goals	Interesting—what's the cost?	Possible—guided by partners

The opportunity cost of time

Spending money versus spending time are perceived differently. The value of time (or sweat equity, as it is sometimes called) is more ambiguous and perishable because time can't be saved for future use. Therefore, losses paid for in time may be experienced as more affordable than losses paid for in money because they can be accounted for more flexibly and are, therefore, seen as being more affordable than ventures paid for in money.

WHAT IS THE BALANCE SHEET FOR SELLING HEALTHIER SANDWICHES?

Income	Expenses	Money questions
From their first venture into hot dogs, they know there is demand.	Ingredients	Do you want fresh ingredients? Could you get yesterday's bread cheaper? Could you cut a deal with a pita manufacturer?
	Pushcart	You already have one, but are you willing to lose the revenue you might have generated selling sausages?
	Time	How do you account for your time?

The couple decides to make pita wrap sandwiches to sell on a pushcart in Boston's financial district. The date is 1997.

Figure 13.2

Graphical Practically Speaking *(continued)*

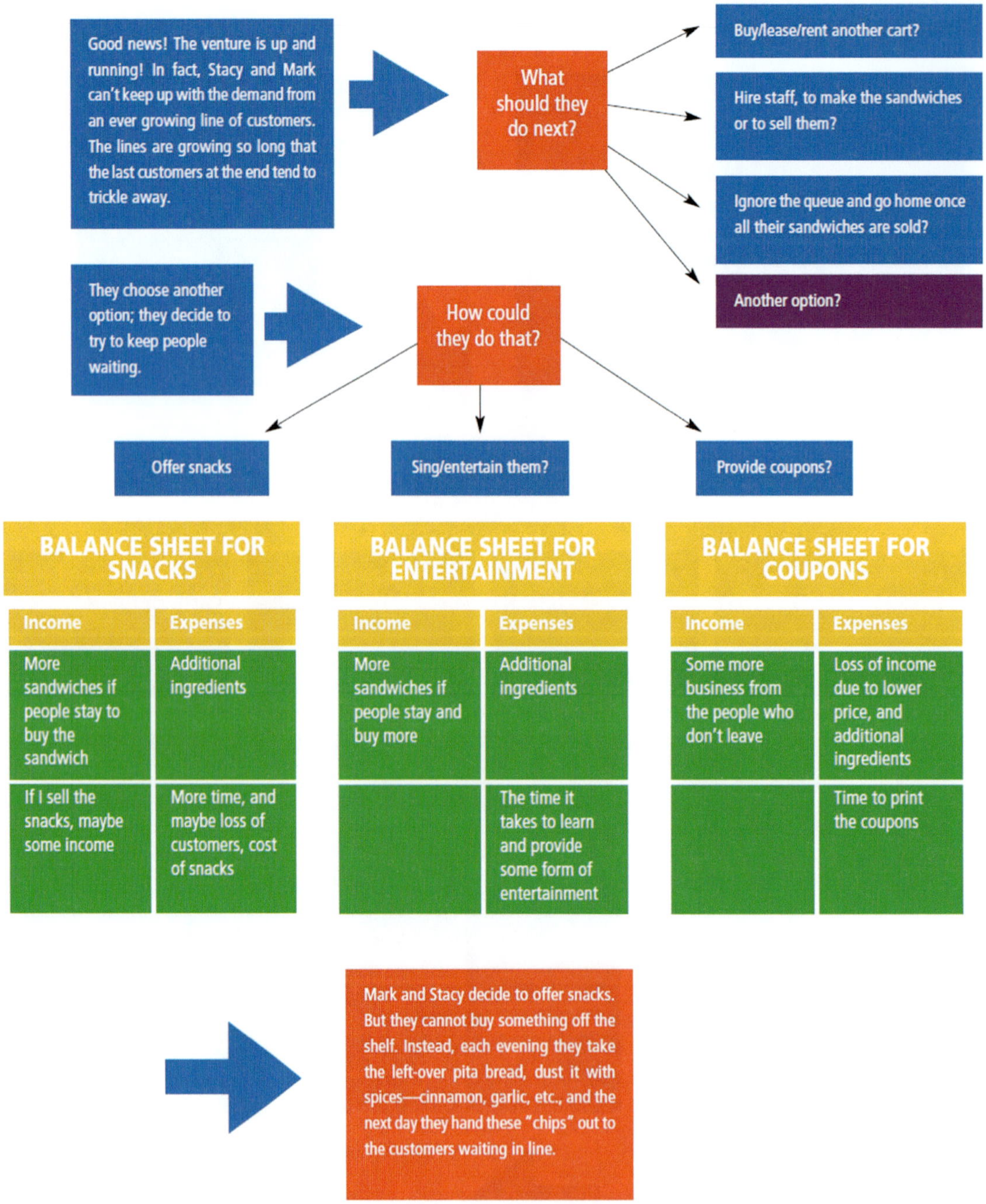

Figure 13.3

Graphical Practically Speaking *(continued)*

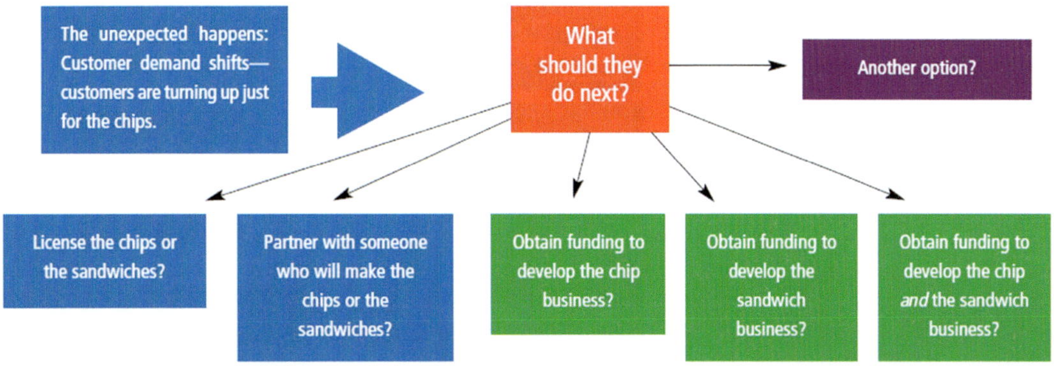

When it's partners you need

When confronted with choice, there is always another option. Sometimes, it's not money you need but a partner.

For Mark and Stacy, this is an easy time to bring on a partner. They have two opportunities, which have created demand, more demand than they have the resources to handle. A partner could add all sorts of resources to their set of means, ranging from broad distribution (a high-end grocery store interested in offering sandwiches), to factory capacity (a bread factory, idle during the day as most baking is done at night).

In addition, money is not always the only motivation for launching a partnership. As these two examples highlight, you may have investors interested for other reasons than money. And in turn, these partners can both offer resources that go beyond money and can also enable the pursuit of new opportunities that were not previously imagined (for example, flavored pita bread produced by the bakery partner to make the sandwiches more unique and exciting).

When it's money you need

It is important to remember that all money comes with strings attached. The relationships you create as you gather investments of all different sorts reasonably require your attention. People involved need to know how things are developing, they often have specific legal rights to be updated, and have a say in some of your major decisions. This relationship work takes real time and sincere attention, not unlike the attention and investment it takes to manage your relationship with a great customer. More money means more of this type of relationship management.

Like all relationships, it's a two-way street: People involved don't just listen to you, you also learn from them and include their resources in your portfolio. We made the case for the value of taking advantage of contingencies earlier in the book and we will look at it again in detail when we talk about contingency. The listening and cooperating involved in working with your investors/lenders/other sources of money can limit the degrees of freedom that you have in dealing with contingencies. Even with great sources of capital and shrewd big thinkers that trust you, the process can slow you down.

Finally, more money often leads to customer interactions that are relatively more directive than collaborative. Imagine you are in the business of selling garlic chips and you find an interested customer. He loves your garlic chips, but will only buy from you if you can modify them into cinnamon chips. If you are sitting on US$10 million in cash, you are imminently less inclined to say yes to that possibility than if you are sitting on US$1 in cash. As a result, you turn the customer away—your business is garlic!

Mark and Stacy are unsure what to do. They stop and think. They speak to other people in the industry, read trade journals, and talk to colleagues and competitors.

Figure 13.4

Graphical Practically Speaking *(continued)*

As a result of their conversations, Mark and Stacy decide to drop the sandwiches and make chips. The market seems to say that they could get bigger faster that way. But they want to do it without asking for funding and without going into a partnership. With their debt still looming, Mark and Stacy look for ways to make chips while spending as little as possible. But they need some things:

- An oven in which to bake the chips
- A space in which to make the chips
- A machine to slice the bread
- Ingredients

What should they do next?

Where do you find money?

Obvious sources

- Friends, family and fools
- Angels
- Venture capitalists
- Banks
- Government and grant sources

Not-so-obvious sources

- Factoring (customers)
- Suppliers
- Professional advisors
- Media
- Non-monetary resources

How to get around the money hurdle:

When dealing with your suppliers, think of negotiating the following:

- delayed payment terms
- payment as a percentage of revenue
- direct capital investment
- paying them in direct services (make them customers)
- using their process/assets/talent during their downtime (use their slack resources)
- getting them to guarantee a line of credit for you at their bank.

When working with customers:

- pay first purchase order (PO) in cash upfront for better pricing
- get a solid PO and then connect to a lender that will accept that as collateral
- use their commercial bank and piggy back on their line of credit (slack resource)
- get them to guarantee a line of credit
- pre-sell them the first year's worth of their purchases.

When going to investors:

- borrow money from them, don't just take investment
- pay them back as a variable cost against a percentage of revenues (not against time)
- get them to guarantee a line of credit
- take investment but negotiate for a "clawback" where you can earn back ownership if things go well.

When hiring employees, think about offering:

- options rather than cash
- percentage of sales rather than base salary.

All of these options can lower the cash-based entry barrier. And when all else fails, use your credit card!

They rent space from a bakery—using the bakery's down time to bake their chips in the bakery's oven. This solves the space, oven, and machine problem. But it does not allow for large-scale production.

Figure 13.5

Graphical Practically Speaking *(continued)*

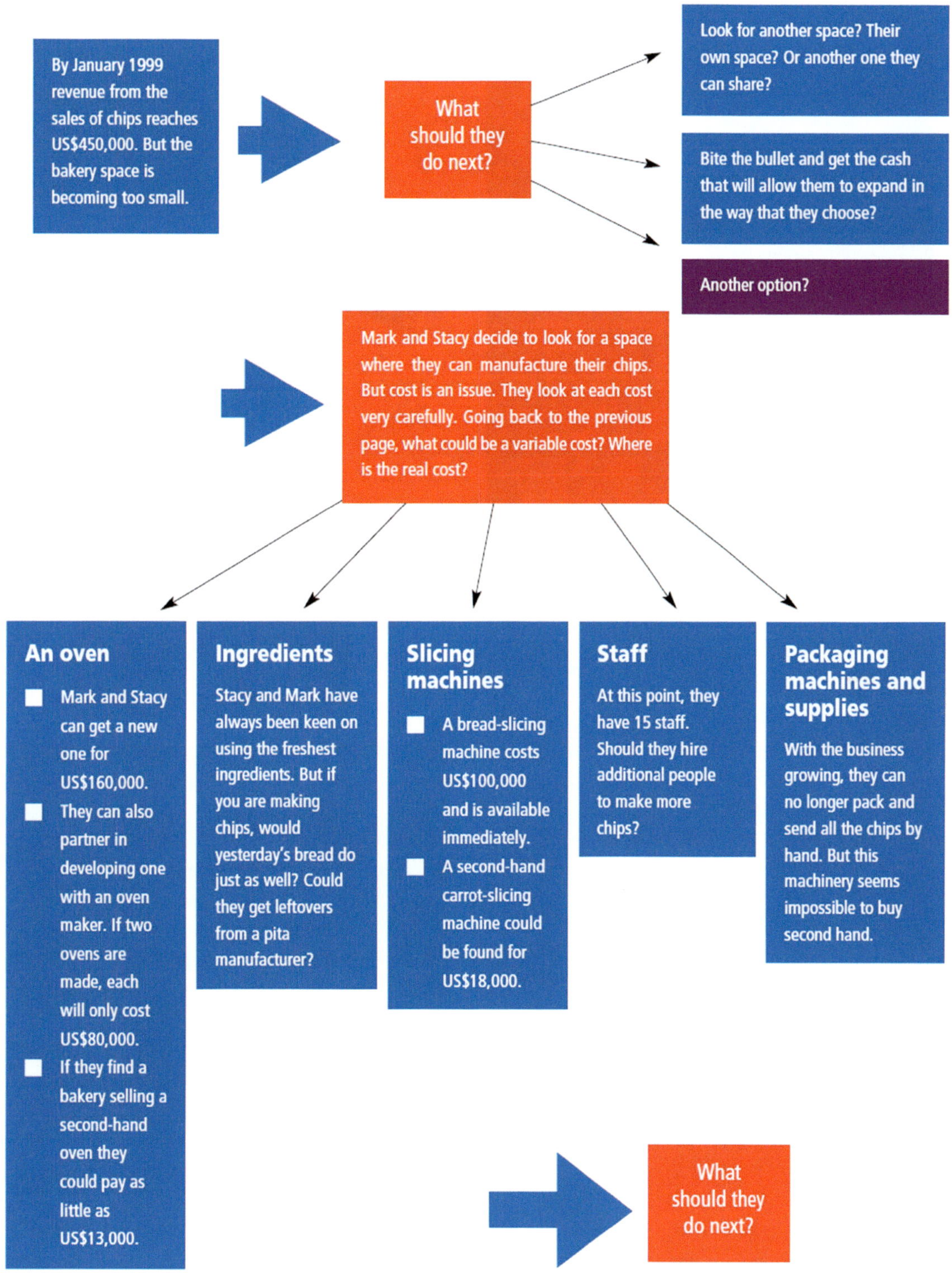

Figure 13.6

Graphical Practically Speaking *(continued)*

Mark and Stacy expand the chip business

- They make Stacy the majority owner of the company so that she is eligible for funding from BankBoston, which has a loan program that assists women in business. They ask for a US$60,000 loan to buy automated packaging equipment and supplies. Six months later they apply for US$500,000. But in exchange for that amount, the bank wants equity, which the couple is not willing to give. They settle for US$300,000.
- They partner with an oven manufacturer to make the oven they cannot find, paying US$80,000—half the original price.
- When they realize they need a second oven, and that the banks will not lend them any more money, they buy a used oven from a bankrupt bakery. They pay for it with their credit card.
- Since they cannot find an automatic slicer at a price they can afford, they buy a 40-year-old carrot-cutting machine from Campbell Soup, which Mark modifies.
- They rent a suburban warehousing space from a contracting company. They spend nothing furnishing it, getting furniture for free from friends and family or making their own.
- They hire Stacy's brother into the company in exchange for a share of the profit.
- When they need more staff than the 15 they have, they hire temporary employees.
- They spend nothing on advertising—instead they give samples away in person at trade shows, cooking demonstrations, public appearances, and grocery stores everywhere across the US.
- They partner with Babson, a Boston area business school focused on entrepreneurship, to hire summer interns to design their website in exchange for them speaking at the school.

The story of Stacy and Mark illustrates the timeless rules of new venture bootstrapping:

- Never buy what you can rent.
- Never rent what you can barter for.
- Never barter for what you can borrow.
- Never borrow what you can get for free.

By 2000 Stacy's Pita Chips is a profitable business with US$1.3 million in revenues (double that of 1999).

Five years later Mark and Stacy sell their pita chips to PepsiCo's Frito-Lay. By then, they are the top-selling maker of pita chips in the US, with revenues of US$60 million and 100 employees.

Figure 13.7

To learn more, visit: https://effectuation.org/EE3/stacy or scan Figure 13.8.

Figure 13.8

Research Roots

Earn versus Burn

Wiltbank et al. (2015) analyzed all the private firms acquired by public firms in the US over a ten-year period. Twenty-seven percent of the acquired firms were created, grown, and acquired on total investments of less than 50,000 US dollars.

Yet when they looked at the data, they did not find a significant discount on the total valuation of those firms with little invested capital, with respect to their terminal valuation at acquisition. Money in did not predict money out.

The big variable that changed with respect to the amount of investment money is the time between founding and acquisition. Investment money accelerated growth and time to liquidity. The finding was so clear in the data that the authors were able to separate the population into a group of "earners" who created value through revenue and cash flows, and "burners" who fueled growth with investment money (Wiltbank et al., 2015).

SELECTING A FUNDING APPROACH

Bootstrapping limits the money entrepreneurs put into fledgling ventures, but that doesn't mean it's without risk. Clearly, bootstrapping entrepreneurs risk underinvesting in a promising opportunity. They may underestimate the upside potential of the market or choose to pursue only one aspect of it, leaving a chunk for someone else.

But entrepreneurs shouldn't look for external funding just because they're afraid of missing out on something.

As normal people, we tend to be overly optimistic in our predictions. Our startups, we believe, will grow rapidly, and so we assume we need a large infusion of cash. The risk is therefore that we will have built a business with more space, more people, more patents, more marketing, and more sales channels than we can sustain with actual revenue.

For most new ventures, bootstrapping is a better fit than outside funding, because of the reduced risk and the obligation of proving the business before a large investment is made. And because of the simple odds against attracting large tranches of institutional investments.

Stuart's Hierarchy of Capital Goodness

Stuart Read, the lead author of the first two editions of this book, has put a lot of thought into the idea that not all money invested into ventures is equal. The source and the related commitments make some types of capital better than others.

Stuart describes it as follows:

> The hierarchy of capital goodness is a rank ordering of the different ways a new venture can receive money. Not every dollar is as valuable as any other dollar. Source matters.
>
> At the top of the hierarchy are paid advance commitments from real customers. It is market confirmation and early revenue which the entrepreneur can use to build the venture. What could be better?
>
> At the bottom of the hierarchy is venture capital. It isn't truly input from the marketplace, and you have to give up equity to someone who is not invested in your success. Moreover, there is a fifty percent chance you will not be CEO a year after you sign the term sheet. Because all term sheets include a board makeup that can allow the board to replace the CEO.

> Clearly there are many other sources of capital, and you could slot them in—or maybe even rearrange some in the middle depending on other factors like (a) who is the partner, (b) does the money come with something else like resources or commitments to using the product, etc.
>
> (*Read*, 2023)

Goodness

- Customer precommitments
- Customer revenue (prepaid)
- Flexible and long payment terms from suppliers
- Grant from a strategic partner
- Small business administration grant
- Loan/lease/long-term quid pro quo deals with partners
- Equity investment from a strategic partner
- Loan from the Small Business Administration (USA)
- Loan from a bank

Not as Good

- Equity investment from angel investors
- Venture capital (in exchange for equity and tough term sheets)

In sum, make a "shopping list" of everything you would buy if you had the money. Then go out and partner with people who have the things you need, in exchange for things other than money.

And even if you do take money from investors, act as though you do not have the money. In other words, continue to bootstrap and partner, even if you have the money.

TAKEAWAY: MAINTAIN CONTROL BY DOING THE MOST WITH THE LEAST

Aspiring entrepreneurs wondering how they'll finance their ventures need to remember that there are countless ways, beyond investment money, to grow a business.

In general, experienced entrepreneurs prefer the cheapest option, so they come up with creative ways of doing things at little cost and risk to themselves. When they do have to seek outside investment, they think carefully about what and whom they need.

Furthermore, it is important to consider that not all money invested into ventures is equal. Commitments that make money redundant, namely, they bring resources that otherwise would need to be purchased with money can be better than money by itself.

By figuring out how to do the most with the least, they are also rewarded with control over their ventures.

So What?

Most startups can find creative ways to avoid external funding. Done right, they retain control and flexibility without betting everything on big predictions.

Think It Through

- What would have happened if Mark and Stacy had chosen different options at each decision point?
- What are the cultural aspects of financing that affect entrepreneurial startups in different communities?

What Now?

For one of your opportunities, before you go looking for money, ask yourself:

- When do you need it?

You probably don't need it all at once. Identify at least three points when you would need a chunk of money. Can you prioritize them? Which point can you reach first for the least resources?

- When does cash flow into this business relative to when you need to pay your largest bills?

Create three ideas for how you can make cash flow in sooner. Create three ideas for how you can delay expenses. Even if it means paying a little extra, or getting a little less, matching ins and outs can be very worthwhile.

REFERENCES

Joyce, J. (1922). *Ulysses*. Shakespeare and Company. https://www.nypl.org/events/exhibitions/galleries/1922-vintage-year/item/14898

Read, S. (2023, July 27). Stuart's Hierarchy of Capital Goodness [Personal communication].

Venkataraman, S. (2002). Ten principles of entrepreneurial creation. *Batten Briefings, 1*(1), 1–5.

Wikipedia. (n.d.). Bootstrapping. Retrieved June 1, 2023, from https://en.wikipedia.org/wiki/Bootstrapping

Wiltbank, R., Dew, N., & Read, S. (2015). Investment and returns in successful entrepreneurial sell-outs. *Journal of Business Venturing Insights, 3*, 16–23. https://doi.org/10.1016/j.jbvi.2015.02.002

CHAPTER 14

Figure 14.1 Textile scraps are stitched together in a co-creative partnership to become a colorful and warm quilt.

The Crazy Quilt Principle

Form Partnerships

In This Chapter

Partners are a source of new means, a source of new ideas, a way of sharing risk, and the people who help you create an opportunity.

How entrepreneurs approach partnerships can be vastly different, depending on the logic employed. In causal logic, the venture's preset goals dictate which partners get targeted. In effectual logic, partners self-select through commitments to co-create the venture in unexpected ways.

DOI: 10.4324/9781003364016-17

ENTREPRENEURS ARE NOT LONE HEROES

Think you can go it alone in starting a business? Think again. We're not saying you must have a co-founder, but you do need other people. More importantly, your business needs other people. In fact, other people—a supplier who can provide raw materials you need, a customer who's interested in what you have to offer, an acquaintance or professional advisors such as lawyers and accountants who introduce you to new potential partners—may end up having a more profound impact on your venture than you'd ever imagine.

We've described how the effectual logic that guides expert entrepreneurs turns traditional causal business logic on its head. This is certainly true when it comes to partnerships. What distinguishes effectual partnerships from causal partnerships is the belief that those who choose to engage with the venture in some way, those who self-select into it by having real skin in the game, ultimately make the venture what it is.

If you start with certain goals in mind, as causal thinkers do, you select partners who help achieve them. *The venture's goals will dictate the partnerships.* This quickly narrows down the world of potential partners.

But if instead you start with a given set of means—who you are, what you know, who you know—and let various ends emerge, *the partnerships create the venture, including its goals and even its markets.* You'll see a partner as someone with another set of means to add to the mix, someone who may end up transforming the venture in a way you could not anticipate. You'll think of a partner not as a partner but as a stakeholder.

The effectual process involves interacting with any and all stakeholders willing to make actual commitments to the project, even though some interactions may result in commitments while others may

Figure 14.2 This image depicts the metaphor of the causal (jigsaw puzzle) and effectual (patchwork quilt) approaches to entrepreneurship. In the middle are hybrid pieces, which is what entrepreneurs do, too, blending approaches to solve problems.

not. This opens up the world of potential partners.

THE PATCHWORK QUILT AND THE PUZZLE

Metaphorically, we contrast effectual and causal approaches using the image of a quilt and a jigsaw puzzle. Making a patchwork quilt differs from putting together a puzzle in at least four ways:

- Unlike the puzzle solver, the quilters determine the pattern. Even when they begin with a basket of random patches, they can choose which patches to use and juxtapose them in a way that is personally pleasing and meaningful. A puzzle can come together in only one way.
- Large quilting projects are usually communal: a good quilter works with others who bring their own baskets of patches along with their tastes and talents. In the process, the quilter must decide who to work with and why, manage various coordination issues, and deal with the unexpected. The puzzle solver may work with others, but this means only that the puzzle may come together more quickly, not that it will be transformed in any way by the contributions of others.
- The uncertainty of what the quilt will look like when it is done is resolved one commitment at a time. Whether it is the quilter deciding alone or a group that decides on a color scheme, a stitch or a border, unlimited possibilities are gradually managed down to a finished result.
- The quilt must be not only pleasing and meaningful, but also useful and valuable—ultimately, its function is to keep people (or pets!) warm or embody their aesthetics. The puzzle just needs to get finished; all the pieces must be in place. The completed picture may be pleasing to look at, but it serves no other purpose.

An effectual logic for building a new firm or a new organization or any type of collaborative institution incorporates similar subjective, intersubjective, and objective elements that make it more analogous to stitching together a patchwork quilt than solving a jigsaw puzzle.

Research Roots

The Intersubjective

For hundreds of years, philosophers have argued about whether we see the world objectively (fact-based and measurable) or subjectively (interpreted or perceived).

But relatively recently, Donald Davidson (2001) proposed a third alternative—that we see the world intersubjectively. What he means by this is that it is nearly impossible to observe anything in isolation and that as human beings we make sense of the world by developing shared understandings.

The concept of the intersubjective acknowledges that we are deeply social beings, and when projected onto the problem of starting new ventures, it explains why partnerships, particularly effectual partnerships, are so important.

By adopting an intersubjective perspective, you can gain a better understanding of the social context in which your business operates and leverage networks and partnerships to co-create value with other stakeholders.

Research Roots

Partnerships and Social Media

Fischer and Reuber (2011) looked at how entrepreneurs use online social media, such as X (formerly Twitter), to connect to stakeholders. What they found is that effectuation is clearly enabled by these new tools and that entrepreneurs use them to develop their businesses.

The primary outcome of using social media was to expand the means an entrepreneur has to work with, but for the tools to be productive, the entrepreneurs had to adopt a community orientation and adhere to community norms.

Later work by Fischer and Reuber (2014) evaluates the role of social media and customer perceptions. They conclude that as much as social media is an important communication channel, ventures that use a "multi-dimensional communicative stream" (in other words, not just rely on social media) are more likely to be able to convince customers of their quality and distinctiveness from the competition.

HOW EFFECTUAL PARTNERSHIPS HAPPEN

Once the entrepreneur has taken stock of her means and affordable loss, she starts to reach out to other people to obtain advice, inputs, knowledge, or help. We term this "the ask" and devote the entire next chapter to it because it is such a central part of effectuation. It is also one of the activities where new entrepreneurs have the most difficulty.

Based on who the entrepreneur knows, potential stakeholders could be friends, family, work colleagues, or random people she meets in daily life. As she finds people who want to participate in the effort to build something (at this point, the "something" may be vague or concrete, but it is always open to discussion), she moves toward obtaining commitments from the people she interacts with.

What counts here is the willingness of stakeholders to commit to the construction process—not their fit or alignment with some preconceived vision or opportunity. Each person who concretely commits something to come on board contributes to shaping the opportunity.

The story of how Anil Parajuli (discussed later in the chapter) blurs the distinction between doctors, tourists, and clients to bring together the stakeholders who run Himalayan Health Care demonstrates the kinds of creative combinations that emerge.

Whatever each stakeholder commits becomes a patch in a growing quilt whose pattern becomes meaningful only through the continual interaction that brings new stakeholders on board. In other words, stakeholders commit resources in exchange for a chance to re-shape the goals of the project and influence the future that will ultimately result.

The process of interacting with stakeholders therefore has two contrasting effects: on the one hand, with each new partner, the means of the venture increase (again, we are not talking only about financial means), enabling new possibilities. On the other hand, as commitments accumulate, the goal of the venture crystallizes, and the direction becomes more specific.

Stakeholder acquisition ends at some point, and there is no more room for negotiating and maneuvering the shape of what will be created. As the structures of the market begin to take visible shape and consistent information becomes available, decision-making naturally shifts from a focus on control and shaping the venture, to one that makes increasing use of prediction in operating the venture.

As we begin to bring this all together, it is useful to see that the interactions between effectual stakeholder partners are based on the other three main principles of effectuation:

- *Available means: Each stakeholder brings new means to the venture.* Each interaction seeks to combine individuals and their various means to create something novel and valuable. In this way, the entrepreneur and the stakeholder select each other.
- *Affordable loss: Each stakeholder strives to invest only what they can afford to lose.* Since it is not clear at the early stages of the effectual process what the pie will be, let alone how much each piece will be worth, stakeholders cannot effectively use expected return as their immediate criterion for deciding what resources to invest. Instead, stakeholders must reconcile within their own minds whether they can live with the loss of what they are contributing to the enterprise. Here, as well, the selection process goes both ways.
- *Surprise: Every interaction contains unexpected contingencies.* If you don't allow contingencies to influence your venture, you end up with purely transactional relationships aimed at reaching a predetermined goal. Although contingencies can undermine the value of current means in achieving given goals, they can also provide opportunities to create new value through those means in pursuit of new goals.

Figure 14.3 contrasts the causal logic approach to partnerships with the effectual approach. Take a moment to think about the various partnerships in your life. Which could be seen as causal partnerships, and which are more effectual in nature? Are some a mix of both?

Why?

	Causal logic	**Effectual logic**
General attitude about others	Competitive (one wins)	Partnership (all win)
Purpose	Benefits from the partnership are greater than the cost and move the venture toward the goal	Co-create with partners to build the future by tapping into shared available means and affordable loss
Source of value	Fair exchange (transactional)	Synergistic increase of value (relationship)

Where to?

	Causal logic	**Effectual logic**
Pathway	The pathway is strictly determined by the goals	The pathway taken is a result of coalescing between committed partners

Who?

	Causal logic	Effectual logic
Partner selection	Carefully chosen to meet goals	Self-selecting (accepting of those who show up and commit)
Selection criteria	Seek partners which meet specific criteria related to goals	Seek diversity of available means and affordable loss
Who determines what?	The venture determines which partners are needed	The partners determine what the shared venture becomes
The role of customers	Despite the importance of customers for the viability of the venture, they are in a category (and hence have specific rules) separate to partners	The idea of customers potentially becoming partners is embraced
Timing	Partners are brought in when needed as dictated by the plan	Partners are brought in from the beginning with the idea that they will help shape the pathway
Variability of partners	The partners vary according to role and timing needed to reach the goal	The team of partners is kept together through shared meaningful purpose and values
Connection of partners to markets	Partnerships are based on and limited to relevance to the planned target markets	More strategic partnerships expand the potential markets for the venture

How?

	Causal logic	Effectual logic
Relationship type	Transaction-focused: exchange based on mutual agreement	Relationship-focused: investment in longer-term benefits for all
Rewards	Seek to retain as much as possible for "my team"	Seek to increase shared benefits for all stakeholders
Focus	On the goal	On the shared journey
Resource commitment by partners	As required to meet goals	Based on what partners are willing to risk (affordable loss)
Extent of participation	Partners are only expected to bring in the expertise for which they were selected	Partners and the perspective they bring into the venture provide additional means with which to address surprises
Dependency	Causal logic is effect-dependent: people are brought in to produce the prescribed effect	Effectual logic is people-dependent: self-selecting stakeholders determine what effect is produced
Basis for trust	Trust is managed through contracts to limit opportunistic behavior of others	Trust is built through making and keeping incremental commitments to the shared journey
Skills required of the entrepreneur	Systematic project management approach	Ability to unlock power of diversity, cultural intelligence, bridge-building
Risk mitigation	Risk mitigation is performed for the venture as a whole; partners are generally seen both as a risk source and solution	Through additional available means and affordable loss, partners provide a highly effective way of mitigating risks

How many/how much?

	Causal logic	Effectual logic
Number of partners	Only those who are considered necessary	Flexible and open
Resources	Common view is that maintaining partnerships can use resources beyond the transactional price paid for goods and services exchanged	Partners bring additional resources (available means) to contribute to reaching shared goals
Participation level and timing	Partners are only called in for the part and time of the plan where they are required.	Always present: interaction between partners and action taken enable creation and constant adjustment of short-term plans

What if?

	Causal logic	Effectual logic
Rewards/gains	As much as possible are retained	Rewards are shared among partners
Perception of uncertainty	Uncertainty is "managed" by planning the timing of involvement of partners	Pre-commitments based on available means and within affordable loss by partners reduce uncertainty
Cost of failure	The cost of failures is generally borne mostly by the venture, its founders, and shareholders	The cost of failures is generally shared among partners who committed their available means within their affordable loss
How failures affect relationship	Shared failures are likely to weaken the relationship with partners	Shared failures are likely to strengthen the relationship with partners

Figure 14.3

Adapted from Sarasvathy (2001, 2009); Read and Sarasvathy (2005); Sarasvathy and Dew (2008); Venkataraman et al. (2012).

If your takeaway from reading this chapter so far is that effectual partnerships encourage you and your venture to go in directions you couldn't have possibly imagined when you started, that's good. Effectuation does not seek to find a single optimal solution. Instead, you and your partners create a new venture that is the result of sufficient conditions as opposed to necessary conditions—one that is the right venture for all of you.

Research Roots

Markets Are Co-Created

Explanations for how markets come into existence cover the entire field of social studies from psychology and sociology to economics and marketing. However, none of these fields agree or offer a comprehensive explanation for the generation of new markets.

Research Roots *(continued)*

In the field of marketing, some researchers have started to adopt the view we use in this book, which is that markets are co-created by supplier and consumer interactions. Vargo and Lusch (2004, pp. 1–17) propose that in developed economies most markets are for services, not products, and that products be viewed as valuable for the services they provide.

In either case, the value of the services provided is realized by customers interacting with the service. The ultimate point at which value is created is when customers interact with a service. Therefore, there is no such thing as firms creating value without interaction with customers. Markets have two active sides to them: they are co-created.

More recent work by Vargo et al. (2023) has evolved to recognize the complexity and emergent nature of some core marketing theories, including markets. Astutely, they summarize the uncertainty this complexity creates as follows:

> That is, they arise, often unpredictably, from interactions within complex and dynamic contexts.

This speaks to the nature of co-creation involving diverse stakeholders: it is dynamic, unpredictable, and inherently unique.

Practically Speaking

Co-Creation Quilt of COVID-19 Vaccines

Spinning Threads of Innovation

In a world struck by a health crisis, the story of COVID-19 vaccines stands out as a vibrant quilt of technologies, people, and organizations, stitched together through global cooperation. Much of the fabric had been woven previously, but required individuals to come together to stitch up solutions and co-create a protective quilt that blankets humanity with hope and health.

Historical Warp: A Different Needle

The fabric of today's vaccine technology is dyed deep with scientific advancements, starting in 1796, when Edward Jenner developed the first successful vaccine by inoculating a young boy with cowpox, which provided immunity against the deadly smallpox virus.

In the nineteenth century, Louis Pasteur made significant contributions by developing vaccines against rabies (1885) and anthrax (1881), using weakened forms of the pathogens. The cholera vaccine was introduced in 1896.

Practically Speaking *(continued)*

The twentieth century saw rapid progress with the development of vaccines against diseases like tuberculosis (BCG vaccine in 1927), diphtheria (1926), tetanus (1938), and the combined DTP vaccine in 1948. Another breakthrough was the polio vaccine, developed by Jonas Salk in 1955.

In the latter half of the twentieth century, vaccines were developed for measles (1963), mumps (1967), rubella (1969), hepatitis B (1981), chickenpox (1996), and rotavirus (1998–1999). The smallpox vaccine led to the declaration of global eradication of the disease in 1980.

The Modern Weft: Spinning Speed With mRNA

Enter the modern era, and the threads take on a new synthetic blend with mRNA technology. Previously on the fringe of vaccine research, mRNA became the golden fiber in the COVID-19 vaccine fabric due to its rapid adaptability and production scalability. Companies like Moderna and Pfizer, in partnership with BioNTech, spun this once-obscure thread into the frontline defense against the pandemic, showcasing how quickly new materials could be woven into public health armor.

Co-Creation in the Loom: Global Collaboration

The loom of COVID-19 vaccine development and distribution was grand, with thousands of weavers co-creating as part of a global ensemble of scientists, healthcare professionals, and government officials. Each brought their thread—be it funding, expertise, or infrastructure—to the table, or rather, to the loom. This collaboration saw unprecedented speeds in vaccine trials, approvals, and rollouts, demonstrating the power of pulling together various strands in parallel toward a common goal.

Knots and Challenges: The Human Factor

In crafting the global quilt of COVID-19 vaccine distribution, the most persistent and intricate knots were not of technical fabric, but rather spun from human threads. These challenges wove a complex pattern of disbelief, mistrust, misunderstandings, greed, and power dynamics, highlighting that the path to widespread vaccine adoption is as much about navigating human nature as it is about scientific innovation.

The rapid development of vaccines, while a scientific marvel, also sowed seeds of skepticism. For many, the accelerated timeline raised questions rather than providing reassurance, leading to a fabric frayed by vaccine hesitancy. This hesitancy was not just a minor snag but a significant hurdle that health campaigns had to creatively and continuously address.

Information—or the lack thereof—can create tangled webs in public perception. Misinformation regarding vaccine safety and efficacy circulated as quickly as the virus itself, creating a tangle which health professionals worked endlessly to address. These efforts were crucial in reweaving trust into the community fabric, ensuring that the public received and understood accurate information.

The vaccine rollout also highlighted the uneven threads of global health equity. Wealthier nations secured large quantities of vaccine doses, leaving lower-income countries with sparse coverage. This disparity showed how greed and geopolitical power could skew the distribution pattern, emphasizing the need for stronger international frameworks to distribute health resources more equitably.

Practically Speaking *(continued)*

The Fragile Weave of Progress

The journey to vaccinate the world is one of co-creation, where every thread and every piece of material count and the human element plays the pivotal role of stitching them together. While the science of vaccination is a thread spun from robust, reliable material, its acceptance and implementation are still delicately woven through the unpredictable and often resistant fabric of human behavior and societal structures. As this tapestry continues to unfold, it serves as a reminder that in the global effort to combat health crises, the needles of technology must be threaded with the equally strong fibers of trust, understanding, and equity.

To learn more, visit: https://effectuation.org/EE3/vaccine or scan Figure 14.4.

Figure 14.4

BI-DIRECTIONAL PERSUASION

Working in an uncertain environment, with a product or service that is yet to be defined, you must be persuasive— and be willing to be persuaded. Being persuasive does not mean that you must be a sales shark. And being willing to be persuaded does not mean that you should be wishy-washy, vague, or opinion-free.

What we do mean is that if you can't convince anyone to work and create with you—be it potential customers, suppliers, etc.—then you have no business. Being persuadable so you can co-create with others is important as well.

In short: interaction between stakeholders creates. And co-creates.

Practically Speaking

A Mountain of Partners

It seems so straightforward. Companies generate revenue and—ideally—return a profit to their owners. Charities, by contrast, do not generate revenue, and certainly not profit. But enter the creative entrepreneur. The term is actually a combination of two words: in French, "entre" means between and "preneur" means taker. Which makes an entrepreneur literally someone who takes from between.

Steep Trail

On a trek in the mountainous country of Nepal, Anil Parajuli met porters from the northern Dhading district. The porters asked for medicine to take back to their village. Curious, Parajuli undertook his first medical assessment trek in 1991. That experience clarified the need to bring medical expertise to the villages of Nepal.

Parajuli then talked with a friend in New York who offered to establish a non-profit and solicit funds in America. He met doctors who, despite visiting Nepal on vacation, were willing to offer their expertise to locals needing medical attention. Pharmaceutical firms with medication to donate found their way to him. And, gradually, an entity that is known today as Himalayan Health Care (HHC) emerged.

Practically Speaking *(continued)*

Collaborative Cure

The model for HHC reflects its partners. Parajuli runs "medical treks" that bring foreign doctors into remote villages to treat the sick, train local healthcare workers, and build awareness about the needs of his country. And generate revenue. If you are a doctor with itchy travel feet and want to perform medicine "in the wild," the rate is about 1,800 British pounds for a two-week trek (you pay for airfare, plasters for blisters, and any other personal expenses).

Self-Selection

Parajuli offers us a unique insight into how entrepreneurs can do so much with what seems like so little. They are not only unconcerned by artificial distinctions, but encourage the people around them to help create opportunities that bridge those distinctions. By letting a volunteer self-select into also being a paying customer, letting a trekker also share her medical expertise, Parajuli opens up the range of people, time, and money resources available to him and his healthcare initiative.

Distinguished Entrepreneur

Parajuli has been leading HHC for over 30 years, building an impressive portfolio of projects with the HHC team. The statistics around people supported and funds raised are as dizzying as the high altitudes of the surrounding mountains, so here's a list of some of their major projects from their 2021 annual report:

Figure 14.5

- COVID-19 Relief for Villages
- Gynecological Training for Village Midwives
- Ilam Hospital Project
- Sanitation Project "One Home One Toilet"
- Nutrition Project
- Village School Program
- Village Income Generation Programs
- JeevanKala (Art for Life)
- Vegetable Farming for Food Security During the Pandemic and Beyond
- Women's Empowerment Through Organic Farming in Rural Nepal
- Young Women's Organic Farming in Rural Nepal

Most importantly, HHC has connected numerous people, organizations, and volunteers to serve the people of Nepal. Customers? Partners? Creators of a venture? Yes.

To learn more, visit: https://effectuation.org/EE3/himalaya or scan Figure 14.6.

Figure 14.6

CREATING MARKETS THROUGH PARTNERSHIPS

Effectuation emphasizes commitments from stakeholders as a way to manage, reduce, and/or eliminate uncertainty in the environment. Each committed stakeholder expands the means available to the venture, making the venture more viable. And each committed stakeholder steers the concept of the venture to one that more people support—increasing the likelihood that the idea is viable.

Partners can come in different shapes and forms—what matters is that they commit to a future in which they all find a stake, and they influence one another's ideas about what shape that venture should take. In an effectual partnership, what matters is that all parties find something in it for them. But the result created is something new for both parties, something beneficial to both, and something neither could have created on their own.

Getting started on building a stakeholder commitment could be the hardest part. Once the conversation has begun, the possibilities begin to unfold.

Practically Speaking

Chobani: A Simple Pot of Yogurt Changes Lives

From the Taurus Mountains to Northern New York State

Hamdi Ulukaya doesn't know his exact birthdate. He was born during a mountain trek as one of seven children in a semi-nomadic ethnic Kurdish family in the Taurus Mountains of eastern Türkiye. His life today, as extremely successful founder of a billion US dollar dairy company based in the United States of America, is a stark contrast to his youth.

But it was Ulukaya's formative years that provided him with the available means to navigate his way in a foreign country and build a successful venture on the effectual foundations of forming partnerships of all types.

Broken English, Broken Factory

Belonging to an ethnic minority, Ulukaya feared persecution for being politically outspoken, so migrated to the United States. He arrived in New York with broken English and just enough money to get started. Later he opened a small cheese shop in the Kurdish tradition.

When a flyer advertising a former yogurt factory came across his desk, he almost threw it away. After touring the lifeless factory (and against the advice of advisors), he took the plunge, purchasing the factory with government loans and grant funding.

Today, the company Ulukaya built (Chobani, which means "shepherd") is a billion-dollar food company that employs over 2,000 people and is one of the fastest-growing food companies of the last decade.

From Ruminants and Rumi to Resettlement and Riches

You might be asking how it is possible for a new arrival from a very different background to be so wildly successful in one of the most competitive consumer markets in the world. And a consumer market unfamiliar with non-sweetened strained yogurt.

Practically Speaking *(continued)*

Like so many "overnight successes," Ulukaya's success comes not just from years of hard work. Ulukaya's formative years in a semi-nomadic family and as a disadvantaged minority created a deep sense of human values, including empathy and other skills to facilitate co-creation with diverse and, in some cases, marginalized communities. In Ulukaya's words from the 2023 interview with Adam Grant: "It had a profound impact on my life. And I carry all those things. The way that people interacted with each other, the worries, how they solved their issues, the life without material things."

An Employer of Choice—Particularly Refugees

Chobani has implemented groundbreaking profit-sharing and parental leave programs for employees, assisting in efforts to attract a diverse workforce and supporting local communities. Ulukaya shared his intentions in a 2023 interview with Adam Grant:

> And we put that in there in day one. And it was going to be a story of everyone. It was gonna be a story of this town, this old factory, the farmers, and it was gonna be a story of another way of conducting business. Maybe you can't change the world with cup of yogurt, but how you make it might.
>
> (*Ulukaya*, 2023)

Ulukaya's personal experience as a Kurdish refugee has shaped his commitment to reducing inequality and improving the lives of refugees and by seeking out refugees to hire, citing them as model employees. In 2015, Ulukaya established new initiatives for improving the lives of the more than 25 million people living as refugees around the world. He believes that refugees can be a solution, not a problem, and that they can help build stronger communities and create economic growth. He has taken a leadership role in the global business community, urging the private sector to do their part in giving refugees employment opportunities.

The Payoff of Diversity: Innovation

Ulukaya's actions demonstrate an understanding that diversity enables innovation and strengthens partnerships. The highly diverse team at Chobani spans all continents and brings new perspectives and ideas to all areas of the company, including product development, enabling the company to create unique products that resonate with customers.

Saying No and Ruffling Feathers

Partnerships are not just about harmony, particularly when you seek to be a values-driven entrepreneur. In fact, it can mean having to say no. This is what Ulukaya told PepsiCo when they wanted to invest in Chobani. He didn't want to compromise the independence of the company, which is not surprising for a Kurdish nomad!

Standing for your values might ruffle feathers and create conflict. Ulukaya's outspoken support for refugees has drawn considerable ire from opponents. He has stood by his values, however, and has even taken legal action against those who have spread false information about his company.

Partners Can Become Family

In late 2023, one of Ulukaya's many partnerships became family when Chobani acquired La Colombe Coffee Roasters, which has done for bottled cold coffee what Chobani has done for strained yogurt in market demand.

Practically Speaking *(continued)*

The relationship began in 2012, when Chobani opened its first branded café in New York City and was looking for a coffee supplier. Being in the neighborhood, literally steps away, La Colombe was the obvious choice. Despite being a tea drinker, Ulukaya fell in love with their coffee and their dedication to quality.

When La Colombe raised capital from a private equity firm, Ulukaya reportedly became concerned that "something very beautiful was about to be ruined for the sake of making profits" (Rainey, 2023) and bought a controlling share of La Colombe.

The relationship has blossomed over the years, with Ulukaya mentoring the growing company with this vision: "What I think we can do is appeal to a large number of people like me who think they don't like coffee—until they taste this one" (Rainey, 2023).

Beyond the clear person-to-person synergies, the move makes manufacturing sense, with great similarities between yogurt and milk coffee processing.

Hamdi Ulukaya's success is a story of effectual entrepreneurship, particularly in his demonstrated ability to co-create with a wide diversity of partners, and his latest move with La Colombe demonstrates how a partner has influenced the direction of Chobani.

To learn more, visit: https://effectuation.org/EE3/chobani or scan Figure 14.7.

Figure 14.7

Figure 14.8 This image of a smiling boss eating yogurt surrounded by happy employees imagines Hamdi Ulukaya celebrating with his team.

Practically Speaking

Mater Iniciativa—Cooking Up the Ecosystem

Anybody can cook food. And Michelin-star chefs can cook up tasty dreams, and gastronomic adventures. Virgilio Martínez Véliz, founder of Central Restaurante in Lima, Peru goes further: "At Central we cook ecosystems."

Quilt Weaver

And it is not only in his restaurant that he cooks them up. He does so through a variety of partnerships across the globe, partnering with Orient Express Hotels, a hospitality and leisure company that operates luxury hotels, train services, and river cruises worldwide, and XCaret Group, a leader in sustainable and socially responsible tourist recreation in Mexico. Martinez's *Lima* restaurants have spread to at least two other continents with multiple locations in London and Dubai.

Practically Speaking *(continued)*

Local Looms

However, the chef's heart is in his home in Peru, where he co-founded Mater Iniciativa, an interdisciplinary team of professionals dedicated to exploring Peru's diverse ecosystems in search of rare and unique ingredients by collaborating with local communities. Mater's outputs extend beyond food to span art, culture, communication, kitchen design, and culinary education and experimentations. In 2018 Martínez opened a laboratory in the middle of the Andes to work with local families to catalog different crops.

By partnering with local farmers, biologists, anthropologists, and other professionals, Martínez has fostered a collaborative environment that drives innovation and discovery, that celebrate Peru's rich biodiversity in a country known for its melting pot of cuisines—Japanese, Creole, and Chifa (Chinese-Peruvian).

Attention to Detail

Yet, these chefs are not afraid to embrace ingredients that are hard to obtain from remote and often difficult-to-access locations. With over 4,000 varieties of potatoes in Peru, some of them are grown at heights of 5,000 meters above sea level. Martínez along with wife Pia Leon and her sister Malena have embraced these obstacles as opportunities to learn and grow. By adapting to the unpredictable nature of their work, they bring us a combined understanding of Peru with an attention to detail reminiscent of unfailing meditators.

Figure 14.9

These chefs urge us to experience even the simplest of ingredients in the most mindful way, single-source salt, for example. As Maris Beck reports in *The Age* (2013):

> In Martinez's restaurant, waiters grate salt at the table like cheese, scratch, chip or break rocks, serve seafood on blocks of salt calculated to lend the exact amount of sodium to the food. Chefs infuse salt with lime, use salts in desserts, cook in salt crust, or make "tiger's milk" to cook vegetables in.

When we think of celebrity chefs, we envision lone artists, dictatorial tyrants ruling their kitchens. But sometimes, as we saw in the case of Claus Meyer, co-founder of Noma (Chapter 10), chefs can be effectual entrepreneurs, stitching together crazy quilts of entire ecosystems.

To learn more, visit: https://effectuation.org/EE3/mater or scan Figure 14.10.

Figure 14.10

Practically Speaking

Virtual John: Till Death Do Us Part? Not!

You might think you have heard it all, but how about co-creation from the grave? How is this even possible? Doesn't co-creation require consent?

Getting to Yes From Beyond

Paul McCartney, one of two living members of the rock band The Beatles, shares his approach to getting consent to include deceased band member John Lennon in a new recording:

> Is it something we shouldn't do? Every time I thought like that I thought, wait a minute. Let's say I had a chance to ask John, "Hey John, would you like us to finish this last song of yours?" I'm telling you, I know the answer would've been "yeah!" He would've loved that.
>
> (*The Beatles*, 2023)

Co-creators and partners, such as The Beatles, produce a great amount of work, some of which is published, recorded, and sold. Much of it, however, just goes into storage, often forgotten, sometimes making it into the hands of collectors or museum curators.

From an effectual logic standpoint, all this is available means, ready to be dusted off and used in creating something new.

Free Birds in Hand

John Lennon recorded the song "Now and Then" on a demonstration cassette tape in the late 1970s after the band had broken up and before his death in 1980. But it was rejected as "rubbish" by George Harrison, fellow band member (Pareles, 2023).

As part of the re-release of new editions of the group's famous "Red" and "Blue" albums in the mid-1990s, the three surviving band members unsuccessfully attempted to resurrect "Now and Then." They were successful, however, in re-mixing and including another "song from the grave," namely, "Free as a Bird."

It was only recently that, with improvements in artificial intelligence technology, the now two remaining members of The Beatles, Paul McCartney and Ringo Starr, were able to stitch together a virtual version of John Lennon.

Quilting Out of This World

Sean Lennon, John's son, agrees with the virtual quilt (The Beatles, 2023):

> My dad would've loved that, because he was never shy to experiment with recording technology.
>
> It's the last song that my dad, and Paul, and George, and Ringo will get to make together.

Practically Speaking *(continued)*

As for the original band member, Paul McCartney is thrilled to thread through his memories:

> All of those memories come flooding back. My god, how lucky was I to have those men in my life and to work with those men so intimately and to come up with such a body of music. To still be working on Beatles' music in 2023: Wow!
>
> (*The Beatles*, 2023)

The world is ready for YOUR re-mix. What do you have lying around in your attic? Get quilting!

To learn more, visit: https://effectuation.org/EE3/virtualjohn or scan Figure 14.11.

Figure 14.11

Practically Speaking

A Messy Collaboration

When was the last time you enjoyed a glass of orange juice from a Tetra Pak carton? Made from a mix of plastic, paper, and aluminum, those containers do a great job of keeping beverages fresh. They're also likely to end up as non-biodegradable waste that burdens landfills, costs money, and puts the squeeze on the environment.

Natural Solution

You may be thinking this story is about recycling used cartons, and perhaps making a business of it. But it's not. That has already been done. Across Europe, the system for collecting and recycling cartons is well developed. Every year, around 25 billion containers end up at recycling plants, where the paper fiber is extracted and remanufactured into new packaging such as cereal boxes.

Residual Problem

Which is terrific … as far as the paper portion of your drink carton is concerned. But what about the plastic and the aluminum? You're not likely to see those in a cereal box. The reason is that the gooey muck left over from the paper part of the recycling process gets dumped into landfills. For a large recycler such as Stora Enso in Barcelona, that means 30,000 tons a year of sludge, costing about 1.3 million British pounds to "tip" into the Earth. Messy.

Residual Opportunity

Unless you are Hans Cool or Gijs Jansen, that is. Where we see mess, they see potential in extracting value from the plastic/aluminum soup left over from Tetra Pak recycling. After talking about this potential in an MBA class, their classmates introduced the pair to Carlos Ludlow-Palafox, a PhD in chemical engineering from Cambridge University working on pyrolysis, a process that gasifies plastic.

Practically Speaking *(continued)*

The partners formed Alucha, a company whose name combines the word aluminum with the Spanish verb "luchar," meaning to struggle. The next step was to manage the struggle by engaging as many committed partners as possible.

Partner Soup

Cool and Jansen's first stop was Stora Enso in Barcelona. After hearing their idea of converting sludge into value, the manager of the recycling mill walked the pair out to a shuttered building in the compound and showed them a dormant machine—a previous attempt at a system for processing plastic/aluminum waste. Could they use the space to try again with different technology?

Cool and Jansen then met with the German aluminum processor Konzelmann. Would they be interested in the grade of aluminum Alucha could extract from packaging? In Austria, the pair talked with GE Jenbacher, maker of generators that run on specialized gas. Might they be interested in co-developing machinery that would burn the gas that results from extracting plastic waste from aluminum waste? As the yeses mounted up, the struggle turned into a business.

Clean Evidence

Since starting in 2004, Cool and Jansen, together with their partners, have faced technical, regulatory and operational struggles—truly earning the core of the firm's name: "luchar."After starting on IESE Business School campus in Barcelona, with funding from the European Union, the firm opened the first plant to recycle plastic-aluminum waste from beverage cartons in the world.

The efforts of the Alucha Team have not gone unnoticed, earning them a special certificate of recognition at the 2015 European Paper Recycling Awards for their development work on paper recycling. In 2019, for their circular solutions efforts, Alucha won AkzoNobel's Paint the Future award.

From the grunge of entrepreneurial struggle, they show us how partners combine to form the glamour of an entrepreneurial venture that creates both profit today and a cleaner environment tomorrow.

To learn more, visit: https://effectuation.org/EE3/alucha or scan Figure 14.12.

Figure 14.12

TAKEAWAY: BUY-IN IS BETTER THAN SELLIN'

We close this chapter with a practical answer to the philosophical question of how you think about the effectual interaction. The answer is simply that buy-in is better than sellin'. In other words, effectual interaction crystalizes with commitment. While it is positive that someone is willing to make a transaction with you, what you really want is a concrete and rational commitment to co-creating an idea with you.

■ ■ ■

So What?

Partners self-select into new ventures and commit different means to the effort. *Without commitments, you don't have a partner; you merely have a potential partner.* Committed stakeholders co-create ventures that don't always look like the original venture you had in mind. You influence them, and they influence you.

Think It Through

- How does viewing everyone as persuadable change your view of the world?
- When "co-creating" an opportunity … who is the entrepreneur? Why?

What Now?

Time for some personal reflection:

- Are you persuadable, willing to reshape your venture with partners in order to gain their commitment to it?
- What are you unwilling to change? Why?
- What potential partners would like to see you succeed? Why?
- How, specifically, will you know if potential partners are actually committed to the relationship in some way?
- Now … go and talk with potential partners. What would it take for them to commit to working with you?

REFERENCES

The Beatles. (2023, November 2). *The Beatles—Now and Then—The last Beatles song* (Short Film). https://www.youtube.com/watch?v=APJAQoSCwuA

Beck, M. (2013, March 9). Gourmet chefs prescribe a single-origin dose of salts. *The Age*. https://www.theage.com.au/national/victoria/gourmet-chefs-prescribe-a-single-origin-dose-of-salts-20130309-2fso8.html

Businessworthy. (2019a, May 9). Hamdi Ulukaya—2019 Oslo Business for Peace Award honouree. https://www.youtube.com/watch?v=D-tCAzezC6g

Businessworthy. (2019b, July 10). Extended interview: Hamdi Ulukaya. https://www.youtube.com/watch?v=QNpvDOoglu0

Chobani. (2017, November 22). Chobani: Embracing cultures. https://www.youtube.com/watch?v=9UUivLyxGNQ

CNN Business. (2015, September 21). Greek yogurt billionaire fills his plants with refugees. https://www.youtube.com/watch?v=44rA8zME8mo

Davidson, D. (2001). *Subjective, Intersubjective, Objective* (Vol. 3). Oxford University Press.

Fischer, E., & Reuber, R. (2011). Social interaction via new social media: (How) can interactions on Twitter affect effectual thinking and behavior? *Journal of Business Venturing*, *26*(1), 1–18.

Fischer, E., & Reuber, R. (2014). Online entrepreneurial communication: Mitigating uncertainty and increasing differentiation via Twitter. *Journal of Business Venturing*, *29*(4), 565–583. https://doi.org/10.1016/j.jbusvent.2014.02.004

Global Citizen. (2019, December 21). Hamdi Ulukaya, Global Citizen Prize Business Leader winner. https://www.youtube.com/watch?v=ZkJ2omMNyOk

History of Vaccines. (n.d.). Vaccine timeline. Retrieved May 22, 2024, from https://historyofvaccines.org/history/vaccine-timeline/overview

Mashed. (2018, August 29). The untold truth of Chobani. https://www.youtube.com/watch?v=dPCZY6nTOWY

Mater Iniciativa. (n.d.). Retrieved December 1, 2023, from https://materiniciativa.com/

Pareles, J. (2023, November 2). The Beatles' "Now and Then": A glimpse of past greatness. *The New York Times*. https://www.nytimes.com/2023/11/02/arts/music/beatles-now-and-then-last-song.html

PBS NewsHour. (2019, June 17). Chobani CEO Hamdi Ulukaya on how businesses can step up for refugees. https://www.youtube.com/watch?v=etGSEIj1Sc0

Plotkin, S. (2014). History of vaccination. *Proceedings of the National Academy of Sciences of the United States of America*, *111*(34), 12283–12287. https://doi.org/10.1073/pnas.1400472111

Rainey, C. (2023, December 15). Chobani buys La Colombe for $900 million (exclusive). *Fast Company*. https://www.fastcompany.com/90997061/chobani-buys-la-colombe-900-million-hamdi-ulukaya-keurig-coffee

Read, S., & Sarasvathy, S. D. (2005). Knowing what to do and doing what you know: Effectuation as a form of entrepreneurial expertise. *The Journal of Private Equity*, *9*(1), 45–62.

Reuters. (2016, June 2). Yogurt maker Chobani rejects PepsiCo's offer for stake in company. https://www.reuters.com/article/business/yogurt-maker-chobani-rejects-pepsicos-offer-for-stake-in-company-idUSKCN0VF028/

Sarasvathy, S. (2001). Causation and effectuation: Toward a theoretical shift from economic inevitability to entrepreneurial contingency. *Academy of Management Review*, *26*(2), 243–263. https://doi.org/10.5465/amr.2001.4378020

Sarasvathy, S. (2005). What makes entrepreneurs entrepreneurial? [Unpublished manuscript].

Sarasvathy, S. (2009). *Effectuation: Elements of Entrepreneurial Expertise*. Edward Elgar Publishing.

Sarasvathy, S., & Dew, N. (2008). Effectuation and over-trust: Debating Goel and Karri. *Entrepreneurship Theory and Practice*, *32*(4), 727–737. https://doi.org/10.1111/j.1540-6520.2008.00250.x

Skoll.org. (2019, October 22). Every single person adds up and becomes something. https://www.youtube.com/watch?v=_sIabCA9QLI

Ulukaya, H. (2023, June 20). "The anti-CEO playbook" with Chobani founder Hamdi Ulukaya (A. Grant, Interviewer). https://www.ted.com/podcasts/rethinking-with-adam-grant/anti-ceo-playbook-with-chobani-founder-hamdi-ulukaya-transcript

Vargo, S. L., & Lusch, R. F. (2004). Evolving to a new dominant logic for marketing. *Journal of Marketing*, *68*(1), 1–17. https://doi.org/10.1509/jmkg.68.1.1.24036

Vargo, S. L., Peters, L., Kjellberg, H., Koskela-Huotari, K., Nenonen, S., Polese, F., Sarno, D., & Vaughan, C. (2023). Emergence in marketing: An institutional and ecosystem framework. *Journal of the Academy of Marketing Science*, *51*(1), 2–22. https://doi.org/10.1007/s11747-022-00849-8

Venkataraman, S., Sarasvathy, S. D., Dew, N., & Forster, W. R. (2012). Reflections on the 2010 AMR Decade Award: Whither the promise? Moving forward with entrepreneurship as a science of the artificial. *The Academy of Management Review*, *37*(1), 21–33. https://doi.org/10.5465/amr.2011.0079

Washington Post Live. (2023, March 14). Chobani CEO on entrepreneurship, immigration and the state of the American Dream. https://www.youtube.com/watch?v=w0JgLNtjsKo

WHO (n.d.). A brief history of vaccination. Retrieved May 22, 2024, from https://www.who.int/news-room/spotlight/history-of-vaccination/a-brief-history-of-vaccination

Wikipedia. (2023). Hamdi Ulukaya. https://en.wikipedia.org/w/index.php?title=Hamdi_Ulukaya&oldid=1166628652

Figure 15.1 Asking to put skin in the game is key in taking part in a team huddle.

CHAPTER 15

Asking Potential Partners to Make Commitments

In This Chapter

Effectual entrepreneurship is less about selling a vision, which is a one-sided exchange, and more about co-creating a vision with others, thus building a mutually beneficial partnership. As such, the effectual ask is a fundamental tool of expert entrepreneurs.

An effectual ask is not selling; its purpose is to get others to co-create with you. This can mean gaining and making commitments to a game that wasn't envisioned at the outset.

The technology entrepreneur Steve Jobs was very skilled at using the effectual ask as a way of taking action: "Most people never pick up the phone and call. Most people never ask. And that's what sometimes separates people who do things from the people who just dream about them."

DOI: 10.4324/9781003364016-18

ASKING: ONE OF THE FIRST ACTIONS

An entrepreneur's first steps with a new idea, the first things she does in taking her idea for a test drive in the real world, almost always involve a partner—someone, as we saw in Chapter 14, who makes a commitment, large or small, to join the entrepreneur in shaping her venture.

How do these partnerships come to be? How does an entrepreneur turn a disinterested bystander into a true stakeholder?

By asking.

Consider the last time you asked someone for something—a date, a favor, some tangible or intangible resource. Chances are you were a bit uncomfortable. Maybe you didn't know how to begin or how to handle the conversation or how to recover from a no.

Many of us cringe at the thought of such situations, while others, especially expert entrepreneurs, become very adept in them. They are not only comfortable asking people for things, but also asking in ways that lead to productive relationships.

Instead of focusing solely on their own immediate need—the thing they're asking for—they continually seek common ground, inviting the other person to ask for what they want. They take the occasion to learn about the other person—how their means and level of affordable loss might dovetail with their own—so they can co-create the future. In short, they look for ways to turn the person they are interacting with into a stakeholder of some kind.

Entrepreneurs are famously fond of taking action rather than planning and cogitating.

Effectuation, the approach we've observed among expert entrepreneurs, is in part a mindset, a way of viewing opportunity and uncertainty. But, ultimately, it's a series of actions.

Asking is one of the very first actions, one of the first things you can do to practice effectuation. And you never stop asking as you grow your ventures and become an expert entrepreneur yourself. Asking—for advice, for help with an idea, for resources, for introductions to other people, for money—is so central to effectual entrepreneurship that we decided to give it a fancy name: "the ask."

Asking should not be a mystery. Each of us likely started asking for all sorts of things from a very young age, yet most of us have probably not mastered the art of "the ask." We can, but first we must learn what "the ask" is—and what it is not. Then we can set out to master the effectual ask.

ASKING IS NOT SELLING

In the popular imagination, entrepreneurs are the consummate salespeople. They are individuals with a compelling vision, who have the communication skills and forceful personalities that get other people to "buy" into their ideas. As we discussed earlier, however, entrepreneurship is less about selling a vision, which is a one-sided exchange, and more about co-creating a vision with others, building a mutually beneficial partnership.

Yet, as we saw in Chapter 14, although you do not need to be an exceptional salesperson to be an entrepreneur, you do need to understand something about the mutual art of persuasion. You need to know how you might persuade others to join you in your adventure. And, just as important, you need to be persuadable yourself.

You must know how to communicate what is most compelling and interesting about your initial idea, but then be open—eager even—to incorporating other people's means and affordable loss, to let other people transform your project and even your vision. It is through such openness to co-creation that entrepreneurs create value. And it is through asking that fruitful partnerships are born.

Causal versus Effectual Ask

To understand the difference between selling and asking, consider the difference between a traditional causal approach and an effectual approach. A causal approach is about gathering the specific means you need to reach a predetermined goal.

Effectuation, in contrast, is about working with a set of evolving means and seeing where you end up. Both approaches require asking for things, but in very different ways.

The causal ask is like a traditional sales pitch:

- You develop a vision.
- You figure out the resources you need to achieve that vision.
- You identify the individuals or organizations who can provide those resources.
- You craft a pitch that can induce them to give you what you want.
- You deliver the pitch, and you either get the resources you're looking for—or you don't.

The effectual ask is the start of a conversation. Your ask may be a "pitch" of some sort, but ultimately you want to get others to give you their pitch in return:

- You decide what you can start doing based on your means and your level of affordable loss.
- You identify individuals and organizations who may be interested in co-creating the future with you. They may be potential customers or suppliers, or they may just be interesting and talented people whose possible role in the new venture is entirely unclear at the start.
- You craft a variety of asks.
- You deliver "the asks" and ask your discussion partner to do the same.
- Through the ensuing dialog, you might end up with commitments—of talent, money, ideas, time—from new stakeholders, whose means may transform your idea. Those stakeholders may then bring on yet other people, who, in turn, will shape the project with their means.

No Failure Approach

Whereas the causal pitch can succeed or fail—you either get what you're asking for or you don't—the effectual ask is flexible enough to not really fail. And unlike the traditional sales pitch, it's not necessarily a one-time thing; you can go back to the same person multiple times with different kinds of asks.

Maybe in an initial conversation you find a person who really likes your idea and is willing to help design an offering. Having established a relationship, you can make follow-on asks, such as asking if she can introduce you to potential customers.

At the end of an effectual ask, you've "sold" yourself as someone others want to collaborate with. But you've probably been doing less talking—especially the sort associated with aggressive selling—and more listening, learning about what potential stakeholders have to offer, *their* visions of your idea, and what they are willing to commit to make those happen.

Be Ready for Surprises

Outcomes of the effectual ask go beyond what you set out to ask for. In fact, the outcome usually is one that neither party to "the ask" may have had in mind at the beginning of the conversation.

One example is when someone changes roles. Your landlord may become your customer. Your customer may become your investor. The company next door may become your provider of internet access or manufacturing capacity.

The effectual ask almost guarantees surprises. After all, you can't know what the other person will say or what their circumstances are. They might respond to your ask with an ask of their own—maybe related to their own passion or a career change they are considering.

Just as they have ideas and resources that they did not realize were valuable to you until you came along and asked for them, you might have something to offer them that you had never dreamed would be valuable for them. The goal of "the ask" is to get others to put skin in the game. You may end up gaining and making commitments to a game you never could have envisioned at the outset.

> Back in the 1790s Adam Smith (1798, pp. 493–494) wrote:
>
> > Different genius is not the foundation of this disposition to barter which is the cause of the division of labor. The real foundation of it is that principle to persuade which so much prevails in human nature … We ought then to mainly cultivate the power of persuasion, and indeed, we do so without intending it. Since the whole life is spent in the exercise of it, a ready method of bargaining with each other must undoubtedly be attained.

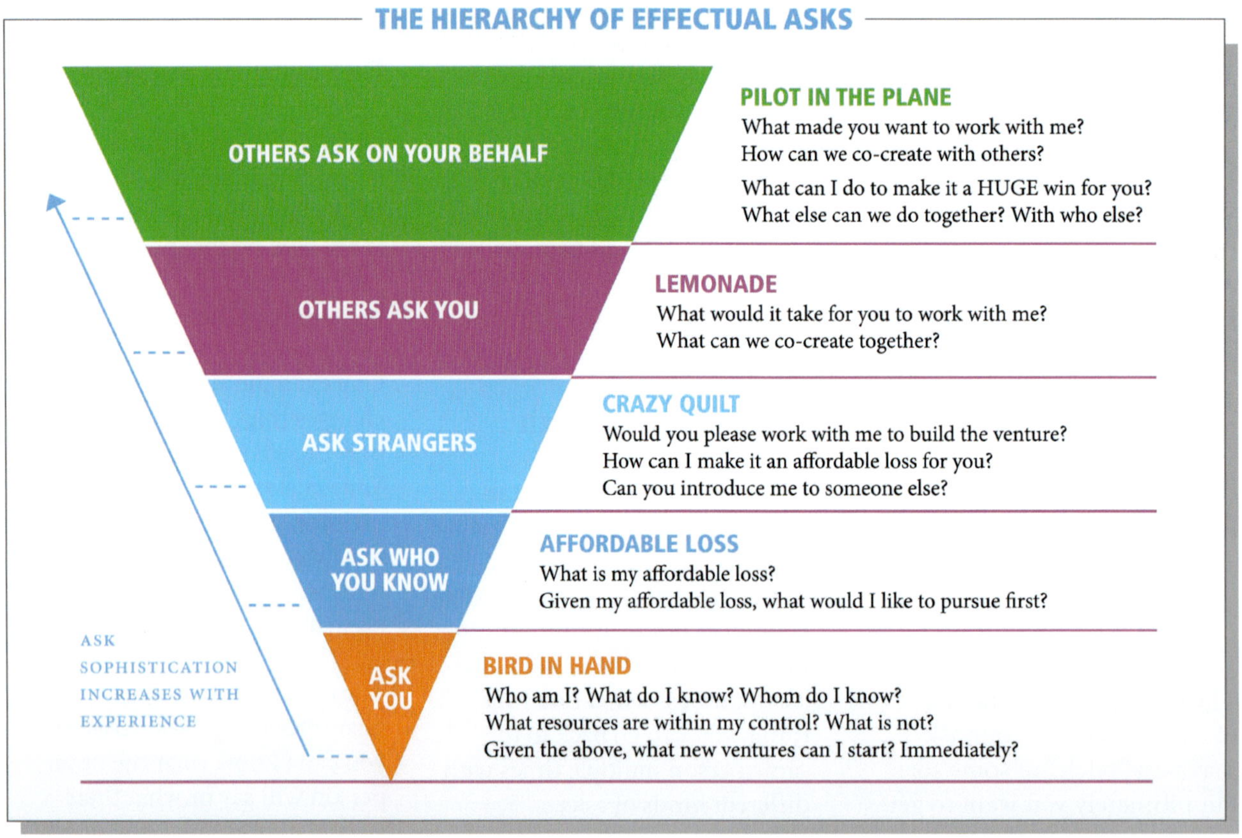

Figure 15.2

THE HIERARCHY OF ASKS

The effectual process begins when entrepreneurs ask themselves what means they have at their disposal and what they're willing to put at risk: "What do I know?" "What do I know that might not appear on my resume?" "Who do I know?" "What can I afford to lose?"

They then turn to potential partners—generally people they know—asking for advice, feedback, assistance of various kinds. These asks give the other person an opportunity to discuss his or her ideas and aspirations. Along the way, the other person may end up asking you for something, asking you to make some sort of commitment. This is how the crazy quilt of committed partners is pieced together.

Ultimately, as your network of committed stakeholders expands, others may make asks on your behalf—a sign of true commitment and partnership in a venture.

BARRIERS TO ASKING

Asking is not necessarily easy. It does not come naturally to many of us. Numerous obstacles—some internal, some external—make it difficult to approach other people for assistance. Here are some of the doubts, insecurities, nagging impressions, and fears that make it easy to procrastinate or not go ahead. If you're aware of them, it's easier to overcome them.

- **Asking will make me seem weak.** It's true: in a culture that values independence and self-reliance, asking for anything—even for directions when you're lost—can be seen as a weakness, an admission that you can't do it all on your own. But the simple truth is that we can't do it all on our own, and why would we want to? As the quote from Steve Jobs at the beginning of this chapter shows, the expert entrepreneurs we've studied understand that they need other people's ideas, insights, expertise, contacts, and other resources to create value. They are comfortable admitting what they don't know and don't have. That understanding is not a weakness but one of their greatest strengths.
- **Asking will make me seem pushy.** What to some people seems pushy will seem brave or creative to others, especially when you ask for permission to pester without being a pest. Most people usually find humor in such candor and are likely to tell you how much "pestering" they are willing to tolerate. The great thing about asking is that you don't necessarily have just one shot at it. If you sense that they are put off or offended by your request, you can step back and engage in a more open-ended conversation about their interests and goals. Ultimately, they may end up asking you for something.
- **How can I ask for something when I have nothing to give in return?** Try to let the other person be the judge of that. You may think you have nothing to offer, but you aren't in the other person's head, so you don't know how they will respond. We know an MBA student who summoned the courage to contact a prominent professional for advice about breaking into his industry. She got his advice, but she also ended up agreeing to help his niece navigate the business-school application process.

She could never have guessed at the beginning of "the ask" that she did have something of value to him. It was "the ask" itself that led to her learning that. The effectual ask is not necessarily a quid pro quo situation, but approaching each interaction openly and truly engaging with the other person will often lead you down unexpected paths and present opportunities for mutual benefit.
Even if the other person is simply generous and you

currently have nothing to offer them in return, it does not mean you cannot return the favor in the future. Or pay it forward to another entrepreneur.

- **I'm afraid the person will say no.** If the answer is no, don't lose heart. Instead, change direction. Rather than ask a yes or no question, try asking open-ended questions that invite conversation and draw on the person's imagination: "How might we be able to work together?" "What would it take to persuade you to collaborate with me?" It's also important to recognize the difference between a flat-out no and a "No, but …" as in "No, I cannot help you with that, but I know someone who might be able to" or "No, I am not particularly interested in that idea, but here's what I am interested in." Sometimes a valuable yes may be hiding within a no.

- **I'm afraid the person will say yes!** If a conversation with a potential stakeholder seems to be heading toward some sort of commitment, even a small one, you are deep into the effectual process. Congratulations! But of course, your work is not over—it is probably just beginning, and it's natural to feel a bit nervous. You will now need to honor this budding partnership by following through on shared commitments and staying open to surprises.

BECOMING AN EXPERT ASKER

The best way to get better at asking and to overcome any fear or anxiety surrounding "the ask" is to practice asking. You can practice asking even if you're not actively building a business. Try to find opportunities in your daily life (asking someone to join you on a fun project or to contribute time and money to a worthy cause) or do a practice run with a friend. Here are some tips to keep in mind as you master the art of "the ask":

- **Tailor a narrative.** Try to create a story that connects your interest with the individual in front of you. That story should be geared toward your possible overlapping interests, but broad enough to let them determine how they might become your collaborator. In creating this story, consider why this person is willing to talk to you in the first place and how their experience aligns with your interests.
- **Start specific.** Go into the conversation with a concrete ask in mind (e.g. for an investment, mentorship, introduction to other people), but keep a mental list of backup asks. Maybe the person doesn't have the time or interest to be an active mentor but would be delighted to introduce you to some of their colleagues. Don't focus so much on what you think you want that you don't hear what the other person is offering.
- **Be a good listener.** Sure, you'll need to do some talking, but the listening is just as, if not more, important. To be truly open to what another person has to offer, you must listen with your full attention.
- **Don't expect a linear path.** It's usually not as simple as asking for something, getting it, going away until the next need arises, and then asking for that next thing. You must allow your vision to be co-opted and be receptive to the other person's vision and means. Remember, it's about building relationships with committed stakeholders, not about getting what you think you need at a given moment.
- **Develop a repertoire of open-ended questions.** "What would you think of …?" "What would it take for you to …?" "How could we work together to …?" "Could you tell me how to …?" "Can you think of a way we could …?" "What do you think is the best way to …?"
- **Set the tone—and then follow through.** Let the other person know at the outset the sort of

conversation you'd like to have: "I'd love to be able to tell you a bit about my idea, and I'd be interested to hear about what you've been working on." And then make sure you live up to that promise.

- **Be open to more than money.** You may think that what you really need is money. But, in fact, you probably need money to buy something, and it may be easier for someone to give you that something than to give you money. For example, after a successful entrepreneur gave a presentation in one of our classes, two of the students asked him to invest in their venture. They needed money, they explained, to fly around the world to promote their idea. Instead of writing a check, the entrepreneur offered the students his many (unused) frequent flyer miles.
- **Think about the exit.** Ideally, the person you're speaking with will make some sort of commitment to your venture. If not, that's okay. Remember that asking is an iterative process. You can end the conversation by asking if it would be possible to talk again in the future (at which point you'd make a different ask) or if the person can suggest someone else you could talk to.

TAKEAWAY: IT'S ABOUT BUILDING, NOT GETTING

Ask and you shall receive? Yes, but what you receive might be something you had not anticipated. The goal of the kind of asking effectual entrepreneurs isn't receiving per se but building by integrating others' means and aspirations with their own and seeing where that leads.

With this in mind, it's time to update the old axiom to something more effectual:

Ask and you shall learn,
Ask and you shall co-create,
Ask and you shall open doors,
and ...
Practice and you shall learn how to ask.

Practically Speaking

Market Queens of Ghana

Co-Creator: Kwabena Obiri Yeboah

When was the last time you went to an open-air, farmers' or crafts market? Did you notice something about the people who seemed to have the most customers swarming around their stand and selling the most goods? Was there a lot of buzz in the air? Probably it was the drone of asking—sellers questioning customers about their needs.

There is definitely a buzz around the markets in Ghana, and it comes from the "Market Queens," the name given to the women who run most of produce markets there (O'Neill, 2016).

Queens Start Small

Despite the grand name, a Market Queen has humble beginnings: like the produce cultivated by farmers, the skills of communication and asking are nurtured within the family, with girls learning from their mothers and grandmothers how to forage for information to understand their future customers.

Practically Speaking *(continued)*

Once it is time to move from their family home, the young women equipped with new skills and a first basket of produce—a type of initial investment from the family—start small: just a simple table at the big, buzzing market. Here they practice the ask with potential customers, gradually increasing their confidence and profits.

Asking is the way these princesses eventually build the relationships that make them queens.

Royal Influence

This might seem like an everyday story, and it is. Yet Market Queens are a significant force in Ghana and have been studied extensively. According to Hendriks (2017), women entrepreneurs in Ghana are more likely to start businesses than men, and they hold a dominant position in markets in Ghana. Despite facing numerous gender-related challenges, these women traders have emerged as influential leaders in the economy. They control the supply side and advocate for their members during negotiations.

Asking to Thrive

Market Queens are also "Ask Drones." In other words, they collaborate with other businesses and organizations, pooling their resources and expertise—just as bees do in a thriving hive. They support each other within their respective commodity groups, helping one another to sell their goods and sharing supplies where necessary.

This co-creative approach can serve as a means of empowerment for women traders, allowing them to achieve greater success in their respective commodity groups. They represent the interest of the members at both local and, in some cases, political levels.

Some Market Queens act as agents for farmers and, in some cases, supply farmers with inputs needed during the farming season—making them sometimes sole buyers of certain farm produce.

Waggle Dance

Just as bees communicate through the waggle dance, Market Queens make their voices heard in a number of ways—building and joining voluntary associations, weaving together significant influence (Asomani-Boateng, 2016). While women in the Ghanaian market strive to build economic power through these organizations, structuring them to work well is not straightforward.

Some Queens abuse power (Katila, 1997; Banful, 1998), while others create conflicts among some stakeholders. However, Scheiterle and Birner (2023) found that a democratic approach to the appointment of the Queens and lack of proof of market manipulation indicate that, overall, Market Queens truly use their power for the betterment of the ecosystem.

Figure 15.3

Practically Speaking *(continued)*

To Compete or Collude: That Is the Question

Economics teaches that the market is all about competition. However, expert entrepreneurs, just like the Market Queens, learn to collaborate and co-create, as much as to compete when needed. Even when the venture grows large and successful, coopetition remains a powerful strategy in the marketplace.

As you start out building your venture, consider: who are the current and potential competitors you can effectually ask to co-create with you?

To learn more, visit: https://effectuation.org/EE3/queens or scan Figure 15.4.

Figure 15.4

Research Roots

Coopetition: Asking Your Competitor to Cooperate

The concept of coopetition involves simultaneous cooperation and competition among firms and is described as an entrepreneurial process that involves risk-taking, exploring and exploiting opportunities, and developing innovative solutions under conditions of uncertainty.

Traditionally, coopetition has been studied from perspectives such as game theory, resource-based views, and network positions. However, recent research, including the work by Galkina and Lundgren-Henriksson (2017), highlights the dynamic and emergent nature of coopetition, aligning it closely with the principles of effectuation.

Case Study: Finnish Media Companies

Galkina and Lundgren-Henriksson conducted a longitudinal case study of three Finnish media companies that engaged in coopetitive relationships. The study revealed that these companies used both effectual and causal logic at different stages of their cooperation.

Initially, based on existing resources and capabilities, the firms took an effectual approach, exploring potential synergies and collaborations without fixed goals. As the coopetition matured and certain outcomes became clearer, they shifted toward more goal-oriented strategies, demonstrating the interplay between effectual and causal logics.

Implications for Entrepreneurial Engagement

Entrepreneurs using effectual logic are more likely to engage in cooperative strategies with competitors, seeing them as partners who can provide complementary resources and capabilities. This approach fosters an environment where trust and mutual benefit are prioritized over strict competitive advantage based on the following conditions:

- Flexibility in partnerships: entrepreneurs employing effectual logic are open to adapting their strategies based on evolving circumstances and the emerging nature of coopetitive relationships to take advantage of unexpected opportunities and respond to changes collaboratively.

Research Roots *(continued)*

- Shared risk and innovation: by cooperating with competitors, entrepreneurs can share the risks associated with innovation and new ventures and leverage collective strengths and resources to achieve mutual benefits.
- Network building: effectual logic emphasizes the importance of building networks and leveraging partnerships. Entrepreneurs who adopt this approach are more likely to create and maintain diverse networks that include competitors, enhancing their ability to innovate and adapt in a rapidly changing market.

Research Roots

The Psychology of Influence

In his bestseller *Influence: The Psychology of Persuasion* (2006), Robert Cialdini looks at what he calls "weapons of influence." We summarize them here.

- *Social proof.* Human beings imitate each other.
- *Authority.* People tend to obey authority.
- *Liking.* People are more likely to be persuaded if they like the person doing the persuading.
- *Scarcity.* Perceived scarcity creates demand.
- *Reciprocation.* If someone does you a favor, you tend to return it.
- *Commitment and consistency.* Once a person has committed, they tend not to back out.

These insights can be applied equally well to "the ask" as they can to more transactional sales kinds of interactions.

Practically Speaking

Gardener's Eden: Is a Cost Always a Cost?

As an executive at diversified mail order retailer Avion Group, Ruth Owades saw an opportunity in the amateur horticulturalist segment, a group that was easy to reach, was extremely loyal if well served, and, most important, had a pressing need: these consumers did not have easy access to specialty gardening equipment.

Ruth proposed the idea of building a mail order business around this need to executives at Avion, but they had no interest. Her next step was to ask if she could develop it on her own. Surprisingly, they agreed.

Practically Speaking *(continued)*

After a brief investigation, Ruth, who had never worked outside the comfortable confines of the corporate world, discovered that investment money for an unproven entrepreneur with an unproven idea was not exactly forthcoming. Ruth's best offer came from a group of four private investors, who were asking for 49% of the company and would require Ruth to provide 25% of the money for the venture from her own bank account. Determined to make it work without the investors' money, she plunged into business, naming her venture Gardener's Eden.

Planting the Seeds

Ruth's first stop was the printer. For a mail order company, the single largest expense is printing and mailing the catalog—this item can account for up to half of the total costs. Ruth needed both a fantastic print job and good financial terms—two elements that are usually mutually exclusive.

So she proposed a scheme in which the printers would bid on her first two catalogs rather than just her first one. This showed the printers that she was willing to make a commitment to them, in exchange for favorable treatment. Her suggestion—a novel one in the industry—was well received. Then, when she went in again and said, "Gee, the other printers are offering me 90-day terms. Can't we do better than that?" The printer gave her six months to pay.

Gardener's Eden needed more than catalogs, however. Ruth asked her utility providers for long credit terms, so she did not have to tie up her cash with deposits for electricity and telephones. She asked for long credit windows with the manufacturers of the exotic gardening items she intended to sell.

She asked both her landlord and her credit card company for unusually low terms and got them. She even pursued her local post office branch, visiting the postmaster again and again until he found a forgotten regulation that enabled her to collect her daily mail without any service charge.

Ruth's strategy was simple: figure out who would benefit from her success, tell them the story about what she was trying to accomplish, and explain to them why they were essential to the venture and how they would be successful when she was.

She asked everyone for everything she needed and found she could do much better than she might have expected. Without using the terminology, she was successfully applying "the ask" and affordable loss to her venture, finding creative ways to reduce her startup costs so she could reduce her risk to only what she could afford to lose. Table 15.1 compares what her costs would have been (using a pitch) versus what they ended up being in the first six months.

Watching Them Grow

Ultimately, Ruth built an environment where everyone around her had a reason to do something special to make her successful, an environment where she had transformed suppliers to the venture into partners with the venture.

Figure 15.5

Practically Speaking *(continued)*

How well did that work for her? Ruth's revenue well exceeded 1 million US dollars when stylish retailer Williams-Sonoma acquired Gardener's Eden less than four years after its launch.

Table 15.1 Ruth Owades' capital expenditures (first six months)

Startup expense item	**Using the pitch** In US dollars	**Using "the ask"** In US dollars
Catalog printing and mailing	100,000	Negotiated for two catalogs and six-month payment terms
Mailing list access	30,800	30,800
Payment for merchandise	75,600	Negotiated long credit windows
Miscellaneous utility and other deposits	4,000	Negotiated no deposit
Other working capital, e.g. mailing supplies, employees, rent	15,000	15,000
TOTAL	**225,400**	**45,800**

To learn more, visit: https://effectuation.org/EE3/eden or scan Figure 15.6.

Figure 15.6

Research Roots

Advice, Decision-Making, Experts, and Social Influencers

Asking for advice is a way entrepreneurs can receive support (or even commitment) from potential stakeholders. Think about your own experience: Who do you turn to for advice and do you follow the advice you are given?

Simple Word-of-Mouth Advice

Economics Professor Andrew Schotter (2003) wrote "Experimental results … indicate that word-of-mouth advice is a very powerful force in shaping the decisions that people make."

In addition, Schotter found:

- Subjects tended to follow the advice of advisors with hardly more expertise at the task than the subject, and this led to better decisions than acting alone.

Research Roots *(continued)*

- Advice does change behavior: subjects played games differently after receiving advice.
- Given a choice between information and advice, subjects tended to opt for advice.
- The process of giving and taking advice tended to foster learning because people tend to give good advice to others, but not necessarily follow it themselves.

Advice Is Now More Complicated

In the meantime, more work has been published on the topic, some of which reflects changes in society, technology, and the view of experts. Consider these two recent papers, which might help explain why people you know are more likely to accept the advice of their neighbor than the advice of a subject expert.

"Errors of Experts": Zhang et al. (2022)

Simply put, the authors postulate that the knowledge and expertise of experts can actually be a barrier to providing advice. They describe how "cognitive entrenchment and reduced perspective taking" makes it difficult for the expert to provide appropriate advice to someone unfamiliar with their field.

You might have experienced this in the classroom: the famous professor, a global leader in their field holding a lecture in front of hundreds of first semester students—all either scratching their heads or sleeping for lack of understanding and engagement.

Intimate Details and Trust: Leite and Baptista (2022)

On the other end of the spectrum, we have the relatively new appearance of social media influencers, some of whom have had significant financial success through endorsing brands, which can be seen as sharing advice.

Leite and Baptista demonstrated in their work how "intimate self-disclosure" of social media influencers builds relationships and creates trust, which then results in increasing the consumer's intention to purchase. In other words, including product placements in "juicy" personal stories can result in greater sales for advertisers.

What Motivation Is Behind the Advice?

Connecting these two results is fascinating: on one hand, we have the assumed well-meaning (but not relatable) expert not convincing the public, and on the other hand, we have the same public accepting purchase advice mainly because they feel the social influencer is relatable: "just like me," although they benefit from advice.

Unfortunately, buyer's remorse (regretting having taken action based on incorrect/inappropriate information) is a clear risk in both situations.

Research Roots

Yes Is Closer Than You Think

Social psychology researchers studied asking for favors from people. For example, in a series of six studies, Francis Flynn and Vanessa Lake (2008) asked students at Columbia University to go out and ask for help from the public.

The tasks included asking people to fill out questionnaires, asking for the use of another person's mobile phone, asking people for directions, etc. One of the studies also examined people in a real situation, asking donors for money for a non-profit organization.

In each study, before they embarked on asking for favors, the subjects were asked to estimate the likelihood of success. For example, they were asked about the time and effort it would take, or the number of people they would have to ask before someone would do them the favor they were asking for.

In all the studies, people overestimated the difficulty of getting other people to do them a favor. In other words, more people are more willing to help than most people believed at the outset.

More recent work by Bohns and Flynn (2021) looked at the effect of empathy and found that empathetic askers tend to have higher expectations that their request will be fulfilled. So, if you don't consider yourself to be particularly empathetic, consider practicing this skill as it could help you not only elicit relevant information about others, but also increase your expectations of being successful in asking.

While we are looking at improving your chances of getting a yes, it is also important what medium (in-person, phone, videocall, email, etc.) you use.

Building on their previous work (2017) indicating that in-person requests are more effective than email, Roghanizad and Bohns (2021) investigated the effectiveness of what they call "richer media channels incorporating audio and video features."

The result? Participants overestimated the effectiveness of requests via richer media channels compared to text requests. More importantly, they underestimated the relative advantage of making requests in person.

What does this mean for you? Depending on the relationship, the circumstances, and your available means, consider switching off the webcam and email and investing in the effort to ask in person.

Figure 15.7

To learn more, visit: https://effectuation.org/EE3/yes or scan Figure 15.7.

Practically Speaking

Asking for Change: From Llanos to AltiPlano

Co-Creator: Patricia Cabero Tapia

As an energetic and ambitious student at the Universidad Mayor de San Andres in Bolivia, Willmar Pimentel wondered if the content of his information technology (IT) courses was keeping pace with the quickly evolving international standard.

Setting Sights Higher

Willmar found the curriculum was stuck, as it were, in the slow-moving tropical lowlands (llanos) of his native Bolivia while the rest of the world was speeding along at 3,500 meters altitude on the high plateau (altiplano). Was he the only one wanting more, wanting change?

Digging around, Willmar came upon the International Collegiate Programming Contest (ICPC):

> The International Collegiate Programming Contest is an algorithmic programming contest for college students. Teams of three, representing their university, work to solve the most real-world problems, fostering collaboration, creativity, innovation, and the ability to perform under pressure. Through training and competition, teams challenge each other to raise the bar on the possible. Quite simply, it is the oldest, largest, and most prestigious programming contest in the world.
>
> (ICPC, n.d.)

Two things became immediately clear to Willmar: the heat of competition would be an ideal way to develop and test their IT skills, and he would need to get many other students interested.

Rippling Asks—All the Way to Chile

Willmar transformed his excitement into a series of asks, rippling like stones dropping onto the glass-like surface of Lake Titicaca, the world's highest navigable lake.

His first ask was of Professor Jorge Teran: would he support a student-led campaign to participate in a regional ICPC competition? Professor Teran was happy to help. Willmar then asked other students to join in organizing internal programming contests.

The initial asks woven together through intense coding work into a growing organization resulted in Willmar traveling with fellow student Alberto Suxo to the 2004 regional ICPC competition in Chile as the sole Bolivian team. Willmar was beginning to soar off the lowlands.

Asking Their Way to the World Finals

Even as Willmar and Augusto were on their way, they realized that he couldn't show up to ICPC World Finals (the "programming Olympics") as a single person or a single team. Hence, Willmar traveled to Brazil to ask the ICPC Regional Coordinator for permission to host the next regional competition in Bolivia.

Practically Speaking *(continued)*

Willmar was asked something, too: He was asked to guarantee that at least 15 student teams from eight different Bolivian universities would participate. And so an ask became a relationship. Willmar agreed and returned home with Bolivia as the designated host for the next ICPC regional round.

That meant asking his askees back home to ask some more. In response, Professor Teran asked other professors to join the ICPC, and together they asked students to sign up, and began working together to prepare them for the competition.

Their co-creative efforts paid off. In 2006, the first regional Bolivian ICPC round brought together 25 student teams from 14 universities from six cities.

Almost There …

Next came the task of building an ongoing structure to train students and organize preparatory and rotating competitions hosted by local universities. The IT professors at these universities therefore asked their deans and program directors for support. The professors also asked the community for sponsors.

Rippling out from Willmar, Alberto, and Professor Teran, many professors and former competitors joined to serve as coaches, judges, and organizers of programming camps.

Figure 15.8

Altiplano at Last

By 2010 Bolivia sent its first team to the ICPC World Round. In the meantime, ICPC programs can be found throughout Bolivia, with participating students developing world-class skills.

Willmar went on to establish the Bolivia Tech Hub Collaborative in 2014, and in 2020, became a member of the Committee for the Promotion of Technological Creativity and Innovation for the Bolivian Ministry of Education.

The ask ripples Willmar set off have reshaped not only the curriculum, but the entire technology ecosystem in Bolivia!

To learn more, visit: https://effectuation.org/EE3/icpc or scan Figure 15.9.

Figure 15.9

So What?

Partners can only select into new ventures when asked. In the early stages of your efforts, open-ended conversations are about building partnerships, not just getting what you want. Help others see what you see, LISTEN to what they want to be a part of, influence each other, and ask for action that seems mutually beneficial. Practice. It's not just selling, it's building.

What Now?

- Are you comfortable with making "the ask"? Are you good at it? Spend some time considering when/where/how you do well asking for advice/money/ideas/introductions.
- For an opportunity you are developing:
  - Consider some things you imagine you need, who might you ask for them? Now step up your game: how might you build a conversation with them that goes beyond just asking for a yes/no for things you need?
  - Consider the "whom you know" of your means ... reach out to some people; develop three different possibilities of how to ask them to engage with you.
  - What "ask" are you most nervous to make? Why? Don't hide from it. Develop your next three ideas for building your way toward that ask.

Think It Through

- Without "asking" how else can a venture proceed?
- How do you know when you should make an effectual ask and when you should make a causal ask?
- How could you build partnerships that can explore both kinds? Or must they be mutually exclusive?

REFERENCES

Asomani-Boateng, R. (2016). Local networks: Commodity queens and the management of organic solid waste in indigenous open-air markets in Accra, Ghana. *Journal of Planning Education and Research*, *36*(2), 182–194. https://doi.org/10.1177/0739456X15604445

Banful, B. (1998). Production of plantain, an economic prospect for food security in Ghana. Bananas and Food Security. Proceedings of an International Symposium Held in Douala, Cameroon, 10–14.

Bohns, V. (2021). *You Have More Influence Than You Think*. WW Norton & Company.

Bohns, V. K., & Flynn, F. J. (2021). Empathy and expectations of others' willingness to help. *Personality and Individual Differences*, *168*, 110368. https://doi.org/10.1016/j.paid.2020.110368

Çelen, B., Kariv, S., & Schotter, A. (2010). An experimental test of advice and social learning. *Management Science*, *56*(10), 1687–1701. https://doi.org/10.1287/mnsc.1100.1228

Cialdini, R. B. (2006). *Influence: The Psychology of Persuasion*. Harper.

Flynn, F. J., & Lake, V. K. (2008). If you need help, just ask: Underestimating compliance with direct requests for help. *Journal of Personality and Social Psychology*, *95*(1), 128.

Fréchette, G. R., Schotter, A., & Trevino, I. (2017). Personality, information acquisition, and choice under uncertainty: An experimental study. *Economic Inquiry*, *55*(3), 1468–1488. https://doi.org/10.1111/ecin.12438

Galkina, T., & Lundgren-Henriksson, E. (2017). Coopetition as an entrepreneurial process: Interplay of causation and effectuation. *Industrial Marketing Management*, *67*, 158–173. https://doi.org/10.1016/J.INDMARMAN.2017.09.004.

Hendriks, T. (2017). Collaboration and competition: Market queens, trade unions and collective action of informal workers in Ghana's Makola market. *Interface: A Journal for and About Social Movements*, *9*(2), 162–187.

ICPC. (n.d.). Retrieved December 28, 2023, from https://icpc.global/static/media/mainLogoMobile.12b91576.png

Katila, S. (1997). Between democracy and dictatorship: The Market Queen institution of Ghanian daily markets. *De Gruyter Studies in Organization*, 269–288.

Leite, F. P., & Baptista, P. de P. (2022). The effects of social media influencers' self-disclosure on behavioral intentions: The role of source credibility, parasocial relationships, and brand trust. *Journal of Marketing Theory and Practice*, *30*(3), 295–311. https://doi.org/10.1080/10696679.2021.1935275

Nyarko, Y., Schotter, A., & Sopher, B. (2006). On the informational content of advice: A theoretical and experimental study. *Economic Theory*, *29*(2), 433–452. https://doi.org/10.1007/s00199-005-0037-7

O'Neill, M. (2016, August 12). In Ghana, women and "Market Queens" dominate the economy. *Vice*. https://www.vice.com/en/article/bjggyd/in-ghana-women-and-market-queens-dominate-the-economy

Roghanizad, M. M., & Bohns, V. K. (2017). Ask in person: You're less persuasive than you think over email. *Journal of Experimental Social Psychology*, *69*, 223–226. https://doi.org/10.1016/j.jesp.2016.10.002

Roghanizad, M. M., & Bohns, V. K. (2021). Should I ask over Zoom, phone, email, or in-person? Communication channel and predicted versus actual compliance. *Social Psychological and Personality Science*, *13*(7), 1163–1172. https://doi.org/10.1177/19485506211063259

Scheiterle, L., & Birner, R. (2023). The myth of the Market Queens: A case study of women and power in Ghanaian markets. *Global Food Security*, *38*, 100703.

Schotter, A. (2003). Decision making with naive advice. *American Economic Review*, *93*(2), 196–201. https://doi.org/10.1257/000282803321947047

Silicon Valley Historical Association. (2011, November 1). Steve Jobs on failure. https://www.youtube.com/watch?v=zkTf0LmDqKI

Smith, A. (1798). *Lectures on Jurisprudence*. Oxford University Press.

Zhang, T., Harrington, K. B., & Sherf, E. N. (2022). The errors of experts: When expertise hinders effective provision and seeking of advice and feedback. *Current Opinion in Psychology*, *43*, 91–95. https://doi.org/10.1016/j.copsyc.2021.06.011

CHAPTER 16

Figure 16.1

The Lemonade Principle

Leverage Surprise

In This Chapter

There is no question about whether the unexpected will present itself in the new venture creation process. The question is when and whether you will take advantage of it.

Many entrepreneurs have "survival" stories that illustrate how even unfortunate contingencies are not only survivable in the short run but can also become springboards for new business opportunities that can be shaped into long-term success.

Effectual entrepreneurs understand what the novelist G. B. Stern meant: "Both optimists and pessimists contribute to our society. The optimist invents the airplane. The pessimist invents the parachute."

DOI: 10.4324/9781003364016-19

WHEN LIFE GIVES YOU LEMONS …

As we will see in the story of ICEHOTEL (Chapter 17), contingencies can mark important turning points for a venture. In the case of ICEHOTEL, rain on ice sculptures was an unpleasant surprise. It wasn't what was meant to happen.

But the ICEHOTEL story illustrates that surprises—even negative ones—can be leveraged in positive ways. Instead of fighting the rain, Yngve Bergqvist did something a little less obvious: in his words, he "invented a new feeling." Rather than trying to preserve something against the forces of nature, he leveraged the natural process, letting the sculptures be destroyed and making something new in their place.

This response epitomizes the lemonade principle, named for the phrase, "When life gives you lemons, make lemonade." It's the idea that in entrepreneurship, as well as in other areas of life, you can often do well by acknowledging and accepting the accidental events, meetings, and information that the environment serves up.

Traditional models suggest the entrepreneurs should envision where they want to go, set goals, and do extensive planning to reach them before venturing into a new business. Although these activities offer some benefits, it is easy to overlook the costs. Rigid plans tend to frame surprises as problems, and so you try to overcome them, as you would any obstacle. But in the meantime, you are missing out on the upside opportunity that surprises—even negative ones—can represent.

Instead of looking at the unexpected as a problem, it can be looked at as a new building block—a resource—for a young enterprise.

> A pessimist sees the difficulty in every opportunity.
> An optimist sees the opportunity in every difficulty.
> *Winston Churchill,*
> former Prime Minister of the United Kingdom

SURPRISES CAN BE VALUABLE

Some of the building blocks might only become obvious once the entrepreneur sets about building the venture. By considering how a surprise might provide a new opportunity, expert entrepreneurs exercise control over the unexpected.

In many ways, the lemonade principle lies at the heart of entrepreneurial expertise. It says that the unexpected is not a cost but a resource that, in the right hands, may become something valuable.

Surprises may be few or many, come early or take their time, and be good or bad. But whatever form they take, whenever they come along, and however frequently they occur, they can be used as inputs into new ventures. Entrepreneurs can't predict surprises (contingencies), and they can't design them, but they can try to exploit them by building their venture to use them.

UNDERSTANDING DIFFERENT KINDS OF CONTINGENCIES

In general, a contingency can be thought of as something that is a mere possibility, something that may or may not happen. Contingencies are, therefore, unnecessary; they are not a logical requirement. Instead, they fall into the realm of pure chance, something that happens without a specific known cause.

But these chance events come in many shapes and sizes, so it is helpful to have a rudimentary way of categorizing them. For instance, though the stories in this chapter are all instances of contingency, in fact they are examples of three very different kinds.

Unexpected People

One category of contingency is accidental interactions with other people. Either you might meet a particular person by pure chance, or the content of your interaction with someone is unexpected and perhaps feels a bit random.

Both kinds of contingency are at work in the encounter between Katalin Karikó and Drew Weissman, who met by chance at the photocopier and struck up a conversation. Neither could have imagined that would be the beginning of a long cooperation which would lead to them being awarded the Nobel Prize in 2023. Research in entrepreneurship suggests that meetings like the one between Karikó and Weissman are far more common than you might think.

Practically Speaking

Persistent Play: Katalin Karikó

Question: what do you do when everything in your venture seems to fail or fall flat?

Answer: you keep doing the doable until a stakeholder self-selects and invests some real skin in the game.

If you think effectual action cannot win you a Nobel prize, think again. Or, better still, ask Katalin Karikó.

First Love

Karikó began work on "Messenger RNA" in her early 20s in a doctoral program in Hungary. At the time, nobody knew whether this research would be of any value, so much so that the project ran out of funding. As Karikó explains: "The Nobel Prize winner who got it for RNA acknowledges that he never thought that RNA will be ever be a medicine" (Karikó, 2021).

Karikó packed up her life (including her husband and daughter) and moved to the United States. Things did not get any easier. After a difficult start and low-level positions to make ends meet, Karikó found work with scientists to synthesize mRNA, insert it into a cell, getting it to follow the instructions set out by the mRNA.

Star Crossed

The success was short-lived. Karikó's scientific sponsor (and source of grant money) left the project. A new sponsor (with funds) she managed to find also moved on. Numerous grant applications and discussions with potential collaborators seemed to lead nowhere. Her decade of passion project became a side hustle.

All her work was digital. But from time to time, she needed to make paper copies. It was at the photocopier that she had a chance encounter with a stranger, Drew Weissman:

> And then I just introduced myself— who I am, and I work here, and I work with RNA. And Drew said that he came from Anthony Fauci's lab. And, of course at that time I didn't know who was [sic] Anthony Fauci.
>
> (*Karikó*, 2021)

Intermission

Drew Weissman had the lab, the funding, and the interest to bring Karikó into his project. Working together on her passion, and following a number of failed attempts, Karikó and Weissman succeeded in introducing mRNA into mouse cells that then produced the long-desired results.

Practically Speaking *(continued)*

You might be tempted to think this was the beginning of the happy ending. But no, life had more lemons to throw at the duo. Academic journals rejected their article submissions and funding dried up again.

Years later, in 2013, after listening to one of Karikó's lectures, the Türkiye-born founder of a German biotech startup called BioNTech offered her a job.

Figure 16.2

Curtain Call

In 2018, BioNTech signed a contract with Pfizer to develop an mRNA-based flu vaccine. Two years later, when the COVID-19 pandemic hit, the BioNTech/Pfizer team was perfectly placed to switch their vaccine work to focus on the new virus. The rest, as they say, is history.

In 2023, Karikó and Weissman won the Nobel Prize in Medicine.

How might the story have developed if Karikó did not have that chance encounter at the copying machine?

To learn more, visit: https://effectuation.org/EE3/mrna or scan Figure 16.3.

Figure 16.3

Practically Speaking

Flaky Surprise

Contingency often takes the form of unexpected people arriving on your doorstep. Consider the history of J. R. Simplot. Simplot built a business storing and sorting potatoes and onions during the Great Depression. As David Silver (1985) recounts:

> [I]n the spring of 1940, Jack Simplot decided to drive to Berkeley, California, to find out why an onion exporter there had run up a bill of 8,400 US Dollars for cull (or reject) onions without paying … The girl in the office said that the boss wasn't in. J.R. said that was fine; he would wait until the man arrived.

Figure 16.4

Practically Speaking *(continued)*

Two hours later, at ten o'clock, a bearded old man walked in. Assuming this was his debtor, Simplot accosted him. But he turned out to be a man named Sokol, inquiring why he was not getting his due deliveries of onion flakes and powder. They sat together until noon, but still the exporter failed to arrive.

As the noon hour passed, Simplot was suddenly struck with an idea. He asked the bewhiskered old trader to a fateful lunch at the Berkeley Hotel. "You want onion powder and flakes," said J.R., "I've got onions. I'll dry 'em and make powder and flakes in Idaho."

Thus, through a chance meeting with Sokol, Simplot found an opportunity. He went on to develop one of the largest agricultural businesses in the US.

To learn more, visit: https://effectuation.org/EE3/simplot or scan Figure 16.5.

Figure 16.5

Unexpected Events

Historians talk frequently about unexpected events—so much so that there is a new genre of counterfactual history, which asks what might have been if such-and-such hadn't happened.

Classic examples of the important role accorded to contingent events can be found in military history. Rain on the battlefield bogged down Napoleon's troops at Waterloo, allowing Wellington to carry the day. And a savage storm scattered the Spanish Armada, saving Elizabethan England from invasion.

Steve Mariotti's mugging and Greg Donovan's sick child are examples of a bad contingent event at the personal level, while Zopa is an example at the level of the economy. On an even grander scale, RocketGirl is an example of contingency on a societal level, when whole cities were locked down during the COVID-19 pandemic. In all cases, the entrepreneur has turned the unexpected situation into something novel and valuable.

Practically Speaking

Surprise Landing

Andrew and Mariya Rovenko, parents of 4-year-old Mia, were almost at the 200-day mark of forced lockdowns in Melbourne, Australia, due to the COVID-19 pandemic and needed a new project, as Andrew describes on his website:

> An unintended photography project, born out of the intended family time in Melbourne's 6th lockdown.
>
> With no more rainbows on the pavements, stuffed animals away from the windows and once vibrant spoonvilles turned sad ghost towns—everyone needed to figure out their own way to keep going. Small things. Small wins. Like making a space helmet for your child fascinated by the night sky. And a suit.
>
> (*Andrew Rovenko* Photography, n.d.)

Practically Speaking *(continued)*

Surprises at Hand

> Too bad that the novelty of a costume doesn't last. Stories, however, seem to have worked since forever. So we took the costume and went looking for stories. The good thing is that stories can be found anywhere, be it 5km travel limit or your bedroom. The bus stop or a laundry.
>
> (*Andrew Rovenko* Photography, n.d.)

Like any child, Mia was so thrilled with her spacesuit that she wanted to keep it on all day, including the permissible regular walks within a 5 kilometer radius of the family home.

And Andrew, like any parent, took pictures of his daughter with his mobile phone and shared them via social media. The empty street made his little girl's walk seem different, other-worldly. He started getting positive feedback from friends, and the project grew, becoming a discovery tour for the whole family.

Here, There, and Everywhere

Strange as the empty cityscapes were, even more surprising for Andrew was how the project was getting international attention and inspiring people.

The surprises continued. Requests for a book started to come in. The crowdfunding campaign for the book reached its goal in 24 hours. And *Rocketgirl* landed in bookstores in October 2023.

Could *Rocketgirl* have come to be without COVID-19? Loneliness and despair need not be the only response to the desolate streets in a pandemic. Sometimes, making a space helmet is what you need to blast off into new worlds.

To learn more, visit: https://effectuation.org/EE3/rocketgirl or scan Figure 16.6.

Figure 16.6

Practically Speaking

Creating During Crisis: Zopa

From all the news stories of economic collapse during the 2009 financial crisis, a casual reader might conclude that at some point society might be reduced to only the most primitive trading activity. With blocked credit markets, corporations and banks could not function effectively, and sometimes the only way to find credit was between individuals, taking us back to the millennia preceding Adam Smith.

Old Ideas, New Opportunities

Not to Giles Andrews. He is not a caveman or even a Luddite. But, as managing director and co-founder of Zopa (short for the negotiating term Zone of Possible Agreement), he is stealing an old idea from our medieval trading ancestors to create a modern business that flourished as a result of the credit crisis and has been growing since.

Practically Speaking *(continued)*

The old idea is person-to-person (with a hip new moniker: P2P) lending. Zopa, founded in 2005, provides a simple online market to connect individual lenders with other individuals who need money. It works a lot like eBay, in that potential borrowers can post their capital needs, be rated on prior transactions and, with luck, be funded by one or many people in the Zopa community.

The Power of People

What makes Zopa tick is that it's everything a bank is not. Here's how it works: say Jamesrw (his Zopa username) is looking to borrow 10,100 British pounds to pay off an existing loan and invest in his advertising consultancy business. He receives money from a large number of people, such as finkerxyz1 (his Zopa username), who lends 20 British pounds at an annual rate of 12%.

Finkerxyz1 distributes tiny loans to many individual borrowers, and spreads lending risk across them all. Andrews knows that most defaults happen on bigger loans, so Zopa limits transactions to 15,000 British pounds, resulting in significantly lower default rates than commercial banking.

In 2021, Zopa announced the end of its P2P lending activities to focus on digital banking. Some "bad apples" in P2P lending had damaged customer trust in the sector, resulting in increased regulation and operating costs reducing investment returns for P2P. Zopa Bank's capital raising announcement of 75 million British pounds in early 2023 shows that they have gone full circle: from old to new to old again.

Figure 16.7

The Business of the Solution

Some people might say that the middle of an economic crisis is not a good time to start a venture. Yet, such venerable companies as Sony and Procter & Gamble were launched in down financial markets. One of the approaches observed in expert entrepreneurs is the ability to invert a problem and imagine how even unpleasant surprises can provide the foundation for new opportunities.

In the same way that Andrews succeeded in an alternative financing model due to failures in the banking industry, crises ranging from energy to malnutrition present opportunities to both make a positive impact and make some money. Which crisis are you going to turn upside down?

Figure 16.8

To learn more, visit: https://effectuation.org/EE3/zopa or scan Figure 16.8.

Practically Speaking

10 US Dollar Surprise

Sometimes contingent events come in unfortunate form. In the case of Steve Mariotti, a mugging at the hands of six teenagers was the chance event. In September 1981, Mariotti was walking on the Lower East Side of Manhattan when a group of youths surrounded him, slapped him, knocked him to the ground, and threatened to throw him into the East River. Their target: a 10 US dollar banknote he was carrying.

Traumatized by the event but determined to make something positive out of it, Mariotti decided to become a high school teacher in a New York City neighborhood in an effort to do what he could to improve the lives of young people in the inner cities.

His experiences teaching high schoolers about making money led him to see the potential in entrepreneurship as a tool for changing people's lives, and he went on to found the National Foundation for Teaching Entrepreneurship (NFTE), which is dedicated to educating kids about the possibilities for using entrepreneurship to better themselves.

To learn more, visit: https://effectuation.org/EE3/nfte or scan Figure 16.9.

Figure 16.9

Practically Speaking

Two Negatives Make Lemonade

Co-Creators: Javiera Salvo Porras and Gonzalo Jiménez-Seminario

Deep in the Chilean mountains, nestled 2,600 meters above sea level, lies a Chilean multidivisional Mining Corporation, CMC, the country's mining powerhouse. Its youngest division, Pablo Neruda (PAN), was born in 2010, with a mission to revolutionize the mining industry and create a gold mine of innovation.

Sleeping Giant

At CMC, the top management team (TMT) embarked on an audacious endeavor to change the mining game. Their goal was to extract value through cutting-edge operations, high-performing teams, and smart technologies. They envisioned a future where collaboration and coordination reigned supreme, and their dreams took shape in the form of the Globally Integrated Operation (GIO) project, by means of which all the mining sites and plants would be both centrally and remotely controlled.

The goal was lofty and laudable. But changing the behemoth proved impossible. Each operation remained fiercely independent, with its own control room, preventing the desired integration.

Practically Speaking *(continued)*

Wake-Up Call

And then, out of the blue, a second lemon! In an unexpected twist of fate, a strike among external contractors erupted, causing chaos and halting mining operations. Suddenly CMC was in danger of having the unions take over not only the mine but also the processing plant. TMT quickly flew in their crack operations team from northern Chile to Santiago. Their mission? To pioneer an integrated remote operation and control!

What was a bureaucratic nightmare became affordable loss. And just like that, innovation broke through the walls of the conservative mining giant. Lesson learned: sometimes two lemons can move even a behemoth to make lemonade.

To learn more, visit: https://effectuation.org/EE3/mining or scan Figure 16.10.

Figure 16.10

Unexpected Information

A third type of contingency is the unexpected arrival of new information. One example of this is information that changes your expectations about the "market," as we see in the Honda example. New information might arrive in many different ways: in the Staples story, Thomas Stemberg's inability to find printer ribbon was a critical bit of information about the potential for an office supply chain in the US.

Practically Speaking

Printed Surprise—The Start of Staples

A terrific example of the role of contingency in a new venture can be found in the history of Staples, the discount office supplies superstore. It was 1985, the Thursday before the July 4 holiday weekend in the US. Having recently lost his job working for a supermarket, Thomas Stemberg was formulating a business plan for a supermarket chain when he ran out of printer ribbon for his printer.

When he went to local stores to buy a new printer ribbon, he found either they didn't have the ribbon he needed, or the store had closed early for the holiday weekend. The simple information that printer ribbon was unobtainable triggered an idea for Stemberg. In a later interview with CNN, he said, "It dawned on me that not only could small entrepreneurs not get stationery at the rate of bigger companies—sometimes they couldn't get it at all."

Because he didn't have the printer ribbon, Stemberg couldn't finish his business plan over the weekend, but it didn't matter. Out of the contingency was born an idea for a venture he wanted to start—a chain of office supply stores valued at 6.7 billion US dollars in mid-2017 when it was taken private and left the NASDAQ stock exchange.

To learn more, visit: https://effectuation.org/EE3/staples or scan Figure 16.11.

Figure 16.11

Practically Speaking

Silly Surprise

Figure 16.12

Perhaps one of the best-known stories of a new venture founded on a contingency is Silly Putty. The substance was actually the result of a failed experiment to create synthetic rubber during World War II in General Electric's New Haven laboratory.

General Electric bounced the idea around for years in search of a practical use, but it wasn't until 1949 that Peter Hodgson, an unemployed advertising agent, encountered the compound as part of the entertainment at a party. Finding the stretchy material was an accident, but Hodgson did what he could with that contingent event.

Unemployed and 12,000 US dollars in debt, he saw potential opportunity and borrowed 147 US dollars to produce a batch of the stuff. He renamed it Silly Putty and used his public relations skills to get it featured in Doubleday bookstores, Neiman-Marcus, and the *New Yorker* magazine. To everyone's amazement, sales took off, and Peter Hodgson laughed all the way to the bank. When he died in 1976, his estate was worth 140 million US dollars.

To learn more, visit: https://effectuation.org/EE3/silly or scan Figure 16.13.

Figure 16.13

Practically Speaking

Scooter Surprise

In the 1960s, when Honda initially entered the US motorcycle market, they aimed to sell large motorcycles. However, in a cost-saving measure their sales team used typical Japanese mopeds to navigate through Los Angeles.

One day, a Sears representative noticed one of the Honda mopeds in traffic and reached out to Honda, suggesting that they explore the potential to sell mopeds in the US. This unexpected call opened a new market opportunity for Honda, and they capitalized on it to significantly increase their sales.

To learn more, visit: https://effectuation.org/EE3/honda or scan Figure 16.14.

Figure 16.14

Figure 16.15

Practically Speaking

Railroad Surprise

Like many of the stories we recount in this book, Railtex leans toward the mundane—after all, short-haul railroading is not exactly the newest or most exciting business venture one could get into. The Railtex story starts in 1977, when Bruce Flohr put 50,000 US dollars of his own money together with 50,000 US dollars from investors to launch a railcar-leasing firm in San Antonio, Texas.

Figure 16.16

Railcar leasing turned out not to be a particularly great idea: five years later, the business was still not profitable and was struggling to stay afloat. The situation forced Flohr and his team to start doing consultancy projects with small railroads as a way of pulling in some extra cash.

The consulting work proved to be a stroke of luck: what they accidentally discovered was that small railroads were badly in need of competent management and marketing. This contingency proved to be a turning point for the firm. Instead of consulting for small railroads, Flohr started buying them, improving their operations, and growing them by marketing freight services to local businesses.

Starting with San Diego & Imperial Valley Railroad, the firm went on to pick up dozens of short-haul lines, going public in 1993 and growing into the largest short-haul railroad operator in the US.

To learn more, visit: https://effectuation.org/EE3/railtex or scan Figure 16.17.

Figure 16.17

Research Roots

Accidental Innovation?

Despite the fact that managers do everything possible to reduce the scope for accidents to happen in the process of developing new products and services, it is well known that "Lady Luck" plays an important role in innovation. Entrepreneurs seem to show more imagination in granting a role for luck in their business ventures. How, then, does an entrepreneur increase the likelihood of favorable surprises occurring on their entrepreneurial journey?

Clues can be found in a paper by Robert Austin and colleagues, who examined how innovators integrate the accidental into their work using 20 case studies ranging across a variety of industries (from shoes to aerospace to Broadway productions).

Research Roots *(continued)*

The researchers found that some innovators not only were open to accidents but also intentionally designed their environment and processes to tempt accidents. In one case, a pottery artist showed the researchers the beautiful artwork he made, describing how he would whack his pots with a stick in order to produce an accidental outcome, saying to himself "Ooh, that's quite wonderful."

The researchers concluded that the biggest driver of innovators being open to accidents was the cost of unproductive accidents. Subjects said that most of the accidents they experienced were not beneficial and that the affordability of the downside dictated the degree to which they could invite the accidental into their work (Austin et al., 2012).

Table 16.1 Positive or Negative, Surprise is a Resource

Unexpected	Entity/project	Contingency	Changed means	New things to do	Novel outcomes
People	mRNA Vaccines	Accidental meeting	New committed co-creation partner	New phase of scientific experimentation	Key to mRNA and vaccine technology, Nobel Prize
	Simplot	Accidental meeting	Knowing someone with a specific need	Produce powdered onions using existing equipment	Opportunity in dried fruits and vegetables
Event	Rocketgirl Chronicles	Pandemic lockdown with child	Search for new activities for child	Make space suit and take pictures in empty cityscapes	Collection of otherworldly images receive awards, become book
	Zopa	2009 financial crisis	Lock of credit markets	Expand person-to-person (P2P) lending	Growth in new areas
	NFTE	Mugged by inner-city youths	Personal fear	Take steps to overcome personal fears	Become a high school teacher in a tough inner-city neighborhood
	CMC	Striking external contractors	Threat of operations being stopped	Put previously rejected remote-control room in action	New production efficiency and profitability
Information	Staples	Unable to easily obtain office supplies	Knowledge of non-availability of products for small businesses	Sell office products to small businesses	Development of Staples retail chain

	Silly Putty	Failed development of synthetic rubber	Pliable putty	Create a toy	A product that has lasted over 60 years
	Honda	Sears wants small Honda scooters	Demand in an unexpected area	Sell scooters	Entry into the US market
	Railtex	Losing money in short-haul rail	Information about why short-haul rail fails	Consulting	A new business model for short-haul rail

In Table 16.1, we organize the eleven stories in this chapter according to what was unexpected. When you see them together, you may find that some of the surprises are positive, and some are negative.

When surprises initially look positive, people often refer to them as "serendipitous" events—good things that happened by accident. If at first glance they appear negative, people often refer to them as examples of "Murphy's Law," the notion that anything that can go wrong will go wrong.

In the next section, we describe how you might think about leveraging contingencies regardless of whether they appear positive or negative.

LEVERAGING CONTINGENCY: THE PROCESS

In the examples we have considered so far, it's important to realize that the contingencies themselves did not automatically shape the direction of their project. Instead, the individuals had to leverage them—they had to behave in a certain way in response to the contingency.

Indeed, entrepreneurs are adept at seizing surprises in an instrumental fashion and figuring out ways to imaginatively utilize them to create new possibilities in the world.

There are several generic ways to think about how to handle contingencies. Consider three common ways and then a fourth, entrepreneurial, way:

- An **adaptive response** involves changing yourself to fit the contingency. For example, Thomas Stemberg could have taken the non-availability of printer ribbon to be a constraint that he would just have to cope with and resign himself to printing his business plan the following weekend.
- A **resource-driven response** involves tapping into networks to find needed resources. Stemberg could have put out a call to his friends and colleagues asking for the required printer ribbon or the availability of a suitable printer. This could well involve negotiating the conditions with them in order to complete the printing task by the predetermined deadline.
- A **heroic response** involves changing the world into a state that you prefer. Stemberg might have treated the non-availability of printer ribbon as an obstacle to overcome and—determined to print his business plan—he might have gone on an all-out campaign to find printer ribbon, spending the whole of the July 4 weekend combing every store within a 50-mile radius of his home

until he found one that carried the printer ribbon he desired.

- An **entrepreneurial response** involves a different approach—using contingencies as resources, as inputs into your entrepreneurial endeavors. Instead of adapting to or overcoming the contingencies the world throws at you, you see contingencies as assets with which you may be able to do something creative. Whereas the adaptive response involves thinking "inside the box," and the heroic response involves thinking "outside the box," the entrepreneurial response is somewhat more subtle—it involves realizing that the "box" has changed and then doing something creative with this new box. Here, the colloquial "box" is seen as an input to the venture.

Sometimes contingencies will be obviously good things; in those cases, the entrepreneur's job is to embrace them and squeeze out the opportunity.

But the most challenging contingencies are those that come in unfortunate or negative forms—such as the mugging of Steve Mariotti in New York City. As that example shows, it is almost always possible to leverage a contingency in some kind of positive way—if you are creative enough. As we've noted, the critical point about contingencies is what entrepreneurs do with them.

Unexpected Responses That Changed the World

In this chapter, we have emphasized that the real source of value in contingencies is the novelty of entrepreneurs' responses to them. The same principles that apply to entrepreneurial ventures also apply to creating value in society as a whole.

A powerful example of this may be found in the story of Indian nationalist Mahatma Gandhi. While still in his twenties Gandhi traveled to South Africa, seeking work as a lawyer. There, to his surprise, he experienced the full range of discrimination directed at Indians in South Africa.

In a series of contingent events, triggered by his race, he was thrown off trains and stagecoaches, and beaten and barred from hotels. These experiences of racism deeply influenced Gandhi and, though he apparently never intended it when he went to South Africa, they led him to begin working as a social activist there.

When the Transvaal government began forcing the registration of Indians in 1906, Gandhi concocted a novel response to the demand: instead of advocating violent resistance, he turned the approach on its head and began promoting the method of non-violent protest for which he subsequently became famous. He urged Indians to burn their registration cards or refuse to register, actions that expressed the deeper novelty in Gandhi's approach, which involved defying the law and suffering the consequences for doing so.

Public outcry over the harsh response of the South African government to peaceful Indian protests eventually forced the authorities to compromise. It was an important symbolic victory for Gandhi and his supporters and proof that unexpected responses can change the world.

Figure 16.18

THE CONTINGENCY PATH

When surprises strike, it is useful to have a structure to guide your thinking and response. Figure 16.19 sketches out the process of leveraging contingencies.

Step 1: Surprise Happens

The first step in the process is the contingency itself, which, as we've discussed, generally takes the form of an unexpected meeting, an unexpected event, or unexpected information.

Step 2: Change of Means

The second step is seeing that a contingency usually changes the entrepreneur's means (who I am, what I know, and who I know), the immediately available resources with which the entrepreneur can take action.

Meeting someone new changes "who you know," and new information while contingent events change "what you know" and perhaps "who you are." In fact, every one of us can be thought of as partly constituted by a long list of contingencies that—in the long run—help form our personality, knowledge, and personal networks.

Think about your own life and all the events, people, and information that have shaped you. Contingencies play a significant role in forming most individuals' means. Therefore, when contingencies occur, entrepreneurs should consider how they alter their means, as a first step toward thinking through how they could be leveraged.

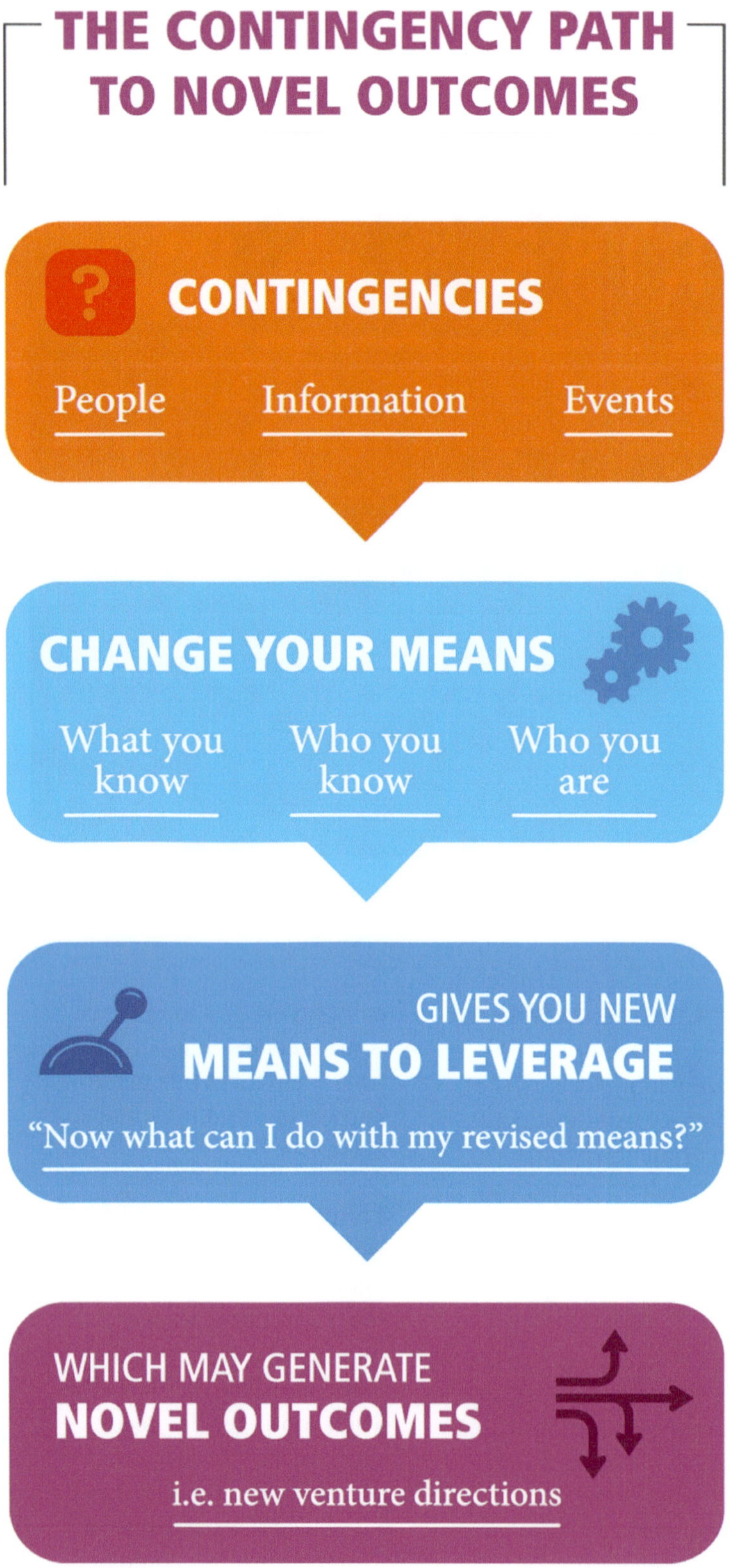

Figure 16.19

Step 3: Forming a Response

The third step in the process is forming possible actions in response to the contingency. The general approach to leveraging contingencies that we outline here fits with some of the most important findings from research on creative problem-solving. This research shows that, in general, there are two keys to being more creative when solving problems:

The first is to consider a lot of solutions. In general, the more potential solutions you consider for a given problem, the more likely you are to find one that's creative. For entrepreneurs, this means imagining lots of different things you might be able to do in response to an unexpected meeting, event, or piece of information.

Very often, there are immediate, obvious, spontaneous responses, such as partnering with someone you just met (as in the case of Karikó and Weissman). In other situations, there is no obvious thing to do, and so the entrepreneur may take some time to imagine various courses of action. For example, Steve Mariotti didn't have to make an instantaneous decision to become a high school teacher—that alternative emerged from his need to face his fears about being mugged.

The second general rule for improving creative problem-solving is to change the way the problem is framed. Entrepreneurs generally do this by inverting the way a contingency presents itself: instead of looking at it as a problem, they turn it on its head and look at it as a (badly disguised) opportunity. For example, Bruce Flohr his own difficulty in the short-haul rail business to other similar businesses and create an opportunity from that realization.

Step 4: Outcome

The final step in the contingency leveraging process is the novel outcome that may be generated. We say "may" because, as with all creative processes, there is no guarantee that a novel, value-creating outcome is going to be forthcoming—it's just a possibility that may occur.

Contingency leveraging is about seizing the unique possibilities that may arise from the interaction between the entrepreneur—with their unique attributes, prior experience, networks, personality traits, etc.—and a particular contingency. These interactions tend to be unpredictable because different people will interact differently with different contingencies. Think about it: something unexpected happens to you, and then you concoct an unexpected response. There is a double novelty in such interactions, which is precisely why they sometimes result in creative moments in the history of entrepreneurial ventures.

> **Research Roots**
>
> **Contingencies as Resources in the Startup Process**
>
> In a series of papers, Susan Harmeling (Harmeling & Sarasvathy, 2013) has argued that a distinguishing feature of entrepreneurship is the way contingencies are treated by entrepreneurs. The notion that chance happenings, accidents, and serendipity may play an important role in new ventures has a long history.
>
> But Harmeling's point is that the key issue is not whether contingencies occur while starting a venture (because they always do) but what entrepreneurs do with them. The entrepreneurial stance is one that is resourceful regarding contingencies. This approach involves leveraging the contingencies that come along (both "good" and "bad") by incorporating them as inputs into the process of "entrepreneuring."
>
> The notion of responding more or less entrepreneurially to contingencies is grounded in the observation that individuals vary in their personal beliefs about the impact of their own agency. Some people perceive more control over their destiny than others do (Harmeling & Sarasvathy, 2013).

MAKING SURPRISES WORK FOR YOU

It may sound paradoxical, but you can prepare for the unexpected. Indeed, there are several things you can do to improve the odds you will experience contingencies that can be leveraged in positive ways. These are activities or ways of thinking that experienced entrepreneurs seem to have internalized and often do reflexively.

Social Networking

New information often arrives through people you know. Therefore, there is an important linkage between social network activity and position and access to new information. To the extent that experienced entrepreneurs have richer social networks, their network connections may expose them to information flows that make them more likely to encounter contingencies.

This suggests entrepreneurs may be able to engage in social networking behaviors which make it more likely contingencies happen to them. Sony's "wandering chairman" brings this to a personal level. It was his wandering between different development teams that connected the two disparate projects that ultimately created the speaker system for the Walkman. So as an entrepreneur, you may be able to increase your exposure to contingencies by deliberately engaging in networking behaviors.

Openness to Experiences

Access to contingencies may also be related to certain personality traits. These may play a role in receptiveness to contingencies and, therefore, the likelihood of leveraging them. Studies of entrepreneurial psychology have found that in general, entrepreneurs score higher on the measure of "openness to experience" than comparable managers.

Openness to experience is defined as intellectual curiosity and the tendency to seek new experiences. Individuals who exhibit those qualities may be more receptive to, and welcoming of, contingent events and information and thus more likely to view them as opportunities for action. In a sense, these individuals display a taste for surprises. Therefore, another way to increase your exposure to contingencies is to deliberately cultivate a taste for new things.

Opportunity Framing

Some research suggests that entrepreneurs are more likely to see the world in terms of the opportunities it presents rather than the attendant threat of changes. This tendency is the opposite of what we generally find among corporate managers, who are overwhelmingly more likely to see threats rather than opportunities in any given scenario.

These different responses are probably related to the way entrepreneurs frame situations and, therefore, what information they tend to see as important. It's unclear what drives people to frame things differently, but one explanation may be that people differ in how they perceive the world and their place in it.

If you view the world as particularly difficult to shape, you are more likely to respond to contingencies by seeing them as a threat and trying to adapt yourself to them. Alternatively, if you view the world as open to transformation, you might see contingency as some kind of cue to shape the future.

TAKEAWAY: HAVE CONFIDENCE IN YOUR OWN ABILITY TO MAKE A DIFFERENCE

Many entrepreneurs have "survival" stories that illustrate how even unfortunate contingencies are not only survivable in the short run but the genesis of new business opportunities and can be the source of long-term success.

Thus, entrepreneurs who have successfully leveraged contingencies in the past justifiably have more confidence in their own agency and, therefore, may have less anxiety about their ability to face the unexpected in the future.

The implication here is that another way to increase your exposure to contingencies is to cultivate your self-efficacy, recognizing and having confidence in your own agency in the world—your ability to make a difference (however small that difference might be).

What Now?

For an opportunity you are developing, identify the surprises that you've taken advantage of. If none, consider the possibility that you aren't actively engaging with your market/partners.

- Ad-lib: imagine one new expertise in your means. Describe one ask you're developing and flip a coin to "determine" the outcome. And add six months of time commitment to what you can afford to commit. Now create three ideas for how to change your opportunity as a result of these surprises.
- Reduce your affordable loss to 500 US dollars. Adjust.
- Win your biggest "ask" and then create an entirely new direction for your opportunity as a result of the new means.
- Consider whether any of these created new directions might be pursued directly.
- Consider whether you are giving luck a chance as you develop your opportunity.

So What?

You will be surprised. There is no way around it. The creative use of a surprise is part of being an entrepreneur. Find ways to learn from surprises, use them as new means, and consider fundamental changes in direction.

Think It Through

- How can you tell if what you're seeing is just "noise" or is an actual signal of something you hadn't anticipated?
- If you pursue all surprises, things may be a mess; how can you choose when to stay the course or deviate?
- How does affordable loss reinforce leveraging surprise?
- What makes a given surprise seem negative rather than positive? Are these things inherent to the surprise?

REFERENCES

Andrew Rovenko Photography. (n.d.). The Rocketgirl Chronicles—Backyard Space Travel. Retrieved January 7, 2024, from https://rovenko.com/

Austin, R. D., Devin, L., & Sullivan, E. E. (2012). Accidental innovation: Supporting valuable unpredictability in the creative process. *Organization Science*, *23*(5), 1505–1522. https://doi.org/10.1287/orsc.1110.0681

Godden, A. (2023, October 2). Nobel prize in medicine awarded to mRNA pioneers—here's how their discovery was integral to COVID vaccine development. The Conversation. http://theconversation.com/nobel-prize-in-medicine-awarded-to-mrna-pioneers-heres-how-their-discovery-was-integral-to-covid-vaccine-development-214763

Harmeling, S. S., & Sarasvathy, S. D. (2013). When contingency is a resource: Educating entrepreneurs in the Balkans, the Bronx, and beyond. *Entrepreneurship Theory and Practice*, *37*(4), 713–744. https://doi.org/10.1111/j.1540-6520.2011.00489.x

Heath, N. (2023, December 26). Tired of baking sourdough, this Melbourne family began an unusual lockdown project—That went viral. ABC News. https://www.abc.net.au/news/2023-12-26/rocketgirl-chronicles-melbourne-photographer-andrew-rovenko/103253728

Karikó, K. (2021, June 10). The unlikely pioneer behind mRNA vaccines (G. Kolata & M. Barbaro, Interviewers). https://www.nytimes.com/2021/06/10/podcasts/the-daily/mrna-vaccines-katalin-kariko.html

Semmler, E., & Cheshire, B. (2022, October 2). A $300,000 redundancy gamble switched Greg's "vanilla life" into rockstar mode. ABC News. https://www.abc.net.au/news/2022-10-03/greg-donovans-gamble-on-the-big-red-bash-music-festival/101466666

Silver, A. D. (1985). Venture capital: The complete guide for investors. https://cir.nii.ac.jp/crid/1130000796919683712

CHAPTER 17

Figure 17.1 An entrepreneur climbs to the light, facing many decisions.

Putting It Together

The Effectuation Process

In This Chapter

Any of the effectual principles (available means, affordable loss, partnerships, and contingencies) can be used on their own. Combined they are a powerful engine capable of generating an infinite set of new artifacts in the world.

There are as many paths as there are entrepreneurs, but effectual entrepreneurs share a common flow—the effectual process—as they co-create with stakeholders based on shared commitments.

DOI: 10.4324/9781003364016-20

This chapter is devoted to explaining the process that connects means, affordable loss, partnerships, and contingencies. There are as many paths as there are entrepreneurs, but effectual entrepreneurs share a common flow as they co-create new ventures with stakeholders.

As we narrate this process, you will recognize each of the steps—each of the principles. The new element to consider in this chapter is the seemingly contradictory set of outcomes that result from a chain of effectual commitments. On the one hand, the process increases the resources available to the venture. On the other hand, it constrains the venture by crystallizing its goals and helping it converge toward something specific.

Here you see the natural tension between effectuation and causation. As the effectual network grows to include more and more of the external world, it tends to become less effectual, slowly turning into a distinct new market.

Up to a certain point, changes in the environment can provide the venture with new means and thus kick-start the cycle again. And any interactions that fail to gain the traction of commitment are put on hold, at least temporarily. But enough successful iterations result in enough commitments, leaving little space for more. The goals have emerged; hence the idea is now a venture.

The venture that results may or may not be what the entrepreneur had in mind at the beginning, and the process may take any number of iterations, so think of the process less as a map and more as an engine.

THE EFFECTUATION PROCESS

We laid out the chapters in this section of the book according to the way entrepreneurs generally work their way through the process. The entrepreneur's means provide the starting point.

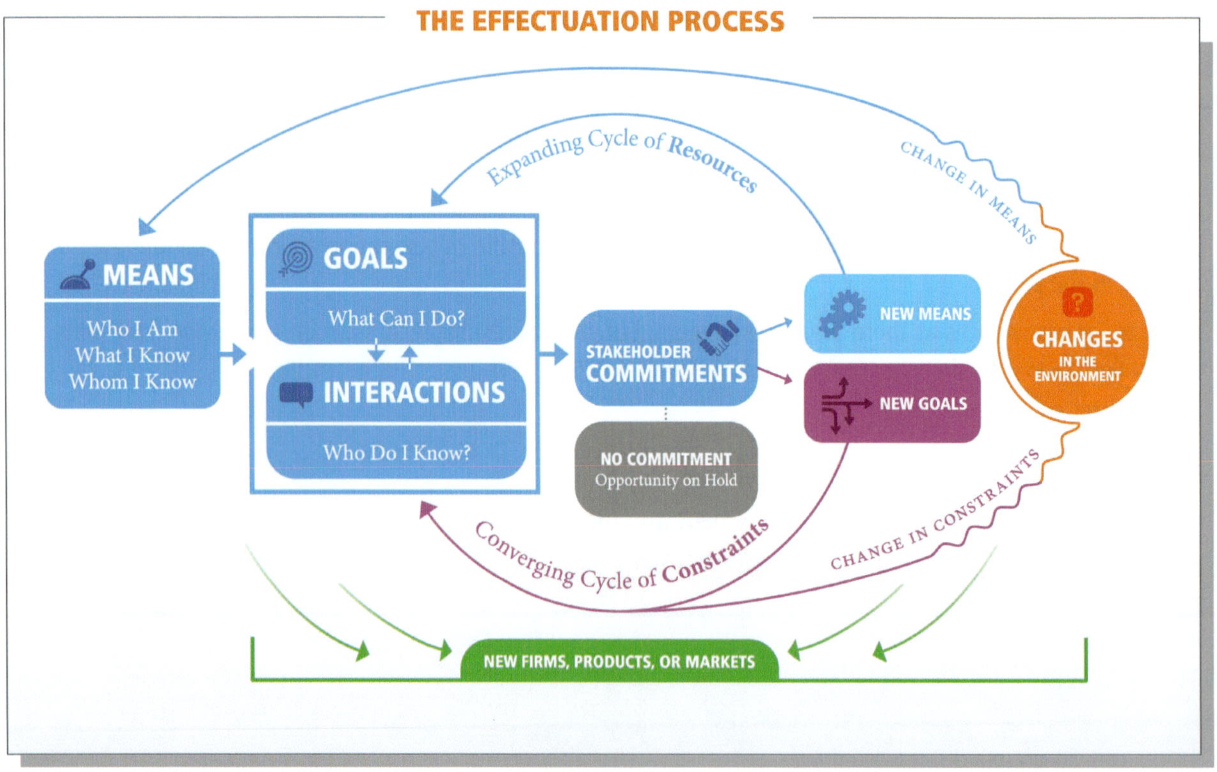

Figure 17.2 The effectuation process is not a map, but rather an engine to turn ideas into reality through co-creation.

The action begins in earnest when the entrepreneur begins interacting with people. Sometimes the starting point of that interaction is an idea, a provisional goal the entrepreneur uses to initiate the interaction. Sometimes the interaction is specifically initiated by asking "what can we do?" as the entrepreneur determines possibilities together with the person she interacts with.

Regardless, each interaction can terminate without a commitment. In that case, the opportunity, as the entrepreneur and that specific person she interacts with envisioned, is on hold.

Alternatively, that interaction might result in a commitment. As we described, those commitments have two effects. One effect of adding a stakeholder to the venture is the addition of that stakeholder's means—the possibilities those means suggest. At the same time, new goals also accompany the commitment, adding to the constraints accumulated by the venture and converging it toward a specific direction.

At any time in this cycle, unexpected events, information, and meetings can change the environment the venture is developing. Those contingencies have similar effects to commitments. On one hand, they present new resources—new means the entrepreneur can use to expand the possibilities of the venture. On the other hand, they present new constraints also, perhaps sending the venture in a more specific direction.

ITERATIONS OF THE EFFECTUATION PROCESS

This process may cycle once or many times. If there are no stakeholders willing to make commitments, it may not even complete a single cycle. But given the room to operate, the process will generate all sorts of outcomes, including unexpected ones.

On our diagram, we indicate new firms, markets, and products as possible outcomes. And by now it should be easy to see how once enough constraints have accumulated, the venture is formed and operational, with all the people, resources, clients, and partners needed to deliver on the commitments that determine its direction.

But the process can also generate new knowledge, new aspirations, new likes, and new dislikes. These too are iterated into future cycles, as the entrepreneur completes the delivery of a venture or product that results from a set of iterations and goes on to create the next product or even the next venture.

TAKEAWAY: THE CONSEQUENCE OF COMMITMENT

The ICEHOTEL example helps us understand how stakeholder commitments shape ventures. The mutual commitments between the first stakeholders (Yngve and the tourist office, the sculptors, the press, the travel agents) forge a network that eventually transforms a budding reality into a new market.

Neither Yngve nor any of his early partners knew what the end product would look like or whether it would be worth anything. Instead, the market was an outcome of the interaction among them. It emerged gradually, as they started making things happen. Through their actions, the stakeholders negotiated the very existence and shape of what would be.

This kind of negotiation proceeds as though everything and anything is possible until the last minute. There is always room for the actual transformation to surprise everyone involved. This is effectuation in action.

Graphical Practically Speaking

Ice Man Cometh

A Hobby Becomes a Business

After five years working for a mining company in a town called Kiruna in Swedish Lapland, Yngve Bergqvist realized what he did not want to do with his life: work for a big company. His colleagues' lack of enthusiasm for the job grated on him. And he found it impersonal and unpleasant having people refer to him by his employee number.

Yngve was an outdoorsman, and as an outlet from his job, he took up river rafting. One day a tourist asked Yngve for a ride on the river. Suddenly, he was in business. He began going to the tourist office on weekend mornings and nearly always found clients. Yngve ultimately resigned from his mining job and gradually expanded the rafting business to 40 summer employees and 30 boats.

But summer in Sweden is short, and rafting on the Torne River in winter is impossible. For starters, the river is frozen solid. Yngve needed to find a winter business to complement his summer earnings. He had heard about Japanese tourists visiting Alaska in winter to see the Northern Lights (Aurora Borealis) and wanted to learn more.

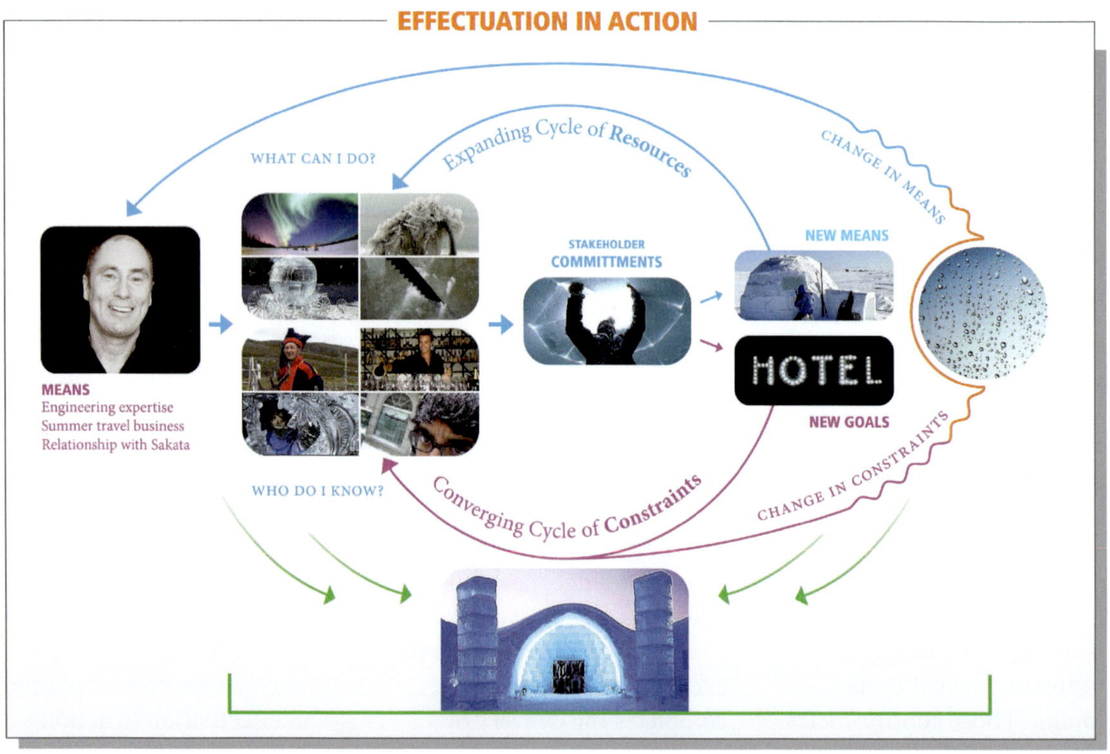

Figure 17.3

Practically Speaking *(continued)*

Sculpting an Icy Future

In 1988, he traveled to Sapporo and Hokkaido, Japan, for the Snow Festivals, and there he met an ice sculptor from Asahikawa. Over beer, the two men planned a winter ice-sculpting workshop in Sweden. The workshop received a lot of press, as numerous international artists, spectators, and local people flocked to a riverfront area of Kruna called Jukkasjärvi.

In recalling the event, Yngve described the evening before as cold and clear. His family was there watching the beautiful ice sculptures take shape, and they were so impressed. The local people in the village were taking photos.

Weathering Change

But then, as Yngve recalled, "The next morning when I woke up, at six, I heard something strange. I couldn't believe it … it was raining, and it was plus seven degrees." The ice workshop was scheduled to start at 11, and the sculptors wanted to know what to do. Rather than trying to preserve something that belonged to nature, Yngve said, "Let it be destroyed and make something new when it is destroyed."

What they made new was the ICEHOTEL. It is a business that is the embodiment of Yngve. It is constructed each winter using ice from the Torne River, where he runs rafting trips, and employs skills learned during his ice-sculpting workshop.

Chilly Partnership

Yngve's friends at the Swedish tourist board then introduced him to Sakata, the owner of a Japanese travel agency named Northern Express. A natural partnership ensued in which Sakata generated interest in Japan for travel to Jukkasjärvi and Yngve provided Sakata's clients with a wholly unique experience in Swedish Lapland, including ice fishing, getting married in an ice chapel, or simply marveling at the art that is the ICEHOTEL itself.

When it rained on Yngve Bergqvist's ice sculpture exhibit, there was more than one way to deal with the unpleasant surprise. Yngve could have gone back to the mines or to the summer canoe job; his employees could have seen the madness in a project that was so dependent on weather and cut their losses.

Instead, some of them picked up their ice-sculpting tools and turned to the guests and press people who had come to see the sculptures. Some chose to learn the art of ice sculpting; others chose to make igloos. When night fell, the group that had been busy building igloos invited others to come and try to spend a night in their creations. Contrary to what they had imagined, it was not cold in the igloos. And it was not dark: in fact, the light coming through the ice made it shimmer in a translucent manner that was almost magical.

Clearly Within Available Means

It is this partnership between ice sculptors and guests that truly launched the ICEHOTEL. There was no money involved, no big venture capitalist cash deal—nothing but a group of people who came back the following year to build another group of igloos.

To illustrate this more completely, we map out the sequence of effectual partnerships that led to the creation of the ICEHOTEL on top of The Effectual Process (see Figure 17.3).

Practically Speaking ***(continued)***

Yngve Bergqvist did not stop with the success of the ICEHOTEL. This first round of business-building provided him with new means. Even from the original ice sculpting exhibit, Yngve wanted his own Swedish icon to be associated with another Swedish icon, the premium vodka brand Absolut.

Absolutely a New Direction

He wrote to Absolut, suggesting a partnership. Initially, Absolut was not interested in partnering with a tree hugger building igloos in the far north of Sweden. Yngve persisted. And as often happens, he was helped by a little serendipity.

Figure 17.4 An enchanting and icy corridor in the ICEHOTEL.

The ICEHOTEL featured a sculpture of a giant Absolut bottle as the centerpiece of its bar. As a result of an ICEHOTEL press release, a picture of the bottle made its way back to Absolut. At first incensed (the sculpture had not received their approval), the company started seeing the potential in a partnership. But their aspirations were much greater than ICEHOTEL.

Together, the tree hugger and the world's fourth largest spirit brand came up with the idea of launching ICEBARS in major cities around the world, using the ice from the Torne River—the very same ice that was used to build the ICEHOTEL.

The bars are kept at a constant temperature of –5°C. A selection of international artists and designers are invited to design the bars, which are transformed every six months. As with the ICEHOTEL, everything is sculpted from ice—the bars, the stools, the glasses, the walls. While the original ICEBAR sits in the ICEHOTEL, today there are ICEBARs in dozens of cities, from Copenhagen, to Tokyo, Las Vegas to Dubai.

Figure 17.5 Snuggling up an ice bed: the new version of hospitality in Swedish Lapland.

Ice in Space?

Thanks to the partnership between ICEHOTEL and Absolut, ice is now the largest export product of that part of Sweden. The success of both ventures could have encouraged Yngve Bergqvist to stop there and focus on running the existing business. But the most unexpected partnership was yet to come.

Kiruna is now home of the Swedish Space Corporation's Spaceport Esrange, which was inaugurated in January 2023. ICEHOTEL has partnered with Virgin Galactic to sell space travel departing from Spaceport Esrange once Virgin Galactic commences operation.

The trips will allow travelers to experience the Northern Lights in the winter or the midnight sun in the summer. Virgin had been looking for accredited space agents to take in bookings, and ICEHOTEL was looking to add new trips to the list of excursions available to guests. And with that a new partnership, and a new business venture, was born. Who knows what is next?

Figure 17.6

To learn more, visit: https://effectuation.org/EE3/icehotel or scan Figure 17.6.

Practically Speaking

Reluctant Billionaire

The Path Is the Goal (in Honor of the Book by Chögyam Trungpa)

What do you do when all you want is to do research you really care about, but no one wants to fund it? This is the story of a real scientist, who definitely did not plan to be effectual, nor did he even want to be an entrepreneur. At his request, we have disguised his name and the name of the publicly traded company he built.

Clear Path

Asian immigrant Wu traveled to the United States as a student of metallurgical engineering. Although thriving as a scientist, he was not fluent in English. The problems he was interested in required large capital investment in laboratory equipment. Neither the university, nor later his employer, a large technology company in Silicon Valley, wanted to invest. All Wu wanted was his lab.

Using a causal approach, he began writing a business plan and seeking funding from private investors. Several investors were impressed with his engineering prowess. But none wanted to invest in a lab. Instead, one of them asked him if he could solve a different problem that one of their investee companies was facing.

Figure 17.7 The ups and downs of the landscape offer many paths through this Tuscan countryside in Italy.

Into the Mist

Wu, of course, did not really want to work on it. But by then, he was exhausted from fundraising efforts. So, he made a deal with the investors. If they would commit to funding his lab after he solved their problem, Wu would resign from his job and tackle it.

As it turned out, commercializing the solution Wu came up with required him to become CEO and lead the company the investors had struggled with. That meant Wu could not find time to build his lab when the investors were later ready to invest in it.

Out of the Woods

It took several years for Wu to train another scientist to become CEO so he could step down and build his beloved lab. For Wu, the 3 billion US dollar company he was forced to build was but a byproduct of pursuing his passion. Along the way he even built a few more ventures, including an institute to foster technology development in his home country.

Sometimes, the goal is the path.

Figure 17.8

To learn more, visit: https://effectuation.org/EE3/path or scan Figure 17.8.

So What?

The effectual process comes together in this chapter. Review Figures 17.2 and 17.3 to ensure that you fully understand the process.

Think It Through

- In hindsight, how might one revise the ICEHOTEL creation story with a causal approach?
- Does that (causal) story sound more familiar? Often, looking back, everything all seems so clear/direct/obvious. The well-known narrative of entrepreneur hero, visionary forecasts, and the like, often hide an effectual process.
- Using the effectual process, can really large new ventures be created? Or does it lead to small incremental ideas?

What Now?

For an opportunity you are pursuing, describe your process so far using the effectual process map.

- How many times around the loop have you traveled?
- What dead ends have you reached?
- What new means have joined?
- What parts of your efforts thus far just don't fit this effectual process?
- Which of the effectual principles have you used the least in your efforts?

REFERENCE

Trungpa, C. (2011). *The Path Is the Goal*. Penguin Random House.

PART IV

I Am an Entrepreneur Now

How Far Can I Go?

Having successfully navigated the confusing, sometimes foggy, sometimes unbeaten tracks of entrepreneurship, you face new challenges. Will you want to stay with your venture as it grows? Will your venture want you to stay as it grows? Though not surprising, the very heuristics that help you create new ventures, markets, and products are something of a liability in a larger firm, a bigger operation, serving a mature market where prediction prevails.

This explains why so many entrepreneurs scale up and then exit the venture for new opportunities. Exiting may mean that the founder resigns from an ongoing operation, or may involve selling the business. Either way, the founder entrepreneur who leads the firm once the firm has advanced into maturity, such as Bill Gates at Microsoft, is something of an anomaly.

Clearly, Gates was able to make the transition from employing non-predictive strategy at the outset to effectively utilizing prediction as Microsoft grew. But most founders leave or are thrown out. These represent two of the three main paths taken by serial entrepreneurs. The third involves starting again at the first chapter of the book.

The point is that successful entrepreneurs have dramatically expanded the means available to them. And so, while some may feel trapped having to run "their baby," the truth is that the range of options available to the successful entrepreneur is not only broader than that; it is significantly broader than when they started "their baby" in the first place. So whatever direction you point your successful venture and your own success in, we hope to have an appropriate section for you.

> Should you shield the valleys from the windstorms, you would never see the beauty of their canyons.
>
> Dr. Elisabeth Kübler-Ross, highly respected international psychiatrist

DOI: 10.4324/9781003364016-21

CHAPTER 18

Figure 18.1 It's easier to split a pizza than a venture, particularly because it is about much more than the dough.

Ownership, Equity, and Control

Manage Stakeholders

In This Chapter

Regardless of whether your objective is to create personal wealth or enduring value for society (or perhaps both), partnerships are critical. A detailed understanding of the needs of the other stakeholders (investors, employees, customers, and others) is needed to structure deals along the dimensions of control and ownership.

The key aspects that underpin the negotiation of any arrangement include determining and articulating the appropriate level of risk, the appropriate amount of control, and equitable provisions for ownership and liquidity.

DOI: 10.4324/9781003364016-22

OWNERSHIP: NOT NECESSARILY CONTROL

As you consider setting up a business and involving various kinds of stakeholders in it—particularly those who will become formal investors in the venture—it is critical to understand the difference between ownership and control. Most people think they are the same. As a result, the natural reaction is to focus on how to retain equity (ownership) in order to retain control.

In this chapter, we challenge you to think more deeply about what you really want from the venture. Do you want ownership? Do you want control? How are they different? Where does each come from? And how does the combination help you design partnerships that work well for everyone involved?

On the surface, the connection between ownership and control seems clear. If you own more than half of the company, you control it, from the day-to-day operations to the overall shape and direction of the new venture—in theory, at least.

Venture capitalists know better. They understand that decision rights are a negotiable matter they establish with the entrepreneur and the terms they build into the contract. For example, they may negotiate specific rights on how the assets of the firm will be distributed in case of liquidity. They can specify when and where the venture can raise subsequent rounds of funding and even the conditions under which they can fire the founding CEO and members of the top management team. Additionally, they have seats on the board with voting rights on a variety of issues. And they can do all this with only a minority ownership share in a venture.

Thus, ownership does not necessarily mean control.

This chapter is intended to help you explore the variety of alternatives you have available in terms of ownership and control. These options give you more choices for structuring partnerships that are low on friction and high on productivity.

WHAT DOES OWNERSHIP BUY?

If ownership does not automatically give you control and decision rights, what does it buy you? The answer: residual claims.

Residual claims are claims to anything of value that remains after all contractual rights and obligations have been fulfilled. In plain English, this means the owners of a venture possess anything that remains after the firm's contracts are met and bills are paid.

For example, if the firm is being liquidated, a variety of creditors, debt holders, preferred shareholders, and others, who have specific rights written down in contracts, get paid before the common shareholders.

> A yes from a potential customer does not come easy. But a yes from an investor does not come easy either. And the yes from a customer is less likely to demand equity and more likely to generate demand.

> **High Control, Low Ownership**
>
> Steve Jobs, who exercised great control over Apple, owned less than 1% of the outstanding shares of the firm when he passed away in 2011.

> **Customers: Often the Best Investors**
>
> **How to Test Your Idea and Get Funding at the Same Time**
>
> Sometimes it's easier to grow your business with customers and suppliers than to raise investment capital. Why can't you just go sell what you're doing to buyers instead of raising money? You might find that you can do exactly that, lending great credibility to your business idea and to your own capabilities.

WHEN AND HOW TO USE EQUITY

Even this specific example shows why the game is not simply about trying to hold as much equity as possible. Instead, you need to think through the subtleties of how to use equity—when to give it away and how much, how to design contractual provisions, and so on.

What the mastery of colors and knives and brushes is to the artist, the mastery of the role of equity, decision rights, time, and cash flows is for the expert entrepreneur. Let's start with some examples of how you can use equity (common or preferred) beyond simply selling shares in your venture:

1. Through appropriate contractual provisions, you can share ownership of the financial returns of the venture without giving up decision rights. In other words, investors and other stakeholders can be entitled to receive a percentage (large or small) of earnings—while having no rights in making management decisions.
2. You can provide equity on a temporary basis, with the right to buy it back if specific milestones are met. This condition is frequently associated with short-term debt or loans.
3. You can offer equity to attract high-potential partners, using equity to align everyone's interests while keeping day-to-day management control through contractual provisions. It is up to you to decide, at any given point, exactly what you want and need in building your venture.

Sometimes you might find the ability to make decisions in the face of unpredictable contingencies more valuable than the ability to control the daily management of the venture. Depending on the direction of the venture, the right to a larger share of the return may be more important than a hold on the day-to-day control of operations.

And yet, at other times, you might want to give away equity to get great people on board and share pieces of the larger pie you co-create with stakeholders.

Ultimately, it is up to you. You can make specific judgments as you build the venture and ensure technicalities are taken care of by good advisors. But it is crucial to understand the subtleties of ownership versus control before you take the plunge.

Practically Speaking

Sharing the Treats Among Investors

Castor & Pollux is a successful organic dog food company. Founded by entrepreneurs with expertise in the pet food business, they chose to bring in a significant amount of angel investment to expand what they saw as a great opportunity. It cost them about one-third of their business, board seats, and the sharing of some decision rights.

Puppy Love

The founders doubled revenue for the first several years, putting the early capital to great use. Over the course of five years, they moved, added facilities, hired more people, changed packaging, and increased marketing.

Practically Speaking *(continued)*

At a certain point, the early investors wanted to cash out their ownership. At the same time, the venture attracted later stage private investors, with additional expertise, who were willing to buy the ownership of those early investors at an attractive price. The entrepreneurs' portion of the venture continued to shrink.

Big Dog

Today, the founders own much less than half of the business, yet they maintain substantial control of the day-to-day operation. Decisions about additional rounds of financing, new board members, new executives, strategic changes to the operation, and major capital expenditures are made with an extended range of stakeholders that includes new investors, original investors, lenders, customers, suppliers, and employees. The founders would add, of course, that all of this activity takes place under the strict oversight of culinary-minded canines.

Figure 18.2

Over to You: What Else Could Castor & Pollux Have Done for Funding?

Imagine you are the founder of Castor & Pollux, looking for capital to expand a growing idea. Think about the following questions and see how many options you can come up with:

- Where might you find other potential sources of funding?
- What do you have to offer them?
- How would you approach them?
- What would they want from you?

To learn more, visit: https://effectuation.org/EE3/castor or scan Figure 18.3.

Figure 18.3

FOOD FOR THOUGHT

There are many alternatives to equity that can encourage people to join you in creating your venture, market, or product. You can offer investors a fraction of revenue or even discounted products instead of equity. You can offer co-founders a sliding scale of salary rather than stock. You can even offer new employees a better title or a nicer office. If you are intent on holding on to equity, you can, if the alternative keeps the stakeholder engaged in the venture. However paranoid you might feel, most outside stakeholders, even venture capitalists, do not want control over your venture—even if they want equity. They want protection from downturns and optimal participation in upturns—the slice of the pie that matches their appetite to invest.

CONTROL WITHOUT OWNERSHIP AND OWNERSHIP WITHOUT CONTROL

We consider control to be the ability to direct the use of any particular resource. When can control be utilized? To what extent? To what end? By what processes? Control is never absolute. Different types of decisions involve different players. Sometimes you only have some influence in a matter, and sometimes you have complete say in a matter. Control is rarely simple.

Ownership is connected to control, but it is not control. A clear example is ownership of public companies: if you have shares in an investment fund, you own a bit of some public companies, but you have very little control over them.

There has been an entire body of academic research around agency theory, which asserts that owners explicitly don't control the operation of the firm but instead subcontract control to agents, such as the CEO. So, it is possible to control a large firm with relatively small amounts of ownership, if any at all.

Then again, what does it mean to "control" a firm? Clearly, if you own 100% of a firm, you have significant control, but even then, you do not have 100% control of the entire venture; you simply have control of how you will lead the venture in reaction to the actions of other stakeholders.

Consider customers versus lenders versus investors versus co-founders and the ownership and control they enjoy in exchange for their commitment to the venture. Customers might have no ownership of your organization, yet exert a lot of control in the form of influence and leverage, especially early on in the life of the organization.

Lenders might not have any ownership of the venture, but they exert significant control in how you use cash and probably little control over anything else. If financial problems arise, however, lenders can take complete control of the organization, without taking complete ownership.

Investors have a range in the extent to which their ownership, purchased by providing cash to you, translates into control. In fact, venture investors are nuanced in the nature of their ownership and the specific rights and situations over which they retain control. And that's the point—there is a range of options in the structure of ownership and the delineation of control.

Figure 18.4

"Congratulations on becoming a partner - your share of company losses are £200,000."

Figure 18.5

Research Roots

Agency Theory

The incentive difference between an owner and a worker has long been appreciated, at least since the days of land barons and feudal farmers. It is the incentive of the worker to be paid as much as possible by the owner to do as little as possible. And it is the incentive of the owner to pay the worker as little as possible and get as much productivity as possible.

Management scholars refer to the owner as the "principal" and the worker as the "agent." The agent works on behalf of the principal. Land barons tried to resolve the incentive difference, the agency problem, by taking only a fraction of the crop that farmers produced. Thus, farmers had some incentive to be productive—the more they produced, the more they benefited.

The same is true today for the sharing of equity. It is the goal of the owner of a venture, be it the founder or the investor, to provide incentives to the agents to be productive. Equity offers a strong incentive, as the agent benefits directly from any value created. There are many other approaches to overcoming the agency problem, ranging from financial rewards, such as raises and bonuses, to less tangible rewards, such as promotions, more interesting work assignments, and public recognition of accomplishments.

Practically Speaking

Steward-Ownership: A Growing Alternative

Co-Creator: Sophia Marie Braun

For the past three hundred years or more, two structures of ownership have dominated economies—namely, for-profit or non-profit. The latter could be organized as corporations, cooperatives, or foundations/trusts. The dominant form in the case of for-profit, generally called firms, consists of some form of limited liability company owned by shareholders. In the case of publicly traded firms, shares can be purchased and sold by anyone in stock markets, subject to the laws of the state/country in which those are incorporated.

From Sharing to Stewarding

Recently, entrepreneurs have begun reshaping this rather uncomplicated organizational landscape with hybrid forms of for-profit and social ventures, including new ways of structuring ownership within each of these.

Steward ownership is one example of such an attempt. As the name suggests, the aim here is to restructure for-profit ventures to enable protecting and nurturing of firm objectives other than financial profit, including stewardship of social values and the health of the planet.

Practically Speaking *(continued)*

In the familiar structure of a for-profit firm, owning a share in a company typically entitles shareholders to a share in the profits of the company as well as certain types of voting rights. In this view, a company is private property, owned by shareholders with rights and responsibilities over its assets, liabilities, and management.

Quilting Together Purpose and Trust

Steward-ownership is an alternative approach to company ownership that can be traced back to the eighteenth century. However, it recently gained a lot of public attention. In 2022, the US outdoor clothing retailer Patagonia, valued at around 3 billion US dollars, switched to steward-ownership.

The Purpose Group

Founded by more than 30 entrepreneurs in 2019, The Foundation for Steward-Ownership (FSO) is an organization advocating for steward-ownership in Germany. The key to steward-ownership is to introduce a layer of "stewards" who have no rights to the financial profits but can intervene with vetoes to ensure long-term values and purpose of the company are not harmed in certain situations such as when a company is sold/acquired or inherited.

FSO is propelled by the Purpose Group, which was co-founded in 2015 by two friends (Armin and Alex) and twin brothers (Achim and Adrian). They are active in four key areas of non-profit work: consulting businesses that want to transition to steward-ownership, managing investments in steward-owned companies, protecting steward-ownership structures in companies, and organizing events to increase awareness about steward-ownership.

SOTRUST

As is common in human history, a similar endeavor had been developing in another domain for a while. Originating in the late 1980s, A group of *Mittelstand* enterprises (German SME sector, mainly family businesses) had been discussing ways to transition their companies from the standard shareholder model into alternative ownership models. Under the name SOTRUST, the group hired two managers in 2014: Till and Gregor.

When they heard about Purpose, Till and Gregor reached out and met with the four co-founders of Purpose. They found that while SOTRUST was connecting theory and practice for discussing a legal problem and coming up with solutions for it, Purpose had created a preliminary solution in the form of steward-ownership. Also, whereas SOTRUST worked with rather traditional *Mittelstand* entrepreneurs, Purpose was engaged with startups, of which many were social businesses.

Invite to Co-Create

Where will this crazy quilt of stewards go in co-creating a new future for enterprise? It depends on who self-selects into the process and how they make lemonade with what the external environment throws at them. If you were to self-select into this new venture, what would be your skin in the game? And how would you seek to shape its goals and outcomes?

To learn more, visit: https://effectuation.org/EE3/steward or scan Figure 18.6.

Figure 18.6

THE PURPOSE OF OWNERSHIP

Ownership is primarily about two things: rewarding risk takers and providing incentives for success. A key difference between these ideas is that the first is about the past and the second is about the future. Ownership tends to go to the people who assume risk when they commit resources to your venture. Obviously, it doesn't have to—people are often compensated directly for their commitments with salary, purchase orders, etc. But early in the life of a venture, sharing ownership is often a way to reward the risk takers.

Early investors will generally not buy the entrepreneur out of a venture entirely. While they may want to capture as large a share of the rewards as possible, they know it's more important to maintain the entrepreneur's motivation and commitment.

There are a lot of rules of thumb about the proper distribution of ownership as a venture grows up. You can do an internet search for the latest opinions, but we offer one basic, not too unusual, and reasonably fair approach as food for thought: one-third to the founding team, one-third to venture investors, and one-third to the employees of the organization.

It doesn't have to be that way—you don't have to spend two-thirds of the equity of your venture to attract resources—but it's not outlandish.

Practically Speaking

A Piece of the Pie

Kenny Burts is a man devoted to key lime pie. Introduced to this regional specialty by his grandfather at the age of 9, he refined his own key lime pie recipe in the mid-1980s and nearly everyone who tasted his pies told Burts he should sell them. When Burts was working as a bartender, he began making pies part time in his apartment. He did everything: marketing, sales, manufacturing, and delivery to individuals and restaurants, all who raved about his product and kept coming back for seconds.

Burts remembers the work that went into his entrepreneurial beginning:

> I was making pies, I was delivering pies and I was tending bar. I was getting two hours sleep a night, setting three alarms and keeping the lights on so that when I woke up, I wouldn't go back to sleep. I knew at that time that nobody in their right mind was willing to do this, but that was my competitive edge. I used to make deliveries as far west as Birmingham, Alabama, 150 miles away, with 1–2 cases of pies. Nobody would have done that—nobody.

Cool Pies, Hot Kitchen

Working like that, Burts had to make a decision. Should he quit his bartending job and commit to squeezing the most out of the key lime pie business? One a stable income, the other his passion. The answer came in a phone call. Through a friend, Burts met executives with California Pizza Kitchen, a national restaurant chain. They liked his pie so much that they wanted to offer it in all their restaurants.

"I knew right then I was ready to take the plunge. I ran down the street to my dad's place and he said, "Son you've got to be careful with big customers—they can make you or break you." He was right. With strong commitment on their part and strong delivery on our part, they made us."

Practically Speaking *(continued)*

Taste for Investment

Prior to the call, the venture had been completely self-funded. But to serve California Pizza Kitchen, Burts began to consider raising capital for a more professional facility than his apartment. Almost immediately, he faced another decision more difficult than selling or making pies:

> I did not have the luxury of financial backing, which forced me to be sure I had a market (and income) before I could do anything. Now I needed to be crystal clear—what was I willing to part with for an investor? If I make a mistake—I had to make sure it would not wipe me out.

Burts built a partnership with an angel investor. An individual who shared (and invested in) his vision, his time horizon, his plans for growth, and his taste for key lime pie. Based on shared vision and objectives, the relationship has remained sweet ever since.

Figure 18.7

Expanding the Pie

Kenny's recipe has worked. In addition to California Pizza Kitchen, Burts was able to build an early partnership with Longhorn Steakhouse before they went public and grow with them as they expanded across the country. Nowadays the company produces six different pie varieties, selling the whopping 2.5 million pies a year through food service companies and over 6,000 grocery and convenience store outlets.

Not to worry, though. In spite of the success, the firm, now called Kenny's Great Pies, celebrated its 35th anniversary in 2024, and it is still making key lime pies according to exactly the same recipe and using the same fresh-squeezed key lime juice that earned his early rave reviews.

To learn more, visit: https://effectuation.org/EE3/limepie or scan Figure 18.8.

Figure 18.8

BUILDING EQUITABLE PARTNERSHIPS

If everyone contributes an equal amount, and receives an equal share of the pie, there is no issue. But what if some partners bring more money, skills, credibility, or contacts than others? How do you divide the equity?

The secret: there is no right answer at the level of detail most entrepreneurs are seeking. What we know is that the split needs to reward people sufficiently for the risks they've taken and motivate them sufficiently to continue to risk their time, talent, and resources on the venture.

Notions of fairness can get mixed into this discussion. Feelings can get hurt. Lawyers can get involved. But in the end, what's most important is stakeholders' level of satisfaction with the agreement.

Where to Start

Start by meeting with a potential stakeholder (investor or key hire—anyone with whom you are negotiating ownership or control) and mutually agreeing on the skill sets and other factors that will be required to make the venture successful in a specified period—say, three years at the most. You'll be listing things like technical capability, sales, raising money, making contacts, running the operation, etc.

Weight the factors on a 0–10 scale. Do this together. If you disagree, talk it through until you agree. The conversation need not get emotional—this is an important process to gain a shared understanding of the business, its key success factors, and the skills available.

Next, take your list of weighted success factors and rate each relevant stakeholder on their ability to bring each success factor to the business. Rate them on the same 0–10 scale. When you're finished, multiply these scores by the weighted factor and you'll have a mutually agreed-upon measure of each person's relative contribution to the success of the business.

And hopefully you'll have done it without any black eyes or injured egos. If you can't agree on what each of you brings to the business, you might want to reconsider whether you have the makings for a successful partnership.

Figure 18.9

Splitting the Pie

Dividing ownership is a stress-inducing topic. It can be legitimately thought of as fighting over a fixed pie—more for you is less for me. And, at some point in the future, if you are successful, real cash will change hands in line with these decisions, highlighting that every percentage point of ownership is connected to a material amount of money.

Even if greed were your only motivation (which we have yet to see), ownership percentage is not what you're trying to maximize. Cash is what you're trying to maximize. Sharing ownership wisely can create more cash than hoarding it. In new ventures, the pie is not fixed. You want to share ownership with talented people, partners, and providers of great resources in order to increase the size of the pie.

The Yellow Sari

In Bollywood movies, when the heroine wears a yellow sari, it usually signifies that something big is about to happen. If there is a yellow sari moment in the entrepreneurship classroom, it has to do with learning how to use equity as a tool in building new ventures. Students confuse equity with (a) control—or the right to make and implement key decisions; (b) piece of the pie—rights to the returns earned; or (c) compensation—for inputs brought into the venture (such as ideas, technical knowhow, money, effort, reputation, etc.).

Figure 18.10

Equity can, and of course should, be used as all of the above. But the important point is that it is not the same as any of these. Equity is like the trump card in a card game. It can substitute for any card in the deck. The key is to know when to use it as what. By assuming in advance that it is any one card, even the Ace of Spades, we may be jeopardizing our chances of winning the game.

Furthermore, in the case of equity in a new venture, as opposed to a trump card in a card game, we can play the trump card again and again and sometimes just temporarily lease or even pawn it with the possibility of redeeming it under circumstances we negotiate.

So, mastering the use of equity is key to how the story of the new venture will turn out. Like the yellow sari—whenever it shows up, the plot is about to change—and the fate of the new venture is literally at stake.

Practically Speaking

Investing in People

Felipe Vergara was a unique student. Not a lot of people born in Barranquilla, Colombia, wind up studying management at the University of Pennsylvania's prestigious Wharton School.

Vergara's path was one of education and entrepreneurship. From an early age, he tutored others in math, science, and languages and, after completing his university studies in Bogota, he founded a firm providing strategic and financial planning services to small businesses.

Mixing education and business with his first-hand understanding of the financial difficulties of attending Wharton, Vergara asked himself a question: Why, if someone could invest in the future value of a firm, could they not invest in the future value of him?

Practically Speaking *(continued)*

Equities r Us

Governments and banks already offered student loans. But loans came with borrowing limits and fixed payments, and often had to be backed by parents' assets or income, all of which challenged applicants from Barranquilla, Colombia, to Columbia, North Carolina.

And students' need for broader access to capital was increasing: according to the Education Data Initiative (Hanson, 2023), in 2023, a four-year undergraduate degree in a public institution costs on average 104,108 US dollars. Private university students pay more than double for a four-year degree, namely, 223,360 US dollars.

When Vergara met Miguel Palacios from the Darden School of Business at the University of Virginia, the answer came in the form of Lumni, a firm that pays a student's current tuition bills in exchange for a percentage of future earnings. Just like a share of stock, only it's stock in you and me. And the future is our careers.

Tomorrow's Markets

A marketplace is the foundation of exchange. In its earliest form, it's a farmer with too many carrots wanting to trade some for a chicken. More recently, it's someone willing to pay money in return for getting a haircut or a hedge clipped.

Today markets enable us to not only trade what exists on the shelves, but also buy and sell future values of everything imaginable, from orange juice to the right to pollute. Markets deliver humanitarian aid—witness UNHCR's Kashmir Relief Note, which provides a return on investments made to reconstruct Pakistan-administered Kashmir following the 2005 earthquake.

Markets also enabled David Bowie to sell the future value of his song royalties. And, with Lumni, that same alternative is open to individual students.

The Circle of Light

To date (2024), Lumni has worked with more than 22,000 students in four countries (Mexico, Colombia, Peru, and Chile), investing 60 million US dollars via 32 discrete funds. Importantly, 84% of those assisted are from low-income families and 45% are female (Lumni, n.d.).

Looking ahead to when his investees turn into his investors is when the future will indeed be even brighter—for Lumni and the rest of us.

lumni
INVESTING IN A BRIGHTER FUTURE

Figure 18.11

To learn more, visit: https://effectuation.org/EE3/lumni or scan Figure 18.12.

Figure 18.12

Figure 18.13

Faces and Wallets

Wallets always come with faces. So why not target faces instead of wallets? Luckily, faces often come with wallets, too, so by starting with your means, particularly the means of who you know, you may generate good leads for investment. And having a relationship with people who invest in you will also make it easier for you to anticipate what kind of interaction your investors will want. Early-stage investments are rarely at arm's length, so no matter what, you get the face with the wallet.

Figure 18.14 Wallets come with faces.

Summary: Ownership and Control in Term Sheet Terms

As you face a term sheet, think about trade-offs along the dimensions of ownership and control:

Ownership

- Ratchet. If there is a down round (valuation lower than the previous), early investors may protect against dilution by adding a "ratchet" to their anti-dilution to adjust the price of their previous investments to the new round.
- Right of first refusal. Major investors get the right to maintain ownership percentage on future financing.
- Liquidation preferences. Major investors get paid first in a liquidity event.

Control

- Directors. The ability to add a person to the board in conjunction with an investment
- Information rights. Monthly or quarterly internal statements—or annually reviewed or audited statements
- Voting rights. Preferred vote with common shares, except as required by law

For more details on the various terms and concepts summarized here, refer to the "Explainer" section at the end of this chapter.

TAKEAWAY: GOOD PARTNERSHIPS MAKE GOOD VENTURES

Regardless of whether your objective is to become very wealthy or to create something of enduring value to society (or perhaps both), partnerships are critical. Structuring partnerships with investors, employees, board members, customers, and even lawyers demands a detailed understanding of the softer side—what each party values in the interaction. And it demands technical proficiency with structuring deals along the dimensions of control and ownership. The key aspects that underpin the negotiation of any arrangement include determining and articulating the appropriate level of risk, the appropriate amount of control, and equitable provisions for ownership and liquidity.

It is important to realize that the spirit on both sides of the agreement is probably more important than the actual text of the agreement. As the venture, the environment, and the constellation of partnerships change, there is much opportunity for re-interpretation of the terms of the agreement, and it is useful to be able to fall back on a shared spirit.

Further, if lawyers have to be brought in to work through differences in understandings of control or ownership, the likely outcome is that nobody wins, so it is good to be able to establish a shared foundation at the start.

Think It Through

- Who really owns the firm (customers, investors, management, society)?
- Why does ownership matter?
- Where does control come from (how much is earned and how much is bestowed)?
- What is the role of the entrepreneur—to control or to own?
- What is the real cost of money?

So What?

Control does not equal ownership—you can get a whole lot of control without ownership, and control rights can be assigned very specifically to different aspects of what your venture is working toward.

Ownership can be used to enable the alignment of incentives around the creation process.

What Now?

Consider your own venture or one you know well:

- What control rights do you need in order to make the venture succeed?
- Can you gain any level of influence or control over those areas without owning anything? You might be surprised how far you can get on this front.
- How will you use equity to align interests and encourage everyone to give their all?
- Who needs equity, and who doesn't?
- What can you do for stakeholders who don't want equity?
- What terms do you really care about if you are going to take an investment? Do you have to be in charge? Are you willing to sell the business?
- Do you need a board of directors? Why? What value do you want to derive from that board? What will it take to build a board that you truly value? How will you attract and reward them (think beyond money)?

EXPLAINERS—THE STRUCTURES OF OWNERSHIP AND CONTROL

Common and Preferred Stock

Both forms of equity provide ownership of a company. They differ in that preferred shares generally: (a) receive dividends at a higher rate; and (b) are repaid before common shares in the event of insolvency or liquidity.

Liquidity Preferences

Often, shareholders will establish a claim on who gets paid first. A one-time liquidation preference means that shareholders get the amount of their investment paid to them first and foremost in the occurrence of a liquidity event. For example, if they invested 1 million US dollars and the business sells for 10 million US dollars, 1 million US dollars is paid to them before any sort of allocation of capital according to ownership percentages is made. A two-times preference would mean that the first 2 million US dollars would go to them, and the remaining 8 million US dollars would be shared among others who participate in the general ownership of the venture.

Dilution Protection

Existing investors may try to protect themselves from dilution of ownership when new investors bring more cash into the company. The most straightforward anti-dilution protection is the right of first refusal (also called pre-emptive rights, or "pro rata"). These establish the right of an investor to invest in the company before new investors, and they may be capped at the amount of investment that would keep their ownership percentage the same (i.e. if they own 20%, they have right of first refusal on whatever shares in the new round it would take to keep them at 20%, but no more).

Sometimes they are not capped, meaning an investor has first rights to all future rounds. A special version of this is called a ratchet, which protects existing investors in the event of a "down round" (when the value of the firm drops over time) by maintaining their ownership percentage even if new investment is brought in at a lower valuation. Anti-dilution enables early investors to retain control as the ownership expands.

Protective Covenants

These are specific rules about what types of votes, and by who, determine specific decisions in the venture. Decisions about new board members, changes in the size of the board, new rounds of financing, executive compensation, stock option plans, major capital expenditures, and so on can be detailed in such a way that the voting rights on a particular topic are not represented by the ownership percentages overall.

The Language of Valuation

With investors, valuation and the distribution of ownership are more explicit than with partners. There are many nuances to the discussion of valuation, and we seek only to mention the main issues here and suggest turning to new venture financing literature for details.

To start with, we need to be clear about the difference between the value of the venture before and after an investment. Pre-money valuation is simply the value of the venture before the investor puts his or her cash into it.

Post-money valuation is the pre-money valuation plus the amount of cash the investors put into the company. Ownership percentages are determined using post-money value as the denominator. For example, if an investor puts 1 million US dollars into a venture with a pre-money value of 2 million US dollars, the investor owns a 1 million US dollar share of a 3 million US dollar business, or one-third of the company (but remember, this doesn't mean the investor controls one-third of it). Investors may want anti-dilution protection to guarantee that they always own their fraction of the business.

A lot of time can be spent negotiating the pre-money valuation of a venture and the terms of the investment. This is understandable, because the higher the pre-money valuation, the less the investment dilutes the current owners' stake, but the less attractive the deal is to new investors.

In that regard, it's just like buying a house: a higher price is great for the sellers and worse for the buyers. But, in this case, the seller and the buyer have to cooperate extensively after the deal has closed. In fact, their ability and desire to cooperate effectively is part of what expands the pie, making consequences of valuation less clear cut than "higher is better" for the seller.

Consider the consequences of a high valuation for future fundraising. An empirical fact: the average series A pre-money valuation for a venture taking on formal venture capital investment is approximately 6 million US dollars. If an entrepreneur is able to raise an angel investment at a valuation of 12 million US dollars, it is significantly more difficult to raise that series A money from formal venture capitalists. This is the case for two reasons: (1) The angel investors object because it results in a dramatic dilution of their ownership percentage; and (2) the VCs object because such a dramatic drop in valuation undermines the ability of the group to grow the pie; it complicates things and can be an easy excuse to say no and move on.

You can search the internet for a litany of advice concerning what the "right" pre-money valuation of a venture should be. These are mostly rules of thumb about how much a patent should be worth or what the value of having a completed product is, along with various milestones that can serve as a guide for valuation. We won't summarize them here.

Two issues dictate valuation in early-stage ventures. The venture needs X amount of cash, and the investor is willing to invest only if he or she can own Y percent of the venture.

For example, an entrepreneur needs to raise 0.5 million US dollars to complete a prototype and win her first major customer. An angel investor prefers to invest in opportunities where she can own around one-third of the business, so long as she has a seat on the board of directors and a say in the hiring of executives. If they were to execute the transaction, the valuation is essentially deduced rather than negotiated: 0.5 million US dollars is one-third of 1.5 million US dollars; thus the post-money is 1.5 million US dollars, and the pre-money is 1 million US dollars.

This may lead the entrepreneur to say, "I don't want to sell my stock at that valuation—1 million US dollars is way too low." Thus, she might like to sell less stock at that valuation; maybe she'd want to raise only 0.25 million US dollars. However, the angel investor would still want to own about one-third of the company. The entrepreneur may have to find a different angel investor to accomplish the goal of selling less stock, because the investment isn't being determined by the valuation. It's often the other way around; the valuation is being determined by the separate preferences of the entrepreneur and the angel investor.

There is a lot written about valuation, and you should review it before you start thinking about a term sheet for raising venture investment.

Term Sheets: Everything Is Negotiable

If investors and entrepreneurs are able to come to an agreement, the specifics are written down on a term sheet. Not all term sheets use all the elements we discuss here. Angel investor term sheets tend to be less complicated than formal VC term sheets.

As the venture grows and goes through multiple funding rounds, different rights are often assigned to different series of preferred stock issuance and to common stock. All the terms are subject to the golden rule: whoever has the gold makes the rules.

When a venture must raise more cash or die, the negotiation power clearly lies in the hands of incoming investors. All terms are then subject to renegotiation. Broadly speaking, good terms align the objectives of the investors and those of the entrepreneurs while protecting the investors from entrepreneurial recklessness (it isn't the entrepreneur's money, so agency risks come into play) and protecting the entrepreneur from investor intrusiveness (because too many chefs spoil the broth).

There are hundreds of actual term sheets to be found floating around the internet or at universities, think tanks, law firms, etc. These term sheets can provide a black and white picture of how ownership is separate from control, and even how ownership can apply to different things.

For example, ownership can change at different levels of upside or downside liquidity events and can even change over time. The details will pile up as your venture grows. Search these topics on the internet and seek legal advice.

The Stakeholders of Ownership and Control

Early-Stage Investors

How early-stage investors learn about entrepreneurs before making an investment:

- *Referrals.* Investors rely on referrals from people they trust who have known the entrepreneur for some time, to understand the ability and motivation of entrepreneur.
- *Interaction.* Investors meet time and again with entrepreneurs. Personal questions are fair game. Do you want to get rich? Do you want power and control? What kind of leader are you? How do you respond to disaster? How do you know?

How early-stage investors think about investing in new ventures:

- *Time.* While you are in a hurry when you're raising money, investors are not. Why hurry? It regularly takes 6 to 12 months to raise investment money, and over that time they can see whether you're delivering on promises and remaining committed to the effort.
- *Committee.* Investors learn from the judgment of other investors, partners in venture capital firms, and other entrepreneurs.

What the Investor Sees in Your Venture

Venture investing is difficult and risky. Investors look at many deals and invest only in those on which they are incredibly bullish. In spite of this, they are wrong more often than they are right and are more likely to lose money than make money on any venture investment.

Angel investors lose money in nearly two-thirds of their investments. The wins have to cover all the losses and take into account the dilution in ownership over time.

You may believe you will sell the business for 100 million US dollars in five years because the opportunity is incredible. An early-stage investor can invest 0.5 million US dollars for one-third ownership, creating a 33 million US dollar return in only five years. Seem obscene? You do the work; they make 32.5 million US dollars.

Reality check. Most likely, you will return less than 0.5 million US dollars to that investor.

Second, in order to grow the company to where you can sell it for 100 million US dollars, you will raise additional capital, and the initial investor might see ownership percentage go from one-third to one-tenth, meaning that they would get 10 million US dollars of the 100 million US dollar exit, a very nice return, 20 times their investment, but nowhere near 33 million US dollars.

Reduce that by the risk that the entrepreneur will not achieve targets, competitive entry, and difficulty of liquidity, and you see why the investor is slow to write a check.

Investor Perspective: Angels

Angel investors often provide seed capital for startups. They will invest less and earlier than VC firms. Typically, they will ask for 20% to 50% ownership. They may invest as little as 1,000 US dollars and more than 5 million US dollars.

Angel investors often feel that the valuation of a company is less than what the entrepreneur has proposed, and given the early and uncertain nature of the opportunity, it is hard to measure and even harder to figure out how to measure. Investors will work with the entrepreneurs' financial projections and use various valuation methods such as transactional value, market value, and return as a multiple of investment.

The valuation methodology most frequently used is backing into exit value. For example, if the company is expected to be worth 50 million US dollars in five years, the company needs to raise a single round of 1 million US dollars to reach that valuation and the investors will require a 10 times cash-on-cash return upon exit— that is, the investors' share must be worth 10 million US dollars in five years. Thus, the investors would need to own 20% of the company, which implies a 4 million US dollars pre-money valuation and 5 million US dollar post-money valuation (this presumes that no further dilutive capital is needed).

It is often said that because angels invest early and small, they miss out on the big wins. But based on our research, that appears not to be true. While the downside of an angel investor is less (from making smaller investments), the upside is as limitless as it is for the venture capitalist, who must invest much larger amounts at later stages in the venture's life. Because angels invest smaller amounts, they can make more investments and increase the chances of a big win.

How Advisory Boards Are Different from Boards of Directors

An advisory board is most useful in providing strategic ideas or feedback on increasing revenue and building your business, with the members not involved in the details of your company.

You go to them, as you would to an old university friend whom you don't see often, to catch up and pick their brains—for a bird's-eye view of your landscape. The members of your board of directors, by contrast, are more like your parents, the people you go to when you are up against it and you need not so much advice, but guidance on a day-to-day basis about how to navigate choppy waters: a lawsuit, for example, or the sale of your company. These people give you the view of your business much closer to the ground (Hoffman, 2003).

Table 18.1

What you need to know about boards	
Why do I need a board in the first place?	If you have a broad-reaching business concept and you want your business to mature, you should consider having a board. You will not possess all the functional skills necessary to make sound judgments consistently. Nor, most probably, will you be able to afford that expertise and skills in the early stages. Having a board of advisors with balanced skills and experience will come in handy. The board can help you with financing and finding new customers. It will provide specific advice, offer wisdom of prior experience, keep you focused on strategy and provide credibility to outside parties such as bankers and investors. Most importantly, it will be there to ensure you make fewer mistakes. Everyone needs to be accountable to someone, and as founder, you will be accountable to the board. As one entrepreneur said, "I needed the board to save the company from myself."
Who should be on my board?	Initially, the board can be made up of insiders if you do not have outside investors. But it is better to have some members on the board whose skills are complementary, not identical, to yours. So, if you have questions, instead of calling professionals such as attorneys and paying them 250 US dollars an hour, you can pick up the phone and call your board member. You try to find people for your board who have been there and done it before.
When do I need the board—at what stage?	Consider having a board from inception. If not, you must have one by the time you want to raise outside capital. In general, the board is there to help with current and strategic issues, but each stage in the development of a new venture calls for different kinds of expertise. Stage → Expertise/need Seed → Financial, legal, business development Emerging management → Industry expertise, market, financial, legal, management Growth → Similar to emerging, add in strategic Mature → Strategic, market, financial, management
Do I need a board of advisors or a board of directors?	An advisory board works fine at the outset. But once you start bringing in cash, it is time to create a board of directors. The members should have specific responsibilities and should be compensated; they can also be fired. In choosing board members, setting expectations up front is important. Your directors constitute your company's governing body and have fiduciary responsibilities for which they can be held legally accountable. Your advisors, by contrast, are high-level strategists or mentors. For small companies, directors are generally shareholders and thus already have an incentive to spend their time on your company. Many companies might compensate advisors with a small token of stock, but most advisors are motivated not by money but by the ability to mentor an entrepreneur.

How do I find people who can sit on my board?	Start with people you know and people who already care about and are deeply involved in your enterprise or industry. Do not take rejection personally. Good people have options, commitments, and not much spare time. When you find someone worthy, share your passion and candidly explore how he or she can add value to your organization. Appeal to someone who would like to help you. Self-selected stakeholders willing to make real commitments of time and interest are best. The key is to find those you want to work with and get them to want to work with you—not by "selling" them on the deal, but by persuading them enough so that they sell themselves.
How do I know whether I have the right people?	Carl F. Frischkorn, a successful entrepreneur, angel investor, and board member at many young companies, talks about his three criteria for choosing which boards to participate in: I have to like the CEO as a person. I need to believe that the person has good ethics and integrity—a person who would listen and also argue. If she wins the argument, then she wins, but if she doesn't, she has to make a change. I think it's fantastic to stand up for what you believe in, but you also need to respond to feedback and then make the changes. I have to like the product, understand the concept and think that the product has good market acceptance and growth opportunity. I have to think that I can add value being involved as an advisor. Sarasvathy (n.d.)

Table 18.2

What you need to do with your board	
What are the duties of directors?	You should create job descriptions for members of the board before bringing them in. In general, the major responsibilities of a board are to: • Participate in policy formulation and financial and strategic planning • Serve as a sounding board for the CEO in major decisions • Evaluate the performance of senior management • Determine the compensation of senior management • Ensure the adequacy of financial controls and monitor compliance with laws and regulations • Advise on succession planning.
How engaged should my board be?	Boards can have varying degrees of engagement. For some companies, boards are passive, functioning at the discretion of the CEO. They only ratify management's decisions. At the other extreme are operating boards, which make all key decisions; management is simply present to implement them. A properly engaged board will provide insight, advice, and support to the CEO. It will oversee both the CEO's and the company's performance and add value to decisions by providing necessary expertise. Good board members will not hesitate to pick up the phone and call people for you or call you on their own initiative when they come across information or possibilities—both positive and negative—important to the survival and health of the business.
What is the best use of my time with the board?	Boards function best when they are tightly managed and have enough diversity of experience. You should bring in people who are neither afraid to question your judgments nor uncomfortable with your right to make final decisions. It's important to communicate with board members as much as you can. Hold four to ten meetings a year. Talk to directors by phone whenever you are in doubt or need a certain expertise. Prior to every meeting, preview key issues with each director and provide a written agenda and information package at least a week in advance. Give your directors bad news quickly and be measured with good news. Taking care of key issues will ensure that your board remains focused and comes to your assistance. Otherwise, you may start seeing your board meetings as a waste of time.

(continued)

How do I compensate board members? What's in it for them?	Signing on as a director is one thing; contributing is another. So, you must keep your board members interested. With advisory boards, the problem is that you can never pay them what they're worth. One way of keeping them interested is to pamper them. Send them free company products, pay for dinner at the best places in town and, if possible, arrange out-of-city meetings and pay for spouses to attend. The best way to keep them interested is by communicating regularly. What's in it for them? It is the pride in helping a promising entrepreneur. To some of them, it will be like a second chance. If you have a formal board of directors, make sure they have some skin in the game. Use stock, warrants, options, and cash to keep their interest. Often, the entrepreneur believes that board members serve simply because they like to. But ultimately, all of us want to be paid for our time. If your advisory board transforms into a real board and you want it to work properly, set aside 3% to 10% of the company as compensation for what they are doing. Do not assume that there is a standard package for compensation. People care about different things, and they often work for strange rewards. This is where it is important to spend sufficient time recruiting board members and to set expectations at the outset. You are building a long-term relationship. Take the time to get to know what each director cares about and why and to share your own passions and motivations.
What are the common conflicts that I should be aware of?	If the board is informal in structure, and it is time to make a real board of directors, compensation issues may arise. The first conflict usually happens over valuation of the director's time and expectations. As the founder, you will be working 365 days a year; your advisors will probably give 5% of their time. So, when there is a question of sharing the pie, you may think they are asking too much. The solution is to be upfront about the issue. The second conflict usually comes if, as founder, you are unable to grow with the company. Running a company at the startup stage requires different skills than running it when it is big and mature. Conflict arises if you are unable to change and your board thinks you are unfit to be the CEO. The only solution is to learn to manage your company well. As long as you are making good decisions, your board members and investors will not want to take the company away from you. They would rather spend 5% of their time on the company and not be involved in day-to-day affairs. Remember, they have other businesses to run, too.

Table 18.3

What you need to know about lawyers	
Do I need a lawyer to incorporate?	Technically, no. A person can incorporate a business without the help of a lawyer. Check your government websites for information; a simple incorporation (called an "S corporation in the US") with one owner and no shareholders might take 20 minutes to register, with minimal fees applied. But it is always better to use professional help when you are not an expert. Good professional advice will save you from making mistakes that may prove costly down the line, especially if you anticipate having investors or selling your company later. There are even online services that take the place of live attorneys. They gather information from clients and automatically draft and customize the articles, bylaws, corporate minutes, stock certificates, and federal forms for each individual business. But because of the automation, it is sometimes difficult to completely customize. For example, creating specific bylaws within the Articles of Incorporation is not possible using most of the online services.

(continued)

How do I find a lawyer?	Ask the people you know and like—your professors, your friends, or someone who is doing business locally. Those people should be able to point you to one or two good lawyers. Talk to at least a couple of people before you decide on the person or firm to go with.
What is the first meeting with a lawyer like? What do I say?	Usually lawyers will not charge you for the first meeting. This is the time to see whether that particular lawyer will be a good fit for you. Remember, the lawyer will also be trying to learn about you and decide whether he or she wants to do business with you. The first meeting involves bringing the lawyer up to speed on your business. What is the product? Who are the customers? What does the future of the business look like? And so forth. Have a set of questions ready for each lawyer. That way, you will be able to compare them before choosing. You should be asking the lawyer's opinion on: • What type of business entity you should choose given the business and its future vision • Any other issues such as patents, copyrights, and other intellectual property rights (depending on the nature of the business, you may need other clearances).
What if I cannot afford to pay the lawyer? Do I offer him or her equity?	To the greatest extent possible, treat a lawyer as a professional service that you pay for. Good and understanding lawyers usually cut startups some slack because they think of working with you as an investment. They expect future returns—repeat business, referrals—when you grow.

REFERENCES

Hanson, M. (2023). Average Cost of College [2023]: Yearly Tuition + Expenses. Education Data Initiative. Retrieved January 11, 2024, from https://educationdata.org/average-cost-of-college

Hoffman, A. (2003, August 6). Going by the board. *BusinessWeek*. http://www.businessweek.com/smallbiz/content/aug2003/sb2003086_8777.htm

Kenny's Great Pies, Inc. "Island Style" Pie Manufacturer, Smyrna. (n.d.). Kenny's Great Pies! Retrieved January 10, 2024, from https://www.kennysusa.com

Lumni. (n.d.). Retrieved January 11, 2024, from https://www.lumni.net/nosotros

Sarasvathy, S. D. (n.d.). *Boards for a New Venture: Putting Together Boards and Working with Them*. Retrieved January 19, 2025, from https://papers.ssrn.com/sol3/papers.cfm?abstract_id=1583303

CHAPTER 19

Figure 19.1 As much as plans can give us comfort in certain times, in uncertain times they are more likely to frustrate progress.

Business Plans and Business Models

In This Chapter

No matter how well-crafted your plan may be, it's taking action and working with committed stakeholders that truly brings your venture to life. It's about turning plans into reality, making things happen, and seeing the tangible results of your efforts.

Aside from acting as a marketing tool for raising investment, one of the best uses of a business plan might be to help you take action. Ultimately, the business plan is nothing more than a tool to help you get your venture going. If it is not helping you do that, then forget it. Forge ahead.

> Plans are worthless. Planning is everything.
>
> *United States President and Army General Dwight D. Eisenhower*

DOI: 10.4324/9781003364016-23

In This Chapter *(continued)*

BUSINESS PLANS TO LEARN

The business plan is one of the most "taught" aspects of entrepreneurship. As a work project, it provides a learning platform that forces entrepreneurship students to spell out all functional areas related to the venture. Everything from financial plans and budgets, assessments, and assertions of market need, the four *P*s (price, product, promotion, and placement) of marketing, key talent needs, risk assessments, competitive details, comparisons, etc. need to be included in a business plan.

BUSINESS PLANS TO COMMUNICATE

The very idea of a business plan may seem contradictory to an effectual approach to building new ventures. Yet, the business plan is difficult to escape in a world of causal investors and other stakeholders seeking the seeming certainty of such plans.

The difference between causal and effectual use of a business plan, therefore, is that in the effectual case, it is not a plan—it is merely a communication tool written over and over again as the venture develops and written differently for different stakeholders. Honesty demands that effectuators do their best in building predictive models, but explicitly clarify that the aim is not to deliver on the plan, but to do what it may take to co-create value for everyone involved.

As such, this chapter will not teach you how to write a business plan. You can go online to find out more, and there are whole books dedicated to the topic. One classic is entitled *How to Write a Great Business Plan* by Bill Sahlman (originally published in the *Harvard Business Review* in 1997, p. 98).

Instead, this chapter is dedicated to the principle of substance over form in thinking through a new business.

SHARING YOUR BUSINESS PLAN

One of the key aspects of business plans is the fact that they are used not only by you (the entrepreneur) as an internal management tool, but also by other stakeholders, in particular your bank (or other financial services firm), your investors, your accountant, your lawyer, business partners (for example, your suppliers), and sometimes even your employees (in ventures that have an "open book" policy). Thus, what business plans do can be much more than just what they do as an internal management tool, which is how they are often portrayed in textbooks.

Sociologists coined the term "Boundary Objects" to describe

the fact that objects like business plans are important bridges across the boundaries between different professional worlds, such as entrepreneurship and banking.

Seen as boundary objects, business plans occupy a special place in communicating and collaborating with stakeholders. Researchers have pointed out that many kinds of objects, both tangible and intangible, can act as boundary objects, with some favorite examples being maps, presentations, business models, and stories. Such objects are intermediaries in the collective work that entrepreneurs and their stakeholders put forth in building new ventures—much more, potentially, than just a plan (Nicolini et al., 2012).

THE SUBSTANCE OF THE BUSINESS PLAN

Emphasizing substance over form is essential because the business plan is largely a marketing tool. We don't mean this in any pejorative sense. You may need a business plan to pitch your venture to various resource providers, and so it must communicate the perspective, insights, and guidance that will help others evaluate and categorize the opportunity.

As with any marketing communication, you must know your audience and the objectives you want to accomplish. Audiences for business plans might include lenders, private investors, potential employees and board members, customers, upstream suppliers, or downstream channel partners.

The form of a business plan really depends on what you intend to do with it—how you plan to address the various interests of these diverse audiences. Here we'll focus on substance and leave the form up to you.

Each audience you're pitching to requires different information and uses the content of the business plan to different ends. Talk to them and find out what they really want to know. Our suggestions in this chapter can help you get started, but we claim no encyclopedic knowledge on the needs and preferences of all those audiences.

Each audience has its own rules and screening procedures which help them process the information you provide much more quickly than you might think. They often have requirements involving minimum revenue levels, industry/technology/sector preferences, different risk factors they are willing to take on, team member details and relationships, or primary customers and marketing channels.

In many instances, you can learn the details of how your audience "screens" and how they rule out plans right up front. Ask what different resource providers want and listen to them—some will fit your venture, some won't.

For example, most banks will not deal with new ventures, most venture capitalists won't deal with pre-revenue businesses, and most angel investors won't invest in ventures valued at more than 5 million US dollars pre-money (often less). Ask and listen.

BUSINESS PLANS TO MANAGE RISK

Our starting premise: business plans are not about selling the upside of your venture. Instead, they are about sharing your mastery of the opportunity, which involves upside, downside, inside, outside, and blindside.

One of the most under-addressed topics in business plans is risk management. No one wants to "spook" potential partners with frank discussions of negative possibilities while in the midst of selling the winning potential of a venture.

Yet, if we take to heart ideas about influencing and being influenced, staying committed means more than goals, working with affordable loss, finding committed partners and leveraging contingencies, then we must also take to heart that things will go wrong. Things we want to happen don't. Things we didn't want to happen do. Murphy's Law applies.

Consequently, your business plan must reinforce your ability to deal with problems, change, disappointment, and so on. Business plans that sell the upside with a mere nod to the risks are considered naïve by good investors and useless by expert entrepreneurs.

Yes, your graphs should go "up and to the right," as Guy Kawasaki (a popular industry pundit and author) jokes about the hockey stick revenue projections entrepreneurs create. But if you stop there, you will be unprepared to deal with the inevitable hard questions coming your way.

Additionally, if you show only "up and to the right" information, you leave the risks to your audience's imagination and miss the opportunity to influence their assessment and learn from their honest feedback about the actual risks.

We've seen countless business plans in which the "worst-case scenario" is still a completely acceptable business, simply with lower sales growth, or the short-term customers go away but you're still okay in the long term, or the whole plan is simply an average of the best case and the worst case. Don't laugh—this is commonplace, and you'll likely do something similar unless you deliberately choose something better. Think through your Murphy's Law plan. Deal with the consequences of receiving a no from everyone you hope will say yes. For example:

Yes:

- Yes, the technical milestone was hit on time.
- Yes, the customer wants to set up a test and then scale out.
- Yes, we just hired the savvy and well-known marketing person we've been chasing.
- Yes, we just brought in an investor who has a lot of relevant expertise.

No:

- If you assume no, what will you do?
- Are there good fallback positions?
- Can you prioritize the pain from different failures?
- Can you take steps to shore up the highest priorities?
- Have you committed to a single solution that could be disastrous for you?
- How can you minimize the damage of negative responses?
- In what ways have you kept things to an affordable loss to help minimize that damage?

Your Murphy's Law plan will not be entirely elegant. Sometimes, the answer to a problem is simply that you will have to work twice as hard to survive. Sometimes, the answer will be that you in fact have no response—and winning that specific yes is mission critical. Lose it and you lose.

Okay. At least you see that. It should also mean that if you win it, you have made a great step forward. Attract more resources with that win. Manage the expectations of investors, and demonstrate your expertise, by considering these topics.

You won't share your Murphy's Law plan with everyone. Different versions of business plans are appropriate for different audiences. It may be that you use it with key leadership, board members, or potential employees in their last decision steps, but not with prospective lenders, members of the press, or potential business partners. It is up to you, but having worked out your thoughts on managing risk is genuinely useful for whatever form of business plan you choose to create.

BUSINESS PLANS TO MANAGE BOTTLENECKS

Potential bottlenecks are also rarely addressed in business plans. You can learn a lot about bottlenecks from ideas in operations management.

The kinds of questions that operations people ask include:

- What is going to be truly difficult about your venture?
- When?
- How will things change over time?
- Where will things get stuck?
- Where are they stuck right now?

Cash is quite often presumed to be the bottleneck for entrepreneurs. This is generally misguided. You must keep asking "why" questions: Why can I not get cash? Chase those causes, dig a little deeper. Those are your real bottlenecks. And once you have gotten to the cause, you may realize that either: (a) there is something about your business that makes it unappealing to an investor; or (b) you don't really need cash at all—you need a machine or a person or a distribution relationship, and finding those resources directly is often easier than finding the cash to go out and buy them.

Research Roots

Useful Tool: The Business Model Canvas

Together with Yves Pigneur (academic focused on the intersection of people and information systems), and based on his dissertation on business model innovation, Alexander Osterwalder co-created the highly successful book *Business Model Generation* with an international team of over 450 collaborators.

The heart of their approach, the Business Model Canvas (BMC), is another example of a popular business book that has made its way into entrepreneurship education for the simple reason that people find it very useful.

What makes the Business Model Canvas such a helpful tool? One can point to several features. It gets users to focus on the key elements of their venture such as value proposition, target segments, partners, and suppliers.

It is therefore a good tool for working through the basic activities entrepreneurs need to undertake in new ventures. The canvas also helps people view a venture as a whole, to check how everything fits—or doesn't fit—together. In other words, it is a useful way of detecting major inconsistencies. It also seems to have just the right amount of structure to help guide users without constraining their ideas too much.

The fact that the Business Model Canvas is a visual tool is undoubtedly what made it popular. It literally brings us a canvas and invites us to physically work on it. In doing so, it helps us to better think through problems by drawing on our powerful visualization skills. In short, the Business Model Canvas works because it's a canvas.

The idea of business models has been around for a long time, but Osterwalder, Pigneur, and colleagues put it into a format that turns something fuzzy into something that can be clearly visualized, hacked-together, worked and reworked, argued about by teams, and ultimately pinned to the wall (Osterwalder & Pigneur, 2010).

To learn more, visit: https://effectuation.org/EE3/canvas or scan Figure 19.2.

Figure 19.2

Research Roots

Seat of the Pants

People will tell you that before you launch a company, you have to write a business plan. So, how is it that so many Inc. 500 CEOs skipped that sober exercise? Research on founders of firms in the Inc. 500 determined that only 40% of the firms in that sample had created a business plan. And of those who had created a plan, 65% said they were doing something significantly different from their original idea. Remarkably, only 12% of the group reported doing formal market research before launching their firms (Bartlett, 2002).

This data is consistent with other research conducted by Amar Bhidé (2000), who investigated a broader sample of new ventures and found that 41% of the founders had no business plan at all, 26% had a rudimentary plan, and only 28% had a formal business plan.

In this regard, notable entrepreneurs that include Bill Gates, Sam Walton, and Jann Wenner are not unique. None of them started with a detailed business plan.

Practically Speaking

The Cube Without a Plan

It's hard to believe that the blockbuster toy that frustrated our childhood and sold almost a hundred million units between 1980 and 1983 is already practically an antique. But what was behind the product that created the first millionaire entrepreneur from the Communist Bloc?

Birth of the Cube

The father of the Cube, Erno Rubik, was a sculptor, an architect, and a teacher of interior design. Spatial relationship problems were his business and realizing them in three dimensions his specialty. In class, he would often build a physical design to make a point—as he did with the Cube. Rubik's Cube was not originally intended to be a blockbuster, or even a toy. It was the presentation of a solution to a structural design problem of surfaces in three dimensions that could be manipulated in any direction.

Inventor Turns Marketer

Technical creations come along all the time. Making a market for them is the job of the entrepreneur. And without such explicit intentions, Rubik started the process by sharing his puzzle with his students and friends. Their attraction to it indicated opportunity. So, when Rubik met Tibor Laczi, a salesman from an Austrian computer company, Rubik was open to what happened next.

Rising to the Challenge

Laczi took Rubik's Cube to the Nuremberg Toy Fair in Germany, where he met British toy specialist Tom Kremer. Kremer shared Laczi's attraction to the cube, and the pair negotiated an order for a million Cubes with the Ideal Toy Company in New York.

Practically Speaking *(continued)*

Rubik set up production in his native Hungary, to feed the escalating demand for his toy. But trying to manufacture high-quality consumer products behind the Iron Curtain in the early 1980s was an insurmountable challenge. Ironically, the wild success of the Cube, compounded by the expense of returned defective Cubes, ultimately led to the collapse of Ideal Toy Company.

A Block of Benefits

The interesting thing about entrepreneurship is that value created in the process finds many homes. Rubik himself came away with about 3 million US dollars. Laczi did well. The Chinese factories that picked up the manufacturing that the Hungarians could not handle did well. The event organizers who held Rubik's Cube solution competitions did well. Retailers selling the product did well. So, even though Rubik himself is the obvious entrepreneur in this story, the other players contributed to the process, and many benefited from it—they are all entrepreneurs.

Figure 19.3

Solving Your Own Puzzle

Fortunately, entrepreneurship is not a Rubik's Cube puzzle. There is only 1 correct answer and 43 quintillion wrong ones for Rubik's Cube. Perhaps quite the reverse is true for an entrepreneur. Starting with what you know and using the partnerships you build may offer 43 quintillion possible paths to success. Rubik had no business plan. The chances of being able to plan what would happen with his Cube were about 1 in 43 quintillion. And even if he had, nobody would have believed him until it was all history.

Consider these questions:

- What was Rubik doing instead of writing a business plan?
- What level of business planning might have helped Rubik?

To learn more, visit: https://effectuation.org/EE3/rubik or scan Figure 19.4.

Figure 19.4

Practically Speaking

Homemade Icon

> Build the people, and they'll build the business.
>
> *Brownie Wise*

It is customary to associate ventures with founders, more often than not inventors of the product of service the venture makes and sells. In case studies used in business schools, for example, the role of stakeholders such as employees, distributors, and others is usually completely ignored.

Practically Speaking *(continued)*

Ideas Are Easy

Let us consider the history of the successful company, Tupperware, literally a household name in the United States and even around the globe. Its founder and inventor, Earl Silas Tupper, had previously started a landscaping company, Tupper Tree Doctors, that went bankrupt during the Great Depression, forcing him to work for 60 cents an hour at DuPont's plastic manufacturing division, Viscoloid.

Throughout his travails during the Depression years, Tupper kept a diary full of ideas for useful inventions: "No Drip" ice-cream cones equipped with a gutter to catch the drippings and funnel them back into the cone, the "Dagger Comb" that came with a clip to fit nicely on bathing suits, and even devised a way to perform an appendectomy without leaving a scar (Kealing, 2016).

Plans Aren't Enough

After a year at Viscoloid, Tupper left to start his own plastics company, producing parts for wartime needs. After the war, when plastic raw materials were in short supply, he pestered his supplier from Bakelite to show him anything else he might have available. The Bakelite rep showed him a smelly, rubbery slag, which was a smelting waste product. Companies like Bakelite and DuPont had no use for it. However, it had one advantage: unlike the more "useful" plastics—it was not brittle. Months of testing and experimentation led him to ways of making the material, polyethylene, that Tupper dubbed "Poly-T: Material of the Future"—flowy, waxy, translucent, colorful, and moldable into a variety of shapes, sizes, and thicknesses.

However, Tupperware, the food storage containers that ensued, were in no way an instantaneous success in the marketplace. Although Tupper managed to get them on to department store shelves, they were not really selling well.

Enter the Fairy Godmother

Well, until single mother Brownie Wise and others she was working with began selling them. Directly to homemakers. And through homemakers. Throwing parties on their patios. And the iconic Tupperware Home Party was born.

In the spring of 1947, a door-to-door sales rep for cleaning products from Stanley Home Products knocked on Wise's door in Detroit. As he badly fumbled his pitch, Wise realized she could do much better. Signing up with Stanley to become a sales rep herself, Wise assiduously gobbled up every bit of sales training they offered through their materials and maxims.

From Hard Lessons to Soft Sells

When Wise became one of Stanley's highest performing salespeople and asked to become a manager, she was rebuffed by the founder, Stanley Beveridge: "Don't waste your time. Management is no place for a woman." Fuming all the way home, Wise vowed to herself, "I'll show him."

And so she did when Gary McDonald, one of her sales associates for Stanley, brought her some Tupperware in excitement that it could be a perfect product for their strategy of selling home products through parties. Others like her in other cities, such as Tom and Ann Damigella in Melrose, Maryland also began selling Tupperware through home parties.

Practically Speaking *(continued)*

Moving Commitment

Brownie Wise set up her own company, "Patio Parties," and was so successful selling Tupperware that she not only began building and training a stable of dealers, but also moved her business—with all her committed dealers uprooting their families in Michigan to move with her—to the warm climes of Fort Lauderdale, Florida.

While the move was far from easy, the team managed to establish themselves in their new homes and even thrive. However, success often brings its own troubles and fights over territories began to develop, even as Tupper drastically changed their rules, increasing prices, and asking Wise and others to terminate and liquidate their independent businesses to work for Tupper Corporation as employees.

Headwinds from Success

The mandate was for Tupperware to be sold exclusively through Tupper's Hostess Division, under the Tupper Hostess Party Plan. Remembering Stanley's rebuff about the inability of women to become managers, Wise accepted the changes and continued to rack in sales for Hostess.

But her successes in selling and managing sales teams did not make for smooth sailing. Not only did she find herself uninvited to area managers' meetings, but also encountered problems with end-of-the-year commissions for her team and a variety of logistical confusions over shipments.

Kite Quilting

Exasperated, in 1951, she called Tupper Corp and demanded to speak to Earl Tupper himself. She would not take no for an answer and the call was put through. Tupper was fully aware that Wise was selling more Tupperware per week than anyone anywhere in the United States. Furthermore, he knew the Hostess Division was collapsing and he needed to find alternative ways to move product. He therefore moved quickly to solve Wise's problems.

Later, when he called to have her come meet with him so he could learn how she managed to do so well with his products, she suggested he come to meet her. Even more important, he would have to meet with everyone, including the Damigellas, who had proven success in home parties before the Hostess debacle.

Wise got her way and the committed team showed up in spite of the terrible seven months of being ridden roughshod by the Hostess Division. "I learned long ago," Wise said, "that a kite rises against, not with, the wind."

As you consider what it takes to build a successful venture, get ready to work with others who want to work with you. But also get ready to deal with the complex, confusing dynamics of forging, nurturing, and enduring stakeholder relationships.

To learn more, visit: https://effectuation.org/EE3/tupperware or scan Figure 19.5.

Figure 19.5

BUSINESS PLAN COMPONENTS

Although difficulties, problems, and risks of a venture are consistently overlooked in business plans, business models are rarely overlooked, but are consistently misunderstood and underspecified. While well-done business plans are primarily useful for potential resource providers, well-designed business models are primarily useful to guiding the entrepreneurial team into action.

There is no one pure definition of what a business plan is, so we'll provide our own. A business plan consists of four components:

- *Revenue model.* What actually generates cash? What does a transaction look like?
- *Operating approach.* How do you do the things it takes to accomplish those transactions?
- *People approach.* What skills and talents are critical? How will you tap into them?
- *Differentiators.* What is unique about what you're doing? Why will it attract resources?

Business Plan Rules

- *Rule number 1.* A business plan is not any one of those components; the business plan is all of them. Underspecified business plans generally detail the revenue model and touch on differentiators, but they overlook the approach to operations and people/talent.
- *Rule number 2.* The map is not the terrain. A business plan is merely a map; it's not supposed to detail every nuance of what your venture is doing. It needs to focus on your key intended activities, on the primary drivers of your business success. If you can't be short and succinct, you haven't yet made your map.

Practically Speaking

Disposable Income

gDiapers makes completely biodegradable and flushable baby diapers based on these business plan elements:

- *Revenue model.* gDiapers generates sales revenue by selling products to grocery and apparel retail chains and to consumers from its website gdiapers.com. Retailers order crate-size shipments with return rights; consumers order starter and refill packs.
- *Operating approach.* The company focuses on the design and marketing of the product and packaging, sourcing the components from suppliers who ship finished, boxed product to the main office.
- *People approach.* Critical talent needs are design, creative marketing in two different arenas (channel marketing and online marketing), and supply chain management. These skills are all in-house, and the company accesses additional talent in technical design through partners.
- Differentiators. The key differentiation is the 100% eco-friendly disposable diaper with unique style. The company has also cultivated relationships with a large group of remarkably passionate users online who help manage channel opportunities and sell products online.

This is clearly a summary of the business, a glimpse at the critical components gDiapers must master to be successful in its current endeavors. However, it offers a clear idea about the risk and opportunities facing this company.

Practically Speaking *(continued)*

Business plans are design exercises, involving intentional design choices as well as emergent insights that result from working with different people. The business plan items (revenue, operations, people, and differentiators) can be considered variables in the equation, and can take different values as you play with the design. Business plan design involves imagining alternatives and getting ideas for alternatives from potential partners. For example, consider these alternatives for gDiapers:

Revenue model:

- Selling store-branded product to chains
- Selling via a network of users holding "diaper and baby play parties"
- Selling through a wholesaler network; no direct relationships
- Exclusively online distribution

Operating approach:

- Full integration: from design to product to marketing to sales
- Exclusively use online marketing and order taking
- Drop shipping only to retailers, no direct handling
- Sourcing from similar operation in different country

People approach:

- Online marketing in-house
- Outside reseller network to retailers
- Open-sourced pants design (product exterior)
- Technical expertise relating to the liner (product interior)

Differentiators:

- Custom pant designs online
- Store branding to encourage channel adoption
- Differentiated focus on "Earth friendly"
- Emphasis on style and functionality
- Position against cloth diapers rather than disposable

Figure 19.6

The list of possibilities is immense and inherently creative. These are merely examples of other legitimate choices that could be part of the gDiapers business plan. These choices about what are and aren't part of the plan are the critical ones.

We hope the earlier parts of this book will help you make these choices in ways that are coherent and actually connected to the preferences and aspirations of your potential customers, partners, and employees.

To learn more, visit: https://effectuation.org/EE3/gdiaper or scan Figure 19.7.

Figure 19.7

The Rocket Pitch

Entrepreneurs have long been challenged to reduce the description of their business to something that could be understood in an elevator ride; hence it was called the "elevator pitch."

The world has gotten faster, and version two of that challenge is the "rocket pitch," something one could understand in the 30 seconds that it takes a rocket to launch. Imagine your business on a single slide, in 30-point font, with a total of four or five bullets. As you look at that condensed summary, ask yourself:

- Who is your audience?
- What are you saying?
- What is that audience hearing?
- What is the one thing you want the audience to walk away with?
- How do you want them to describe it to others?

Remember that every pitch that fails gives you an idea for how to make the next one better. You should never make the same pitch twice as pitching is as much about your learning as it is about gaining commitments.

Figure 19.8

MANAGING PREDICTIONS

Another necessary element in most business plans is a demand forecast. This assumes you have described what customers seem to want, you've learned about other relevant companies and what they were able to accomplish, and you've learned about the size of different markets. This builds an answer to the question: What do you think you can accomplish with your opportunity over the next few years?

How you build your prediction logic, starting at the top or starting at the bottom, is a matter of opinion. Top-down forecasting is simply estimating the overall size of the market, looking at what might be feasible in terms of market share and customer adoption, and doing the math.

In our opinion, this sort of predictive work all too often leads to grossly high-demand forecasts. Top-down forecasts lead to statements like this: "We only need to get a 1% market share and we'll be really successful." These statements leap over the important logic of how the venture will obtain 1% market share and undermine the credibility of entrepreneurs.

Bottom-up forecasts look at things in a more micro fashion, causing you to ask the following questions:

- Which customers (name them!) can you actually reach this year?
- How many customers can you keep in your sales process simultaneously?
- If you added four salespeople, what happens to that number?
- Can you list the prospects you need to approach for each year you're forecasting in order to make those numbers real?
- What is the revenue you can actually generate right now?
- What are the bottlenecks keeping you from doubling your sales over the next 12 months?

- Can the bottlenecks be eliminated so your sales forecast is legitimate?

These types of forecasts are consistently lower and more credible, but many entrepreneurs don't feel that it gives justice to the true potential of their opportunity.

Here is the painful reality: both types of forecasting typically lead to demand forecasts that simply don't get hit. Many investors, and all bankers, barely pay attention to forecasts made by entrepreneurs. Early-stage investors will use them to broadly characterize the overall size potential of the venture—small, medium, and large, if you will.

More important than either top-down or bottom-up forecasting is the more direct analysis relating to your business model. It's not the macroeconomics of the top-down approach or the micro level of the bottom-up forecast. It is the economics of your business model, constructed with an understanding of the contribution margin of a typical transaction. To build your own, answer the following questions:

- What kind of marketing/ sales investment is required to win a customer?
- What type of inventory will you have to build to attract sales?
- What drives your product costs?
- Are your gross margins fragile?
- What are the potential service requirements after you make a sale?
- Over the course of a year or two, what level of cash flow are you generating from your lead customers?
- How many customers do you need to sell to break even?
- How many transactions are needed to break even?
- Are there business model changes that can materially change these transaction-level economics?

If you can get clarity at this level of analysis, the needs facing your venture will be significantly clearer, and because this type of analysis involves less prediction (not zero prediction, just less prediction), it is less risky to use in your decision-making. (Of course, keep in mind that garbage in equals garbage out. You have to do real work to identify your product costs, selling and service costs, and validate your pricing.)

Alternative Predictions: A Case for Scenario Thinking

Co-Creator: Moataz Darwish

Entrepreneurial ventures are particularly susceptible to an uncertain future. It is a bumpy, long, and risky adventure taking an idea through validation to scaleup and finally maturity.

Risk is not only inherent in the business model hypotheses, but also in hypotheses made about the general environment and the future in terms of potential customers, products, technology, and operations.

The traditional (causal-logic-driven) approach to risk involves working hard to constantly improve the input data and the models used in forecasting and prediction. But being a linear process that cannot reflect all variables, the predictions made do not stand up well to the test of uncertain futures.

A complementary tool is scenario thinking, which seeks to develop alternative plausible futures. The process employs systems thinking to identify the root driving forces in the environment, which will likely shape the venture going forward to develop multiple alternative futures.

By exploring the resulting alternative scenarios, effectual entrepreneurs can identify new opportunities and make decisions based on the available means, affordable loss, and co-creation partners, rather than relying on a predetermined plan to reach a singular (causal) goal. This approach leverages existing strengths and relationships to create innovative solutions in uncertain environments.

Practically Speaking

A Lick of the Old Block

As you might recall from Steve Jobs' speech about connecting dots in Chapter 10, entrepreneurs are known for seeing patterns in seemingly unconnected things. Perhaps Chick Olsson's hobby of painting (and his occupation as agriculturist and economist) enabled him to cleverly connect the following dots across technologies, interests, and locations.

Lick Blocks Are Healthy

You might be wondering about the strange title of this *Practically Speaking*. Lick blocks are brick-shaped cakes of nutrients designed to improve the health of livestock, re-creating the behavior of animals to seek out minerals in their habitat. Animals with a supplemented diet are healthier, produce stronger offspring and more milk, and command better prices when sold.

A Poor Diet Leads to Nasty Emissions

In northern Laos, most buffalo eat poor-quality grasses and thus emit relatively large amounts of methane. It has been found that by adding specific ingredients to their diet, the gut microbiome of buffalo (and many other animals) can be improved, thereby reducing the amount of greenhouse gases (specifically methane) they emit.

Challenge of Offsetting Emissions

Organizations seeking to offset their carbon emissions can face challenges, particularly when they are city-bound and don't have opportunities to set up extensive solar panels or wind turbines. A case in point is the Australian law firm, Bennett and Philp, who, through an independent audit, determined that their carbon emissions in financial year 2020–2021 were 119 tons. Located on the fifth level of an office tower in downtown Brisbane, solar panels and wind turbines are definitely not a viable way of reducing emissions.

User Doesn't Pay

When was the last time you paid your search engine for internet queries you made? It is unlikely you have ever had to pay anything for that service, despite using it regularly. Compare this to the typical user-pays revenue model: you purchase a product or service and pay the price requested by the seller. So, returning to the search engine, who is covering the costs of your internet queries? Advertisers.

Figure 19.9

Practically Speaking *(continued)*

Happy Farmers, Happy Lawyers, and Happy Planet

By now you might have guessed where this is headed. Chick and his son Daniel designed a business model under the name AgCoTech, which connects those dots to reduce carbon emissions and increase food security and incomes of buffalo farmers in northern Laos.

AgCoTech's approach is relatively simple: the farmers receive the emission-reducing lick blocks free of charge in exchange for verified carbon credits, which are sold to third parties seeking carbon offsets or traded in global carbon markets.

The satisfied customers on both ends of the exchange share their thoughts (AgCoTech, n.d.):

> We have received some blocks from the project and now our cattle look healthier and grow faster. Before the emission control blocks it was difficult to bring the cattle home at night, today they return home more easily because they know the emission control blocks are waiting for them (Mr. Lae, Farmer from Nongchong Village).
>
> AgCoTech's approach is unique—with a focus not only on reducing emissions, but also positively impacting the social and economic circumstances of Laotian farmers and improving animal welfare. There must be real and meaningful action to preserve this planet, and our partnership with AgCoTech will allow us to contribute (Lance Pollard, Managing Partner, Bennett & Philp Lawyers).

So next time you pay for something outright, consider who might be interested in paying for you, to reach their own goal. This thought experiment might lead to some interesting ideas, or at least make you aware of dots that can be connected, re-connected, or even removed.

To learn more, visit: https://effectuation.org/EE3/lickblock or scan Figure 19.10.

Figure 19.10

ATTRACTING RESOURCES THROUGH METAPHOR AND ANALOGY

The process of attracting resources to new ventures is rife with contradictions. One of these is the desire to demonstrate that the venture is truly innovative and the need to provide evidence that it will work. New + proven = really tricky (oxymoronic, really).

Well-designed business plans help deal with this challenge. They allow you to use metaphors and analogies to other companies and industries as evidence to support the value and feasibility of your novel offering. What industries and companies provide metaphors and analogies? The ones that share important features of your business model.

Using the example of gDiapers, what industries or companies would be relevant?

- Branded apparel (children's specifically)
- Non-food products for sale in grocery retail (e.g. other baby products or video rental)
- Design/marketing outfits (e.g. Nike)
- Companies with a complicated mix of online

and offline sales (e.g. Barnes & Noble or BMG)
- Companies that use suppliers for technical innovation (e.g. Dell)
- Companies positioned as eco-friendly (e.g. Seventh Generation)
- Obviously, other diaper companies (e.g. Huggies and Pampers).

Some of these will provide more robust analogies than others. Certainly, you can imagine more. Come up with a list to provide analogies for your company; let's call this your peer group. Now, you can study these companies, looking for evidence to support what you're trying to do.

What evidence does your peer group provide that:

- Customers will adopt a product like yours?
- Your venture can grow as fast as you want to show in your plan?
- Your particular business model choices are "state of the art?"
- Your business model is robust enough to endure mistakes?

If you were to tell the story of your peer companies, their key mistakes and successes, what would be the important learning points? If you've done a good job of connecting key components of your business model to those of the peer group, you'll be surprised by how much you can learn. Adjust your strategy and share some of what you've learned in your business plan.

TRACTION: WHEN THE RUBBER MEETS THE ROAD

Of course, there is no evidence quite as good as your own successes to prove that the novelty of your business venture is valuable. This evidence is commonly referred to as traction. Traction is what connects the power of a car engine to the road—it's what leads to forward motion (in this case, you and your team are the horsepower). Every yes you win is a point of traction. Without traction, the effort you put into executing your business plan is akin to spinning your wheels. No one wants to put resources (time, money, relationships, or talent) into a business that's going nowhere.

Business plan competitions can be outstanding learning experiences. The winners of these competitions consistently have genuine traction that differentiates their efforts from hypothetical plans, and they demonstrate their potential for success—they aren't just spinning their wheels.

Sometimes, you can't get traction until you've attracted certain resources. You might need an engineer to finalize the prototype. You might need cash to order enough product for your first sales test. Traction can be a serious chicken and egg problem.

Remember affordable loss? You need to prioritize and pursue accomplishments, within your levels of affordable loss, which constitute traction. This is an art, and so it takes practice, but keeping this concept in mind will help you focus on progress and make sense of the small victories you accumulate as you proceed.

ESCALATION OF COMMITMENT

A well-specified business plan that includes interesting thoughts and strategies for dealing with risk and surprise, and emphasis on traction and gaining ground with customers, partners, employees, and investors can materially change how you proceed as an entrepreneur.

It can increase the emotional commitment you have to the work you've done thus far. This increased commitment to your plans, to the goals you now have in mind, and to delivering on the support you may have won from customers, partners, employees, and investors can prematurely pull you away from the principles of entrepreneurship we've been discussing in this book.

Your willingness to think of new ways to use your means, leverage contingency, stay connected to your affordable loss, and truly focus on committed partnerships can wane if you are not careful. Timing is everything. As your venture develops, you will need to focus on goal-driven activities more and more, on delivering what everyone has agreed to deliver.

This is different from the notion of "escalation of commitment." Escalation of commitment involves an emotional response to the material resource investments that constrain your ability to change direction. Beware of this.

Entrepreneurs often become less willing to pursue the opportunities that reveal themselves through their work with customers, partners, employees, and investors.

Venture capital investors are a common example of this. Venture capital investors get involved because they intend to execute on the vision, strategy, and opportunity championed by the entrepreneurs. With new cash resources available, the entrepreneurs focus on exploiting the opportunity. If the opportunity turns out to be valuable, the additional funds enable the entrepreneurs to develop it faster and give the entrepreneurs an advantage over competitors.

On the other hand, if the opportunity does not materialize, it is hard for the entrepreneurs to change directions because the escalation of commitment to the specific opportunity associated with the venture capital investment limits flexibility.

We don't know one right way to resolve this tension. There is value in focus sometimes. There is value in flexibility at other times. We do know that if you don't explicitly deal with escalation of commitment bias, you likely will not make a fully informed choice, and may both overinvest in a failing path or fail to move to a new path—either way constraining your ability to succeed.

Research Roots

Rewards to Entrepreneurs With Venture Capital Investors

Only a tiny fraction of new ventures ever raises venture capital (VC), but those that do sometimes turn into very valuable firms. Economists Hall and Woodward (2010) analyzed almost all the US firms funded by venture capital from 1987 to 2008.

There were 22,004 cases in total. Of these, 2,015 (9%) held initial public offerings of their stock, 5,625 (26%) were acquired, and 7,572 (34%) exited with zero value. At the time the study was done, 6,792 (31%) still existed as independent businesses.

The study is interesting because it documents what rewards entrepreneurs receive from seeing a firm through from VC investment to exit. In the typical venture-funded firm, the entrepreneur receives a submarket salary and keeps a substantial ownership interest in the firm.

In 75% of cases, that ownership interest was worth zero at exit, while 1% received over 100 million US dollars. Venture capital-funded entrepreneurship is, therefore, a low-probability/high-return game. This is epitomized by Google, which delivered the largest single entrepreneurial payoff in Hall and Woodward's (2010) sample of firms at over 1 billion US dollars.

Practically Speaking

The Wind and the Plan

"New-age traveler" is a euphemism for a hippie, a house trucker, or even a vagrant. It's not the community typically associated with the next generation of business leaders. But then again, solutions to climate change don't seem to come from traditional business leaders. This may explain in part why Dale Vince, an ex-traveler himself, is considered an influential "green" entrepreneur.

Measuring the Zephyr

Committed to a low-impact lifestyle, Vince's journey into business began with building small-scale windmills to serve his personal energy needs and limit his dependency on commercial power. One of the most complex pieces of the puzzle was reliably measuring the environment in order to identify a location that provides consistent wind to drive turbines.

Not finding adequate solutions on the market, Vince started crafting wind-monitoring towers in 1991 and, in 1992, founded Western Windpower. Though Vince has continued his own expedition, Western attracted orders from clients like Scottish Power and later changed its name to Nexgen Wind, a market leader in wind monitoring equipment in the United Kingdom.

A Powerful Gust

Armed with knowledge of wind measurement and power generation, Vince applied for permission to establish a wind farm in the UK, and in 1992 gained approval. Just three years later, he founded Ecotricity (originally the Renewable Energy Company), offering the radical alternative of "green" electricity to both household and business customers.

By the end of 2007, Vince's firm was operating 12 wind farms, representing 10% of England's wind energy, 46 GWh/year of renewable electricity, and savings of around 46,000 metric tons of CO^2 emissions as well.

His accomplishments have been duly recognized. Vince has been presented with the second highest civilian award in the United Kingdom, the "Officer of the Most Excellent Order of the British Empire" (OBE) for services to the environment, a Queen's Award for Enterprise, and an Ashden Award for sustainable energy, and he made the list of the world's Top 100 Eco-Heroes. But this is really just the start of the story.

Figure 19.11

Contingency in the Air

Fewer new-age travelers roam Europe today, and green energy is no longer a radical idea. With the external environment, Vince himself has changed. His networks, his knowledge, and even his assets have changed. And as is often seen with serial entrepreneurs, he reconfigured his available means to create his next opportunity.

Practically Speaking *(continued)*

His focus became a prototype electric sports car based on the Lotus Exige called "Nemesis," which makes sense not only in light of Vince's relationship with sustainable energy, but also because Lotus is an Ecotricity customer with a wind-powered automobile factory in Norfolk, England.

Vince sums up his philosophy as follows: "The one thing I have learned is that you have to be flexible, you have to continually reappraise that which you hold to be true because things change internally and externally."

Regeneration

And what lies ahead? Certainly, no specific business plan. Vince is a vegan, a keen advocate of organic farming, and is still committed to a low-impact, self-sufficient life. And not being constrained to a plan means Vince can stay open to options that range from micro-generation of electricity at home, to creating software that manages home power consumption, to his latest (2023) venture: renewable energy-powered jets.

Maybe he is also the creator of something else—the plan to not have a plan.

To learn more, visit: https://effectuation.org/EE3/wind or scan Figure 19.12.

Figure 19.12

Research Roots

A Great Debate: Business Planning

Business planning is one of the most ubiquitous aspects of entrepreneurship education, but researchers have not agreed about the benefits of planning for the performance of new ventures. Over many years of research, studies have generated inconsistent results, with some indicating a negative relationship between planning and firm performance, while others a positive relationship or no relationship.

The benefits of planning are thought to occur from using resources more efficiently and from making better-informed decisions. Critics counter that entrepreneurs can put their time to better uses than planning (e.g. establishing relationships with new customers) and that planning introduces cognitive biases that limit an entrepreneur's flexibility.

Research by Brinckmann and colleagues (2010) sought to cut through the confusion by analyzing the combined results of 46 previously published studies involving over 11,000 small firms in total. Results indicated that on average planning does have a positive relationship with performance.

The benefits of planning, however, are significantly lower for new firms than for established firms. This may be because new firms face a more uncertain environment than established firms do, as well as more ambiguity about exactly what products they will offer and which customers they will serve. These factors may limit the returns to planning.

Overall, these results suggest taking a contingent view of business planning where the right question to be asking is, "What is a business plan useful for in my venture?" and tailoring your planning approach accordingly (Brinckmann et al., 2010).

Practically Speaking

A Model for Healthy Change

Kiran Mazumdar-Shaw is something of a modern business folk hero. She started her own life sciences firm in a garage at the age of 25 on a shoestring of 10,000 Indian Rupees (about 120 US dollars). At that time, the idea of a woman chief executive officer in India was as remote as the idea of an Indian competitor taking away significant market share from the pharmaceutical behemoth Pfizer.

Today, her venture Biocon is a multinational publicly listed pharmaceutical provider in Bangalore. As of 2023, the firm employs more than 23,000 people, offers therapies in the areas of oncology, diabetes, and immunology, and is working hard on a breakthrough oral formulation of insulin. Mazumdar-Shaw has won just about every entrepreneurial award on the planet, and she is recognized as the wealthiest (self-made) woman in India.

Business Change

But that's not what this story is about. It is about what happens next. It is easy to script romantic endings for business legends. She might retire to a private island. She might fancy art or theater and create a charity with her enormous wealth. Or she might do something as surprising as creating another successful firm.

Indeed, she did start again, taking what she had learned about business—and what she had learned about wellness—and applying those lessons to one of the most pressing social problems facing India: the lack of available healthcare for the 15% of the population (nearly half a billion souls) that fall below the poverty line, earning less than 2 US dollars a day.

Business Clarity

It would be easy for someone like Mazumdar-Shaw to simply throw money at the problem. With Biocon equity worth approximately 2.8 billion US dollars (late 2023), she has plenty to throw. But she is a self-titled "compassionate capitalist," who spent her career learning that profit can be a solid foundation for impact, sustainability, and progress.

When Mazumdar-Shaw turned her sights to social purpose, she meant business. "Innovation and commerce are as powerful tools for creating social progress as they are for driving technological advancement," she says. "The only difference is that when they are put to use for social progress, the implementation is a lot cheaper, a lot more people benefit, and the effect is more lasting."

Business Impact

Mazumdar-Shaw created two platforms to enable caring capitalism. The first is a foundation called Arogya Raksha Yojana (translated as "Health Help"). Its mission is to run small rural clinics that serve a local radius of the population. The second is the Mazumdar-Shaw Cancer Center, a state-of-the-art facility in Bangalore. Each delivers quality healthcare using a uniquely social business model.

Practically Speaking *(continued)*

Micro Insurance

India has neither universal healthcare nor government-backed health insurance. Without those mechanisms, any significant treatment of injury or illness for a member of a poor family would mean financial ruin or, more likely, foregoing treatment. But with family plans ranging from 25 to 750 US dollars a year, even low-income citizens can get the peace of mind and financial coverage to seek professional healthcare through Arogya Raksha Yojana.

Figure 19.13

Social Pricing

At Mazumdar-Shaw's high-tech cancer center in Bangalore, fixed costs are substantial, and micro insurance would not cover them. So, she created a "subsidized convenience" pricing plan, enabling her to serve (wealthy) patients at full price between the hours of 8 a.m. and 5 p.m., (middle income) patients with more flexibility than money between the hours of 6 p.m. and 10 p.m. at half price, and offer the services of the center to the poor for free in the middle of the night.

Business Health

By creating healthy patients and healthy profits, Mazumdar-Shaw also shows us the path to healthy change. For her, business is not good or evil; it is merely a means that can be applied to many purposes—and even at the same time. She shows us the cycle of the entrepreneur, continually creating with everything and anything available at hand. And she challenges us to improve the health and purpose of our own work.

To learn more, visit: https://effectuation.org/EE3/biocon or scan Figure 19.14.

Figure 19.14

TAKEAWAY: WHETHER YOU PLAN OR NOT, STAKEHOLDERS MATTER

We hope you are both more confident in how to create a business plan if you want to, or to operate without one if you want to. Clearly, there are plenty of failed businesses both with and without business plans. And there are many successes with and without them as well.

But all of them require you to take action. And all of them require you work with stakeholders. With or without a plan, you can build a venture. But no matter how well crafted your plan, nothing happens without taking action. Or without committed stakeholders.

Aside from acting as a marketing tool for raising institutional investment, one of the best uses of a business plan might be to help you take action and bring stakeholders on board. Not everyone needs the support of a plan to get going, but if it is something that helps you do so, then take advantage of it. Remember that, ultimately, the business plan is nothing more than a tool to help you get your venture going. If it is not helping you do that, then forget it. Forge ahead.

■ ■ ■

So What?

Great business plans are different for the different purposes to which they are put to use. One size does not fit all. Above all, they need to be compelling, not legalistic or focused on your divine predictions of the future.

If you are doing it right, you will learn about your venture as you create different versions of your business plan. This planning work will help you create an entrepreneurial culture as your venture grows up (Chapter 20).

Think It Through

- What things can you really plan?
- Is there something else that a business plan might provide—confidence to the entrepreneur?
- How do the ideas of escalation of commitment and business planning intermingle?

What Now?

- How simply can you explain your current opportunity?
- Summarize your current plan down to short phrases to answer these three questions: What do you sell? To whom do you sell? Why do they buy from you?
- Detail one transaction for your current business model; the timing, costs, pricing, and customer decisions around a typical transaction. Does your business plan effectively communicate this level of mastery, or is it focused only on big ideas and bold predictions?
- Identify the audiences that will need to see a plan from you. What will you emphasize differently to each of those audiences? What do you want each audience to believe as a result of understanding your plan?

REFERENCES

Acko, T. (2021, June 9). Aarogya Raksha: Eligibility, coverage, benefits. Acko General Insurance. https://www.acko.com/health-insurance/aarogya-raksha/

AgCoTech. (n.d.). Retrieved December 14, 2023, from https://agcotechglobal.com/

Bartlett, S. (2002, October). Seat of their pants. *Inc. Magazine*. http://www.inc.com/magazine/20021015/24772.html

Bhidé, A. (2000). *The Origin and Evolution of New Businesses*. Oxford University Press.

Biocon. (n.d.). Retrieved December 12, 2023, from https://www.biocon.com/

Brinckmann, J., Grichnik, D., & Kapsa, D. (2010). Should entrepreneurs plan or just storm the castle? A meta-analysis on contextual factors impacting the business planning–performance relationship in small firms. *Journal of Business Venturing, 25*(1), 24–40. https://doi.org/10.1016/j.jbusvent.2008.10.007

Clarke, Alison J. (2001). *Tupperware—The Promise of Plastic in 1950s America*. Smithsonian Books.

Dale Vince OBE—The Green Pilot—Platinum Media Group. (2023, November 2). https://www.platinummediagroup.co.uk/platinum-business-magazine/2023/10/dale-vince-the-green-pilot/

Ecotricity. (n.d.). Retrieved December 18, 2023, from https://www.ecotricity.co.uk/

Food and Agriculture Organization of the United Nations. (2022, October 20). Livestock and enteric methane. https://www.youtube.com/watch?v=VFkqrrRYK0A

Hall, R. E., & Woodward, S. E. (2010). The burden of the nondiversifiable risk of entrepreneurship. *American Economic Review, 100*(3), 1163–1194.

Kealing, B. (2016). *Life of the Party: The Remarkable Story of How Brownie Wise Built, and Lost, a Tupperware Party Empire*. Penguin Random House.

Kumar, M. (2023, July 17). One-tenth of India's population escaped poverty in 5 years—Government report. Reuters. https://www.reuters.com/world/india/one-tenth-indias-population-escaped-poverty-5-years-government-report-2023-07-17/

Nicolini, D., Mengis, J., & Swan, J. (2012). Understanding the role of objects in cross-disciplinary collaboration. *Organization Science, 23*(3), 612–629. https://doi.org/10.1287/orsc.1110.0664

Osterwalder, A., & Pigneur, Y. (2010). *Business Model Generation: A Handbook for Visionaries, Game Changers, and Challengers*. John Wiley & Sons.

Sahlman, W. A. (1997). How to write a great business plan. *Harvard Business Review*. https://ieeexplore.ieee.org/iel3/46/14446/00660335.pdf

Truu, M. (2023, April 15). Inside the rise and fall of Tupperware's plastic empire. ABC News. https://www.abc.net.au/news/2023-04-16/tupperware-plastic-container-inspired-generations-of-fans/102224914

Tupperware Brands. (2023, October 17). Tupperware Brands announces CEO transition and board refreshment. https://ir.tupperwarebrands.com/news-and-events/press-releases/2023/10-17-2023-123037763

Wikipedia. (2023). Mineral lick. https://en.wikipedia.org/w/index.php?title=Mineral_lick&oldid=1189362232

Figure 20.1 A whimsical take on how founders need to match the growth of their venture or risk a crash.

CHAPTER 20

The Venture Grows Up

Create an Entrepreneurial Culture

In This Chapter

Understanding expert entrepreneurial approaches and applying them to the large firm offers a new perspective on the questions facing executives charged with innovation and growth.

As techniques to deal with complex concurrent uncertainty, effectual approaches offer insight into developing new products and entering new markets as well as promoting and training people inside a large firm.

Even when odds are against the large firm that aspires to be entrepreneurial, there are ways to overcome the three main structural barriers of prediction, structure, and process to acting entrepreneurially within a large organization.

DOI: 10.4324/9781003364016-24

THREE STRUCTURAL BARRIERS TO ENTREPRENEURIAL THINKING

It is the relentless business paradox: entrepreneurs dream of building a venture that becomes successful, enduring, and large. And yet executives from successful, enduring, large firms flock to business schools with the objective of somehow making their organizations and themselves entrepreneurial. There are enough large firms out there to reassure us that the entrepreneurial dream is possible. But will executives be forever unfulfilled in their quest?

It is important to acknowledge at the outset that the deck is stacked against large firms that aspire to be entrepreneurial. There are three positive attributes of big companies and their people that directly conflict with the approaches employed by expert entrepreneurs:

- *Prediction.* Firms become large typically because they are able to successfully create markets for their products or services. This success generates all sorts of positive reinforcement, like reliable revenue, a known brand, and a large client base. It also generates history.
  Successfully selling the same product in the same market/s year after year enables, encourages, and reinforces the use of prediction based on that history. Throughout the value chain, from raw material providers to distributors, the patterns generated from a history of success offer useful planning tools for further refining and expanding the business.
  Ironically, the reliance on prediction undermines managers' ability to pursue new opportunities—the uncertain ones that enabled them to grow in the first place.
- *Structure.* Scale must be managed. When a startup is selling only a few units, a single entrepreneur or a tight team can oversee the whole operation. But as the firm adds volume, moves into more geographic locations, supports more clients, works with more suppliers, and seeks to standardize delivery, the structure grows stronger and less nimble.
  As it grows, the organization develops into specialized units within a hierarchy or a matrix, building structure under a small number of decision-makers at the top. Structure separates decision-making from action taking—the tasks expert entrepreneurs perform quickly, concurrently, and iteratively.
- *Process.* Process is a word with both positive and negative connotations. It is a natural result of the successful growth of a new venture and an asset to a large firm.
  Not everyone can interact with everyone else, so there is a want and a need for rules, policies, and procedures that enable the structure to function smoothly and in concert. Yet, many processes design newness—the source of opportunity—out of the system.

A potential entrepreneur reading this might look at these attributes of large firms and be reassured by the reasons they chose NOT to work for a big firm and, instead, become an entrepreneur in the first place. But these are some of the mechanisms that enable firms to become large and successful.

In fact, entrepreneurs aspiring to grow their ventures need to heed both the benefits and costs of prediction, structure, and process.

Surely, capitalizing on a market the firm worked to create cannot be undesirable. What the entrepreneur implicitly objects to is that these attributes do not generate novelty. They do not free the organization to create. And the reason for the entrepreneurial disdain of prediction, structure, and process is that these elements emerge in more mature environments, while entrepreneurs operate in the uncertain setting of venture, market, or product creation.

Our research identified the effectual principles expert

entrepreneurs use for creating new ventures in uncertain situations. As we outline those principles throughout the book, we contrast effectuation with the predictive approaches better suited to mature organizations. For clarity, we sometimes describe effectuation and causation as either/or. But many situations have elements of both uncertainty and maturity. And as the venture grows and the market matures, the use of causation or prediction becomes more prominent in the decision-making around the firm.

Our objective here is to take the best of expert entrepreneurial thinking and redesign prediction, structure, and process in a large-firm setting in order to free parts of the organization to work on creating the next market, product, or service—creating the longer-term future of the large firm.

> What we need is an entrepreneurial society in which innovation and entrepreneurship are normal, steady and continual.
>
> *Peter F. Drucker,* author, educator, and management consultant

Figure 20.2

THE POWER OF PREDICTION

When we present a business problem to expert entrepreneurs, one of the things we notice is how little they use prediction to try to solve it. While creating new ventures, entrepreneurs learn not to rely on history for making decisions. Confident (wrongly or rightly) that they can change the environment, they focus instead on actions that will create a future where they will benefit.

Of course, entrepreneurs are not the only experts out there. There are expert doctors, chess players, taxi drivers, and even expert corporate executives. The same logic applies. Over the course of time (at least ten years) and practice, expert corporate managers learn heuristics that work well in a large-firm environment. One of those is prediction.

Institutionally, prediction is forced on corporate executives. From forecasts to budgets, from personal objectives to customer satisfaction levels, historical data is used as a baseline for planning and goal setting—because it works.

Plotting the sales growth over previous years to predict sales this year in order to plan staffing levels and production gives a good and useful result. The institutional mandate is therefore reinforced by the fact that prediction is sufficiently useful, and it is what corporate executives learn. In fact, corporate executives learn prediction so well that it becomes the hammer they use in any situation, regardless of whether the problem is a nail or not.

In an experiment, we presented senior corporate executives with a decision-making scenario. It started in a very mature industry and involved strategic decisions over multiple years for a fictitious refrigerator manufacturer named Frigus. For half the executives, the company and the industry stayed mature over time. Little changed. The same competitors made the same products, and the same consumers bought them.

For the other half of the executives, the environment became uncertain: competitors merged, new competitors entered, new technologies appeared, and new consumer segments and new distribution channels arose.

In both situations in the experiment, we measured the extent to which executives based their decisions on prediction. As you might expect, in the mature situation, executives used prediction more and more as the scenario unfolded.

What you might not expect is that as soon as executives were presented with the uncertain situation, they chose prediction even more! In other words, executives faced with uncertainty took many more actions based on prediction than their peers making the decisions in the mature environment.

Despite the obvious disconnect between what had happened historically and what they were currently faced with, expert managers, unsure of what to do next, defaulted to the predictive tools they knew best.

Are corporate executives destined to deploy the hammer of prediction in any situation? No. The key is awareness. The understanding that prediction is only one of many possible tools. Enabling executives to see their own decision-making bias helps to sensitize them to the need to fit strategy, and more importantly their strategic mindset, to changes in the environment.

In the refrigeration company simulation experiment, we analyzed two more elements that meaningfully influenced the ability of corporate executives to venture beyond prediction when faced with uncertainty.

The first was how they viewed the situation. When they found the company's industry and competitive environment threatening, they resorted to prediction even more heavily. But when these factors were viewed instead as an opportunity, executives were able to shift more quickly to approaches similar to those used by our expert entrepreneurs.

The other factor relates back to expertise. Those executives who had experience in uncertain situations (new locations, new products, new markets) were able to shift more quickly to non-predictive approaches when they saw prediction wasn't working.

So, helping corporate executives reframe threats as opportunities and rotating them through positions where they will face uncertainty seems like a good way to keep people in large firms open to entrepreneurial heuristics.

Table 20.1 provides some ways executives and entrepreneurs differ in their view of typical business situations.

Table 20.1 Contrasting Perspectives: Executives and Entrepreneurs

	Expert executives (causal prediction)	**Expert entrepreneurs (effectual control)**
View of opportunities	*Defined and narrow.* Corporate policies restrict options. Typically, only opportunities adjacent to or supporting the core business are considered.	*Diverse and negotiable.* Everything from product offering to target market is negotiable. Tend to consider investments unrelated by business area, size, customer, or nature of product.
Potential funders	*Few and restricted.* New opportunities often have prespecified budget lines and a single point of approval. This limits both the ability to get a project started and to change the direction of a project as the opportunity unfolds.	*Many and flexible.* The diversity in the investor population gives entrepreneurs a market of potential funders. They can stage and mix and match funding as goals and commitments change.
Return criteria	*Large impact on the bottom line.* For a 20 billion US dollar company, a minimum meaningful impact might be 1 billion US dollars, precluding consideration of smaller opportunities, and forcing the firm to make a few large bets.	*Positive return.* Level of investment can be scaled to the size of the opportunity, so the range of "interesting" can be broad. Moreover, opportunities can be reshaped and made larger through effectual entrepreneurial action.
Outlook	*Measured in quarters and not easily abandoned.* Large public firms answer to the stock market and inevitably manage toward quarterly earnings reports. Once funded, a project is typically supported unless faced with overwhelmingly negative results. In fact, vested interests in funded projects can result in denial of negative news.	*Measured in years and multiple commitments.* Incoming stakeholders propel changes. Even a venture capitalist-funded startup might raise four to six investment "rounds" prior to liquidity. Each new investment requires that significant milestones be achieved with the last investment and offers a checkpoint to adjust direction.
Value added by funder	*Infrastructure and synergy.* The large enterprise offers distribution, brand, manufacturing, and administrative support to the venture. These assets are typically helpful only after the opportunity has been created.	*Innovation in rearrangements of means-ends frameworks.* The need to accommodate incoming stakeholders sets in motion an engine of innovation in shaping new opportunities. Even investors bring relationships that might generate customers, partnerships, or future investors.

Research Roots

Effectuation as Business

Several scholars have built businesses with effectuation itself as the product. Thomas Blekman built a consulting practice around effectuation and contributes his insights in books that explain how larger corporations can be more effectual (Blekman, 2011), and more specifically, how to organize for effectual behavior (Blekman & Konijnenburg, 2012).

Michael Faschingbauer built a coaching practice around effectuation and has distilled many of his insights regarding effectual action and decision-making (Faschingbauer, 2021).

Fashingbauer and René Mauer have also collaborated to deliver intensive private seminars and workshops on effectuation, helping people create and implement projects over time—work that has generated a number of new insights into the different ways effectuation encourages people to think, act, and interact differently (Mauer et al., 2014).

Research Roots

Congrats, You Raised a Bunch of Money! Sorry You're Fired

While at Harvard Business School, Professor Noam Wasserman taught a course on the conflicts founders encounter on their entrepreneurial journeys. His research and learnings from teaching the course are summarized in his award-winning book *The Founder's Dilemmas.*

Wasserman argues that entrepreneurs often face a choice about whether they want to be "rich" or be "king." To grow a company to the point of becoming very valuable, founders usually need outside money, but bringing in outside investors means surrendering control of the firm.

In a survey of 212 US startups that made it to IPO, fewer than 25% of founders led their firm to IPO. In fact, 50% of founders were no longer CEO by the time the firm was three years old. Most of these founders were pushed out of the firms they created in ways they didn't like, well before they thought it was their time to go.

Wasserman points out that many outside investors (such as venture capitalists) will often insist on bringing in a professional CEO to run firms they invest in. It is part of "professionalizing" the firm by putting in place a management hierarchy and formal processes such as financial controls (Wasserman, 2013).

THE STRENGTH OF STRUCTURE

How we think and how we organize are intimately connected. So, it is natural that managers comfortable with prediction would build structures that reinforce and streamline the repetition of activities. By itself, this is not bad. However, this can instill a growing bias for prediction and against uncertain, yet innovative, opportunities.

Consider the following situation:

There is a proposal for a new product on top of the stack of papers on your desk. You left it there last night, knowing how important it is for the company to generate new opportunities. Before you even look at it, questions enter your mind.

How will you get this approved by the division president? Are the numbers in the proposal big enough to get her attention? Are the numbers in the proposal so big the team can never achieve them? If it is approved, can the team execute fast enough to beat competitors? If it fails, will you lose your job? If it is so successful it eats into the margin on the firm's existing profitable products, will you lose your job, or maybe avoided as a spoiler?

Next to the new proposal on your desk sits a budget for a small marketing outlay on an existing product. Your gut tells you to pick up the marketing budget and ignore the new product idea for yet another day. Too many financial hurdles. Too much personal risk. Too much uncertainty. You start telling yourself, the not-so-new could be spun as new, too. A much easier sell.

You reach, and …

Research Roots

The Elements of the Internal Market

Three core elements can be used to make any company more market-like:

- *Autonomy.* Give employees the freedom to pursue what they perceive to be interesting ideas.
- *Rewards.* Make sure that whoever creates an innovation derives some benefit.
- *Psychological safety.* Offer the assurance that if an employee has an idea, explores it and it fails, the employee won't be fired or penalized for it.

In a study, Read et al. (2013) looked at around 6,000 firms representing some 2.5 million employees. They found these three elements—autonomy, rewards, and psychological safety—significantly related to innovation. But the element that stands out, with its relationship to innovation twice as significant, is psychological safety.

The study shows that the most important factor in creating a culture that promotes innovation is supporting employees and allowing them to weather the storm of failure. People should feel safe trying out innovative, experimental ideas without fear of being penalized for doing so.

Specifically, companies aspiring to be entrepreneurial have to figure out how to institutionalize failure as an opportunity for organizational learning. After all, not every project will result in a positive financial outcome, but there will always be a positive knowledge outcome (Read et al., 2013).

RESTRUCTURING STRUCTURE

What is it about the organizational structure of a large firm that guides decisions like this one down the incremental path, refining existing products and discouraging the creation of new ones?

The new venture environment is simply more fertile for the process of opportunity creation. It is easy to see why leaders like Ross Perot left IBM to create Electronic Data Systems, and

Steve Wozniak left HP to create Apple, instead of developing those opportunities within their large firms. But the entrepreneurial environment shows us that structure can be used to encourage, rather than inhibit, opportunity creation.

Figure 20.3

Research Roots

Threat Rigidity

Researchers have shown that when faced with a situation people find threatening, people artificially limit the range of options available to them, typically to the approaches they have already been using—they become rigid in the face of the threat. However, when the situation is viewed as an opportunity, people see many more possible solution options and become much more creative with the possibilities (Staw et al., 1981).

Research Roots

Asking in the Corporate Environment

In the courtroom, lawyers abide by the rule of: "Never ask a question you don't know the answer to." Unfortunately, many businesspeople follow the same philosophy. This limits innovation and creative thinking. And it leaves many corporate managers feeling hamstrung by constraints.

If the solution to this is asking, why don't more corporate managers do this? Because they fear the unknown, what might happen if they are to go off-script? So much of a corporate manager's role is based on planning and executing those plans, that there is no room left for improvisation.

Asking, however, can actually lead one to have more control over outcomes than just moving forward with forecasted assumptions. Here are a few steps you can take toward becoming a successful asker in a corporate setting:

- *Start small.* Start making small asks of people you have a collegial relationship with. For example, ask another manager to combine efforts with your team on a project. Or ask an external partner you work with to collaborate with you in a new way.
- *Manage expectations.* If you are going to make a bigger ask or enter into a more open-ended conversation, prepare your colleague ahead of time. Since the default communication style in the corporate environment is causal, it can catch people off guard when one communicates in a more open, co-creative way. Letting someone know ahead of time that you want to have a different type of conversation, one that is open and allows both of you to explore possibilities, increases the likelihood of your ask getting thoughtful consideration rather than just surprise.
- *Listen.* After you make the ask, listen closely to the response. Hear the words, but also hear what the person is not saying. If they answer "no," or refuse to engage, is it because they feel they do not have decision-making authority?
- *Seek out others who are open.* If you do hit an impasse with an individual who is uncomfortable co-creating with you, seek those in their organization who may be so inclined, or who might have the managerial latitude to creatively address your ask.
- *Report back.* Build a culture of asking in your team and within your organization by sharing your ask stories. Share both successes and failures. Talking about your ask journey will grow your confidence as you see the positive outcomes generated—from both your successes and failures. And it will encourage others to get out and start asking as well (Whiffen, 2015).

Research Roots

Transacting Within Hierarchies

Oliver Williamson's book *Markets and Hierarchies* (1975) presents a comprehensive analysis of the economic organization of activities within firms and markets, focusing on the theory of transaction cost economics.

Research Roots *(continued)*

Williamson posits that the structure of firms—whether they are more market-like or hierarchical—significantly influences their efficiency and the way they handle transactions. This theory is crucial in understanding how firms decide whether to produce internally or outsource activities, which can have implications for entrepreneurship and venture creation.

A core idea in Williamson's work is that market-like structures often promote efficiency through competition and price mechanisms, while hierarchical structures can reduce transaction costs by improving coordination and reducing uncertainty.

The benefits of hierarchical structures—formalizing decision-making and resource allocation—are likely to have the disadvantage of preventing decision-makers from identifying opportunities in the natural uncertainty outside the established structures of the firm.

Williamson argues that transaction costs—costs incurred during an exchange of goods or services—can be optimized through the structures and hierarchies of firms. This operational efficiency drives profitability, thus is critical for entrepreneurs once they have market acceptance to structure their new venture to minimize transaction costs and enhance operational efficiency.

ENTREPRENEURIAL STRUCTURE: THE INTERNAL MARKET

The new venture environment works as a market. Most large firms work as hierarchies. But imagine if the opportunity creation function within a large firm could be restructured to operate more like a market. Markets already exist within some companies.

Founded in 1902 as a mining company, and now multi-billion-dollar innovation giant, 3M uses a market-like system to manage employee time; employees are given one day a week to work on whatever ideas they like.

One of 3M's more than 60,000 products is the Post-it Note. Art Fry, a 3M employee, was part of the team that invented what might have been thrown out as a failed product, a glue that did not stick well. But because the 3M structure provided him and others in the firm time to work on it nonetheless, the Post-it became one of 3M's biggest successes.

Another example is Koch Industries, a large privately owned US corporation trading in oil and fertilizers. It practices "market-based management," which gives employees decision rights and performance-related pay.

And in Silicon Valley, employees at highly successful Google can use 20% of their time to work on whatever projects they want.

The core idea is that in addition to its existing products, a large corporation should also encourage a portfolio of differentiated opportunities across technology or market commonalities. Ideas might originate anywhere, but the logic of the structure can still nurture them at an appropriate level so their potential can be realized with minimal risk.

An internal market can function on some or all of the following principles derived from the experiences of expert entrepreneurs:

- *Open the market to all potential innovators.* Offer time, freedom, or autonomy to people who have the drive to explore new opportunities. Provide structure so that anyone with an idea can submit a proposal for funding.

- *Open the market to all potential investors.* Anyone with profit-and-loss responsibility in the firm can apply to manage a fund. Investment returns are included in the profit/loss results of the investor's business unit. Fund sizes are set annually (at the most frequent). Decision-making for investing in new projects is distributed outside the CEO office, potentially even to outsiders—for example, individuals from the venture capital industry might be permitted to invest in internal projects; and employees might bring startups from outside for potential investment from their employers or through a variety of B2B partnerships.
- *Encourage iterative opportunity development.* The initial funder of the project is not permitted to exclusively provide follow-on funding. Other funders (internal and external) must participate. This has several implications. First, external funders such as venture capitalists, partners, or customers can help validate an opportunity. Second, internal funders have to be cooperative and quick to compete with external sources of funding for the best new opportunities. Third, this approach restrains the "escalation of commitment" that initial funders can fall into—throwing good money at an opportunity that is clearly bad.
- *Eliminate minimum investment sizes.* Investments can be scalable based on the industry and the opportunity. This encourages people to fund projects that don't initially impact the bottom line and encourages people not to prematurely overfund uncertain projects; instead, add funding iteratively as the opportunity is proven.
- *Make everything negotiable (within the philosophy and values of the company).* Just like in entrepreneurial finance, ownership, salary, amount of funding, nature of the business plan, milestones, and much more are all jointly agreed by funders and creators. Equity in opportunities can be bought and sold both in internal and external markets at market rates. Intellectual property owned by the firm can be secured by the new opportunity team, and vice versa.
- *Support projects that compete with the core business.* And share company resources that might complement the new venture. Better for competition to come from inside than outside.
- *Embrace failure.* Offer employees the assurance that if they explore an idea and it fails, they won't be fired or penalized. Build a culture and a structure that uses failure as a mechanism for learning, not for weeding out employees. Scott Cook, the founder of software firm Intuit, sees failures as part of the process: "In business, every failure is just a stepping stone towards success."

After bringing many of these principles inside the firm, HP established a close relationship with Silicon Valley venture firm Foundation Capital, to learn how to manage opportunities from venture capitalists and exchange ideas about future trends.

And, while it might be no surprise that Microsoft regularly meets with venture capitalists to shop opportunities too small for the software giant to bring to market, the trend is one that extends to companies in more traditional industries. Internal market elements drive new products at firms that include Coca-Cola and Citigroup and give energy to talent management at American Express.

Table 20.2

Safety in failure within large organizations: Questions and answers	
How should a professional negotiate a margin of failure with the boss?	The employee should consider expectations and affordable loss. Setting outrageous expectations for a new project or a new product may help get resources approved, but makes it difficult to deal productively with any shortfall in the results. Be realistic with the boss. Second, and particularly with highly uncertain projects, evaluate the level of affordable loss, or the level of downside that the individual and the firm can tolerate. If managed effectively, failure will never get to a point where the project generates losses that the individual or the firm can't afford. This helps to make the post-mortem of failed projects less of an emotional exercise and something people can learn from objectively.
Should failures be discussed before or after they happen?	Failure should be discussed in advance in the context of where the pitfalls may lie (so that they can be avoided or leveraged) and in terms of how much will be invested in the project. A project can still be considered successful as long as it stays within the predefined affordable limit—a key insight for being able to redefine losing as successful with a large organization. Also, every project deserves an "after-action review"—a chance to look at what the team liked and did not like about the project, what was learned from the project, and how to take that learning into the organization and into the next iteration of the project.
How can a manager make it safe for his or her team to innovate?	Walk the talk. Learn from his or her own failures. Share that learning with the team. Conduct "after-action reviews" with the team for all projects. Promote people who have been able to learn from failure and communicate those stories. This is clearly not something that can be put into a policy manual—it is an enacted part of a team or firm culture.

Practically Speaking

Breath of Fresh Air

Adventurers from New York to Nepal have long appreciated Gore-Tex. The material's seemingly paradoxical ability to keep the weather out while enabling perspiration to escape enables a wide range of functional and comfortable outerwear. Noting that the firm which delivered this innovation, W. L. Gore & Associates, was established in 1958, we take a closer look at how the company has stayed entrepreneurial for such a long time.

No Climate for Innovation

W. L. "Bill" Gore started his career at DuPont in 1945 and joined a team finding applications for a novel polymer called polytetrafluoroethylene—Teflon, to the rest of us. Bill experimented with the material as a tough, heat-resistant coating for wiring, an application he felt offered great potential given the likely rise of the computer.

Convinced of its technical merits, he tried unsuccessfully to persuade DuPont to develop Teflon-coated cable. Frustrated, in 1958 he created his own firm with his wife Vieve in their basement. W. L. Gore & Associates' cable product created a market. Within ten years, the firm employed more than 200 people, and Gore cable was used on a mission to the moon.

Practically Speaking *(continued)*

Fabric of Life

Strong competition in the cable industry kept Bill and his son Bob focused on innovation. Continuing to work with Teflon, the pair figured out how to heat and stretch the material so it could be woven as fabric, and Gore-Tex was born. But even before that, Bill had started carefully crafting W. L. Gore & Associates' organization so it could embrace innovation in the way his previous employer had not.

The Committed Associate

Employees of W. L. Gore are called associates. In the non-hierarchical "lattice" structure, Gore empowered all his employees with the same level of authority. Leaders could emerge only if other associates committed to follow them, and associates had the choice of which projects to work on. The intent and outcome of the structure was to enable good new ideas to grow organically at the discretion of the team. And the teams also had the support of Gore, as he let them do just about anything that would not jeopardize the entire company.

Smaller Sizes

Gore quantified optimal team size and constructed his organization accordingly. He felt that when a team at a manufacturing facility exceeded 150 people, two things happened. First, the team lost a sense of cooperation, shifting decision responsibility from "we" (the team) to "they" (some anonymous bureaucracy). Second, accomplishment per person started to decrease. Consequently, when manufacturing teams exceeded 150 people, Gore split the operation in two.

Patently Successful

The approach works. W. L. Gore & Associates has created innovative products in areas you probably know, such as clothing and shoes, and in many more that range from guitar strings to dental floss, space suits to surgical sutures. Gore is one of the 200 largest private firms in the US, and consistently makes Fortune's annual list of the "100 Best Companies to Work For" in the United States. In 2023, the company generated 4.8 billion US dollars in sales, has thousands of patents, and has more than 13,000 employees worldwide. The company continues to defy the common expectation that large cannot also be entrepreneurial.

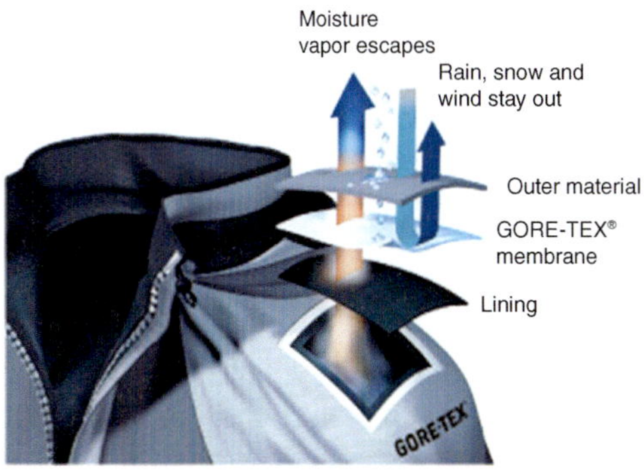

Figure 20.4

Practically Speaking *(continued)*

Gore Application Questions

- What are some potential pitfalls of the Gore model?
- How does the Gore model help us think about managing spin-offs?
- In what situations might the Gore model offer benefit?
- Which aspects of the Gore model seem most compelling to your organization?

To learn more, visit: https://effectuation.org/EE3/gore or scan Figure 20.5.

Figure 20.5

Staying Entrepreneurial

W. L. Gore splits the firm every time the number of employees exceeds 150 in order to ensure that every "company" within Gore continues to operate entrepreneurially.

Practically Speaking

A Guide to the Process

Despite the popular malignment of process, it has an intended function: to help organize, coordinate, and facilitate the actions of many individuals within a large organization. The problem is not the process, but the implementation of the process—what it is actually intended to accomplish.

To provide a view into a different possible implementation of process, consider the story of insurance software provider, Guidewire. When John Seybold and his partners founded Guidewire in 2001, he knew little more about the insurance industry than an informed consumer. But as chief technology officer of the upstart company, he also knew he and the team had to learn quickly if they were going to convince mainstream insurers to scrap their aging mainframes and adopt Guidewire's Java-based solutions.

Process Objective: Flexibility

The team members looked at the problem and made a decision. Above all, they would be flexible—flexible product, flexible business model, and flexible organization. They expected to gain insights every day from customers, partners, and competitors, and they wanted to be able to immediately benefit from everything they learned.

Practically Speaking *(continued)*

Process Implementation: Sprint

Guidewire organized around small, nimble project teams. But here comes the twist: a project team's assignment lasts only a month. At the start of a month, each "sprint team" picks from the list of the most important tasks to be tackled. The team selects a leader for the month and devours the task. At the end of the month, the team wraps up the project, reflects on its progress, reprioritizes, picks a new task, and the process starts all over.

The key to keeping the whole organization moving toward success is the "master backlog" list of projects. As new ideas are generated and new requests come from customers, they are added to the backlog. No changes to priorities are made during a monthly sprint. But at the start of each new month, the organization reprioritizes the entire backlog and assigns only those tasks that top the list to the next month's sprint teams.

At the end of each month, each team has a specific deliverable—something that must be completed, tested, documented, and ready for a customer. In fact, it is the customer who reviews the deliverable and decides whether to accept it or not. Doing this forces the team to focus on creating something usable and complete, thus giving the customer a strong voice within the organization.

Every day, each sprint team meets for ten minutes in the morning at their whiteboard to discuss what it did the previous day and what it hopes to accomplish today. Individual priorities and performance are as transparent as team performance. Completely transparent. At the end of each month, the teams examine the process to discuss what worked well, what did not work, and what they want to change when they reassemble for the next month's sprint.

Process Outcome: Innovation

The success of the process can be demonstrated in the numerous industry awards and client references Guidewire has garnered. But John Seybold describes an unexpected benefit:

> When we first did this, I thought seeing the huge backlog and the small projects we finished in a month would discourage the team. But exactly the reverse happened. They said wow—we're in control and look at what we did. It was a real morale booster, and it has continued to be.

As of 2023, Guidewire employs more than 3,000 people and counts more than 540 international insurers in 40 countries in its growing customer base—successful, but still small compared with the insurance giants they sell to. Nonetheless, this process has continued to scale and work for Guidewire.

Figure 20.6

If you are skeptical about this version of process within a large organization, you may be interested to know that virtually all Guidewire's large, conservative clients in the insurance industry use precisely this approach, learned from Guidewire, within their teams implementing Guidewire's software.

Practically Speaking *(continued)*

Guidewire Application Questions

- How easy is it for you to terminate a dead-end project?
- Do you have a place for the customer in your organization?
- What kind of people will this kind of organization attract?
- Do you have a regular way to revise and optimize teams?
- Is your organization generating innovation at the rate you expect?
- Do your employees feel they make a visible and measurable contribution toward the success of your firm?
- Do you have the visibility you need in the innovation process in your organization?

To learn more, visit: https://effectuation.org/EE3/guidewire or scan Figure 20.7.

Figure 20.7

PRINCIPLES OF PROCESS

Process generally does what it is designed to do. What Guidewire demonstrates is that it is possible to offer insight into developing new products and entering and shaping new markets. More subtly, they offer ideas on selecting, promoting, and training people inside a large firm as well as insight into what might help entrepreneurs stay with the venture as it grows into a large firm.

Guidewire has important implications for the strategic planning process inside large firms—particularly for acquisitions of startups and corporate venture funds. Furthermore, experiences from Guidewire inform research and development partnerships and technology licensing.

Even when the odds are against the large firm that aspires to be entrepreneurial, there are ways to overcome the three main structural constraints and design a process that enables rather than inhibits innovation. As you think about your own organization, it is not necessary to do everything Guidewire has done. Elements of the process, such as monthly priority reviews or customer acceptance of deliverables, can be implemented in an organization without moving to small sprint teams.

Also, an entire large organization need not be re-engineered to have the same process. Teams, groups, cells, or divisions charged with creating new opportunities might design their own process in the same way teams within insurance firms implementing Guidewire software decided to. Regardless of what the actual implementation looks like, it is liberating to consider how you might change the rules of the organization to encourage entrepreneurial action.

DIFFERENT STRUCTURE, DIFFERENT OUTCOME

Let's return to the new product proposal still sitting on your desk. Imagine the firm runs an internal market, and you have a block of real money and time to invest in real opportunities. It is separate from your operating budget. Your peers also have funds of different sizes; they, too, may invest to create opportunities. In fact, you may be competing with one of them for a piece of ownership of the proposal on your desk.

This fund is dear—you had to apply for it from treasury and you carry it on your unit's profit and loss. You will benefit both financially and professionally if you can turn it into something. Instead of a large research and development budget, it is a source of innovation for your business unit. How would that change which proposal you reach for—the new product or the marketing outlay for the existing one?

Research Roots

Enduring High-Performance Ventures Create High Social Value

In *The Illusions of Entrepreneurship*, Scott Shane (2008) surveys research on small businesses in order to highlight that the general public and economic policymakers tend to hold many misconceptions about entrepreneurship.

One interesting misconception is the idea that new ventures are a public good because they generally create jobs. The truth is that a few new ventures that grow larger and endure 16 years or longer (Hathaway & Litan, 2014) are responsible for most of the job growth.

This reinforces the core idea in this book—that learning principles used by expert entrepreneurs who have demonstrated an ability to launch enduring, high-performance ventures is not only good for you but also good for society because it is the enduring, high-performance ventures that also create high levels of social value.

TAKEAWAY: A FRESH LOOK

Understanding expert entrepreneurial approaches and applying them to the large firm offers a new perspective on the questions facing executives charged with innovation and growth. Clearly, these approaches offer insight into developing new products and new markets. More subtly, they offer ideas on selecting, promoting, and training people inside a large firm as well as insight into what might help entrepreneurs stay with the venture as it grows into a large firm. They have implications for the strategic planning process inside a large firm—in particular for acquisitions of startups and corporate venture funds. They also inform research and development partnerships and technology licensing.

Even when the odds are against the large firm that aspires to be entrepreneurial, there are ways to overcome the three main barriers consisting of prediction, structure, and process, to acting entrepreneurially within a large organization.

So What?

Large organizations are built to withstand entrepreneurial efforts involving the effectual principles laid out in this book. But in order to continue to grow, they need specially designed solutions to overcome their over-reliance on research, prediction, and big bets in the pursuit of new opportunities.

Think It Through

- What might help entrepreneurs stay with the venture as it grows into a large firm (Bill Gates and Mark Zuckerberg are exceptional; most founders leave or are forced out as the venture grows)?
- Is there an optimal size for any firm?

What Now?

- In your organization, at what number of employees does your "achievement per employee" level off (e.g. Gore)?
- How will you change selection and promotion of people inside a larger firm, considering these ideas?
- If you were to create an "internal market" for opportunities, who would be your "buyers," who would be your "sellers," and what would a transaction look like?
- Identify two existing research and development partnerships and/or licensing relationships that seem to be built upon these effectual ideas (they may have snuck in). Can you identify how they came to be, and how you might initiate, run, or re-design others more effectually?
- Think about what you are going to tell your Chief Financial Officer (CFO) when she asks for revenue projections on a project to develop a new product.

REFERENCES

Blekman, T. (2011). *Corporate Effectuation: What Managers Should Learn From Entrepreneurs!* S. D. U. Uitgeverij. https://cir.nii.ac.jp/crid/1130000794441940736

Blekman, T., & Konijnenburg, R. (2012). *Orkestratie van Effectuation: Het Organiseren van ondernemend gedrag.* BIM Media BV.

Faschingbauer, M. (2021). *Effectuation: Wie erfolgreiche Unternehmer denken, entscheiden und handeln.* Schäffer-Poeschel.

Hathaway, I., & Litan, R. E. (2014). Declining business dynamism in the United States: A look at states and metros. *Brookings Institution, 2.* https://www.brookings.edu/wp-content/uploads/2016/06/declining_business_dynamism_hathaway_litan.pdf

Mauer, R., Baker, T., & Welter, F. (2014). Thinking different. In T. Baker & F. Welter (eds.), *The Routledge Companion to Entrepreneurship.* Routledge.

Mayer-Haug, K., Read, S., Brinckmann, J., Dew, N., & Grichnik, D. (2013). Entrepreneurial talent and venture performance: A meta-analytic investigation of SMEs. *Research Policy, 42*(6–7), 1251–1273.

Read, S., Dew, N., & Margery, P. (2013). Innovation by design—The hybrid organization. *Kindai Management Review, 1*(1), 67–79.

Read, S., Sarasvathy, S., Dew, N., & Wiltbank, R. (2016). *Effectual Entrepreneurship.* Routledge.

Shane, S. A. (2008). *The Illusions of Entrepreneurship: The Costly Myths That Entrepreneurs, Investors, and Policy Makers Live By.* Yale University Press.

Staw, B. M., Sandelands, L. E., & Dutton, J. E. (1981). Threat rigidity effects in organizational behavior: A multi-level analysis. *Administrative Science Quarterly, 26*, 5014524.

Wasserman, N. (2013). *The Founder's Dilemmas: Anticipating and Avoiding the Pitfalls That Can Sink a Startup.* Princeton University Press. https://doi.org/10.1515/9781400841936

Whiffen, S. (2015). Assets to action. Unpublished paper.

Williamson, O. E. (1975). *Markets and Hierarchies, Analysis and Antitrust Implications: A Study in the Economics of Internal Organization.* Free Press.

PART V

Applications of Effectuation

You will have noticed that not all examples of effectual logic in this book are entrepreneurs. In this next section, we delve deeper into the idea that effectuation is a way of describing human decision-making and human action, which can be applied as easily to the starting of a new venture as it can to the solving of a problem in the world.

And though we take on only the topics of how firms communicate their unique identity (Chapter 21), how people deal with technology when creating ventures (Chapter 22), and how the entrepreneurial method is similar to the scientific method (Chapter 23), we hope you will consider these chapters your gateway out into the wide world. And as your voyage faces uncertainties not detailed in this book, we hope you figure out how to apply some elements of effectuation to help you on your way.

> Whatever you can do or dream you can, begin it.
> Boldness has genius, power and magic in it.
>
> *Johann Wolfgang von Goethe*, writer, philosopher, and statesman

REFERENCE

Goethe, J. W. von. (1875). *Italienische Reise*. Hempel.

DOI: 10.4324/9781003364016-25

Figure 21.1 Your fingerprint is your identity. In the same way, the identity of your venture is your brand.

CHAPTER 21

Brand as Venture Identity

Marketing You

In This Chapter

New ventures start without a brand. But all start with something more central, potentially more useful, free, and within the entrepreneur's control: An identity.

In small, founder-led ventures, the identity of the founder and the identity of the venture are largely the same thing. This illustrates another way an entrepreneur's means are important, showing the imprint an entrepreneur leaves on a venture she creates, and how that can affect the trajectory of the venture.

DOI: 10.4324/9781003364016-26

IT ALL STARTS WITH IDENTITY

As the prospective founder, owner, manager, and first employee of a new venture, you may well look with awe at the world's greatest brands. Names like Apple, Coca-Cola, Spanx, Toyota, Alibaba, and Tata must give employees at these organizations an incredible advantage in the market. And here you are with nothing but an idea and a little inspiration (perhaps enhanced by the caffeine from that Coca-Cola).

The purpose of this chapter is to think about marketing a new venture. Not from the perspective of the things you don't have (a recognizable brand, a large communications budget, and a team of PR people), but from the perspective of what you do have: an identity. An identity not only prepares you to start taking action without spending money, but also helps set a foundation for what the brand will be as the venture grows, what messages to communicate, and the product or service areas the firm might or might not occupy.

We should say at the outset that no single identity is necessarily better than another. Consider the following two examples. Cypress Semiconductor, based in San Jose, California, makes programmable chips for custom computers that go into everything from automobiles to medical devices. Founder and CEO T. J. Rogers, named one of America's toughest bosses by *Fortune Magazine* in 1993, exercises with his direct reports at lunch and has a license-plate holder that reads, "Cypress: We eat nails."

Contrast that with the Vermont Teddy Bear Company, a folksy outfit known for people calmly sipping tea during meetings and sponsoring guns-for-bear exchanges. What do the two companies have in common? Both are enormously successful. Both have a strong identity. And for both, the identity of the firm, an extension of the founder's identity, helps attract employees and partners and provides a basis for choosing which activities make sense for the business and which don't. Yet, their identities could not be further apart.

Clearly, there can be as many company identities as there are entrepreneurs; the question is how to create and use yours.

IDENTITY SHARING: VENTURE AND ENTREPRENEUR

There are many opinions about what venture identity means. We think of venture identity as the "persona" of a firm, designed to be consistent with and facilitate the attainment of business objectives. Venture identity is not a brand. Venture identity is not a logo. It is the philosophy, values, norms, and personality of the firm. Brand and logo usually reflect parts of the venture's identity, but only parts of it. When the venture starts, those elements of logo and brand don't exist at all.

So, at the start, personal identity and venture identity are largely the same thing. This illustrates another way an entrepreneur's means are important, and also the imprint an entrepreneur leaves on a venture she creates, and how that can affect the trajectory of the venture.

Research Roots

IDENTIFY YOURSELF

It has long been known that non-pecuniary motivations are an important reason why some individuals take the plunge into entrepreneurship. Fauchart and Gruber (2011) probe the nature of these motives, finding many ventures to be expressions of the founders' self-identities. Based on a sample of 49 founders who had created businesses in the sports equipment industry, the researchers found three basic categories of founder identities. They describe these as:

- *Missionaries.* These are founders that are advancing a cause, believe in contributing to a better world, and see their firms as instruments of that cause.

Research Roots *(continued)*

- *Communitarians.* These are founders that see themselves as supporting their communities by bringing something useful to them, often based on their knowledge of community needs.
- *Darwinians.* These are founders that view business as business, and themselves as professional, competitive players seeking to make money.

Fauchart and Gruber (2011) note that several of the founders they interviewed were hybrids of two or three of the pure identities, which is consistent with the view that many entrepreneurs have a complex set of motives for founding a venture.

YOU ARE THE IDENTITY; THE IDENTITY IS YOU

It will be of little surprise, after reading about "means" in Chapter 10, to learn that your means are directly connected with the identity of your venture. Never is this truer than when you are the sole employee of the venture, but it continues to be true as the venture grows.

The reason is that your startup's identity could not be created by the marketing department (even if you had one) in a vacuum. Rather, it reflects the systematic and often mundane internal and external actions that employees (or the sole employee) of the firm take every day. But simply taking action does not guarantee that a desirable or coherent identity will emerge. To achieve that, you must authentically reflect your personality and values in your actions.

Research Roots

BRIDGING THE GAP

As this book edition goes to press, increasingly there are calls to address the perceived gap between the values and needs of society and those demonstrated by large, influential businesses and institutions.

This is not a new issue; Freeman and Auster addressed it in their 2015 book *Bridging the Values Gap: Business and Society in Transformation.* They argue that skepticism and mistrust toward corporations is partly due to the "values gap"—the discrepancy between what society expects from businesses in terms of ethical behavior, environmental stewardship, and social responsibility, versus what businesses prioritize, often profitability and shareholder value.

To close the gap, the actions of the company must reflect genuine values and ethical considerations of its people—founders, employees, and other stakeholders such as suppliers, customers, and the community.

Freeman and Auster advocate for increased dialogue and engagement with stakeholders to understand diverse perspectives and values, thereby identifying common ground and (re-)building trust between businesses and society.

This engagement is fundamental to the experimentation phases of a new entrepreneurial venture and when the team and structures are directly controlled by the founders. The challenge arises as the business grows, responsibilities are delegated, and the direct influence of the founders wanes.

It is therefore up to founders to lead the team consciously and authentically by modeling ethical and values-driven behavior, thus creating a culture which fosters open communication, transparency, and integrity within the organization, particularly as it grows in size and impact on the wider community.

Your Venture Reflects You

Your firm's identity best reflects your authentic personality. It must be consistent whether directed at customers, partners, employees, media—any stakeholder who has contact with the company. Of course, when you have been successful at co-creating your venture with stakeholders, this consistency emerges naturally. The goal is to succinctly understand, down to the level of individual words, the core principles of the company, principles that help stakeholders relate to the value proposition of the firm. It has to be unique, and it has to be genuine. HP, for example, has distilled it to a single word—"Invent"—which goes all the way back to the founders working together in a Palo Alto garage. What will it be for you?

Practically Speaking

Frida Kahlo—The Art of Pain

When we consider our identity, most of us do not hark back to an accident. Yet, in reality, identity is sometimes forged from the lowest points in life. Mexican artist Frida Kahlo (1907–1954) was only 18 when she was involved in a serious bus accident, leading to devastating injuries that left her bedridden for long periods. This came on top of her childhood encounter with polio which left her with a limp for the rest of her life.

Lemons in Hand

As she turned to paint to cope with her pain, she squeezed her experiences of pain and physical confinement along with the skills she had learned assisting her photographer father to mix together a whole new palette of visual composition. Not only of the world she lived in, but also her own identity—as a woman and a living contradiction of mixed ancestry. "I paint my own reality," she once said (Herrera, 1983).

Mixing Colors

As mentioned in *Britannica* (2024), "Kahlo was born to a German father of Hungarian descent and a Mexican mother of Spanish and Native American descent. Later, during her artistic career, Kahlo explored her identity by frequently depicting her ancestry as binary opposites: the colonial European side and the indigenous Mexican side."

The latter led her to dress in Tehuana style, vibrant colors and indigenous Mexican jewelry, that she captured in the self-portraits that have come to characterize her work.

Moving Tapestry

Kahlo defies the myth of the lonely artist. Along with her husband, monumental muralist Diego Rivera, and the leading surrealist André Breton, she helped shape the Mexican Renaissance. She was integral to the development of "Méxicanidad," an artistic and intellectual movement that aimed to redefine Mexican identity post-revolution.

Practically Speaking *(continued)*

Even the house Kahlo and Rivera constructed embodied their enterprise. It consisted of separate individual spaces connected by a bridge, which became the gathering place for artists and political activists from around the world.

Sometimes, living your inner truth is your greatest competitive advantage—not only for the present, but for the ages.

To learn more, visit: https://effectuation.org/EE3/frida or scan Figure 21.3.

Figure 21.3

Figure 21.2

Practically Speaking

Augusto Teodoro: Love at First Loss

Co-Creators: Edmilson Lima and Rose Mary Almeida Lopes

What would you do when you finish last in the first race you run? And you are in terrible pain? Maybe quietly move to another sport? Grimly persist to beat the odds? Or simply fall in love with the sport that humiliated and injured you? Surprisingly, that's what the now successful sports entrepreneur and torchbearer for the 2016 Olympic Games in Rio de Janeiro, Augusto Teodoro did—fall in love.

Losing Odds

Augusto had a difficult start. Coming from a poor family, he started working menial jobs early to support his family and save money for university studies. When he finished last in a 6-kilometer race, Augusto fell in love with the sport and decided to study physical education.

Leading Gains

Augusto was elected to the role of vice president of all athletic activities for students at his university, motivating him to organize the "Industrial Olympic Games" in his hometown of Nova Friburgo, Brazil.

Practically Speaking *(continued)*

His love of sports was contagious. Other runners sought to work with him to make sports an intrinsic component of quality of life in the community, leading to the foundation of the Friburguese Runners' Association.

Running Ventures

Equipped with his degree, Augusto began teaching physical education to pay the bills. But his heart was in sports venturing. Quilting together with his widening network in the community, Augusto opened a gym, a side business selling sports equipment, and, eventually, a business running sports events.

Working with five other entrepreneurs, Augusto established swimming classes and hydrotherapy sessions for disabled people using the pool of a local hotel.

Racing for Impact

Through a multitude of ventures over time, Augusto has influenced hundreds of people to become healthier through sports, including some participants who were able to overcome major health challenges such as depression, chemical dependence, and chronic illness.

Some people run for the medal and fame. Others for money and the adrenalin rush. But when you fall in love, you lose yourself. And gain the world. In Augusto's case, that world is a healthy community and entrepreneurial co-creation.

Who better to be a torchbearer for the 2016 Rio Olympic Games?

To learn more, visit: https://effectuation.org/EE3/augusto or scan Figure 21.4.

Figure 21.4

IDENTITY IS THE SUM OF MANY SMALL ACTIONS

Once you understand the persona of your venture, it is easy to see how your daily actions either reinforce or undermine it. A major life sciences company with an identity built around safety made the decision to buy Volvos for its company-owned cars. That may not have been the most cost-effective decision, but it certainly is the one most consistent with the company's identity.

Mark and Stacy Andrus (see Chapter 13) employed their own re-use desires to make pita chips from day-old bread, and then proceeded to do their marketing by giving away their own product (initially, they used pita chips to keep people in line for sandwiches, and once they moved into the snack business full time, they used the pita chips as their primary revenue generator).

Practically Speaking

Margaritaville: Neverending Song

Over the course of his life, the US pop singer Jimmy Buffett released more than 30 albums, selling over 20 million records (so last century!). But like the other Buffett (Warren), Jimmy is an investors' idol as well.

Surprise Hit

Whereas Buffett's entrepreneurial success never made the pop charts like some of his noisier competition, the silent facts speak for themselves: "People are always shocked when they find out how big we've gotten. We just kept quietly doing our thing. Not saying much. And now—bam!—here we are" (Barnes, 2016).

Buffett on Buffett

What's behind this success? Branding. His namesake and investment guru Warren E. Buffett (not related to Jimmy) endorses it: "He understands his brand, which has a substantial reach. One of the secrets to his success is that he never really loses any fans" (Barnes, 2016).

So how can you have a winning brand after 30 albums? You stick with what the audiences continue requesting, even if you may not think it is your best (or deepest) song. For Buffett that is the 1977 (!) hit "Margaritaville," which earned him the following popular image, as summarized in this obituary in *The New York Times* (Friskics-Warren, 2023):

> Peopled with pirates, smugglers, beach bums and barflies, Mr. Buffett's genial, self-deprecating songs conjured a world of sun, salt water and nonstop parties animated by the calypso country-rock of his limber Coral Reefer Band. His live shows abounded with singalong anthems and festive tropical iconography, making him a perennial draw on the summer concert circuit, where he built an ardent fan base akin to the Grateful Dead's Deadheads.

Singing Is Feeling Is Branding Is Selling

You might still be wondering how Jimmy Buffett turned a song about a sad story of a fellow looking deep into the glass while lamenting the loss of a girlfriend into a lucrative business empire.

Mindy Grossman, highly experienced consumer goods executive and CEO of the Home Shopping Network from 2006 to 2017 which featured hundreds of Margaritaville-themed items over the years, shares her analysis: "The stroke of genius was making Margaritaville a feeling, not a place. If you don't take the name so literally, growth could be endless" (Barnes, 2016).

The power of music to elicit emotions is well known, but Jimmy Buffett and his business partners took it a step further, basically branding a set of emotions created by a single song. They started with restaurants, then expanded to resorts, drinks, and merchandise licensing—and the sweet sound of profits continues to echo through even empty concert venues.

Practically Speaking ***(continued)***

Entrepreneurial High Note

In a *New York Times* article from 2016, author Brooks Barnes explains the wider implications of Buffett's approach:

> In some ways, with his approach to concert merchandise and tour sponsorship in the 1980s, he created the model of musician-as-entrepreneur that managers for artists like Madonna and Dave Matthews have pursued more recently. Other singers have parlayed their personas into business empires—Dolly Parton, for instance, with her Dollywood theme park, Dixie Stampede dinner theaters, Dolly slot machines and "Coat of Many Colors" merchandise—but none are as singularly sprawling as Mr. Buffett's Margaritaville.

Figure 21.5

As you venture out, ask yourself: what is your Margaritaville?

To learn more, visit: https://effectuation.org/EE3/margaritaville or scan Figure 21.6.

Figure 21.6

BE CONSISTENT

Every day presents opportunities for actions that are not consistent with the corporate identity. Whether it's making a hire, launching a product innovation, writing a press release, or forming a partnership, managers need to hold the action up against the corporate identity. If it is not coherent, don't do it.

One of the uses of a good corporate identity is that it helps managers figure out what the company is "not." In the 1970s, Pierre Cardin had an identity tied with luxury. But Pierre Cardin has slipped a long way from the cover of the fashion magazine *Vogue*, where it once was, to the discount stores where it is today. Pierre Cardin failed one corporate identity test after another, infusing chaos and irrationality into what could have remained an iconic fashion brand.

Looking at new opportunities, partners, and customers from the perspective of the identity of your new venture can offer an efficient way to select activities that are a good fit as well as those that are not.

IMPLEMENT BEYOND THE LOGO

Identity is much more than a logo. Over the years, Apple Computer, the computing pioneer, has consciously become Apple (notice "Computer" is conspicuously absent), the hip provider of trendy lifestyle technology. In the process, the company's design firm, Mark Anderson Design, worked on literally hundreds of projects to make the shift.

Some identity-reinforcing (or -creating) actions, such as letterhead, corporate signage, and product packaging might be obvious. But other projects, like designing the annual report, press releases, and even the appearance of company offices, might not be so obvious. Corporate identity is a message that benefits from reinforcement at every opportunity.

Another example is Starbucks Coffee Company. A brief text outlining the mission statement is printed on the back of every partner's (employee's) business card, ensuring that employees and their business partners are regularly reminded of the Starbucks corporate identity. It is a powerful and inexpensive way to communicate using space otherwise left blank.

Practically Speaking

Terry Heckler: Creator of Enduring Brands

Terry Heckler, founder of Heckler Branding in Seattle, Washington, has helped create dozens of successful brands from scratch—ranging from Redhook Beer and Jansport Backpacks to Panera Bread and Starbucks, one of his earliest adventures in brand building.

Heckler's adventures, chronicled on his company's website, give us a glimpse of how his firm constitutes brand from identity—often starting with the founder.

A Cup of Starbucks, Not a Cup of Pequod

Contrary to popular wisdom, Starbucks was not founded by Howard Schultz, who came in much later to become the driving force behind the growth of the company. The original Starbucks, a tiny shop in Seattle's Pike Place market that sold imported fine roasted coffee beans, was founded in 1971 by three friends: Gordon Bowker, Jerry Baldwin, and Zev Siegl—a writer, a literature teacher, and a history teacher, respectively.

All three founders were fans of *Moby Dick* and so wanted to name their company Pequod, the name of Captain Ahab's ship in what, in their opinion, was the greatest American novel. Heckler pointed out to them that nobody would ever buy a cup of Pequod and suggested instead the name Starbos—the name of a local mining camp in the Northwest during the 1800s.

In fact, Heckler described his vision of "the quintessential moment of use" of the product—a miner's hand reaching for a green can of coffee inside the camp's tent in the beautiful cool and damp surroundings of Mount Rainier in the rainy Northwest. The three friends jumped on the name because it evoked the name Starbuck, first mate on the Pequod!

Figure 21.7

Practically Speaking *(continued)*

And so a great brand began its journey as a patchwork stitched together from the romantic dreams and values of its founders and roughly blessed by a young commercial artist who would go on to become a kingmaker in his own right. Heckler Branding has not only created successful brands for a number of new ventures that went on to embody strong corporate identities as the fledgling ventures grew into global brands, but also helped rebrand existing companies and create brand extensions as they expanded their horizons.

Figure 21.8

Figure 21.9

Panera: Food as It Should Be

Take the case of the St. Louis Bread Company, Panera, which hired Heckler Branding to redefine the brand, articulate its mission and values and identify core attributes. Again, the Heckler vision of the quintessential moment of use can be observed in the logo and all design aspects associated with the name and the stores. The website describes the core of the identity as follows: food as it should be.

> The central image of the logo was a painterly line illustration of a woman with flowing hair caressing a loaf of bread. She came to be known as "Mother Bread" and symbolized the core essence of the brand's differential. Interestingly, the process of making sourdough bread requires a small piece of the dough used to make the previous batch of bread dough. This starter piece is often called the "mother." Whenever Panera opens stores in a new region, a piece of the original starter that was created in the 1980s is lovingly carried to the new bakery to ensure that original Panera quality and character will rise again and again.
>
> (*Panera*, n.d.)

Will You Sew for Me ... and Marry Me?

The story of Jansport Backpacks also reveals the importance of the quintessential moment of use. The company was founded in the 1960s by Murray Pletz and his cousin Skip Yowell, who won a design competition sponsored by Alcoa for an aluminum flexible frame backpack.

Since neither of them knew how to sew, Murray induced his girlfriend, Jan Lewis, by offering not only to name the company after her, but also to marry her. When ski-maker K2 Corp bought the company in 1972 and tried to change its name, all the employees resigned. They wanted to work for Jansport and not for something called K2. When hiking in the Alps, it was Jan's name they wanted to point to on their customers' backs. K2 gave in and retained the name Jansport.

Heckler's philosophy of the quintessential moment of use is not a mystical one—it is utterly pragmatic and focused on the user as co-creator of the brand.

To learn more, visit: https://effectuation.org/EE3/heckler or scan Figure 21.10.

Figure 21.10

IDENTITY INFLUENCES DECISIONS

Personal identity is people's conception of themselves and how they relate or belong to broader social categories. Entrepreneurs often explain their actions and decisions in terms of their identities ("what kind of person I am"), rather than their goals or preferences ("what I want and like"). Sometimes the identity has to do with being an entrepreneur, however idiosyncratic that might be; in other cases, it comes from other areas of their lives—such as religious faith, political affiliations, childhood traumas, aesthetic pursuits, or even loyalties to sports teams.

Identity often plays an important role in decisions, especially important life decisions (such as starting a new career in entrepreneurship) and can be especially helpful in situations of high uncertainty.

We find powerful examples of this in great literature, such as the fable of Don Quixote. In Quixote's case, knowing what a knight would do in any circumstance makes him decisive even when the consequences are uncertain. His decision-making ability is deeply rooted in his sense of identity—in knowing who he is and what a person like him should do.

In other words, identity consists of having a strong affinity for particular ways of living and deciding, rather than for any particular consequences. Entrepreneurs, in general, appear to realize the value of creating and sustaining strong identities, which can guide them when it is not otherwise clear what they should do. Identities may be fictive or real, freely chosen or constructed, good or evil.

Often, entrepreneurial identities develop incrementally in the course of building a venture—think of how the identities of Bill Gates and Steve Jobs both changed and became more pronounced as their entrepreneurial careers unfolded.

With Steve Jobs fresh in your mind, consider how his strong personality divided opinions on him and his work. Similarly, while Elon Musk enjoyed an initial period of admiration, he has, over time, shown the complexity of his personality and thus faced more criticism.

Practically Speaking

The Identity Spectrum

When we consider identity in entrepreneurship, names like Elon Musk and Steve Jobs immediately come to mind. Both have achieved remarkable success, and infamous notoriety. But it is easy to forget both started with co-founders that helped shaped their first ventures. Steve Wozniak (and Ronald Wayne) in the case of Apple and in the case of Elon Musk's Zip2, his brother, Kimbal Musk, and a friend, Gregory Kouri.

But more inspiring and useful to learn from could be the identities of others who infused their values into their ventures to break down barriers and glass ceilings, including Jamshedji Tata, founder of the more-than-a-century-old Indian conglomerate bearing the family name.

Lasting Returns on Identity

Recently ranked first in the "Hurun Philanthropists of the Century" (2021), Tata's contributions go beyond significant returns on investments year after year. His total contributions since his first major endowments in 1892 equaled 102 billion US dollars in 2021.

Practically Speaking *(continued)*

Endurance Athletes

Imagine you're doing business in a country under a colonial power. All around you are millions of poor, illiterate people. You have many pressing problems. What would explain your decision to write a letter urging your son to: "Be sure to lay wide streets planted with shady trees, every other of a quick-growing variety. Be sure that there is plenty of space for lawns and gardens. Reserve large areas for football, hockey, and parks. Earmark areas for Hindu temples, Mohammedan mosques, and Christian churches."

Legacy Letter

Jamshedji Tata wrote this in a letter to his son Dorab. The cynical may dismiss this as the grandiose dreams of a powerful and wealthy old man. Yet, while Jamshedji did not die a wealthy man and even though only one of his four dream projects was realized in his lifetime, the others were posthumously realized because he never failed to see the connection between family, community, and country identity. And that identity has pervaded the Tata companies for decades after his passing.

Sublime to the Ridiculous? Not So Fast!

But identity need not only be serious and social. Sometimes, it can be fun and even frivolous, yet end up solving frustrations that impact lives day after day. Sara Blakeley has been celebrated for her positive attitudes. In an interview with *Times of Startups,* she attributes it to her father who taught her to celebrate failure:

> Growing up, he would ask us what we failed at that week. If we didn't have something, he would be disappointed. It changed my mindset at an early age that failure is not the outcome, failure is not trying. Don't be afraid to fail.
>
> (*Times of Startups*, 2016)

This lesson was particularly poignant as Blakely lost 11 people due to various causes before she was 30. Mortality became a motivating factor that moved her from selling telefax machines door to door to becoming the world's youngest self-made billionaire in 2012. Not to mention a female entrepreneur making a product primarily for women.

Footloose in Florida

Her idea for Spanx came to her in a rather ordinary moment. She wanted to wear white pants to a party with nothing showing below them. So she cut the feet off her pantyhose. Like most successful ideas, it came from customer frustration—Blakely was her own first customer. However, once she began wearing the footless hose, she began finding a long list of frustrations that this product could overcome.

Oprahtic Quilting

Not being new to hustling (remember what it takes to sell fax machines door to door), Blakely began creating buzz for Spanx. Her marketing and advertising budget? The princessly sum of zero US dollars. The company leveraged networking, social connections, and customers' word of mouth.

Practically Speaking *(continued)*

Knowing that Spanx's target customers also loved *The Oprah Winfrey Show*, Blakely sent her prototypes to the show along with a handwritten note. The prototype caught the attention of the person responsible for Oprah's wardrobe. After wearing Spanx, Oprah loved it so much, she featured Blakely on her "Favorite Things" episode.

And the rest, as they say, is history.

To learn more, visit: https://effectuation.org/EE3/spectrum or scan Figure 21.11.

Figure 21.11

IDENTITY ACTION PLAN

Creating a plan for how to communicate your corporate identity is a straightforward process. It takes quite a bit of work, but there is no magic to it:

Step 1: Articulate Your Corporate Identity

The goal is to reduce the elements of corporate identity to a few key words. These reflect the unique philosophy, values, norms, and personality of the firm that will inspire potential customers, employees, and partners. Articulating this identity is not something you do on your own. It is something you do with all stakeholders, inside and outside the firm:

- Ask yourself why you started the venture.
- Ask your co-founders why they joined you in the venture.
- Ask your customers why they (would) buy from you.
- Ask your partners why they work with you.

Step 2: Assess Your Current Actions

Are the things you do every day aligned with the identity you want to create and communicate? One easy way to start a personal assessment is by using your own "to do" list, email inbox, or telephone call log. With your key identity ideas in mind, go through the list and underline actions that are consistent with the identity you defined and cross out actions that are not. This should prepare you to generate ideas around questions such as:

- What current activities reinforce the elements of your corporate identity?
- Is there anything you do that conflicts with your corporate identity?
- What new activities might you initiate to communicate or reinforce your corporate identity?

Step 3: Put Your Corporate Identity to Work

Identity is a differentiator for your venture. At the start, it may be the only differentiator. You need to figure out how to use that uniqueness to help you accomplish your objectives. The following list suggests some examples with corresponding questions. It is by no means complete, but our hope is that it will serve as a starting point as you consider your own context:

- *Obtain/retain customers.* Do your existing customers have a way to share their enthusiasm for your identity with you?
- *Differentiate.* Is it clear to your stakeholders how your identity clearly distinguishes your offering from that of your competitors?
- *Build partnerships.* What potential partners might be willing to help you achieve your objectives because

they share your values and elements of your identity?

- *Improve visibility.* Are there members of the press and analyst community who relate to your identity and are willing to bring their passion to disseminating your message?
- *Add new products or markets.* In what new areas might your identity give you a competitive advantage?

Three Thoughts on Firm Names

Perhaps the most obvious connection between personal identity and venture identity is naming the firm after yourself (McKinsey & Co., for example). Beyond that, the name can still communicate much about the identity of the venture. LinkedIn does as good a job of illustrating the value of a social network for professionals as Costco does of setting the expectation of finding low prices.

Should the Firm Name Be the Same as the Product Name?

There is no right answer. The logic for making the names the same is that stakeholders have a hard enough time learning a single new name, so why spend the effort teaching two?

Companies like Oracle (the name of the firm and of the firm's core database software product) illustrate the simplicity of this approach. Firms interested in creating a portfolio of products separate the two and may focus on product brands more than on the company brand, such as Proctor & Gamble as the company behind many famous consumer brands such as Pampers, Oral-B, and Vicks.

Who Is Going to Use Your Name, and Is It Suited to the Different Applications?

Think about all the people who are going to use your name. If they speak a different language, what does your name mean in their language? Consult the dictionary and native speakers of that language.

If the press is a big part of your marketing effort, will they write you up in a comparison list with your competitors? If so, choose a name at the start of the alphabet. Will you speak your firm name to a lot of people? If so, it is best spelled easily. Will your name go onto consumer packaging? If so, keep it short and think about the graphic elements of the letters (lots of curves—S, O, G—versus lots of angles—L, E, A).

How Can You Ensure Your Firm Name Is Unique?

This has gotten easier and harder at the same time: easier because you can search the internet for the word(s) you are hoping to use and see what comes up and check an internet registration site to see whether and how the word is being used.

Harder because everyone else can do this, too, and so there has been an explosion of site registrations and new company names. If you want something unique, you are going to have to be creative, search other languages, combine pieces of existing words, or even add special characters.

"As our new company logo, I'm not quite sure it's sending out the right message."

Figure 21.12

TAKEAWAY: IDENTITY IS SOMETHING YOU CREATE EVERY DAY

Creating a plan for how to communicate your corporate identity is a straightforward process.

- Start by articulating your corporate identity: what makes you unique and will inspire stakeholders to work with you?
- Next, assess your current actions for alignment with your identity and consider what else you can do to communicate and reinforce your corporate identity.
- Finally, put your corporate identity to work as a differentiator to help you accomplish your objectives.

As you move ahead and build your corporate identity, you will be able to continue to take greater and greater advantage of identity as a brand. Keep in mind that corporate identity is something you create every day through the things you do, and it should provide you with an advantage in communicating with every stakeholder who touches your venture.

So What?

A corporate identity is nothing more complex than a reflection of what you stand for on a daily basis. Shaping this identity, reinforcing it through actions, and communicating it effectively are central to the value you are creating. And it gives you a competitive advantage.

Think it Through

Irrelevance is the enemy of every startup. With so much activity and so many new ideas and new firms and new products coming out every day, the job of breaking through all that noise to make your firm relevant to your customers, your employees, and your partners is challenging.

As you use social media, public relations, and word of mouth to promote your current effort, begin to formulate your own theory of cutting through the noise:

- What ideas have been most successful in getting your attention?
- Were those ideas presented consistently?
- How many times do you think the entrepreneur had to tell her story?
- What channels of communication are most effective?

What Now?

- What are the elements of value in your identity?
- Can you distil them into a single word? At most five?
- What can you do to communicate and accentuate your identity?
- How can you use identity as a foundation for marketing in your venture?
- What parts of your overall opportunity does this identity enable you to ignore? (And not just the obvious choices that simply don't fit.)
- Is your identity tied to a single product? Does that seem problematic?
- What other opportunities are suggested under the umbrella of that identity?
- What is it about your venture's identity that inspires you to come to work in the morning?
- What is it about your venture's identity that inspires your customers, suppliers, and employees to work with you?

REFERENCES

Barnes, B. (2016, April 23). Jimmy Buffett's "Margaritaville" is a state of mind, and an empire. *The New York Times*. https://www.nytimes.com/2016/04/24/business/media/jimmy-buffetts-margaritaville-is-a-state-of-mind-and-an-empire.html

Britannica. (2024). Frida Kahlo | Biography, Paintings, Self-Portrait, Accident, Husband, & Facts. https://www.britannica.com/biography/Frida-Kahlo

De Cervantes Saavedra, M. (1877). El ingenioso hidalgo Don Quijote de la Mancha: Compuesto por Miguel de Cervántes Saavedra (Vol. 1). Tip. La Mercantil de D. José R. y Rodriguez.

Fauchart, E., & Gruber, M. (2011). Darwinians, communitarians, and missionaries: The role of founder identity in entrepreneurship. *Academy of Management Journal*, *54*(5), 935–957. https://doi.org/10.5465/amj.2009.0211

Freeman, R. E., & Auster, E. R. (2015). *Bridging the Values Gap: How Authentic Organizations Bring Values to Life*. Berrett-Koehler Publishers.

Frida Kahlo and Diego Rivera—Art Gallery NSW. (n.d.). Retrieved December 15, 2023, from https://www.artgallery.nsw.gov.au/artboards/frida-kahlo-diego-rivera/mexicanidad/item/801bdg/

Frida Kahlo: Paintings Analysis, Biography, Quotes, & Art. (n.d.). Retrieved December 15, 2023, from https://www.fridakahlo.org/

Friskics-Warren, B. (2023, September 2). Jimmy Buffett, roguish bard of island escapism, is dead at 76. *The New York Times*. https://www.nytimes.com/2023/09/02/arts/jimmy-buffett-dead.html

Heckler Branding. (n.d.). Retrieved December 15, 2023, from https://www.hecklerbranding.com

Herrera, H. (1983). *Frida: A Biography of Frida Kahlo*. Harper & Row.

Jones, P., Ratten, V., Klapper, R., & Fayolle, A. (2019). Entrepreneurial identity and context: Current trends and an agenda for future research. *The International Journal of Entrepreneurship and Innovation*, *20*(1), 3–7. https://doi.org/10.1177/1465750319825745

Panera. (n.d.). Retrieved May 1, 2010, from www.panera.com

Procter & Gamble. (n.d.). Retrieved December 15, 2023, from https://us.pg.com/

Times of Startups. (2016, May 7). How Sara Blakely lost her way to a billion dollars. https://timesofstartups.com/inspiration/sara-blakely-lost-way-billion-dollars/

Wikipedia. (2023). Jimmy Buffett. https://en.wikipedia.org/w/index.php?title=Jimmy_Buffett&oldid=1190995126

CHAPTER 22

Figure 22.1 This antique printing press is the result of entrepreneurship, has enabled many entrepreneurs, and has trapped others not willing to adapt their approach to a changing world.

Technology

Means, Outcome, or Trap?

In This Chapter

We explore ways of applying effectual logic to various problems and at different points in the venture creation process.

Making technology the goal indicates a causal (predictive) approach to problem-solving—this is the domain of engineers. In contrast, expert entrepreneurs see technology as available means. They work with what they directly control to move forward, hence, do not need to make predictions.

Technology can also be a trap. Making a specific technology the core of a business venture isn't necessarily a problem … until it prevents the venture from adapting to the changing world (particularly customers and competitors) around it.

DOI: 10.4324/9781003364016-27

TECHNOLOGY: MEANS OR OUTCOME?

Technology poses an interesting question to entrepreneurs. Is it a type of available means? Is it an outcome? Can technology be developed effectually? Can a causally developed technology go to market using an effectual approach? The short answer is yes.

The purpose of this chapter is to explore some of the different ways of applying effectuation to different problems, and at different points in the process of creating a new venture.

Although this chapter is designed to help you with technology, we hope it will also encourage you to think about how effectuation applies to other specific kinds of firms. Service firms or capital-intensive businesses, for example, have unique challenges that might benefit from effectual thinking. And while those are only mentioned in this book, we offer them here to provide ideas for areas where you might see if you can apply effectuation on your own.

For now, we focus our attention on two areas where effectuation intersects with technology as summarized in Table 22.1. The first considers the situation where effectuation is applied to commercializing an existing technology. And the second looks at a situation where an effectual approach is used to develop a technology.

TECHNOLOGY AS A MEANS

As much as the common belief is that a patent is a stepping stone to success, the statistics are more sobering.

According to the World Intellectual Property Organization (WIPO), 16.5 million patents were globally active in the year 2021. An estimate by the director of public affairs for the US Patent & Trademark Office deemed only 0.2% of active patents in the USA to be commercially viable, in other words, having a return to at least justify the cost of applying for and maintaining the patent (Klein, 2005). Even a more generous estimate of 10% would indicate that the number of commercially viable active patents is only 1.65 million.

While the pessimist may say that patenting is wildly unsuccessful and the optimist may say that patent lawyers have a great business, the effectuator (someone applying effectuation) looks at these technologies that made it through the long and expensive process of becoming patented and are still available for commercialization and sees a healthy set of possibilities—a rich set of means—the starting points of new possibilities.

Before we continue, we note that the patent authorities are not the only place to find new available means in the form of technology. The corners of corporate R&D labs, university research, and even amateur inventors expand the possibilities of hidden technology means further still.

Research Roots

Lead Users

The notion of lead users became popular in marketing in the 1990s as an antidote to the problem of rapidly changing markets and competition from new products. Despite rationally managed new product development processes and sophisticated market research, marketers knew the failure rate of new products was greater than 90%.

Based on earlier work, however, researchers already knew that in many fields users not only knew much more about their needs than market researchers, but in many instances actually developed most of the innovations in their industry.

Research Roots *(continued)*

For example, 82% of commercialized scientific instruments were developed by users rather than producers. And the origin of many new firms was linked to the commercialization of products users had developed for themselves, often as enthusiasts. For example, mountain bikes and desktop computers were both commercialized in the 1970s by entrepreneurs who started off as mountain bike and computer enthusiasts (Von Hippel, 1986).

While marketers have tried to use lead users as a needs-forecasting laboratory for what users more generally are going to need in the future, entrepreneurs recognize they can't afford the luxury of trying to predict which users provide signals of what the market more generally is going to want.

More recent research draws the connection with effectuation and lead users who are willing to make a commitment (Coviello & Joseph, 2012), updating both the interaction with these users and the product innovation process more generally (Berends et al., 2014).

Research Roots

In Praise of Venturesome Users

Early stakeholders are crucially important in effectual ventures, none more so than lead users. Yet, economic and management thinking largely fails to do justice to the role that lead users play in new ventures. In a wonderful book and series of articles, Amar Bhidé describes the vital role played by the venturesomeness of lead users for the development of new firms.

Bhidé points out that lead users are important partners with entrepreneurs because they often shoulder some risk when they try new products and services. They may not know whether a product is going to work, let alone work well for them.

Users also face uncertainty about the value of a new product, particularly if a critical mass of other users are needed to make the product (and venture) viable. Many new products also require considerable learning before users can get full value out of them, including acquiring a taste for them. And finally, lead users may risk a considerable downside if a venture fails completely, leaving them without any product support in the future.

For all these reasons, lead users are co-developers of new products and services in the true sense of the word: they have "skin in the game." As Amar Bhidé (2009) reminds us, their willingness to be involved, to play a venturesome role in the genesis of new firms, is a vital enabler of the entrepreneurial process.

Research Roots

Effectuation Improves R&D Project Performance

Brettel et al. (2012) transfer the principles of effectuation in corporate research and development management and show, using a survey of 400 research and development projects, that research and development managers tend to use effectuation in more uncertain projects and that using effectuation improves the performance of these projects.

Table 22.1 Technology as Both Means and Outcome

	Entity	Effectual aspect of the process	Outcome
Effectual technology commercialization (technology as means)	CD	Finding stakeholders willing to commit to a use for the invention	Not only the creation of the audio CD, but also its application in computer data storage
	Novozymes	Building a network of partners to turn the invention into a business	Re-organization of an engineering group to include individuals who perform the entrepreneurial role
Effectual technology development (technology as outcome)	GenShock	Using the means of potholes in Boston roads as the basis of a new technology	An innovation that turns bumps in the road into green energy
	Voxiva	Applying means of experience in refugee communications systems to healthcare	An inexpensive, simple, and accessible means of providing certain kinds of healthcare

Practically Speaking

Thank You for the Music

Quick trivia question: what was the first audio title etched with lasers on a compact disc (CD)? Answer: ABBA's *The Visitors* in 1982. Since this historic moment in culture and technology, more than 200 billion compact discs have been sold, and the format has provided a foundational element for the digital music revolution, as well as a friendly way of storing large quantities of data that has greatly enhanced computer functionality. But where did the CD originate, and how can it help us think about innovation?

A Sound Invention

The answer to the first question is more modest than you might expect. James T. Russell, from the state of Washington (USA), is an engineer and an audiophile. As much as he loved music, his technical education reminded him that every time he listened to a vinyl record, the friction from the needle degraded the recording material and over time reduced the quality of the sound.

Practically Speaking *(continued)*

Russell had designed and built the first electron beam welder, so when he joined Battelle Laboratory in 1965, he had already thought of combining his audio problem with his electron solution to create a recording device that would never touch the material and could deliver top-quality music even after thousands of hours of playback.

No Noise in the Market

From a technology perspective, Russell was successful. He patented the first digital-to-optical recording and playback system in 1970. In the process of refining it, Russell earned another 25 patents for himself and Battelle. But, for the next 12 years, the invention went little further than the patent office. Battelle, which had 25 years earlier invented the dry copy process and licensed it to Xerox, was unable to persuade the market to listen to the possibilities offered by its new compact disc.

Invention to Innovation

Eli S. Jacobs, a New York venture capitalist, captivated by Russell's invention, formed a company called Digital Recording Corporation (DRC), which provided funding to Battelle to continue research and development and adapt the technology to store and play video.

But it was not until Philips and Sony got involved that enough pieces came together to turn the CD into an innovation. Philips owned Polygram Records, so it had access to both music content and distribution. Sony added credibility, which established an industry standard around Russell's CD format.

And while Sony and Philips extended their fortunes by weaving CD technology into the computer storage industry, Russell, Battelle, and DRC were not able to profit from the invention until 1988, four years before the patents expired.

Figure 22.2 James T. Russell, inventor of compact disc (CD) technology

Unexpected Entrepreneur

Two useful insights are audible in this story. The first is that even large firms can act entrepreneurially. Philips and Sony were able to do what Russell, Battelle, and DRC could not—create a market. And while scientists or creative people can invent, it is entrepreneurs who innovate by making markets for new ideas.

Practically Speaking *(continued)*

The second insight is a more subtle entrepreneurial activity: the process of transformation. Applying something invented for one thing (CD audio) to something completely different (computer data storage). Like so many things in the world (Edison created the original phonograph using components from the telephone and the telegraph), it turned out that CDs have multiple purposes. Doing something unexpected with technology to create a market is what makes an entrepreneur.

To learn more, visit: https://effectuation.org/EE3/compactdisc or scan Figure 22.4.

Figure 22.4

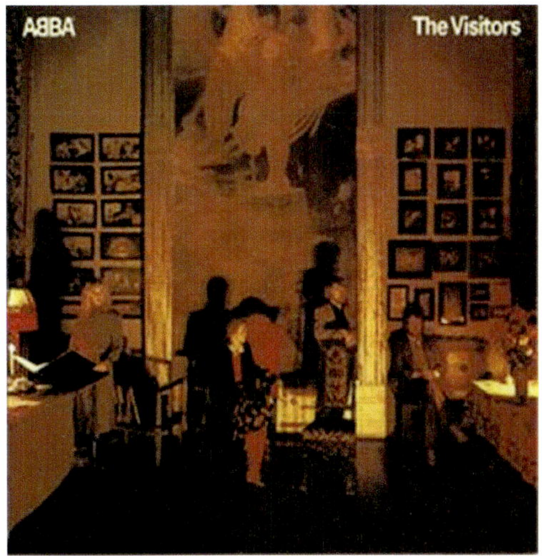

Figure 22.3

THE ENGINEER AND THE ENTREPRENEUR

While we may poke fun at the pessimist and the optimist above, there is a meaningful difference in the way engineers and the way (effectual) entrepreneurs view the same technology (one clear example is presented in the story of the CD, as mentioned in this chapter).

For an engineer, functional technology is a solution to a problem. And the job that needs to be done is the realization of a technology that addresses the problem in a way that is sufficiently better than what is currently available. The rest, as engineering or mathematics faculty may write on the board after starting the solution to a complicated problem, is Q.E.D. (abbreviation for the Latin phrase "quod erat demonstrandum"—"that which was to be proven"). As anyone who has seen those letters written on the board knows, however, the hard work is about to begin.

In contrast, entrepreneurs see the job that needs to be done as that of building a bridge between a technology and its application to something valuable in the world. Indeed, as mentioned, the "entre" part of entrepreneur means "between" in French, so it's actually part of the job description. Technology may offer a foundation for one end of the bridge, but it's unclear as to where the other end of the bridge will ultimately lead.

In some ways, an engineer can be likened to the predictor—the person trying to make a forecast of an uncertain future and then optimizing a single solution for that future. The engineer or/and the predictor may be correct. And when they are, the returns are grand. But statistically speaking, their chances of guessing or predicting correctly in an uncertain environment are perhaps 3,000/1,500,000 or about 0.2% if we take the patent data as representative of this strategy.

For an effectual entrepreneur starting with a technology, the concept of means is more flexible. As we saw in Chapter 10, the means you begin with enable you to start the effectual process. But by the time the process starts generating goals and products and firms and markets, you will use some of your means and not others. You will combine them with the means of others to create novel combinations.

And so, instead of seeing a specific technology as a solution to a single problem, that technology is only a starting point for an effectual entrepreneur, as a vehicle to initiate conversations with prospective stakeholders; something that may or may not be used in the product, firm, or market artifact that results from the process. And something that is available to be deformed, adapted, or exapted during the process (see Chapter 11).

Like effectuation in general, this approach simply increases the odds of finding a viable solution. Not only does it enable more possible solutions, it also engages the stakeholders in the process to bring enhancements or adaptations to the technology that are selected as a function of attention, which may reflect the interest of a broader market.

One of the greatest risks for technologists is falling in love with their technology to such an extent that they fail to even see opportunities for transforming it into actual products and markets. But when technologists genuinely strive to transform themselves into entrepreneurs, amazing new futures become possible for all of us.

Moreover, when the effectual process is done right, new technologies may emerge from existing ones.

> Technology is a word that describes something that doesn't work yet.
> Douglas Adams, author of *The Hitchhiker's Guide to the Galaxy*

Practically Speaking

Fuel Proof

Google offers a tool called "Trends," which shows the number of searches on a keyword over time. According to Google Trends, from 2004 to the end of 2023, internet searches for the term "biofuel" peaked in April 2008, which, coincidentally, was the date an article entitled "Scientists want to stop using food to make biofuel" was in the news. If internet searches are an indication of public sentiment, interest in biofuel has therefore fallen to approximately 25% of the peak level in 2008.

Whatever politics, preferences, or conspiracy theories might be at work here, the fact remains that despite any historical correlation between biofuel production and food prices, first-generation biofuels based on corn, soy, and rapeseed have lost public appeal and will likely not provide a singular solution in our search for sustainable energy sources.

End of the story? Not for Per Falholt, chief scientific officer at Novozymes. Previously, biofuel was only made by physically grinding corn, breaking down the starch into sugar with enzymes, converting the sugar into ethanol with microorganisms, and distilling the ethanol. Per's research team of 150 scientists, in seven different locations around the world, designed the enzymes converting waste corn stalks or wood chips into clean fuel—the second generation of biofuel technology.

Technically, Novozymes is successful. Novozymes is at the center of the process. From their expertise, they know that other vegetation also offers the sugars necessary to make energy, and they created a second generation of enzymes capable of producing "cellulosic" biofuels based on refuse or crops such as switchgrass, grown on marginal land.

Practically Speaking *(continued)*

But there is a cost. Corn, rich in sugar, converts easily into fuel. Corn stalks require more effort and consequently more cost to convert, but the conversion of both corn and stalks was more expensive than fossil-based fuels until recently. Like any alternative product, biofuels need to be competitive for consumers to switch.

Must Per and his team wait patiently until the price of oil makes biofuels competitive to embark on the next chapter of the story? Not necessarily. While scientists invent, entrepreneurs shape, package, and deliver an innovation that is useful and valuable. For Per and his scientific team at Novozymes, this means changing from white lab coat to white dress shirt to transform second-generation biofuel technology into a business. Their new tasks:

Re-Engineer Partnerships

First-generation biofuel production involves a long "value chain" of partners: farmers, grain processors, processing plants, financiers, and oil companies. Second-generation biofuel can start with waste, while the third- (algae-based) and fourth-generation (microorganisms) biofuels are also underway, meaning an evolving list of partners.

That long chain of partners might now include organizations ranging from paper companies and municipalities that would pay to dispose of corn stalks and wood chips, to owners of marginal land where the acreage is not profitably cultivated today. Any of these partners could benefit by working with Novozymes to design new business models around biofuel.

Reconsider the Customer

If you buy corn to make fuel, you build large factories to drive down processing costs with volume production. If you help cities or companies save money disposing of waste, smaller distributed facilities located near that waste might be desirable. And while input is a cost in the first generation, it is maybe free or even a source of income in the second. Partners may also buy the finished product, as activities like paper processing have significant energy demands.

Re-weight Involvement

Today, Novozymes is a technology supplier to only a single step in the process. The firm counts on external entrepreneurs to turn its inventions into innovations. Though this limits risk, it also limits the company's ability to shape the market. In the next biofuel generations, Novozymes needs to go beyond existing partnerships with grain processors and oil companies to build business models for cities or even design processing plants for industry in order to ensure its invention becomes the catalyst of a genuine innovation.

Figure 22.5

Practically Speaking *(continued)*

Biofuel illustrates the power entrepreneurs can have over markets. The fate of next-generation biofuels, certainly part of the answer to the problem of greenhouse gas emissions, lies in the hands of the entrepreneur as much as the technologist. As with everything technical, from internet search engines to hybrid car engines, the real innovation lies in creating the opportunity.

One of the approaches observed in expert entrepreneurs is the ability to invert a problem and imagine how even unpleasant surprises can provide the foundation for new opportunities. Problems ranging from climate change to malnutrition present transformation opportunities to make both impact and money.

To learn more, visit: https://effectuation.org/EE3/biofuel or scan Figure 22.6.

Figure 22.6

Research Roots

Partners Over Patents: Open Innovation

The popular idea of open innovation (Chesbrough, 2003) encourages entrepreneurs to make technologies widely available so customers, partners, and suppliers can co-create with the entrepreneur.

TECHNOLOGY AS AN OUTCOME

Throughout this book, we talk about outcomes of the effectual process in terms of products and firms and markets. And while those terms cover a lot of ground, the chapters in this section of the book more precisely describe the variety we intend.

In the next chapter, for example, the markets that result from effectuation might not be traditional commercial markets you expect from a business school class, but markets in social change and markets in human hope. Here, too, we are careful to include technology as a specific class of outcome that might result from an effectual process. That said, it is a special class of technology that results from an effectual process. It is technology that already has some of the hard work done—the work of engaging the stakeholders who are critical in turning that technology invention into a useful and valuable innovation.

In principle, the transformation of means and partnerships into a new technology happens in the same way effectuation happens generally. An entrepreneur starts with what they have. They interact with others. Stakeholders make commitments according to affordable loss. Contingencies are embraced. And, ultimately, those commitments aggregate to form the pieces necessary to create a valuable outcome.

In practice, some special aspects of creating technology effectually merit further discussion.

The first is specific to means. Technology lends itself to solutions to a wide variety of problems. A visionary technologist might imagine teleportation, clean energy from particle physics, or curing cancer with nanomachines.

The effectual approach to developing a technology starts more modestly. Certainly, an entrepreneur begins with aspirations that might include, for example, a clean energy future. But the difference lies in the doing. Instead of starting with particle physics, the example we highlight in this chapter starts with potholes and the energy lost by a vehicle every time it hits a bump in the road. That insight is local and more amenable to practical "doing."

So, when you read the story of GenShock, consider how the entrepreneur's unique means of being in Boston, being at MIT, realizing the problem in a vehicle, and then working on a solution for a vehicle make the creation of the GenShock technology more manageable, and more feasible with existing or modest resources.

One element of creating technology using effectuation lies in the application of means—the pragmatic approach to starting a project with things that are reasonably readily at hand. The second is working with partners. Though the lone inventor is perhaps as romanced a notion as the mythical entrepreneur (Chapter 1), even Thomas Edison worked extensively with collaborators inside his firm and with industrial partners outside his firm to bring his innovations to light.

Continuing with the GenShock example, one of the problems facing the entrepreneur is where to start. Building a technology that turns potholes into energy is something that could be useful to anyone from automobile manufacturers to public transit operators, to commercial transport companies, or to the government and military.

Letting stakeholders self-select into the technology development process connects development with commercialization. It increases the likelihood that the technology that results from the process will be more than invention—it will be a useful innovation that is designed to be adopted.

One final note on developing technology effectually. It is also possible to take an effectual approach to organizing and leading a technology firm. We cover that topic in our discussions of Guidewire and W. L. Gore (Chapter 20) and refer you to those stories and ideas when you are ready to put all the pieces together.

Practically Speaking

Shocking Venture

Quick math test. If an average passenger car gets 22.5 miles per gallon (or 9.6 kilometers per liter), but only uses about 15% of the energy from fuel to move the vehicle and its passengers and power its accessories, how far could a perfectly efficient passenger car travel on a gallon of fuel? In case you don't happen to have a calculator handy, the answer is an even 150 miles to the gallon (or 63.8 kilometers per liter)—a big improvement. But what happens to the other 85% of the energy? Some is lost to heat. Some is lost to aerodynamic drag. And some forms the basis of entrepreneurial opportunity.

Impactful Idea

As a student at Massachusetts Institute of Technology (MIT) in Cambridge, Massachusetts, Shakeel Avadhany had plenty of opportunity to consider these facts while idling in Boston area traffic. But it was the infamous Boston potholes that launched his venture, ClearMotion (originally named Levant Power). Bouncing down the street, Avadhany realized that these bumps not only cause headaches, but also cost fuel efficiency. The shock absorbers in his car were turning vibration into lost heat. His solution? Capture the energy. Build a shock absorber that generates electricity for the battery or other uses.

Practically Speaking *(continued)*

Harnessing Harvest

If Avadhany can achieve the midrange of the 1% to 6% efficiency he hopes for, his idea could cut fuel use by more than 250,000 barrels in the US alone. Every day. More math says that if every car in the world were equipped with ClearMotion GenShocks, it would save drivers 15 billion US dollars per year at an oil price of 40 US dollars per barrel. (In early 2024 the average oil price is closer to 80 US dollars per barrel.)

Small solutions to big problems can generate enormous opportunities. And though ClearMotion is still relatively small, they are on a positive trajectory. In late 2022, ClearMotion received 39 million US dollars in a third round of capital and, in late 2023, began constructing its first overseas manufacturing facility near Shanghai, China.

Powering Partners

Avadhany cannot drive down this road alone. In addition to building technology, he has also built partnerships with the US Army, testing his technology in military vehicles for performance and durability, and with Battelle National Labs to explore the possibilities of using his technology in capturing ocean energy. Together with resources, both these partners guide him to places where there is a need for his technology—effectively creating demand and product at the same time.

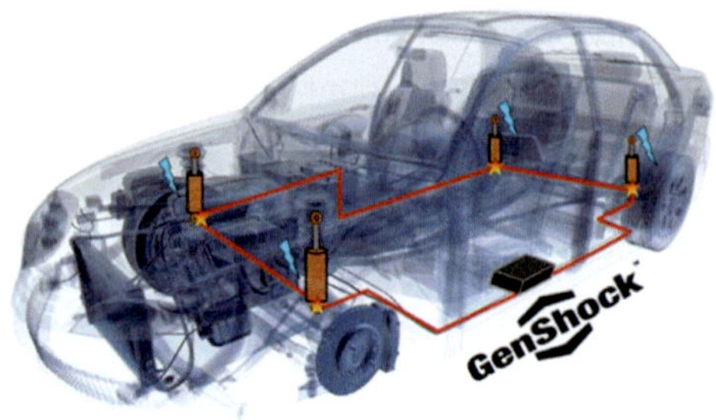

Figure 22.7

Open Road

Should entrepreneurial ideas at the intersection of energy and automobiles intrigue you, it might be interesting to know where the remaining opportunities lie. If universally adopted, Avadhany's GenShock could take at most 6% out of the "rolling resistance" figures. That leaves 94% of the harvest open to other entrepreneurs with clever solutions. Certainly, there will be bumps, but it is the job of the entrepreneur to turn those into opportunity.

To learn more, visit: https://effectuation.org/EE3/shock or scan Figure 22.8.

Figure 22.8

Practically Speaking

Health of Nations

Consider a few of the mega trends in the world today. Healthcare costs are significantly outpacing inflation or economic growth and 25% of the global population has no access to healthcare at all. At the same time, there are more mobile phones in the world than people. It is not hard to fit these facts together and imagine a business that uses technology to deliver better, less expensive, and more widely available healthcare. It is so clear, perhaps, that you may be wondering why you haven't done it yourself.

Entrepreneurial Shape

The answer is that you are not Paul Meyer. In the weeks after the Balkans conflict ended, Meyer founded IPKO, the first and largest internet service provider in Kosovo. It provided critical communications for civilians and aid workers. And a healthy return for Meyer.

Before that, Meyer was in West Africa, setting up computer systems to help reunite refugee children with their families. Deploying connectivity and computers in rugged, developing regions, knowing how information flows in these environments, and understanding the people who need and use the information are assets unique to Meyer.

Vital Action

But it is important to see exactly how this knowledge helps him. Ideas are cheap and plentiful. It is action that creates opportunities. With three co-founders, Meyer formed Voxiva in March 2001. The mission was to create a business that uses technology to deliver better, less expensive, and more widely available healthcare.

And the action—the important part—was to distil simple elements of the healthcare delivery process into text messages. Whether collecting data on the spread of communicable disease or helping pregnant mothers through preparations for childbirth, Voxiva turned a (relatively) cheap mobile phone into a readily available doctor. Anywhere and everywhere, for example:

Peru. The first deployment in 2002, in the sparsely populated Andean foothills, showed that Voxiva could make contagious disease information, previously updated monthly on paper, instantly available, reducing costs by 40%.

Iraq. In 2003, Voxiva won an 815,000 British Pound contract to deliver a system for monitoring the spread of disease across the country as the population recovered from war.

Rwanda. In the spring of 2004, the firm focused its attentions on HIV/AIDS, deploying an information system across the country. The initiative was so successful it led to expansion in South Africa, Nigeria, Madagascar, and Uganda, and garnered support from Columbia University.

India. In February 2004, Voxiva launched an initiative to monitor the spread of Japanese encephalitis in India. The initiative was so compelling that it drew Madhu Krishna from her position directing the Bill and Melinda Gates Children's Vaccine Program in India to join the startup.

Practically Speaking *(continued)*

United States. Emerging and war-torn economies are not the only beneficiaries of better, cheaper, and more available healthcare. Voxiva's Text4baby, the largest mobile health service in the US, provides information to more than 150,000 mothers a week.

Mexico. Care4life is Voxiva's mobile-enabled diabetes education and management service. It was initially developed in partnership with Instituto Carlos Slim de la Salud, and was also launched in the US.

In 2017 Voxiva merged with Sense Health to become WellPass, which was later acquired by Welltok. In 2021, Virgin Pulse, part of Richard Branson's portfolio, acquired Welltok. Paul Meyer has traveled a very long way—and through many technologies—in his mission of communications to extend health coverage.

Entrepreneurial Condition

So, do you have to be Paul Meyer to achieve this kind of impact? The answer is no, but there are at least two things to learn from him. Anyone could have undertaken what Voxiva set out to do in 2001.

And the first takeaway is the importance of action. The second takeaway is less obvious, that is, how dependent action (and outcome) is on the person who takes it. Someone with experience in a big pharmaceutical company might have taken action with corporate partners. Someone more social might have enabled peer-to-peer support instead of information delivery and data capture. What would you have done?

Figure 22.9

Figure 22.10

Figure 22.11

To learn more, visit: https://effectuation.org/EE3/voxiva or scan Figure 22.12.

Figure 22.12

TECHNOLOGY AS A TRAP

As we have already noted, technology can be an excellent solution to problems. But technology can also be a trap. Making a specific technology the core of a business venture isn't necessarily a problem … until it prevents the venture from adapting to the changing world (particularly customers and competitors) around it.

Depending on your age, location, and preferences, it is likely that you have not recently bought a loose bundle of large sheets of paper printed with a wide variety of articles on various topics (in other words, a "newspaper"). But it is likely that you have accessed a wide variety of articles on various topics NOT printed on paper.

According to the Pew Research Center, a social science think tank based in Washington, DC, revenue from advertising and subscriptions for US newspapers reached a high of 60.2 billion US dollars in 2005. This was estimated to have fallen to 21.4 billion US dollars in 2022. In that period, many newspapers went out of business and others suffered, laying off thousands of employees. Very few have thrived.

What does this have to do with technology? If you are running a newspaper and base your entire business model on producing, printing, and delivering sheaves of paper to readers, you are facing increasingly vigorous competition from other sources of news, particularly via the internet.

Some news organizations have not just survived; they even thrived in this same period. They applied the idea of the late Harvard professor Clayton Christensen—that the "job to be done" is to keep their customers informed, regardless of the technology used. So, they use various media and approaches to meet this need, from online articles to podcasts, to videos, even to live in-person events.

Netflix, known today as a global streaming entertainment giant, started out solving a simple problem (late fees!) related to a specific technology (digital video discs, DVDs), but adapted its business model to changing customer needs and technological possibilities. Over the last 20 years, Netflix has demonstrated how it has not been trapped by technology. Will their success continue? One key factor is their ability and willingness to continue adapting and co-creating as the world changes around them.

Practically Speaking

Netflix: Streaming Through Calm and Storm

Netflix, co-founded by Reed Hastings and Marc Randolph in 1997, has demonstrated adaptability and innovation in the rapidly evolving world of entertainment technology and customer preferences. Netflix has not just been successful at delivering entertainment to its customers, it has also evolved into a major producer of content.

In the Mail, Not the Mall

Netflix began as a DVD rental service, offering a novel mail order rental system that solved the inconvenience of late fees and limited selection that plagued traditional video rental stores such as Blockbuster. Hastings famously cited his own experience of being fined 40 US dollars for a late return of a rented movie, which sparked the idea for Netflix.

Practically Speaking *(continued)*

Swapping Streams

Replacing streams of envelopes carrying DVDs, in 2007, Netflix introduced video streaming services, using a subscription-based service. This shift was a response to rapid advancements in internet technology and changing consumer preferences, favoring immediate access to entertainment.

Hastings and Randolph recognized the potential of streaming technology to provide instant access to content on demand. Hastings reported that they didn't name the company "DVDs by Mail" because the founders expected the internet to evolve to handle large bandwidth for video content.

Flywheels: Local and Global

In 2013, Netflix launched its first original series, *House of Cards*, which proved to be a massive hit. The model here went beyond content delivery to a deeper dive into customer preferences through collection and analyses of data that would in turn propel content development. This became the flywheel to expand content globally in multiple languages.

Choppy Waters

As always, life after success can bring its own challenges. While a variety of old and new competitors surge in streaming, licensing and regulatory issues also swell, both in the US and abroad. The task ahead is to continue to innovate fast-moving technologies and environments, while holding steady on the tiller.

So what about those DVDs? Believe it or not, Netflix maintained the physical DVD service until September 2023, having sent out five billion DVDs over the years. But the last batch were one-way deliveries: No need to return it—and there is certainly no late fee!

To learn more, visit: https://effectuation.org/EE3/netflix scan Figure 22.13.

Figure 22.13

Research Roots

Scientific Discovery and Entrepreneurial Innovation

Building on the work of technology historians such as Joel Mokyr and Robert Friedel, a book by Matt Ridley (2015) argues that core scientific research is not strongly connected with commercial innovations or with economic growth.

His book *The Evolution of Everything: How New Ideas Emerge* reviews historical scientific developments (e.g. Prince Henry's fifteenth-century investments in the science of mapmaking, nautical skills, and navigation) and current ones (the identification of the Higgs boson, which is a major advance in quantum physics).

Ridley compares these efforts with "garage-style" innovations from the likes of Thomas Edison. His conclusion is that despite the large investments in scientific research, the economic results of technological innovation result from efforts that are closer to the ground, closer to the customer, and are in essence more entrepreneurial than they are scientific.

TAKEAWAY: EFFECTUATION AS A TECHNOLOGY

As you begin to think about building your own venture to deliver interstellar flight or providing the next huge trend in smart phones, consider this. Throughout this book, we work to make the case that effectuation is a general process: an engine that enables the co-creation of new artifacts in the world. You may choose to apply that engine to a new venture, a new technology, or, as we describe in the next chapter, a technology for addressing social problems in the world.

Think it Through

Technology is only one example of a resource available to new ventures seeking a unique point of differentiation. This chapter opens up questions about any such resource, from a specialized business model to the ownership of a unique piece of land. Are those outcomes or inputs? And depending on how you look at them, how do you manage them?

So What?

Technology can be a valuable element in the effectual process, regardless of whether effectuation is applied to the development of the technology, or to the commercialization of technology that was created using a more causal R&D approach.

What Now?

Consider each of the different paths.

- Look at a series of existing technologies and imagine how you might use each as a "means," a starting point in the effectual process.
- Look at a series of existing problems in the world, problems that have not yet seen a compelling technology solution. Imagine how you would pursue a solution to each—starting with an effectual approach.

REFERENCES

Berends, H., Jelinek, M., Reymen, I., & Stultiëns, R. (2014). Product innovation processes in small firms: Combining entrepreneurial effectuation and managerial causation. *The Journal of Product Innovation Management*, *31*(3), 616–635. https://doi.org/10.1111/jpim.12117

Bhidé, A. (2009). The venturesome economy: How innovation sustains prosperity in a more connected world. *Journal of Applied Corporate Finance*, *21*(1), 8–23. https://doi.org/10.1111/j.1745-6622.2009.00211.x

Brettel, M., Mauer, R., Engelen, A., & Küpper, D. (2012). Corporate effectuation: Entrepreneurial action and its impact on R&D project performance. *Journal of Business Venturing*, *27*(2), 167–184.

Chesbrough, H. W. (2003). *Open Innovation: The New Imperative for Creating and Profiting From Technology*. Harvard Business Press.

Coviello, N. E., & Joseph, R. M. (2012). Creating major innovations with customers: Insights from small and young technology firms. *Journal of Marketing*, *76*(6), 87–104. https://doi.org/10.1509/jm.10.0418

Google Trends. (n.d.). Biofuel. Retrieved December 19, 2023, from https://trends.google.com/trends/explore?date=all&q=biofuel&hl=en

Kang, L. (2023, August 17). Nio Capital-backed ClearMotion begins construction of its 1st plant to produce suspension systems. CnEVPost. https://cnevpost.com/2023/08/17/clearmotion-begins-construction-of-1st-plant-changshu/

Klein, K. E. (2005, November 9). Smart answers: Avoiding the inventor's lament. *Business Week*.

Liao, R. (2022, September 7). ClearMotion to switch on in-car metaverse in China. *TechCrunch*. https://techcrunch.com/2022/09/07/china-nio-capital-chassis-motion-control-company-clearmotion/

MobiHealthNews. (2018, September 12). Welltok acquires Wellpass (formerly Voxiva) to build out Medicaid, government business. https://www.mobihealthnews.com/news/welltok-acquires-wellpass-formerly-voxiva-build-out-medicaid-government-business

Pew Research Center. (n.d.). Newspapers fact sheet. Pew Research Center's Journalism Project. Retrieved December 20, 2023, from https://www.pewresearch.org/journalism/fact-sheet/newspapers/

Ridley, M. (2015). *The Evolution of Everything: How New Ideas Emerge*. HarperCollins.

Science Direct. (n.d.). Fourth generation biofuels. Retrieved December 19, 2023, from https://www.sciencedirect.com/topics/engineering/fourth-generation

Ugwu, R. (2023, August 24). Netflix says you can keep their DVDs (and request more, too). *The New York Times*. https://www.nytimes.com/2023/08/24/arts/netflix-dvds.html

US Department of Energy. (n.d.). Alternative Fuels Data Center: Fuel prices. (n.d.). Retrieved December 19, 2023, from https://afdc.energy.gov/fuels/prices.html

Von Hippel, E. (1986). Lead users: A source of novel product concepts. *Management Science*, *32*(7), 791–805. https://doi.org/10.1287/mnsc.32.7.791

World Intellectual Property Organization. (2022). WIPO IP facts and figures 2022. https://www.wipo.int/publications/en/series/index.jsp?id=36

CHAPTER 23

Figure 23.1 Entrepreneurship can be a tool for sustainable growth and social change. Working in harmony with natural rhythms and available means can produce bountiful results.

Social Change and Markets in Human Hope

In This Chapter

We put forth the idea that equity markets can and should be open to all ventures (for providers and recipients of capital), regardless of their profit orientation. In fact, we raise the provocative possibility that the profit/non-profit categorization is an unnecessary and unhelpful distinction. We also look at the incremental nature of change and how small changes can sometimes make a big difference.

DOI: 10.4324/9781003364016-28

WHY NOT MARKETS FOR HUMAN CAPITAL?

Throughout this book we have addressed many aspects of the entrepreneurial process and demonstrated the power and value of market mechanisms to channel value creation. When it comes to non-profit organizations, the prevailing sense is to not want to apply the same market forces to solve problems such as poverty and inequality.

Yet, all markets rely on human capital, the capacity in human beings to build, exchange, and grow value. That capacity in turn depends on removing barriers to hope and access to social and institutional mechanisms which allow that hope to be transformed into new purposes worth achieving.

In this chapter we examine how and why the effectual process can build market mechanisms within the non-profit and public sectors. We further explore the idea that equity markets can and should be open to all ventures and for providers and recipients of capital to those ventures, regardless of their profit orientation. In fact, we raise the provocative possibility that the for-profit/non-profit categorization is an unnecessary and unhelpful distinction.

Furthermore, we contend that equity markets are particularly useful for investors in human capital, the core of all value creation.

SCIENCE ENABLES, ENTREPRENEURS MAKE PURPOSE

The practice of entrepreneurship has developed greatly, aided by the introduction of formal entrepreneurship education programs. It is now commonplace to learn about and use the approaches borrowed from the scientific method, in particular hypothesis testing and experimentation in venture creation.

While the scientific approach built to deliver testable predictions is an important and useful tool in tackling big problems in the world, it is not the only logic available to us. As expert entrepreneurs learn through years of experience, we can approach big problems from the opposite direction—namely, working with things within our control to co-create rather than predict. Whereas the scientific method emphasizes the objective, the entrepreneurial method leverages the intersubjective. Entrepreneurs actively engage with the world and with others who want to work with them for disparate reasons and objectives of their own.

It is also important to recognize that despite the application of scientific tools such as hypothesis testing and experimentation, the scientific approach cannot determine the purpose of the venture. Combined with the individual purposes of founder(s), purposes get shaped and co-created through intersubjective interactions with committed stakeholders who come with their own varying objectives. The effectual process, therefore, becomes a powerful tool for shaping new purposes, not merely to come up with new ways to achieve pre-existing purposes.

The chain of logic described above is from the second edition of the seminal work *Effectuation: Elements of Entrepreneurial Expertise*, which is also the source of the following summarizing statements (Sarasvathy, 2022, p. 245):

> **That is why it is important to distinguish experimentation from effectuation, finding from making, exogenous goals from endogenous ones.**
>
> **The scientific method enables us to put the universe to work to achieve our purposes. But the entrepreneurial method helps us co-create purposes worth pursuing.**

As noted, the purpose of an entrepreneurial venture is both highly individual and intertwined with the founders' circumstances. While the term social entrepreneurship has become more widely used in recent times, the fact is that all entrepreneurial ventures compel founders to learn the importance of being enmeshed in the real world and in continual committed interactions with others.

BLURRING THE LINES BETWEEN CHARITY AND BUSINESS

Mercy Corps is an organization devoted to helping people in crisis—a worthy, though not unusual sounding, non-government organization (NGO), until you take a closer look. Mercy describes its mission as "helping turn crisis into opportunity for millions around the world." And when you notice that the staff is made up of engineers, financial analysts, project managers, public health experts, and logisticians, the news that the organization acquired a commercial bank (Mercy Corps acquired Andara Bank in Indonesia in 2008) starts to make sense.

By blurring the lines that distinguish a charity from a business, Mercy Corps offers us one introduction to the idea of the social entrepreneur. Improving access to microfinance in Indonesia supports the organization's mission. Making money in the process does not detract from it. When we consider this in some depth, we realize that creating revenue-generating products and services can free social entrepreneurs from the need to pursue donors and instead fully focus on actually solving the problems they set out to solve in the first place.

Mercy Corps is just one example of an organization that challenges the artificial and unhelpful distinction between a for-profit venture and a charity. And when you look around, revolutionaries can be found everywhere in the financial services industry, from Muhammed Yunus, creator of Grameen Bank, to the team behind Kiva, a person-to-person micro-loan website.

To gain insight into whether the separation thesis that entrepreneurs must choose between doing well and doing good is valid, we go back more than 200 years to the story of Josiah Wedgwood. As founder of the famed Wedgwood pottery works, he is associated with the accumulation of great wealth, but is also an entrepreneur, who clearly saw his purpose to be much more than wealth generation through the production of fine porcelain. His active engagements with propelling social mobility and slave emancipation are just a few instances.

Practically Speaking

Josiah Wedgwood: Social and Financial Strength in Porcelain

Josiah Wedgwood, an eminent eighteenth-century potter, exemplifies a socially minded entrepreneur whose business practices were deeply intertwined with social investment and reform. As the founder of the Wedgwood pottery company, he not only revolutionized the pottery industry but also used his business as a platform for social change, illustrating that for socially minded entrepreneurs, the boundary between for-profit ventures and social ventures is virtually non-existent.

Wedgwood's entrepreneurship journey was marked by innovative practices in both product and social domains. He pioneered new pottery techniques, such as the famous Jasperware, and implemented high standards of quality and design.

Practically Speaking *(continued)*

Smart Investment in People and Pathways

Wedgwood built a village, Etruria, for his workers, providing them with comfortable housing and a healthier environment. Furthermore, Wedgwood created a school to teach unskilled laborers the craft of fine porcelain painting.

His motives were not solely altruistic; they were strategic. There were not enough skilled artisans to meet the demand for Wedgwood pottery. His investment in the workforce ensured their well-being and, consequently, their efficiency and loyalty.

Wedgwood undertook several major public works projects, digging the canals that connected the River Trent with the River Mersey. Again, a strategic measure to safely transport finished delicate porcelain since the bumpy roads of Stoke-on-Trent were simply too risky.

Pottery as a Message

His business acumen was matched by a profound sense of social responsibility. Wedgwood was an ardent abolitionist, and he used his pottery as a medium for social commentary. One of his most famous pieces was the "Am I Not a Man and a Brother?" medallion, created for the Society for Effecting the Abolition of the Slave Trade.

This medallion, bearing an image of a chained slave, became a powerful symbol in the abolitionist movement and, through Benjamin Franklin, was distributed in the United States of America. Wedgwood demonstrates his conviction in a letter he wrote Franklin in February 1788: "It gives me great pleasure to be embarked on this occasion in the same great and good cause with you, Sir, and I ardently hope for the final completion of our wishes" (Wedgwood, 1788).

Figure 23.2 An imagined scene depicting a barge filled with Wedgwood porcelain traveling down a canal on its way to market.

Even a Stake in Scientific Impact

It is interesting to note that the Wedgwood fortune also funded Wedgwood's grandson, Charles Darwin, as he made a voyage that would generate what scientists claim to be the most significant advancement in scientific thinking of the millennium.

Wedgwood's approach to stakeholder investment highlights that the essence of doing business successfully, whether for-profit or not-for-profit, lies in a unified strategy that values social impact alongside financial success. And perhaps more important, what we find is that the same underlying entrepreneurial method is at work in both cases.

To learn more, visit: https://effectuation.org/EE3/wedgwood or scan Figure 23.3.

Figure 23.3

Comparison of Three Approaches to Investment—For Profit, for Charity and for Impact

People creating social change do the same things we associate with "for-profit" entrepreneurs. So, everything thus far in the book is relevant to entrepreneurs regardless of whether the legal form of the venture is for-profit or not.

With the purpose of helping people improve their situation, the approach taken varies. The traditional charity approach speaks to the redistribution of wealth to address human and environmental needs, as is described in the stories of Jane Addams and Neiva Guedes.

In contrast, Mohammed Yunus built Grameen Bank as a market to invest in human potential while also providing a return on investment, thereby making it sustainable. The success of Grameen propelled a growing revolution in microfinance and impact investment. Related to that are notions such as social business and social entrepreneurship. Another profit-driven, yet stakeholder-focused, example is Raiffeisen Bank, which seeks to provide financial services that benefit its members while also serving the wider community.

Our short tour of examples in this section ends with Sunlabob, focused on bringing electricity to remote communities. The venture has been profit-driven from the outset, which enabled it to raise capital to expand its socially minded reach.

We are not seeking to judge the various approaches, but rather acknowledge that there are many ways to reach similar goals, and that all can be considered examples of social entrepreneurship.

Practically Speaking

Jane Addams: Social Entrepreneur Pursuing Peace

Jane Addams (1860–1935), a prominent figure in the history of social work and women's suffrage in the United States, embarked early on a pathway focused of social activism, entrepreneurship, and the promotion of peace.

Addams' sense of purpose was deeply rooted in her belief in democracy and social equality, envisioning a society where every individual had the opportunity to develop their potential. She was committed to social reform, emphasizing the interconnectedness of individual and communal well-being. Addams' purpose was not just to aid the poor, but to create a society where every person could thrive.

Hull House: Hub of Social Reform

Inspired by her visit in 1887 to Toynbee Hall in London, a settlement house, Addams and her friend, Ellen Starr, founded Hull House in Chicago in 1889. It was more than just a shelter; it aimed to bridge the gap between the privileged and the underprivileged, providing a hub for social reform and community support. Hull House offered various services, including educational courses, arts programs, and legal aid, fundamentally altering the approach to social welfare in the United States of America.

Practically Speaking *(continued)*

Social Innovation for the Community

Addams' work at Hull House was pioneering in several ways. She introduced the concept of community-based social work, focusing on the empowerment of the local community. Hull House became a center for research, public health initiatives, and labor union support, as well as offering an extensive array of services, including the first public playground in Chicago, an art gallery, a public kitchen, and a bathhouse.

Challenges in Sustainability

Despite its achievements, Hull House faced significant challenges in sustainability. Relying heavily on donations and the goodwill of benefactors, it was vulnerable to economic downturns and shifting philanthropic interests. The challenge of ensuring consistent funding highlighted a key vulnerability of social entrepreneurship reliant on external funding. Addams herself grappled with these challenges, once stating, "Private beneficence is totally inadequate to deal with the vast numbers of the city's disinherited" (Addams, 1910, p. 310).

Making Even Bigger Waves

It could be that the dependency of Hull House funding on outside sources moved Addams (applying effectual logic) to move her attention to matters within her control. Being a staunch advocate for women's rights, Addams' activism extended beyond voting rights to include women's education and their role in peace movements, which naturally extended to her vocal opposition to World War I and leading her to co-found the Women's Peace Party in 1915.

Figure 23.4 What Hull House in the 1890s with its two founders at the entrance might have looked like.

Nobel Peace Prize and Lasting Legacy

In recognition of her relentless efforts in promoting peace and social justice, Jane Addams (together with Nicholas Murray Butler) was awarded the Nobel Peace Prize in 1931 "for their assiduous effort to revive the ideal of peace and to rekindle the spirit of peace in their own nation and in the whole of mankind" (The Nobel Peace Prize, 1931, n.d.).

Although the entity she founded, Hull House, faced challenges in sustainability, Jane Addams' legacy in community-based social reform is undeniably profound, particularly in the face of economic and societal challenges.

To learn more, visit: https://effectuation.org/EE3/addams or scan Figure 23.5.

Figure 23.5

Practically Speaking

Taking Flight: Hyacinth Macaw Institute

Co-Creator: Rose Mary Lopes

Most likely you have encountered a problem and thought to yourself, "someone should fix that!" Entrepreneurs decide to be that "someone" and take action. When Neiva Guedes first discovered that the bird species Hyacinth Macaw was on the brink of extinction due to illegal trafficking, habitat destruction, and lack of knowledge about the species, she decided she would take action.

Birthing Macaws and a Career

Instead of seeing obstacles, she saw an opportunity to make a purposeful change, one which would become her career. Little was known about the reproduction of the Hyacinth Macaw at the time, so Guedes started on a journey of scientific discovery in trips to the nesting sites on the Miranda River of Pantanal, Brazil, which is a gateway to the surrounding glades rich in wildlife such as jaguars, macaws, giant otters, pantanal caimans and jabirus, the symbol of wetlands.

To study the reproductive behavior of the Hyacinth Macaws, Guedes sought support from local farmers, rural communities, conservationists, and international researchers. Her work focused on investigating the nests, marking, registering, and monitoring movements of the birds. Over time, her efforts evolved into a study project for her Master of Science in Biology degree at the University of São Paulo.

Building the Nest

Guedes' efforts were formalized in the founding of the Hyacinth Macaw Institute (HMI), located in Campo Grande, Brazil, which is dedicated to preserving and studying the Hyacinth Macaw and other endangered birds.

HMI manages the bird's environment, produces artificial nests, looks after abandoned eggs and chicks, and, above all, publicizes the importance of keeping the Hyacinth Macaws free and flying in the wild. Through its research, education, and advocacy, HMI has succeeded in transforming the narrative around the Hyacinth Macaw, whose vulnerable population has reportedly doubled in the time of the project (Schlossman, n.d.).

Not Just Vulnerable Birds …

Despite the significance of the project and its success, the Hyacinth Macaw Institute itself is vulnerable, relying on the unstable funding of grants and donations to support a significant part of its operations.

How is this story different from any other entrepreneurial venture? To recap: a woman with a purpose uses science and an entrepreneurial approach to solve a man-made problem.

Practically Speaking *(continued)*

Figure 23.6 Hyacinth Macaws in the wild in Pantanal, Brazil

In the profit-making world, the first investors provide the initial capital to solve a problem, which is then sold to customers, which generates profits, which are returned to the investors—a sustainable loop.

But what about in social or non-profit ventures? Usually, they depend on the goodwill of others to fund their initial and ongoing work.

So, considering the situation of Neiva Guedes and the Hyacinth Macaw Institute, what could they do to continue their environmental sustainability mission while also being financially sustainable? Or, in other words, how could Neiva Guedes turn HMI into a profitable venture without compromising its essence?

To learn more, visit: https://effectuation.org/EE3/macaw or scan Figure 23.7.

Figure 23.7

Practically Speaking

Grameen: Birth of Microbanking

Founded in Bangladesh by Muhammad Yunus, a professor of economics, Grameen Bank has revolutionized the concept of banking for the poor, transforming it into a vehicle for societal upliftment.

A Small Loan Becomes a Business

Yunus's journey to establishing Grameen Bank began during a famine in Bangladesh in 1974. Struck by the stark contrast between the classroom theories of economics and the grim realities of poverty, Yunus lent a small amount of money to a group of impoverished artisans. This act laid the groundwork for what would later become Grameen Bank.

Grameen Bank's business model proves that a bank can make profits while building communities. Unlike traditional banks that rely on collateral for loans, Grameen extends credit based on trust and future cash flows. This revolutionary approach is grounded in the belief that even the poorest of the poor can be bankable if given the opportunity.

Practically Speaking *(continued)*

The Money Comes Back

While supporting the general idea of charities in the community, it has disadvantages, according to Yunus: "Charity money goes out, does that wonderful thing, but the money doesn't come back. It is only a one time use of your money" (Hoover, 2016). Grameen Bank is not a charity; it is what Yunus describes as a "social business," a bank from which "the money goes out, does the work, and it comes back" (Hoover, 2016).

The bank's lending strategy is unique. Loans are small, often less than 200 US dollars, and are geared toward entrepreneurs who are too poor to qualify for traditional bank loans. These micro-loans have empowered millions, especially women, to start or expand small businesses, leading to income generation and improved living standards.

In results published in 2013 by Alam and Islam, a survey of 85 women entrepreneurs receiving loans from Grameen Bank clearly substantiated the tangible and intangible benefits—from family financial survival to increased influence in family financial decision-making to increased savings.

Small Loan, Big Impact

The impact of these small loans is magnified when viewed through the lens of community development. As individuals grow their businesses, they employ others, increase local spending, and contribute to the community's overall economic health. This model has demonstrated that financial sustainability and community development are not mutually exclusive objectives. In fact, Grameen Bank's repayment rates are exceptionally high at 99% (Grameen Australia, n.d.), a testament to the effectiveness of lending based on future cash flows and social accountability.

Moreover, Grameen's approach fosters a sense of collective responsibility. Borrowers form groups, and loan repayment depends on each member's success, creating a system of mutual support and accountability. This structure not only ensures financial sustainability but also strengthens community bonds.

Grameen Bank's pioneering model of microbanking, conceptualized from Yunus's visionary approach to addressing poverty, demonstrates that financial services, when designed with a social purpose, can be both profitable and transformative for communities.

To learn more, visit: https://effectuation.org/EE3/grameen or scan Figure 23.8.

Figure 23.8

Practically Speaking

Swiss Precision: Making Cooperatives Work in Banking

Raiffeisen Bank, the third-largest player in the Swiss banking market, serves as an example of balancing the interests of its members and community while maintaining financial sustainability in a cooperative bank model. The bank's structure involves its cooperative members actively in decision-making, ensuring an exceptional proximity to clients and a strong emphasis on local/regional markets.

Fine-Tuned Machine

In terms of financial performance and market reach, Raiffeisen is significant. It serves more than 42% of the Swiss population, with one in every five mortgages in Switzerland originating from Raiffeisen. This extensive reach is supported by the densest branch network in the country, demonstrating its commitment to accessibility and local presence while offering a complete suite of digital banking services.

Raiffeisen has shown a commitment to sustainability, expanding its range of pension and investment products to include more sustainable options. This includes the launch of the "Futura Impact" asset management mandate, which aims for a positive environmental and social impact, demonstrating a balance between financial goals and broader societal contributions.

Representing All Stakeholders Can Be Challenging

The bank has faced challenges as well, such as the legal proceedings against its former chairman, which highlighted governance issues. These incidents underline the importance of strong governance and ethical leadership in maintaining the trust and credibility essential to a cooperative bank's success.

Despite these challenges, Raiffeisen's financial performance remains strong. For instance, the cooperative bank reported double-digit profit growth in the first half of 2023, demonstrating its ability to be financially robust while adhering to its cooperative principles. This profitability, coupled with its commitment to the community and sustainable banking practices, suggests that Raiffeisen is able to balance profitability with social responsibility effectively.

To learn more, visit: https://effectuation.org/EE3/raiffeisen or scan Figure 23.9.

Figure 23.9

Practically Speaking

The Bright Entrepreneur: Sunlabob

As an expatriate working in Laos for a German development organization during the late 1990s, Andy Schroeter observed that nearly half the population was off the electricity grid and that the cost for the kerosene needed to run lamps was one of the highest expenditures for a household. He realized that an answer could be the basis of a bright opportunity with the potential to make both money and social progress.

Building Change

Schroeter did not have funding from a venture capitalist, nor did he have a novel technology solution. Laos was recovering from 20 years of war, and the government wasn't exactly set up to foster entrepreneurship. But instead of seeking charitable contributions or support from a large non-governmental organization, Schroeter formed Sunlabob in 2000 with his own means. The mission of the firm was to operate as a profitable, full-service energy provider selling hardware and providing energy services for remote areas where the public electricity grid does not yet reach.

Simple Trade

At this point, you might be expecting a dramatic story of innovation—how Schroeter invented a robust and inexpensive fuel cell, wireless energy transmission, or perhaps cold fusion for the villagers of Laos. The reality is somewhat less glamorous but a lot more practical. Schroeter takes the most suitable alternative energy products available in the global marketplace and adapts and installs them in Laos. He is a reseller, an integrator, and a (very) local distributor. These are business ideas as common as the sunlight that powers most of what he delivers.

Entrepreneurial Energy

While it is easy to equate the power of the entrepreneur with the creation of a radical new product or technology, people like Schroeter show us the real job of a founder of a new venture—crafting a market opportunity by hand.

Someone has to get up in the morning and find solar panels, thermosiphon heaters, or wind turbines that will perform well in the rugged environment of Laos. Someone has to build an economic model so that customers in a country where annual per capita income is 986 US dollars can realistically afford these products.

Someone has to hire the people who can install and maintain the systems. And someone has to organize the company vacation to Vietnam for those same employees. Schroeter shows us that there is no magical invisible hand of the market that does this: it is the visible hand of the entrepreneur that made Sunlabob happen.

Practically Speaking *(continued)*

Powering Growth

As Sunlabob moves ahead, the hand of the entrepreneur continues to be visible. The venture is commercially successful—having installed thousands of systems throughout Laos—and it has been recognized for its social impact, winning a series of awards, including the prestigious Schwab Foundation Asian Entrepreneur of the Year award at the 2010 World Economic Forum.

Real Impact. Real Business. Real Simple.

In addition to serving the entire country of Laos, with venture capital funds, Sunlabob expanded services using the franchising model into Uganda, Cambodia, and Tanzania and will soon be operating in Afghanistan. It also established a subsidiary in Singapore to serve the markets in Southeast Asia.

Entrepreneurs adapt to changing circumstances, and in 2019 Sunlabob moved its headquarters to the United Kingdom and now offers:

> a full range of renewable energy services from consultancy to hardware supply and turnkey solutions. Today, we're proud to serve governments, development agencies, NGOs and the private sector, helping to deliver sustainable renewable energy projects from Africa and Asia to the South Pacific.
>
> (*Sunlabob*, n.d.)

Figure 23.10

Sunlabob has remained true to its mission: operate as a profitable, full-service energy-provider selling hardware and providing energy services for remote areas where the public electricity grid does not yet reach. The sustainable approach of Andy Schroeter and his team has clearly allowed Sunlabob to power on over time and space.

To learn more, visit: https://effectuation.org/EE3/sunlabob or scan Figure 23.11.

Figure 23.11

ADVANTAGES (FOR INVESTORS) OF EQUITY MARKETS

Every system has weaknesses and unscrupulous players exploit these and cause misery. In spite of this, on the whole, open markets have been strong enablers of value creation.

Therefore, in assessing their efficacy, we need to dive a bit deeper. From an investor's perspective, the specific aspects that can be particularly useful for the creation of markets for human hope consist in the following, as Sarasvathy (2022, pp. 226–227) argues:

Competing Models

Public equity markets allow me to systematically explore, analyze, and evaluate a variety of competing models in particular industries or technologies. Similarly, I would like to be able to choose between competing

models for eradicating poverty, illiteracy, and other human ills. Even within a single model, different entrepreneurs may execute differently or come up with entirely different innovations. Hayek (1984) argued that competition fosters innovation and increases the dimensionality of the commodity space. Publicly traded equity in human hope will similarly foster quick imitation and diffusion of valuable innovations as well as induce the creation of new models to solve social problems.

Monitoring

Public equity markets also help me monitor my investments. Through quarterly reports using standardized formats and metrics, I am able to keep track of my investments in terms of management changes, new strategic initiatives, financial performance, and so on. I would like to be able to do that with my investments in Afghan women or inner city education, but for now I have to rely on the occasional newsletter or solicitation for more donations. Furthermore, it is virtually impossible to compare how my money is performing in the various initiatives to which I have made contributions. I would also like to be able to turn on CNBC to hear about the latest techniques in dealing with human misery and listen to entrepreneurs make their pitches as to why their models are better, faster, or cheaper in solving these problems.

Liquidity

Once I have given money to a particular charity, it simply vanishes. Stock market bubbles notwithstanding, I enjoy the ability to liquidate my investments when I need the cash and invest again when I have some idle funds in the bank. I understand and am delighted by the fact that Mohammed Yunus did not want my money. But I would like to fund another Yunus in another venture, maybe on another continent or in another domain of human hope—someone who has the drive and energy and mother wit to put my money to work in the world. And by having his stock publicly traded, I need not depend on him to return my money when I do need to use it. I can merely sell my equity to another investor like me.

Upside Potential

Of course, it is possible that non-loss ventures will fail just as for-profit ventures do. That is already true of non-profit and social ventures today. Again, stock market bubbles notwithstanding, a case could be made that it is harder to lose money in the stock market than in philanthropic investments. Yet, billions of dollars are given every year to social causes without expectation of financial return. An upside potential, therefore, need not be a necessary condition for investments in non-loss ventures. But that does not mean an upside potential is *unlikely*. In fact, how can it possibly be profitable to invest in new technologies if it is not profitable to invest in human beings? It is clear that some ventures have potential while others do not. That is true in every technology, industry, and human activity. But what is the reason for classifying some types of human hope as marketable and others not?

Figure 23.12 Dome of the Bolsa de Comercio (stock exchange) in Santiago, Chile.

The next three Practically Speaking organizations take a closer look at how entrepreneurs can build their ventures within existing market structures while fulfilling their socially driven mission. First up is Mohammed Yunus sharing the learning he and his team at Grameen Bank acquired as they incrementally built the venture. This is followed by a connection between disaster-struck Kashmir and a French bank, followed by the efforts of the OneWorld Health team to improve the lives of underserved populations.

Practically Speaking

Grameen Bank—Part 2—Principles and Practices

In a presentation at Darden School of Business at the University of Virgina in 2004, Mohammed Yunus outlined the following principles and practices of Grameen Bank (GB), which were developed while building the bank.

Looking back, he noted that almost all are the inverse of standard banking practices. Considering that traditional banks are ultimately built to serve shareholders, it is logical that Grameen Bank, built to serve those considered "unbankable," would take a very different approach, as summarized by Sarasvathy (2022, pp. 223–225):

Principles and Practices Embedded in the GB Experience:

Start with a problem and not with a solution. Yunus explained that with the founding of GB, he had given up the bird's eye view of academics and had instead adopted the worm's eye view: "I may not see the larger context and all the theoretical issues any more. But I see the little problems; and I see them clearly and in great detail." As a result, his solutions are precise and uniquely adapted to each situation. GB's website insists that "a credit system must be based on a survey of the social background rather than on a pre-established banking technique." The solutions are *designed,* leveraging locality and contingency to the fullest.

Lend to the poorest of the poor. Conventional banks do not lend to the poor; the poor are GB's primary stakeholder-customers. And it is not merely the high-potential poor who constitute GB's market. GB welcomes and works with any and all, including the poorest of the poor. Consider, for example, GB's recently instituted "beggar program." Yunus pointed out that they began with generational beggars – those whose families had been beggars for three or more generations. These beggars would go door to door and ask for small quantities of rice. GB found that they make good salespeople, so GB gave them the option of trading goods in return for the rice. One case was particularly telling—the case of beggars without legs. But, as Yunus pointed out, these beggars already had "strategic locations"—or else they could not have survived on begging. It turned out that they had good sales potential too. Both beggar programs have achieved considerable success as investments.

Lend without collateral. The bulk of GB's investments are made on the basis of affordable loss. GB's loan amounts are often so miniscule that it is not cost effective to write and enforce contracts. This is one of the main reasons conventional banks consider poor borrowers "unbankable." Yet, as other microfinance operations have also shown, the world's poorest are often the most credit-worthy: repayment rates for GB are close to 100 percent. On its website, GB announces another reversal of conventional banking theory—namely, the transformation of "the vicious circle of 'low income, low saving and low investment' into a virtuous circle of 'low income, injection of credit, investment, more income, more savings, more investment, more income'."

Practically Speaking *(continued)*

The bank comes to the customer; customers do not go to the bank. Since GB lends primarily to women (also a reversal of banking practices, which tend to be biased against women), it has had to deal with what are normally seen as insurmountable cultural problems. In Bangladesh, as in other cultures, women not only earned no income—many had literally never touched money. Turning them into active participants in new markets in credit and empowering them to seek economic self-sufficiency involves going door to door—listening, understanding, learning, and building trust by walking in their shoes and even living in their shadows. Yunus described how this has been accomplished—not by the wholesale rejection of their cultural values (for example, through lectures on the rights of women) but through little practices that require them to take small steps (such as requesting the husband's permission for the wife to handle small amounts of currency). Each particular step involves minimal investments (monetary and otherwise) that individuals can decide whether they can "afford to lose," as it were. And so, to use James's words, by piling "grain on grain of willful choice like a very miser," new habits were formed, leading eventually to new "fields of action."

GB *invests* in people without whom neither the venture nor the economy can fly. It takes its stakeholders' problems and needs as design constraints, and not as obstacles in the development of markets and economies. Yunus mentioned illiteracy as a case in point. He said that when designing computers and other appliances, modern engineers do not give up on blind customers; instead, they develop Braille keyboards or voice-activated mechanisms. Similarly, he suggested using technology and other means to design *around* illiteracy. "Just because she is illiterate does not mean she is not intelligent" he repeated. He mentioned several instances of how the world had underestimated the potential of these "Bonsai" women to create value and wealth, "It is so easy to throw away human potential, unvalued and unused!"—a lament that Julian Simon would have heartily endorsed.

Think in terms of non-loss ventures, not non-profit ventures. This principle represents the ultimate reversal apparent in GB's principles. Toward the end of the speech, Yunus called for two things: capital markets for social causes (to be examined a little later in this chapter) and non-loss ventures as opposed to non-profit ventures. Non-loss ventures will not have profit maximization as their objective function; instead, they will have *not making a loss* as a constraint on their (social) objective function.

Here a shortened, more pointedly effectual-logic version of the previous Grameen Bank principles:

Adapted Effectual-Logic-Driven Principles and Practices of Grameen Bank

Start with a problem and not with a solution.

Listen closely to your customers' problems and incrementally develop tailored solutions using your available means and within your affordable loss.

Lend to the poorest of the poor.

Work with anyone, identifying and working with their available means to move forward.

Practically Speaking *(continued)*

Lend without collateral.

Invest resources in your customers based on your affordable loss.

The bank comes to the customer; customers do not go to the bank.

Meet your customers (and other stakeholders) where they are, communicating to find a shared and committed path forward.

Think in terms of non-loss ventures, not non-profit ventures.

Ensure growth (or at a minimum, sustainability) of your venture by not making a loss.

To learn more, visit: https://effectuation.org/EE3/gbprinciples or scan Figure 23.13.

Figure 23.13

Practically Speaking

Kashmir Relief Note: Example of Market in Human Hope

In 2005, a massive earthquake struck the Kashmir region in the mountains of India and Pakistan. Eighty-seven thousand individuals perished in the quake and three million survivors needed to rebuild their lives. The international aid organizations rushed in with supplies and food. And were joined by entrepreneurs.

Notes Instrumental for Relief

Marc Freudweiler is the founder of a Swiss derivatives trading firm named Derilab. Freudweiler saw both the humanitarian need to rebuild the Kashmir region and the economic benefit that would result. Kashmir had been a productive area before the quake. Repairing the infrastructure would enable the businesses destroyed by the quake to resume the creation of value. Freudweiler talked with people at the United Nations High Commission on Refugees (UNHCR), and the Kashmir Relief Note was born.

The Note represented a completely novel idea—that the public might invest in humanitarian relief and receive a return on its money. The specific outcome was a financial instrument that directs part of the investment into refugee relief and part of the investment into businesses that are likely to increase in value as the region rebuilds. Investors could direct funds to the crisis and could generate a return. Doing what we ought does not have to conflict with doing what we can.

A recent review of Freudweiler's social media (Freudweiler, n.d.) provided the following update on the project:

Practically Speaking *(continued)*

The financial instrument was issued in May 2006 and matured in May 2011, generating a 18.72% performance for the investor. The beneficiary UNHCR received a coupon of 2% at inception to support the relief effort. The issuer was Société Générale.

To learn more, visit: https://effectuation.org/EE3/kashmir or scan Figure 23.14.

Figure 23.14

Figure 23.15 A photo of the devastation caused to houses of Bakalot in Kashmir Pakistan by a powerful earthquake in October 2005. While some houses appear to be still standing, many are flattened completely.

Practically Speaking

On the Pharma: Victoria Hale and OneWorld Health

The next time you pick up a prescription, take a look at the price of the product—not the portion you pay after reimbursements, but the actual price. Pharmaceuticals are expensive. And that translates into good business: the pharmaceutical industry had significantly higher profit margins than other industries in the period from 2000 to 2018 (Ledley et al., 2020). And with the aging population driving demand, global pharma sales reached 1.48 trillion US dollars in 2022 (Mikulic, 2024).

Counter Intuition

An opportunity of that scale attracts entrepreneurs by the score, but none quite like Victoria Hale. She chose to make pharmaceuticals that don't make money. Yes, you read that correctly. Her firm, Institute for OneWorld Health, described itself as a non-profit pharmaceutical company. OneWorld is her solution to the problem facing people in countries such as India who simply cannot afford many modern pharmaceutical treatments—clearly a worthwhile endeavor, one whose foundation is worth understanding.

Practically Speaking *(continued)*

Recycling Science

Hale comes from the industry. She has a Ph.D. in pharmacology from the University of California San Francisco (one of the top medical schools in the US), and she has worked for both the US Food and Drug Administration and Genentech. Those experiences enabled her to see "opportunity" where others saw waste. Every day, patents on profitable pharmaceuticals expire, enabling anyone to produce and distribute the compound without paying a royalty. Every day, research and development projects are canceled because the resulting product could not find a profitable market. While useless to large pharma firms, these events could offer technology at a price OneWorld and its customers could afford.

Taking the First Step

Also known as "black fever," kala-azar (formally visceral leishmaniasis) is a disease transmitted by sand flies. If left untreated, the resulting internal organ damage is nearly always fatal. Half a million new cases are estimated worldwide annually, largely in India, Bangladesh, and Nepal. Starting with an "off-patent" antibiotic, OneWorld assembled partners from the commercial, non-profit, and government sectors to develop, test, and approve paromomycin—a compound capable of curing a black fever victim for less than 10 US dollars. Paromomycin distribution started in 2007 in India, and if Hale has her way, the compound could eradicate the disease completely.

Making the Opportunity

Entrepreneurs are often described as "creative," but perhaps "creators" is a more apt term. Had Hale not dragged a solution from the dustbins of pharma and built partnerships to create a new business model that gets cheap remedies to "unprofitable" markets, it is unlikely that the need would be served today. In other words, while so many aspiring entrepreneurs search for opportunities waiting to be discovered, real entrepreneurs roll up their sleeves to make opportunities that make the world we live in.

In the meantime, Victoria Hale has moved on to other opportunities. OneWorld has evolved as well, and as a non-profit venture builds treatment capacities (both physical clinics and medical training) to serve its mission "To provide quality, affordable healthcare to people in need."

To learn more, visit: https://effectuation.org/EE3/oneworld or scan Figure 23.16.

Figure 23.16

Three Claims and Call for Action to Future Changemakers

We close this section with three claims and a call for action made by Sarasvathy (2022, p. 227):

> **Relying on the alternate assumption that all economic value ultimately derives from human beings, *even-if* some human beings may at times be a burden on others, I make the following claims:**
>
> **The Markets-for-All Thesis:**
>
> **It is feasible and valuable to open up public equity markets to all ventures without creating separations between for-profit, non-profit, and "social" ventures.**
>
> **The Non-Loss Thesis:**
>
> **It is possible to design all ventures, involving every facet of human hope, with a strong non-loss constraint.**

The Human Hope = Economic Value Thesis:

Over the long run, open equity markets and non-loss ventures will lead to increased economic income and growth for all ventures and their stakeholders, including the ones outside these markets.

Each of the above three theses can also be seen as a call to action for entrepreneurs seeking to co-create social value through the use of tools and techniques already in use in the for-profit sector.

Practically Speaking

Ronni Kahn and OzHarvest: The Metamorphosis of Food Waste Into a Butterfly

Ronni Kahn, the queen of the Australian promotional events scene, established OzHarvest in 2004 with a seemingly simple mission: to stop good food from going to waste. In the meantime, her social venture has become an influential force in addressing United Nations Sustainable Development Goals (SDGs).

Kahn's journey exemplifies the concept of the butterfly effect in social entrepreneurship, where a small initiative aimed at reducing food waste has cascaded into significant impacts across various critical areas of human and environmental well-being.

Food for Thought

Ronni Kahn ran a successful events company and was increasingly disturbed by the amount of still fresh and safe food being thrown away by the hospitality industry. Motivated by a desire to reduce waste, she began by redistributing surplus food from her company to homeless shelters. One thing led to another, and over time she found herself rescuing food from other caterers, supermarkets, farmers, and food manufacturers.

What started as "doing the right thing" became her sole focus and led her to found OzHarvest. Her approach was not about meticulously planned outcomes, but about starting with available means and allowing the pathway to emerge organically.

Beyond Imagination

When Ronni took the first step (or first flap of butterfly wings), she couldn't have known how far-reaching the effects this would have over time. In a presentation (Social Good Summit Australia, 2019), she outlined how the work of OzHarvest impacts on the following SDGs:

1. **No Poverty (SDG 1)**: By providing food to those in need, OzHarvest directly contributes to alleviating poverty. The OzHarvest website states, "Every $1 invested in Food Rescue returns $7.70 as charity agencies can redirect valuable funds from buying fresh, nutritious food to other essential services." This value is calculated in terms of meals provided, savings to the charity sector, and the environmental benefit of diverting food from landfills.
2. **Zero Hunger (SDG 2)**: OzHarvest has delivered millions of meals to Australians facing food insecurity, which also nourishes communities.

Practically Speaking *(continued)*

3. **Good Health and Well-Being (SDG 3)**: Beyond hunger relief, OzHarvest promotes healthy eating through educational programs. Kahn's team educates people about nutrition and food preparation, thus addressing health and lifestyle diseases related to diet.
4. **Quality Education (SDG 4)**: OzHarvest's FEAST program for primary school students teaches about food waste, sustainability, and healthy eating, fostering a future generation conscious of these critical issues.
5. **Responsible Consumption and Production (SDG 12)**: Kahn's initiative has been a trailblazer in advocating for sustainable food practices. She successfully campaigned for changes in Australian food donation liability laws, removing barriers to surplus food donations by businesses.
6. **Climate Action (SDG 13)**: By diverting food from landfills, OzHarvest reduces methane emissions, a potent greenhouse gas. This contribution to combating climate change is a significant extension of Kahn's original vision.
7. **Partnership for the Goals (SDG 17)**: Collaboration is central to OzHarvest's success by engaging with governments, businesses, and other NGOs, they demonstrate how partnerships can amplify impact.

Figure 23.17 Distributing the harvest.

Ronni Kahn's journey with OzHarvest shows how small actions can trigger a butterfly effect. Starting with what she had—an awareness of food waste and a network in the hospitality industry—Kahn's actions and interactions led to outcomes far beyond what she or anyone could have imagined at the start.

To learn more, visit: https://effectuation.org/EE3/ozharvest or scan Figure 23.18.

Figure 23.18

EFFECTUAL ACTION FOR SOCIAL CHANGE

Enough theory! Let's visit entrepreneurs building hope in their own ways, through the nourishing integration of refugees in new communities, to educating new generations in technology and social interaction, to a princess promoting womens' sport, to cleansing conversations while waiting for the laundry.

Practically Speaking

Food Integrates: Refugees Sharing Culture

Food is a universal language that transcends borders and cultures. A trend seen across the globe involves innovative social ventures using food as a bridge, bringing together migrants to share their native cuisine with their host community.

Such ventures not only introduce diverse culinary experiences, but also promote integration, provide economic opportunities, provide a space for social interaction, and boost the self-worth of the migrants involved.

Food is not just about sustenance. It's about stories, traditions, and connections. Migrant-focused culinary ventures worldwide are harnessing the power of food to create economic opportunities and build bridges, showing how entrepreneurial ideas can be just a meal away.

Figure 23.19 A refugee-run restaurant on a snowy day.

Some examples from around the world:

Name	Location	Web address
Heart & Parcel	Manchester, England	https://heartandparcel.org/
Über den Tellerrand (Beyond the Plate)	Began in Berlin, now with satellites in Germany, Austria, Czech Republic, and Columbia	https://ueberdentellerrand.org/
HummusTown	Rome, Italy	www.hummustown.com
Living Soil, Local Seed	Mardin, Türkiye	https://ebrubaybarademir.com/en/living-soil-local-seed/
Newcomer Kitchen	Toronto, Canada	https://newcomerkitchen.ca/about-newcomer-kitchen/
Kitchen 66	Tulsa, Oklahoma, USA	www.kitchen66tulsa.com
United We Eat @ Home	Missoula, Montana, USA	https://unitedweeatmt.org/
Flavors From Afar	Orange County, California, USA	www.flavorsfromafar.co
Grassroots Future	Hong Kong, Hong Kong SAR	https://grassrootsfuture.org/
Plate It Forward	Sydney, Australia	www.plateitforward.org.au
Free to Feed	Melbourne, Australia	www.freetofeed.org.au
UNESCO Refugee Food Festival	International	www.unesco.org/interculturaldialogue/en/interculturaldialogue/good-practices/refugee-food-festival

Practically Speaking *(continued)*

To learn more, visit: https://effectuation.org/EE3/foodintegrates or scan Figure 23.20.

Figure 23.20

Practically Speaking

Technology Camps Teaching More Than Science

Rana El Chemaitelly is a mother of three; an independent businessperson who ran her own digital photography company for 12 years until the service became a commodity; an engineer with a bachelor's degree in mechanical engineering and a master's degree in engineering management; and an instructor at the American University of Beirut, Lebanon.

Before you read on, close your eyes for a moment and consider how you might combine these available means to form the basis of a new venture.

Inputs in Design

Now, with your own possible solution in mind, consider two observations that influenced El Chemaitelly's thinking. The first was that she found her students at the American University unprepared for their studies in engineering and unsure of what they might do with their education when they graduated. And the second was that her own seven-year-old son was so captivated by video games that he was missing out on many of the social aspects of childhood.

Prototyping Progress

El Chemaitelly transformed her resources and observations into an initiative called "The Little Engineer" (TLE). Launched in her home in 2009, while tires burned and riots raged in other parts of the city, TLE was intent on teaching hands-on science and technology to kids in an interactive and positive environment. After school, TLE provided robotics, energy and engineering instruction, challenges, and competitions to creative little engineers.

Practically Speaking *(continued)*

Building Up

What started as a cottage project became a fully-fledged venture. Today, TLE has in-person and online programs for students of all ages. In 2012, TLE partnered with Airbus Middle East and has offered programs to thousands of students in 12 countries in the Middle East, Africa, and South Asia. All this has been noticed, with El Chemaitelly receiving a number of international social impact awards.

Building the Future

Like Ronni Kahn with food waste, there are at least two things that El Chemaitelly offers us in understanding social entrepreneurship and the role of near decomposability (ND) in how local action can create global impact.

Figure 23.21 A rendition of a robotics camp in downtown Beirut—the mixing of old and new worlds.

The first is how many different possibilities exist, even from a modest starting point. Compare your original idea with what she has actually done. Imagine how you might take another completely different direction from the same starting point. Good ideas and available resources are plentiful, but it is what the entrepreneur does that matters. And then consider the longer-term implications of her efforts.

Second, notice that El Chemaitelly is not just in the business of teaching engineering. She is in the process of shaping engineering education, just as Ronni Kahn is not merely tackling food waste. She is shaping our relationship to food, waste, and the future. And Josiah Wedgwood did not just make pottery. He built social mobility. And Mohammad Yunus did more than provide loans. He provided ways to build markets in human hope for generations of poor illiterate women.

To learn more, visit: https://effectuation.org/EE3/engineers or scan Figure 23.22.

Figure 23.22

Practically Speaking

Princess Reema: Nudging Social Change

Princess Reema bint Bandar Al Saud of Saudi Arabia stands out as a notable figure due to her approach to inducing incremental social change in a conservative society. Her work resonates strongly with the principles of near decomposability, a concept popularized by Herbert Simon (2002).

Near decomposability, as proposed by Herbert Simon, suggests that complex systems can be understood as a hierarchy of subsystems, which are relatively independent in the short run but interdependent in the long run.

Figure 23.23 A Saudi Arabian princess watches a women's track and field event.

Princess Reema's initiatives in Saudi Arabia exemplify this theory. For instance, her involvement in the Saudi Arabian Women's Sports Authority and her push for the inclusion of physical education in girls' schools were incremental steps that addressed specific subsystems—sports and education—within the broader societal system. These efforts, while seemingly isolated and incremental, contributed cumulatively to the long-term goal of empowering women and shifting societal norms.

Her advocacy for women's participation in the workforce and sports has had a tangible impact. Her efforts in the Saudi Arabian General Sports Authority have been pivotal in normalizing women's presence in these traditionally male-dominated spaces. These actions, although small in isolation, collectively symbolize a significant shift in societal attitudes toward women's roles.

Figure 23.24

To learn more, visit: https://effectuation.org/EE3/princessreema or scan Figure 23.24.

Practically Speaking

Orange Sky: Clean Clothes and a Chat

Orange Sky, an innovative venture based in Australia, exemplifies a transformative approach in addressing challenges faced by homeless people. Founded in 2014 by Nicholas Marchesi and Lucas Patchett, this non-profit organization revolutionized the concept of aiding the homeless by offering free laundry services and showers in mobile vans.

The core philosophy of Orange Sky extends beyond the immediate benefits of clean clothes and showers; it is grounded in restoring human dignity and fostering personal empowerment.

Orange Sky's impact is far-reaching. For instance, a clean set of clothes and the opportunity to maintain personal hygiene significantly enhance the chances of someone securing a job interview. This idea is supported by the theory of "scarcity mindset," where individuals struggling with basic needs have limited mental bandwidth to pursue opportunities (Mullainathan & Shafir, 2013). By alleviating this burden, Orange Sky enables individuals to focus on long-term goals like employment, achieving stable income, and ultimately being able to afford housing.

Figure 23.25 A cleansing conversation is the important work of Orange Sky.

Furthermore, Orange Sky fosters community and social connections through its services, which are pivotal for psychological well-being and social inclusion. The informal conversations that occur around the vans serve as a catalyst for building relationships and community support networks, crucial elements for sustainable social reintegration.

To learn more, visit: https://effectuation.org/EE3/orangesky or scan Figure 23.26.

Figure 23.26

Strength in Numbers: Co-Creation and Collective Action

A core principle of effectual logic is co-creation, which applies to all entrepreneurial action, regardless of the profit motive. In fact, while entrepreneurship is often seen (at least in early phases) as a relatively lonely undertaking, dealing with societal problems is, by its very nature, more of a "team sport," making the term "collective action" particularly descriptive.

In the following Research Roots, Sarasvathy and Ramesh (2019) investigate Nobel laureate Elinor Ostrom's work on collective action and provide practical guidance for tackling sustainability issues using effectual logic.

Research Roots

Collective Action Requires Stakeholder Commitments

Perhaps you have heard the term "collective action" in connection with a worker's strike. This relatively common example is usually an indication of negotiations breaking down, yet another way of using collective action can be preventative—to preserve shared or common resources.

We are familiar with the core problem of shared resources: unless there are rules everyone follows, it is human nature for each individual to act in their own self-interest, which often conflicts with the interests of the group as a whole.

This concept was given the name "tragedy of the commons" by ecologist Garrett Hardin in his 1968 essay, "The tragedy of the commons." It refers to situations where individuals, acting in their own self-interest, deplete a shared limited resource, leading to its degradation or depletion.

Hardin used the example of herders sharing a common pasture, each with their own self-interest in mind, leading to overgrazing and the destruction of the resource. This concept highlights the challenges of managing common resources and the potential need for collective action or regulation.

Elinor Ostrom (1933–2012), a political economist, challenged the conventional wisdom that common resources are inevitably overexploited due to the "tragedy of the commons." Ostrom's research emphasized the capacity of communities to self-organize and manage their resources sustainably through collective action and institutional design. In 2009, she became the first woman to receive the Nobel Prize in Economic Sciences for her contributions to our understanding of economic governance.

In a recent paper, Sarasvathy and Ramesh (2019, p. 405) took a closer look at Ostrom's work and concluded that:

> Our analysis allowed us to bring together Ostrom's institutional analysis and development framework and effectuation to show how effectual entrepreneurs transform market failures into sustainable solutions by self-selecting stakeholders. The resulting integrated model of collective action serves both as a practical guide for entrepreneurs seeking to tackle sustainability issues.

Referring to Ostrom and Walker (2000), Sarasvathy and Ramesh (2019, p. 408) take this a step further, writing: "According to Ostrom, collective actions are mechanisms that transform tragedies of the commons to opportunities by coordinating or organizing based on rules that individuals can agree on, monitor, and mutually sanction."

For socially minded entrepreneurs, Sarasvathy and Ramesh highlight the very practical implication of their work, namely, that effectual entrepreneurs applying Ostrom's institutional analysis and development (IAD) model of collective action can help structure enduring stakeholder commitments.

Sarasvathy and Ramesh (2019, p. 413) provide the following clear guidelines on the stickiest part of co-creation, negotiating with stakeholders to reach lasting commitments for collective action:

> IAD design principles lead to enduring commitments to collective action and sustainable entrepreneurship. When negotiating with stakeholders, effectuators must pay attention to:
>
> 1. Defining clear group boundaries.
> 2. Matching rules governing use of common goods to local needs and conditions.
> 3. Ensuring that those affected by the rules can participate in modifying the rules.

Research Roots *(continued)*

4. Making sure the rule-making rights of community members are respected by outside authorities.
5. Developing a system, carried out by community members, for monitoring members' behavior.
6. Using graduated sanctions for rule violators.
7. Providing accessible, low-cost means for dispute resolution.
8. Building responsibility for governing the common resource in nested tiers from the lowest level up to the entire interconnected system.

Bookmark this page: whenever you have stakeholders, you need commitments to move forward, which requires negotiations. Perhaps these eight points will help you move forward together.

Inspiring Effectual Action

Climate change, political polarization, income inequalities, refugees and asylum seekers—the enormity of the challenges in today's world is inescapable. We all need, at times, inspiration. Where can we find such inspiration? Let us consider quotes from inspiring people and match them up with each of the five principles of effectuation.

"Hope is not the conviction that something will turn out well, but the certainty that something makes sense, regardless of how it turns out."—Václav Havel, author and former president of the Czech Republic. This evokes the bird-in-hand principle because it focuses on doing the doable that is worth doing without defining the project in terms of outcome goals.

"There are those that look at things the way they are, and ask why? I dream of things that never were, and ask why not?"—George Bernard Shaw. This works well with the affordable loss principle and the "why not pitch" we described in Chapter 12.

"You'll never have to chase someone who wants to walk with you."—Mandy Hale. Although meant as advice for single people seeking love, this quote captures the crazy quilt principle rather nicely.

"The impediment to action advances action. What stands in the way becomes the way."—Marcus Aurelius, *Meditations*, Book 5.20. Stoic philosophy is rife with discussions about the role of adversity in leading a meaningful life. Lessons from Stoics work particularly well for using the lemonade principle.

Finally, to make sense of the pilot-in-the-plane principle, we turn to a quote from Nelson Mandela's inauguration speech:

> *Our deepest fear is not that we are inadequate*
> *Our deepest fear is that we are powerful beyond measure*
> *It is our light, not our darkness, that most frightens us.*
> *We ask ourselves:*
> *"Who am I to be brilliant, gorgeous, talented, fabulous?"*
> *Actually, who are you not to be.*

The deep idea here is that every human being is and can be a co-pilot capable of steering their own destiny. Taken together, then the future is indeed shaped and co-created by what people choose to do. And expanding that idea further, we can see that effectual entrepreneurship is about unleashing that which is "powerful beyond measure" in "our light" as human beings.

Research Roots

Near Decomposability as the Key to Hope

Co-Creators: Philippe Silberzahn and Dominique Vian

How can a single individual have any hope of making an impact on the world? Given the size and complexity of issues, it's no wonder that many feel helpless. Yet, history shows us that "small is big," i.e. many big changes happened when a single individual started to act small using, most often unknowingly, the principles of effectuation.

The Sum of Many "Smalls" Is Big

"Big" really means anything from gaining a degree of control over one's life to creating new products, new firms, and new markets to addressing more global issues such as poverty or global warming. But how can "small" become "big"? In other words, how does a series of local means-effect associations using the principles of effectuation eventually have a global impact?

That's where "near decomposability" (ND) comes in. ND is a property of complex systems. It was first described by Herbert Simon, a pioneer in economics, organization theory, and artificial intelligence, and also the supervisor of Saras Sarasvathy's Ph.D. which led to effectuation. According to him, in a complex system, "the whole is more than the sum of its parts; not in a metaphysical sense, but in a strong, pragmatic sense" (Simon, 1996, p. 172).

Not Only Food Decomposes

The McDonald's restaurant chain is a good illustration of ND in the context of organizations (Sarasvathy, 2009). With more than 40,000 outlets, most of them independent franchises, serving about 70 million customers daily in more than 100 countries, McDonald's is admittedly a very complex organization.

Because these outlets are almost independent, they are legally autonomous and therefore only loosely connected to the company. They alone determine, for example, who to hire or how to redesign their parking (The link between the brand and the parking is weak). Yet, they relay national advertising campaigns and must observe strict company standards on a large range of issues, such as food safety, recipes, etc. (The link between brand and food safety is strong.)

Despite the strong local autonomy of its restaurants, McDonald's has an identity specific to the group, i.e. to the company itself and to all its franchisees; it is much more than just a network of independent restaurants. Within the McDonald's social artifact with its own identity, there are therefore strongly interacting and weakly interacting subsystems (Sarasvathy, 2009).

Links Abound

What characterizes an ND system is that while all components are linked (think employees and consumers of MacDonald's), it is possible to distinguish subsystems made of components that are strongly linked with each other (think sales team and consumers). Such subsystems are almost, but not totally, autonomous—hence the term "near." The term "near decomposable" therefore means that it is possible to partially decompose a system into homogeneous subsystems, but not completely because these subsystems remain connected to the whole.

Research Roots *(continued)*

Near decomposable systems are distinguished from non-decomposable systems. For instance, reducing the weight of the burger packaging includes elements that are causally related. By definition, these can only be changed all at once. If systems are large, non-decomposable tasks become intractable.

Modular Systems: Completely Decomposable

Near decomposable systems are also distinguished from completely decomposable, also called modular, systems. A modular system is characterized by the fact that, on the one hand, the modules (or subsystems) are objectively identified a priori, while on the other hand the system is designed so that the number of links between these subsystems is minimal. A watch is made up of several subsystems, but the knowledge associated with these subsystems and their links is perfectly determined as, for instance, between the battery and the movement.

Infinite Linkages of Social Systems

Unlike modular systems, social systems such as markets, organizations, and "issues" (e.g. poverty) are open. This means that the number of their subsystems is potentially infinite, which also means that the number of links between these subsystems is potentially infinite, and these are unknowable in their entirety. For instance, poverty is a complex issue linked to, of course, economic development, but also education, women's rights, infrastructure, political situation, climate, psychology (people's beliefs about work and economic development), international trade, geopolitics, etc. Some of those components interact weakly and others strongly.

Modularity and ND play opposite roles: while the purpose of modularity is to minimize the number of links by design, that of ND is to take advantage of them to create new possibilities of association. It provides the entrepreneur with a way to increase the number of links to consider: instead of having a binary choice between either zero (independent) or one (dependent or causal), the choice becomes a large range from weak to strong (nearly independent to nearly dependent).

Hope Springs From Local Action With a Global Impact

The use of ND makes possible a local action with a global impact. Working on a local, relatively autonomous subsystem is advantageous: because it is small and local, the entrepreneur can have a certain degree of control over it. The identification of a subsystem on which to act is a way to address bounded rationality, i.e. the impossibility for the entrepreneur to consider the whole issue, as it quickly becomes too big and too complex.

Yet, thanks to ND, the entrepreneur knows that the subsystem is linked to the global system. Thanks to ND, the emerging artifact is robust: change is local, at the level of a subsystem. Hence, if the change is not successful, only the subsystem is impacted; the failure remains affordable because it is at the local level (affordable loss principle). If the change is successful, the local piece is reworked, and the global artifact evolves as a result.

Research Roots *(continued)*

Contingencies: Connection to Effectual Logic

ND also allows exploitation of contingency, i.e. unexpected events (lemonade principle). If a surprise strikes, it can be taken advantage of at the local level. One does not need to wait and evaluate the global impact, and the evaluation of the potential impact is easier at the local level than at the global level.

This is where ND and effectuation connect. ND enables the identification of relatively independent subsystems, while effectuation allows for the identification of possible links between subsystems, providing a basis for means-effect association. For instance, education is an eventual means to foster women's rights as a possible effect, with in turn economic development as a possible effect.

Quilting Involves Stitching and Tearing

Sarasvathy and Simon (2000) put it nicely as follows:

> While effectuation stitches together pieces of entrepreneurial fabric into economic quilts that continue to make sense in an interactive and dynamically changing environment, near-decomposability identifies lines of ''tearing'' so that pieces can be re-worked in synchrony with the overall pattern as the needs imposed by the environment change.

Hence the origin of the quilt as a metaphor for the effectual process. A quilt is made of pieces of fabric. One doesn't know in advance who will turn up for a quilting session, and what type of fabric they will bring. Once the pieces are on the table, participants discuss what to do with them (available means principle and co-creation principle). When an additional participant joins with a new piece, new possibilities emerge. The overall artwork can be reworked thanks to the new piece. Small groups can gather to work on parts of the piece without losing sight of the overall intention—say, making a bed cover.

Sarasvathy and Simon (2000, p. 1) add: "Just as effectuation creates rapidly evolving artifacts that exploit interdependence to exploit locality and contingency, ND in the structure of such systems exploits independence to exploit the same locality and contingency."

In conclusion, Effectuation is the set of principles regular people use to make big changes in the world, and near decomposability is the property that makes the use of these principles effective. Enabling "small is big" is the key to hope that change is possible for regular folks who want to act.

Research Roots

Social Entrepreneurship in Perspective

Social entrepreneurship has a long and illustrious history dating back at least to the nineteenth century when some Victorian industrialists recognized the need to combine social progress with economic success. Therefore, early models for social entrepreneurship include the great American chocolatier Milton Hershey and the British Quaker firm Cadbury's (also a chocolatier), both of whom sought to combine the creation of social value with their commercial successes.

Research Roots *(continued)*

Addressing Failures to Meet Social Needs

Research on social entrepreneurship highlights that what is common in all kinds of social entrepreneurship is a drive to create social value rather than just personal or shareholder wealth. Social entrepreneurs are usually creating something new, whether accidentally or deliberately, whether that's in the non-profit or for-profit sector. It also has been noted that social entrepreneurs are addressing social problems often perceived as failures of commercial market forces to meet social needs, or government failures to meet them.

Mobilizing Resources a Challenge

One important issue highlighted by research on social entrepreneurship is challenges in mobilizing resources for new social ventures. When ventures are created on a not-for-profit basis, they are limited from attracting startup capital the way for-profit entrepreneurs do. They may also rely heavily on the value of non-pecuniary compensation by their staff. For-profit ventures may face fewer constraints in these regards. Entrepreneurs, therefore, face important decisions about whether pursuing a not-for-profit or a for-profit model is the best way to achieve the ultimate social mission of a venture (Mair & Marti, 2006).

Taking Action to Marry Social Change and Profit

What holds us back from accomplishing what Hale (OneWorld) and Yunus (Grameen Bank) demonstrate can be done? How might we encourage more people to realize that they don't have to choose between doing something socially productive and making a profit?

Here are some ideas for action:

- *Change the tax code.* Perhaps the answer lies in making social enterprise more attractive at a regulatory level—reducing the tax burden on income from products or services provided by organizations that deliver social good. Tax codes vary across countries and even local governments, but one theme is reasonably consistent: taxation schemes clearly delineate between charity and for-profit enterprise. A graduated approach that appreciates the spectrum of different business models might serve to encourage more firms to serve the common good by making a profit.
- *Take political action.* The separation of these two realms is enforced at the political level, perhaps needlessly. While one arm of the government is focused on bringing money in through taxation, a completely different arm is focused on pushing money out to socially beneficial programs. What if these two bodies were to collaborate? What if they set up a scheme that allowed people like Hale and Yunus to take on the social needs of the community while at the same time generating a profit?
- *Teach and preach.* Educators hold sway among the educated populace. There is certainly more opportunity to open the dialog about ways to break down the artificial separation between charity and profit. Whether accomplished through an indirect Socratic dialog kind of an approach, or a more promotional direct sales style, the opportunity exists.

- *Entrepreneurship*. But where are the revolutionaries? Will this problem be resolved by the top-down approach the first three alternatives represent? Probably not—which is why we focus on the power of the entrepreneur. As a maker of new worlds, the entrepreneur is not bound by assumptions such as "Doing something socially productive can't also make money." Why not? If there is an interest in doing both, the only question for the entrepreneur is how.

TAKEAWAY: DOING WHAT WE OUGHT; DOING WHAT WE CAN

Hopefully, after reading this chapter, you come away with the appreciation that whether a firm is for-profit or not-for-profit is a design decision that's made by you. And that the same principles apply regardless. So, what are you going to do?

- Change the world?
- Make money?
- Why choose?

Think It Through

- How can we make government more entrepreneurial so it might be more supportive of some of these efforts?
- Unless you are taking gifts, why not be a for-profit venture?

So What?

Entrepreneurship can generate sustainable solutions to social problems while reducing the need to raise donations or wait for legislation. By closing the value loop, you can raise investments and earn returns rather than count on the generosity of individual contributions or the government taxation process.

What Now?

Closing the value loop

- When you find a cause that turns you on, an injustice you want to correct, or a social problem you want to solve, think like a for-profit entrepreneur:
  - Who are your key stakeholders?
  - What is the value proposition for each of them?
  - How can you create a product or service that the stakeholders would want to pay for?
  - How can the beneficiaries of your product/service become your investors?
  - How do you close the value loop through time so that the benefits pay for the costs, even as you make a decent living at it?
  - In short, what is your business model?

REFERENCES

Addams, J. (1910). *Twenty Years at Hull-House With Autobiographical Notes*. Macmillan.

Alam, M. S., & Islam, S. (2013). Performance of women entrepreneurs of Grameen Bank with special reference to Grameen generalized system. *International Journal of Business and Economic Development* (*IJBED*), *1*(2). https://www.ijbed.org/cdn/article_file/i-2_c-17.pdf

Bacon, F. (1620). *Novum Organum*. Clarendon Press.

Bill & Melinda Gates Foundation. (2006). Developing a safe, inexpensive cure for "black fever." https://docs.gatesfoundation.org/documents/iowh.pdf

Candel, J. J. L., Breeman, G. E., & Termeer, C. J. A. M. (2016). The European Commission's ability to deal with wicked problems: An in-depth case study of the governance of food security. *Journal of European Public Policy*, *23*(6), 789–813. https://doi.org/10.1080/13501763.2015.1068836

Carlos III University of Madrid. (n.d.). "Butterfly chaos effect" discovered in swarms and herds of animals. Phys.org. Retrieved January 25, 2024, from https://phys.org/news/2023-06-butterfly-chaos-effect-swarms-herds.html

Cavalcanti, M. F. R. (2021). Social entrepreneurship and social change: A practice-based study in non-governmental organizations. *RAUSP Management Journal*, *56*(2), 170–185. https://doi.org/10.1108/RAUSP-05-2020-0091

Center for International Development. (2013, November 12). GEM13: Sendhil Mullainathan on Scarcity. Retrieved January 26, 2024, from https://www.youtube.com/watch?v=fBPzc9NsggU

Davis, A. (2000). *American Heroine: The Life and Legend of Jane Addams*. Rowman & Littlefield.

Donatelli, L. (2020, March 8). Neiva Guedes—Homenagem no dia Internacional da Mulher. Cristófoli. Retrieved January 31, 2024, from https://www.cristofoli.com/biosseguranca/neiva-guedes-homenagem-no-dia-internacional-da-mulher/

Finews. (2023, August 23). Raiffeisen boosts profits as all units contribute. Retrieved January 26, 2024, from https://www.finews.com/news/english-news/58923-raiffeisen-1h23-profit-aum-switzerland

Freudweiler, M. (n.d.). Marc Freudweiler—Profile in LinkedIn. Retrieved January 29, 2024, from https://www.linkedin.com/in/marcfreudweiler/?originalSubdomain=ch

Grameen Australia. (n.d.). History. Retrieved January 30, 2024, from https://grameen.org.au/history/

Hajo, C. M. (2015, November 3). Did she really say that? Jane Addams quotes on the Web—Jane Addams Papers Project. https://janeaddams.ramapo.edu/2015/11/did-she-really-say-that-jane-addams-quotes-on-the-web/

Hansmann, H. (2000). *The Ownership of Enterprise*. Harvard University Press.

Hardin, G. (1968). The tragedy of the commons: The population problem has no technical solution; it requires a fundamental extension in morality. *Science*, *162*(3859), 1243–1248. https://doi.org/10.1126/science.162.3859.1243

Hayek, F. A. (1984). Competition as a discovery procedure. In C. Nishiyama & K. R. Leube (eds.), *The Essence of Hayek* (p. 257). Stanford University Press.

Hoover, S. (2016, November 22). Muhammad Yunus: Charity with a business engine. CFA Institute Enterprising Investor. https://blogs.cfainstitute.org/investor/2016/11/22/muhammad-yunus-charity-with-a-business-engine/

Hsu, C. (2005, November 31). Entrepreneur for social change. US News and World Report.

Knight, L. W. (2006). *Citizen: Jane Addams and the Struggle for Democracy*. University of Chicago Press.

Ledley, F. D., McCoy, S. S., Vaughan, G., & Cleary, E. G. (2020). Profitability of large pharmaceutical companies compared with other large public companies. *JAMA*, *323*(9), 834–843. https://doi.org/10.1001/jama.2020.0442

Mair, J., & Marti, I. (2006). Social entrepreneurship research: A source of explanation, prediction, and delight. *Journal of World Business*, *41*(1), 36–44.

Mikulic, M. (2024, January 10). Global pharmaceutical industry. Statista. https://www.statista.com/topics/1764/global-pharmaceutical-industry/

Mullainathan, S., & Shafir, E. (2013). *Scarcity: Why Having Too Little Means So Much*. Times Books.

OneWorld Health. (n.d.). Retrieved January 31, 2024, from https://oneworldhealth.com/

Orange Sky Australia. (n.d). Retrieved January 26, 2024, from https://orangesky.org.au/

Ostrom, E. (1990). *Governing the Commons: The Evolution of Institutions for Collective Action*. Cambridge University Press.

Ostrom, E., & Walker, J. (2000). Neither markets nor states: Linking transformation processes in collective action arenas. In D. C. Mueller (ed.), *Perspectives on Public Choice: A Handbook* (pp. 427–471). Cambridge University Press.

Ostrom Workshop. (2021, June 30). 1. What is polycentric governance? A quick answer—Professor Michael McGinnis. https://www.youtube.com/watch?v=ybVMOLveaS8

OzHarvest. (n.d.). Retrieved January 26, 2024, from https://www.ozharvest.org/

Plesse, R. H. (2016, March 30). Clean streets: The mobile laundry service helping Australia's homeless. *The Guardian*. https://www.theguardian.com/cities/2016/mar/30/clean-streets-mobile-laundry-service-australia-homeless-orange-sky

Portrait—Raiffeisen. (n.d.). Retrieved January 26, 2024, from https://report.raiffeisen.ch/en/portrait/

Raiffeisen Bank. (n.d.). Markets, clients and services. Retrieved January 25, 2024, from https://www.raiffeisen.ch/rch/de/ueber-uns/markets/investor-relations/about-us/markets-clients-and-services.html

Rosa, R. (2020, April). Alumni em destaque: Neiva Guedes e o Instituto Arara Azul. https://www.alumni.usp.br/alumni-em-destaque-neiva-guedes-e-o-instituto-arara-azul/

Roy, E. A., & Jong, E. de. (2018, November 6). Cleaning up: Mobile laundry for the homeless goes international. *The Guardian*. https://www.theguardian.com/world/2018/nov/06/cleaning-up-mobile-laundry-for-the-homeless-goes-international

Sabzian, H., Shahriari, N., & Nejad, M. G. (2023). Unraveling the butterfly effects in social dynamics: Insights from agent-based modeling. arXiv. http://arxiv.org/abs/2312.07914

Safian, B. (n.d.). How the word "no" inspires change, with Princess Reema bint Bandar Al Saud. Masters of Scale. Retrieved February 1, 2024, from https://mastersofscale.com/episode/how-the-word-no-inspires-change-princess-reema/

Sagan, C. (2002). *Cosmos*. Random House.

Sarasvathy, S. (2009). *Effectuation: Elements of Entrepreneurial Expertise*. Edward Elgar Publishing.

Sarasvathy, S. (2022). *Effectuation: Elements of Entrepreneurial Expertise* (2nd ed.). Edward Elgar Publishing.

Sarasvathy, S., & Ramesh, A. (2019). An effectual model of collective action for addressing sustainability challenges. *Academy of Management Perspectives*, *33*(4), 405–424. https://doi.org/10.5465/amp.2017.0090

Sarasvathy, S., & Simon, H. (2000). Effectuation, near-decomposability, and the creation and growth of entrepreneurial firms. First Annual Research Policy Technology Entrepreneurship Conference.

Schlossman, M. (n.d.). Hyacinth Macaw (Anodorhynchus hyacinthinus). Extinction. Retrieved January 31, 2024, from https://www.extinction.photo/species/hyacinth-macaw/

Sharma, N., Devalkar, S. K., & Sohoni, M. G. (2021). Payment for results: Funding non-profit operations. *Production and Operations Management*, *30*(6), 1686–1702. https://doi.org/10.1111/poms.13336

Simon, H. A. (1962). The architecture of complexity. *Proceedings of the American Philosophical Society*, *106*(6), 467–482.

Simon, H. A. (2002). Near decomposability and the speed of evolution. *Industrial and Corporate Change*, *11*(3), 587–599.

Simon, J. L. (1996). *The Ultimate Resource 2*. Princeton University Press. https://doi.org/10.1515/9780691214764

Social Good Summit Australia. (2019, August 29). Ronni Kahn AO/ Founder & CEO OzHarvest. https://www.youtube.com/watch?v=PKIWSzbe8Aw

Strategy—Raiffeisen. (n.d.). Retrieved January 26, 2024, from https://report.raiffeisen.ch/en/strategy/

Sunlabob. (n.d.). Retrieved January 29, 2024, from https://www.sunlabob.com/

The Aspen Institute. (2013a, August 2). Scarcity: Why having too little means so much (full session). https://www.youtube.com/watch?v=29yi-5226rs

The Aspen Institute. (2013b, September 27). Scarcity: Why having too little means so much—Sendhil Mullainathan. https://www.youtube.com/watch?v=GCZAZRFSCx8

The Institute—Instituto Arara Azul. (n.d.). Retrieved January 31, 2024, from https://www.institutoararaazul.org.br/en/the-institute/

The Little Engineer. (n.d.). Retrieved January 31, 2024, from https://thelittleengineer.com/

The Nobel Peace Prize 1931. (n.d.). NobelPrize.Org. Retrieved January 29, 2024, from https://www.nobelprize.org/prizes/peace/1931/summary/

US Department of State | Diplomatic Reception Rooms. (n.d.). Anti-Slavery Medallion, Am I Not a Man and a Brother. Retrieved January 30, 2024, from https://www.diplomaticrooms.state.gov/objects/anti-slavery-medallion-am-i-not-a-man-and-a-brother-3/

Wanzenböck, I., & Frenken, K. (2020). The subsidiarity principle in innovation policy for societal challenges. *Global Transitions*, *2*, 51–59. https://doi.org/10.1016/j.glt.2020.02.002

Wedgwood History & Heritage—The Story—Wedgwood®. (n.d.). Retrieved January 30, 2024, from https://www.wedgwood.com/en-us/welcome-to-wedgwood/the-wedgwood-story

Wedgwood, J. (1788, February 29). Benjamin Franklin Papers—From Josiah Wedgwood (unpublished). https://franklinpapers.org/framedVolumes.jsp?vol=45&page=424

Wikipedia. (2023). Raiffeisen (Switzerland). https://en.wikipedia.org/w/index.php?title=Raiffeisen_(Switzerland)&oldid=1189377322

Wikipedia. (2024). Jane Addams. https://en.wikipedia.org/w/index.php?title=Jane_Addams&oldid=1198167384

Wójcik, D. (2015). The butterfly defect: How globalization creates systemic risks and what to do about It. *Journal of Economic Geography*, *15*(1), 250–252. https://doi.org/10.1093/jeg/lbu043

Young, H. (1995). *The Genius of Wedgwood*. Victoria & Albert Museum.

Yunus, M. (2004, November 20). Grameen Bank. Ruffin Lecture Series of the Olsson Center for Applied Ethics, Darden School of Business at the University of Virgina.

Conclusion

DEAR READER,

In the introduction to this book, we promised that you would discover that there is a science to entrepreneurship—a common logic we have observed in expert entrepreneurs across industries, geographic locations, and time.

When you start a new venture—for-profit or not, individually or within an existing organization—you are not only trying to make a good living; you are engaged in expanding the horizon of valuable new economic opportunities.

This book is designed to help you do that from start to finish. And in form and content, the book embodies the expert entrepreneurs' logic—bold, systematic, pragmatic, and at all times full of energy, mischief, and fun.

If you believe we have delivered on our promise, we would like to conclude by extracting a promise from you in return, namely, that you keep Carl Sagan and the Blue Dot in mind and seek to co-create a better world, one that you will reveal as you move forward together.

The picture above is the only one of its kind. When the first (and only) human-made object to leave the solar system, the Voyager spacecraft, crossed into the vast space between us and the rest of the universe, it turned its camera to take a picture of earth from outside the solar system. Carl Sagan wrote about this picture in a moving way:

> Look again at that dot. That's here, that's home, that's us. On it everyone you love, everyone you know, everyone you ever heard of, every human being who ever was, lived out their lives.
>
> The aggregate of our joy and suffering, thousands of confident religions, ideologies, and economic doctrines, every hunter and forager, every hero and coward, every creator and destroyer of civilization, every king and peasant, every young couple in love, every mother and father, hopeful child, inventor and explorer, every teacher of morals, every corrupt politician, every "superstar," every "supreme leader," every saint and sinner in the history of our species lived there—on a mote of dust suspended in a sunbeam.
>
> … The Earth is the only world known so far to harbor life. There is nowhere else, at least in the near future, to which our species could migrate. Visit, yes. Settle, not yet. Like it or not, for the moment the Earth is where we make our stand.

In this book you have learned that you need not wait for the right technology or the proper resources or the massive machinery of governments or the feeble hope of the next election to rebuild your life and the world in which you seek to live. You can start today—with who you are, what you know, and who you know—and invest nothing but what you can afford to lose to begin building pathways for your stakeholders to self-select into your valuable new venture. And together you can co-create a better world, one that neither you nor they can yet fully imagine.

So, get started on your (ad) venture and make your stand on this pale blue dot. And beyond.

Bon voyage!

BEFORE YOU GO ...

We wrote this book for you and are keen to hear what you think of it: what you like, what you don't like, suggestions for future editions, and what impact it has had on your entrepreneurial story. Visit https://effectuation.org/EE3/feedback or scan the following QR code. Thank you in advance for sharing and co-creating with us!

Overview of "Practically Speaking" Sections

Practically Speaking

In every chapter, you will find brief stories of new ventures matched to the topics of the chapter. Every entrepreneurial story illustrates at least one of the principles described in this book. If you choose to focus on just the "Practically Speaking" stories, you can skip from one to the next and quite literally tour the entrepreneurial world.

Alternatively, use this overview to select specific stories based on their description, entity, entrepreneur, or geography.

To access the following list in sortable format, visit https://effectuation.org/EE3/practically or scan this code:

Chapter	Title	Description	Entity / Cause / Project	Name(s) of entrepreneur(s)	Learn More Link	Country
1	Asma Khan: From Arranged Bride to Social Force	A homesick migrant unable to cook becomes a beloved celebrity chef in the UK.	Darjeeling Express	Asma Khan	https://effectuation.org/EE3/asma	Great Britain
1	Howard Schultz and His Rising Star	Despite declining coffee consumption and after many mistakes, Starbucks becomes a cultural phenomenon.	Starbucks	Howard Schultz	https://effectuation.org/EE3/starbucks	USA
1	Arianna Huffington: A Woman With New(s) Perspectives	Leveraging existing connections to build a diverse team of co-creators makes Huffington Post a success in the challenged media space.	Huffington Post	Arianna Huffington	https://effectuation.org/EE3/arianna	USA
1	The Blind Leading the Blind	Two friends turn their disability into a global success: a screen reader for the vision impaired.	NVDA	Jamie Teh & Mick Curran	https://effectuation.org/EE3/blind	Australia
2	Turning a Hobby Into a Business	Building a loft bed for his son becomes a business and employer, delivering lofts across the USA.	College Bed Lofts	John Vence	https://effectuation.org/EE3/hobby	USA
2	Old Godmother Spices Things Up	A street vendor's chili sauce is so popular it makes her one of the richest women in China.	Lao Gan Ma	Tao Huabi	https://effectuation.org/EE3/godmother	China
2	Focus on the Food, Just Not With Your Eyes	Blind dates are different at this restaurant where you can't focus on the food with your eyes.	unsicht-Bar	Axel Rudolph	https://effectuation.org/EE3/unsichtbar	Germany
2	Trash to Cash	Back to the beginning: Turning plastic waste into crude oil make business and environmental sense.	Agilyx	Kevin DeWhitt	https://effectuation.org/EE3/agilyx	USA
2	Everyone Is Doing It	Healthy competition with your neighbor reduces electricity bills and optimizes capacity.	Opower	Dan Yates & Alex Laskey	https://effectuation.org/EE3/opower	USA
3	Dragon Lady	Woman in minivan collects enough to become "Queen of Waste Paper" and major paper producer in China.	Nine Dragons	Yan Cheung	https://effectuation.org/EE3/dragon	China

3	Business in a Bowl	College student turns part-time job into a breakfast and snack food empire, one munch at a time.	Carman's Muesli	Carolyn Creswell	https://effectuation.org/EE3/muesli	Australia
3	Chill Out in Tradition	The story of a traditional drink developed into business opportunities in cultivation, processing, export, and hospitality.	Fiji Kava	Zane Yoshida	https://effectuation.org/EE3/kava	Fiji
4	Boing-Boing	Instead of retiring, this scientist and inventor deployed his unique skill set to write science books for children.	Boing-Boing	Larry Hench	https://effectuation.org/EE3/boing	USA
4	Billions Without Blank Checks	With a day job, this founder built his venture to be self-sustaining and simple, which was the recipe for growth.	eBay	Pierre Omidyar	https://effectuation.org/EE3/ebay	USA
4	A Model Business	What started as an art project became a business, and didn't cost this entrepreneur an arm and a leg.	Mannequin Madness	Judi Henderson-Townsend	https://effectuation.org/EE3/mannequin	USA
4	The Making of Sears	A mistaken delivery led this entrepreneur to find innovative ways to bring goods to customers and build a national retail chain.	Sears Roebuck	Richard Sears	https://effectuation.org/EE3/sears	USA
4	Venturing In Sync	Authenticity was the basis for this singer to build a distinct brand which carried over into social projects and philanthropy.	Annie Lennox	Annie Lennox	https://effectuation.org/EE3/lennox	Great Britain
4	How to Learn to Let Go	Knowing what he could afford to lose gave this entrepreneur the confidence to quit his day job and build his venture.	Browning-Ferris	Tom Fatjo	https://effectuation.org/EE3/waste	USA
5	Persist Easy; Swerve Hard	Not dogged determination in the face of adversity, but a combination of persistence and flexibility led this entrepreneur to success.	Easy Auto	Padmasree Harish	https://effectuation.org/EE3/easyauto	India
5	Making Sweet Success Out of Bitter Failure: Milton Hershey	After three failures in the confectionary business, sweet success was found in chocolate innovation by this entrepreneur.	Hershey's	Milton Hershey	https://effectuation.org/EE3/hershey	USA

Chapter	Title	Description	Entity / Cause / Project	Name(s) of entrepreneur(s)	Learn More Link	Country
5	Sheila Johnson: Under the Thorns	The confidence and courage to become a successful entrepreneur in media, sports, and hospitality only came after surmounting high barriers.	Black Entertainment Television	Sheila Johnson	https://effectuation.org/EE3/sheilajohnson	USA
5	Failing Up to the Top: Apple Computer	Applying learning from failures to the next product generation won this company a reputation of industry-leading innovation.	Apple		https://effectuation.org/EE3/appleflops	USA
6	The Unlikely Story of Freitag	Two brothers make hip bags out of old truck covers, reducing waste, making an environmental fashion statement, and generating worldwide sales.	Freitag	Markus and Daniel Freitag	https://effectuation.org/EE3/freitag	Switzerland
6	Your Amigo: Navigating Uncertainty Without Maps	Going where the big companies wouldn't, these three founders navigate the complex environment of Brazilian favelas to deliver on time.	Carteiro Amigo	Pedro, Elaine, and Silas	https://effectuation.org/EE3/amigo	Brazil
6	U-Haul, or Transforming Uncertainty Into Success	Despite being impossible on paper, within four years, a young couple built a nationwide one-way trailer rental company.	U-Haul	Anna and Leonard Shoen	https://effectuation.org/EE3/uhaul	USA
7	Duh! Why Doesn't This Exist Already?	Despite the bumpy ride, this company has created opportunities to generate income from private cars and for passengers to travel inexpensively.	Uber	Travis Kalanick and Garrett Camp	https://effectuation.org/EE3/uber	USA
7	Something From Nothing	Cycling through various products and markets, this company literally turns throw-aways into raw materials while making a profit.	TerraCycle	Tom Szaky	https://effectuation.org/EE3/terracycle	USA
7	Curry in a Hurry	A myriad of business possibilities provides more chances to try out ideas, thus increasing the likelihood of success.	Curry in a Hurry		https://effectuation.org/EE3/curry	Global

7	An Overwhelming Urge	On the hunt for yoghurt and cheese, two women create the first buffalo dairy in Laos, which also improves local incomes.	Laos Buffalo Dairy	Susie Martin	https://effectuation.org/EE3/buffalo	Laos
7	Making a Market Out of a Joke	People love their pets, particularly when they are easy to look after. Enter the Pet Rock, a low-maintenance friend.	Pet Rock	Gary Dahl	https://effectuation.org/EE3/petrock	USA
8	The Seasons of Bar Semente (Seed Bar)	Like a gardener, this entrepreneur takes control and adapts the business model to the circumstances and seasons of its environment.	Bar Semente	Aline Brufato	https://effectuation.org/EE3/semente	Brazil
8	The Magic of Control at the Circus	How do you take a circus into the uncertainty of a world tour? By mastering control—and the show itself.	Cirque du Soleil	Guy Laliberté	https://effectuation.org/EE3/cirque	Canada
8	The Power of Control	This entrepreneur turned piles of waste rice husks into the first electrical connections for thousands of rural families.	Husk Power	Gyanesh Pandey	https://effectuation.org/EE3/husk	India
9	A Clean Start (Means)	A married couple takes stock of their available means and wants to make everyday healthy products, namely, organic soap.	GoodKaarma	Ea and Stephen Greenwood	https://effectuation.org/EE3/kaarma	Estonia
9	Drawing the Future, Sketch by Sketch (Affordable Loss)	An artist enters new territory and starts a livestreamed drawing class for children during the pandemic lockdown and lifts spirits.	DrawTogether	Wendy McNaughton	https://effectuation.org/drawtogether	USA
9	Surprise in a Glass (Contingencies)	Beer used to flavor whisky barrels was meant to be thrown away, until someone tasted it. Now it is a top-selling microbrew.	Innis & Gunn	Dougal Sharp	https://effectuation.org/innis	Scotland
9	Good Pill Hunting (Partnerships)	Counterfeit pharmaceuticals can be dangerous, which moved this entrepreneur to create an innovative authenticity verification system.	mPedigree	Bright Simons	https://effectuation.org/mpedigree	Ghana

Chapter	Title	Description	Entity / Cause / Project	Name(s) of entrepreneur(s)	Learn More Link	Country
10	Many Happy Returns	Through entrepreneurial action a stack of used envelopes became a business offering a range of ecologically responsible postal solutions.	Eco Envelopes	Ann DeLaVergne	https://effectuation.org/EE3/ecoenvelopes	USA
10	New Venture Recipe	For this entrepreneur, international culinary success started with a first step, involved many partnerships, little planning, and learning from the process itself.	Claus Meyer	Claus Meyer	https://effectuation.org/EE3/clausmeyer	Denmark
10	The Bird Not in Hand	Resilience developed from surviving a brutal regime has served entrepreneurs who crossed the border to South Korea well.	Ju Chang Yang	Ju Chang Yang	https://effectuation.org/EE3/northkorea	South Korea
10	Connecting the Dots	The "dots" of experience and skills are collected before knowing how they might powerfully fit together one day.	Apple	Steve Jobs	https://effectuation.org/EE3/jobs	USA
10	Cordon Blue	A star chef collaborates with local and international organizations to provide immediate food relief in disaster zones around the world.	World Central Kitchen	José Andrés	https://effectuation.org/EE3/wckitchen	USA
10	Destination Unknown	Needing to pay their rent, these three roommates offered an air mattresses and breakfast as rustic accommodation and people actually showed up.	Airbnb	Joe Gebbia, Brian Chesky, and Nathan Blecharczyk	https://effectuation.org/EE3/airbnb	USA
10	Up the Wall	An unemployed medical school graduate imports wacky toys which become an overnight fad—not his career plan!	Wacky WallWalkers	Ken Hakuta	https://effectuation.org/EE3/wallwalkers	USA
11	A Window Into Precision Dumplings	Dumplings, a ubiquitous food, were the focus of innovation for this entrepreneur, who built an international chain of restaurants.	Din Tai Fung	Yang Bing-Yi	https://effectuation.org/EE3/dumpling	Taiwan

11	Mollydooker: The Serious Science of Fun	Recipe for international success: the fun nature of this wine brand attracts customers while science and systems assure exceptional quality.	Mollydooker	Sarah Marquis	https://effectuation.org/EE3/mollydooker	Australia
11	Transforming Stone Into Water: The Birth of the Zen Gardens	Japanese Zen gardens demonstrate the application of effectual logic to overcome constraints, transform limited available means, and innovate in challenging circumstances.	Zen Gardens		https://effectuation.org/EE3/zengarden	Japan
11	Dust, Sweat, and New Ventures	Hardly a glamorous topic, but sweaty feet propelled this man to find a solution to his problem . . . and build an international shoe brand.	Geox	Mario Moretti Polegato	https://effectuation.org/EE3/geox	Italy
12	Delivering a Venture	By engaging this entrepreneurial team in Kenya to run tedious errands, you can buy time, a precious resource.	Petty Errands	Steve Kiruri	https://effectuation.org/EE3/petty	Kenya
12	Partners' Affordable Loss	A bunch of friends each investing a small amount made a big difference and enabled this shop to take off.	Bacania Veche	Marius Tudosiei	https://effectuation.org/EE3/marius	Romania
12	Affordable Loss for an Unaffordable Loss	Skipping school was an affordable loss for this teenager concerned about climate change: an investment which became a movement.	Fridays for the Future	Greta Thunberg	https://effectuation.org/EE3/greta	Sweden
12	Diving Deep in Affordable Loss	Knocking out someone to save their life? It's a calculated risk when 13 boys are stuck in a Thai cave.	Thai cave rescue	Richard Harris	https://effectuation.org/EE3/cave	Thailand
13	Stacy's Pita Chips	This food business was built on literally thin resources without external funding and turned it into serious dough.	Stacy's Pita Chips	Stacy Madison	https://effectuation.org/EE3/stacy	USA
14	Co-Creation Quilt of COVID-19 Vaccines	The story of COVID-19 vaccines is a vibrant quilt of technologies, people, and organizations, stitched together through global cooperation.	Various	Various	https://effectuation.org/EE3/vaccine	Global

Chapter	Title	Description	Entity / Cause / Project	Name(s) of entrepreneur(s)	Learn More Link	Country
14	A Mountain of Partners	This healthcare initiative removes barriers to enable interested co-creators to contribute as they choose to a shared vision.	Himalayan Health Care	Anil Parajuli	https://effectuation.org/EE3/himalaya	Nepal
14	Chobani: A Simple Pot of Yogurt Changes Lives	A tough nomadic childhood in the mountains of Türkiye taught this entrepreneur about building partnerships—and successful businesses.	Chobani	Hamdi Ulukaya	https://effectuation.org/EE3/chobani	USA
14	Mater Iniciativa—Cooking Up the Ecosystem	This venture actively engages with local communities, ecosystems, and ingredients to create a sustainable model for culinary innovation and entrepreneurship.	Mater Iniciativa	Virgilio Martínez Véliz	https://effectuation.org/EE3/mater	Peru
14	Virtual John: Till Death Do Us Part? Not!	Could some of your available means be re-mixed, re-recorded, re-released, or serve a new purpose for a new audience?	The Beatles	John Lennon	https://effectuation.org/EE3/virtualjohn	Great Britain
14	A Messy Collaboration	The entrepreneurial struggle can get really messy, particularly when you are building a profitable recycling venture with many partners.	Alucha	Hans Cool and Gijs Jansen	https://effectuation.org/EE3/alucha	Spain
15	Market Queens of Ghana	The "Market Queens" of Ghana reorganized the value chain to benefit members, adapt constantly, and are a key economic force.	Market Queens in Ghana		https://effectuation.org/EE3/queens	Ghana
15	Gardener's Eden: Is a Cost Always a Cost?	Partnering with suppliers enabled this entrepreneur to make her limited startup capital go more than four times further.	Gardener's Eden	Ruth Owades	https://effectuation.org/EE3/eden	USA
15	Asking for Change: From Llanos to AltiPlano	An initial ask of a professor set this student on an unpredictable career trajectory while positively influencing many others around him.	Bolivian ICPC Team	Willmar Pimentel	https://effectuation.org/EE3/icpc	Bolivia

16	Persistent Play: Katalin Karikó	Funding issues, surprises, difficult science, and even after technical breakthroughs, lack of attention and support didn't keep this scientist from success.	mRNA Technology	Katalin Karikó	https://effectuation.org/EE3/mrna	USA
16	Flaky Surprise	An unpaid bill and a chance encounter set this entrepreneur on the path to creating one of largest agricultural firms in the world.	Simplot	J. R. Simplot	https://effectuation.org/EE3/simplot	USA
16	Surprise Landing	A space-obsessed daughter, homemade helmet, and many eerie photographs in pandemic-struck Melbourne attracted worldwide attention, awards, and became a book.	Rocketgirl Chronicles	Andrew, Mariya & Mia Rovenko	https://effectuation.org/EE3/rocketgirl	Australia
16	Creating During Crisis: Zopa	This venture identified market demand for an online market connecting individual lenders and borrowers and met success . . . until it was out-regulated.	Zopa	Giles Andrews	https://effectuation.org/EE3/zopa	Great Britain
16	10 US Dollar Surprise	A traumatizing mugging leads this teacher to address the root problem and work on improving the lives of inner-city youth.	National Foundation for Teaching Entrepreneurship (NFTE)	Steve Mariotti	https://effectuation.org/EE3/nfte	USA
16	Two Negatives Make Lemonade	This mining giant learns that innovation thrives on taking risks, seizing opportunities, and turning setbacks into steppingstones—sounds entrepreneurial!	Chilean Mining Corporation (CMC)		https://effectuation.org/EE3/mining	Chile
16	Printed Surprise—The Start of Staples	No printer ribbon on the weekend becomes the beginning of a chain of office supply stores later valued at billions.	Staples	Thomas Stemberg	https://effectuation.org/EE3/staples	USA
16	Silly Surprise	A failed attempt at creating synthetic rubber becomes a hit toy when an advertising executive got his hands on it.	Silly Putty	Peter Hodgson	https://effectuation.org/EE3/silly	USA

Chapter	Title	Description	Entity / Cause / Project	Name(s) of entrepreneur(s)	Learn More Link	Country
16	Scooter Surprise	When potential customers call wanting to buy, you know you have something good: the story of this Japanese scooter company.	Honda		https://effectuation.org/EE3/honda	Japan
16	Railroad Surprise	Instead of consulting for small railroads, this entrepreneur bought and managed them to growth and success.	Railtex	Bruce Flohr	https://effectuation.org/EE3/railtex	USA
17	Ice Man Cometh	A rained-out ice sculpture festival almost sent this entrepreneur back to employment. Instead he built his future with partners, one ice block at a time.	ICEHOTEL	Yngve Bergqvist	https://effectuation.org/EE3/icehotel	Sweden
17	Reluctant Billionaire	A scientist just wants his own research laboratory and had to build a billion-dollar company to finally get it.	Anonymous	Anonymous	https://effectuation.org/EE3/path	USA
18	Sharing the Treats Among Investors	These entrepreneurs maintain substantial control of their venture, although they sold most of the business to investors.	Castor & Pollux		https://effectuation.org/EE3/castor	USA
18	Steward-Ownership: A Growing Alternative	Steward-ownership seeks to ensure long-term and purpose-driven decision-making in organizations and is gaining in popularity.	Foundation for Steward-Ownership (FSO)		https://effectuation.org/EE3/steward	Germany
18	A Piece of the Pie	This home-based pie venture went national with the help of a like-minded investor, who shares in the sweet rewards.	Kenny's Great Pies	Kenny Burt	https://effectuation.org/EE3/limepie	USA
18	Investing in People	This firm pays a student's tuition bills in exchange for a percentage of future earnings: dividends on career success.	Lumni	Felipe Vergara	https://effectuation.org/EE3/lumni	Colombia
19	The Cube Without a Plan	This hit toy demonstrates a familiar story: the inventor is brilliant, but the commercial success is shared by many.	Rubik's Cube	Erno Rubik	https://effectuation.org/EE3/rubik	Hungary

19	Homemade Icon	This great invention basically went unsold until a woman created an entire sales approach specific to customer needs and interests.	Tupperware	Brownie Wise	https://effectuation.org/EE3/tupperware	USA
19	Disposable Income	The business model of this diaper company is tightly linked to the preferences and aspirations of customers, partners, and employees.	gDiapers		https://effectuation.org/EE3/gdiaper	USA
19	A Lick of the Old Block	This entrepreneur connected seemingly unrelated dots: farmers in Laos, companies seeking carbon offsets, and the nutrition of buffalos.	AgCoTech	Chick Olsson	https://effectuation.org/EE3/lickblock	Laos
19	The Wind and the Plan	Starting out with green power, this entrepreneur has changed with the times and winds, creating new opportunities in the process.	Ecotricity	Dale Vince	https://effectuation.org/EE3/wind	Great Britain
19	A Model for Healthy Change	She turned a garage-based life-sciences firm into a multinational. How? She innovated to solve healthcare problems and make a profit.	Biocon	Kiran Mazumdar-Shaw	https://effectuation.org/EE3/biocon	India
20	Breath of Fresh Air	Although founded in 1958, this firm remains highly innovative and entrepreneurial by carefully cultivating its corporate culture and team size.	W. L. Gore & Company	W. L. Gore	https://effectuation.org/EE3/gore	USA
20	A Guide to the Process	Process is necessary but can hinder progress. This venture delivers results differently through small, flexible, month-long project teams.	Guidewire	John Seybold	https://effectuation.org/EE3/guidewire	USA
21	Frida Kahlo—The Art of Pain	This woman took the bitter lemon of a life-changing accident and turned it into a vibrant canvas of self-expression and cultural representation.	Frida Kahlo	Frida Kahlo	https://effectuation.org/EE3/frida	Mexico
21	Augusto Teodoro: Love at First Loss	Despite finishing last in his first race, this man kept running, influencing countless others to become healthier through sports.	Augusto Teodoro	Augusto Teodoro	https://effectuation.org/EE3/augusto	Brazil

Chapter	Title	Description	Entity / Cause / Project	Name(s) of entrepreneur(s)	Learn More Link	Country
21	Margaritaville: Neverending Song	This singer became an entrepreneur by branding the feeling of a song and selling that emotion through events, hospitality, and merchandise.	Margaritaville	Jimmy Buffett	https://effectuation.org/EE3/margaritaville	USA
21	Terry Heckler: Creator of Enduring Brands	A branding guru follows the pragmatic idea of "moment of use" to focus on the user as co-creator of the brand.	Heckler Branding	Terry Heckler	https://effectuation.org/EE3/heckler	USA
21	The Identity Spectrum	Two very different entrepreneurs infused their values into their ventures to break down barriers and glass ceilings.	Tata Group and Spanx	Jamshedji Tata and Sara Blakeley	https://effectuation.org/EE3/spectrum	Global
22	Thank You for the Music	Compact disc technology shows that large firms can act entrepreneurially and that a single technology can have many applications for entrepreneurial exploitation.	Philips, Sony, Battelle	James T. Russell and Eli S. Jacobs	https://effectuation.org/EE3/compactdisc	Global
22	Fuel Proof	Biofuel technology has evolved, but those iterations can only move beyond experimentation if entrepreneurial minds transform them into viable market opportunities.	Novozymes	Per Falholt	https://effectuation.org/EE3/biofuel	Denmark
22	Shocking Venture	Small improvements to fuel efficiency generate enormous opportunities for this vehicle component supplier.	Levant	Shakeel Avadhany	https://effectuation.org/EE3/shock	USA
22	Health of Nations	What action an entrepreneur takes is highly influenced by who they are, as the pathway of this healthcare-focused venture demonstrates.	Voxiva	Paul Meyer	https://effectuation.org/EE3/voxiva	USA
22	Netflix: Streaming Through Calm and Storm	This venture started by "just" delivering entertainment, but as technology evolved, it did as well, becoming a major producer of content.	Netflix	Reed Hastings and Marc Randolph	https://effectuation.org/EE3/netflix	USA

23	Josiah Wedgwood: Social and Financial Strength in Porcelain	This potter invested in stakeholders to build a venture which produced great financial success as well as lasting positive social impact.	Wedgwood Porcelain	Josiah Wedgwood	https://effectuation.org/EE3/wedgwood	Great Britain
23	Jane Addams: Social Entrepreneur Pursuing Peace	This highly successful woman focused on social activism, entrepreneurship, and the promotion of peace, but also recognized the vulnerability of depending on philanthropy.	Hull House	Jane Addams	https://effectuation.org/EE3/addams	USA
23	Taking Flight: Hyacinth Macaw Institute	A purposeful woman uses science and an entrepreneurial approach to solve a problem of environmental sustainability, but how to make it financially sustainable?	Hyacinth Macaw Institute	Neiva Guedes	https://effectuation.org/EE3/macaw	Brazil
23	Grameen: Birth of Microbanking	This pioneering model of microbanking demonstrates that financial services, when designed with a social purpose, can be both profitable and transformative for communities.	Grameen Bank	Muhammad Yunus	https://effectuation.org/EE3/grameen	Bangladesh
23	Swiss Precision: Making Cooperatives Work in Banking	This member-owned Swiss bank seeks to balance the interests of its members and community while maintaining financial sustainability.	Raiffeisen Bank		https://effectuation.org/EE3/raiffeisen	Switzerland
23	The Bright Entrepreneur: Sunlabob	This energy-provider selling hardware and services to remote areas of Laos is profitable while meeting community needs, allowing it to evolve and grow.	Sunlabob	Andy Schroeter	https://effectuation.org/EE3/sunlabob	Laos
23	Grameen Bank—Part 2—Principles & Practices	The principles of this stakeholder-focused bank are logically the inverse of standard banking practices which serve shareholders.	Grameen Bank	Muhammad Yunus	https://effectuation.org/EE3/gbprinciples	Bangladesh

Chapter	Title	Description	Entity / Cause / Project	Name(s) of entrepreneur(s)	Learn More Link	Country
23	Kashmir Relief Note: Example of Market in Human Hope	This idea enables the public to invest in humanitarian relief and receive a return on its money—almost 19% in fact.	Kashmir Relief Note	Marc Freudweiler	https://effectuation.org/EE3/kashmir	Switzerland
23	On the Pharma: Victoria Hale and OneWorld Health	This entrepreneur turned off-patent pharmaceuticals into life-saving treatments for those in need.	OneWorld Health	Victoria Hale	https://effectuation.org/EE3/oneworld	USA
23	Ronni Kahn and OzHarvest: The Metamorphosis of Food Waste Into a Butterfly	One woman's desire to reduce her company's food waste leads to positive impact on seven of the seventeen UN Sustainable Development Goals.	OzHarvest	Ronni Kahn	https://effectuation.org/EE3/ozharvest	Australia
23	Food Integrates: Refugees Sharing Culture	These social ventures bring together migrants to share their native cuisine with their host community and spark new entrepreneurial opportunities.	Various		https://effectuation.org/EE3/foodintegrates	Global
23	Technology Camps Teaching More Than Science	This cunning plan to get her son away from video games became a venture running hands-on science and technology camps in Lebanon and beyond.	The Little Engineer	Rana El Chemaitelly	https://effectuation.org/EE3/engineers	Lebanon
23	Princess Reema: Nudging Social Change	This incremental approach to social change has facilitated a broader shift in norms and attitudes toward women's roles in Saudi society.	Saudi Arabian Women's Sports Authority	Reema bint Bandar Al Saud	https://effectuation.org/EE3/princessreema	Saudi Arabia
23	Orange Sky: Clean Clothes and a Chat	This venture offers clean laundry, a shower, and a chat to restore the dignity of homeless people as a step toward better perspectives.	Orange Sky	Nicholas Marchesi and Lucas Patchett	https://effectuation.org/EE3/orangesky	Australia

Overview of "Research Roots" Sections

Research Roots

There is an enormous body of academic research on entrepreneurship—far too much for us to include in a book you could actually carry in your hand. So, we searched for foundational research that has shaped thinking over the years and contemporary research that reflects current knowledge to date. In the context of a chapter, we summarize the key points of a research stream in "Research Roots" to give you an idea of what other scholars are working on and to offer directions for further reading.

To access a more detailed version of the following list, visit https://effectuation.org/EE3/researchroots or scan this code:

Chapter	Title	Description
1	What Is Entrepreneurship, Really?	One perspective: entrepreneurship is about the activities undertaken, not necessarily the person or their personality.
2	Innovation Adoption	Five things can help innovators assess if their idea is likely to gain adoption.
3	The Lean Startup	No more elaborate business plans and long ramp-up: lean is about doing just enough to create a viable venture.
3	Funding via the Masses	Crowdfunding spreads the financial risk and helps ventures get a kick start.
3	Keeping Cool Under (Financial) Pressure	Little cash, but still good decisions: research indicates that scarce resources are not bad for decision-making.
4	Who Actually Plunges?	Data indicate that people create their own source of income through entrepreneurship often due to a lack of job opportunities.
5	Amy Edmondson: "Right Kind of Wrong"	Understanding your failures can help increase the number of intelligent failures you need to make to move ahead.
5	Persist, but Know When to Quit	Equipping yourself with quitting tools will help you know when to persist and when not.
6	Frank Knight	This economics teacher of Nobel laureates created the notion that entrepreneurs manage uncertainty, which justifies profit.
6	Adam Smith	He explained that rational self-interest and competition can lead to economic well-being and prosperity, thus justifying free trade and capitalism.
6	The Future That's Already Happened	By studying demographic patterns, you can identify opportunities aligned with the needs and wants of certain groups.
6	Expert in Forecasting? An Oxymoron	Research indicates that entrepreneurial skills are more likely to be the reason for success and not ability to predict accurately.
6	Blue Ocean Strategy	This strategy plays a different game: create markets and generate uncertainty, not react to uncertainties in the environment.
6	Entrepreneurs and Risk: It's Complicated …	We don't yet have a clear picture on the risk tolerance of entrepreneurs, including because their self-perceptions might not be accurate.
6	Real Options	Manage the risk of failure by making small initial investments. You are buying into the option of making larger investments later.
7	New Combinations	Schumpeter defined "the carrying out of new combinations" as the essence of entrepreneurship.
8	On the Importance of Control	People want a sense of control by knowing what they can and cannot change—from bodily functions to global issues.
8	A Short History of Contemporary Human Rights	Human rights have evolved over centuries, driven by individuals taking action and advocating for basic freedoms and dignity.
8	Slow Disruption	Innovation is not a sudden, revolutionary event, but a series of incremental advancements which can cumulatively result in significant disruption.

8	The Power of Networks	Research suggests that entrepreneurs should focus on building diverse, flexible, and trust-based networks to achieve their goals.
8	Learning Helplessness and Optimism	The interplay between Learned Helplessness and Learned Optimism highlights the importance of individual action in gaining control in the face of uncertainty.
9	Why Study Expert Entrepreneurs?	By studying expert entrepreneurs, we can understand the thought patterns used to develop opportunities in uncertain environments.
9	Measuring Effectuation	Academics have developed a methodology to measure the use of both effectual and causal logic in new venture creation.
9	Supersizing the Entrepreneurial Mind	Entrepreneurs are adept at expanding their minds by engaging with aspects of their material, physical, and social context.
9	Entrepreneurs Made Through Education	Education (regardless of source) is the biggest predictor of entrepreneurial success.
9	The Surprising Differences Between Expert and Novice Decision-Making	To learn how to make decisions, turn to the experts who are experienced in identifying patterns and reacting accordingly.
9	Talent Is Overrated?	There seems no way around it: talent is developed through deliberate practice; it does not come from innate skill.
10	The Corridor Principle	Corridor Principle: Pursuing one opportunity leads to other opportunities (in the corridor) which could not have been previously imagined.
10	Six Degrees of Separation	Humans are highly interconnected: Your network and the network of your network extends to everyone on the planet.
10	One Technology—>Eight Entrepreneurs—>Eight Different Ideas	Despite the same technological starting point, because of their unique knowledge and experience, each entrepreneur takes a different path forward.
11	Creative Templates	Idea generation is not magic; it's method. Research determined that five creative templates are the source of 70% of all new product ideas.
11	Exaptation	Despite the name, exaptation isn't painful. It's the process of asking "what else can I do with this thing?" to identify potential opportunities.
11	Adam Smith and Novel Combinations	About 250 years ago, Adam Smith recognized the power of observation and combining similar and dissimilar things.
11	Design Thinking	There is overlap with effectuation and design thinking, particularly in the process of turning available means into something valuable.
11	How to Fly a Horse	Key insight on innovation: Success depends on "… how we respond to the adversity of creation."
12	Mental Accounting	Limited mental bandwidth is why we categorize our money into short-term expenses and long-term savings, even if the cost varies.
12	Affordable Loss	Estimating possible losses can help entrepreneurs evaluate which opportunity to pursue.

13	Earn Versus Burn	The amount of money invested does not predict payout, but investment money accelerates growth and shortens time to liquidity.
14	The Intersubjective	It is nearly impossible to observe anything in isolation: we make sense of the world by developing shared understandings.
14	Partnerships and Social Media	We knew what these academics have since proven: social media and technology are catalysts for developing partnerships.
14	Markets Are Co-Created	Markets are complex, dynamic, unpredictable, and involve co-creation among diverse stakeholders, making new market generation difficult to explain.
15	Coopetition: Asking Your Competitor to Cooperate	Simultaneously cooperating and competing is an entrepreneurial process of risk-taking, exploring, and exploiting opportunities in uncertainty.
15	The Psychology of Influence	Robert Cialdini defines the following as "weapons of influence": social proof, authority, liking, scarcity, reciprocation, and commitment and consistency.
15	Advice, Decision-Making, Experts, and Social Influencers	Changes in society, technology, and experts make receiving advice complicated, so be sure to consider the motivation of the giver.
15	Yes Is Closer Than You Think	People are more willing to help than is generally thought, but consider the medium (in-person, phone, etc.) to improve outcomes.
16	Accidental Innovation?	According to research, unplanned surprises, or accidents, can be beneficial, if you can control the downside.
16	Contingencies as Resources in the Startup Process	Being entrepreneurial involves leveraging the contingencies that happen (both "good" and "bad") by making them inputs for the next step.
18	Agency Theory	Venture owners can incentivize their agents to be productive by offering equity, bonuses, promotions, interesting projects, and recognition.
19	Useful Tool: The Business Model Canvas	This single-page business planning template enables easy visualization, discussion, and reworking by teams, making it a favorite among entrepreneurs.
19	Seat of the Pants	Research shows that about 40% of founders create a business plan, and those who do write one usually end up building something very different.
19	Rewards to Entrepreneurs With Venture Capital Investors	Hugely successful venture capital-backed firms are very rare. Seventy-five percent of founders exit VC-funded ventures with nothing besides experience and stories.
19	A Great Debate: Business Planning	Planning is good; the plan not necessarily. Ask yourself how a business plan could be useful and act accordingly.
20	Effectuation as Business	Effectual logic is used to create new things, and it can also be what is sold, as a number of authors and advisors have done.
20	Congrats, You Raised a Bunch of Money! Sorry You're Fired	Outside funds are usually required to build a valuable venture, but that also means surrendering control. Is the trade worth it?
20	The Elements of the Internal Market	Innovation requires autonomy, reward, and psychological safety, so how can companies institutionalize using failure as an opportunity for organizational learning?

20	Threat Rigidity	People become rigid when threatened, but when the situation is viewed as an opportunity, people become more creative with the possibilities.
20	Asking in the Corporate Environment	Managers tend to not ask because they fear the unknown and going off-script. Asking, however, can lead to having more control over outcomes.
20	Transacting Within Hierarchies	How firms decide whether to produce internally or outsource activities can have implications for entrepreneurship and venture creation.
20	Enduring High-Performance Ventures Create High Social Value	Most job growth comes from few high-performing ventures. Learning the principles of expert entrepreneurs can help you build one of those job-makers.
21	Identify Yourself	Ventures are reflections of their founders. This research found three basic categories: founders driven by cause, founders supporting communities, and founders seeking money.
21	Bridging the Gap	Founders who lead consciously and authentically by modeling ethical and values-driven behavior create a culture of communication, transparency, and integrity.
22	Lead Users	Engaging with lead users can assist marketers to understand more, but they don't necessarily represent the market as a whole.
22	In Praise of Venturesome Users	Lead users can play a venturesome role in the genesis of new firms and making them a vital enabler of the entrepreneurial process.
22	Effectuation Improves R&D Project Performance	Research and development managers tend to use effectuation in more uncertain projects, which improves the performance of these projects.
22	Partners Over Patents: Open Innovation	Open innovation encourages freely sharing technologies so customers, partners, and suppliers can co-create with entrepreneurs.
22	Scientific Discovery and Entrepreneurial Innovation	This book concludes that despite the large investments in scientific research, the economic results of technological innovation come from entrepreneurial efforts.
23	Collective Action Requires Stakeholder Commitments	Effectual entrepreneurs can apply Ostrom's institutional analysis and development model of collective action to facilitate structuring enduring stakeholder commitments.
23	Near Decomposability as the Key to Hope	"Small is big": Many big changes start when a single individual takes action, which, due to "near decomposability" links, has ripple effects.
23	Social Entrepreneurship in Perspective	The challenge of mobilizing resources for new social ventures creates a question for entrepreneurs: which financing model best fulfills the mission?

Image Acknowledgments

CHAPTER 2 GOOD IDEAS ARE EVERYWHERE

- Figure 2.5 Photo courtesy of Unsicht-Bar

CHAPTER 3 MOST VENTURES REQUIRE LITTLE STARTUP CAPITAL

- Figure 3.6 Wikimedia Commons

CHAPTER 4 THE PLUNGE DOESN'T HAVE TO BE A PLUNGE AT ALL

- Figure 4.2 Photo courtesy of Can of Worms Enterprises
- Figure 4.5 © Mannequin Madness. Photo courtesy of Mannequin Madness
- Figure 4.7 By Winchester Journal, Indiana—*Winchester Journal,* January 5, 1888, p. 3, Public Domain, https://commons.wikimedia.org/w/index.php?curid=66283222

CHAPTER 5 FAILING AS THE WAY FORWARD

- Figure 5.3 Based on data from the US Bureau of Statistics, 2024
- Figure 5.7 Photo courtesy of EasyAuto © Stuart Read
- Figure 5.10 Photo by Stuart Read with permission of Hershey's
- Figure 5.13 Photo by Bronayur at the English-language Wikipedia
- Figure 5.16 "Newton MessagePad 120 opened" by Nzeemin—Own work. Licensed under CC BY-SA 3.0 via Commons

CHAPTER 6 PREDICTION, RISK, AND UNCERTAINTY

- Figure 6.2 Courtesy of the International Naval Research Organization—history.navy.mil
- Figure 6.3 By United Press International, photographer unknown
- Figure 6.5 GV Students, CC0, via Wikimedia Commons
- Figure 6.8 Photo courtesy of Isabella Nunes Pereira
- Figure 6.10 Westport Wiki, CC3, via Wikimedia Commons

CHAPTER 7 OPPORTUNITIES ARE CREATED AS WELL AS DISCOVERED

- Figure 7.6 Image courtesy of TerraCycle, CC 2.0, via Wikimedia Commons
- Figure 7.7 Image by Pexels from Pixabay
- Figure 7.11 Photo courtesy of Gentile Entertainment Group, https://petrock.com/

CHAPTER 8 MANAGING UNCERTAINTY THROUGH CONTROL

- Figure 8.2 Photo courtesy of the Office fédéral

de météorologie et de climatologie MétéoSuisse

- Figure 8.5 Photo courtesy of Aline Brufato

CHAPTER 9 THE EFFECTUAL LOGIC OF EXPERT ENTREPRENEURS

- Figure 9.2 Photo courtesy of GoodKaarma
- Figure 9.5 Photo courtesy of Innis & Gunn
- Figure 9.7 Photo by Evan-Amos made available through Wikimedia Commons
- Figure 9.8 Photo made available through Creative Commons

CHAPTER 10 THE BIRD-IN-HAND PRINCIPLE: START WITH WHAT YOU HAVE

- Figure 10.3 Photo courtesy of EcoEnvelopes
- Figure 10.5 Photo courtesy of City Foodsters
- Figure 10.11 Photo courtesy of World Central Kitchen/ WCK.org
- Figure 10.13 Infographic courtesy of Anna Vital, fundersandfounders.com

CHAPTER 11 TRANSFORMING MEANS INTO SOMETHING VALUABLE

- Figure 11.2 © Teri Read
- Figure 11.7 Photo courtesy of Mollydooker Wines
- Figure 11.8 Photo courtesy of Masuo Koogure, 1997
- Figure 11.9 Photo courtesy of Masuo Koogure, 1997
- Figure 11.12 Photo courtesy of Geox

CHAPTER 12 THE AFFORDABLE LOSS PRINCIPLE: INVEST LITTLE, LEARN A LOT

- Figure 12.2 © Petty Errands
- Figure 12.4 © Mihai SIMIONICA Start & Grow

CHAPTER 15 ASKING POTENTIAL PARTNERS TO MAKE COMMITMENTS

- Figure 15.5 © Teri Read Photo

CHAPTER 16 THE LEMONADE PRINCIPLE: LEVERAGE SURPRISE

- Figure 16.12 Photo provided courtesy of Crayola LLC, used with permission. © 2010 Crayola. (Silly Putty® is a registered trademark of Crayola LLC)
- Figure 16.15 Photo courtesy of Honda
- Figure 16.17 Photo by Joseph Sohm–Visions of America/ Getty Images

CHAPTER 17 PUTTING IT TOGETHER: THE EFFECTUATION PROCESS

- Figure 17.4 Photo courtesy of ICEHOTEL
- Figure 17.5 Photo courtesy of ICEHOTEL

CHAPTER 18 OWNERSHIP, EQUITY, AND CONTROL: MANAGE STAKEHOLDERS

- Figure 18.2 Photo courtesy of Castor & Pollux
- Figure 18.4 © vikiri – Fotolia.com
- Figure 18.5 © Patrick Hardin – www.cartoonstock.com
- Figure 18.7 Photo courtesy of Kenny's Great Pies
- Figure 18.9 © John Morris – www.cartoonstock.com
- Figure 18.11 © Lumni Corporation

CHAPTER 19 BUSINESS PLANS AND BUSINESS MODELS

- Figure 19.3 Image by Booyabazooka, Wikimedia Commons
- Figure 19.6 Photo courtesy of gDiapers
- Figure 19.11 Photo courtesy of Ecotricity

CHAPTER 20 THE VENTURE GROWS UP: CREATE AN ENTREPRENEURIAL CULTURE

- Figure 20.3 Photo made available through Pixabay, by denvit
- Figure 20.4 Image courtesy of GORE-TEX®
- Figure 20.6 © Stuart Read

CHAPTER 21 BRAND AS VENTURE IDENTITY: MARKETING YOU

- Figure 21.8 Photo courtesy of Panera Bread
- Figure 21.9 Photo courtesy of Jansport
- Figure 21.12 © Tim Cordell—www.cartoonstock.com

CHAPTER 22 TECHNOLOGY: MEANS, OUTCOME, OR TRAP?

- Figure 22.7 Image courtesy of Levant
- Figure 22.9 © Voxiva
- Figure 22.10 © Voxiva
- Figure 22.11 © Voxiva

CHAPTER 23 SOCIAL CHANGE AND MARKETS IN HUMAN HOPE

- Figure 23.10 © Sunlabob

CONCLUSION

- Blue Dot: Photo courtesy of NASA/nasaimages.org

Index

Note: Bold page numbers refer to tables; *italic* page numbers refer to figures and ***bold-italic*** page numbers refer to boxes.